MICROARCHAEOLOGY

The archaeological record is a combination of what is seen by the eye and the microscopic record revealed with the help of instrumentation. The information embedded in the microscopic record can significantly add to our understanding of past human behavior, provided that this information has not been altered by the passage of time. *Microarchaeology* seeks to understand the microscopic record in terms of the types of information embedded in this record, the materials in which this information resides, and the conditions under which a reliable signal can be extracted. This book highlights the concepts needed to extract information from the microscopic record. Intended for all archaeologists and archaeological scientists, it will be of particular interest to students who have some background in the natural sciences and archaeology. This book

- emphasizes the nature of the materials in which information is embedded and the problems associated with extracting a real signal,
- provides a comprehensive list of the types of information embedded in the microscopic archaeological record, and
- offers an in-depth overview of the use of infrared spectroscopy for analyzing the microscopic record, the only one of its kind available.

Stephen Weiner is director of the Kimmel Center for Archaeological Science at the Weizmann Institute of Science in Israel. He is the author, with Heinz A. Lowenstam, of *On Biomineralization* and has published more than 250 scientific journal articles.

Microarchaeology

BEYOND THE VISIBLE
ARCHAEOLOGICAL RECORD

Stephen Weiner

Weizmann Institute of Science

CAMBRIDGE UNIVERSITY PRESS
Cambridge, New York, Melbourne, Madrid, Cape Town, Singapore,
São Paulo, Delhi, Dubai, Tokyo

Cambridge University Press
32 Avenue of the Americas, New York, NY 10013-2473, USA

www.cambridge.org
Information on this title: www.cambridge.org/9780521705844

First published 2010

Printed in the United States of America

A catalog record for this publication is available from the British Library.

Library of Congress Cataloging in Publication data

Weiner, Stephen, 1948–
Microarchaeology : beyond the visible archaeological record / Stephen Weiner.
  p. cm.
Includes bibliographical references and index.
ISBN 978-0-521-88003-9 (hbk.) – ISBN 978-0-521-70584-4 (pbk.) 1. Archaeology –
Methodology. 2. Microscopy. 3. Antiquities – Analysis. 4. Excavations
(Archaeology) I. Title.
CC75.7.W45 2010
930.1–dc22   2009026783

ISBN 978-0-521-88003-9 Hardback
ISBN 978-0-521-70584-4 Paperback

Contents

Preface   *page* xvii

1 Archaeology, Archaeological Science, and
   Microarchaeology   1
   Archaeology Is a Difficult Science   3
   Historical Perspective   4
   Archaeological Science   5
   The Microscopic Record   6
   Tool Kit for Deciphering the Microscopic Archaeological
       Record   8
   The Importance of Integrating Microarchaeology with
       Macroarchaeology   8
       The ideal solution to this problem   9
       The reality   10
   On-Site Laboratory   10
   The Concept of This Book   10
   Conclusions   12

2 Information Embedded in the Microscopic Record   13
   Archaeobotanical Record   16
   Dating   18
       Perspective on techniques used for dating materials
           from archaeological sites   18
       Radiocarbon dating   19
       Uranium series dating   21
       Dendrochronology   21
       Trapped charge dating: Thermoluminescence (TL),
           optical stimulated luminescence (OSL), and
           electron spin resonance (ESR)   22
       Dating by fluoride uptake   23

Obsidian hydration dating   23
Amino acid racemization dating   24
Dating by archaeomagnetism   25
Life History Reconstruction of Individuals   26
Paleodiet Reconstruction   27
Stable isotope paleodiet reconstruction   28
Strontium contents of human bones   29
Molecules trapped in ceramics (residue analysis)   29
Paleoenvironmental Reconstruction   30
Micromorphology   30
Archaeobotany   31
Rare earth elements   31
Pollen   32
Stable isotope compositional variations   32
Paleogenetics   33
Paleomigration   35
Pottery Contents   35
Provenience and Procurement Strategies   36
Provenience studies   36
Limited sources   37
Obsidian   37
Amber   37
Soapstone (Steatite)   37
Marble   38
Metals   38
Abundant sources   39
Pottery   39
Flint (Chert)   40
Procurement strategies   40
Season of Occupation   41
Archaeobotanical remains   41
Rhythmic growth   41
Site Formation Processes   42
Site Spatial Organization   43
Weaning Age   44

3 Completeness of the Archaeological Record   46

How Bad Is the Archaeological Record?   47
The Almost Complete Record   47
The Incomplete Record: Conceptual Framework for
        Assessing the Missing Record   51
Macroscopic versus microscopic records   51
Time frame   52

The driving forces of degradation   54
  Mechanical disturbances   54
  Hydrological regime and chemical reactions   54
Materials that degrade   56
  Organic material   57
  Minerals   59
Minerals rearranging at the atomic level   61
Summary of the conceptual framework for estimating
    the missing record   62
  Time frame   62
  Agents of degradation   62
  Assessing the extent of degradation   62
  Conclusions   62
Practical applications of the conceptual framework   63
Future Prospects for Improving Our Understanding of the
    Missing Archaeological Record   66

4 Common Mineral Components of the Archaeological
   Record   68

Minerals and Mineral Identification   70
  Optical mineralogy   70
  X-ray diffraction   70
  Infrared spectroscopy   71
  Raman spectroscopy   71
  Chemical elemental analyses   72
Size and Shape of Mineral Particles   72
In Situ Assemblages of Minerals (Micromorphology)   73
  Zhoukoudian Layer 10 (China): Are these
    anthropogenically produced ashes?   74
Calcite and the Calcium Carbonate Mineral Family   76
  Calcium carbonate pH buffering capacity   77
  Calcite and aragonite: Similarities and differences   77
  Possible origins of calcite in archaeological sites   78
    Geogenic calcites   78
    Pyrogenic calcites   79
    Biogenic calcites   79
  Possible origins of aragonite in archaeological sites   80
  Diagenesis of calcite and aragonite   80
  Embedded information   81
    Aragonite and calcite: Assessing the preservation
    state of the minerals in a site   81
    Differentiating among geogenic, biogenic, and
    pyrogenic calcites   81

Cemented sediment: Recrystallized wood ash or a
geogenic cement?   82
Carbonate Hydroxylapatite   83
Atomic structure   84
Stability field   85
Diagenesis   86
Embedded information   86
Identifying areas in a site that had high organic
contents   86
Differentiating between biogenic and geogenic
carbonate hydroxylapatites   87
Paleoclimate reconstruction   87
Using authigenic phosphate minerals for identifying
strata in which bones have dissolved   88
Polymorphs of Silicon Dioxide   88
Quartz and flint/chert   88
Silica   89
Silicon dioxide polymorphs produced at high
temperatures   90
Diagenesis   90
Quartz   90
Silica   90
Microcrystalline quartz in flint and chert   90
Embedded information   91
Provenience of quartz   91
Provenience and procurement strategies of flint and
chert   91
Dating of flint tools   92
The Clay Family   92
Clay structures and classification   93
Identifying clay minerals   94
Clay and organic materials   94
Diagenesis   95
Embedded information   96
Better preservation in clay-rich sediments   96
Clay provenience   96
Was the clay exposed to elevated temperatures?   97
General Implications of Mineral Assemblages for Site
Preservation   97
Assessing the Completeness of the Archaeological Record   98

5   Biological Materials: Bones and Teeth   99

Biomineralization: Archaeological Perspective   99
Bone and Bones   101

Bone the material: The hierarchical structure   102
    Level 1: The basic constituents   102
    Level 2: The mineralized collagen fibril   106
    Level 3: The fibril arrays   106
    Level 4: The packing motifs of fibril arrays   107
    Level 5: Osteonal bone   107
    Level 6: The spongy to compact bone continuum   108
    Level 7: Whole bone   108
Porosity   109
Diagenesis of bone the material   110
    Mineral diagenesis   110
    Organic matrix diagenesis   112
    Microbial and fungal diagenesis   113
The pseudomorph and cast issue   115
Timescales for bone diagenesis   115
Bones lying on the soil surface   115
Buried bones   116
Burned bone   117
Embedded information   118
    Migration pathways   118
    Paleodiet reconstruction   119
    Paleogenetics   121
    Paleoenvironmental reconstruction using rare earth
        elements   122
    Radiocarbon dating   122
    Reconstructing aspects of an individual's life history   123
Teeth   123
    Enamel: The hierarchical structure   124
        Level 1: The basic constituents   124
        Level 2: Crystal arrays (prisms)   126
        Level 3: Reticulate three-dimensional network of
            prisms   126
        Level 4: Graded changes in structure   126
        Level 5: The whole enamel layer   126
    Dentin: The hierarchical structure   126
        Level 1: The basic constituents   127
        Level 2: The mineralized collagen fibril   127
        Level 3: The fibril arrays   128
        Level 4: The packing motifs of fibril arrays   128
        Level 5: The tubules and peritubular dentin   128
        Level 6: The whole dentin component of the tooth   128
    Whole teeth   129
    Cementum   129
    Dental calculus   130

Diagenesis of teeth   130
  Enamel diagenesis   130
  Dentin diagenesis   131
Embedded information   132
  Enamel   132
  Dentin   133
  Cementum   133
  Dental calculus   134

6 Biological Materials: Phytoliths, Diatoms, Eggshells,
   Otoliths, and Mollusk Shells   135

Phytoliths   135
  Phytolith material   136
  Phytolith formation and morphology   137
  Information categories obtained from phytolith
      assemblages   139
    Taxonomy   139
    Plant categories   140
    Plant parts   140
  Strategy for studying phytoliths in an archaeological
      context   141
    Reference collection   141
    Sampling and analysis   142
  Diagenesis   143
  Embedded information   145
    Fuel use at a site   145
    Identifying ancient irrigation practices and/or
        rainfall   145
    Genetic information   146
    Identifying plant taxa brought to the site   146
    Paleodiet   147
    Paleovegetation ecology   147
    Radiocarbon dating of phytoliths   148
    Reconstructing relative amounts of plant materials
        used   148
    Use of space   148
  Final comment   149
Diatoms   149
  Cell wall composition   150
  Diagenesis   150
  Embedded information   150
    Ancient irrigation practices   150
    Provenience of pottery   151
    Reconstructing the paleoenvironment   151

Avian (Bird) Eggshells   151
  Basic morphology and structure   151
  Diagenesis   152
  Embedded information   152
    Dating using amino acid racemization   152
    Reconstructing the paleoenvironment   153
    Radiocarbon dating   153
Avian Gizzard Stones   154
Otoliths   154
  Morphology, ultrastructure, and mineralogy   154
  Diagenesis   156
  Embedded information   156
    Reconstructing the paleoenvironment   156
    Season of occupation of a site   157
Mollusk Shells   157
  Taxonomy   159
  Shell ultrastructure and mineralogy   159
  Mineral phase   160
  Organic matrix   162
  Embedded information   162
    Dating   163
    Reconstructing the paleoenvironment   163
    Season of occupation   164
    Site preservation   164

7 Reconstructing Pyrotechnological Processes   165

Basic Concepts of Heating and Cooling   166
Order and Disorder in Solids   167
Ash   168
  Composition of ash   169
Ash from Wood and Bark   170
  Diagenesis   172
    pH above 8   172
    pH below 8   173
  Identifying ash produced by burning wood
    and bark   174
  Embedded information   175
    Demonstrating control of fire by humans   175
    Fuel types used for fires   176
    Radiocarbon dating   177
    Thermoluminescence and electron spin resonance
      dating   177
    Type of wood used for fires   177
Charcoal and Charred Materials   178

Molecular structure of modern wood charcoal produced
    in natural fires   179
Molecular structure of fossil wood charcoal from
    archaeological sites   181
Diagenesis   182
Embedded information   183
    Impact of fires produced by humans on the local
        vegetation and soils   183
    Ink   183
    Identification of charred organic material in
        sediments   184
    Radiocarbon dating   184
    Seed and fruit identification   184
    Wood identification   184
Plaster and Mortar   185
    Binders   185
        Calcite binder   186
        Gypsum   188
        Hydraulic plaster and mortar   188
    Aggregates   189
        Proportions of aggregates and binders   189
    Identifying plaster and mortar   190
    Diagenesis   190
    Embedded information   191
        Radiocarbon dating   191
        Reconstructing production procedures and functions   192
        Refractory materials produced by heating carbonate
            rocks   193
        Residue analysis   194
        Specific features in a site   194
Ceramics and Pottery   194
    The essentials of pottery manufacture   195
        Raw materials   195
        Temper   195
        Fluxes   195
        Shaping and decorating   196
        Drying   196
        Firing conditions   197
    Diagenesis   198
    Embedded information   198
        Provenience and trade   198
        Production areas   200
        Manufacturing processes   202
        Refractory ceramics   205
Concluding Comment   206

8   Biological Molecules and Macromolecules:
    Protected Niches   207

    Brief Overview of Different Biomolecules of Interest in
            Biomolecular Archaeology   208
        DNA   209
        Proteins   210
        Polysaccharides   210
        Lipids   211
    Historical Perspective   211
    Protected Niche 1: Intracrystalline Macromolecules   212
        Embedded information   214
            Amino acid racemization dating   214
            Paleoenvironmental reconstruction   214
            Radiocarbon dating   215
    Protected Niche 2: Macromolecules inside Intergrown
            Biogenic Crystals (Crystal Aggregates)   215
        Embedded information   217
            Paleodiet reconstruction   217
            Paleogenetic information   218
            Radiocarbon dating   218
    Protected Niche 3: Molecules Preserved in Ceramics   219
        Optimize environmental preservation conditions   220
        Optimize ceramic porosity   220
        Optimize ceramic material type   221
        Embedded information   222
            Vessel contents   222
            Radiocarbon dating   222
    The Enigmatic Preservation of Starch Grains   222
    Where Were There Once Large Concentrations of Organic
            Materials?   223
    Preserved Organic Molecules: Are They Really in Context
            and Not Intrusive?   225
    Possibility of Finding Other Protected Niches for Organic
            Molecules   225

9   Ethnoarchaeology of the Microscopic Record: Learning
    from the Present   227

    Microartifacts: The Ethnographic Evidence of Their
            Usefulness   228
    Controls   230
    Ethnoarchaeology of the Microscopic Record   231
        Inferences on the microscopic record of Aliabad based
            on macroscopic observations   232
        Features outside house complexes   232

Features inside house complexes   234
Inferences on the microscopic record of an Eskimo
    winter house based on macroscopic observations   236
Wood pile and the hearth   237
Dump of bone splinters   237
Areas of human waste disposal   237
Animal Dung: Merging of the Archaeozoological and
    Archaeobotanical Microscopic Records   237
Identifying and Characterizing Livestock Enclosures   239
Phytolith and Charcoal Microscopic Records in Sarakini,
    Northern Greece   240
  Phytoliths   240
  Charcoal   243
Activity Areas Using Phosphate Concentrations:
    Ethnoarchaeological Verification   244
Concluding Remarks   244

10 Absolute Dating: Assessing the Quality of a Date   245

Understanding a Date: The Communication Gap Problem   247
Solution to the Communication Gap Problem   248
Designing a Program for Dating a Site   249
  Calibration   249
  Context   250
    The macrocontext   250
    The microcontext   251
    Context for trapped charge dating   252
  Choice of sample type   254
  Number of samples to collect and analyze   255
  Prescreening for sample preservation and purity   256
    Bone collagen   256
    Charred organic material for radiocarbon dating   258
  Purifying the sample   258
    Charcoal purification   258
    Collagen purification   259
Analyzing the Results: A Team Effort   259
Radiocarbon Laboratory Measurements: Are There Biases?   259
Future Prospects   260

11 Reading the Microscopic Record On-Site   261

Benefits of an On-Site Interactive Laboratory   261
On-Site Laboratories for the Analysis of the Macroscopic
    Record   262
Choice of Instruments for On-Site Analysis of the
    Microscopic Record   263

Basic considerations   263
Choice of instruments   264
  Binocular microscope   264
  Petrographic microscope   264
  Wet-sieving apparatus for charred materials   264
  Fourier transform infrared spectroscopy   265
  X-ray fluorescence spectrometer   265
  Raman spectroscopy   266
  UV-visible spectrophotometer   266
  Mapping and three-dimensional reconstructions   267
  Photography   268
Operation of the Laboratory   268
Useful Work Program for the On-Site Interactive
       Laboratory   269
  First visit to the site   269
  Operation of the on-site laboratory during excavation
       seasons   270
  Identifying problems   270
  Solving an identified problem   270
  Controls   270
  Further analyses in the home laboratory, data
       analysis, and synthesis   271
Examples of Questions to Ask about the Microscopic
       Record of a Site   271
  What components are missing because they were not
       preserved or because they were not brought to the
       site?   271
  What fuel was commonly used at the site?   271
  Are there indications of pyrotechnological activities
       other than making fires?   272
  Where is the site on the rural-urban continuum?   273
On-Site Artifact Conservation   273
Future Trends   273

12 Infrared Spectroscopy in Archaeology   275

Sample Preparation   276
Points to Note   277
  Sampling   277
  Grinding   277
  Reproducibility   277
  Quantification   277
  Background subtraction   278
  Artifacts due to the quality of the KBr pellets   278
Interpretation of the Spectra: Some General Pointers   278

Mineral, macromolecule, or small organic molecules?   278

Mixtures of compounds   279

Shifting of peak maxima   279

Variations in peak widths   280

Sharp peak at 1,384 wavenumber   281

Infrared Microscopy   281

Available literature   281

Library of archaeologically relevant infrared spectra   281

Overviews   282

1. Polymorphs of calcium carbonate   282

2. Calcite disorder: Distinguishing between calcites formed by different processes   284

3. The apatite family: Hydroxylapatite, carbonate hydroxylapatite, and carbonate fluorapatite   286

4. Crystallinity of bone, dentin, and enamel: The splitting factor   289

5. Burned bones   292

6. Authigenic phosphate minerals   295

7. Silicon dioxide polymorphs: Quartz, flint (chert), silica (opal), and other polymorphs   297

8. Clays   300

9. Clay exposed to elevated temperatures   303

10. Calcium oxalates   306

11. Collagen: State of preservation   307

12. Wood and olive pit preservation   309

13. Natural organic materials: Resin, copal, amber, gum, bitumen, and humic and fulvic acids   312

14. Presence of soluble salts in sediment samples   315

Appendix A: Identifying Minerals Using Microchemical Analysis   317

Appendix B: Identifying Minerals and Compounds Using Infrared Spectra: Table of Standard Minerals and Compounds for Which Infrared Spectra Are Available   320

References   327

Index   373

Color plates follow page 174.

Preface

The familiar archaeological record is the record that we see with the naked eye. The record that we do not see with the naked eye is as large and as fascinating as the visual macroscopic record. Instruments are needed, however, to reveal this microscopic record. The aim of this book is to provide archaeologists interested in exploring both the macroscopic and microscopic records with broad-ranging and basic conceptual information on the types of information that may be embedded in the microscopic records of their sites, the conditions under which this information can be extracted, and the means for assessing the reliability of this information. This is not a book about methods, nor a book about materials chemistry (although both are important); rather, it is a book about archaeology beyond the visual record. I have therefore called this book *Microarchaeology*.

For many years now, the trend in archaeology, and especially in prehistory, has been to excavate less but to extract more information from the archaeological record. This not only involves making better use of remote sensing and global positioning systems and better documentation of the macroscopic record, it also involves extracting as much information as possible from the microscopic record. It is hoped that this book will facilitate access to the microscopic record for all interested archaeologists and enable the specialists and archaeological scientists to obtain a broader view of the potential of the microscopic record. The book does not simplify the problems involved, but an attempt is made to explain the issues as well as possible. In fact, while writing the book, I had in mind as a reader an advanced undergraduate or graduate student studying both natural sciences and archaeology. I hope that this book will encourage many more students to choose this field of research. I can promise entry into a wonderfully interesting world.

If this book has a special tone, then it can probably be attributed to the unique training that I received from my former PhD supervisor, who also became a colleague, collaborator, and close friend: the late Professor Heinz A. Lowenstam. He taught me how to enjoy revealing nature's secrets and introduced me into the rich world of mineral formation by organisms, or *biomineralization*. I dedicate this book to the memory of Heinz Lowenstam.

I would like, first and foremost, to acknowledge my wife, Nomi Weiner, who understands and enthusiastically supports all my efforts to explore my two professional worlds: archaeology and biomineralization. I would also like to acknowledge the lifelong support that my late father, Motty Weiner, gave me in pursuing my scientific career as well as the support I have received from my children Danya, Noa, and Allon.

I was introduced into the world of archaeology by Ofer Bar-Yosef, who spent a year with me at the Weizmann Institute of Science in the late 1980s. Together with our colleague Paul Goldberg, we have worked together ever since. I owe much to both of them as well as to all the colleagues with whom I worked in the Kebara and Hayonim Caves in Israel. I am also particularly thankful to Elisabetta Boaretto and Ruth Shahack-Gross, two of my colleagues at the Kimmel Center for Archaeological Science at the Weizmann Institute. Over more than a decade of collaboration, we have established the framework for educating a new generation of archaeologists trained in both the natural sciences and archaeology. These students are also trained to work in the field and in the laboratory. Much of this book reflects the spirit of the Kimmel Center for Archaeological Science. I am also grateful to all the students and postdocs who have and are working at the Center. Finally, I want to acknowledge the support of Helen Kimmel and the late Martin Kimmel for recognizing that archaeology and archaeological science do contribute significantly to our self-concepts and that pursuing these endeavors is important. The Kimmel Center for Archaeological Science is a tribute to their vision.

I would like to thank Haya Avital for preparing all the figures. I would also like to thank the following colleagues for reading various chapters: Lia Addadi, Elisabetta Boaretto, Adi Eliyahu, Panagiotis Karkanas, Dvory Namdar, Lior Regev, Ruth Shahack-Gross, Clive Trueman, and Georgia Tsartsidou.

Stephen Weiner
Weizmann Institute of Science
Rehovot, Israel
May 2009

1

Archaeology, Archaeological Science, and Microarchaeology

The archaeological record is mainly composed of materials related to past human behavior. Some of these are visible to the naked eye – the so-called macroscopic record – and some require instruments, such as microscopes or spectrometers, to be seen and characterized. This is the so-called microscopic record, and the study of this record is referred to here as *microarchaeology*.

The macroscopic record is composed of strata, buildings, graves, floors, and so on, as well as artifacts such as pottery, bones, stone, and metal tools. The microscopic record is composed of the materials of which the macroscopic artifacts are made, as well as the sedimentary matrix in which the artifacts are buried. Thus the investigation of the archaeological record as a whole involves the integration of both the macroscopic and microscopic records. It incorporates activities that span the humanities, social sciences, and natural sciences, with the former two disciplines being focused mainly on the macroscopic record and the latter discipline being focused mainly on the microscopic record. Herein lies a problem: the different parts of the archaeological record are studied by investigators with diverse backgrounds and approaches. Often lacking is an integration of these different worlds.

In this book, the focus is on the archaeological information that can be extracted from the microscopic record and, in particular, from the materials commonly found in most archaeological sites such as ceramics, bones, rocks, ash, and sediments. The process starts in the field, where problems are identified, preliminary analyses are carried out, and samples are collected for further analysis. It then proceeds to the laboratory and finally returns to the field to better understand the results in terms of their archaeological contexts. Even though the idea is simple and certainly not new, in practice, it is by no means straightforward to integrate information from different subdisciplines, collected by different investigators using different methods. One requirement is that the archaeological contexts under study be well defined and understood by all involved. Another essential requirement is that the quality of all forms of data be evaluated so that the weight given to high-quality data is much more than the weight given to low-quality data. When independent lines of evidence point to the same conclusions, then the real benefit of integrating all the data is obtained, and the conclusions reached are well grounded. These concepts are not unique to archaeology, but are common to all scientific approaches to solving problems.

The term *scientific* conjures up different concepts in different archaeologists' minds, as it does in different scientists' minds. A definition of *science* I like is from a plaque I photographed in a small museum in Udaipur, India (Figure 1.1). The reference to "verified terms" encapsulates the essence of science, and the "bubbling with excitement" characterizes the way it should be. Of course, there are more formal definitions, such as the following: "the ultimate goal of any science is construction of an axiomatized theory such that observed regularities can be derived from a few basic laws as premises" (Watson et al., 1984, p. 14). It helps, however, to keep things simple. Following ideas popularized by Richard Feynman (1998), an appropriate definition of science in the context of archaeology is the extent to which the uncertainty of a given observation can be assessed. Reading texts can be scientific if the information is evaluated, based, for example, on assessing the reliability of the sources and obtaining independent lines of information. Field archaeology is scientific if the observations are recorded in a manner such that the site structure can be later reconstructed, and for this to occur, the stratigraphy has to be well substantiated based on different lines of evidence, and so on. A radiocarbon date is the product of a scientific process not only if the accuracy and precision of the date are reported, but also if the uncertainty involved in determining the context from which the sample was taken and an assessment of the sample purity are reported prior to analysis (Chapter 10).

Science does not, of course, confine itself to the dry facts, and the word *truth* is never used in so-called polite scientific circles as this implies that there is no uncertainty, and such a condition never exists. Almost every scientific article has a results section, in which the new data are presented together with an assessment of the degree of uncertainty, and if this also includes numbers, the measurement error (uncertainty) is reported. The results section is followed by a discussion section, in which the implications of the data are interpreted and thoughts about the broader implications are presented. The same format should be appropriate for most archaeological studies and is often used. The main difference I discern between many archaeological studies and studies in other fields of the natural sciences relates to the manner in which the uncertainty of the observations is addressed (or ignored) and the extent to which the archaeological community is willing to, or expects authors to, speculate – often more than in most natural sciences.

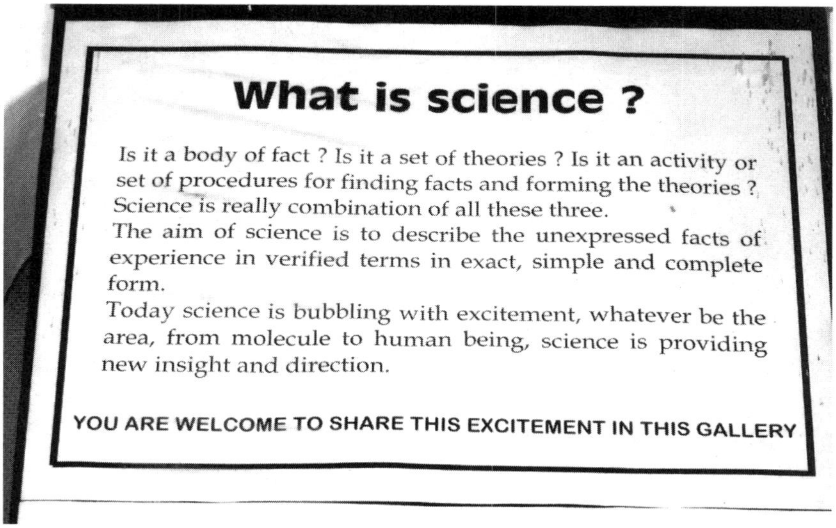

What is science ?

Is it a body of fact ? Is it a set of theories ? Is it an activity or set of procedures for finding facts and forming the theories ? Science is really combination of all these three.

The aim of science is to describe the unexpressed facts of experience in verified terms in exact, simple and complete form.

Today science is bubbling with excitement, whatever be the area, from molecule to human being, science is providing new insight and direction.

YOU ARE WELCOME TO SHARE THIS EXCITEMENT IN THIS GALLERY

Figure 1.1
A photograph of a plaque in a two-room science museum in Udaipur, Rajasthan, India.

This difference falls into the realm of tradition and is not inherent to the subject itself, and probably also reflects the fact that almost all archaeologists are trained in the humanities or social sciences, and not the natural sciences.

The practice of archaeology is indeed scientific. Archaeological studies in which the observations are carefully made and supported in different ways, and are then interpreted in terms of other well-established observations that are consistent with or not consistent with the new observations, are good science. Many of the ideas expressed in this chapter are also described by Weiner (2008).

ARCHAEOLOGY IS A DIFFICULT SCIENCE

E. O. Wilson (1998), in his book titled *Consilience*, wrote, "Everyone knows that the social sciences are hypercomplex. They are inherently far more difficult than physics and chemistry, and as a result they, not physics and chemistry, should be called the hard sciences. They just seem easier because we can talk with other human beings but not with photons, gluons, and sulfide radicals" (p. 183). Archaeology is even more difficult than the social sciences as humans from the past can only "speak" through the material remains that are excavated.

The recognition that, among all the historic natural sciences, archaeology is probably the most difficult field is a first essential step in figuring out how best to approach and at least partially solve some of these very challenging problems. Furthermore, recognizing the difficulty brings with it a lowering of expectations as to what problems can be solved at a given time, and an appreciation for archaeological studies that succeed in firmly putting well-substantiated observations into the pool of common knowledge. This lowering of expectations might well make archaeology more boring as excessive speculation will be looked down upon, but on the other hand, it will encourage the best in archaeological research.

HISTORICAL PERSPECTIVE

In the book titled *A History of Archaeological Thought*, Trigger (1989) identifies the beginnings of scientific archaeology with the work of the Danish scholar Christian Jürgensen Thomsen (1788–1865). Thomsen knew that in general, artifacts of stone were produced before those of bronze, and bronze artifacts were produced before iron artifacts. The problem that Thomsen solved was finding a systematic way to identify stone artifacts produced in the Bronze Age, or bronze artifacts produced in the Iron Age, and so on. He did this by paying attention not only to the material of which the artifact was made, but also to shapes and decorations (seriation), and he paid particular attention to assemblages of artifacts excavated in closed contexts. In this way, he could arrange the artifacts into chronological sequences. The method is, of course, predictive and can be reproduced by anyone using the same criteria on different materials – all characteristics of a sound scientific approach.

Another Dane who contributed most significantly to the beginnings of archaeology was Jens J. A. Worsaae (1821–1885). He followed in the footsteps of Thomsen (they both worked in what is now the National Museum of Denmark in Copenhagen) and tested Thomsen's approach by associating the stratigraphy of archaeological sites to the assemblages found in different layers. Trigger (1989) also notes the complementary contribution of Scandinavian Sven Nilsson (1787–1883), who had studied under the famous French paleontologist Cuvier. He introduced the use of ethnographic specimens to shed light on the functional use of artifacts excavated from archaeological contexts.

The development of Scandinavian archaeology in the scientific tradition, according to Trigger, was not based on the model developed earlier by paleontologists and geologists for arranging fossils into a relative chronology, but rather, was inspired by social-evolutionary theories of the Enlightenment. Denmark was, in fact, one of the first countries to adopt these ideas, which were developed in France. The Scandinavian approach to archaeology spread to other small countries in Europe (Scotland and Switzerland, in particular) but did not immediately impact those studying the archaeological record in Britain and France, who, for the most part, adopted the paleontological approach to studying human fossils and associated artifacts. This approach is also, of course, based on the scientific method.

Thus the foundations of modern archaeology from the very beginning are well entrenched in the scientific method: the Scandinavian approach that developed out of the field of history, the French and British approaches that developed from the field of paleontology, and the use of ethnographic models that later came to be associated with the field of anthropology. The focus was, and still is, on understanding past cultures based on preserved material remains.

The chemical analysis of ancient artifacts started in the 18th century. Many famous chemists analyzed such artifacts. A fascinating description of these early studies is given in the first chapter of Pollard and Heron (2008). Many of the studies carried out in the 19th century also addressed archaeological problems such as provenience and dating. One of the first attempts to date artifacts was based on the fluoride contents of bones (Middleton, 1844). It was not uncommon to ask a chemist to analyze samples from an excavation to resolve a specific problem. This was done, for example, to determine whether certain black-colored samples from Zhoukoudian, China, were composed of charred material to better understand the use of fire (Black, 1931; Oakley, 1970). A better-known example is the work of the chemist Oakley, who, together with the anthropologist J. S. Weiner, exposed the Piltdown forgery based on chemical analyses of fossil bone (Weiner, 1955). For the first half of the 20th century, these studies appear to have made little impact on the overall nature of the research carried out in the field of archaeology.

This situation changed dramatically, however, with the development, by Libby et al. (1949), of the absolute dating technique using radiocarbon. This not only enabled an independent check of the relative chronologies that, to this day, serve as the foundation for much of archaeological research, but also provided the first absolute chronology. The importance of radiocarbon dating in archaeology is now hardly disputed, although the manner in which it is applied is often scientifically compromised (with dates that do not fit preconceived ideas finding their way into lists of unpublished data filed in drawers; Chapter 10). Since the advent of radiocarbon dating, a plethora of other analytical techniques, in addition to dating techniques, have been applied to solving archaeological problems. The result is that today, an excavation can be investigated based not only on what can be seen with the naked eye (the macroscopic record), but also using all the information that can be extracted using microscopes and various other analytical tools (the microscopic record). The integration of the macroarchaeological record with the microarchaeological record (microarchaeology) results in a better understanding of the entire archaeological record.

ARCHAEOLOGICAL SCIENCE

If all archaeology is inherently scientific, and has been since the early 19th century, then clearly, referring to a subfield of archaeology as "archaeological science" makes no sense. Even though conceptually, there is no such subfield, when archaeologists refer to "archaeological science" and/or "archaeometry," they do have something specific in mind. This something is encapsulated in the types of papers that are published in the two journals that bear these names. These papers, for the most part, involve analyses of materials from archaeological sites, with, of course, their archaeological contexts and the implications of the results for the broader picture – as in all scientific studies.

Irrespective of the illogicality of calling a subfield "archaeological science," even though the whole field is itself based on the scientific method, the facts on the ground are that with the majority of archaeologists being trained in the humanities, their access to the microscopic record is often not direct, but via a so-called archaeological scientist, and vice versa. This situation has been exasperated by the tendency of some archaeologists to emphasize aspects of archaeology that are more meaningful or significant, and do not, as Hodder (1999, p. 14) so aptly stated, say something about the past that is "true."

THE MICROSCOPIC RECORD

The archaeological record, even under fairly favorable conditions, preserves little of the complexity and diversity of a site during occupation (Chapter 3). Even robust architecture does not withstand the ravages of time well. Many materials, particularly of plant origin, are hardly ever preserved, and what is preserved is often altered to some extent. Reconstructing human behavior is thus a major challenge. This situation is often exacerbated by the manner in which excavations were, and often still are, carried out. Kathleen M. Kenyon (1960) pointed out, in the context of her archaeological projects in the Near East, that excavation has "big potential prizes – temples, palaces and royal archives – and also a large and cheap labour force available, and therefore minutiae of archaeological observation were ignored" (p. 14). In the almost 50 years since she published this statement, excavation practices have improved enormously, and so have the possibilities of learning more from the "minutiae" of the microscopic record.

The microscopic record has a huge amount of "space" below the submillimeter scale that is not visible to the naked eye. The physicist Richard Feynman gave a prophetic lecture in 1959, titled "There's Plenty of Room at the Bottom," in which he explained the implications of the fact that between the millimeter scale and the scale of atoms, there are seven orders of magnitude. The example he gave was that if you magnify the head of a pin 25,000 times, the area of the pin is so large that the entire *Encyclopedia Britannica* can be written on it. From the point of view of archaeology, this large "space" potentially contains much embedded information that can be used to better understand the record.

To better appreciate the size of the "space" available in the microscopic record, consider the following. If you stand in front of a section in an archaeological excavation and focus only on a mollusk shell easily visible to the naked eye, and you start zooming in on the shell structure

x1000   x7.5

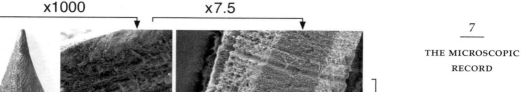

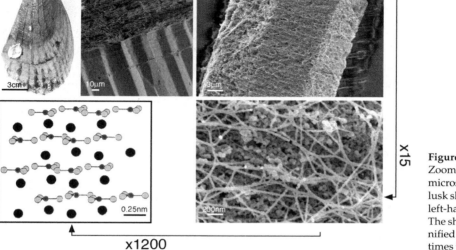

x15

x1200

Figure 1.2
Zooming in to the
microstructure of a mol-
lusk shell, starting in the
left-hand upper corner.
The shell has to be mag-
nified about 135 million
times to see the atoms.

(Figure 1.2), you will easily see, at a magnification of 1,000 times, the layered structure: for example, prisms on the outer side and pearly nacre on the inner side. At a magnification of around 7,500 times, you will see the surface structure of one prism. If you slightly etch the prism surface and examine it at a magnification of around 110,000 times, you will see that it is composed of protein spheres attached to chitin fibers. We would still need to zoom in another 1,200 times to see the atoms themselves. There are seven orders of magnitude in scale between the visible shell and the atoms. There really is a lot of room at the bottom (Feynman, 1998)!

What can be learned about an archaeological section by turning up the magnification? In the case of the mollusk shell, you can find out whether the original shell components are still preserved (at low magnifications). At higher magnifications, you learn that some of the organic macromolecules are occluded inside the mineral phase. These occluded molecules are known to be relatively well preserved (Collins et al., 1991), and together with the preserved mineral phase, they could therefore be used to study the paleoenvironment in which the mollusk lived, the temperature of the water, and the season of death (Chapter 8). Much of this work is done using stable isotopes, namely, analyses at atomic resolution (Chapter 2).

One of the main purposes of this book is to provide access to the microscopic world of the archaeological record and, by so doing, make it easier for the archaeologist to extract the embedded information and thus obtain a better understanding of the archaeological record under investigation.

TOOL KIT FOR DECIPHERING THE MICROSCOPIC ARCHAEOLOGICAL RECORD

An integral part of the training of an archaeologist is to acquire a set of skills that makes it possible to extract information about past human behavior from an excavation in an orderly and systematic manner. This requires excavation skills; the ability to define loci, strata, and so on; and the ability to identify the major classes of materials that are often encountered: pottery, bones, charcoal, and so on. The archaeologist is also trained to differentiate between records that are mixed and/or altered, as opposed to those that are in primary, so-called sealed contexts. In essence, archaeological training can be described as providing the student a "tool kit" for reliably extracting and interpreting information from the archaeological record. This training is, for the most part, confined to the macroscopic record. The training should apply just as much to the microscopic record; however, deciphering the microscopic record is complicated by the fact that instruments are needed to reveal it. The modes of operation of these instruments need to be understood, as do the results they provide. The results also need to be understood in terms of their strengths and weaknesses (uncertainty) and, of course, in relation to the whole archaeological record.

I therefore advocate that the tools that should be in the "tool kit" of modern archaeologists not be confined to those useful for deciphering only the macroscopic record, but also the microscopic record. It is hoped that this book will provide an accessible framework for archaeologists to learn more about the tools available for deciphering the microscopic record.

Kenyon (1960) referred to the "big potential prizes" of an archaeological excavation as temples, palaces, and royal archives. Archaeologists of the next generation may well include in their list of big potential prizes materials so well preserved that they contain, for example, archives rich in genetic material, or a material that can provide a radiocarbon or dendrochronological date with an error of less than ±20 years, or a sherd that can reveal the recipes of past cooks based on preserved molecules within its pores. To find these "molecular treasures," archaeologists will need good insight into both the macroscopic and microscopic records of the sites they investigate.

THE IMPORTANCE OF INTEGRATING MICROARCHAEOLOGY WITH MACROARCHAEOLOGY

Faced with the reality that archaeological problems are difficult to resolve with a reasonable degree of certainty, it is clear that it makes sense to exploit every possible means for solving these problems. This interdisciplinary approach to the archaeological record has been an integral part of modern archaeology from the 19th century. It, too, has its roots in Denmark, with the work of Worsaae (Trigger, 1989, p. 82), who used all the diverse materials available for interpreting the archaeological remains of shell middens close to the present Danish coastline. Worsaae headed a team that included a biologist and a geologist. They reconstructed the paleoenvironment, the season of occupation, the presence of domesticated dogs, and the distribution of hearths. They also conducted experiments by feeding bones to dogs to understand the preponderance of the midshafts of long bones (Trigger, 1989).

The inherent problem with integrating the macroscopic and microscopic records is that more often than not, the archaeologists studying the macroscopic record are not also involved in studying the microscopic record, and vice versa. There are two communities of archaeologists, which usually meet not at scientific meetings where results are discussed, but briefly in the field, where the so-called archaeological scientists visit for a few days to obtain samples. There is a widening communication gap, especially as the analytical techniques used by the archaeological scientists become more diverse and sophisticated, making it even more difficult for archaeologists trained in the humanities to critically evaluate the quality of the data provided and the degree of uncertainty of the conclusions. The archaeological scientists do not usually spend enough time at the excavation to really appreciate the subtle problems related to defining the uncertainty of context and the stratigraphic problems that are the basis for any interpretation of the data, whether they are from the macroscopic or the microscopic record.

The ideal solution to this problem

Ideally, the basic training of all archaeologists should include both natural sciences and archaeology so that the graduate of such a program is at home intellectually in both disciplines. These new-generation archaeologists, like many archaeologists today, can and should also have their own specialties such as lithics, ceramics, bones, micromorphology, and so on. The difference will be that they will be able to pursue the questions they ask seamlessly, from the macroscopic to the microscopic record and back, taking full advantage of their knowledge of the natural sciences and archaeology. Thus, for example, a specialist in ceramics may not only document the typology, ornamentation, and so on, but may also examine the ultrastructure of the ceramic using a scanning electron microscope and use X-ray diffraction to identify the possible presence of minerals formed at high temperatures to better understand production conditions. The latter studies will be based on an understanding of the kinetics and thermodynamics of phase transformations and other factors. An archaeozoologist may not only classify the bones, reconstruct the number of individuals represented, and so on, but may also analyze the bones to reconstruct migration pathways using strontium isotopes or reconstruct ancient diets using stable isotope analyses of collagen, if, indeed, the collagen is well preserved. The basis for these studies is an understanding of bone structure, mineral and bone organic matrix formation, and the stabilities of these materials over time.

The reality

The above scenario is indeed the ideal solution. Perhaps the more realistic solution is that this integrated training will allow all archaeologists to communicate at a meaningful level, irrespective of whether the data being analyzed are derived from the macroscopic or the microscopic records. It will allow some to work in both arenas. At the very least, it should allow all archaeologists to have the basic knowledge to know, for example, not only that a flint tool can be used for provenience studies or for determining whether the raw material was derived from the surface or below the ground, but also the principles of the application and, most important, the conditions necessary to evaluate the uncertainty of the data obtained. This involves a subtle understanding of preservation conditions, archaeological context, local geology, and so on. In other words, all archaeologists should be able to ask the right questions and should be able to understand and evaluate the uncertainty of the results. One of the major objectives of this book is to facilitate this process by making the information needed to access the microscopic archaeological record more accessible.

ON-SITE LABORATORY

The place where this integrative approach to archaeology begins is on-site, not only for understanding and documenting the macroscopic record, but also, at least in part, the microscopic record. The iterative process of asking a question, gathering data, and then, in light of the new data, reformulating the question is at the heart of the scientific method of excavation. This can be done most effectively when some analytical capability is available in the form of an on-site laboratory (Figure 1.3). For more details on the concept and practicalities of operating on-site laboratories, see Chapter 11.

THE CONCEPT OF THIS BOOK

The overall aim of this book is to provide both the conceptual framework and the knowledge necessary for extracting as much information out of the microscopic record as possible. This is achieved by the following:

1. Presented are many, if not most, of the types of information that can be extracted from the microscopic record (Chapter 2).
2. Also given is a review of the common materials found in excavation sites that potentially contain this embedded information, highlighting the potential for diagenesis to alter the signal. This includes geogenic minerals (Chapter 4), biogenic minerals (Chapters 5 and 6), and pyrogenic materials (Chapter 7).
3. Background information is provided to allow the archaeologist to assess whether material preservation conditions are such that the information of interest is likely to be preserved, and if so, how reliable the "signal" measured may be. This subject is addressed in general in Chapter 3, and more specifically, with respect to the preservation of biological molecules, in Chapter 8, and dating in Chapter 10.
4. Ethnoarchaeology is a valuable approach to better understanding the archaeological record and developing new analytical tools. The potential of the ethnoarchaeological approach for the microscopic record is discussed in Chapter 9.
5. The major benefits and practicalities involved in operating an on-site laboratory are discussed in Chapter 11.
6. I regard infrared spectroscopy as one of the most powerful analytical tools for investigating the microscopic record. Chapter 12 provides detailed information on how to use this tool in archaeology.

Many of the chapters conclude with a section listing the possible types of embedded information that can be extracted from the microscopic record. It is hoped that the book will provide archaeologists interested in exploring the microscopic record with useful information and insights. The book may also enable students well versed in archaeology and the natural sciences to easily enter into the fascinating world of microarchaeology.

Figure 1.3
On-site field laboratory in operation. *Left*, The field laboratory at Tell es-Safi, Israel. The transportable Fourier transform infrared spectrometer is visible. *Right*, The field laboratory at Tel Dor, Israel. A portable X-ray fluorescence spectrometer is in the foreground, and a Fourier transform infrared spectrometer is in the background. Behind the table is a small petrographic microscope.

CONCLUSIONS

Archaeology involves solving difficult problems. Providing answers with the smallest degree of uncertainty requires the exploitation of all possible sources of information, both from the macroscopic and the microscopic records. For this to occur, archaeologists need to be familiar with both natural sciences and archaeology, and then to use this knowledge in an integrated manner to solve these challenging problems. It is hoped that this book will contribute to achieving these goals.

2

Information Embedded in the Microscopic Record

The macroscopic record (what you see with the naked eye) and the microscopic record (what you "see" with the aid of technology) together constitute the archaeological record. All the information that we can learn about past human behavior is embedded in this combined record. The first requirement for exploiting the microscopic record is to have an overview of the types of information that can be obtained from the record, and to understand the basic principles on which this information is based; the subject of this chapter.

This chapter provides brief overviews of many, but not all, of the different categories of information that are embedded in the microscopic record. The chapters following this chapter provide information on various common materials that are present in archaeological sites, underlying mechanistic processes that influence the preservation of these materials, and at the end of each chapter or subsection, more information is given on the embedded information that can be extracted from these materials. Emphasis is placed on the concepts rather than the methods. For a review of the most common methods used to extract information from the microscopic record and the principles on which these methods are based, see chapter 2 of the work by Pollard and Heron (2008).

It is noteworthy that many of the methods used to extract information from the microscopic record were not developed by archaeologists. They were developed mainly by chemists, geochemists, botanists, and others for their own purposes and were later adapted and applied to archaeological problems. There is still much potential for archaeologists, especially those trained in the natural sciences, to develop new methods to probe the microscopic record. These methods can be tailored to the needs of archaeology. For more information on many of the topics covered in this chapter, refer to the *Handbook of Archaeological Sciences* (Brothwell and Pollard, 2001). This is an excellent source of information. For easy reference, Table 2.1 lists the main types of information embedded in the microscopic archaeological record.

Table 2.1. Overview of the main categories of information embedded in the microscopic archaeological record (in alphabetical order).

Category	Method	Material	Embedded information	Chapter
Archaeobotany	Optical and electron microscopy	Charred and mineralized remains (phytoliths)	Plant types and parts that were brought to the site for consumption, construction, medicinal purposes, etc.	6, 7
Dating	Radiocarbon	Bone collagen, wood, charred materials	Absolute date (±0.3% at best) up to about 10,000 years BP. Generally around ±50–100 years after calibration. Maximum limit: around 50,000 years BP.	5, 7, 8, 10
	Uranium series dating	Speleothems, travertine	Absolute date (±10%) from hundreds to about 500,000 years	
	Dendrochronology	Charred or uncharred wood with rings	Generally less than ±50 years, and in some cases around 10 years	
	Thermoluminescence	Burned flint tools, ceramics	Absolute date (±10%–15%) up to about 1 million years	7
	Electron spin resonance	Tooth enamel	Absolute date (±10%–20%) up to about 1 million years	5
	Optical stimulated luminescence	Sediment grains, building stones	Absolute date (±10%–15%) from hundreds to around 200,000 years	4
	Fluoride uptake	Bone	Mainly relative ages	5
	Obsidian hydration dating	Obsidian	Absolute date (±10%–15%) up to about 100,000 years BP	
	Amino acid racemization	Eggshells and land snail shells	Absolute date (±10%–15%) up to about 1 million years BP	6
	Archaeomagnetism	Kiln wall sediments, lava flows	Absolute date up to thousands to millions of years	
Life history reconstruction	Incremental growth lines	Teeth, cementum, otoliths	Developmental stages, age at death, stress events	5, 6
Paleodiet reconstruction	Stable carbon and nitrogen isotopes	Bone collagen and mineral	Relative proportions of basic food types	5, 8

Category	Method	Material	Embedded information	Chapter
	Strontium concentrations	Bone mineral	Differentiates trophic levels, e.g., proportion of meat in a diet	5
	Stable small molecule assemblages ("residues")	Ceramics	Pottery use, diet reconstruction, trade	7, 8
Paleoenvironmental reconstruction	Stable oxygen isotopes, trace and rare earth element concentrations	Mollusk shells, otoliths, diatoms, bone mineral	Regional and local environment reconstruction, paleoclimate, seasonal variations	5, 6
Paleogenetics	DNA sequences, protein sequences	Bone	Genetic affinities of humans and other animals	5, 8
Paleomigration	Strontium isotopes, oxygen isotopes	Bone and enamel minerals	Movement of humans during their lifetimes	5
Pottery contents	Stable small molecule assemblages ("residues")	Ceramics	Contents of organic matter in ceramic vessels, diet, trading	7, 8
Provenience and procurement strategies	Petrography, trace element analyses, cosmogenic isotopes	Ceramics, flint, obsidian, marble	Trade routes, human interactions, technological capabilities	4, 7
Season of occupation	Rhythmic growth deposits	Mollusk shells, cementum, otoliths	Sedentary vs. migratory human behavior	6
Site formation processes	Micromorphology, sedimentological methods	Sediments	Identifying the biases and completeness of the record	3
Site spatial organization	Phosphate and lipid concentrations	Sediments	Areas where organic matter accumulated, was stored, or was used	4, 8
	Phytolith concentrations and types	Phytoliths, sediments	Activity areas, plant use, use of domestic animals	4, 6
	Spherulites	Sediments	Herbivore dung accumulations, fish processing	3
	Microartifacts	Flint, bone, and other artifact microfragments	Activity areas	
Weaning age	Stable nitrogen isotopes	Bone collagen	Reduction and cessation of breast milk in a baby's diet	5, 8

Note: The last column lists the chapters in which more information can be found.

The following are short overviews of the main categories of information embedded in the microscopic record. Note that there are, in addition, a variety of techniques used that are relevant to archaeology but are not usually based on the analyses of materials from archaeological sites. These are not included in this chapter. The references given in these overviews tend to be from more general sources. The chapters in this book where more detailed information is available are noted in Table 2.1.

ARCHAEOBOTANICAL RECORD

Plant remains are almost totally absent in the macroscopic archaeological record, even though they are a major component of almost every ethnographic setting. Fortunately, the microscopic record does contain plant remains. These plant remains are among the most valuable components of the microscopic record.

The major components of the microscopic archaeobotanical record are charred plant materials, pollen grains, and mineralized siliceous bodies (phytoliths) produced by many plants (Figures 2.1c and 2.1d; Piperno, 2006). The only common plant remains usually seen with the naked eye in an archaeological site are large fragments of wood charcoal, charred pits (Figures 2.1a and 2.1b), and other relatively large charred seeds (Jones and Colledge, 2001). Furthermore, the remains of macroscopic charred wood also need to be studied with microscopes to reveal their tissue structures and, from this, the taxonomic identity of the species of tree from which the wood was derived (Jones and Colledge, 2001; Lev-Yadun, 2007; Weiss and Kislev, 2007). Thus the microscopic record is the major source of information on the archaeobotanical record.

The archaeobotanical record of an archaeological site includes the remains of plants eaten by humans, plants brought to the site as fodder for animals, plants used for various constructional and other functional purposes, and plants that naturally grew at the site. One objective of an archaeobotanical study is to identify the plant taxa that were used by the site occupants. This, in turn, provides information on diet, subsistence strategies, medicines, the territorial range covered by the site occupants, the plants that domestic animals ate, and much more. The charred organic remains (mainly seeds, fruits, wood, and a form of soft tissue called *parenchyma*, common in roots; Jones and Colledge, 2001) are particularly valuable for this purpose as detailed examinations of the preserved structures using optical and/or electron microscopes enable taxonomic identification, often down to the species level. Charring effectively prevents microbial breakdown of the plant material, but charred materials are still susceptible to chemical breakdown due mainly to oxidation (Cohen-Ofri et al., 2006). One problem is that the circumstances under which a plant becomes charred, although not well understood,

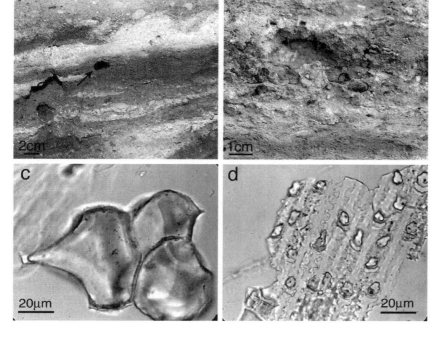

Figure 2.1
Common preserved
forms of plant remains in
the archaeological record:
a, wood charcoal (arrow)
embedded in a hearth
(Kebara Cave, Israel);
b, charred olive pits in an
ash layer (Tel Dor, Israel);
c, *d*, siliceous phytoliths.

can hardly be expected to be such that the charred remains are representative of the plants that were used on-site. For more information, see Chapter 7.

A major source of botanical information is the phytolith record (Piperno, 2006). As the phytoliths are mainly composed of mineral (silica) and are robust, they have a greater chance of being preserved as compared to the charred remains. The phytolith record should therefore be more representative of the plants brought to the site than the record of charred remains. One problem with phytolith analyses is that not all plants produce phytoliths, and hence the phytolith record is biased toward those that do, and especially toward those that produce many phytoliths such as the grasses. Another problem is that phytolith morphologies often cannot provide taxonomic information down to the genus or species level. Phytolith morphologies do, however, provide information on whether the phytoliths were derived from wood/bark, grasses (wild or domesticated), flowering parts (inflorescence), leaves, hairs, and so on (Albert et al., 2003b). This is certainly useful information for archaeology. Phytoliths that were derived from burned plant material used mainly for fuel can be distinguished from those derived from plant material that degraded at ambient temperatures (Elbaum et al., 2003). For more information, see Chapter 6.

Under certain unusual environmental conditions, the original organic material can escape microbial degradation and be preserved. Where this happens, the information obtained on the archaeobotanical record is much more complete. In very dry areas, desiccated macroscopic and microscopic plant remains are preserved. The almost complete absence of liquid water restricts the microbial activity. Another environment that restricts much of the microbial activity is one in which oxygen is absent. Under these conditions, relatively stable molecules can survive such as the outer exine layer of pollen (Stanley and Linskens, 1974) and the lignin of wood. In such locations, pollen can constitute a major source of information on the archaeobotanical record (Jansonius and McGregor, 1996; Kühl and Litt, 2003). Pollen is produced by plants in huge amounts, and individual pollen particles often have morphologies that are characteristic of the plant that produced them. They are also small and light enough to be transported large distances by the wind. They are usually not an integral part of the record of an archaeological site, but where preserved, they often provide invaluable information on the regional vegetation. Finally, many plants store starch in the form of tightly packed granules. For reasons that are not clear, these often survive in environments where the only other plant remains are charred or mineralized. They, too, have characteristic morphologies that enable taxonomic identification (Piperno, 2006).

General references. Jones and Colledge (2001); Zohary and Hopf (2001); Piperno (2006); Weiss and Kislev (2007)

DATING

In a historical science like archaeology, the dating of events being investigated is of paramount importance. Relative dating using comparative morphologies and typologies of archaeological artifacts, such as ceramic vessels, and metal and stone tools, was developed in the early 19th century. It was only in the 1940s, with the development of the radiocarbon dating technique by Libby and colleagues (1949), that it became possible to systematically relate the relative chronological framework to an absolute chronological framework. The effective range for radiocarbon dating is currently around 50,000 years. For periods beyond this range, the more commonly used absolute dating techniques are all based on measurements of trapped charges in crystals. These methods use thermoluminescence (TL), electron spin resonance (ESR), and optical stimulated luminescence (OSL) to measure the various trapped charges. There are, in addition, other dating techniques, which are often used under special circumstances.

Perspective on techniques used for dating materials from archaeological sites

In terms of broad applicability, as well as accuracy and precision, radiocarbon dating is by far the best dating technique available to archaeologists. Radiocarbon dating is based on radioactive decay, which is not influenced by chemical or environmental conditions. Dendro-chronological dating, using pieces of wood with preserved growth rings, is even more accurate and precise than radiocarbon. The obvious limitation is the availability of suitable samples. Uranium series decay is also based on radioactive decay and indeed provides accurate and precise measurements over a much larger time range than radiocarbon. Its major limitation is that for archaeological purposes; it can currently only be reliably used on speleothems and travertine.

The trapped charge dating techniques (TL, ESR, and OSL) are based on complicated reactions involving the interactivity of radiation with solid materials and also require a so-called zeroing event to reset the reaction process. Thus the precision is relatively poor compared to radiocarbon dating, but the effective dating ranges are much larger, and many of the materials used are commonly found in archaeological sites.

Several archaeologically relevant dating techniques are based on chemical reactions. These include obsidian hydration, amino acid racemization, and fluoride uptake into bones. These techniques suffer from being influenced not only by the amount of time elapsed, but also by other environmental and structural parameters. In each case, however, there are special circumstances in which they can be reliably applied, and even though they may not be the first choice, they should not be automatically rejected.

Finally, archaeomagnetism is a technique that can be very effective, provided that the archaeological site under investigation is located in a region where the local variations in the geomagnetic field have been calibrated as a function of time.

For a complete review of almost all dating techniques applicable to archaeology, see Aitken (1990). The following sections contain brief overviews of many of the dating methods used in archaeology. Chapter 10 focuses on radiocarbon and trapped charge dating methods, and especially on approaches to dating using these methods that can improve the impact of the dates obtained for better understanding the archaeological record.

Radiocarbon dating

The basis for the method is that the radioactive isotope of carbon (^{14}C) decays at a constant rate such that after $5{,}730 \pm 40$ years, half of the original concentration remains. Thus, if the original concentration is known, then a measurement of the ^{14}C in the object to be dated provides the age of the object. The material to be dated has to not only contain carbon, but also only carbon that was derived from carbon dioxide in the atmosphere and was incorporated into the material at the time it was formed. Thus all organic matter, charred or uncharred, can

Figure 2.2
Example of a ^{14}C analysis before calibration
(peak on vertical, y-axis)
and after calibration
(black-filled peaks, x-
axis) using the OxCal
program (Bronk Ramsey,
2003). The double set
of curves (showing the
margin of error) is the calibration curve. The peak
on the Y-axis is a typical
result obtained with a
characteristic precision
of ±30 years. When this
peak is projected onto
the calibration curve and
all the errors are taken
into account, the result-
ing calibrated date is
shown in black. The cal-
ibration curve is based
on data from Reimer
et al. (2004b) and the
calculation using Bronk
Ramsey (1995) and Bronk
Ramsey (2001). (*See color
insert following page 174
for this image in color.*)

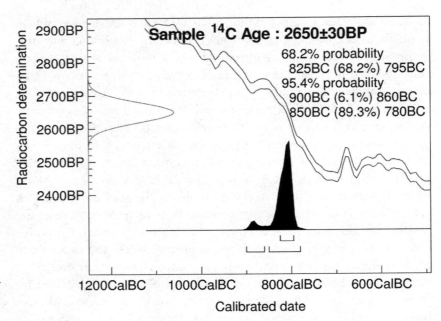

be dated because the carbon is incorporated from the atmosphere via the photosynthetic pathway, and even if the original plant material is eaten by another animal, its ^{14}C content is transferred into the organic material of the animal that ate it. Minerals that contain carbon, such as calcium carbonate or carbonate hydroxylapatite in bone, can also be dated, pro-vided that they incorporated only atmospheric carbon dioxide during their formation and did not exchange any of the carbon after burial. This requirement is usually not fulfilled and carbon containing minerals are therefore rarely dated.

Another precondition for dating using ^{14}C is that the original con-centration of the ^{14}C pool be known. In general, this is the concentration of ^{14}C in the carbon dioxide of the atmosphere. As a first approxima-tion, the present-day concentration can be used (as Libby did). Past ^{14}C concentrations in the atmosphere have varied, however. Over the last 30 years or so, a huge effort has been made to measure these variations, and the result is that today, dates obtained can be accurately corrected for atmospheric fluctuations back to 28,000 years, and with less accu-racy and precision, back to almost 50,000 years (Hughen et al., 2004). Figure 2.2 shows an example of a ^{14}C analysis after calibration. The ability to calibrate radiocarbon concentration measurements with such high accuracy and precision is an incredible achievement. The calibra-tion makes it possible to obtain dates for the last 10,000 years or so with a precision of ±0.2%. For the last 10,000 years, this translates into an error of a few tens of years, depending on the number of repeat analyses performed and, most important, on whether the material being dated formed within a few years (so-called short-lived materials). A lump of wood charcoal is often not a good sample for dating in this respect as it may have formed over tens of years and might be derived from an inner part of the tree that formed tens or even hundreds of years before the sample was burned and incorporated into the archaeological record. The date obtained is the time elapsed since the tree formed the wood and not when the wood was charred (Schiffer, 1986).

General references. Aitken (1990); Hughen et al. (2004); Boaretto et al. (2008, 2009a)

Uranium series dating

Uranium, like radiocarbon, is a radioactive chemical element and therefore decays over time. In this decay process, one of the isotopes formed is thorium-230 (^{230}Th). Thorium is relatively insoluble compared to uranium. It, too, is radioactive and has a half-life of 75,400 years. The mechanism for dating is based on the different solubilities of uranium and thorium. Being relatively soluble, uranium is initially incorporated into the sample to be dated when it is formed. Thorium then "grows" into the sample with time. Thus the ratio of uranium to thorium is a direct measurement of the time elapsed since the sample formed. This ratio can be measured accurately with a mass spectrometer, and errors as small as ±1% can be obtained. The effective dating range with this error is between 1,000 and 100,000 years, and if a larger error is acceptable, this can extend to 500,000 years (Aitken, 1990). It is thus an excellent dating method.

The applications in archaeology are, however, limited by the fact that the only materials that can be reliably dated are speleothems and other calcitic deposits that form in caves as well as travertines that form around springs. Much effort has been expended to date bones and teeth using the uranium series, but presumably, because of the disorder in their carbonate hydroxylapatite crystals (Chapters 4 and 5), they do not generally behave as "closed" systems (Pike et al., 2002).

General reference. Schwarcz (1980)

Dendrochronology

Many trees that live in regions where the seasons are well differentiated do not grow continuously, but rather, produce annual rings. The rings vary in thickness according to regional climatic conditions. Thus a careful analysis of the thickness variations of a set of rings from the original or charred wood is often unique. Dendrochronologists have taken advantage of this to obtain absolute dates of pieces of wood by comparing the tree ring signature of the sample to be dated to a master curve (Douglass, 1921, 1941). If the comparison does not produce a unique solution, then the analysis can be aided by radiocarbon-dating several of the rings and then searching for the match in a better defined region of the master curve. If a good match is found, this type of dating can be even more precise than radiocarbon dating. In fact, if the piece of wood being dated still has the outer bark, and hence the last formed ring is still preserved, then the dating can be as precise and accurate as one year. The master curve of overlapping tree ring records extends back more than 11,000 years (Stuiver et al., 1986).

In practice, applying dendrochronological dating to material from archaeological sites is not easy. Trees do not produce rings in the tropics. Thus the technique applies mainly to temperate climate regions. The first requirement is that a master curve for the regional area exists, and these to date exist mainly from Europe, North America, and a few other regions such as New Zealand (Norton and Ogden, 1987). Not all tree species are sensitive to environmental changes, and those that are sometimes produce false rings or, in some years, do not produce a growth ring at all. This, too, has to be factored in. Fossil wood samples with at least 80 rings are required if a reliable match to the master curve is to be obtained (Aitken, 1990).

General references. Aitken (1990); Baillie (1995); Nash (1999)

Trapped charge dating: Thermoluminescence (TL), optical stimulated luminescence (OSL), and electron spin resonance (ESR)

These dating methods are all based on essentially the same mechanism: the accumulation of various types of trapped charges inside the crystal lattice of minerals due to the effect of radiation impinging on the mineral (Grün, 2001). The age is obtained by determining the amount of radiation per unit time (dose) that the sample was exposed to radiation. The key requirement is that all the original trapped charges were somehow removed at the time of burial. In the case of TL and OSL dating, the amount of trapped charge is based on the quantity of light emitted when the sample is heated or exposed to light, respectively, whereas in the case of ESR dating, the trapped charge is measured directly. The sources of radiation that produce the charge are mainly from uranium and thorium in the sample itself, and from uranium, thorium, and the radioactive isotope of potassium in the surrounding sediments. To obtain a date, the concentrations of these elements have to be measured in the sample and the surrounding sediments. Thus the determination of a date is dependent on a number of different analyses, each with its associated error. Furthermore, it is assumed that the radiation concentrations have not changed over time – an assumption that, due to diagenesis in the sediments, is not always valid (Mercier et al., 1995). The result is that the precision of these dating methods is around ±10% at best.

The materials that are usually dated by thermoluminesence are flint tools that were heated by humans for one reason or another. The heating event eliminates all the previous traps, and the dating is only based on traps that accumulated since the heating event. The material that provides the most reliable dates using ESR is tooth enamel because the crystals are large and relatively stable. Modern enamel does not contain uranium. The uranium is incorporated after burial, and thus the date reflects the time elapsed since burial and is dependent on the manner in which the uranium enters into the enamel crystals. For OSL, the most common materials measured are grains of quartz and/or feldspar that, prior to burial, were exposed to sunlight. The exposure to sunlight removed the previous trapped charges, which are sensitive to exposure to light. OSL can be used for dating certain sediments and for dating stones in buildings (Liritzis, 1994). For more information on trapped charge dating, see Chapter 10.

General references. Valladas et al. (1988); Aitken (1990)

Dating by fluoride uptake

The carbonate hydroxylapatite mineral in modern bone is relatively unstable compared to synthetic or geologically formed carbonate hydroxylapatite (Chapter 3). One of the ways in which modern bone mineral becomes more stable is by taking up fluoride ions from its surroundings. These fluoride ions replace the hydroxyl ions, and the resulting mineral, called carbonate fluorapatite or francolite, is more stable than the carbonate hydroxylapatite itself. This process thus continues for long periods of time, provided that fluoride is present in the groundwater.

The reaction occurs on the bone surface and is thus governed by diffusion laws. The reaction is also probably influenced by other diagenetic processes that bone mineral undergoes with time (Chapter 5), and fluoride uptake is thus far from being only dependent on time elapsed. Even though fluoride dating of bone is perhaps the oldest application of chemical analyses in the field of archaeology (and paleontology; Middleton, 1844), it is rarely used today, except for relative dating (Schurr and Gregory, 2002). Perhaps the best known application of this method was the use of fluoride in bone to prove the Piltdown forgery (Oakley, 1948; Weiner, 1955).

Obsidian hydration dating

Freshly cleaved obsidian exposes surfaces that are not stable under ambient temperature conditions. The surface reacts with water in the environment to produce a hydration layer with a thickness in the range of micrometers. This reaction is controlled by diffusion, and its rate can be theoretically and empirically modeled (by comparison to other associated materials dated by radiocarbon or other direct methods; Friedman and Trembour, 1983). The relation between hydration layer thickness and diffusion rate is the basis for determining the time elapsed since the obsidian artifact was buried and hence exposed to water. This relation was first observed by Friedman and Smith (1960). The effective dating range is from a few hundred to a few million years (Friedman and Trembour, 1983).

Perhaps the main advantage of obsidian dating is that it is simple and inexpensive to prepare and measure samples. The measurements are made on thin sections using an optical microscope. Thus many measurements can be made. The hydration layer thickness is influenced by the local temperature fluctuation range, the humidity in the sediments, the specific type of obsidian being dated, and other less important factors (Hull, 2001; Rogers, 2008). In practice, this means that the method can be most effectively applied in regions where a large bank of calibrated data on diffusion rates already exists, such as in North America and Central America, unless, of course, an effort is made to produce a new database from scratch for a specific region.

General references. Friedman and Trembour (1983); Aitken (1990); Hull (2001)

Amino acid racemization dating

Amino acids, the building blocks of proteins, have two possible structural configurations: left handed (L) and right handed (D). The L–amino acid and the D–amino acid are mirror images of each other. Only the L racemers are incorporated into proteins. With time, and as the protein degrades, the initial 100% L composition transforms into a more stable equilibrium mixture of ideally 50:50 L:D racemers. Abelson (1955) proposed that this transformation process could be used for absolute dating using amino acids that are preserved in fossil-mineralized tissues such as bones, teeth, and shells. The time dependence of this reaction was later demonstrated by Hare and Abelson (1967).

The rate of racemization is, however, dependent on many other factors besides the time elapsed since the mineralized tissue was formed such as temperature, pH, bound metals, and the neighboring amino acids in the protein polymer. The racemization rate is also strongly influenced by whether the amino acids being analyzed are still part of the protein polymer or are located at the ends of the polymer or are present as free amino acids (Kriasakul and Mitterer, 1978). It is therefore not surprising that it has proven to be very difficult in practice to use racemization for absolute dating. What is surprising is that there are two mineralized tissues that have been demonstrated empirically, by calibration with radiocarbon dating, to provide reliable dates (with an error of approximately ±10%). These are eggshells (Brooks et al., 1990) and land snail shells (Goodfriend, 1987). It is still necessary to calibrate the results obtained against absolute dates for a particular region (mainly because of the complex temperature fluctuation history), but once this is done, the analyses do seem to provide reliable ages. The effective dating range is from hundreds of years to a million or more years (Aitken, 1990).

General references. Aitken (1990); Johnson and Miller (1997); Goodfriend et al. (2000)

Dating by archaeomagnetism

The direction and intensity of the earth's magnetic field vary over the earth's surface and with time. The variations with time can be as much as $10°$ within a century. If these variations are calibrated as a function of time for a specific region, then this calibration curve can be used as a method for dating unknown samples. This concept was first proposed by Gheradi (1862) and was later developed by Thellier (1938) and Aitken (1958).

Archaeological applications take advantage of the fact that iron oxides are common impurities in clay. When a heated clay is cooled, the magnetic minerals, such as iron oxides, preserve the direction of the earth's magnetic field. The heated clay sample can then be analyzed, and the direction of the earth's magnetic field at that geographic location can be determined. A calibration curve then provides the date or dates when the magnetic field was aligned in this direction at that location. Samples that can be dated in this way are the floors and walls of kilns. The accuracy and precision can be remarkably good if the calibration curve is itself accurate and precise. For example, a brick kiln was dated to AD 1700 with an error of around ±10 years or better (Casas et al., 2007). The effective dating range is up to several thousand years, depending on the local calibration curve.

Another application of the earth's magnetic field for dating is based on the fact that the whole field has undergone a series of reversals, when the north pole becomes the south pole and vice versa. These reversals can be detected by analyzing sediment samples and/or lava flows. Twenty-one such reversals have occurred over the last 5 million years, and the dates of these reversals are well known. The most recent reversal occurred some 780,000 years ago. Thus, if a series of reversals can be identified in or around an archaeological site, then the age of that site can be determined.

Samples for archaeomagnetic analysis need to be extracted in such a way that their original orientation is determined. This is usually done by a specialist, and for kiln samples, it is often necessary to take many samples.

General references. Leute (1987); Aitken (1990)

LIFE HISTORY RECONSTRUCTION OF INDIVIDUALS

It is of much interest to obtain information on events and/or behavior patterns that occurred to an individual during his or her lifetime such as change in diet, stress events, or migration from one location to another. This capability depends on the availability of skeletal material that was deposited at different times during the lifetime of an individual. There are two approaches: to microsample different parts of the skeletal material that were deposited at different stages of the individual's lifetime, or to directly observe incremental growth patterns and obtain information on development rates or events such as birth or weaning.

The bone of many animals, including humans, is continuously remodeled. This remodeled bone is called *osteonal* or *Haversian* bone (Figure 2.3). Thus, at any given time, the average age of the bone material can be assessed. For adult human bones that remodel relatively quickly (e.g., the iliac crest), this can be less than 10 years, whereas for slowly remodeling bones (e.g., the midshaft of the femur), this can be around 30 years (Jowsey, 1961; Price et al., 2002). Within this period, it is possible to differentiate between the most recently deposited bone and two stages of bone deposited earlier, based on whether individual osteons are whole (most recent) or disrupted (Figure 2.3). This would cover usually the last one or two decades of the individual's life span, depending on the age of the individual at death.

Teeth, on the other hand, do not remodel. They do, however, form at different times during development (Hillson, 1986). The enamel and most of the dentin of an individual tooth form within a few months of each other. There is, however, a deposit of dentin around the pulp cavity (secondary dentin) that forms continuously after the tooth erupts (Saleh et al., 1993). Thus, by microsampling these two forms of dentin, two time points can be obtained from one tooth. By sampling teeth that develop at different times, additional time points can be obtained.

Tooth enamel and dentin do contain rhythmically deposited growth line increments. In primates, these can be used to reconstruct life history events such as the day of birth, the identification of serious illnesses or environmental stresses, if the tooth was still developing at the time of death, and the age at death (Smith et al., 2006). Highly resolving analytical techniques can provide information on daily variations during the time the tooth was formed.

Thus teeth and, to some extent, osteonal bone provide opportunities for reconstructing life history events of individuals. There are microsampling devices that are capable of removing samples of around 100 micrometers in diameter – the size of an average osteon, or several samples within a tooth. The types of chemical analyses that could be of interest are strontium isotopes and possibly also the oxygen isotopes of the bone phosphate, as a means of determining whether an individual

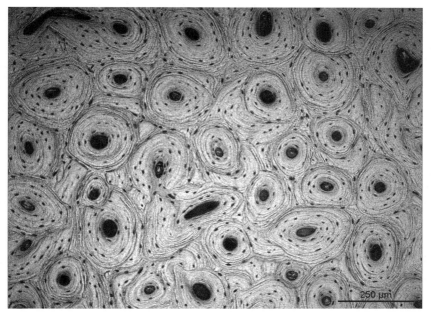

Figure 2.3
Light microscope image of the polished surface of osteonal bone from a horse. Note that the last formed "generation" of osteons is complete, the previous generation is cut by another osteon, and the earliest material present is in the interstices between osteons. Courtesy of Dr. Ron Shahar.

migrated from one region to another. Stable isotopes of carbon and nitrogen from bone or dentin collagen could provide information on changes in diet. For more information, see the appropriate sections in this chapter.

PALEODIET RECONSTRUCTION

The term *paleodiet* refers specifically to the food that humans ate. As humans are omnivores, all edible materials can be a component of the human diet, and thus reconstructing the details of this diet is almost impossible. There are two approaches to this problem: direct and indirect. The direct approach is to identify preserved plant remains (such as charred materials and phytoliths) on the site that were clearly gathered and stored for human consumption, as well as bones of animals that were raised or hunted for food. The difficulty is being sure that these materials do really relate to human diet. Under rare circumstances, human coprolites may be preserved (Rhode, 2003). The botanical remains from such coprolites are obviously directly related to diet. The indirect approach is to obtain more general information that is related to diet. This can be based on analyses of the relatively stable small molecules that are often trapped inside the pores of ceramic vessels used for preparing or storing food, the strontium contents of human bones, and/or the stable carbon and nitrogen isotopic compositions of organic material (collagen) extracted from human bones. These indirect approaches have the advantage that there is usually no doubt that these values somehow relate to human diet. The disadvantage is that even under the best of circumstances, only information of a general nature can be obtained. The following sections contain brief overviews of the three indirect paleodiet reconstruction methods.

Stable isotope paleodiet reconstruction

As isotopes of an element have the same chemical properties, but only differ slightly in mass, the stable isotopic composition of the food ingested by an animal is almost, but not quite, the same as that of the food itself (DeNiro and Epstein, 1978; van der Merwe and Vogel, 1978). This means that irrespective of whether nonhuman animals or humans eat plants directly, or eat the flesh of other animals that ate plants, the isotopic composition of the organic material of the consumer basically reflects the original plant source at the base of the food chain. In the case of the element carbon, the isotopic composition of this plant source varies mainly according to the type of photosynthetic system the plant used (Park and Epstein, 1961). The common photosynthetic systems are the C_3 system for plants from more temperate climates and the C_4 system used mainly by grasses and shrubs adapted to higher temperatures and more arid regions. Nitrogen is incorporated into biological tissues through fixation by bacteria and other soil microorganisms. The factors that control the isotopic fractionation of nitrogen are less well understood than for carbon but basically reflect the extent of precipitation (mainly rainfall) in a particular area, with extreme values being recorded from animals under heat stress (Sealy, 2001).

The organic matter of choice for these analyses is the protein collagen, which is often preserved in human bones. Because the collagen is embedded inside the mineralized tissue, it has a better chance of surviving diagenetic alteration and contamination than most other organic materials in an archaeological site. The purity of the extracted collagen does, however, have to be carefully checked prior to the analysis as contaminating organic matter can change the result significantly.

Even if both nitrogen and carbon isotopes are measured, it is still very difficult to reconstruct much about an animal's diet, let alone a human's diet, and obtain useful information. There have been, in the past, a few unique opportunities to do this such as tracking the introduction of maize, a C_4 plant, into the diet of humans, which was previously predominantly based on C_3 plants (Vogel and van der Merwe, 1977). Stable nitrogen isotopic composition also provides information on the component of marine-derived food in the diet (Schoeninger and DeNiro, 1984). For bones from purely terrestrial environments, the collagen nitrogen isotopic composition is influenced by local climatic variations and the physiology of the herbivores lower down on the food chain (Ambrose, 1991).

One way of improving the information obtained from isotopic analyses is to analyze the individual amino acids that make up the collagen protein as each has its own biosynthetic pathway, and thus the extent of carbon and nitrogen fractionation differs (Hare et al., 1991). Furthermore, some amino acids are not synthesized by herbivores, but rather, are ingested and used as such directly from the plants. They thus maintain information specifically relating to the input of the plant component of the diet. Another useful handle is the fact that some plants have very low concentrations of certain amino acids. Thus the isotopic composition of this amino acid can be used to obtain information on other sources of nutrition. An example is the amino acid lysine, which is present in very small amounts in corn and wheat but is abundant in legumes (Lehninger, 1982). By using single amino acid isotopic compositions in this way, and integrating this information with independent archaeobotanical evidence from charred seeds and phytoliths, a more informative reconstruction of past human diets may be possible.

General references. Katzenburg and Harrison (1997); Sealy (2001)

Strontium contents of human bones

An additional input on an aspect of human diet can be obtained from the strontium content of human bone mineral, provided, of course, that it is well preserved. Strontium has a similar chemistry to calcium. Strontium is, however, discriminated against in the mammalian digestive tract and during excretion in the kidneys. This does not occur in plants. Plants thus have high Sr:Ca ratios, whereas herbivores have lower values, and carnivores have even lower values (Elias et al., 1982). Thus a comparison of Sr:Ca ratios in human bones from a particular locality could reflect the relative proportions of meat in an individual's diet. If a time series is analyzed within the skeleton (different teeth, parts of teeth, and bone osteons formed at different times; see previous section on life history reconstruction), this could track a change in the meat component of the diet during the lifetime of an individual.

General reference. Sealy (2001)

Molecules trapped in ceramics (residue analysis)

When food is stored or cooked in ceramic vessels, some of the molecules diffuse into the pores of the ceramic. These molecules are relatively protected mainly from biological degradation, and the more stable molecules can be preserved. These are mainly lipids, and in particular the fatty acids: low-molecular-weight organic molecules with a very stable backbone composed of linked CH_2 groups and, at one end, a charged COO^- carboxylic group. These molecules can often be extracted from the powdered ceramic and analyzed. There are many different molecules of this type, and the assemblage of molecules extracted from one vessel is sometimes indicative of the contents of that vessel

(Condamin et al., 1976). Often, however, the assemblage extracted is not sufficiently well preserved to be useful, or the vessel was used for many different purposes and the assemblage of molecules is not informative. Some of these problems can be partially resolved by also measuring the stable isotopic composition of the extracted molecules (Stott et al., 1999).

General references. Evershed et al. (2001); Sealy (2001)

PALEOENVIRONMENTAL RECONSTRUCTION

Reconstructing aspects of the past environment around a site is an integral part of archaeology. There are many key events in human history that have been influenced by changes in climate, and the interplay between climate and human behavior is always in the background in terms of understanding cultural changes. Paleoenvironmental reconstruction is a huge field that lies mainly within the realm of geochemistry. Geochemists deal with past climatic changes in the oceans and on the continents. The past marine environment is somewhat easier to reconstruct as it is more homogeneous than on the continents. Archaeologists are mainly interested in the regional and local continental paleoenvironmental conditions, especially the paleoclimate. Of particular interest are opportunities for reconstructing the on-site paleoenvironmental conditions. Some of these are briefly reviewed in the following sections.

Micromorphology

Probably the most direct and powerful approach to reconstructing the past local environments on-site is by the examination of the texture of the sediments deposited at specific locations around the site. This is done by embedding the undisturbed sediments in a polymer and then making thin sections for examination in an optical microscope (Figure 2.4). This approach is known as *micromorphology* (Courty et al., 1989). The information obtained can be used, for example, to identify paleosoils, areas where lakes or ponds existed, sediments deposited by the action of wind, the presence of running water such as streams and ditches, sediments that were reworked by humans, and much more. Some of the key textural properties that are used for differentiating between these environments are the presence or absence of finely laminated sediments (usually indicating sediment deposition under water), a graded sequence of particle sizes (often indicative of wind deposition), preferred orientations of the sediment components (due to running water), and the presence of a mix of unsorted microartifacts (implying a dump deposit). The information obtained is often crucial for the interpretation of the local archaeology and can provide insights into the local climate.

6.5mm

Figure 2.4
Photomicrograph of
embedded sediments
from Layer 10 in Zhouk-
oudian, China, showing
the presence of finely
laminated bedding,
which is indicative of
a fluviatile deposition
environment. Courtesy of
Dr. Paul Goldberg.

General references. Courty et al. (1989); Goldberg and MacPhail (2006)

Archaeobotany

The plant remains preserved on-site were either brought to the site
by humans and/or domestic animals or grew on the site. Either way,
the wild plants (as opposed to the domesticated plants) do reflect the
paleoenvironment in the immediate vicinity of the site, and in the site
itself. Only charred plant remains are commonly preserved, or the stable
minerals that many plants produce (phytoliths; see the previous section
on archaeobotany). Pollen can also sometimes be preserved on-site,
but more often, pollen is found only in oxygen-limiting environments,
where it is better preserved (see the following section on pollen).

Rare earth elements

It is of much interest to understand the ecological setting of an archaeological site and, in particular, open-air sites that are located in changing environments. Such information can be used to address questions
concerning the relations among climate, local environment, and occupation horizons within a site. Opportunities to link local environmental
conditions to the archaeological site using material from the site itself
are limited. One promising approach is the use of a group of related
but different chemical elements (the rare earth elements, REE) that are
incorporated into bone soon after burial (Lozinski, 1973). The relative
concentrations of the REEs in the pore waters of the sediments in which
the bones were buried reflect well the composition of the sediments, and
this, in turn, is influenced by the depositional history of the sediments.
Thus profiles of REEs adsorbed into fossil bones are an indication of the
local paleoenvironment.

The REE profiles do not provide specific information on the actual environment; rather, they can be used more as fingerprints to detect different environments within a stratigraphic horizon or to contrast environments from different times as preserved in the profiles of bones from different horizons. This approach has been applied around the site of Olorgesaillie in southern Kenya (Trueman et al., 2006). This site was in the proximity of a lake. Bones from four different horizons were analyzed, and they could all be clearly differentiated. Furthermore, even within one stratigraphic horizon, different local depositional environments could be identified.

This ability to "fingerprint" bones in this way has other interesting applications. For example, if bones were redeposited in different stratigraphic layers, then a REE analysis could differentiate between a mixed assemblage of bones and bones that were deposited more or less simultaneously (Trueman et al., 2005). There are probably many other circumstances in which such "fingerprinting" of bones can be applied in archaeology.

Pollen

One of the most effective means of reconstructing the paleoenvironmental and/or paleoclimatic conditions in the region around a site is by examining the changes in the pollen record – a subject that was pioneered by Von Post (1944). The reason is that pollen is distributed widely by wind transport, and as pollens from different species have distinctive morphologies, their sources can be identified. Thus the major pollen-producing plants in a fairly wide geographic region can be identified. Pollen, as opposed to most other organic materials, contains an unusually stable outer wall (Stanley and Linskens, 1974), and thus it tends to preserve better, especially in environments devoid of oxygen. These are mainly organic-rich water-lain deposits such as in swamps and lakes. The past pollen record can be examined from cores extracted from these environments, and the changes can be compared to the pollen distribution from today. This is a most effective way of reconstructing past paleoclimates, as reflected by variations in the geographic distribution of plants.

General reference. Jansonius and McGregor (1996)

Stable isotope compositional variations

Variations in relative proportions of stable isotopes are due to the differences in the mass of the isotopes, as their chemical properties are identical. When a mineral forms from a saturated solution, more of the heavier isotope enters the mineral as compared to its concentration in the aqueous solution. The extent to which this occurs (called *fractionation*) is also influenced by temperature. This was first recognized by Urey (1947), who used this temperature dependence to reconstruct past temperatures of the oceans based on the oxygen isotopic compositions of fossil mollusk shells that formed in the ocean in the past (Epstein et al., 1953). Even though the mollusks do not precipitate their shell minerals in direct contact with seawater, their physiological processes, for unknown reasons, do not eliminate this temperature-dependent isotope fractionation. This is not the case for many other marine animals (see the review of Weiner and Dove, 2003).

The oxygen isotopic composition of a mollusk shell depends both on temperature and the isotopic composition of the water in which the mollusk lived. Thus analyses of mollusk shells can only provide past temperature information if the isotopic composition of seawater is known. On the other hand, the isotopic composition can be used to identify the specific environment in which a mollusk lived. As some very common mollusks, such as the blue mussel, *Mytilus edulis*, can live in both marine and estuarine environments, their shell isotopic compositions can be used to reconstruct the environment around a coastal site or to determine where the mussels were collected.

The oxygen isotopic compositions of biogenic minerals formed by terrestrial animals is indirectly related to the composition of their drinking water. This has been demonstrated for bones of animals that are obligate drinkers (Luz et al., 1984). The drinking water is almost always rainwater, and its oxygen isotopic composition is influenced by the local climate. Thus bone mineral oxygen isotopic composition is a valuable parameter for reconstructing local terrestrial climates.

For animals that can survive on the water they imbibe through the plants they eat, such as ostriches, bone oxygen isotopic compositions reflect the source of the water of the plants they eat. It has been shown that this is the case for their eggshell isotopic compositions (Ayliffe and Chivas, 1990). This, in turn, can reflect the environment in which the ostriches lived.

General reference. Taylor et al. (1991)

PALEOGENETICS

The possibility of actually obtaining DNA sequences of genes that existed in the past opens up exciting opportunities in archaeology, such as comparing and contrasting coexisting human populations, including Neanderthals and anatomically modern humans; determining whether information was transferred by population exchange or communication; and documenting population migrations. There are also specific questions that can be addressed that relate to the mechanisms of plant and animal domestication, possible human involvement in extinctions of animals, and, I am sure, many more. The first major steps to transform this dream into a reality were taken in the 1980s by Alan Wilson and Svante Pääbo (Higuchi et al., 1984; Pääbo, 1985). Powerful new molecular biological techniques were developed that propelled the field forward (Pääbo et al., 1989), and the first demonstration that some DNA could be preserved in fossil bone was by Hagelberg et al. (1989). A new field (called *ancient DNA*, or simply aDNA) was created. A series of papers followed over the next decade, some of which proved to be far too optimistic. More serious problems were also identified that showed that if the aDNA was damaged, then erroneous information could be obtained (Gilbert et al., 2003b). Such studies brought this field into line with all other applications in archaeology by showing that if you do not take diagenesis into account, the embedded information you obtain can be misleading. To put it more crudely, garbage in is garbage out. The principles of the main approaches used are briefly described in the following paragraphs.

Genetic information resides in the sequence of the four nucleotides that make up DNA. This information can be extracted by directly sequencing the DNA itself, or by determining the amino acid sequence of a protein. In vivo, the protein sequence is determined by the genomic DNA via the genetic code. Obtaining a sequence of a fossil protein is very difficult as the molecule needs to be more or less intact and available in relatively large amounts. One of the first indirect partial sequences of a fossil protein was obtained from a mollusk shell millions of years old (Weiner et al., 1976). Only recently, using mass spectrometry, has the entire sequence of a fossil bone protein been obtained (Nielsen-Marsh et al., 2002).

It is much easier to obtain a sequence from preserved DNA, mainly because of the incredibly versatile and powerful polymerase chain reaction (PCR) procedure. In essence, this procedure allows a specific portion of the DNA to be singled out using specially prepared small pieces of DNA (primers) that bind to the target DNA sequence of interest. They then act as starting points for the polymerase enzyme to make a copy of only this portion of the DNA. The copy is then separated from the original by raising the temperature, and then the process is repeated, and two copies are made of these molecules. Thus every cycle doubles the number of copies produced, and after some tens of cycles, enough material is available to obtain a sequence. A problem arises from the fact that the enzyme can also duplicate damaged DNA and hence incorporate mistakes that cannot easily be differentiated from true Darwinian mutations. Furthermore, the damage tends to occur at the same locations as the Darwinian mutations, presumably because of weaker local structural features in the DNA. It seems that, as always, the best way around this problem is to analyze only well-preserved DNA. Another way is to analyze as many sequences as possible and then use other criteria to sort out the original sequences from the damaged and contaminated sequences. This was done using a parallel sequencing technique and resulted in the sequencing of around a million base pairs of Neanderthal DNA – an incredible achievement (Green et al., 2006).

PALEOMIGRATION

A fascinating question in reconstructing past human behavior is whether some individuals in a population migrated to the area where they were buried or lived their whole lives in the area. Ericson (1985) first proposed using strontium isotope ratios to address this problem, based on the fact that strontium isotope ratios vary between regions with different rock types (the ultimate source of the strontium). In addition, as strontium is a heavy element, there is essentially no separation (fractionation) of the isotopes as they pass from the rocks to the soil, and then into the food chain.

More detailed studies have revealed that reality is somewhat more complicated, but it is still possible to use this valuable tool. Problems arise from the fact that even in a given ecosystem, the ratios do vary significantly, depending on the local soils and the manner in which the plants incorporate strontium. Price et al. (2002) have proposed a practical approach for resolving these problems by comparing animal bone and snail shell strontium isotope ratios with those of human bones from the same time period within the site. The incorporation of strontium into these mineralized tissues is a means of providing a sort of baseline for the local variations. It is then fairly easy to differentiate between the local and migrant human populations at a given site. To minimize problems of bone diagenesis, which can also affect the results, Price and colleagues recommend analyzing tooth enamel.

The oxygen isotopic compositions of bone and tooth mineral are indirectly related to the composition of the drinking water. This has been demonstrated for animals that are obligate drinkers (Luz et al., 1984). The drinking water is almost always rainwater, and its oxygen isotopic composition is influenced by the local climate. Thus, if migration involved moving from one climatic region to another, then bone and/or enamel mineral oxygen isotopic compositions can also be used to document this change (Britton et al., 2009).

General reference. Price et al. (2002)

POTTERY CONTENTS

Ceramic vessels were widely used for storage, cooking, and transport. Thus the determination of the vessel contents when it was in use can provide invaluable information on agricultural and industrial products, diet, trade, and many other aspects of human behavior. Only on rare occasions are the actual contents preserved in vessels either as a charred residue or in some degraded form. It has been demonstrated, however, that some of the molecules that were present in the vessel penetrate into the pores of the vessel wall, and in this relatively protected environment, the more stable molecules may survive (Chapter 8). These can be extracted and analyzed (so-called *residue analysis*). This was first demonstrated by Condamin et al. (1976).

The molecules that are most often preserved are lipids. These are low-molecular-weight hydrophobic molecules that are relatively resistant to microbial or chemical breakdown. They are sparingly soluble in water but can be extracted with organic solvents. They are common components of both plant and animal cells, and the specific molecule types can be indicative of different organic sources. They are not always present in ceramics, and in fact, in certain climatic regimes, it is not easy to find sites in which they are sufficiently well preserved to provide reliable information. Furthermore, if the vessel was used for cooking, then it is likely that molecules from a variety of sources entered into the ceramics, and they are further degraded by the cooking process itself. Residue analysis is therefore more likely to provide useful information for storage and transport jars as well as specialty containers for perfumes, drugs, and so on.

General reference. Evershed et al. (2001)

PROVENIENCE AND PROCUREMENT STRATEGIES

Provenience studies

Provenience in an archaeological context usually refers to the geographic location of the source of the raw material for producing an artifact such as flint and obsidian for stone tools, clay for pottery, ores for metals, steatite (soapstone) for vessels and beads, amber for ornamentation, and marble for sculptures and building construction. The interest in determining the sources of these artifacts is to be able to reconstruct pathways that link human groups in different regions, and can thus often provide an indication of trade routes. The basic strategy for identifying the location of the source of the material is to use a chemical fingerprint that varies sufficiently between all possible sources so that the fingerprint of the artifact can be matched to one or only several of these sources. This can be relatively straightforward if the possible sources are limited, but it is a huge task if the sources are numerous. In such situations, hundreds, if not thousands, of analyses of all possible sources in a region are required. It becomes even more complicated if the material is processed in some way or if materials from different sources are mixed, as often occurs for metals and, sometimes, for ceramics.

The term *provenience* is synonymous with the term *provenance*. In art history, *provenance* refers to the history of the object. I therefore choose to use the term *provenience* to refer to the initial source of the material used for producing the artifact, and *provenance* for its history until burial. This distinction is quite common, but not universal.

Provenience studies can be subdivided into two categories: those in which the potential sources for a given region are limited, and those in which the sources are abundant. The strategies used and the information obtained are quite different.

Limited sources

Where limited sources are available, attempts are made to fingerprint every possible source in a given region. If a match can then be made between the artifact and the source, trade routes can be established with a reasonable degree of certainty.

OBSIDIAN

Perhaps the best known and most specific provenience studies are those that involve the sourcing of obsidian. The first studies by Renfrew and colleagues (1966) were in the Near East and Mediterranean regions. The possible sources are located on various Greek islands or in Sardinia, central Anatolia, Armenia, Hungary, Slovakia, and possibly even Ethiopia and Kenya (Lambert, 1997). Obsidian was also used extensively in Central and North America for producing tools. The possible sources have also been well characterized in these areas (Bowman et al., 1973). The chemical fingerprinting is most often based on trace element analyses using neutron activation analysis (NAA) or inductively coupled plasma optical emission spectrometry (ICP-OES).

AMBER

Amber is a fossil plant resin composed of a variety of different organic molecules. The most common chemical fingerprint used for amber provenience studies is its infrared absorption spectrum. This was shown to contain specific regions characteristic of ambers from different geographic regions and, in particular, one form of amber from the Baltic region (Beck et al., 1965). It has proved to be a useful technique, but in some cases, the results are not unequivocal (Angelini and Bellintani, 2005). Figure 2.5 shows this fingerprint region for five amber samples. There are differences, but it has to be demonstrated that these are unique to a specific area.

SOAPSTONE (STEATITE)

Soapstone is a soft silicate mineral that was widely used for producing both utilitarian objects, such as bowls, and figurines (Lambert, 1997). Luckenback et al. (1975) have characterized many of the possible sources of soapstone in the eastern part of the United States based on a specific group of trace elements, namely, the rare earth elements (REEs). Similar studies have been performed in Britain (Moffat and Butler, 1986).

MARBLE

Marble was used in the Mediterranean region since the Neolithic. It was extensively used by the Greeks and Romans. The possible sources of marble around the Mediterranean are, however, numerous and not easily fingerprinted. Trace element compositions vary within even a single quarry and thus cannot be used for provenience studies. Variations in the stable isotopic compositions of oxygen and carbon are useful, and many of the quarries around the Mediterranean were analyzed, and most could be unequivocally identified (Herz, 1992). By combining stable isotope analyses with petrography, more resolution between quarries can be obtained, as was demonstrated by a study in Mesoamerica (Luke et al., 2006).

METALS

Metals commonly used in the past (gold, silver, copper, iron, tin, mercury, and lead) were produced from ores with relatively limited distributions. It is thus feasible to determine the provenience of specific sources, and from this to reconstruct trade and exchange pathways. Furthermore, because of the importance of metals for many basic aspects of a developing society, these trade routes reflect many economic, social, and military aspects of past societies (Rheren and Pernicka, 2007). Proveniencing metal sources is not easy; a breakthrough came in the 1960s with the application of lead isotope analyses (Brill and Wampler, 1965; Grögler et al., 1966). As lead is a heavy chemical element, the proportions

Figure 2.5
The specific region in the infrared spectrum (shaded) of amber that is indicative of its provenience. The amber samples are from the following regions: *a*, Dominican Republic; *b*, Baltic; *c*, Dominican Republic; *d*, Israel; *e*, United States (New Jersey). The region shown was identified by Beck et al. (1965) as being indicative of provenience. Samples courtesy of Dr. A. Nissenbaum.

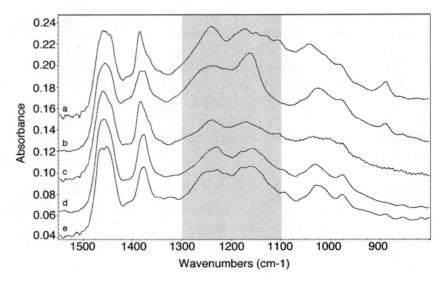

of its isotopes do not change during the extraction (primary production) and manufacturing procedures. A major effort thus ensued to fingerprint the possible sources of ores. These focused on Cyprus (Stos-Gale et al., 1997) and southeastern Europe (Pernicka et al., 1997). This body of information enables the effective proveniencing of metals found in many archaeological sites to specific quarries or local areas in these regions. If, however, the metals have been recycled and the sources are mixed, the method cannot be applied.

A particularly interesting provenience problem in the Old World is the source of tin for producing bronze. There are very few known tin sources in southwestern Asia, where bronze was first used in the third millennium BC, and it was proposed that tin was imported to this area from central Africa, England, Germany, and various other distant locations. In 1989, a tin mine was found in the Taurus Mountains (Turkey), with archaeological artifacts dated by radiocarbon to the Early Bronze Age (Yenner et al., 1989).

Abundant sources

POTTERY

Pottery is produced from clay-rich sediments. Ethnographic studies indicate that these can usually be found within a 10-kilometer radius around a site (Arnold, 1985). Thus the rationale behind proveniencing pottery ceramics is that the site location is more or less the source location, and the presence of ceramics that are not local indicate that they have been transported as vessels from some other location. Trade routes can thus be reconstructed by identifying the sites where the imported vessels were produced.

An inherent problem in ceramics proveniencing is that the original raw material may be processed to remove some of the coarser fraction and concentrate the clay. Furthermore, because these are local deposits that are relatively abundant, the variability can be large, and thus the uncertainty of the provenience assignment can also sometimes be large. Despite the difficulties, the analysis of the bulk trace element composition by NAA or ICP-OES does often provide a characteristic fingerprint that can effectively distinguish local from imported ceramics, and often also possible source locations (Sayre and Dodson, 1957). This is achieved by comparing the results to a large data bank of ceramic trace element compositions. The second approach is to use petrography to characterize mainly coarse, poorly fired ceramics (Peacock, 1967; Goren et al., 2004). The assemblage of coarse components, and sometimes also the clay-sized components, is then compared to the local sediment compositions in a given region. If these are well known and sufficiently variable, this approach is also effective. Obviously, a combination of both is even better (Schubert, 1986). Surprisingly little attention has been paid to the possibility that diagenesis affects pottery provenience studies (see Chapter 7).

FLINT (CHERT)

Flint is relatively abundant in some regions, and absent in other sometimes very large regions. Determining provenience is thus difficult. Furthermore, in the regions where flint is available, sources are quite variable in terms of color and texture. Color and texture therefore are often not reliable indications of the source of the raw material, although in some regions, these properties have proved to be useful (Della Casa, 2005). The microstructure or petrography of the flint can be more helpful, especially if fossil remnants of the siliceous organisms from which the flint originally formed are still preserved (Navazo et al., 2008). This, too, is often not the case. The most effective method for fingerprinting flint is by trace element analysis using NAA or ICP-OES. Among the trace elements, variations in the rare earth element (REE) compositions sometimes prove to be the most effective means of differentiating between possible sources of flint (Segal et al., 2005). Here, too, there is an inherent problem, as the fingerprint reflects the conditions of formation, and these can be quite uniform for flints formed during the same geological period in relatively large geographic regions (Navazo et al., 2008). Thus the fingerprint often only differentiates between flints of different ages from the same region. Despite the difficulties, provenience studies are carried out and seem to provide detailed information.

Procurement strategies

Procurement strategies refer to the manner in which the raw material was obtained at the source: surface collection, shallow mining, or deep mining. These studies are not usually associated with the microscopic record, as they most often involve documentation of ancient mining activities at the source itself. An approach to this problem for lithic tools was developed based on the fact that rocks exposed to cosmic radiation produce minute amounts of certain cosmogenic isotopes in situ. If, however, the rock was buried at a depth greater than 2 meters, then this process does not occur. Thus the presence of the in situ–produced cosmogenic isotope indicates that the rocks were either present on the surface or just below the surface for long periods of time, as opposed to having been mined from depths below 2 meters. This method can only be applied to lithic tools that were left in a cave after use, where they were shielded from cosmic radiation exposure. Boaretto and her colleagues developed and applied this method for flints. They showed that the cosmogenic isotopes were not lost from the flint over time, and that indeed, different procurement strategies could be inferred using tools found at the site, without having to locate the source from which they were derived. This approach also enables a comparison of procurement strategies over time in a given prehistoric cave site (Verri et al., 2004, 2005; Boaretto et al., 2009b).

General reference. Wilson and Pollard (2001)

SEASON OF OCCUPATION

Archaeological sites may not have been occupied throughout the year, but rather, on a seasonal basis. The basic strategy for identifying seasonal or year-round occupation is to analyze the remains of resources that are available only in a specific season or determine the season during which the resource item was collected. Even though this approach only provides firm evidence for the season of procurement, it does not necessarily mean that during the remaining seasons, the occupants were not at the site (Deith, 1983b). It is often assumed that evidence of this type is indicative of seasonal occupation. There are a variety of different resource types that can be used to address this issue, both macroscopic (such as the bones of animals that migrate on a seasonal basis) and microscopic. Among the latter are the following.

Archaeobotanical remains

Archaeobotanical remains of annual plants, and in particular, seeds and fruits, can provide perhaps the most direct evidence for seasonal occupation. This is based on the fact that these plants only produce seeds and/or fruits in specific seasons. Thus the presence of an assemblage of such remains would constitute good evidence that the site was occupied during that season (Riley, 2008).

Rhythmic growth

Rhythmic growth of skeletal materials offers another approach to determining season of occupation. Many marine mollusks that live in the intertidal zone add new growth increments to their shells on a daily, or sometimes even twice daily, basis, depending on the tides (Rhoads and Lutz, 1980). The thickness of these growth bands varies with the water temperature and hence with the seasons. Thus a microscopic examination of thin sections or sometimes even the surface of the very edge of the shell can reveal the season in which the animal died (Coutts, 1970; Quitmyer and Jones, 1997). If there is clear evidence that the mollusk was collected by humans, based usually on the accumulation of shell middens, then the season of death is assumed to correspond to the season of occupation of the site. If the seasonal nature of the rhythmic growth deposits are not clear, an alternative is to analyze the oxygen isotopic composition of the growth increments. As these vary with change in water temperature, the season in which the last growth increments were deposited can be determined (Deith, 1983a).

Otoliths are mineralized bodies produced by fish for sound perception, gravity sensing, and acceleration detection. In the common teleost fish, the otoliths produced in the larger of the three chambers are usually composed of aragonite, and in the smallest, of vaterite (Lowenstam and Fitch, 1981; Lowenstam and Weiner, 1989). Figure 2.6 shows a photograph of a typical otolith. The large otoliths are commonly identified in archaeological sites, and they usually have well-defined growth rings. These are deposited in such a way that dark and light bands correspond to different seasons. Examination of fracture surfaces of otoliths from an archaeological site in New Zealand demonstrated the effectiveness of this approach and that the results are consistent with the determination of season of occupation using mollusk shells from the same site (Higham and Horn, 2000).

Tooth cementum is the outer layer of the tooth root that interfaces with the bone of the mandible through the periodontal ligament. Herbivores that have diets that vary according to the season use their teeth in different ways, based on the mechanical properties of the food they eat. The tooth is pushed deeper into the socket if the food is relatively hard, or the tooth rises if the diet is mainly composed of a softer food. This change is reflected in the structure of the cementum (Lieberman, 1993). Thin sections of well-preserved cementum of certain herbivores do show periodic structural differences that correspond to seasonal depositions. These can be used to determine season of occupation, provided that the cementum is well preserved (Stutz, 2002).

General reference. Rhoads and Lutz (1980)

SITE FORMATION PROCESSES

Any interpretation of the archaeology of a site must take into account the manner in which the site formed and the manner in which it transformed over time. The reason is that what is preserved today is generally just a small remnant of what was once at the site when it was occupied. Without understanding this transformation or site formation process, it is not possible to evaluate the biases that have been introduced over time. Even more important, it is not possible to evaluate what is absent from the record because humans never brought these materials to the site or because they were degraded and lost over time. This is a huge subject that defies a short synopsis. In fact, much of this book is about aspects of site formation processes, especially as they pertain to the microscopic record (Chapter 3, in particular).

Conceptually, it is helpful to divide the subject into the processes responsible for the buildup of the site and those responsible for its transformation over time. Formation processes can be natural, such as

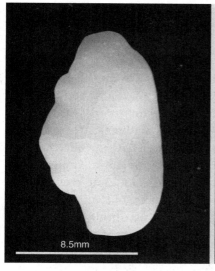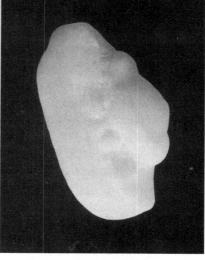

8.5mm

Figure 2.6
Photographs of two sides
of the same otolith from
the sacculus of the fish
Coryphaenoides acrolepis.

sediment transport and deposition due to wind or water, or due to the activities of the humans and other animals on the site, such as importing of construction materials, burning of fuel that produces ash, dung accumulation, and much more. Formation processes can also involve loss of material from the site by, for example, wind or water transport, with the result being that part of the record is absent. This absence is not easy to discern as it is usually represented by only an interface (referred to in geology as an unconformity).

Transformation (diagenetic) processes can be biologically mediated due to the mechanical actions (e.g., burrowing) of relatively large organisms or the metabolic activities of mainly bacteria and fungae. They can also be chemically mediated whereby changing conditions cause less stable components of the record to dissolve and be removed from the site, or they can reprecipitate in a more stable and less insoluble form. Of course, combinations of all the above can and do occur. A good analogy for archaeology are the varied processes responsible for soil formation (Holliday, 2004).

The key tools used for reconstructing site formation processes in general, and especially regarding the microscopic record, are micromorphology and materials characterization, especially minerals. See Chapter 3 for more details.

General references. Schiffer (1983); Stein and Farrand (2001); Holliday (2004); Goldberg and MacPhail (2006)

SITE SPATIAL ORGANIZATION

Reconstructing the different ways in which an area was used at a particular time (spatial organization) is a major theme in many archaeological projects. Binford's (1983) ethnographic studies do, in many respects, set the stage for these types of observations in the archaeological record. Indeed, the distribution of macroscopic artifacts can, in certain contexts, be very informative. Often, however, the macroscopic artifacts are deliberately not left in place (O'Connell, 1987). On the other hand, the microscopic artifacts are too small to be a hazard or a nuisance and are more likely to enter into the substrate than the macroartifacts (Gifford, 1978). The distribution of the microartifacts may therefore better reflect the manner in which the area was used (O'Connell, 1987). Microartifacts can, however, be redistributed by burrowing organisms and various natural processes that affect the sediments. Examples of microartifacts that can effectively be used to reconstruct aspects of the spatial organization of a site are the fragments of flint produced during knapping, the siliceous components of plants (phytoliths) that are not easily degraded, fish scales, small teeth and bones, and calcitic spherulites that are present in the dung of many herbivores (Canti, 1997). Calcitic spherulites have also been identified in the intestinal tracts of fish (Wilson et al., 2009).

Another form of microartifact is a stable molecule or an assemblage of stable molecules whose distribution also reflects one or more human activities. These chemical artifacts are widely used in archaeology. One of the earliest applications of chemical signals for site spatial analysis was the mapping of phosphate concentrations in an area, both to identify the boundaries of an archaeological site (Arrhenius, 1931) and within the site, to determine different activities (Woods, 1977). Phosphate is an integral component of all cells and therefore is a marker for biological activity. Thus the presence of high phosphate concentrations reflects an area that once contained large amounts of organic material. It should, however, be noted that not all organic matter contains phosphate, and phosphate concentrations can vary from almost zero to very high concentrations, depending on the type of organic matter deposited. The reason why phosphate is a marker is that after the organic matter is oxidized and the carbon-containing components are converted into carbon dioxide, the phosphate remains. It readily reacts with many of the available cations in the sediments and forms a relatively insoluble mineral phase. There are other stable molecules that can, in principle, also be used for determining spatial organization such as fatty acids. They are usually used to determine the contents of a vessel and not for mapping different activities in an area of the site. This, however, can be done, as was demonstrated in a study of plaster floors (Barba, 2007).

General references. Gifford (1978); Chapter 8

WEANING AGE

The age and duration of weaning of infants can provide valuable insights into aspects of the social and economic status of a society.

Several methodological approaches have been proposed to address this issue, such as Sr/Ca ratios in bone mineral (Sillen and Smith, 1984) and tooth enamel (Humphrey et al., 2008), but the one that seems to be most reliable is the measurement of the stable nitrogen isotopic compositions of the bone and dentin collagen of the infant. The reasons why this parameter is sensitive to weaning is that during the first few years of life, the infant's diet shifts from placental nourishment (essentially reflecting the mother's diet) to breast-feeding, and then back to the same foods that its mother eats. Katzenberg (1993) first developed this application based on principles developed by Fogel et al. (1989), namely, that ^{15}N is concentrated in a mother's milk relative to her diet, and that the utilization of breast milk by the baby further increases the ^{15}N concentration. Thus, during the period of breast-feeding, the ^{15}N concentration is high, but as breast milk is substituted for other foods, the ^{15}N concentration decreases. If the decrease is abrupt, the transition to other foods must have been within a very short time. If not, it implies that the process was gradual. For more details on the applications of this method, and for a model to better understand the data, see Millard (2000).

It should also be noted that the same approach can be applied to the weaning of domestic animals. This provides information on the animal husbandry practices at that time (Makarewicz and Tuross, 2006).

General reference. Millard (2000)

3

Completeness of the Archaeological Record

It is not easy to forget that the familiar macroscopic archaeological record is missing a huge amount of information when compared to the same site when occupied. Any interpretation of the excavated record thus requires a serious assessment of what is missing, and in particular, differentiating between what is missing because it was never present or because of degradation (*diagenesis*). The microscopic record is, in many respects, the key to understanding the missing part of the archaeological record. The focus of this chapter is on better understanding the completeness of the whole archaeological record through the microscopic record.

Darwin (1859, chap. 9) addressed the issue of completeness in the context of paleontology when he wrote about the "imperfection of the fossil record." Darwin recognized that the fossil record was a direct source of information for evaluating his theory of evolution and was concerned that an uncritical reading of this record would compromise his hypothesis. He was particularly concerned with the fact that fossils rarely show any morphological change over time and hence contradicted his predictions. Gaps exist in the fossil record, and any reading of the record obviously needs to take this into account. In fact, it is not only the gaps that can cause confusion, but also the quality of the record: the proportion of past life that is not recorded, the information content of the record that is preserved, the bias that this introduces, and so on (Kidwell and Holland, 2002).

Darwin, I guess, chose the term *imperfection* to emphasize what is missing. T. H. Huxley (1863, p. 18) referred to "the completeness or incompleteness of those records themselves." I prefer the more positive approach and use the term *completeness*. Either way, we are dealing with what is missing and the quality of what is preserved.

The completeness of the archaeological record is just as pertinent an issue to archaeology as the completeness of the fossil record is to paleontology – perhaps even more so, because over and above the loss of information due to natural processes, direct human "interventions" often destroy part of the record. Even the relatively short timescale of the archaeological record ("just" 6 or so million years) compared to the paleontological record does not simplify matters much because during this time period, major climatic fluctuations occurred, and as a consequence, so did changes in preservation conditions. Furthermore, many of the processes that degrade the fossil or archaeological records occur on much shorter timescales. In her introductory chapter to *Archaeology in the Holy Land*, Kathleen Kenyon (1960) writes that "one has only to consider one's own surroundings to see how incomplete the picture would be if all objects of organic materials had disappeared. Even solid structures, when abandoned, comparatively soon start to crumble under the effects of time and weather" (p. 12).

This chapter aims at synthesizing a more coherent approach to assessing what is missing and the quality of what is preserved – the completeness of the archaeological record.

HOW BAD IS THE ARCHAEOLOGICAL RECORD?

Even though there is obviously no unique answer to this question, it is interesting to consider the following observations made by Robbins (1973) on the macroscopic material culture items of a traditional, occupied Turkana homestead in Kenya and a homestead that was abandoned a month or so before the investigation. Two-thirds of the items in the occupied homestead were composed entirely of organic materials that were most unlikely to be preserved. Of the remaining one-third, 21% were composed of a combination of perishable organic materials and more durable materials. Only 8% of the macroscopic items found in the occupied homestead were preserved in the abandoned homestead, and of these, none were functional. Furthermore, they constituted a very poor representation of the material culture of this Turkana family. This loss only one month after abandonment reflects mainly the fact that items of value were not left behind. In contrast, items not visible to the naked eye are left behind. Although these were not included in this study, they could well include the microscopic remains of durable items that were either produced or broken on-site such as stones, bones, glass, clay, and metal objects. It can be expected that the microscopic record is more representative of at least the durable materials used during occupation.

THE ALMOST COMPLETE RECORD

The complete record can be defined as all the materials present in ethnographic contexts. If this record, without the living organisms, were somehow preserved, the record that would be presented to future archaeologists could be described as pristine. This is the starting point.

As it is invaluable to understand as much as possible about the starting point, this is one of several good reasons to study ethnographic contexts from an archaeological perspective. There are many others (Chapter 9).

Archaeological sites that preserve the almost pristine record are rare. It is therefore difficult to study them in a systematic manner and draw general conclusions. On the other hand, from the perspective of embedded information in the microscopic record, these exceptionally well preserved sites are often treasure troves for biomolecular archaeology. The molecules that are preserved can be used for reconstructing the genetics of humans and other animals, migrations, diet, and much more (Chapters 2 and 8). It is also helpful to examine the unusual circumstances that result in organic matter being very well preserved, as this provides insight into the agents that are responsible for the more common degradation of organic and inorganic materials.

One of the best documented cases of an almost complete record is that of the so-called Tyrolean Ice Man (Ötzi), whose body was found at 3,210 meters above sea level in a glacier in the Tyrolean Alps in 1991 (reviewed in zur Nedden et al., 1994). The body was radiocarbon-dated to the Neolithic period between 3350 and 3150 BC (Bonani et al., 1994). The unique location of the body in a shallow depression prevented it from being sheared by the moving ice, and its fortuitous discovery soon after it appeared on the glacial surface prevented major degradation of the soft tissues. In essence, preservation conditions cannot get much better than this. The man's hard and soft tissues were analyzed, including his DNA (Rollo et al., 2006). Analyses of his bones, teeth, and intestinal contents provided information on where he came from and where he moved about during his life (Müller et al., 2003). The pollen on the surface of his clothes revealed the path he took on his last trip into the Alps, and his equipment provided an amazing glimpse into the tool kit of a Neolithic man. It included a bow, 14 arrows, a fur quiver, a leather satchel, flint blades of various types, a fragment of a hollow bone, an axe with a copper blade glued with plant resin to a handle, a white stone disk with a hole in it, grass cords, and more (zur Nedden et al., 1994). Findings such as this are like windows that allow us to obtain an almost real glimpse into the world of the past.

Both the temperature of the ice and the solid state of the ice (and in particular the absence of liquid water) contributed toward the unique preservation of the body by more or less totally inhibiting biological degradation of the organic molecules and minimizing chemical degradation. Extreme desiccation also severely inhibits biological activity and hence slows down the breakdown of organic matter. The spectacular preservation of organic materials in Egyptian tombs is probably the best known example. Here, presumably, I would guess that the combination of the generally dry climate and the location in a tomb that prevented even occasional wetting episodes explains why these materials are so well preserved.

Many deserts do receive rainfall from time to time, and this enables microbial and fungal degradation of organic materials. In Egypt, and probably in many other desert environments, the water drains away rapidly due to the porous nature of the sand in which the organic matter is located (Renfrew and Bahn, 1991). This may minimize microbial action. The Atacama Desert in northern Chile almost never receives any rain. Water from the melting snow of the Andes runs down into this desert. These rivers are a vital source of water in an environment where rain does not occur. If the plant and animal organic matter that forms in this environment is buried out of contact with liquid water, conditions for preservation are ideal. Indeed, there is spectacular preservation of organic materials, including desiccated human bodies that were mummified prior to burial (Aufderheide et al., 2005). Such extreme desiccation may also result in macromolecules, such as DNA and proteins, being preserved.

In other deserts, there are locations, such as caves or rock shelters, where organic material may be protected from wetting during rainfall. One such site is a small cave (Qumran 24) located a kilometer or so from the Dead Sea. Figure 3.1 shows photographs of the deposits from

Figure 3.1
Views of the upper part of the stratigraphic section in Qumran 24 cave, showing layers of preserved organic materials from about 6,000 years BP. The upper right-hand photograph is a close-up view of the top of the section, and the bottom right-hand photograph is a higher-magnification view of some of the organic-rich layers. Twigs and leaves can be seen. Scale bar: 20 centimeters. The site was excavated by Avi Gopher, Ran Barkai, and colleagues.

the upper part of a section dug into the sediments, which are more than 6,000 years old. The whole section contains abundant organic matter still in the form of fibers, twigs, leaves, and so on. While examining some of the sediments with a binocular, I noted the presence of occasional halite (sodium chloride) crystals. Clearly water never wetted these sediments, as these crystals would have dissolved immediately. The total absence of liquid water may be the key to preservation of this kind and could well explain the preservation of the Dead Sea Scrolls themselves, which were found in caves just a few kilometers to the south.

It is interesting to note that even though this cave is located in a desert where the present-day vegetation is sparse, organic matter is still a major component of the section. In more temperate regions, if, for some reason biological activity did not degrade the organic component, it would probably be the dominant component of the sediments.

The Dead Sea Scrolls provide another insight into extraordinary preservation of organic matter. The scrolls were stored in ceramic jars inside caves (de Vaux, 1973). The ends of the rolled-up parchment (composed mainly of the protein collagen) that were most exposed to the humidity of the atmosphere were severely degraded. The relatively well preserved parchment was located in the core of the rolled-up scroll. This parchment was less degraded, presumably because the outer parts of the roll acted as a desiccant that lowered the humidity in the core. In the case of the Dead Sea Scrolls, the major degradation is probably not due to biological activity, but rather to chemical breakdown. It was demonstrated that the collagen near the edges had lost much of its original helical structure to become gelatin (Weiner et al., 1980). This is a chemical process. Water molecules are important agents for chemical change, and in this case, the molecules that reached the scroll edges were probably transported into the jars in the form of vapor and not as a liquid.

Waterlogged environments are often cited as locations for pristine preservation (Renfrew and Bahn, 1991). Indeed, human and other animal bodies as well as abundant plant materials are often preserved macroscopically in these environments (Glob, 1965). Degrading organic matter lowers the pH, and many minerals, including the mineral of bone, dissolve (Glob, 1965). At the molecular level, however, the preservation of the remaining organic matter is usually far from pristine. The good macroscopic preservation is in large part due to the absence of oxygen in the water and the resultant lowering of microbial activity. The oxygen is absent because it is removed by the degrading organic matter, including the organic artifacts of interest archaeologically. The plants that accumulate in the bogs contain molecules that can stabilize degrading organic matter by chemically cross-linking different macromolecules (such as proteins and polysaccharides) together. This process is called *tanning*, and tanning is known to be an important component of bog body preservation (Stankiewicz et al., 1998). Even though this stabilizes the macromolecules, tanning also makes the macromolecules less accessible to analysis at the molecular level. Pristine preservation of artifacts from waterlogged environments is therefore unlikely.

An analysis of pristine preservation conditions leads to the following conclusions:

51

THE INCOMPLETE
RECORD:
CONCEPTUAL
FRAMEWORK FOR
ASSESSING THE
MISSING RECORD

1. Organic material is a major component of the pristine record, even in a desert environment where relatively little vegetation exists a priori. Organic matter would certainly have been much more abundant in temperate and tropical climates, had it been preserved.
2. Biological activity is mainly responsible for the breakdown of this organic matter.
3. Biological activity can probably only be stopped altogether when liquid water is eliminated from the system. This can occur by freezing, or in very dry areas, where even the occasional rain does not reach the organic material.
4. Chemical degradation can proceed when water vapor is present and in the absence of liquid water. Chemical degradation can be slowed down if some of the organic matter acts as a desiccant, protecting the remaining organic matter.

THE INCOMPLETE RECORD: CONCEPTUAL FRAMEWORK FOR ASSESSING THE MISSING RECORD

As so little is generally preserved in the archaeological record, the natural tendency is to focus on what is preserved and not on what was lost. This is a valid approach, and it is also a practical approach, as the material that is preserved can, of course, be analyzed. This initially led to emphasis being placed on site formation processes that accounted mainly for the material that was preserved (Schiffer, 1987). The missing part of the record is much more difficult to evaluate, even though it is important. Furthermore, the missing record may be missing because it was degraded and lost, or because it was never present – an important distinction to be made when interpreting the record. The state of preservation of the materials that do survive needs to be assessed to know whether reliable embedded information can be extracted from them. The quality of the remaining record is thus another important issue. In this section, I will address these related problems by trying to identify common underlying mechanisms of degradation (diagenesis) that can be used to at least partially reconstruct the missing part of the record and assess the preservation states of materials that do survive.

Macroscopic versus microscopic records

The degradation/diagenetic trajectories of the macroscopic and microscopic records diverge almost immediately after the site is abandoned by its occupants. It can be assumed that nothing of value that can be seen will purposely be left on-site – a process referred to as *gleaning* (Schiffer, 1987). This process directly affects the macroscopic record, and not the microscopic record. After abandonment by the original occupants, the site will often be used by other humans, and if not by them, by animals. This secondary use of the site can affect both the macroscopic record, by introducing new materials into the site, and the microscopic record, especially if the secondary use involves domestic animals or storage of plants, both of which increase the organic matter content of the site. In addition, the macroscopic materials that do remain begin to degrade and enter into the microscopic record.

The strategy proposed here for reconstructing the missing component of the whole archaeological record mainly involves the microscopic record – the part that is not visible to the naked eye. The microscopic record is less disturbed and also likely to contain remains of the degraded part of the macroscopic record. Despite the fact that these processes are also diverse and site-specific, an attempt will be made to define a conceptual framework that can be more generally applied to reconstruct aspects of the missing record.

Four different components enter into this conceptual framework:

1. the time frame of degradation
2. the driving forces of degradation – mainly water, chemical reactions, and mechanical agents
3. the materials that degrade – both organic and inorganic (minerals)
4. how the minerals that remain record information on the state of preservation of the site

Even though the four components are all interconnected, it is helpful first to consider each separately and then integrate them into a conceptual framework.

Time frame

In many respects, the time frame is the key to understanding the underlying mechanisms of degradation. The presence of partially broken-down, abandoned structures, especially in rural areas, is familiar worldwide. Figure 3.2 shows examples from Greece, China, and India, which include both stone buildings and mud brick buildings. The constructions within these villages degrade rapidly, and usually, very little remains within tens to a few hundred years after abandonment. Often parts of the village are degrading, whereas other parts are still occupied. After this rapid period of degradation, the site enters into a pseudo-equilibrium with its environment, and although the state of preservation only deteriorates, the rate of degradation is slower. The time frame for degradation can thus be divided into two: a rapid period, lasting usually less than a century, and a long period of slow degradation. The importance of the rapid degradation phase has been well recognized in paleontology and, later, in archaeology. In fact, it has been given a name of its own: *taphonomy* (Eframov, 1940).

The major process responsible for the rapid degradation phase is probably the biological destruction of organic matter. Organic matter degrades very fast in terms of the archaeological timescale. The self-evident fact that huge piles of leaves do not accumulate under trees is one of many "logical" lines of reasoning that this must be the case. A comparative study of seven different mixtures of organic matter and sediments showed that under aerobic conditions (compasting), most of the organic matter was degraded into a gas phase within about three weeks at 28°C. The process then continues more slowly for months (Bernal et al., 1998). Anaerobic processes are much slower. A study of organic matter–sediment mixtures in a reactor showed that anaerobic degradation reached a steady state only after about 75 days at 28°C (Vavilin et al., 1996). Ethnoarchaeological observations of animal

53

THE INCOMPLETE
RECORD:
CONCEPTUAL
FRAMEWORK FOR
ASSESSING THE
MISSING RECORD

Figure 3.2 Photographs of partially degraded structures from ethnographic settings. *Top left*, A two-story stone building from the village of Sarakini, located in the Rhodope Mountains, northern Greece. The upper story comprises a storeroom (in the foreground) and a living room (in the back), and in the lower story are stables and pens for horses and sheep or goats. This house was in use about 50 years before the photograph was taken. *Top right*, A small stone building a few kilometers away from Sarakini village. This was used as a domestic abode during the summer. It was in use 20 years before this photograph was taken. *Bottom left*, Mud brick houses in Hunan Province, China. The one in the foreground is used as a storehouse, although judging from the structure around the opening, this is probably a secondary use of the building. *Bottom right*, An abandoned part of a building still in use (Rajasthan, India).

enclosures in abandoned Maasai villages demonstrated that after 30 or 40 years, a dung pile that was originally about a meter high could be visually identified only as a black layer below the sediment surface (Shahack-Gross et al., 2003). As most organic matter degrades within months or years, from the archaeological perspective, biologically mediated degradation of organic matter is fast and very efficient. In fact, it is so efficient that any organic matter that escapes destruction probably has a special niche where it can be protected (Chapter 8).

The driving forces of degradation

MECHANICAL DISTURBANCES
The effects caused by the activities of burrowing organisms (*bioturbation*), such as earthworms, various insects, certain mammals, and birds, can cause serious damage to the archaeological record. Their activities are mainly mechanical. Bioturbation can be a major cause for the incompleteness of the record.

Geogenic processes are also sometimes very destructive. One of the best examples is the damaging effect of cycles of freezing and thawing that are common in temperate environments (Courty et al., 1989). Flowing water and wind can also redistribute materials. At the microscopic level, dissolution of soluble minerals followed by deposition of more stable minerals results in the filling of voids within the sediments. This can seriously disturb the original microscopic record. On the other hand, mineral deposition can stabilize the record at the macroscopic level such as with the formation of a cemented sediment.

Finally, anthropogenic processes can also contribute significantly to the degradation of a site. Leaving aside deliberate episodes of destruction, the common activities of building foundations, digging pits, "robbing" building materials from an earlier period for reuse, plowing, and even straightforward trampling by humans (Gifford-Gonzalez et al., 1985) all contribute mechanically to the degradation of a site.

These mechanical disturbances are discussed in detail by Courty et al. (1989), Rapp and Hill (1998), and Goldberg and MacPhail (2006). Mechanical disturbances are, however, site-specific, and within a site, they vary greatly from one location to another. It is therefore difficult to generalize about mechanical disturbances, even though they are usually very important.

HYDROLOGICAL REGIME AND CHEMICAL REACTIONS
Water is a key agent in diagenesis. In extremely dry environments, chemical reactions and biological activity slow down significantly, and the record can be very well preserved. Normally, however, water is not limiting, and both biological activity and chemical reactions proceed. Biological activity also requires a source of energy, namely, organic

matter. Chemical reactions depend on the presence of water molecules (liquid and/or vapor) and the presence of ions, many of which are released by the microbial degradation of the organic matter.

In general, every mineral will dissolve to some extent when in contact with water. The less stable minerals will dissolve more than the more stable ones. If the water in the microenvironment surrounding the mineral is stagnant, the mineral will only dissolve until the ions released reach a certain concentration, and then the situation will remain in chemical equilibrium. If, however, the water in the sediment is flowing, and the new water replacing the old water contains fewer dissolved ions, then the mineral dissolution process is continuous. Under these circumstances, the mineral dissolves until it disappears completely. Thus the extent to which the water moves through the sediments is a key factor in preservation. This is referred to here as the *hydrological regime*.

The extent to which water flows through a sediment is influenced to a great extent by the nature of the pores in the sediments and the pressure exerted on the water due to the difference in height between the source of water and the outflow location. This was formulated into a law (Darcy's law). If the pressure is normalized, then the flow rates of different sediments can be measured experimentally to determine the so-called hydraulic conductivity. Sediments can vary enormously, with the two extremes being unconsolidated, course-grained sediments having very high flow rates and clays with very low flow rates (Tindall and Kunkel, 1999). The reasons that clays have very low flow rates are that the clay particle sizes are small and hence the porosity is low, and the surface area is large. The large surface area results in an increase in the interactions between water molecules and the clay surfaces. These interactions also slow down water movement. Thus, as a rule of thumb, sediments with large amounts of clay will have reduced flow rates. This, in turn, implies that in general, preservation of minerals, and even macromolecules, is likely to be better in clay-rich sediments. A rough correlation between bone preservation and clay content was noted (Weiner and Bar-Yosef, 1990).

When water enters into the sediments from the surface, it will flow downward through the sediments by the force of gravity, until it fills all the accessible pores. Sediments with water-filled pores are referred to as the *saturated zone* or the *phreatic zone*. In the *unsaturated zone*, or *vadose zone*, above the phreatic zone, the water exists as a liquid phase, a vapor phase, and as thin films that adhere to the particle surfaces. The path by which water will flow through the vadose zone into the phreatic zone depends on the extent to which the pores are connected. Some pores are isolated and may be filled with liquid water all the time, whereas others are transiently filled after a rainfall. This will influence the extent to which a mineral will dissolve; minerals exposed to flowing water will dissolve more rapidly than those around isolated pores. Water in

55

THE INCOMPLETE
RECORD:
CONCEPTUAL
FRAMEWORK FOR
ASSESSING THE
MISSING RECORD

the vadose zone also flows, and the extent to which it flows is defined by Darcy's law, namely the hydraulic pressure, and the porosity of the sediments (Tindall and Kunkel, 1999).

It is not obvious (to me) whether preservation of the archaeological record will be better in general in the phreatic or vadose zone, as water flows in both. The key factors are probably the flow rate in the sediments and the amounts of water entering and leaving the sediments.

Less discussed, it seems, is a microscopic process that occurs on soil surfaces, and especially when a site is excavated. The soil surface and/or balks (walls of sediments that are left standing following excavation) are exposed to an atmosphere that is relatively dry compared to the sediments that constitute the balk. The result is that the water close to the sediment surface evaporates, and the soluble salts that were dissolved in this water crystallize. Capillary action draws more water to the surface, and the process repeats itself. This deposition of new crystals is not only unrepresentative of the sediment composition, but also, the growth of the crystals can mechanically displace some of the original fine-grained components of the sediments as well as artifacts. This destructive process due to salt crystal formation is well known in masonry and wall plasters (Rapp and Hill, 1998). Nitrates are common constituents of this surface deposit. Nitrates can easily be detected in an infrared spectrum (see Overview 14 in Chapter 12). In certain chalky deposits, this evaporitic deposit can reach thicknesses of several centimeters or more and, after a short time (years), can totally obliterate the surface of the original section. Sometimes this deposit actually stabilizes the section and can discourage birds and other animals from burrowing into the section. The sampling of sediments from such a section requires removing the surface deposit and exposing the original sediments.

Materials that degrade

Almost all the common materials that are present in ethnographic settings degrade. The mineral quartz is perhaps the one exception. Quartz is so stable that nothing, or almost nothing, happens to it in archaeological environments. The other common materials (such as clay minerals, calcium carbonate minerals, carbonate hydroxylapatite, silica, and charred and uncharred organic materials) are all affected in one way or another by chemical and/or biological activities. In terms of understanding degradation processes, it is useful to separate the degradation of organic matter from the degradation of all other common materials, including the degradation of charred organic matter. The reason is that when uncharred organic matter degrades, it releases mainly acids, which can have a radical effect on the preservation of the other materials. Furthermore, as organic material is initially present in large amounts, this is often the driving force for site degradation.

ORGANIC MATERIAL

It can be assumed that almost all sites, when occupied, contained large amounts of organic material, not only as construction materials or stored food and fodder, but within the sediments due to human and animal activities. Furthermore, after abandonment, the site is often used secondarily by other humans and/or animals, and during this period, more organic matter can be introduced in the form of dung, remains of stored crops, and so on. Almost all this organic matter degrades. A key component of the conceptual framework presented here is that this breakdown of organic matter is a major driving force in the rapid degradation stage of the site.

57

THE INCOMPLETE
RECORD:
CONCEPTUAL
FRAMEWORK FOR
ASSESSING THE
MISSING RECORD

In general, the soil organisms that contribute most to organic matter degradation are bacteria, fungi, protozoans, algae, plants, and a variety of other animals, including earthworms, ants, and termites (Waksman, 1952; Alexander, 1977; Oades, 1989). The breakdown process essentially involves the conversion of small and large organic molecules into their most fundamental components, which are mainly the gases carbon dioxide and methane and various soluble molecules, such as alcohols and organic acids (Bolan et al., 1991). Water is also produced in the process. All these products are mainly the result of oxidation, and they form when the microorganisms are active in an oxygen-containing aerobic environment. This process is often referred to as *compasting* This mode of degradation takes place in most environments in which microbial breakdown of organic matter occurs. If oxygen is limiting or totally absent, then other microbes are active and use different chemical pathways to break down the molecules. This anaerobic process results in the formation of many partially broken-down organic products, some of which are acidic (Gujer and Zehnder, 1983). In fact, one of the steps in anaerobic breakdown of organic matter is called *acidogenesis*. Thus an important consequence of anaerobic degradation processes is that the pH of the local environment decreases. Note that during the initial stages of degradation, the pH may rise, due in part to the formation of ammonium carbonate (Kirchmann and Witter, 1992).

There are no well-defined rules that can predict when aerobic or anaerobic degradation will occur. We only know for sure that when the oxygen source is limited, anaerobic activity ensues. Many factors can limit the oxygen supply, but perhaps the most important in archaeological contexts is when large amounts of organic matter are initially available, the first aerobic attack will use up all the oxygen, leaving the remaining organic material available to the anaerobic organisms, provided that new sources of oxygen are not introduced. The exclusion of oxygen depends on the extent of water flow in the local environment, the degree of bioturbation that occurs during the aerobic cycle, the rate of sediment accumulation, and probably many other factors.

All this is relevant to the archaeological record because even though aerobic degradation leaves only a minor chemical imprint on the record, it acts rapidly and efficiently and results in the almost total removal of all uncharred organic materials. Anaerobic processes are slower and do leave an imprint, due in part to the consequences of the pH drop. We can thus exploit the chemical changes due to anaerobic degradation to reconstruct areas within a site where large amounts of organic matter once existed such as animal enclosures, waste dumps, dung-processing and storage sites, latrines, sewers, and food stores.

Microbes have developed an incredible arsenal for breaking down organic matter, and from the archaeological perspective, almost everything can be broken down by them with the help of specialized enzymes. Chemical stability of the molecules seems to be of little consequence. For example, the biogenic polymer chitin, which is very common in the arthropods (insects) and many other animals, is so stable that it can be boiled for hours in sodium hydroxide. Almost all other organic molecules break down under such conditions, yet chitin survives. This incredible stability has not resulted in chitin being a common component of sediments. On the contrary, it is very difficult to find fossil chitin because microbes have no problem rapidly breaking it down (Hood and Meyers, 1977).

One important class of organic polymers that does seem to be difficult to break down microbially is lignin (Scheffer and Cowling, 1966; Buxton and Russel, 1988). Lignin is the name given to highly cross-linked, large polymers that are rich in aromatic groups (Zhang and Gellerstedt, 2001). After cellulose, lignin is the most common component of wood. Poorly preserved fossil wood contains much higher proportions of lignin than cellulose because lignin is less likely to degrade (see Overview 12 in Chapter 12). It has been noted that the major components of the humic substances in soils have similar properties (Inbar and Chen, 1990), and these also accumulate in soil because microbes have difficulties breaking them down. Although most of the humic substances form de novo in soil (Hayes, 1998), some may be derived directly from the breakdown of wood (Tan, 2003). Note, too, that some classes of small organic molecules are also relatively resistant to degradation. These are mainly the fatty acids. They are often the most abundant molecules extracted from ceramic sherds (Evershed et al., 2001; Chapter 8).

An important class of organic material that cannot be degraded biologically is charred materials. Charred materials do, however, degrade chemically by oxidation over long periods of time (Cohen-Ofri et al., 2006). It is for this reason that charcoal, charred seeds, and charred fruits are commonly found in archaeological sites.

Organic matter also contains various chemical elements, such as sulfur and phosphorus, that are usually not converted into gases. These remain in the sediments. If the degradation conditions are anaerobic, then the sulfur converts into a sulfide ion, which in turn readily reacts, mainly with iron, to form minerals such as pyrite. If oxygen is present, then the sulfur is in the form of sulfate. This can bind to cations to form relatively soluble mineral products, such as gypsum, that are usually not preserved (Doner and Lynn, 1977). Phosphorus is always bound to three or four oxygen atoms to form a phosphate moiety and, on release from the organic molecule, reacts with cations, such as calcium, iron, and aluminum, to form relatively insoluble minerals (Moore, 1984). As these minerals are relatively insoluble, they tend to remain close to the location where the original organic matter was located. Thus concentrations of phosphate in the sediments are usually good indications that high concentrations of organic matter were once present at that particular location within a site (Herron, 2001). This was one of the first applications of chemical analysis in archaeology, and it is still widely used (Chapter 8).

MINERALS

The archaeological record is composed almost entirely of minerals: the minerals that are the major components of artifacts (bones, ceramics, stone tools, etc.) and the minerals in the sediments. Thus almost all information on the missing record needs to be extracted from minerals. The less stable minerals are of most interest in this regard as these are more likely to record diagenetic changes. The less stable minerals are mainly the carbonates, the phosphates, and silica (opal). The more stable clays and quartz are unlikely to change much in most archaeological contexts.

Stability and solubility are two sides of the same coin (in thermodynamics; Everett, 1959). Solubility is measured by allowing the mineral to dissolve in water with different concentrations of certain ions, including hydrogen ions. The hydrogen ion concentration is defined by the pH of the solution, and the lower the pH, the more acidic is the solution. When the mineral stops dissolving and comes to equilibrium (i.e., the rates of dissolution and mineral growth are equal), then it is stable under these conditions, and its solubility can be measured. Solubility measurements can be used to calculate the stability field for each mineral with respect to all the various parameters that influence its stability. There are usually several such parameters, and a two- or even a three-dimensional plot is usually inadequate (Kittrick, 1977). Figure 3.3 is an example of a two-dimensional stability field plot relevant mainly to prehistoric caves (Karkanas et al., 2000).

From Figure 3.3, it can be inferred, for example, that if the phosphate mineral montgomeryite forms in the sediments, then the conditions are such that carbonate hydroxylapatite is not stable. This in turn implies that bones, which are composed of carbonate hydroxylapatite, have

59

THE INCOMPLETE
RECORD:
CONCEPTUAL
FRAMEWORK FOR
ASSESSING THE
MISSING RECORD

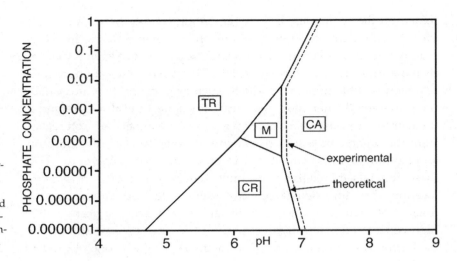

Figure 3.3
Stability relations for carbonate hydroxylapatite (CA), montgomeryite (M), crandallite (CR), and taranakite (TR) as a function of phosphate concentration (more accurately, activity) and pH, after fixing the concentrations (more accurately, the activities) of Ca, K, and Al. This is based on Karkanas et al. (2000), using data from Nriagu (1976). The experimental curve for carbonate hydroxylapatite solubility was determined by Berna et al. (2003).

dissolved. Furthermore, if montgomeryite forms, rather than crandallite, then the phosphate concentrations in the sediments were relatively high. This could be an indication that bones dissolved in this location, and if so, the presence of authigenic montgomeryite might actually be the "memory" of the lost bones (Karkanas et al., 2002).

Using this logic, we can define a mineral reaction cascade that is relevant to many archaeological sites (Figure 3.4). The ordinate is a measure of how soluble the mineral is, and the abscissa shows variations in pH. Variations in pH are chosen because they are an indirect measure of microbiological activity. Bacteria and fungi produce organic acids, such as acetic acid and formic acid, especially under anaerobic conditions. These metabolic processes all tend to reduce the pH of the water in the sediments. The starting pH is usually around 8: the value that is essentially fixed by the dissolved bicarbonate-carbonate ions in the water that originated from carbon dioxide in the atmosphere and/or dissolution of calcite. This calcite may be geogenic (limestone, dolomite, etc.), biogenic (shells), or, as often occurs in archaeological sites, pyrogenic (ash). Thus a clear-cut trend in early diagenesis is for the pH to decrease in areas where large amounts of organic material were originally present. Furthermore, depending on the type of organic material, more or less phosphate will be released, and it will readily react to form relatively insoluble minerals. The results of these diagenetic processes are that the less stable, more soluble mineral phases in the site will be the first to dissolve, and their ions will either be transported out of the site if the hydrological regime is vigorous, or if not, other more insoluble minerals will form in their place. In general, the more soluble minerals are the carbonates, and the less soluble ones are the phosphates.

Minerals rearranging at the atomic level

61

THE INCOMPLETE
RECORD:
CONCEPTUAL
FRAMEWORK FOR
ASSESSING THE
MISSING RECORD

Dissolution of one mineral and the reprecipitation of a different mineral is a manifestation of major changes in the chemical environment. More subtle changes can occur without a change in mineralogy. These changes are also thermodynamically driven in the sense that a less stable, more soluble phase is replaced by a more stable, less soluble phase. Many biologically produced carbonates, and possibly bone mineral as well, form via a highly unstable amorphous precursor phase that subsequently crystallizes into a more stable phase (Weiner et al., 2005; Mahamid et al., 2008). The stable phase, however, still contains many imperfections, and if conditions change, then these imperfections cause the crystal to dissolve locally and/or rearrange its atoms such that the imperfections are eliminated and a more stable phase is produced. This process can be monitored using infrared spectroscopy (see Chapter 4 and Overview 2 in Chapter 12). A similar process occurs for bone mineral that is also initially relatively unstable (see Chapter 5 and Overview 4 in Chapter 12). Although it has not as yet been documented, I suspect that amorphous silica (opal) may also undergo subtle changes such as losing tightly bound water molecules. It is therefore possible to monitor changes in imperfections in different localities within a site and differentiate between well-preserved and less well preserved areas. If the primary mineral has undergone atomic rearrangement, then it might well lose some of its embedded information.

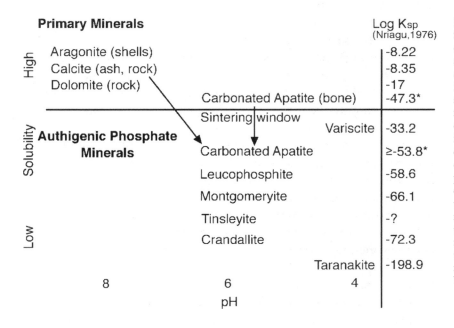

Primary Minerals

			Log K_{sp} (Nriagu, 1976)
High	Aragonite (shells)		-8.22
	Calcite (ash, rock)		-8.35
	Dolomite (rock)		-17
	Carbonated Apatite (bone)		-47.3*

	Sintering window		
		Variscite	-33.2
Authigenic Phosphate Minerals	Carbonated Apatite		≥-53.8*
	Leucophosphite		-58.6
	Montgomeryite		-66.1
	Tinsleyite		-?
	Crandallite		-72.3
Low		Taranakite	-198.9

8   6   4

pH

Solubility

Figure 3.4
Scheme showing the common primary and secondarily formed authigenic minerals found in archaeological sites. Arrows designate known examples of one mineral transforming into another due to changing chemical conditions – mainly lower pH due to organic matter degradation. The solubility products of the minerals are shown on the right-hand side. The more negative the value, the more insoluble is the mineral. Adapted from Weiner et al. (2007).

Summary of the conceptual framework for estimating the missing record

TIME FRAME

Following abandonment, a site undergoes rapid degradation over a period of tens and possibly hundreds of years. This is followed by a long period during which either very little happens or slow degradation occurs. Thus the initial degradation period is often the period that determines the overall state of preservation of the site. The degradation trajectory followed is very much influenced by the organic component of the inhabited site, and thus the "signature" of the absent organic matter is imprinted on the site.

AGENTS OF DEGRADATION

Sites in which a large component of the structural materials and sediments was organic are most affected by its degradation. Organic degradation results in both mechanical destabilization and chemical destabilization. The chemical effects of organic matter degradation are more predictable than the mechanical effects – they are small if the degradation processes are aerobic and much greater if they are anaerobic. As the latter conditions arise in areas of high organic matter concentrations, these should leave a clear chemical imprint. It is difficult to generalize about mechanical destabilization processes as these are diverse and site-dependent. Mechanical destabilization together with other site-dependent factors, such as the hydrological regime, the climate, and bioturbation, can contribute significantly to site degradation and loss of information.

ASSESSING THE EXTENT OF DEGRADATION

Minerals change their properties as a function of changing chemical and hydrological conditions. An extreme response is that they dissolve and reprecipitate in a more stable form. Sometimes the original mineral remains, but only the exposed external and internal surfaces readjust to new microenvironmental conditions. A less extreme response is that minerals become more ordered by losing foreign ions initially present in the structure and/or by eliminating discontinuities or dislocations. This ordering results in the mineral becoming more stable. The overall result is that a detailed characterization of the mineral assemblages as well as the atomic order within the minerals can be used to evaluate the state of preservation of the site. This information can then be used to assess the missing part of the archaeological record.

CONCLUSIONS

The preceding sections provide a practical framework for assessing the completeness of the archaeological record. If the most soluble primary minerals are preserved in their initially disordered state, then it can be assumed that at least in that local environment within the site, other more stable minerals are also preserved. If, however, the more soluble minerals are absent, then the extent to which the pH dropped, which in turn is a rough measure of how much organic matter was present, can be estimated by the types of minerals that form in their place. Clearly this is not a complete description of diagenesis or a means of estimating the entire missing record. It is hoped that it provides a conceptual basis that can be improved and expanded. This conceptual framework does, however, emphasize that there are ways to reconstruct the missing record. We need more analytical tools for this purpose.

Practical applications of the conceptual framework

There are many practical ways in which this framework can be translated into observations and analyses that can be made on minerals from an archaeological site. It is in fact very helpful to carry out many of these observations and analyses on-site (Chapter 11), to be able to focus the excavation on the better preserved areas within the site. The following are some examples:

1. Aragonite is usually the most unstable mineral that can survive in archaeological sites. It is usually biogenic. Terrestrial snail shells and freshwater clams as well as many marine mollusks all form aragonitic shells. If these shells are still composed entirely of aragonite, then more stable minerals, such as calcite, should be well preserved. If they are partially or entirely calcitic, this implies that conditions are such that calcite may also be poorly preserved. Thus analyzing the mineralogy of mollusk shells on-site is a very useful index of preservation conditions (see Chapters 4 and 6 and Overview 1 in Chapter 12).

2. The calcite formed biologically and the calcite formed via the hydration of calcium oxide (plaster and wood ash) have different infrared spectra ($v_2:v_4$ ratio; see Overview 2 in Chapter 12). This property is therefore easily monitored on-site and can be used to map subtle changes in preservation conditions. Furthermore, if the ash and plaster are well preserved, they may well contain embedded information.

3. Carbonate hydroxylapatite that forms in the sediments is in the form of nodules. These nodules form when phosphate is released from degrading organic matter and reacts with calcium. This occurs at roughly between 7 and 8 pH units. Carbonate hydroxylapatite is also formed biologically in bone. The latter has very small and disordered crystals as compared to its authigenic counterpart. X-ray

diffraction or infrared spectroscopy can be used to monitor this dis-order in bone. If the extent of disorder is similar to that in modern bone, then the crystals are well preserved. If it is similar or the same as in authigenic carbonate hydroxylapatite, they are not well pre-served. This disorder can be used to assess whether the information embedded in the bone mineral is likely to be preserved (see Chapter 5 and Overview 4 in Chapter 12).

4. A good starting point for assessing the state of preservation of a site is to determine whether bones are present everywhere. If not, then search for authigenic phosphate nodules in areas where bone is absent. The presence of authigenic phosphate nodules in the sed-iments implies that bone has probably dissolved because most of them form between 6 and 7 pH units. If bones are absent and these areas contain primary calcite (such as ash or plaster), this indicates that the pH was always around 8, and that the absence of bones is because bones were never at that location. This logic was first applied in Kebara Cave (Weiner et al., 1993). For more details, see Chapter 5.

5. If authigenic phosphate minerals, such as taranakite or variscite, are present, then the pH was once very low as these minerals only form under low-pH conditions (Figure 3.4). Such low-pH conditions are most probably due to very large amounts of organic materials having degraded at this location.

6. The distribution of charcoal can also be informative in terms of preservation conditions. In Kebara Cave, charcoal is found in abun-dance where taranakite is present, but it is almost totally absent where calcite and carbonate hydroxylapatite are present (Rebollo et al., 2008). Thus charcoal distribution may also be indicative of paleo-pH conditions and past concentrations of organic materials. A possible reason for this is discussed in Chapter 7.

7. Calcium-containing rocks, such as limestone, chalk, and dolomite, are, in effect, very large reservoirs of calcium. Their surfaces there-fore "monitor" the changing chemistry of the solutions in the sedi-ments over long periods of time by the formation of reaction rims. If phosphate is released into the environment, it will readily react with the rock surface, and if the rock surface is exposed to acidic con-ditions in the presence of phosphate, different authigenic minerals will form on its surface (Figure 3.5). It can therefore be informative to analyze scrapings of rock surfaces to detect authigenic minerals. This can conceivably be a way of detecting caves or rock shelters whose roofs have since collapsed as the rocks that were in the sed-iment (not the roof fall) should still have the authigenic phosphate mineral imprint on their surfaces from the guano that formed when the cave was intact and used by bats and/or birds.

Figure 3.5
Photograph of a section through a large dolomitic rock buried in the Upper Paleolithic sediments of Kebara Cave, Israel. The surfaces of this rock have been severely altered due to chemical reactions. The reaction rim covers the entire surface of the rock, but is clearly visible at its base. For more details of the mineralogy of this reaction rim, see Schiegl et al. (1996). Scale bar: 20 centimeters.

8. Tilted strata are surprisingly common in many archaeological sites (Figure 3.6). In caves, tilted strata could be due to underlying sediment falling through a sinkhole in the floor of the cave. Another mechanism that could account for tilted strata in caves and open-air sites is that large amounts of organic matter were initially present in the underlying sediments, and this organic matter was subsequently removed by biological activity after burial. This possibility can be tested by determining the concentrations of phytoliths per unit weight of sediment or, if the organic matter contained much phosphate, by the presence of authigenic phosphate minerals. The

Figure 3.6
Tilted strata from Iron Age deposits at Tel Dor, Israel. Some of the white layers are composed almost entirely of phytoliths, which in turn implies that these were once organic-rich layers. The organic material has all degraded. For more details of phytolith-rich layers, see Albert et al. (2008). Scale bar: 20 centimeters.

former presence of large amounts of organic materials can be indirectly inferred from increased concentrations of phosphate in the sediments.

9. Strata that are rich in clay tend to have reduced hydrological activity. This in turn leads to better chemical preservation. If, for example, well-preserved bones are sought, then attention should be paid to clay-rich strata.

FUTURE PROSPECTS FOR IMPROVING OUR UNDERSTANDING OF THE MISSING ARCHAEOLOGICAL RECORD

Charcoal has the propensity to adsorb ions and small organic molecules in relatively large amounts. It is possible that these ions and organic molecules contain archaeologically relevant information. As the charcoal is formed de novo, all the adsorbed moieties must be from the period following its formation. Charcoal is thus potentially a "recorder" of the organic molecules produced in the site. If these could be extracted and identified, they might provide information on degraded dung, fodder, food, and so on. In areas where specific activities took place, such as wine or olive oil production, the extracted molecules may be characteristic of these activities.

Clay also adsorbs ions and organic molecules. These adsorbants, however, may be from prearchaeologically relevant periods. On the other hand, if, for example, the pH was lowered significantly due to locally degrading organic matter, the very old organic molecules and ions may be released, and then when the pH rises, the exposed clay surfaces may adsorb archaeologically relevant molecules. These molecular assemblages may also have interesting archaeological signals.

Silica (opal) is a relatively stable mineral phase, even though it is disordered at the atomic level. It may well be that it does dehydrate and become more ordered over time and that these changes can also be used to monitor different states of preservation. This could be very helpful as silica is more soluble as pH increases (in contrast to carbonates and phosphates), and dehydrated silica could reflect areas with relatively high pH microenvironments. These are not common. In the early stages of degradation of dung, the pH can rise (Kirchmann and Witter, 1992). We measured pH values of around 9 for freshly degrading bat guano.

Iron-containing minerals may record areas that, in the past, were devoid of oxygen. Under these reducing conditions, the iron changes its charge state, and as a result, characteristic minerals are formed. If these altered iron minerals are preserved even after oxidizing conditions return, their presence would be an indication of past anaerobic conditions.

In a broader context, it seems that one of the most challenging problems to be addressed is the differentiation between primary activities, when the site was occupied, and secondary activities, after it was abandoned. Despite the fact that the site layout and infrastructure reflect the primary activities, in terms of the microscopic record, the last deposited materials are most likely to be the ones that enter into the archaeological record, and these are derived mainly from secondary activities.

FUTURE PROSPECTS
FOR IMPROVING OUR
UNDERSTANDING
OF THE MISSING
ARCHAEOLOGICAL
RECORD

4

Common Mineral Components of the Archaeological Record

Much of the hard work of an excavation involves removing the sediments from the site to reveal the architecture and/or the artifacts. Most of what is being removed in these buckets is the microscopic record – the archaeological record that is not visible to the naked eye. It often contains a wealth of important archaeological information in the form of microartifacts, biologically produced minerals, organic matter, and the minerals that make up the sediments themselves. Much can be learned about the archaeological record from these microscopic components, including from the minerals themselves: the subject of this chapter.

The potential information content embedded in minerals can be conveniently understood by analogy to the information content of a short text (Figure 4.1). Chemical elements are the basic components of a mineral. In most minerals, they are present in specific proportions (the chemical formula). Chemical elements often have different masses (isotopes), even though their chemical properties are identical. Furthermore, in certain minerals, chemical elements that have similar chemical properties can substitute some of the major chemical elements in the mineral. Both isotopic composition and chemical element substitutions (the substitutions are often referred to as trace elements) can provide archaeologically relevant information such as for radiocarbon dating, paleodiet reconstruction, and much more (Chapter 2).

The identification of the assemblage of minerals in a sediment can provide information on the source of the sediment, the manner in which it was transported to the site, and the modes of deposition at the site (site formation processes). If chemical conditions in the sediments change with time, then some of the minerals may dissolve, and other new minerals (authigenic minerals) may form in their place. The identification of authigenic minerals can provide information on the paleochemistry of the sediments. This in turn may have relevance to the states of preservation of the artifacts (Chapter 3). Some minerals change their atomic structure if exposed to elevated temperatures. This property can be used to reconstruct ancient pyrotechnological practices (Chapter 7).

Even though a list of the minerals present in a sediment is in itself informative, much more information can be obtained if the spatial associations of these minerals are still maintained. This can be achieved by embedding the undisturbed sediment in a polymer and then cutting the hardened block into thin sections for examination using a petrographic microscope or a scanning electron microscope (SEM). The examination of such undisturbed samples is called *micromorphology* (Courty et al., 1989). The information obtained is of particular importance for reconstructing site formation processes. The study of site formation processes is the domain of geoarchaeology, and several excellent and comprehensive books are available on the subject (Rapp and Hill, 1998; Stein and Farrand, 2001; Garrison, 2003; Holliday, 2004; Goldberg and MacPhail, 2006).

Minerals in archaeological sites can be produced in four different ways. *Geogenic minerals* are derived from some geological source such as the breakdown products of igneous rocks. *Authigenic minerals* are those that form in situ in the sediments as a result of changing chemical environments. *Biogenic minerals* are produced by organisms. *Anthropogenic minerals* are the products of human activities. Most of these are formed at high temperatures and can be referred to as *pyrogenic minerals.*

The archaeological record contains a myriad of different minerals, with the more exotic ones often providing key insights into trade, human technical skills, rituals, and so on. Disproportionate attention has been paid to the more unusual minerals. (For information on some less common minerals, see Chapter 12.) In this chapter, and in this book in general, the focus is on the minerals commonly found in archaeological sites: quartz and various siliceous minerals, clays, carbonates, and

---

Inorganic World

In reality most of what is being removed in these buckets is the microscopic record – the archaeological record that is not visible to the naked eye. It often contains a wealth of important archaeological information.

Letters = elements

Words = minerals

Sentences = mineral assemblages

Page = undisturbed sample of sediment

Organic World

CCHCHN CHOCN CHCHCH CONH

Letters = C,H,N,O,S

Words = small molecules

CHN-CHCHCHN-CHOCHO-CHCCNH---

Sentences= large molecules (proteins, polysaccharides)

Figure 4.1
This analogy compares the atoms that make up a mineral to the letters that make up a word. Words contain much more information than a listing of the number and types of letters in the word. The associations of the minerals, as seen in bulk mineralogical analyses, can be compared to sentences, and undisturbed blocks of sediments, as seen in petrological thin sections, can be compared to the text on a page. The bottom portion shows the analogy for organic molecules.

phosphates. These are the minerals that are usually encountered on a day-to-day basis at an excavation. They can provide much information on human behavior and usually determine the preservational state and hence the completeness of the archaeological record of a particular site. Much can be learned from a detailed analysis of the different minerals that make up the sediments. This chapter provides basic information on exploiting these common minerals in archaeology. Chapter 7 deals in more detail with minerals produced by pyrotechnology, and Chapters 5 and 6 focus on common biogenic minerals in archaeology.

MINERALS AND MINERAL IDENTIFICATION

Minerals are composed of chemical elements (atoms). Different minerals may have the same chemical elements, but they are organized into different structures. Each structure is unique. The structure in turn determines the stability of the mineral and often also the conditions under which it forms. Thus a large amount of information can be obtained, both on the origin of the sediment and on the depositional environment, if the mineral type is known. Each mineral has a name. The name identifies the type of mineral. The use of an accepted and widely used nomenclature opens the way for communication between scientists and facilitates comparative studies. Sloppy use of mineral names causes confusion. An example of a mineral classification system is the one proposed by Ferraiolo (1982). In this book, I use the updated version of this classification system (Ferraiolo, 2008). Following are the common methods used for mineral identification.

Optical mineralogy

The oldest and still very useful method for mineral identification is *optical mineralogy*. It involves the use of a special optical microscope known as a *petrographic microscope*. A unique property of a petrographic microscope is that it has two polarizers above and below the sample, which make it possible to conveniently differentiate between crystalline and amorphous minerals. This microscope can be used to identify minerals in the form of grain mounts (i.e., sediment dispersed on a microscope slide) and in thin sections (sediment embedded in a polymer and then ground to a thin layer some 30 microns thick). Examples of optical mineralogy books that also explain the appropriate methods for mineral identification are Heinrich (1965) and Nesse (1991). Note that the same microscope can be used to examine phytoliths and pollen.

X-ray diffraction

X-ray diffraction has, for the most part, replaced optical methods for mineral identification. The advantages of X-ray diffraction are that it can differentiate reliably between thousands of different crystalline mineral types. Furthermore, by collecting the data in various ways, additional information can be obtained on the extent of disorder within the lattice, substitutions of one element for another, precise measurements of distances between atoms, and more. When powders are analyzed, the method usually requires several milligrams of material and sophisticated instrumentation.

As diffraction by X-rays is derived from the manner in which the X-rays interact with a regularly ordered array of atoms, only crystalline minerals can be identified. Furthermore, if the mineral is crystalline, but the crystals are very small, then the diffraction pattern also becomes diffuse and difficult to use for mineral identification. These are two weaknesses of X-ray diffraction for mineral identification, especially in the archaeological context, where amorphous and disordered minerals are common.

Infrared spectroscopy

Infrared spectroscopy can be used for mineral identification (Farmer, 1974). Infrared spectroscopy is widely used in the field of mineralogy, but surprisingly, not as much in related fields such as geology, pedology, and archaeology. Infrared spectroscopy has the major advantage of being able to identify both crystalline and amorphous minerals as well as many organic materials, and only tens of micrograms are required. The instrument usually costs much less than an X-ray diffractometer. Infrared spectrometers are also small enough and sufficiently robust to be used on-site (Weiner and Goldberg, 1990). The difficulty with infrared spectroscopy is that the interpretation of the spectra is often complicated, especially when mixtures of minerals are present. Chapter 12 contains a description of how to use infrared spectroscopy as well as short descriptions of 14 different applications in archaeology.

Infrared spectra can also be obtained through a microscope that, in principle, enables the identification of mineral grains in thin sections. In practice, this proves to be difficult as the section has to be very thin to obtain transmission spectra, or if reflectance spectra are obtained off the specimen surface, then the spectra are less reproducible and often somewhat distorted. The infrared microscope has the potential of combining the advantages of micromorphology and infrared spectroscopy and, if the problems can be resolved, could have a major impact on the field of archaeology. Progress is being made (Berna and Goldberg, 2008).

Raman spectroscopy

Raman spectroscopy can be used for identifying minerals. Raman spectroscopy has the advantage of being nondestructive, and portable

Raman spectrometers are available. Raman spectra can also be obtained through a specially adapted microscope from areas as small as a few square microns. The major problem that I have encountered with the use of Raman spectroscopy for analyzing excavated archaeological materials is that the presence of humic substances adsorbed onto the minerals causes the sample to fluoresce strongly, and in most cases, this makes it impossible to obtain a Raman spectrum. Some exceptions are the analysis of charred materials (Alon et al., 2002) and, of course, the study of archaeological materials that were never buried in sediments. To date, one of the major applications of Raman spectroscopy is in the field of pigment analysis of paintings (Bell et al., 1997).

Chemical elemental analyses

An effective, albeit indirect method for identifying mineral type is by quantitative analysis of the chemical elemental composition using wavelength or energy-dispersive spectrometry (WDS or EDS) detectors in a SEM, or by using a dedicated electron microprobe. The strategy is to calculate the elemental proportions (stoichiometry) of the suspected mineral based on the analysis and compare them to the known stoichiometry of the mineral. If the fit is good, then it is reasonable to assume that this is indeed the mineral type. The problem is that mixed mineral phases, or minerals that are somewhat disordered and have many substituting trace elements, do not provide unequivocal answers. As this approach is not widely used, Appendix A, at the end of the book, explains this method in detail.

SIZE AND SHAPE OF MINERAL PARTICLES

The manner in which the sediments and the artifacts were transported to the site is a key issue in understanding site formation processes. For example, if both the sediments and the artifacts were transported to the site by natural processes, then the interpretation of the artifact assemblage is quite different from the case in which the artifacts were brought to the site by its occupants and the sediments were transported by natural processes. Much can be learned about these aspects of site formation processes by studying the size distribution of the minerals that make up the sediment and their shapes (Goldberg and MacPhail, 2006). This is a basic approach used in sedimentology, and the processes that determine different particle size distributions are relatively well understood. Particle size distributions can, for example, differentiate sand that was deposited by rivers as opposed to dune sand, or wind-blown loess from particles deposited in standing water (Rapp and Hill, 1998). An assemblage dominated by large particle sizes is one that was sorted by high-energy environments such as river transport or by strong winds, resulting in dune formation. Airborne dust (loess) has a characteristic particle size distribution. Sediments that are deposited under water are usually composed mainly of small, fine-grained particles (Rapp and Hill, 1998). If sediments are derived from a combination of sources, this differentiation is not applicable. Furthermore, the physical separation of particles (usually, by sieving) can be affected by practical difficulties (particle aggregates, differently shaped particles passing through the same sieve size, etc.). Despite the difficulties, the analysis of mineral sizes and shapes can provide key information on the ways in which the sediments were deposited in the site. For more information, see Goldberg and MacPhail (2006).

Note some confusing terminology. Sedimentologists use very specific terms for describing particle size ranges (*boulder, cobble, pebble, granule, sand, silt,* and *clay*; Goldberg and MacPhail, 2006, table 1.1). These are common terms that also have general connotations. In the context of defining minerals in sediments, much confusion arises with the term *clay*. For example, a sedimentologist will describe a very fine grained sediment as clay, without implying that it is composed only of clay minerals. Another basic terminology issue that arises in the archaeological context is the loose use of the term *soil*. *Soil* refers to the products of in situ weathering and biological processes that take place at the surface of the earth, whereas *sediment* is a much broader term that encompasses the products formed by many different processes (see Goldberg and MacPhail, 2006, chap. 3). Soils are important in certain archaeological sites (Holliday, 2004), but all sites contain sediments.

IN SITU ASSEMBLAGES OF MINERALS (MICROMORPHOLOGY)

The gap between the macroscopic and the microscopic archaeological record is, to a large extent, filled by the analysis of undisturbed sediments and anthropogenic materials using an optical microscope. The technique is called micromorphology and essentially involves stabilizing, if necessary, the sediment with a polymer, then cutting and grinding a slice of the sample into a 25- to 30-micrometer-thick section and examining it using a petrographic polarizing light microscope. This is certainly one of the most valuable tools available for investigating the archaeological record. An excellent book on this subject is Courty et al. (1989).

Micromorphology can provide direct information not only on the assemblage of minerals present in a sediment, but also on their spatial relations with respect to each other (Matthews et al., 1997). This is almost literally like reading a page out of the sedimentary record. There is often no other alternative source for information of this kind.

The types of information available can be roughly divided into three: (1) natural processes responsible for the formation of the sediment,

(2) the contribution of anthropogenic materials and identifying structural disturbances due to the activities of humans, and (3) some insights into the diagenetic processes that have affected the sediments after deposition. Often the information obtained is dynamic, in the sense that a sequence of events can be deduced.

Micromorphology has several rather serious limitations. As even the largest thin sections are just a few centimeters on a side, the question of how representative the results are is always a major issue. It is thus very helpful to use micromorphology in conjunction with mineralogical analyses of loose sediments; the latter, using infrared spectroscopy, is rapid, and many samples can be analyzed. This provides a better perspective for the interpretation of the thin sections.

Another problem is that often, not all the components in a thin section can be identified. This problem is exasperated by the fact that we naturally tend to see only what we know in an image. The implication is that the more experience the practitioner has, the better the interpretation of the thin section is likely to be.

Ideally, the combination of microscopic examination with a means of identifying the components would be invaluable. Both Raman and infrared spectroscopy can be used in combination with light microscopes, and this should be the best solution to the problem. To date, however, both instruments have proved to be difficult to use in this way (see the preceding discussion and Chapter 12).

Another approach is to examine key areas in a thin section using a SEM fitted with a back-scattered electron detector and an elemental analyzer. The former provides information on the spatial distribution of different materials and the latter on the elemental composition of each material. The elemental composition can then be used to infer the mineral identity (see Appendix A). This is not always unequivocal but can certainly limit the possibilities and provide useful information. Furthermore, the samples examined in the SEM preserve the spatial relations between minerals and thus provide insights into the site formation processes.

A good way to obtain a better appreciation of the potential of micromorphology and associated mineralogical analyses is through an example. The following section is an example of an application of micromorphology, as analyzed by Goldberg et al. (2001).

Zhoukoudian Layer 10 (China): Are these anthropogenically produced ashes?

Zhoukoudian (Peking Man site) is one of the first hominid sites discovered in Asia and one that has produced many bones of *Homo erectus*. The first locality to be excavated at the site (starting in the 1920s and called Locality 1) had several strata within its approximately 45-meter-thick section that contained quartzite tools, implying that these were

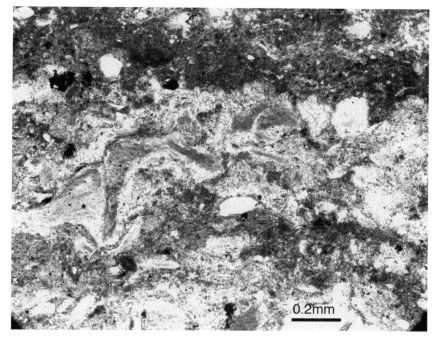

Figure 4.2
Photomicrograph of the
thin section from the
lower unit of Layer 10 in
Locality 1, Zhoukoudian,
China. From Goldberg
et al. (2001).

occupation levels. The oldest of these is from Layer 10. Layer 10 is also famous because it was often cited as being one of the oldest sources of solid evidence for the deliberate use of fire (Renfrew and Bahn, 1991). Interestingly, the first description of the lower part of this layer does not mention the possibility that these were ashes. In fact, only the finely laminated nature of the sediments was noted (Teilhard de Chardin and Young, 1929). Four years later, Black et al. (1933) interpreted this deposit as being the product of burning, noting the presence of ash and charcoal and numerous stone artifacts. Goldberg et al. (2001) and Weiner et al. (1998) reexamined the part of the layer still preserved based on field observations, micromorphology, and mineralogical analyses.

Layer 10 can be divided into upper and lower units. The lower unit is composed of the bedded red, yellow, and dark brown silty layers noted earlier. In the exposed section, no quartzite fragments or debitage were noted in the lower unit, but they were present in the upper unit. Figure 4.2 is a photomicrograph of part of the lower unit. Goldberg et al. (2001, figure 9c) describe the thin section as follows:

... the bedding becomes less well defined, more contorted and chaotic, and there is a greater proportion of rip-up clasts (compared to the base of the unit). Moreover the sediment is locally cemented by micrite (microcrystalline calcite), embedding numerous yellow-brown siliceous plant tissues that range from individual, rectangular cells, up to millimeter size grains of aggregates of tissues. In some places calcite has been replaced by yellow-brown, isotropic phosphate. Finally, many voids and vertical cracks are filled with translocated reddish brown clay, that is similar to that found in Layer 11. (p. 195)

The major mineral components of this layer (based on infrared spectroscopy) are clay, quartz, and carbonate hydroxylapatite (dahllite). The elemental analysis of the clay from the embedded section using EDS shows that the clay is illite, with unusually large amounts of iron. Quartz is probably responsible for the red and yellow colors of some of the sediment layers.

The depositional environment deduced from the presence of alternating fine laminae of dark organic matter and light-colored silt and clay is standing or slowly flowing water. Iron-rich illite is known to form in such environments. The sediments were wet when deposited and were deformed when wet, based on the distorted nature of the layers and the presence of vein fillings, void coatings, and intercalations of clay. The presence of cracks suggests that from time to time, the sediments also dried out. Finally, the presence of authigenic carbonate hydroxylapatite suggests that this sediment was infiltrated by a phosphate-rich solution after deposition. This phosphate may have been derived from the occupation layer immediately overlying this deposit. This scenario, based on micromorphological and mineralogical analyses, is not compatible with the formation of anthropogenic ash and charcoal.

Interestingly, the upper unit of Layer 10 has a totally different character. The thin section shows that it is not finely laminated, but rather, more massive, and that it contains red clay aggregates, small rock fragments, and coprolite fragments. The sediment was probably derived from loess. The presence of authigenic carbonate hydroxylapatite implies that there was a local source of phosphate. A significant proportion of the bones collected from the exposure were burned (Weiner et al., 1998). Weiner et al. (1998) concluded that the close association in this layer of burned bones, quartzite debitage, and phosphate mineral points to an occupation by hominids who were capable of using fire. Obviously, had this layer also contained ashes, the strength of this conclusion would be better.

This study clearly shows that micromorphological analysis, especially in conjunction with mineralogical and elemental analyses, can be an invaluable tool for reconstructing site formation processes.

The following is a review of the properties of the four families of minerals most commonly found in archaeological sites. The focus here is on the geogenic and authigenic members of these families. The biogenic minerals are discussed in Chapters 5 and 6, and the pyrogenic minerals are discussed in Chapter 7.

CALCITE AND THE CALCIUM CARBONATE MINERAL FAMILY

Calcite is the most stable member of the calcium carbonate family of minerals. Calcite is also by far the most common form of calcium carbonate found in archaeological sites. It can be geogenic, biogenic, or pyrogenic in origin. Aragonite is the second most stable form of calcium carbonate. The most common form of aragonite in archaeological sites is of biological origin. Aragonite can also, under certain circumstances, be formed pyrogenically (Lippmann, 1973). The other members of the calcium carbonate family are vaterite, the two hydrated forms monohydrocalcite and ikkaite, and the group of so-called amorphous calcium carbonates. The latter are widely used by many organisms as a transient precursor phase in the formation of biogenic calcium carbonate (Addadi et al., 2003). Monohydrocalcite has been observed in the dung of an extant animal enclosure in a Maasai village (Shahack-Gross et al., 2003). An excellent comprehensive book on the calcium carbonates is Lippmann (1973). In this section, only calcite and aragonite will be discussed.

Calcium carbonate pH buffering capacity

If calcite or aragonite is allowed to dissolve in water until equilibrium is attained, then the pH of the water will be close to 8.2 (Stumm and Morgan, 1970). The dissolved carbonic acid, bicarbonate, and carbonate in water act as a buffering system that tends to maintain the pH around 8.2, even if relatively large amounts of acid or alkali are added. As calcite is so common in the sediments of archaeological sites, its presence will buffer the pH of the water in the sediment to around 8.2. This has important implications for preservation of other components of the archaeological record, for example, bone mineral is stable at this pH (Berna et al., 2003), whereas the silica of phytoliths are relatively soluble at this pH compared to lower pH values (Fraysse et al., 2006).

If calcite is absent in the sediments, the implications for preservation of the archaeological record are far-reaching. The absence of calcite (and other buffering components) can reduce the buffering capacity, and the water in the sediments of the site may become acidic (Weaver et al., 2004) due mainly to the degradation of organic material (Bolan et al., 1991). This in turn implies that the bones will not be preserved, and the calcitic ash and plaster/mortar will also not be preserved. On the other hand, the silica phytoliths are more stable. For more details, see Chapter 3.

Calcite and aragonite: Similarities and differences

Calcite and aragonite are both composed of only calcium carbonate. They differ with respect to the arrangement of their atoms (and are therefore called polymorphs; Figure 4.3). They both have a layered structure, and their calcium ions are in almost identical locations. The main difference is that in calcite, there is a single layer of carbonates, and in aragonite, the layer is staggered and the carbonate moieties are rotated with respect to each other (Lippmann, 1973).

At ambient temperatures and pressures, calcite is less soluble, and hence more stable, than aragonite. Thus aragonite will dissolve more readily than calcite (Lippmann, 1973). The presence of aragonite in the sediments is therefore a good indication that the calcite distribution is also not affected by differential dissolution during diagenesis (Weiner et al., 2007). At elevated temperatures (around 100°C), the reverse is true, and aragonite becomes the more stable polymorph in solution (Lippmann, 1973). This is the reason why the scale that forms in a kettle is composed of aragonite. Aragonite precipitates out of evaporating seawater at ambient temperatures and pressures because Mg ions in seawater prevent calcite nucleation, and as a result, only aragonite forms (Kitano and Hood, 1962). Under certain circumstances, calcite can also form from seawater, but this calcite will contain large amounts of magnesium (Lippmann, 1973).

In a pure solution saturated with respect to calcium carbonate, the calcite crystals that form have a rhomb shape, with very smooth surfaces. In contrast, aragonite forms much smaller crystals that are elongated and are often present as intergrown clusters or aggregates (Figure 4.3).

Possible origins of calcite in archaeological sites

GEOGENIC CALCITES

Geogenic calcites can be an inherent component of the natural sediments of the area in which the archaeological site is located. These calcite crystals could have been brought to the area by wind (calcite is a major component of loess; Courty et al., 1989) or could have been derived from the breakdown of the underlying bedrock, if it is limestone or chalk. Calcite can also form authigenically in the sediments, particularly in the soils from arid and semiarid environments (Holliday, 2004). In caves located in karstic environments, calcite can precipitate from water percolating through the sediments into the cave. As the water enters the cave, some evaporates, and a part of the dissolved carbon dioxide is lost. This raises the saturation level of calcium carbonate, resulting in the formation of calcite, usually in the form of stalagmites, stalagtites, and a variety of other forms (Hill and Forti, 1997). The calcite that forms in this way has many different names, depending on its morphology, color, and so on (Hill and Forti, 1997). In and around many cave sites, the sediments are cemented into a hard composite material, and the cementing agent is calcite. The origin of this calcite could be de novo precipitation from groundwater, or the calcite could be formed by a diagenetic process involving dissolution and reprecipitation of calcitic wood ash (Karkanas et al., 2007).

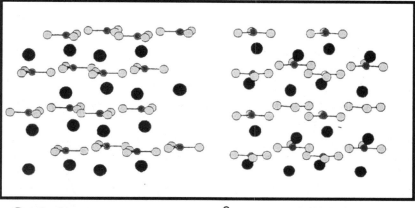

Calcite   ● Ca^{2+} c   Aragonite

○—●● CO_3^{2-} a

Figure 4.3
Top left, Scanning electron microscope images of single crystals of calcite, showing their characteristic rhombohedral shape. *Top right*, Needle- or acicular-shaped crystals of aragonite that precipitated abiologically in the past from the water of the Dead Sea. Note their tendency to form clusters. *Bottom*, The atomic structures of calcite and aragonite. The arrows show the directions of the *c* and *a* crystallographic axes of the projections.

PYROGENIC CALCITES

In archaeological environments, there are two major sources of pyrogenic calcite: the burning of wood and the production of lime plaster and/or mortar. Wood often contains abundant crystals of whewellite (calcium oxalate monohydrate). When the wood is burned, the calcium oxalate loses carbon monoxide and is converted into calcite at temperatures between 430° and 510°C (Pobeguin, 1943). If this calcite is heated to around 800°C, carbon dioxide is lost, and calcium oxide (CaO) forms. The CaO rapidly reacts with the carbon dioxide in the atmosphere and forms calcite (Humphreys et al., 1987; Brochier and Thinon, 2003). When limestone is heated above around 800°C, it also decomposes to form CaO. In lime plaster formation, the calcium oxide is usually deliberately immersed in water to form calcium hydroxide. When the latter is allowed to dry in the atmosphere, it reacts with atmospheric carbon dioxide to form calcite (Boynton, 1980). For more information, see Chapter 7.

BIOGENIC CALCITES

Biogenic calcite is not usually abundant in archaeological sites. One fairly common source, especially in prehistoric sites, is bird eggshells.

At sites near the coast, various mollusk shells may be present that are composed mainly of calcite (such as oysters) or that contain calcite in one or more of their shell layers. Calcite in the form of travertine may form in the proximity of springs. Its formation is often biologically mediated by various algae (Courty et al., 1989). Some calcitic cave deposits may also be biologically mediated (Courty et al., 1989). For more information, see Chapter 6.

Possible origins of aragonite in archaeological sites

The aragonite in archaeological sites is mainly biogenic and is derived from the shells of terrestrial gastropods (land snails), freshwater bivalves (clams), and, for sites near the coast, certain marine mollusks (Chapter 6). Aragonite is a polymorph of calcium carbonate that usually precipitates out of evaporating seawater. Thus coastal sites may have a conglomerate with an aragonitic cement and sometimes also a high-magnesium calcite cement (Milliman, 1974). The natural equivalent of this process of conglomerate formation is called *beach rock*: slabs of quartz grains and other debris that are cemented mainly by aragonite (Milliman, 1974). Aragonite can also be formed from an aqueous solution at high temperatures (Lippmann, 1973). In fact, the deposits produced in kettles used for boiling water are composed of aragonite. The presence of aragonite in sediments may, under certain circumstances, be indicative of a high-temperature formation process (Chapter 7).

Diagenesis of calcite and aragonite

Compared to most minerals in archaeological sites, calcite and aragonite are relatively soluble. This means that if the chemical environment changes and becomes undersaturated with respect to aragonite only or both aragonite and calcite, some of the carbonate mineral phase will dissolve until saturation conditions are restored. If undersaturated conditions are maintained and all the calcite and aragonite dissolves, then another, more stable/insoluble phase will precipitate. This is the basis for Ostwald's Rule of Stages (Ostwald, 1896), namely, that the mineral that forms will be more stable than the mineral that dissolved. This transformation process can take much longer for more insoluble minerals. Highly insoluble minerals can survive for extended periods even under conditions in which they should dissolve, that is, outside their stability field. A demonstrated archaeologically relevant example is the persistence of the highly insoluble phosphate mineral taranakite in cave sediments that were initially rich in guano, even though the current conditions are not within its stability field (Shahack-Gross et al., 2004).

As biogenic and pyrogenic calcites are more disordered than their geogenic counterparts, these calcites will dissolve, and following

Ostwald's Rule, a more ordered/stable phase will form. In this case, it can be more ordered calcite. If biogenic or pyrogenic aragonite dissolves and reprecipitates, the product could conceivably be a more ordered aragonite but is usually an ordered calcite. It is well known that fossil aragonitic shells dissolve and reprecipitate as calcite (Boggild, 1930). If aragonite is heated above 500°C, it will begin to convert into calcite (Lippmann, 1973).

This process of dissolution and reprecipitation can take a different course if other ions are present in the solution that readily form complexes with the dissolved ions. A common example is the phosphate ion that reacts with calcium to form the calcium phosphate mineral carbonate hydroxylapatite (also called dahllite). If magnesium is present in solution, it can inhibit the formation of calcite and cause aragonite to form (Kitano and Hood, 1962; Lippmann, 1973).

Embedded information

ARAGONITE AND CALCITE: ASSESSING THE PRESERVATION STATE OF THE MINERALS IN A SITE

Assessing the completeness of the archaeological record is an essential first step in interpreting the record. A good starting point is to analyze the mineral composition of as many land snails or freshwater clams as can be found from different strata. The reason is that they are composed of aragonite, the calcium carbonate polymorph that is less stable than calcite. Thus, if the shells are all still composed of pure aragonite, it can be assumed that the calcite from the same area is also well preserved, and the calcite distribution should reflect the manner in which it was deposited. If the mollusk shells are composed of both aragonite and calcite, or only calcite, this means that preservation conditions are less good, and the calcite record needs to be interpreted with caution. For more details on this concept, see Chapter 3, and for an example related to snail shell preservation, see Chapter 6.

Note that even though aragonite may be preserved, this does not imply that the aragonite crystals or primary calcite crystals have not been diagenetically altered. Biogenic and pyrogenic calcites and aragonites are initially inherently disordered and will therefore tend to recrystallize. In the process, they may well exchange their isotopes and trace elements (Buchardt and Weiner, 1981).

DIFFERENTIATING AMONG GEOGENIC, BIOGENIC, AND PYROGENIC CALCITES

As calcite is often a major component of the sediments in archaeological sites, it is of much interest to determine whether it is derived from a geogenic source (such as loess) or a pyrogenic source (such as ash or plaster). Biogenic calcite is not common in archaeological contexts and usually has a characteristic macroscopic morphology (e.g., eggshell fragments). There are two approaches to this problem: analyzing calcite crystal morphology and remnant atomic disorder.

Crystal morphology. One way to differentiate between geogenic and pyrogenic calcite is by examining crystal morphology in thin sections using a light microscope. The geogenic calcite crystals are relatively large and often adopt a characteristic rhomb shape. The pyrogenic calcite crystals formed in wood ash are usually very small and have a rather characteristic, so-called micritic appearance. They do, however, sometimes retain the shape of the original calcium oxalate monohydrate (whewellite) crystals from which they were originally derived. These are referred to as *pseudomorphs*. In wood, the calcium oxalate crystals are often elongated and have a rectangular cross section (known as *raphides*; Figure 4.4). Others have tetrahedral or prismatic shapes (Scurfield et al., 1974). If leaves and other organic matter containing calcium oxalate crystals were burned, then the calcite pseudomorphs of these crystals may adopt other characteristic shapes (Franceschi and Horner, 1980). Thus the presence of characteristically shaped calcium oxalate pseudomorphs, especially when still preserved in ordered arrays reflecting their original organization in the plant tissue, is a good indication of an ash-derived deposit (Karkanas et al., 2007). Calcite crystals in lime plaster are also very small but usually do not have characteristic shapes and have a homogeneous micritic appearance (Courty et al., 1989).

Atomic disorder. The study of biological calcite formation processes has revealed that many different invertebrate phyla produce calcite via the initial formation of an amorphous calcium carbonate precursor phase (Beniash et al., 1997; Addadi et al., 2003). The arrangement of the atoms in the mature product is still, however, not as ordered as the atoms in a calcite crystal grown slowly from solution. This "frozen-in" remnant disorder can be detected by X-ray diffraction (Pokroy et al., 2004) but is relatively easily characterized by infrared spectroscopy using the changes in the ratio of two peaks in the infrared spectrum (see Overview 2 in Chapter 12). It was also demonstrated that the calcite in lime plaster produced via the formation of calcium oxide also has remnant disorder, as compared to geogenic calcite (Chu et al., 2008), and that this disorder differs from the disorder in biogenic and geogenic calcites (unpublished observation). Note, however, that this disorder can be lost if the calcite crystals have dissolved and reprecipitated during diagenesis.

CEMENTED SEDIMENT: RECRYSTALLIZED WOOD ASH OR A GEOGENIC CEMENT?

Wood ash is a major component of the sediments of many archaeological sites, in particular, prehistoric caves (Weiner et al., 2007). Being pyrogenic, it is disordered and will tend to dissolve and reprecipitate. The resulting sediment will become cemented and transform into a hard, composite, rocklike material. Cemented sediments are fairly common in caves and are often referred to as breccia, even though they do not have angular inclusions – the characteristic feature of a breccia. In Qesem Cave, Israel, the cement of the "cave breccia" was shown to be derived from wood ash (Karkanas et al., 2007). The phenomenon of wood ash recrystallizing and forming a cemented sediment could well be widespread in archaeological sites.

Cemented sediments may also form if the groundwater is saturated with respect to calcite, and as a result calcite precipitates within the sediment. This calcitic cement may not differ from the cement derived from wood ash, unless, as was the case in Qesem Cave, pseudomorphs of the calcium oxalate crystals are preserved. It could also be expected that a wood ash–derived cement would contain charcoal fragments and/or siliceous phytoliths. Neither of these components, however, preserve well in the relatively high pH conditions of water in equilibrium with calcite, so their absence is not proof that the calcite cement was not derived from wood ash. I have noted at some sites that the cemented sediments often contain bones, whereas the associated loose sediments do not. This could be explained by the formation of the cement soon after sediment deposition. As this recrystallization process transforms the more soluble ash calcite into less soluble geogenic calcite, the ash-derived calcitic cement would be less likely to dissolve than the original ash. Furthermore, the presence of the calcitic cement would assure that the pH remains well above 7 – conditions under which bone mineral does not dissolve. Thus the presence of such wood ash–derived cements could provide information on the use of fire and insight into the diagenetic processes.

CARBONATE HYDROXYLAPATITE

Many different minerals contain calcium and phosphate, and among these are a group of minerals that have the same basic atomic organization, namely, the so-called apatite family of minerals (Nriagu, 1984).

Figure 4.4
Modern wood ash embedded, polished, and then observed with a scanning electron microscope. Remnants of charred organic materials (rounded and elongated structures) as well as small crystals can be seen. The crystals adopt the shapes of the original calcium oxalate crystals that were present in the wood. After burning, they are composed of calcite.

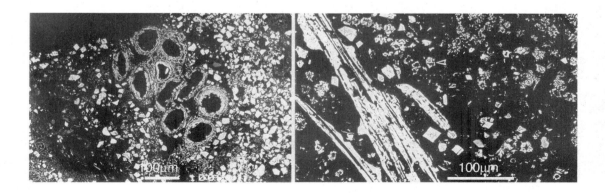

One of the members of this group is particularly important in archaeology: carbonate hydroxylapatite. The reasons are that this is the mineral present in mature vertebrate bones and teeth (Chapter 5), and authigenic carbonate hydroxylapatite commonly forms in sediments when calcium carbonate reacts with phosphate in solution (Chapter 3). Fluoride can enter into the mineral lattice of buried carbonate hydroxylapatite with time. This carbonate fluorapatite can also be found in archaeological sites.

These mineral phases, like all minerals, have formal names, and unfortunately, some minerals are referred to by different names. In this book, I follow Ferraiolo (2008), who uses the names *carbonate hydroxylapatite* and *carbonate fluorapatite* (Ferraiolo, 2008). There is total confusion in the literature regarding the nomenclature of carbonate hydroxylapatite. It is sometimes called *dahllite*, following McConnell (1952, 1969). It is often referred to as *hydroxylapatite* or *hydroxyapatite*. In fact, these are the names given to the noncarbonated form, which rarely, if ever, is present in archaeological sites and is not formed biologically. The carbonate mineral in bones and teeth is not hydroxyapatite. The mineral phase of bones and teeth, or its authigenic counterpart, is also sometimes referred to as *calcium phosphate*, which is totally misleading as this could refer to many different minerals. The term *carbonate apatite* is also sometimes used, even though bone mineral does contain some hydroxyl groups (Cho et al., 2003).

Atomic structure

The atoms in pure hydroxylapatite are organized in a specific, symmetric manner to form a crystalline phase (Figure 4.5). The extent of this order is disturbed mainly by the fact that about 4 to 6 weight percent of the mineral is carbonate (Legeros et al., 1987). Many of these carbonates replace some of the phosphate and hydroxyl groups (Rey et al., 1989; Legeros, 1991). As the phosphate has a tetrahedral shape (a phosphate atom surrounded by four oxygens) and the carbonate has a planar shape (a carbon atom surrounded by three oxygens), this replacement introduces disorder into the crystal. Carbonates could also be located on the crystal surfaces, where perhaps, because they are surrounded by only three oxygens, they somehow stabilize the structure.

Fluoride mainly substitutes hydroxyl groups. Fluoride does not, however, occupy exactly the same locations as the hydroxyl groups, but rather, resides in a more symmetrical location, and hence the resulting carbonate fluorapatite is more stable than carbonate hydroxylapatite (Newesely, 1989). This in turn implies that carbonate fluorapatite is less soluble than carbonate hydroxylapatite (Legeros, 1991). An implication of this increase in stability is that if fluoride is present in the groundwater of an archaeological site, then it will be incorporated into the crystal

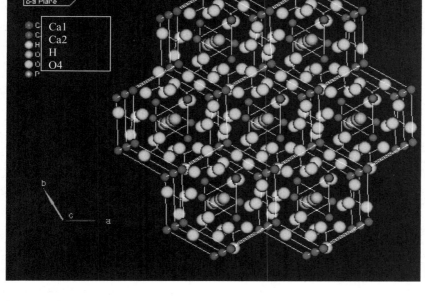

Figure 4.5
Atomic structure of hydroxylapatite. Kindly obtained from Professor Leng Yang, Hong Kong University of Science and Technology; prepared with permission using CaP Model software, produced by the Hong Kong University of Science and Technology. (See also color insert for this image in color.)

lattice. The presence of fluoride in carbonate hydroxylapatite can be qualitatively detected using infrared spectroscopy (see Overview 3 in Chapter 12).

In my experience, carbonate fluorapatite is not abundant in archaeological sites. It could well be that fluoride ions are present in low concentrations in many geogenic carbonate hydroxylapatites, but their presence is not readily detected by X-ray diffraction or infrared spectroscopy. More sensitive methods, such as ion-specific electrodes (Dressler et al., 2002), are more suited for detecting small amounts of fluoride. Note that the term *fluorine* refers to the gas and *fluoride* to the ion.

Stability field

Carbonate hydroxylapatite is stable above pH 7. The precise pH that determines its stability is a function of the concentrations of other ions in the solution in which the mineral is present such as phosphate and aluminum (Karkanas et al., 2000; for more information, see Chapter 3). The stability fields of biogenic and geogenic carbonate hydroxylapatites are not identical because the biogenic mineral is less ordered and the crystals are generally smaller than the geogenic mineral (Berna et al., 2003). Thus there are conditions under which biogenic carbonate hydroxylapatite will dissolve and reprecipitate as geogenic carbonate hydroxylapatite (Chapter 3). Below pH 7, carbonate hydroxylapatite dissolves, and other more stable phosphate minerals form under appropriate conditions.

Diagenesis

Authigenic/geogenic carbonate hydroxylapatite is much less susceptible to diagenetic alteration than bone carbonate hydroxylapatite
because bone crystals are de novo generally much smaller and less ordered at the atomic level, and are hence more soluble (Berna et al.,
2003). Authigenic carbonate fluorapatite is even more stable because
of the presence of the fluoride ions. To my knowledge, no diagenetic
studies have specifically targeted authigenic carbonate hydroxylapatite,
and perhaps more surprising, no use has specifically been made of this
material for extracting environmental information such as groundwater
isotopic composition. Much is known, however, about the diagenesis of
biogenic carbonate hydroxylapatite (Chapter 5).

Embedded information

IDENTIFYING AREAS IN A SITE THAT HAD HIGH ORGANIC CONTENTS

Authigenic carbonate hydroxylapatite forms as a result of phosphate
ions readily reacting with calcite or aragonite crystals in the sediments.
The phosphate is thus "fixed," or stabilized in place. The presence of
authigenic carbonate hydroxylapatite in sediments is therefore an indication that phosphate was once present in the environment at this specific location. This is of much interest archaeologically because the major
source of phosphate (other than dissolving bones) is organic matter. In
archaeological sites, sewers, garbage pits, latrines, animal enclosures,
dung accumulations, and so on, would all be expected to have authigenic carbonate hydroxylapatite in their associated sediments, provided
that calcium carbonate is or was present in the sediments. In the absence
of calcium carbonate, other cations may react with the released organic
phosphate to form different phosphate minerals such as crandallite,
montgomeryite, leucophosphite, and taranakite. All these have been
detected in sediments that were once rich in organic matter (Karkanas
et al., 2000). If authigenic carbonate hydroxylapatite or other phosphate
minerals are not detected, this does not necessarily imply that this was
not an organic-rich environment. The reasons may be that the phosphate is still part of an organic complex and/or that the original organic
matter contained only small amounts of phosphate. The absence of
detectable carbonate hydroxylapatite could also be due to the fact that
the phosphate mineral concentration is below the detection limit of the
method being used. In this case, it would be preferable to use a sensitive colorometric assay to detect phosphate, rather than identifying the
mineral phase. An example is the method reported by Rypkema et al.
(2007).

Note, too, that the presence of authigenic phosphate minerals more
stable than carbonate hydroxylapatite (such as the minerals referred to

previously) does not unambiguously imply that organic-rich environments were present in these locations as well. The reason is that these more stable minerals form under conditions at which bone mineral is not stable, and bone mineral could therefore have dissolved. Therefore these authigenic phosphate minerals could have formed either from organic phosphate or from phosphate derived from dissolved bones.

DIFFERENTIATING BETWEEN BIOGENIC AND GEOGENIC CARBONATE HYDROXYLAPATITES

Crystals of carbonate hydroxylapatite formed in vitro are rather similar in size and shape to those formed in vivo: both are small and plate shaped (Ziv and Weiner, 1994). During diagenesis, the biogenic crystals of bone increase in size and in atomic order (Trueman et al., 2003). This is well expressed by increasing values of the splitting factor measured from infrared spectra (see Overview 4 in Chapter 12). Very few studies have been conducted that examine changing crystal morphologies with time. There are indications that they tend to become more elongated and needlelike (Reiche et al., 2002; Trueman et al., 2003). It is therefore difficult to differentiate between geogenic (authigenic) and biogenic fossil carbonate hydroxylapatite crystals, unless, of course, the biogenic crystals are still part of a bone fragment. One theoretical possibility for differentiating between the two after the crystals are dispersed is by measuring the oxygen isotopic composition of the phosphates. If the original composition is preserved, then it should reflect, at least in the case of mammals, that the crystals formed at elevated temperatures (Luz and Kolodny, 1989).

PALEOCLIMATE RECONSTRUCTION

The oxygen atoms bound to the phosphate (as opposed to those bound to the carbon) in carbonate hydroxylapatite are less likely to be exchanged with oxygen in the water from the surroundings. The phosphate oxygen isotopic composition can therefore be expected to be relatively well preserved. The isotopic composition of the phosphate oxygen reflects the isotopic composition of the water from which the crystals formed (Longinelli, 1965). This indirectly is a function of climate (Luz and Kolodny, 1989). Bone phosphate oxygen isotopic composition has been used for paleoclimate reconstruction (Bryant et al., 1994; Chapter 5), but not authigenic carbonate hydroxylapatite. As authigenic carbonate hydroxylapatite forms at ambient temperatures and directly from the water in the sediment, it should produce a good environmental signature of rainwater oxygen isotopic composition. If, however, the authigenic phosphate mineral dissolves and reprecipitates during diagenesis, then exchange may occur due to biologically mediated exchange of the phosphate oxygen when in solution (Blake et al., 1997).

USING AUTHIGENIC PHOSPHATE MINERALS FOR IDENTIFYING STRATA IN WHICH BONES HAVE DISSOLVED

Bones dissolve below a pH of around 7. It is of much interest to know whether strata in which bones are absent can be attributed to the bones having dissolved or to human or animal behavior that excluded the deposition of bones at that location. One approach is to determine whether other authigenic phosphate minerals that are more insoluble (and hence more stable) than carbonate hydroxylapatite are in the sediments under investigation. If so, it can be concluded that the conditions existed for bones to have dissolved, and bones may once have been present. On the other hand, if more soluble minerals are preserved in the sediments, such as primary ash calcite, it is unlikely that the bones would have dissolved. Weiner et al. (1993) used this approach in Kebara Cave, Israel. Another possible refinement to this approach is to note whether the authigenic mineral montgomeryite formed, as opposed to crandallite. Both form under more or less the same pH conditions, but montgomeryite forms when phosphate concentrations are high, and crandallite forms when they are low. Thus the presence of montgomeryite in confined contexts in a stratum may well be indicative of bones having dissolved (Karkanas et al., 2002).

POLYMORPHS OF SILICON DIOXIDE

This family of minerals is composed of a variety of polymorphs that have the composition of silicon dioxide (SiO_2), with or without associated hydroxyl groups and water molecules. Quartz is the most crystalline and stable form of silicon dioxide. At the other end of the spectrum is the polymorph silica (also known as *opal*). It has a disordered structure that also incorporates hydroxyl and water moieties (see Figure 6.1 for a schematic of its structure). Between these two end members are several partially ordered forms known as opal-A and opal-CT (Kastner et al., 1977) as well as two polymorphs that form at high temperatures and ambient pressures: tridymite and cristobolite. These polymorphs can be found in some products of pyrotechnology (Chapter 7). For more information on these minerals and their infrared spectra, see also Overview 7 in Chapter 12.

Quartz and flint/chert

In the archaeological context, it can be said that quartz is forever. Quartz rarely, if ever, undergoes any structural changes at the atomic level. The ultimate source of most of the quartz in an archaeological site is eroded igneous and metamorphic rocks. The quartz is often transported long distances from its source and, as a result, undergoes mechanical abrasion. The shape and size of the quartz grains can thus reflect its provenience (see the following Embedded information section). Quartz is not formed biologically.

Quartz can also be produced in a totally different way. When accumulations of biogenic silica (mainly from diatoms, radiolarians, and sponges) are buried for long periods of time, the elevated temperatures and pressures cause the silica to dissolve, migrate through the sediments, and reprecipitate in a microcrystalline form around some nucleus (Calvert, 1974). The product is called *chert*, or if it has a gray to black color, it is usually called *flint*. As the quartz crystals are small and intergrown, the chert fractures very smoothly in a manner that resembles glass. It is this unique property that makes chert/flint such a desirable raw material for the production of stone tools. It would be very interesting to better understand, in a quantitative manner, the fracture properties of flint and determine whether flint knappers could have subconsciously selected for this property.

It is interesting to note that the infrared spectrum of chert/flint is not identical to that of large-grained quartz (see Overview 7 in Chapter 12). As the main difference in the infrared spectrum is a shift in the major peak location, rather than a broadening of this peak, this disorder is probably due to a compositional and/or structural change compared to quartz derived from igneous rocks.

It has been shown that much of the silt-sized quartz in sedimentary rocks, such as mudstones, may also have been derived from the diagenetic crystallization of silica, and not, as is generally thought, from igneous rocks (Schieber et al., 2000).

Silica

Silica (opal) has no long-range order and is therefore referred to as having an *amorphous* structure. This term usually implies that it is isotropic in polarized light and does not diffract X-rays. It does not imply that its atoms are not at all ordered. They do have short-range order, with the silicon atoms being surrounded by four oxygen atoms in a tetrahedral arrangement – the characteristic motif of all silicates.

Silica is produced today, as it was in the past, in huge quantities by organisms. The main producers are the single-celled photosynthetic organisms called diatoms, the marine zooplankton called radiolarians, some marine sponges, and many different higher plants that live on land and in freshwater (Lowenstam and Weiner, 1989). This biogenic silica rarely accumulates in sedimentary deposits as it tends to dissolve both in seawater and in soils (Loucaidies et al., 2008). Paradoxically, silica in the form of phytoliths is often found in high concentrations in archaeological deposits. The reason for this is not known (see Chapter 6 for more details). Authigenic silica can also be formed as a result of the breakdown of clays or as a reaction product that forms at ambient temperatures in hydraulic cements (Chapter 7).

Silicon dioxide polymorphs produced at high temperatures

Quartz undergoes a series of transformations at high temperatures. The polymorphs formed can be identified by X-ray diffraction and infrared spectroscopy (see Overview 7 in Chapter 12). In the absence of fluxes, the stable form of quartz, namely, α-quartz, converts to β-quartz at 573°C. The latter converts to tridymite around 870°C, and at temperatures above about 1250°C, cristobolite forms (Deer et al., 1992). These high-temperature polymorphs are sometimes present in ceramics. As fluxes can change these transformation temperatures, the presence of a particular high-temperature polymorph can only be used as a rough indication of firing temperature of the ceramic.

Diagenesis

QUARTZ

In archaeological contexts, quartz is almost always stable. Mechanical abrasion during transport can reflect the provenience of the quartz (Rapp and Hill, 1998).

SILICA

At ambient temperatures and pressures, the solubility of silica is 17 times higher than quartz, and all the other polymorphs have intermediate solubilities. Silica dissolution rates are lowest at very acidic pH values (around 3) and increase with increasing pH (Fraysse et al., 2006). Silica is not always stable in archaeological contexts. As its solubility increases with increasing pH, it is susceptible to partial or complete dissolution, especially in carbonate-containing sediments that are buffered to a pH above 8. Despite this, authigenic and biogenic silica are usually preserved in archaeological sites but may show signs of surface etching.

MICROCRYSTALLINE QUARTZ IN FLINT AND CHERT

It is rare to observe any chemical alteration of flint from archaeological sites. However, flint is not inert, and it does undergo both mechanical and chemical alteration, particularly on its surface. This is described in some detail by Burroni et al. (2002). I observed flint tools that were partially replaced by carbonate hydroxylapatite in Kebara Cave, Israel. Even in this cave, the phenomenon was rare.

Embedded information

PROVENIENCE OF QUARTZ

The source of most quartz grains are igneous and metamorphic rocks that have undergone weathering. Quartz is usually just one product of such weathering and is often associated with other weathered products such as clay. In sediments from high-energy environments, such as beach sand and sand dunes, the less stable minerals and the ones with smaller particle sizes are effectively removed, and quartz is often the major component. The examination of quartz grain size, shape (especially roundness), and the proportion of strained quartz grains (using optical petrography) can provide information on the provenience of the sediments (Greensmith, 1963; Goldberg and MacPhail, 2006). This approach can be used in archaeology by comparing these properties to those of quartz grains in the surroundings of the site. This would be of particular interest if the quartz sand was deliberately brought to the site as a raw material for construction or for the production of glass.

PROVENIENCE AND PROCUREMENT STRATEGIES OF FLINT AND CHERT

Most flint in archaeological contexts was brought to the site by humans. This in turn raises the questions of where it was brought from and how it was extracted at the procurement site – questions of much interest, especially in prehistory (Chapter 2).

Determining flint provenience is based on correlating a suite of properties of the flint assemblage at the site with flint sources in the environment around the site. The properties that can be used are color; texture; the presence of microfossils, as seen in thin sections; and variations in trace element contents (Della Casa, 2005; Navazo et al., 2008). The effectiveness of this approach is a direct function of the nature of the local flint; if there are abundant sources and their properties are diverse, then the task is very difficult. If only a few sources are available and they have distinct characteristics, the provenience of flint from a site can be more easily determined.

It is also of much interest to identify the procurement strategies used to obtain the flint for producing tools. This provides some insight into the extent to which the quality of the material was taken into account by the knappers, and the effort that was made to procure the best-quality material. The simplest procurement strategy is surface collection. As flint extracted from beneath the surface has better properties for knapping than surface-exposed flint (Barber et al., 1999), at some point in time, humans began extracting this underground flint. These procurement strategies can be identified by measuring the concentrations of the cosmogenic ^{10}Be isotope in the flints from cave sites (Verri et al., 2004). The principle involved is that if the flint is exposed to cosmic radiation for long periods of time, then [10]Be is produced inside the flint. This occurs in flints lying on the surface for tens or hundreds of thousands of years. As this type of cosmic radiation does not penetrate more than 2 meters beneath the surface, flint without [10]Be must have been derived from a source deeper than 2 meters below the surface or from a ledge somehow protected from cosmic radiation. The reason why only flint from caves can be analyzed is that after the flint had been used for knapping, it must not be exposed to cosmic radiation in order to prevent more [10]Be from being produced. A cave is usually such an environment (Verri et al., 2004, 2005). It has been shown that the flint used for different tool types in the Lower Paleolithic site of Qesem, Israel, was obtained using different procurement strategies (Boaretto et al., 2009b).

DATING OF FLINT TOOLS

Natural radiation that impinges on flint from the surrounding sediments or emanates from within the flint causes electrons to be activated to higher energy levels. These are often trapped and can be released by heating. This release also results in light being emitted and this so-called thermoluminescence (TL) can be measured. If the flint tool was heated when it was produced or used, then the trapped charges are all released. They start to accumulate again after the tool is buried. The amount of trapped charge that then accumulates is proportional to the time since the flint tool was heated. This is the basis for using TL for dating flint tools (Chapters 2 and 10).

THE CLAY FAMILY

Clays are one of the major components of soils and therefore of most sediments in archaeological sites. They are also the major component of mud bricks and hence accumulate in vast quantities in sites where these were used extensively (Rosen, 1986). Clays are also the most common raw material used for producing bricks and ceramics.

The abundance of clays on the earth's surface is due to the fact that they are the major breakdown product of minerals produced in the interior of the earth at high temperatures and pressures. The type of clay produced reflects both the starting material and the conditions under which this diagenetic breakdown process occurred. Most clays are also very fine grained and hence easily transported by water and wind. They can thus be separated physically from the other mineral breakdown products (particularly quartz). Because of their small particle size, clays tend to deposit in low-energy environments such as standing water bodies and shallow seas.

Clay-rich sediments have "plasticlike" properties (Kingery and Francl, 1954), arising from the fact that clays are generally fine-grained, plate-shaped particles that tend to bind relatively large amounts of

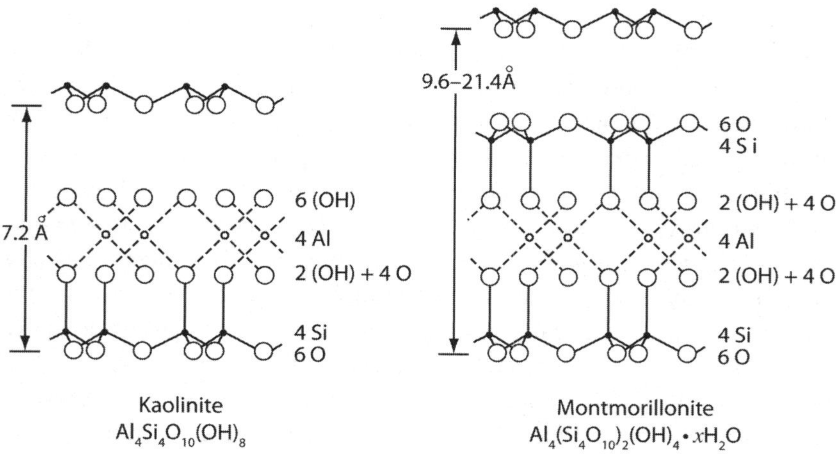

Kaolinite
$Al_4Si_4O_{10}(OH)_8$

Montmorillonite
$Al_4(Si_4O_{10})_2(OH)_4 \cdot xH_2O$

Figure 4.6
Schematic of the structures of two of the common clay minerals, showing the single-layer sheet of kaolinite and the double-layer sheet of montmorillonite. Adapted from Mason (1958).

water. Sediments with these "plastic" properties were named "clays" long before mineralogists recognized that these minerals all have basic common structural features at the atomic level. The clays belong to a family of minerals called *sheet silicates* (also known as *layered silicates*). This family includes minerals such as the common biotite and muscovite. For more information on clays, see Dixon and Weed (1977) and Deer et al. (1992).

A source of confusion is that the term *clay* is also used in sedimentology to describe a specific range of particle sizes, irrespective of the minerals that may be present within this size range. For more information on clays from an archaeological perspective, see Henderson (2000, chap. 4) and Rapp and Hill (1998, chap. 8).

Clay structures and classification

There are basically two different layer types that make up the sheet silicates in general, including the clay family of minerals. These are layers or sheets composed of silicon atoms that bind four oxygen atoms to form a tetrahedron, and layers of aluminum atoms that bind eight oxygen atoms to form an octahedron. These two layer types alternate, and each layer shares some of the oxygens. The different layer arrangements are an important feature that defines the particular clay mineral (Figure 4.6).

The clay minerals are usually divided into five groups, as follows: (1) the kaolinite group, (2) the illite group, (3) the smectite group, (4) the vermiculite group, and (5) the palygorskite group. The first three groups include most of the commonly found clays. This rather tidy classification based on atomic structure is compromised by the fact that in many clay deposits, the clay types are mixed and hence very difficult to characterize. Furthermore, the silicon atoms can be partially substituted by aluminum, and the aluminum atoms in the octahedral sites can be partially substituted by magnesium and iron. The charge imbalance that these substitutions cause is redressed by the interleaving of other cations between layers such as calcium, sodium, or potassium. Another difficulty is that many clays either do not have any long-range atomic order, or their particle sizes are so small that their periodic atomic structures cannot be easily identified. These so-called amorphous clays are apparently a lot more common than was previously recognized and are difficult to classify. Yet another complication is that clays can easily occlude many other ions and organic molecules, in addition to water molecules. These generally reside between the sheets. They not only change the clay composition, but also its swelling properties. So it has been, and still is, a challenge to classify and characterize clays. A whole community of mineralogists devote themselves to this challenge. A brief overview of information on clay structures and mineral properties is given by Deer et al. (1992).

Identifying clay minerals

A reliable identification of a clay mineral more often than not requires a combination of analytical methods:

1. Chemical analysis provides quantitative information on the atoms present in the sample. For example, a ratio of silicon to aluminum of 1 is a good indicator that kaolinite is a major component.
2. X-ray diffraction (powder) is used mainly to determine the distances between layers (7 Ångstroms for the kaolinite group; 10 Ångstroms for the illite group, 15 Ångstroms for the smectite group, and 14.5 Ångstroms for the vermiculite group). The most common form of clays is actually a mixture of illite with some smectites (usually montmorillonite). The presence of mixtures changes the layer spacing, as measured by X-ray diffraction.
3. Differential thermal analysis (DTA) can also be used to distinguish between clay mixtures as it is sensitive to water loss and phase changes on heating.
4. Infrared spectroscopy can provide general information on the dominant clay types (see Overview 8 in Chapter 12).

Clay and organic materials

An integral part of soil formation is the involvement of plants and their breakdown products. Thus clays that form during this process are exposed to organic matter and are influenced by their breakdown products. This is a complex process that varies significantly in different climatic regimes (Righi and Meunier, 1995). For our purposes, it can be assumed, unless proved otherwise, that clays have some strongly bound organic molecules. A very general trend is that in more tropical and hotter climates, less organic matter remains associated with the clays than in temperate and colder climates. This organic matter is very difficult to remove completely, even by oxidation. One important implication in archaeology is that the presence of clays in a sample of charcoal, for example, can significantly alter the radiocarbon content, and hence the age obtained (Chapter 10).

Diagenesis

The oldest soils are found in the tropics. Their major components, irrespective of the rock type from which they were derived, are kaolinite and hydroxides and oxides of iron and aluminum (mainly goethite, hematite, and gibbsite; Righi and Meunier, 1995). Thus these are the most stable end products of diagenesis of rocks in general and are the major and characteristic components of the red soils that are distributed around the world in the tropics. Above and below these tropical zones are soils that form in arid and desert zones. They are dominated by quartz, but in areas where a major clay component is present, it is smectite. With increasing latitude, the clay components include both illite and smectite, often associated with carbonate minerals. The organic component also increases. At even higher latitudes, the organic component is more prominent, and the acidity of these sediments can result in the formation of more amorphous and hence more soluble clay components. The stable clay components are a mix of vermiculite and various mixed-layer clays. In fact, soils at high latitudes are often dark colored because of the presence of organic matter (Righi and Meunier, 1995). Much of this organic matter was stabilized by having been burned (Schmidt et al., 2002; Eckmeier et al., 2007). Thus the sequence of clay types encountered with increasing latitude also more or less reflects their relative stabilities.

There are, however, too many contributing factors for clay type variations in a sediment profile to be used as an indicator of climatic change. One such variable is the nature of the parent rock from which the clay was derived. Another is that during soil formation, clays move up and down the profile in a process called *illuviation*.

Clay can also break down into disordered, noncrystalline forms under natural conditions, such as the degradation of volcanic ash (Wada, 1977), and also as a result of specific conditions that may occur within archaeological contexts. For example, phosphate can react with clay. This will tend to occur under acidic conditions. The original clays lose cations and tend to become more like kaolinite, and silica as well as various relatively insoluble phosphate minerals form (Nriagu, 1976). The latter type of reaction is probably responsible for the formation of noncrystalline clays in the lower strata of Hayonim Cave, Israel

(Weiner et al., 2002), including the formation of authigenic silica (Karkanas et al., 2002). Clay can also lose some of its crystalline order when exposed to elevated temperatures. This change can provide a rough estimate of the temperature to which the clay was exposed (see Overview 9 in Chapter 12).

Embedded information

BETTER PRESERVATION IN CLAY-RICH SEDIMENTS

One of the many unusual physical properties of clays is that they tend to retain water, and because of their small particle size, they block pores and hence do not allow water to pass through freely (Righi and Meunier, 1995). Thus a clay-rich layer acts as a surface on top of which groundwater flows (Goldberg and MacPhail, 2006), and where it intersects the ground surface, springs often develop. For the same reasons, clay-rich sediments in archaeological sites tend to minimize the movement of water. Water is an "aggressive" reagent chemically in the sense that it removes ions and hence induces minerals to release more ions. Thus water moving through the sediments promotes dissolution. It also promotes oxidation of organic matter in that the newly arrived water usually contains more oxygen if it recently originated at the surface. The result is that preservation of certain minerals and organic matter tends to be better if the associated sediments are rich in clay. This was noted for bone preservation by Weiner and Bar-Yosef (1990) and may be the case for ash, plaster, and other artifacts composed of relatively soluble minerals.

CLAY PROVENIENCE

The wide use of clays for construction purposes and for the production of bricks and ceramics raises the issue of the locations of the local sources of clays for a particular site. Finding these sources in turn raises the broader issue of the nature of the local landscape at the time of occupation. Ethnographic studies show that suitable sources of clay for ceramics are usually available within 7 kilometers of a site (Arnold, 1985, 2005). Actually proving that a particular location was indeed the source of clay used at a certain time is not easy, bearing in mind how difficult it is even to identify clay minerals. This is often complicated by the fact that the question of provenience arises in relation to clay sources for ceramics, and hence the clays of interest have been heated to high temperatures. Thus, for provenience purposes, it is often more practical to look for other stable minerals that may be associated with the clay and are not affected by heating, or compare the overall chemical compositions of all the minerals (Chapter 7). In a study of constructed clay hearths produced around 30,000 years ago in Klisoura Cave 1, southern Greece, the presence of the same assemblage of local rock types in a nearby paleosol and in the constructed hearths was used to identify the source material (Karkanas et al., 2004).

WAS THE CLAY EXPOSED TO ELEVATED TEMPERATURES?

Clay structure does change when heated above about 400°C (Rama-swamy and Kamalakkannan, 1995). Clay, however, is an excellent insulator, and the heat does not easily penetrate into the clay layer, unless the heating is for an extended period of time (Bellemo and Harris, 1990). A natural brush fire or the act of making a fire on a clay-rich sediment substrate for several hours may, at most, alter the upper millimeter or so of the surface clay (personal observations). It was thus a surprise to discover, in our systematic analyses of the sediments of Tel Dor, Israel, that large volumes of sediments were exposed to elevated temperatures and clearly had altered structures as a result. Some of these sediments were altered during a major destruction phase on the tell, where many other indications of an intense conflagration were evident (Berna et al., 2007). Other sediments were heated to high temperatures as a result of metal-casting activities. We were not, however, able to identify specific causes for heating of many of the other heat-exposed sediments.

The altered structure can be identified by X-ray diffraction, nuclear magnetic resonance (NMR), and Raman and infrared spectroscopy (Farmer, 1974; Shoval, 1993; Bray and Redfern, 1999). As different clay types respond to heating in different ways, it is helpful to "calibrate" the local clay types, especially if a rough estimation of temperature of exposure is of interest (Berna et al., 2007). Another way to estimate the temperature of exposure is to reheat the sample in an oven and record the temperature at which mineral phases become unstable using DTA (Cole and Hoskins, 1957; Karkanas et al., 2004) or infrared spectroscopy (see Overview 9 in Chapter 12).

GENERAL IMPLICATIONS OF MINERAL ASSEMBLAGES FOR SITE PRESERVATION

Quartz, clay, and the carbonate minerals calcite and aragonite are often the major components of the sediments of archaeological sites. They determine the prevailing pH conditions and the intensity of water flow through the sediments. These parameters influence mineral solubility and whether oxygen dissolved in the water is freely available or limiting. Oxygen availability in turn influences the microbial activity that results in more or less degradation of the organic material. This network of interactions, in essence, defines the preservational conditions of a site (Chapter 3).

In assessing the preservational conditions of a site or locations within a site where quartz, clay, and the carbonate minerals are the major mineral components of the sediments, it is helpful to know if all three major mineral components are present. If they are, then preservational conditions can be expected to be relatively good. If one of the three major components is absent and the sediments are not cemented, then there may be significant consequences in terms of preservation:

1. In the absence of carbonates, the water in the sediments is not buffered and the pH can drop to acidic conditions, and the bones will dissolve. On the other hand, the silica will be stable, and as microbial activity decreases somewhat at low pH, organic matter may be better preserved.
2. In the absence of quartz, the flow of water through the sediments decreases, and this generally creates conditions for better preservation of the more soluble carbonate and phosphate minerals.
3. In the absence of clay, the flow of water through the sediments increases significantly, and the more soluble carbonates and phosphate minerals may dissolve.

It is fairly rare that two of the three major components are absent in the sediments. If two are in fact absent, the preservational consequences may be far-reaching. A sediment dominated by quartz has no buffering capacity, and water passes through the sediments with ease. This will result in dissolution of the carbonate and phosphate minerals, and in loss of organic material. A sediment dominated by carbonates also has a high water throughput, and although the carbonates and phosphates will most likely be preserved (bear in mind that the less stable pyrogenic and biogenic minerals may dissolve), organic matter is unlikely to be preserved. Finally, if clay is the only major component, water will not pass through the sediments easily, and organic matter will tend to preserve better, particularly if the pH is acidic and the microbial activity decreases.

ASSESSING THE COMPLETENESS OF THE ARCHAEOLOGICAL RECORD

The common clay, carbonate, and phosphate minerals can provide key information on a fundamental issue often overlooked in archaeological studies, namely, whether the archaeological record of a particular site contains all the components that were buried at the site, or whether some materials have been lost during diagenesis. Obviously, this information is necessary before an interpretation of the record can be made. See Chapter 3 for more details of how these common minerals as well as the associated biogenic and authigenic minerals can be used to address the key issue of completeness of the archaeological record.

5

Biological Materials: Bones and Teeth

Biologically produced mineralized materials are an important component of the archaeological record. The most common biogenic materials found in archaeological sites are bones, teeth, mollusk shells, eggshells, otoliths, and plant phytoliths. The fact that they are mineralized greatly increases their chances of being preserved, and as they are biologically produced, they contain much embedded information of interest to archaeology.

BIOMINERALIZATION: ARCHAEOLOGICAL PERSPECTIVE

The biogenic mineralized materials common in archaeological sites are part of a much larger group of mineralized materials produced by a wide variety of organisms, ranging from bacteria to man (for overviews, see Lowenstam and Weiner, 1989; Simkiss and Wilbur, 1989; Dove et al., 2003). More than 65 different minerals are known to be produced biologically. These include minerals that, at the atomic level, are highly disordered such as amorphous silica (opal), amorphous calcium carbonate, and amorphous calcium phosphate. Most biogenic minerals are relatively ordered at the atomic level and are thus crystalline. Common crystalline biogenic minerals include the carbonate minerals (such as calcite, aragonite, vaterite, and monohydrocalcite), the calcium phosphate mineral carbonated apatite, oxides (such as the magnetic mineral magnetite), calcium oxalates, and more. For a partial list, see Appendix B. Biogenic minerals usually have shapes that are quite distinct from their inorganic counterparts and are often aligned into arrays. Biogenic mineral assemblies almost always have intimately associated organic components, some of which are responsible for controlling mineral formation.

The mineralization process, like all biological processes, is orchestrated by cells. They produce the microenvironment in which mineral formation takes place. This can be within cells, and the mineralization site is defined by a membrane, or outside cells, where the mineralization site is usually defined by a macromolecular organic matrix (Lowenstam and Weiner, 1989). The macromolecules of the extracellular organic matrix can usually be divided into two groups: the framework macromolecules and the macromolecules that are involved actively in controlling mineral nucleation, growth, and inhibition. Examples of framework macromolecules are type I collagen in bone and dentin, β-chitin in mollusk shells, and α-chitin in crustaceans. The mineral-controlling macromolecules are often highly acidic, being rich in the amino acid called aspartic acid. The carboxylate side group of this amino acid can interact with cations, such as calcium, and in this way, the assemblage of aspartic acid-rich proteins can perform their various mineral-controlling functions. Some of these organic materials form an envelope or organic matrix around the mineral particles (intercrystalline matrix), and some are actually occluded inside the mineral phase during its formation (intracrystalline matrix) (Weiner and Addadi, 1997). From the archaeological perspective, the intracrystalline matrix constitutes a protected niche in the sense that these molecules are likely to be relatively well preserved in the archaeological record as they are essentially sealed off from the environment (Chapter 8). Occluded macromolecules from fossil mineralized materials can provide paleogenetic information, as well as information on paleodiet and paleoenvironments.

Over the last decade, it has become apparent that many of the minerals formed biologically are initially deposited in an amorphous form, and only subsequently crystallize (Weiner et al., 2005). The crystallization process is often not complete, and the mineral phase of even the mature mineralized tissue is more disordered than the nonbiogenic counterpart of the same mineral (Addadi et al., 2003). This small difference may result in biogenic minerals dissolving more easily during diagenesis. The extent to which this disorder is preserved can be used to evaluate the state of preservation of the biogenic mineral phases of interest in the archaeological record (Chapters 3 and 4).

Some mineralized tissues are produced almost continuously over the lifetime of the organism. A good example is the shell of the mollusk. These mineralized tissues thus record changing physiological conditions of the animal, and even more important from the archaeological perspective, they may record the changing environmental conditions in which the animals live. They thus offer opportunities to reconstruct aspects of the paleoenvironment. For more information on this aspect of biomineralization, see Dove et al. (2003).

Thus biologically produced materials potentially contain much embedded information that can be exploited in archaeology. In this chapter, two of the most well-investigated biological materials, bones and teeth, are described. In the chapter that follows, the other archaeologically important biological materials – eggshells, mollusk shells, otoliths, and phytoliths – are discussed.

The structure of a mineralized tissue is the key to a better understanding of preservation and diagenesis. Knowledge of diagenesis is necessary to use the information embedded in the structure for archaeological purposes. Thus the pertinent aspects of structure are first discussed, followed by diagenesis, and finally, the embedded information.

BONE AND BONES

Bones are usually the most common macroscopic, biologically produced materials found in archaeological sites. The bones from relatively large mammals preserved in a site are generally derived from animals that were killed and eaten, whereas the bones of small mammals are, for the most part, from rodents living on-site. Small mammal bones can also be brought to specific areas of a site by birds of prey such as owls. Coastal sites and sites near freshwater bodies often contain large numbers of fish bones. These, too, are assumed to be from fish caught for food. Bones can also be used to produce bone tools of various types. For the last 15,000 years or so, dogs have lived in a symbiotic association with humans (Tchernov and Valla, 1997). They have almost certainly reduced the number of bones that enter into the archaeological record. Ethnographic studies attest to the fact that very few bones survive the scavenging of dogs (Kramer, 1982; Chapter 9). Despite this, bones are found, and it is of much interest to understand the circumstances under which bones escaped scavenging.

The study of bones from archaeological sites is a well-developed field within archaeozoology. Much has been written about the analysis of bone assemblages to deduce the past hunting behaviors of humans and/or their use of domestic animals. These studies can be seriously biased if certain bones are differentially preserved as compared to others, and/or bones are lost due to diagenesis in some parts of a site. Furthermore, the study of cut marks, fracture surfaces, and so on, can also be affected by state of preservation. Bone diagenesis can be discerned even at the macroscopic level. Many archaeologists describe bone preservation at their sites or in certain areas within the site, at least in terms of being well preserved or poorly preserved. This can rarely be done for mollusk shells. This reflects the fact that bones, as compared to shells, can undergo rather severe diagenesis, and their appearance and mechanical properties change remarkably. I have noticed another difference: whereas the original shell material may often be lost completely, leaving only the cast of the shape of the shell in the sediment (a so-called pseudomorph), this almost never happens with bones. There is something inherently different between these two materials. Bone diagenesis is thus an important subject, and one that has been investigated in detail.

In English, the terms *bones* and *bone* are used in a rather confusing way. The term *bones* refers to the objects, and the term *bone* is often used to refer to the material of which these objects are composed. Bearing this in mind, it should be noted that despite the huge number of morphological forms of bones, and the fact that they may fulfill different functions (such as load bearing in the case of long bones, and protection in the case of skull bones), variability in the types of bone material is rather limited (Currey, 2002). In fact, it is helpful to think of bone, the material, as a multipurpose material (Weiner et al., 2000), a sort of "concrete" of the vertebrate skeleton, in that basically, the same material is used for many different functions. Bone structure varies according to the length scale at which the structure is examined. Bone is thus a hierarchically organized material. In bone, the material also varies in structure, to some extent, from one location to another, even within the same bone. Bone is thus also a graded material. Understanding structure is the key to better understanding diagenesis and the information embedded in the structure. The following is a brief overview of the hierarchical structure of bone the material.

Bone the material: The hierarchical structure

Weiner and Wagner (1998) have organized bone material into seven hierarchical levels of organization. As this scheme has been fairly widely accepted, I will follow it here. The hierarchical scheme is illustrated in Figure 5.1.

LEVEL 1: THE BASIC CONSTITUENTS

The basic constituents of bone are mineral, organic matter (the *organic matrix*), and water. The relative proportions of these constituents are not fixed and can vary considerably between bones (Figure 5.2). The average mineral content of a particular bone is under strict biological control. Most bones have mineral contents that range from 60 to 70 weight percent (circle in Figure 5.2). Furthermore, the mineral phase continues to form even after it is initially deposited. The forming mineral phase replaces some of the water in the material (Robinson, 1979). The formation of new mineral occurs in vivo all the while that the specific bone volume is not removed and replaced by new bone (the latter process is called *bone remodeling*). Remodeling occurs continuously in vivo. Bone mineral formation continues after death during diagenesis. Thus the inherent driving force behind the increase in mineral content both in vivo and after burial is the mineral phase itself, and hence its properties are key to understanding many aspects of bone the material, and its diagenesis.

Mineral phase. The mineral phase of fresh bone is called carbonate hydroxylapatite (Ferraiolo, 2008; for more information on this mineral, see Chapter 4 and Overviews 3 and 4 in Chapter 12). There is growing

Level 7: Whole bone

Level 5: Osteonal and circumferential lamellar bone

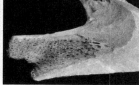

Level 6: Compact and trabecular (spongy) bone

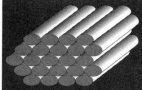

Parallel arrays

Woven fiber structure

Lamellar structure

Root dentin structure

Level 4: Structural types

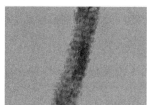

Level 2: Mineralized collagen fibril

Level 3: Mineralized collagen fibril array

Level 1: Crystals

Level 1: Collagen fibrils

Figure 5.1
Hierarchical organization of bone from level 1, the basic constituents, to level 7, the whole bone (Weiner and Wagner, 1998).

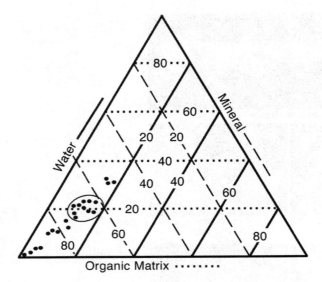

Figure 5.2
Relative proportions of
water, mineral, and col-
lagen in bone (weight
percent). The circle represents the composition of
most mature bones. The
figure was adapted from
Lees (1987).

evidence that the first-formed mineral phase in bone is amorphous
calcium phosphate, and that this phase subsequently crystallizes into
the mature phase via other crystalline intermediates (Crane et al., 2006;
Olszta et al., 2007; Mahamid et al., 2008).

The crystals in mature bone are extremely small. They are mostly
plate shaped and have average dimensions of $50 \times 25 \times 2\text{--}4$ nanometers (Weiner and Price, 1986; Lowenstam and Weiner, 1989; Figure 5.1,
level 1). Thus the entire crystal is only about 10 to 15 atomic layers thick.
This means that many of the atoms are disordered as they "feel" the surface, where the regular three-dimensional atomic order is interrupted.
Thus the small size of the crystals (and hence the very high surface to
bulk ratio of the crystals) is one source of disorder in the crystal. Note
that the surface area of bone crystals is around 240 square meters per
gram (Weiner and Price, 1986), which is similar to the surface area of
clay minerals. A second source of disorder is derived from the fact that
many of the tetrahedral phosphate moieties are substituted by planar
carbonates. The disorder in the mineral phase affects its stability and
hence its solubility. Berna et al. (2003) measured subrecent and fossil
bone mineral solubilities under close-to-natural conditions and indeed
found that subrecent bone mineral is much more soluble than fossil bone
and well-crystallized synthetic carbonate hydroxylapatite crystals. This
difference in solubility implies that the driving force for mineral maturation in bone in vivo is the inherent disorder of the mature mineral
phase. Following Ostwald's Rule of Stages (Ostwald, 1879), the more
disordered phase will tend to transform into a more ordered and hence
more stable phase. Thus with time, crystal size increases, along with
atomic order. These changes in crystallinity can be monitored by X-ray
diffraction patterns of powders (Burnell et al., 1980; Legeros, 1991) and
by infrared spectrometry (see Overview 4 in Chapter 12).

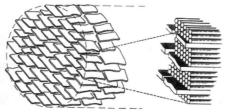

100nm

Figure 5.3
The crystals in bone are organized in layers: *left*, high-resolution scanning electron micrograph of the fracture surface of bone showing the layered mosaiclike pavement arrangement of the plate-shaped crystals; *right*, schematic showing the relation of the crystals to the collagen fibril structure. The small cylinders in the right-hand-side schematic represent the triple helical molecules, and the plates are the crystals. In the left-hand-side schematic, only the crystals are shown, and not the triple helical molecules located between the crystal layers. The crystals are located in the grooves of the collagen fibril. This scheme is not drawn to scale.

Organic phase. The organic phase of modern bone usually constitutes about 20% by weight of the material. The major constituent (about 90% by weight) is the protein type I collagen (Termine, 1984; Veis, 2003; Figure 5.1, level 1). This is also the major constituent of skin and other soft tissues in vertebrates. In fact, type I collagen is the most abundant protein in vertebrates. The remaining 10% by weight of the organic matrix of bone is a complex assemblage of other proteins, proteoglycans (proteins associated with polysaccharide chains), and various lipids. Among the noncollagenous proteins (NCPs) is a group of relatively acidic proteins that are thought to play a direct role in mineralization (Veis, 2003). After type I collagen, the second most abundant protein is osteocalcin (also referred to as bone Gla protein; Hauschka et al., 1975). The Gla term signifies the presence of a most unusual amino acid in this protein (called γ-carboxyglutamic acid, or Gla). It is interesting to note that some of these proteins (including osteocalcin, but excluding collagen) are intimately associated with the mineral phase and cannot be extracted, unless the mineral phase is dissolved (Termine et al., 1981). This has important ramifications with regard to diagenesis, where the mineral phase apparently affords such proteins relative protection from breakdown (see the subsequent discussion).

Type I collagen forms a fiber. It, too, has a hierarchical structure (Veis, 2003). The basic building block of the collagen fiber is the triple helical molecule, which is composed of three very long proteins twisted together. The triple helical molecule is about 300 nanometers long and has a diameter of about 1.5 nanometers. The triple helical molecules in bone are organized into two-dimensional sheets, with the unique characteristic that along the fiber axis, there is a gap between the ends of the triple helical molecules in one sheet and the beginnings of the triple helical molecules in the next sheet. Furthermore, this gap or hole is systematically staggered in the fibril axis direction (Hodge and Petruska, 1963; Veis, 2003). The staggered arrays of two-dimensional sheets are organized into a three-dimensionally ordered (or crystalline) array such that the holes are aligned in one direction to form long, thin grooves (Katz and Li, 1973). This structure constitutes the "fibril," and it usually has a diameter of about 80 to 100 nanometers. In bone, fibrils tend to align themselves into even larger ordered arrays (called *fibers*), which can be variable in size.

LEVEL 2: THE MINERALIZED COLLAGEN FIBRIL

The building block of the material bone is the mineralized collagen fibril. The crystals nucleate in the gap region and immediately grow to fill the flat, extended groove within the collagen fibril (Fitton Jackson, 1956; Traub et al., 1992). As the grooves are aligned to form parallel arrays across the fibril, so are the plate-shaped crystals within the grooves (Weiner and Traub, 1986). Thus the crystals essentially form a series of mosaiclike pavements (Figure 5.3). Perhaps the hallmark of crystal organization in relation to collagen fibrils is the alignment of the c-crystallographic axes of the crystals with the collagen fibril axis (Schmidt, 1936).

The crystals continue to grow over months or years (until they are remodeled). This additional growth mainly takes place between layers of triple helical molecules (Arsenault, 1991) and also in the space between fibrils. Even in the latter, however, the crystals appear to be arranged, for the most part, in the same layered motif as within the fibrils.

In some parts of the bone, the ongoing crystal growth results in crystals intergrowing to form crystal aggregates (Weiner and Price, 1986). The aggregates were identified by treating a fine bone powder with a strong oxidant that removed all exposed organic matter. If all the crystals are surrounded by organic matrix, then the bone particles should disaggregate completely into single crystals. Only poorly mineralized bones totally disaggregate. Mature bones with more than about 60% by weight mineral only partially disaggregate. The remaining aggregates can constitute up to about 50% by weight of the original bone powder (Weiner and Price, 1986). Although their biological significance is not known, they have important implications with regard to the preservation of embedded archaeological information. The intergrown crystal aggregates occlude collagen, presumably some of the NCPs, and DNA, and because they are protected from the surroundings by the mineral, they are relatively well preserved. The aggregates thus constitute a protected niche, where some macromolecules reside. For more information, see Chapter 8.

LEVEL 3: THE FIBRIL ARRAYS

Type I collagen has the ability to self-assemble into three-dimensional ordered arrays of triple helical molecules. These triple helices are not only aligned along their long axes, but also, their gap and overlap regions are aligned laterally. This is evidenced by the extension of the banding pattern across many fibrils (Figure 5.1, level 3). As the three-dimensional collagen structure dictates the location of the crystals, the end result is that the crystals inside the collagen fibrils are also aligned in three dimensions within the array.

LEVEL 4: THE PACKING MOTIFS OF FIBRIL ARRAYS

There are four common ways in which the packing of fibril arrays occurs (Weiner and Wagner, 1998); these are shown in Figure 5.1 (level 4). The simplest packing arrangement is essentially the extension of the order of the array itself to form an extended array. This structural type is characteristic of mineralized tendon and parallel-fibered bone found commonly in bovids. The opposite organization, namely, the disordered packing of fibril arrays, is common in newly formed fetal bone (woven bone) and during wound repair (Xu et al., 2003). It is almost never present in mature bone as remodeling removes this bone type and usually replaces it with so-called lamellar bone. Lamellar bone is by far the most common structural type in mature bone. It has a highly complex structure (Giraud-Guille, 1988; Weiner et al., 1999b) that is thought to provide bone (the material) with the ability to withstand mechanical challenges more or less equally from different directions. It can thus be mechanically effective in many different locations within a bone (hence the analogy with concrete). The fourth common structural type is characterized by fibril arrays being misaligned in two-dimensional planes but aligned in the third dimension. This structural type is characteristic of intertubular dentin (the material that forms the bulk of vertebrate teeth; Kramer, 1951).

It is therefore at the fourth level of hierarchical organization that bone the material is adapted to mechanical function. Hence, at this level, many interesting phenomena occur that provide insight into the relations between structure and function. For example, the initially formed lamellar bone has a parallel layered organization (called *circumferential lamellae*). This structural type is, however, removed during remodeling and is replaced by essentially the same lamellar bone, except that it is now organized into cylinders (called *osteonal* or *Haversian* bone; Figure 5.1, level 6). The mechanical advantages seem to lie not with the elastic properties, but more with beneficial fracture properties (Liu et al., 2000). It is interesting to note that even in bovids, where the first formed structural type is a combination of parallel fibered bone and lamellar bone (the combination has also been given a name: *plexiform* or *fibrolamellar* bone), this bone type is also remodeled to form osteonal bone. The beneficial properties of plexiform bone apparently lie in its ability to be produced rapidly (Currey, 2002) and also to be strong in the load-bearing direction.

LEVEL 5: OSTEONAL BONE

New bone can be deposited on existing surfaces or within the bone material itself. In both cases, the bone type is lamellar bone. If it is laid down on an existing surface, the lamellae are more or less parallel to the surface (forming circumferential lamellar bone), whereas if it is internal, they line the insides of the channel to form cylindrically shaped osteons (also called Haversian systems; Figure 5.4 and Figure 5.1, level 5). Internal remodeling is an important attribute of bone as it essentially enables the bone material to renew itself continuously.

Although generalizations are always inaccurate when it comes to bone (and, I guess, most other subjects), it has been noted that the bones of small mammals and birds tend to remodel less intensively than do the bones of large mammals and large birds (Currey, 1984). Much of the bone is still in the form of the primary circumferential lamellar bone. It thus appears that there are some mechanical advantages of remodeled osteonal bone over the bone that it replaces (usually, circumferential lamellar bone).

LEVEL 6: THE SPONGY TO COMPACT BONE CONTINUUM

At the scale of hundreds of microns, bone can adopt a more massive structure (called *compact* bone) or have an open pore system (called *spongy*, *trabecular*, or *cancellous* bone; Figure 5.1, level 6). In fact, there is no sharp demarcation between these two types, and in reality, they form a continuum. The materials that make up the two end members are not consistently different, except that spongy bone tends to remodel somewhat faster than compact bone, and hence its mineral content, on average, is less than in compact bone (Currey, 2002). Both are mostly composed of osteonal bone.

LEVEL 7: WHOLE BONE

It is at this level that bone the material becomes bone the object. Much has been written about the shapes of bones in relation to their functions, and this forms the heart of much of archaeozoological and physical anthropological research. Much still remains to be understood about shape-function relations in modern bones. For example, the contribution of spongy bone to whole bone function is still not well understood.

Figure 5.4
Scanning electron microscope image using a back-scattered electron detector. The differences in gray scale reflect different densities. Thus the youngest bone with the least amount of mineral is the darkest. The young bone is confined to the most recently formed osteons. Courtesy of Dr. Rizhi Wang.

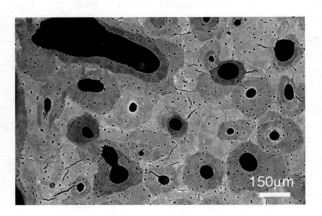

Table 5.1. Porosity of modern bovine bone and modern deproteinated bovine bone measured by mercury porosimetry.

Size range of pores (nm)	Modern bone		Modern deproteinated bone	
	Measured porosity (cm³/g)	Total porosity (%)	Measured porosity (cm³/g)	Total porosity (%)
2.8–4.0	0.0141	32	0.0377	10
4.2–100	0.0177	40	0.3114	85
100–36,500	0.0127	28	0.0196	5

Source: Data are from Nielsen-Marsh and Hedges (1999).

For a fascinating early account of this topic, see D'Arcy Thompson's (1942) classic book *On Growth and Form*.

Although bone the object is the main preoccupation of archaeozoologists, I would propose that bone the material become a bigger part of archaeozoological research. Bone material structure can provide insights (especially at level 4) into the function of extinct species and perhaps also information on the manner in which bones may have been used differently in the past within a species. Although mechanical material properties cannot be measured directly in fossil bones (because of diagenesis), they can be inferred through structure. As questions of interest to archaeologists/archaeozoologists are usually not the same as those of interest to researchers in modern bone biomechanics, archaeozoologists will probably have to investigate many of the relevant mechanical-structural relations themselves using modern bone.

Porosity

Porosity is important for understanding bone diagenesis (and biomechanics). At the visual macroscopic level, it is obvious that spongy bone has a much higher porosity than compact bone. In terms of exposed surface area, the difference between compact bone and spongy bone is not that significant. The reason is that both compact and spongy bone contain myriads of pores of different sizes; the vast majority of which are nanometers in scale. In untreated bone, most of the pores are less than 6 nanometers in size. There are also pores with sizes concentrated around 100 and 10,000 nanometers (Nielsen-Marsh and Hedges, 1999). The former most likely correspond to the canaliculi, which are small channels that permeate compact bone, and the latter to the blood vessels. The abundant pores (less than 6 nanometers in size) are located at the level of the mineralized collagen fibril arrays. This is well demonstrated by removing the collagen. A comparison of porosity in intact and deproteinated bone is shown in Table 5.1. The overall porosity of deproteinated bone is about eight times more than the intact bone. The major increase that occurs as a result of deproteination is in the pore size range of 4.2 to 100 nanometers, and in the latter, most of the pores are less than 50 or so nanometers. These results imply that as collagen is degraded and removed from the bone during diagenesis, the fossil bone will become much more porous and, as a result, will have a higher surface area for interacting with the water in the environment. Fossil bone lacking collagen will thus be more susceptible to diagenetic alteration (see the next section).

Diagenesis of bone the material

Diagenesis of bone involves a suite of complex processes that affect bone differently at different length scales. Counterintuitively, the extent of bone diagenesis does not usually correlate well with the time elapsed since burial. This is mainly due to the fact that much happens very quickly during the initial phases of matrix breakdown, and after that, the process is mainly influenced by the microenvironment in which the fossil bone resides (Trueman et al., 2008). For an overview of bone diagenesis, see Hedges (2002), and for a more historical perspective on the preserved organic components in bone and other fossils, see Wyckoff (1972).

MINERAL DIAGENESIS

The same forces that drive the changes in crystals in vivo, namely, the tendency to increase internal order and crystal size, also drive mineral diagenesis after death. Our bone crystals continue to grow long after we have died. The diagenetic process is enhanced by the microbial and chemical breakdown of the organic matrix as this significantly increases the porosity of the bone at the nanometer level (Nielsen-Marsh and Hedges, 1999), and the crystals are more exposed to the local aqueous environment. As this can vary, bone mineral diagenesis can follow different trajectories. The key to understanding possible diagenetic trajectories is the solubility of fossil bone mineral.

Berna et al. (2003) measured the solubilities of subrecent and fossil bones under conditions that more or less reflected natural conditions, by leaving the samples open to the atmosphere during the experiment. Figure 5.5 is a plot of phosphate concentrations versus pH for carbonate hydroxylapatite. The lines (isotherms) are the boundaries between conditions under which the mineral is stable (to the right of the isotherm) and conditions under which the mineral will dissolve (to the left of the isotherm). The isotherm for subrecent bone is on the right (A–A' in Figure 5.5), and the isotherm for highly crystalline synthetic hydroxylapatite is on the left (B–B' in Figure 5.5). This clearly shows that subrecent bone mineral is much more soluble than the same mineral in the form of large, atomically well-ordered crystals.

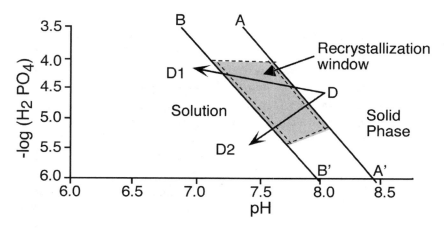

Figure 5.5
Plot of phosphate con-
centrations against pH.
The conditions under
which bone crystals dis-
solve and reprecipitate is
called the *recrystallization
window*. Note that if the
conditions are at point
D, then bone mineral is
stable. If they change and
the pH decreases, but the
phosphate concentration
increases (line D–D1),
then all the while that
the conditions within the
recrystallization window
prevail, the bone crystals
will become larger and
more ordered, and even-
tually, when line B–B' is
crossed, the mineral will
dissolve. If the trajectory
that is followed is along
line D–D2, then even
in the recrystallization
window, bone crystals
may lose some mineral.
Adapted from Berna et al.
(2003).

It can be deduced from Figure 5.5 that subrecent bones (buried for about 20 years, but still having the collagen content of modern bone) are stable if the pH is above 7.6 to 8.2. This in turn implies that bones that are associated with calcite in the sediments will not dissolve as calcite buffers the pH to around 8.2. This explains why bones are usually preserved in a calcitic cemented sediment, provided that the calcitic cement formed early after burial. If the conditions are such that even the most stable form of carbonate hydroxylapatite dissolves, namely, to the left of the isotherm for synthetic carbonate hydroxylapatite (B–B'), all the bone mineral will dissolve. This means that in practice, bones dissolve in almost any environment with a pH of less than 7.2.

What happens to a bone crystal if the pH or the phosphate concentrations change such that the crystal is now in the stability field to the left of the A–A' isotherm for subrecent bone? The bone crystal will dissolve and, as a result, locally raise the phosphate concentration (and calcium concentration) in the associated solution. As the new conditions are still within the stability field for carbonate hydroxylapatite, a new crystal of carbonate hydroxylapatite will form that is slightly more ordered than the one that just dissolved. Thus, in this area of the stability field diagram, the more stable crystals grow at the expense of the less stable ones, but the mineral type does not change. Berna et al. (2003) therefore referred to this area of the stability field as the *recrystallization window* (Figure 5.5).

Berna et al. (2003) pointed out that if the bone is buried in an aggressive hydrological regime, such that groundwater passes through the bone fairly rapidly, some of the ions from the dissolved crystals will be removed, and the bone will lose mineral. If the hydrological regime is fairly stable, then most of the dissolved ions will reprecipitate within the confines of the bone. This can occur in clay-rich sediments, and indeed, better preservation of bones in such sediments has been noted (Weiner and Bar-Yosef, 1990). One important implication of the recrystallization window is that even though the macroscopic morphology of the bone remains unchanged, the internal crystal population can change. This change in the mineral phase can be monitored by infrared spectrometry. See Overview 4 in Chapter 12 for more details.

Many changes occur to bone mineral moving through the recrystallization window, all of which increase the stability of the crystals. The crystals increase in size (Trueman et al., 2003). The plate shape, which does not reflect the hexagonal symmetry of the crystal lattice, tends to become needle shaped (Reiche et al., 2003; Trueman et al., 2003). The carbonates, some of which substitute phosphates, are reduced in content, resulting in the mineral phase having a composition closer to pure hydroxylapatite. Fluoride ions, if present in the surroundings, are taken up into the crystal lattice because the fluoridated form of this mineral phase is more stable than the nonfluoridated form. Fluoride replaces the hydroxyl groups (Parker and Toots, 1970; Newesely, 1989). The fluoride does not, however, occupy exactly the same locations as the hydroxyl groups, but rather, resides in a more symmetrical location. Hence the resulting carbonate fluorapatite (francolite) is more stable (Newesely, 1989).

ORGANIC MATRIX DIAGENESIS

It is difficult to predict the conditions under which the organic matrix constituents of bone are preserved. Breakdown of the organic material can be caused by bacteria and fungi and/or chemical reactions. For biological breakdown, water is necessary, and oxygen is usually required. If either is limiting, then the rate of breakdown can be reduced or stopped altogether. Chemical breakdown probably involves mainly hydrolysis. In theory, water could be a limiting factor in chemical breakdown. Bearing in mind that relatively few molecules of water are needed, it is unlikely that even in the driest conditions, the absence of water can prevent hydrolytical degradation.

It has been observed empirically that proteins that are more closely associated with the mineral phase, such as osteocalcin and many of the more acidic NCPs, do tend to be preserved under conditions in which collagen is not preserved (Hare, 1980; DeNiro and Weiner, 1988a; Tuross et al., 1989b). One indication that this is the case is that these macromolecules cannot be extracted from modern bone without dissolving the mineral phase (Termine et al., 1981). This implies that the mineral is somehow protecting these macromolecules. It has also been noted that collagen and DNA are preferentially preserved within the crystalline aggregates of bone (DeNiro and Weiner, 1988b; Salamon et al., 2005). Here the reason for preferential preservation is almost certainly due to the occluded macromolecules being completely sealed off from the environment by the intergrown crystals (Chapter 8).

The first step in collagen degradation probably involves the loss of the triple helical conformation (Collins et al., 1995). The unfolded form of collagen has a name of its own: *gelatin*. The unfolding of collagen to gelatin can be mediated by elevated temperatures and changes in pH (Collins et al., 2002). The temperature at which unfolding of collagen occurs in fresh bone is around 155°C, as compared to 60° to 70°C in skin (Kronick and Cooke, 1996). However, the loss of some of the chemical bonds that stabilize the collagen fibril can lower this melting temperature (Nielsen-Marsh et al., 2000). A method to semiquantify the proportions of collagen and gelatin in parchment using X-ray diffraction was developed by Weiner et al. (1980) and applied to the study of the Dead Sea Scroll parchments. Once unfolded, the gelatin is much more susceptible to chemical hydrolysis and also to enzymatic cleavage during microbial attack.

In conclusion, the hierarchical organization of bone the material at level 1 is probably most important for understanding diagenesis as much of the embedded information in bone is at this level. In my experience, there is rarely a correlation between mineral preservation and matrix preservation in fossil bone. This suggests that the factors that influence the preservation of the two major constituents of bone are, for the most part, different.

MICROBIAL AND FUNGAL DIAGENESIS

At hierarchical level 4, bone the material has different microstructures. Thus it can be asked whether certain bone structural types tend to preserve better than others. I am not aware that this occurs. The significance of this level for diagenesis probably lies in the fact that this level includes all structures in the micrometer to tens of micrometers range. Bacteria and fungi are also in this size range. It is conceivable that different bone structural types offer different extents of access to bacteria via existing pores. Here there might be a case for suggesting that osteonal bone may be more susceptible to bacterial breakdown as this bone type contains many canaliculi, through which bacteria can move. Many fungi and bacteria that attack bone have the ability to completely dissolve and remove both the mineral and the matrix constituents. In fact, they tunnel their way through the bone and destroy its original microstructure. These tunnels may remain empty, and as a result, porosity increases (Jans et al., 2004). Thus bones degraded in this way can retain their macroscopic form, but at the scale of tens of micrometers, the original microstructure is, in part, destroyed. Surprisingly, the part that is not affected by the tunneling may contain relatively well-preserved bone, with intact collagen.

Degradation of bone as a result of microbial and fungal attack appears to be much more prevalent in temperate climatic zones, as opposed to warmer climatic zones (Hedges, 2002). In fact, in temperate climates, bone preservation is often dominated by microbial and fungal activity, evidenced mainly by the presence of abundant tunnels inside the bone (Hackett, 1981). This is strange as soil microbial activity increases exponentially with increasing temperature (Edwards, 1975). The various categories of microbial degradation are described by Jans et al. (2004).

The lack of oxygen prevents fungal activity and most (but not all) bacterial activity. Such oxygen-limiting anaerobic conditions occur in organic-rich environments as most of the oxygen is removed during the oxidation of the large amount of organic material. Examples of such environments are peats, bogs, and certain submarine environments. The problem for bone survival under these conditions is that organic material breakdown results in a lowering of the pH, and if this falls below 7.2, then the bones will dissolve. If a body is buried, then in essence, a local anaerobic and low-pH microenvironment around the bones will develop. This should affect bone diagenesis. Although earlier studies were equivocal in this regard, Jans et al. (2004) did show that human bones were more porous and showed more evidence of microbiological attack than animal bones from the same site. Interestingly, the increase in pore size occurs at the nanometer scale, reflecting, presumably, collagen loss, as well as at the micron scale, due presumably to bacterial channeling.

Microbial degradation may also be reduced if liquid water is absent (as opposed to water vapor in the air). This does occur in some deserts (e.g., the Atacama in Chile), and indeed, dessicated human bodies are found in this region (Post and Donner, 2005). The rate at which microbial attack occurs is estimated by Hedges (2002) to be, for the most part, within 500 years after burial. In the Overton Down experiment, it was noted that after 32 years, only one in four buried bones was subjected to microbial attack (Nielsen-Marsh and Hedges, 1997).

It is interesting to note that at the Neolithic site of Bercy (France), bones from the immersed (waterlogged) region of the site contained more collagen than those from the region above the water table. They also differed with respect to porosity and crystallinity. The differences cannot be ascribed unequivocally to one specific environmental parameter or, for that matter, to microbial attack, but presumably, in part, they reflect the more stable and less aerobic conditions of the waterlogged environment, as opposed to the region above the water table (Reiche et al., 2003).

Preferential destruction of spongy bone, as compared to compact bone, can occur as a result of differential mechanical breakdown due to trampling, gnawing, bone marrow removal, and so on. It is unlikely that differential preservation at this level can be due to the difference in surface areas between spongy and compact bone in terms of chemically and biologically mediated diagenesis.

The pseudomorph and cast issue

A curious observation is that bones are almost never preserved as casts, or as pseudomorphs that maintain their macroscopic shape, but are composed of different materials. This is in contrast to mollusk shells, which are often preserved as pseudomorphs or casts. Pseudomorph formation probably involves (1) burial in a fine-grained sediment, (2) dissolution of the biogenic mineral phase, and (3) replacement of the biogenic mineral phase at a very fine scale by the sediment in which it is buried. My guess is that the first two stages should be no different for mollusk shells and bones. The replacement of the dissolving mineral phase by sediment may, however, be far more complicated in bone than in mollusk shells. Bone has many internal pores, whereas the outer surface of bone is generally free of pores, and hence access to the interior for the replacing phase is limited. Mineral removal would also be accompanied by much collapse and subsequent loss of the ability of the sediment to replicate the bone structure.

Timescales for bone diagenesis

Much has been written about the taphonomy of bones (as opposed to bone the material) as they pass from the in vivo environment into the fossil/archaeological record (Behrensmeyer and Hill, 1988). As this is a complex process that involves both microorganisms and chemical alterations, the rates at which this occurs will be highly variable. Intuitively, it can be guessed that as the biological processes of degradation require energy sources, these will occur rapidly when nutrients are available from the surroundings and/or the bone matrix itself. The changes that occur over longer timescales are probably driven mainly by chemical processes. Trueman et al. (2008) propose an insightful model for bone diagenesis rates, namely, that the initial rapid rate of diagenesis is related to the degradation of collagen. This exposes the crystals to the environment, causing them to change rapidly. The slower, long-term changes then reduce the available surface area as crystals grow and additional phosphate or other material enters into the bone pores (Trueman et al., 2008). It is conceivable that much of the biological attack on bone mineral also occurs in the early phase, when collagen serves as a source of nutrients for microbes.

Bones lying on the soil surface

Intuitively, it would seem that bones lying on the soil surface should be fairly stable, except for direct exposure to the sun's radiation and to rain, and that most of the breakdown that occurs is mechanical, due to scavenging. This is not necessarily the case.

Behrensmeyer (1978) collected an invaluable set of bones lying on the soil surface at Amboseli National Park, Kenya. Bones from the same individual kill sites were collected periodically over a period of some 20 years. Although the main focus of this long-term study was to examine the taphonomic fates of each kill site, the materials of the collected bones have also been analyzed.

The sizes of bone crystals from the Behrensmeyer collections were measured indirectly by X-ray diffraction line width broadening (Tuross et al., 1989b) and directly from images obtained in the transmission electron microscope (Trueman et al., 2003). These studies showed that in some bones, the crystals were larger after just 10 to 20 years (Figure 5.6). They also showed a linear correlation between mean crystal length and the infrared spectrometry splitting factor (see Overview 4 in Chapter 12), indicating that the splitting factor reflects, in part, change in crystal size. The importance of these observations is that these changes took place in bones lying on the soil surface in less than 20 years. Changes in the bone mineral splitting factor were also noted in bones from northern Israel that were lying on the surface for between 2 and 11 years (Stiner et al., 1995). The protein contents of bones from Amboseli also declined rapidly after burial (Tuross et al., 1989b).

Trueman et al. (2003) documented the presence of a variety of authigenic minerals within the pore spaces of the bones, some, but not all, of which were phosphate minerals. One of the minerals identified was barite. The barium could only have been derived from the soil itself. Furthermore, there was a crust of authigenic minerals that formed due to evaporation (which included the evaporitic mineral trona) on the upper bone surfaces. These observations led Trueman et al. to propose that bones lying on the surface actually wick up the groundwater. The water then evaporates on the upper surface of the bone. The driving mechanism for this type of diagenesis is the rapid passage of water through the bone to its surface. This is probably why the bone material is altered so rapidly. The extent to which this would occur depends both on the soil chemistry and the climate.

These studies show that bone mineral lying on the soil surface can change within a very short time after death. Changes also occur over long periods of time.

Buried bones

The vast majority of bones in an archaeological site are buried. How they become buried is often not clear, and the rates at which burial occurs are presumably variable. Human intervention can, of course, make burial an almost instantaneous process such as deliberate burying of kin, filling up of a garbage pit, use of bone-containing sediments for substrates for building, and so on. In caves, the burial rate is greatly enhanced when bats and birds are present due to the rapid accumulation of guano.

Although it is impossible to generalize about rates of diagenesis of buried bones, it is reasonable to assume that if the microenvironment in which the bone is buried does not change, diagenesis will, at some point, cease. If the conditions then change, it may begin again along another trajectory.

Burned bone

The term *burned bone* refers to bones that were somehow exposed to temperatures that caused charring and/or oxidation of the organic matter, and recrystallization of the mineral phase. Bones change their color due to charring and recrystallization. The colors themselves can be used as a practical and visual guide to the approximate temperature of exposure (Shipman et al., 1984; Stiner et al., 1995; Table 5.2). If the exposure temperature exceeds 650°C, then all the organic matter is converted into carbon dioxide, the bone loses its mechanical integrity, and the bone crystals recrystallize (Nicholson, 1993; Stiner et al., 1995). The resultant calcined bone has a white color. This process can be monitored by infrared analysis (see Overview 5 in Chapter 12). The white calcined bone is usually not preserved in the archaeological record because it easily disintegrates into a powder. As the minimum temperature required for bone calcination is well within the temperature range in the open-flame region of a fire, bones tossed into a fire are likely to be calcined. Cremation of a human body is not, of course, the same as tossing a bone into a fire. The major end product in terms of the bones is, however, much the same, namely, a powder composed of recrystallized bone mineral.

It is, however, often not easy to differentiate between black bones that are black due to charring and those that are black due to staining with manganese and other oxides. This can be done using infrared spectroscopy (Shahack-Gross et al., 1997; see also Overview 5 in Chapter 12). It is also sometimes difficult to differentiate between bones exposed to fairly low temperatures and weathered bone. In most cases, no single criterion is definitive, but rather, several independent criteria need to

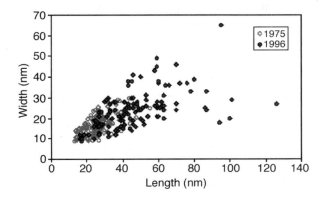

Figure 5.6
A plot of the lengths and widths of crystals extracted from bones from a rhinoceros. One bone was collected soon after the animal was killed, and the other 21 years later. Adapted from Trueman et al. (2003).

Table 5.2. Color and mineralogical changes that take place when bone is exposed to elevated temperatures.

Burn code	Description of the bone	Organic matrix color[a]	Splitting factor
0	Not burned (cream to tan)	Cream	2.6–2.9
1	Slightly burned	Yellow	3.0
2	Lightly burned	Partly black	3.2
3	Fully carbonized (black)	Completely black	3.8
4	Partially calcined (more black than white)	Black and white	3.6
5	Mostly calcined (more white than black)	Black and white	3.6
6	Calcined (white)	No insoluble residue	7.4

[a] Color after the mineral has been dissolved in 1N HCl.
Source: Data are adapted from Stiner et al. (1995).

be used. These could include color, the state of the mineral phase, the presence of charred residues, and microscopic cracking and shrinkage.

Identifying burned bone in the archaeological record provides information on the use of bones (e.g., for fuel or nutrition; Schiegl et al., 2003) and indirectly on the use of fire. Furthermore, as burning at high temperatures (calcination) can destroy the bone or make it more susceptible to mechanical breakdown, burning can change the preserved bone assemblage significantly and thus affect conclusions drawn about past human behavior from the archaeozoological record. Bone can also be exposed to high temperatures after burial, when a fire is made in the immediate vicinity. Finally, burned bone will not retain information embedded in the organic matrix and will only retain selective information in the mineral phase. It is therefore important to identify burned bone.

During a cremation, some of the bones are certainly exposed to temperatures well above 600°C for hours and thus become calcined. Under these conditions, Holden et al. (1995) observed that crystal growth occurs between 600° and 1,000°C, and above 1,000°C, local melting and fusion of crystals can occur. Furthermore, under these conditions, a high-temperature form of calcium phosphate, called tricalcium phosphate, may be produced (Grupe and Hummel, 1991). These properties may be indicative of cremated bone, as opposed to bone burned in cooking fires. During cremation, all bones do not spontaneously disintegrate into a powder, but they do undergo significant shrinkage and have characteristic cracks (McKinley and Bond, 2001).

Embedded information

For additional details on aspects of these subjects, see Chapter 2.

MIGRATION PATHWAYS

The proportions of two of the isotopes of strontium (^{87}Sr:^{86}Sr) in rocks vary as a function of age of the rocks and the formation processes of rocks when they are produced deep in the earth's crust. The range of variation in the ratio is from 0.700 to 0.750. This variation is orders of magnitude larger than the instrument analytical error, and there is therefore generally no difficulty in differentiating between much smaller differences. Some of the strontium in the rock dissolves and enters the groundwater. This strontium is then taken up by the soil and biomass and enters the food chain, where, in the case of vertebrates, it eventually ends up in the bone. Throughout this process, the strontium isotope ratio does not change as the mass difference between the two isotopes is so small. The result is that the $^{87}Sr{:}^{86}Sr$ ratio in bones and teeth reflects the characteristics of the geological terrain on which the vertebrate lives. This interesting relation between bone and local geology, first recognized by Ericson (1985), has been used for reconstructing migratory pathways.

If, during its lifetime, an animal migrates from one geological environment to another, this will be recorded as a change in the strontium isotope ratio of the skeleton. As bone continuously remodels in vivo, at any given time, most bone analyzed will represent the last decade of a person's life, whereas teeth form during early development and thus record the habitation environment during the early part of an animal's lifetime. See the review by Price et al. (2002).

The relation between geological substrate and bone turns out to be more complicated than first envisaged (Price et al., 2002). Detailed studies of strontium isotope variations in local environments show that it can vary significantly among different plants and animals (Sillen et al., 1998; Blum et al., 2000). This in turn means that even animals and humans living in the same location can have quite variable ratios in their bones. Indeed, this has been observed (Bentley et al., 2003). It is thus often difficult to reliably identify the migrants from the locals. Price et al. (2002) proposed that the best way to do this is to measure the variability in the strontium isotope ratios of a population of animals, such as small mammals, and also measure the ratios in bones and tooth enamel of humans. Only values of tooth enamel that exceed by one standard deviation the spread of the human and small mammal ratios should be considered as migrants.

The fact that bone mineral is more susceptible to diagenesis than enamel may affect the results. Bone mineral readily adsorbs ions from the groundwater in the sediments. Thus there might well be a diagenetic overprint of the strontium added to the bone after burial. If the bone is not in an environment that is representative of the local area, this could confuse the interpretation of the data. It could also be responsible for differences between the ratios in enamel and bone as enamel is much less likely to be influenced by diagenetic processes.

PALEODIET RECONSTRUCTION

Stable isotopes of bone collagen. The carbon and nitrogen stable isotopic composition of the food an animal eats is reflected in the isotopic composition of the organic matter that the animal produces (DeNiro and

Epstein, 1978; van der Merwe and Vogel, 1978; reviewed by Sealy, 2001). This is the basis for paleodiet reconstruction based on stable isotopes. Although this approach is widely used, its resolving capability in terms of diet is not good as the isotopic variability of the foods eaten is limited. This is further compromised by the fact that most animals, including, of course, humans, are omnivores. If, however, this information can be integrated with information from charred seeds found at a site, and to some extent the phytolith types, then a better understanding of paleodiet can be obtained. For more information on the types of questions that can be addressed using stable isotopes, see Chapter 2 and Sealy (2001).

A requirement for paleodiet analysis is that the fossil organic material analyzed should be the same in all samples. Bone collagen fulfills this requirement and indeed is the material most commonly used. The signal is compromised if the collagen is not pure. Thus the same approach used for selecting and characterizing pure collagen for radiocarbon dating can be used for paleodiet reconstruction.

The information on paleodiet obtained by analyzing the whole collagen molecule can be significantly improved if the amino acids that make up the collagen are analyzed separately (Hare and Estep, 1983). The reason is that each amino acid forms via its own synthetic pathway and hence has its own unique isotopic composition. Furthermore, some amino acids are only formed by plants and are incorporated as such into the collagen of animals that eat the plants. The amino acid composition of these amino acids is thus a direct reflection of the input of that particular plant or group of plants. The analysis of the isotopic composition of individual amino acids requires a dedicated instrument and considerable know-how (Hare et al., 1991).

Strontium:calcium ratios. Strontium and calcium are similar in terms of their chemical properties. Calcium is, however, preferentially extracted in the mammalian digestive tract, and strontium is preferentially removed in the kidneys. Thus strontium is depleted relative to calcium in the tissues of herbivores compared to the plants they eat. Furthermore, as the same process exists in carnivores, their tissues are even more depleted in strontium compared to the tissues of herbivores. Thus the Sr:Ca ratio in tissues should reflect the Sr:Ca ratio in the bedrock and the trophic level of the animal that produced the tissue (Sealy, 2001). The most convenient fossil tissues to analyze are bones and teeth. It was indeed demonstrated that bone Sr:Ca ratios in human populations do reflect diet (Brown, 1973; Schoeninger, 1979). Detailed studies have shown, however, that the ratio is also affected by the type of calcium-containing food that was eaten. This is reviewed by Sealy (2001).

The Sr:Ca ratio in fossil bone is directly affected by the deposition of diagenetic calcite in the bone and is also affected by the recrystallization process of the bone mineral itself. These problems can be alleviated, but only to some extent, by removing the more soluble calcite from the bone with a weak acid (Tuross et al., 1989a; Sillen, 1991). It is thus not straightforward to apply Sr:Ca ratio analysis to reconstruct aspects of diet. Under well-controlled conditions, this method has revealed interesting information. Good examples are the studies of Sr:Ca ratios in young humans (Sillen and Smith, 1984) and in the tooth enamel of young baboons (Humphrey et al., 2008) to identify the age and duration of weaning. This is based on the facts that the Sr:Ca ratio in human milk is very low and physiological discrimination against Sr develops only after three to four years. Cremated bone has been shown to provide reliable Sr:Ca ratios (Grupe and Hummel, 1991).

Burned and cooked bone. Differentiating between bones that were exposed to high temperatures and those that were not exposed to high temperatures can potentially provide information on cooking practices, bone disposal practices, the use of bone as a fuel, cremation practices, and even the management of fire (see the preceding section on burned bone). Whether the bone is boiled in water or the meat around the bone is cooked in an open fire, the temperature of the bone rarely exceeds around 200°C. To date, no irreversible changes to bones exposed to these relatively low temperatures have been identified that would make it possible to differentiate between cooked and uncooked bone. Changes in the collagen fibril structure have been observed in cooked bone, but it would be difficult to unequivocally use this to prove that fossil bone was cooked (Koon et al., 2003).

PALEOGENETICS

DNA. Fossil bone was first shown to contain DNA by Hagelberg et al. (1989). Since then, bone is the major source of ancient DNA for applications in archaeology. One reason is that bones, unlike other mineralized tissues, such as shells, enamel, or even dentin, contain cells within the material itself. Thus, after burial, there is a much greater chance that some of this DNA will be preserved. The power of molecular biological methods for extracting, amplifying, and sequencing DNA is such that even if tens of molecules of a particular segment of DNA are preserved, then the DNA sequence can often be obtained (reviewed by Brown, 2001). It is, however, not necessarily the exact same sequence that was present in the living animal as damage during diagenesis can cause changes to the DNA, and the analytical methods do not distinguish between the damaged sequence and the original one (Gilbert et al., 2003a). It is thus imperative to obtain the best-preserved DNA possible from a suite of bones. In fact, if the DNA obtained is not sufficiently well preserved, then it is perhaps better not to sequence it at all and be misled. There is a protected niche in bone where better-preserved DNA (as compared to the rest of the bone) can often be extracted (Salamon et al.,

2005). This is within crystal aggregates (Chapter 8). These are areas of the bone where the crystals have intergrown. Some collagen, NCPs and DNA, are trapped within these intergrown aggregates. For more information on ancient DNA, see Chapter 8 and Brown (2001).

Proteins. The amino acid sequence of a protein is a "readout" of the DNA sequence of the gene that encodes for that protein. Thus the sequence of a fossil protein records paleogenetic information. The tools for sequencing proteins are not as powerful as those available for determining DNA nucleotide sequences, and a prerequisite for obtaining an amino acid sequence is that the majority of the extracted protein molecules be intact. The first complete sequence of a fossil protein was published only in 2002 (Nielsen-Marsh et al., 2002).

PALEOENVIRONMENTAL RECONSTRUCTION USING RARE EARTH ELEMENTS

Bone mineral has a very high surface area and surface properties that readily adsorb foreign ions. Thus a bone buried in sediments or even lying on the soil surface will adsorb the ions dissolved in the groundwater. The so-called rare earth elements (REEs) are among the adsorbed ions. The REEs are grouped together in the chemical periodic table, and they thus have similar but slightly different chemical properties. Their relative concentrations reflect well the composition of the sediments, and this in turn is influenced by the depositional history of the sediments. Thus profiles of REEs adsorbed into fossil bones are an indication of the local paleoenvironment. In reality, they do not provide direct information on the type of environment, but more on changing local environments with time (Lozinski, 1973; Trueman et al., 2005). As REEs are, in effect, a fingerprint of the local environment, a useful application of REE analysis of bones is to identify or exclude any postburial mixing in disturbed sites (Plummer et al., 1994).

RADIOCARBON DATING

There are three potential sources of carbon in bone that could, in principle, be used for dating: the collagen, the NCPs, and the carbonate in the mineral phase. To date, only the collagen provides reliable dates, and this is on condition that the collagen is not contaminated (van Klinken, 1999). For reasons that are not obvious, the NCPs as an assemblage do not provide reliable dates (R.E.M. Hedges and S. Weiner, unpublished observations, 1985), and it is probably far too difficult to extract and purify a single component from this assemblage for dating. As the original mineral phase readily undergoes recrystallization (see the preceding discussion), the carbonate in the mineral is generally not used for dating. It has, however, been shown that the carbonate of the mineral phase of cremated bone can provide reliable radiocarbon dates (Lanting and Brindley, 1998). This could be due to the large and relatively stable crystals that form at high temperatures during the recrystallization process and/or to the carbonate that remains being located in a more stable site within the crystal lattice. Difficulties that can be expected are that not all bones are subjected to the same conditions during cremation and during burial. It is thus difficult to know for sure when the carbonates have or have not exchanged.

Collagen in bones and tooth dentin is often better preserved in the temperate, more northern latitudes, and less so in the arid and tropical zones (van Klinken, 1999). In the warmer Mediterranean climate or in south China, even though bone collagen in general is less well preserved, some of the bones at a site do sometimes contain collagen (Yizhaq et al., 2005; Boaretto et al., 2009c). This implies that the microenvironment in which the bone is located plays an important role in collagen preservation. Furthermore, it means that if sufficient bones from a site can be tested for collagen, there is a chance that some will be found. Bones can be tested for collagen relatively easily (Chapter 10), and the purity of preserved collagen can be assessed by infrared spectroscopy (see Overview 11 in Chapter 12). For more details on radiocarbon dating, see Chapter 10.

RECONSTRUCTING ASPECTS OF AN INDIVIDUAL'S LIFE HISTORY

As bone continuously undergoes remodeling while the animal is alive, osteons have different ages. This can be revealed by back-scattered electron imaging in the scanning electron microscope (Figure 5.4). In general, at any given time, three or four "generations" of osteons can be discerned within any volume of osteonal bone (Figure 5.4). This offers the opportunity to sample bone of different chronological ages and reconstruct aspects of an individual's behavior over his or her life span. The time points that three or four generations of osteons represent vary according to the bone type but are most likely to be from the last 10 or so years of their lives (Price et al., 2002). This type of microanalysis could be applied to paleodiet reconstruction by extracting collagen from different osteons or to migration times by measuring Sr isotopes (for both, see the preceding discussions). Microdrilling and other microsampling techniques are capable of sampling individual osteons (Liu et al., 1999). By combining bone information with sampling of certain teeth that formed at different stages of an individual human's lifetime, an additional two or three time points can be obtained.

TEETH

Vertebrate teeth have different morphologies that reflect the different functions they perform during food processing (Lucas, 2004). All vertebrate teeth have the same basic design, namely, the bulk of the tooth is composed of relatively pliant materials (various types of dentin), and the enamel working surface is a very hard and stiff material. The tooth resides in the alveolar bone, and the interface between the tooth and the bone is composed of the periodontal ligament and a mineralized tissue called *cementum* (Figure 5.7). The core of the tooth is hollow (*pulp cavity*). This is where the odontoblast cells that form the tooth dentin reside. These cells have processes that extend into the dentin almost all the way to the base of the enamel layer. The processes are located in tubules. The dentin thus contains a dense array of tubules about 1 to 2 microns in diameter.

From the materials point of view, dentin and cementum are special types of bone material as their building blocks are the mineralized collagen fibril. They differ from other bone structural types at hierarchical level 4, described earlier. There are two main types of dentin: peritubular dentin, which is a hard and relatively collagen-free material that surrounds the tubules only in the tooth crown, and intertubular dentin, the remaining material. Enamel is a unique material that does not resemble bone. There are two types of enamel: the common enamel and enameloid, which is formed by certain fish. A single tooth thus contains a variety of different materials. For more information, see Lowenstam and Weiner (1989) and Nanci (2003).

A major difference between tooth materials and bone is that tooth materials do not undergo remodeling in vivo. In many teeth, secondary dentin continues to form over long periods of time, reducing the size of the pulp cavity. Different teeth form at different periods of time during the development of an individual (Hillson, 1986). Teeth thus contain materials produced at different time points during an individual's lifetime. This property, together with the diversity of materials within an individual tooth, offers many opportunities to extract information from teeth for archaeology. For a detailed discussion of teeth in relation to archaeology, see Hillson (1986).

The following sections are brief overviews of the main materials in teeth, described in terms of their hierarchical levels of organization.

Enamel: The hierarchical structure

LEVEL 1: THE BASIC CONSTITUENTS

About 99% by weight of mature enamel is composed of crystals of carbonate hydroxyapatite – the same mineral that is present in bone and dentin. Enamel crystals are very long (tens of microns or more; Figure 5.8) and have widths and thicknesses in the range of 20 to 60 nanometers (in human enamel; Daculsi et al., 1984). They are huge compared to bone and dentin crystals. A helpful way to envisage the difference is that if a single enamel crystal were cut into slices 2 to 4 nanometers thick in the direction perpendicular to the crystal long axis, each slice would be roughly the size of an average bone crystal. The

Enamel
"Soft" Zone
Dentin
Pulp
Gums
Alveolar Bone
Cementum

Crown
Root

Figure 5.7
Schematic of a cross section of a tooth.

large size of enamel crystals in itself makes them a lot more stable (and hence less soluble) than bone and dentin crystals.

The organic matrix comprises about 1% by weight of the enamel (compared to about 20% by weight in bone and dentin). There is no collagen in enamel (only in fish enameloid; Lowenstam and Weiner, 1989). The mature enamel matrix is composed mainly of a variety of relatively acidic proteins. During the formation of enamel, the major protein component is amelogenin. It fulfills a structural/regulatory role in the formation of the crystals. Amelogenin is, however, subsequently broken down by enzymes, and the crystals grow into the newly available space (Veis, 2003). This results in the mature material being much harder and stiffer than bone and dentin (see Figure 8.4).

Figure 5.8
Scanning electron micrographs of rat incisor enamel, *left*, showing the three-dimensional arrangement of prisms, and, *right*, at higher magnification, the individual elongated crystals that make up a prism can be seen. Reproduced from Jodaikin et al. (1984).

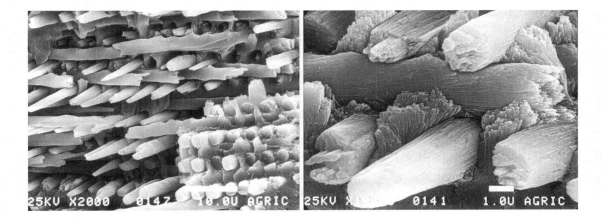

LEVEL 2: CRYSTAL ARRAYS (PRISMS)

The very long, spaghetti-shaped crystals are arranged into bundles (usually called *prisms*; Figure 5.8). These are about 5 micrometers in diameter, and each prism contains hundreds of crystals. An individual prism and its constituent crystals may span the whole width of the enamel layer. In forming enamel, each crystal has its own envelope of organic matrix. As the enamel matures, this envelope is broken down and removed almost completely. See Boyde (1997) for more structural information.

LEVEL 3: RETICULATE THREE-DIMENSIONAL NETWORK OF PRISMS

Most enamel structures contain three interwoven arrays of prisms (Figure 5.8). This forms an extremely complex three-dimensional structure. Often, two of the prism arrays are much larger than the third. This unique structure results in a material that is very stiff (Wainwright et al., 1976) but also capable of deforming during mastication (Zaslansky et al., 2006b). At this level, there is much variation between enamel types, and it is presumably at this level that the structures are adapted to specific functions.

LEVEL 4: GRADED CHANGES IN STRUCTURE

It has been observed in hardness measurement profiles that the surface of the enamel has the maximum hardness and that hardness steadily decreases toward the base of the enamel layer at the interface with dentin (Meredith et al., 1996). This must reflect structural variations that are, to date, not well understood. In some teeth, the prisms change direction just below the outer surface such that they are all aligned perpendicular to the outer surface. This might be one reason why the outer surface is harder than the inner enamel.

LEVEL 5: THE WHOLE ENAMEL LAYER

The distribution of the enamel layer on the surface of the tooth as well as its thickness can vary a lot between teeth of the same species and between species. In some teeth, the enamel covers the whole exposed surface, whereas in others, it is present only on one or several surfaces. Polished sections of enamel reveal well-defined growth increments that can be analyzed sequentially for regular or sporadic changes that occur during the lifetime of the individual (Hillson, 1986).

Dentin: The hierarchical structure

The bulk of the tooth is composed of a dentin type called *intertubular dentin*. It is the only dentin type in the tooth root. In the tooth crown, however, there is an additional dentin type called *peritubular dentin* (Miller, 1954). Peritubular dentin surrounds the tubules. Figure 5.9

shows the two types of dentin. The following sections contain a brief description of the hierarchical organization of dentin.

LEVEL 1: THE BASIC CONSTITUENTS

The dentin crystals are composed of carbonate hydroxyapatite, and they are plate shaped. The major framework protein is type I collagen, and the third major component is water. In all these respects, intertubular dentin is identical to bone. The major difference between intertubular dentin and bone is in the assemblage of NCPs. Some of these, including the most abundant NCP (usually called *phosphophoryn*), are present in intertubular dentin, but not in bone (Veis, 2003). Phosphophoryn was also the first of the unusually acidic proteins to be discovered that characterize invertebrate and vertebrate mineralized tissues (Veis and Perry, 1967).

A most important difference between intertubular dentin and bone is that in intertubular dentin, the crystals do not appear to continue growing after they reach a certain size, whereas in bone, larger crystals continually grow at the expense of smaller ones, and mineral mass increases. The reason for this difference is difficult to understand, as in bone, I proposed that crystal growth was driven thermodynamically because the de novo biogenic crystals were very small and disordered compared to synthetic counterparts. Assuming that this explanation is correct, it implies that the microenvironment around the dentin crystals differs from the microenvironment around bone. The differences could lie in the matrix structure and/or in the chemistry of the solutions in contact with the mineral phase.

LEVEL 2: THE MINERALIZED COLLAGEN FIBRIL

The mineralized collagen fibrils in intertubular dentin have the same structure as those in bone, namely, they are composed of layers of plate-shaped crystals aligned in parallel arrays across the fibril (Figure 5.3).

Figure 5.9
Scanning electron microscope images of human tooth dentin. *a*, Low-magnification view showing the tubules and, between the tubules, the intertubular dentin. Note that the collagen fibril arrays are oriented more or less perpendicular to the tubule direction (Kramer, 1951). *b*, Higher-magnification view showing an individual tubule surrounded by a dense layer of peritubular dentin about a micron or so thick. Scale bars: 5 micrometers.

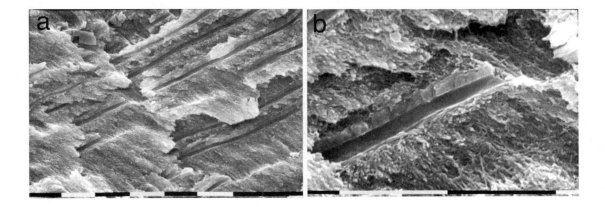

LEVEL 3: THE FIBRIL ARRAYS

In intertubular dentin, the adjacent mineralized collagen fibrils are generally not aligned around their long fibril axes, nor are they in register along the collagen fibril (Wang and Weiner, 1998). This is quite different in bone, where they are aligned in three dimensions.

LEVEL 4: THE PACKING MOTIFS OF FIBRIL ARRAYS

Most of the mineralized fibrils have their fibril axes aligned in one plane. This plane is roughly perpendicular to the overall surface of the tooth and is locally perpendicular to the tubule direction (Kramer, 1951; Figure 5.9). This structural arrangement differs from all the other structural types found in bone.

LEVEL 5: THE TUBULES AND PERITUBULAR DENTIN

The intertubular dentin is riddled with elongated tubules that extend from the pulp cavity almost to the dentin-enamel boundary (Figure 5.9). In vivo, these tubules contain extensions of the odontoblast cells that line the inner surface of the pulp cavity and, of course, water. They are 1 to 2 micrometers in diameter. The presence of the tubules means that intertubular dentin has a higher surface area than would be expected from a solid bulk material, and the tubules are large enough for bacteria to move through them. These are properties that may well affect diagenetic processes in dentin.

The crystals of peritubular dentin type are the same or similar to those in intertubular dentin in terms of composition, shape, and arrangement (Weiner et al., 1999c), but in contrast to the latter, mature peritubular dentin contains little or no collagen and a different assemblage of NCPs. The matrix content is much smaller than intertubular dentin, and peritubular dentin is therefore much denser than intertubular dentin. Detailed observations of the boundary reveals a gradation between the two dentin types. It is not known exactly how peritubular dentin forms, but one proposal is that the primary collagenous matrix is broken down and removed, and the crystals continue to form (Weiner et al., 1999c). It is interesting to speculate that the analog of peritubular dentin in bone is the crystal aggregate fraction as the latter also contains intergrown, plate-shaped crystals.

The dense structure of peritubular dentin may protect the associated matrix macromolecules. This could imply that they are relatively well protected during diagenesis.

LEVEL 6: THE WHOLE DENTIN COMPONENT OF THE TOOTH

At this level, root dentin differs from crown dentin in that only the crown contains peritubular dentin. Another difference between the root and the crown is that in crown dentin, a zone of around 50 to 200 micrometers below the dentin-enamel junction has a structure quite different from bulk dentin. The tubules do not have a lining of peritubular dentin, they often bifurcate, and the collagen fibril orientations can vary to the extent that some are even perpendicular to those in bulk intertubular dentin (Zaslansky et al., 2006a). This zone may also undergo diagenetic changes that differ from bulk dentin.

Whole teeth

The macroscopic variability of tooth morphologies within the oral cavity, and between species, is well documented (Hillson, 1986). The design strategies of teeth can vary significantly. For example, many herbivores have teeth that are designed to wear down with use (*hypsodonty*), as opposed to teeth that are designed to function with their original shape throughout the lifetime of the individual (*brachydonty*). The relations between whole-tooth morphology, tooth microstructure, and tooth function are not well understood. This information could be invaluable for better understanding the functional implications of past changes in tooth morphology such as the cusp arrangements in hominid teeth. Tooth morphology–structure–function relations could be a most productive area of investigation for paleoanthropology.

Cementum

Cementum is the mineralized tissue that is deposited on the surface of the tooth root. It connects the tooth to the alveolar bone of the mandible through a nonmineralized tissue called the periodontal ligament. Mineralized type I collagen is the major building block of cementum. Cementum is therefore one of the members of the family of bone materials. Cementum structure (corresponding to level 4 in the hierarchical scheme for bone structure described earlier) has a woven-type texture, with large, thick collagen fibrils (known as Sharpey's fibers), oriented more or less perpendicular to the tooth surface, and thinner, so-called intrinsic fibers, oriented more or less orthogonal to the Sharpey's fibers (Figure 5.10). For a review, see Lieberman and Meadow (1992).

An important feature of cementum in terms of archaeological applications is the wavy structure of the Sharpey's fibers (Figure 5.10). This reflects the position of the tooth in the mandible socket, which is in turn a function of the nature of the diet of the animal. This was demonstrated experimentally by feeding goats alternating hard and soft diets (Lieberman, 1993). In many herbivores, diet changes of this type occur seasonally in nature. Thus bands of differently oriented collagen fibers reflect seasonal changes in diet. Thus the number of such seasonal increments can provide information on the age of the animal and the season of death (see the subsequent section on embedded information).

Dental calculus

Dental calculus is mineralized dental plaque. The plaque is composed of hundreds of different species of microorganisms that adhere to the tooth surface and are embedded in a matrix composed of bacterial products and constituents of the saliva (Ten Cate, 1989). Various calcium phosphate minerals are found in dental calculus, including brushite, octacalcium phosphate, and carbonate hydroxylapatite (White, 1997). Dental calculus is present in almost all individuals in human populations that do not carry out regular dental hygiene treatments (White, 1997). It can therefore be expected that dental calculus was widespread in past populations. It has been observed in Neanderthals (Figure 5.11). It is often assumed that the formation of dental calculus is related to diet. This relationship, if it exists, is clearly not a simple one (Arnay-de-la-Rosa et al., 2009).

Diagenesis of teeth

There is a general impression that teeth are less susceptible to diagenesis than bone. This is certainly correct with respect to enamel, but probably not with respect to the dentin, unless, under certain conditions, the enamel affords the dentin some protection. The exception is possibly peritubular dentin, which is much denser than intertubular dentin and may well be better preserved than intertubular dentin or bone from the same location.

ENAMEL DIAGENESIS

Relatively little is known about enamel diagenesis as compared to bone diagenesis. It is often correctly assumed that because enamel crystals are so much larger than those in dentin and bone and are more ordered at the atomic level, they are less susceptible to diagenesis. It is sometimes

Figure 5.10
Scanning electron microscope fracture surface of the cementum, with the dentin on the right. The thick Sharpey's fibers are clearly seen oriented more or less perpendicular to the dentin. Note that they have a wavy appearance, indicating differences in fiber orientation.

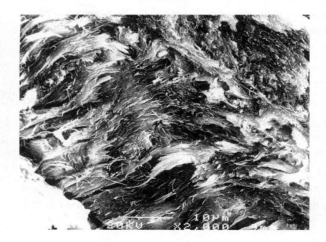

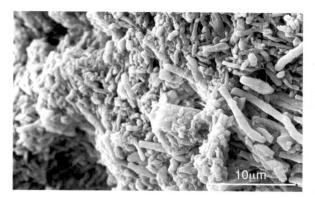

Figure 5.11
Scanning electron micro-
scope fracture surfaces
of dental calculus from
a juvenile Neanderthal
from the cave of Combe-
Grenal, France: *left*, section through the entire
thickness, showing areas
composed of differently
shaped bacteria and areas
with only mineral; *right*,
higher-magnification
view of one area, show-
ing bacteria with coccal
(round) and bacillary
(rod-shaped) morpholo-
gies. In collaboration
with M. D. Garralda,
B. Arensburg, and
B. Vandermeersch.

even tacitly assumed that enamel does not undergo diagenesis. This is not correct.

Perhaps the most familiar proof that enamel crystals do undergo diagenetic change is from electron spin resonance (ESR) dating. The ESR signal is obtained from uranium that enters into the enamel crystals due to diagenetic alteration (Schwarcz and Grün, 1992). Uranium is not present in fresh teeth, whereas most fossil teeth do contain uranium. Exchange of ions and/or isotopic exchange processes can occur in fossil enamel (Lee-Thorp, 2002), as can the uptake of fluoride ions (Michel et al., 1996). Infrared spectroscopy has been used to document changes in the relative distributions of carbonate groups between the A and B sites in fossil enamel (Sponheimer and Lee-Thorp, 1999). Changes in crystal shape and substructure have also been observed (Dauphin et al., 2007). There is thus abundant evidence that enamel can and does undergo diagenesis.

Many studies of fossil enamel have, however, confirmed that enamel is generally less affected by diagenesis than bone and dentin (see references in Lee-Thorp, 2002). Enamel is therefore an important mineral-ized tissue in archaeology as it may more faithfully preserve embedded information.

DENTIN DIAGENESIS

Intertubular dentin. The diagenesis of intertubular dentin should be more or less the same as bone diagenesis, at least up to hierarchical level 4, where the tissues differ with respect to their structural organization at the micron level. Even at higher levels of organization, it is not obvious why intertubular dentin preservation should differ from the other bone types in terms of diagenetic pathways.

Peritubular dentin. This tissue is essentially composed of intergrown carbonated apatite crystals that occlude an assemblage of proteins (with little or no collagen) that are, at least in part, different from those in the intertubular dentin (Weiner et al., 1999c; Gotliv et al., 2006). It can therefore be expected that both the mineral phase and the occluded macromolecules will be better preserved than in intertubular dentin.

Embedded information

ENAMEL

Dating. Enamel has been shown empirically to be the most suitable material for ESR dating (Schwarcz and Grün, 1992). Enamel can also be used for uranium series dating. In fact, the combination of both techniques allows for a more reliable date (Grün et al., 2005). For more information, see Chapter 2.

Life history reconstruction. Thin sections examined in polarized light reveal rhythmic growth lines both in the enamel and in the dentin. These represent daily deposits during the time that the tooth was forming. Thus the information obtained is the time it takes to form the tooth crown and/or the age at death, if the tooth was still being formed when the animal died (Boyde, 1963). Calibrations with animals of known age show that this can be very accurate (Smith et al., 2006), although in fossil material, this may be affected by preservational state. In addition, major disruptions often represent singular stress events in the life of the animal such as a birth event in females or episodes of environmental stress.

This approach has been used to reconstruct tooth development in early hominids (Benyon and Wood, 1987) as well as age at death of various juvenile hominids (Dean et al., 1993).

Migration. The strontium isotopic ratio of enamel can be used to identify migrations of humans and other animals. As the enamel does not undergo remodeling, the values obtained reflect the local environment of the individual during the early years of its life. By comparing the enamel strontium isotope ratio to that of bone from the same individual, more time points can be obtained. An elegant application of this method was the identification of a fallow deer in a Roman site in England, which was most likely brought to that site as a young fawn, possibly even from Europe (Sykes et al., 2006). Another good example of this application is demonstrated by Price et al. (1994). For more information, see Chapter 2.

Paleoclimate reconstruction. The oxygen components of the phosphate of enamel crystals reflect the drinking water isotopic composition (Longinelli, 1984; Luz et al., 1984). In some animals that derive all their water from drinking, this in turn reflects the isotopic composition of the groundwater. In animals for which some or all of their water intake is through the plants they eat, then the phosphate oxygen isotopic composition reflects the plant water isotopic composition (Luz et al., 1984). In the former case, the oxygen isotopic composition is in turn a measure of rainwater. This, finally, is the link to paleoclimate.

The same link to paleoclimate also exists for the oxygen isotopic composition of the carbonate component of the enamel crystals. In fact, it has been shown that the two are correlated (Bryant et al., 1996) and

that the same partitioning found in modern animals can be retained in
fossils (Bocherens et al., 1996).

Trace element concentrations in enamel can reflect the paleoenvironment in which the enamel lived. This has been demonstrated in
modern populations and applied to fossils (Sponheimer and Lee-Thorp,
2006).

Paleodiet reconstruction. The isotopic composition of the carbon of
the carbonate component of enamel crystals contains information that
pertains to paleodiet. Like the carbon isotopic composition of organic
matter, it, too, reflects the diet of the animal. The reason is that this carbon
is derived from the blood bicarbonate, which in turn is derived from the
diet (Lee-Thorp, 2002). In enamel, most of the carbonate is located within
the crystal. Thus enamel crystal carbon isotopic compositions should be
less susceptible to diagenesis. Indeed, studies of relatively old material
have proven this to be the case (Al-Shorman, 2004). Clearly, however,
this will not always be the case, and independent criteria need to be
obtained to prove that the signal is preserved (Lee-Thorp, 2002).

DENTIN

As dentin is a member of the bone family of materials, the information
embedded in dentin is similar to the information embedded in bone (see
the preceding discussion and Chapter 2). Peritubular dentin, however,
offers some unique opportunities for analyzing a mineralized tissue that
should be relatively well preserved compared to intertubular dentin
because it is composed of intergrown, dense carbonate hydroxylapatite
crystals. The question is whether these properties can be exploited to
extract embedded information, bearing in mind that the peritubular
dentin is localized around the tubules and is only 1 or 2 micrometers
thick. A peritubular dentin–enriched fraction can be extracted from
a powder of crown dentin (Weiner et al., 1999c). This is achieved by
treating the powder with the strong oxidizing agent sodium hypochlorite and sonicating the powder extensively. This combined treatment
tends to disaggregate the intertubular dentin and leave the peritubular
dentin more or less intact. It is conceivable that like in bone, DNA may
be trapped inside peritubular dentin, and this, too, could be useful for
ancient DNA analysis. Another approach would be to use a focused
ion beam ablation technique that selectively volatilizes the peritubular dentin and the products are analyzed in a mass spectrometer. This
has been used to specifically analyze the trace element and amino acid
compositions of peritubular dentin (Gotliv et al., 2006).

CEMENTUM

Seasonally deposited bands in cementum occur especially in ungulates,
which have a diet that changes significantly between seasons. This is
most common in temperate climates. The potential of using these bands

to assess the age of an animal was first recognized by Laws (1952). As cementum is a mineralized tissue, this approach can be applied to fossil mandibles in which the teeth are present (Saxon and Higham, 1969). The normal method used is to prepare thin sections of the tooth-mandible interface and examine them in polarized light using a petrographic microscope (Lieberman and Meadow, 1992). This is by no means a straightforward analytical method. It has been shown that diagenesis can result in incorrect interpretations (Stutz, 2002).

DENTAL CALCULUS

The analysis of microfossils trapped in dental calculus produced by humans as a means of reconstructing diet has the obvious advantage that there can be no doubt that these materials were part of the diet. With this in mind, several studies involving the identification of phytoliths from dental calculus were carried out (Lalueza Fox et al., 1996). Encouragingly, phytoliths were found, but in such small amounts that it is difficult to know the significance of the find. A study of both phytoliths and starch grains from the dental calculus of five human teeth from the middle Holocene in Syria revealed a relatively large number of starch grains, and a few phytoliths (Henry and Piperno, 2008). The presence of starch grains occluded inside fossil dental calculus has been confirmed (Hardy et al., 2009). Although the sources of most of the starch grains have not yet been identified, the potential for using dental calculus for paleodiet reconstruction is clearly demonstrated.

The formation of dental calculus may be somehow related to the diet of individuals. This relationship is, however, not straightforward (Arnay-de-la-Rosa et al., 2009). It was observed that dental calculus was more prevalent in individuals buried near the altar in an 18th-century church in the Canary Islands. This could relate to the diet of these higher-social-class individuals (Arnay-de-la-Rosa et al., 2009).

6

Biological Materials: Phytoliths, Diatoms, Eggshells, Otoliths, and Mollusk Shells

Mineralized biological materials in an archaeological site can potentially provide much information on past human behavior. Many of the organisms that produced the mineralized materials were brought to the site by humans or their domesticated animals, and the mineralized material itself often has embedded information about the past environment around or within the site. Bones and teeth are the "traditional fare" of archaeological studies involving biological materials (Chapter 5). Eggshells, mollusk shells, fish otoliths, diatoms, and plant phytoliths are other biological materials often found in archaeological sites that can also contribute in many ways to the reconstruction of past human behavior. Phytoliths, in particular, are often abundant in archaeological sites and provide information about a key component of human life that is usually not visible to the naked eye, namely, the archaeobotanical record.

This chapter is a continuation of Chapter 5. Here phytoliths, diatoms, eggshells, fish otoliths, and mollusk shells are discussed. Each section ends with a list of the embedded information that can, under certain circumstances, be extracted from these materials.

PHYTOLITHS

Plants produce a variety of different minerals, including two forms of calcium oxalate, silica, calcite, aragonite, vaterite, amorphous calcium carbonate, and various organic crystals (Lowenstam and Weiner, 1989). The term *phytolith* strictly refers to all the minerals that plants produce. In archaeology, the term *phytolith* has, for the most part, become synonymous with one category of minerals produced by plants, namely, those composed of the mineral silica (also known as opal; Piperno, 2006). Siliceous phytoliths are not the most abundant mineralized materials produced by plants but are usually the most durable biogenic plant material in archaeological sites. The most abundant mineral type produced by plants is calcium oxalate (Simkiss and Wilbur, 1989). The

136

BIOLOGICAL
MATERIALS:
PHYTOLITHS,
DIATOMS,
EGGSHELLS,
OTOLITHS, AND
MOLLUSK SHELLS

oxalates are, however, rapidly recycled, and the result is that with few exceptions (e.g., Reinhard and Danielson, 2005), calcium oxalates do not accumulate in sediments in archaeological sites (or, for that matter, in sediments in general). Silica, on the other hand, is chemically relatively stable and is less prone to biological degradation. Siliceous phytoliths are often present in high concentrations in sediments from archaeological sites. This section therefore focuses on siliceous phytoliths, referred to here simply as phytoliths. An excellent source of information on phytoliths is the book by Piperno (2006).

Phytolith material

Phytoliths are composed of almost 100% silica (opal), and the remainder (around 0.03% by weight) is organic material (Harrison, 1996). The basic structural unit is the silicate moiety composed of an atom of silicon surrounded by four oxygen atoms. Silica in polarized light displays no birefringence, and in an X-ray beam, it produces no reflections. This shows that it has no long-range atomic order. Silica is therefore referred to as being structurally amorphous. In addition to the silicate moieties, some of the oxygen atoms are in the form of hydroxyl (OH^-) groups, and some are part of tightly bound water molecules (Perry, 2003; Figure 6.1). The presence of these hydroxyls and water molecules can be readily discerned in the infrared spectrum (see Overview 7 in Chapter 12).

Silica, like most amorphous minerals, almost always forms into small spherical bodies some tens of nanometers in diameter (Perry, 2003). When these spherical bodies are ordered into a crystalline, three-dimensional structure, the structure interferes with light to produce a characteristic luster. This is common in geogenic opals. Most biogenic forms of silica are not that well ordered (Perry, 2003). The surfaces of the particles are enriched in hydroxyl groups and tightly bound water molecules (Figure 6.1). When phytoliths are heated, some of the water molecules and hydroxyl groups are driven off. As the water content is linearly proportional to the refractive index (Kokta, as cited in Heinrich, 1965), heating of phytoliths causes a change in the refractive index. This change is the basis for a convenient method for determining whether phytoliths were burned (Elbaum et al., 2003). This has many applications in archaeology.

The hardness of phytolith silica is of considerable interest because it has been assumed that phytoliths cause tooth abrasion in herbivores. Teeth of grazers recovered from archaeological sites commonly show striations on their enamel surfaces, which are attributed to the abrasive action of phytoliths. The hardness of phytoliths was originally reported to be higher than the hardness of enamel (Baker et al., 1959). This, however, was not confirmed, and in fact, phytoliths are softer than enamel (Sanson et al., 2006). Abrasion of tooth enamel by phytoliths is therefore

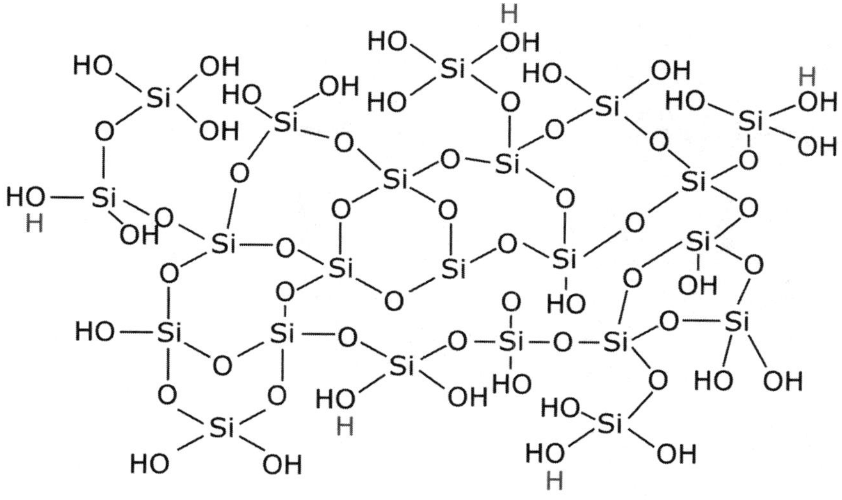

Figure 6.1
Schematic of the disordered atomic structure of silica (opal), showing the presence of hydroxyl groups and water molecules close to the particle surface. Adapted from Perry (2003).

not an important factor. Phytoliths may, however, still cause abrasion of tooth dentin, which is much softer than enamel. As many herbivores use both dentin and enamel surfaces for mastication, phytoliths abrasion of dentin could be important.

Phytolith formation and morphology

The silica produced by plants can be deposited at various locations: between the cell wall and the cell membrane, within the cell itself, or outside the cell (Blackman, 1969). The silica often replicates the structure of the cell wall, as can be seen in light micrographs in Figures 6.2a–6.2c. In some cases, the whole cell silicifies and the shape of the phytolith is the shape of the cell (Figure 6.2f). This can be more clearly seen in scanning electron microscope images of phytoliths (Figure 6.3). As the morphologies of many phytoliths partially or totally replicate the shapes of the plant cells, phytolith morphologies are often characteristic of the plant taxon, or even a part of the plant within a specific taxon. Phytoliths can thus be used for identifying plant taxa.

Not all plants produce phytoliths with characteristic morphologies, and many plants do not produce phytoliths at all. The phytoliths in plant tissues are not arranged in a way that they form a pseudoskeleton. This does not imply that they do not cause the plant tissues to be stiffer. It is known that isolated aggregates in soft tissues can have this effect (Koehl, 1982). Phytoliths are thought to fulfill other functions as well, such as protecting the plant against herbivores (McNaughton and Tarrants, 1983), pathogens, and parasites (El Hiveris, 1978); improving drought resistance (Lux et al., 2002); enabling mechanical movement, such as the ability of wheat seeds to dig themselves into the ground (Elbaum et al., 2007); and probably more.

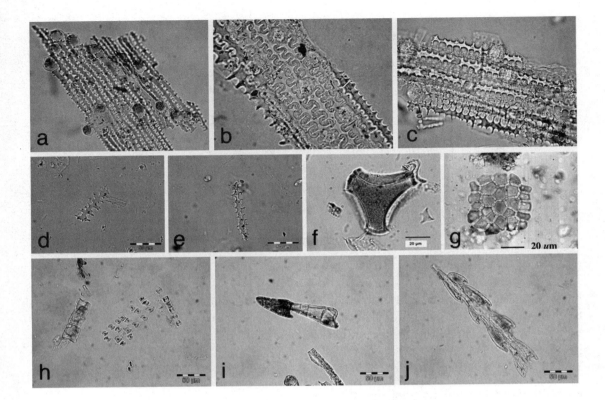

Figure 6.2

Light microscope images of plant phytoliths: a-c, multicell phytoliths from, *a*, the inflorescence of *Avena sterilis*, *b*, husk of *Triticum monococcum*, and, *c*, the inflorescence of *Triticum dicocum*; d-e, dendritic phytoliths from, *d, Triticum monococcum* and, *e, Secale cereale*; *f*, bulliform-shaped phytolith from the leaves of *Sporobolus consimilis*; *g*, a multicellular structure from the leaves of *Ceratonia siliqua*; *h*, short-cell phytoliths from leaves of *Cynodon dactilon*; *i*, prickle phytolith from leaves of *Avena sterilis*; *j*, prickles from the epidermis cells of the leaves of *Avena sterilis*.

An important attribute of phytolith formation is that the main control over phytolith formation in most plants is genetic, and not environmental (Hodson et al., 2005; Piperno, 2006). This means that phytolith-producing plants distributed over relatively wide geographic areas produce the same phytoliths in similar amounts and deposit them at the same anatomical locations. This makes it possible to extrapolate observations on phytolith morphologies and concentrations in the plant tissue from one region to another, and hence to draw general conclusions about the plants that form phytoliths. Piperno (2006) provides excellent tables summarizing this information. There is, however, an "environmental overprint" that reflects silicon availability and/or water availability to the plant. This influences the extent of phytolith production by an individual plant (Sangster and Parry, 1969; Madella et al., 2002). This environmental effect has been demonstrated experimentally (Yoshida et al., 1959; Miller Rosen and Weiner, 1994).

The specific anatomical sites that undergo silicification vary greatly within a plant and between plants (Figure 6.2). To date, about 600 or so different phytolith morphologies have been identified from plants worldwide. For convenience, these are often referred to as morphotypes. A typical survey of phytoliths in archaeologically relevant plants around an archaeological site will often produce 100 or more morphotypes. Not all phytoliths, however, have specific morphologies. In some cases,

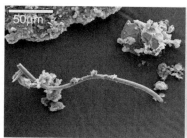

phytolith morphologies from a particular tissue are variable. It is therefore helpful to classify phytolith assemblages into consistent-morphology phytoliths and variable-morphology phytoliths. As a common source of the latter is wood and bark (Figure 6.4), the presence of a high proportion of variable-morphology phytoliths in a sample is often a good indication of phytoliths originating from wood (Albert et al., 1999).

The classification of the morphotypes is complicated. It is obviously important for the advancement of the field that a universal classification system be adopted so that comparisons can be reliably made between studies. An international effort is under way, and a standardized nomenclature is being developed (Madella et al., 2005).

Information categories obtained from phytolith assemblages

The key to exploiting phytoliths for reconstructing aspects of past human behavior is to understand the types of information that can be obtained by studying assemblages of phytoliths in archaeological sediments. The three main categories of information are taxonomy, broad classifications of plant categories, and differentiation of plant parts.

TAXONOMY

Much of the phytolith literature emphasizes the potential for identifying the taxa of the plants that were brought to the site using the morphologies of the phytoliths in the sediments. This is certainly one important application of phytoliths, but for many plant taxa important

Figure 6.3
Scanning electron micrograph images of three different types of phytoliths, showing their three-dimensional shapes.

Figure 6.4
Phytoliths and siliceous aggregates from wood: *left*, variable-morphology phytoliths (blocky shapes) and constant-morphology phytoliths (cylindrical shaped) from the wood of *Quercus ithaburensis*; *middle*, spheroid psilate–shaped phytoliths (center of image) and cylindrical-shaped phytoliths characteristically found in wood; *right*, siliceous aggregates (dark material) in the wood of *Ceratonia* sp. The siliceous aggregates shown range in size from around 10 to 50 micrometers.

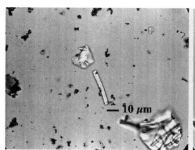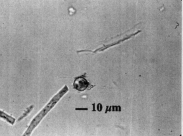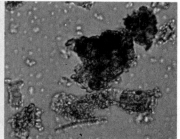

140

BIOLOGICAL
MATERIALS:
PHYTOLITHS,
DIATOMS,
EGGSHELLS,
OTOLITHS, AND
MOLLUSK SHELLS

in archaeology, phytolith morphologies are not taxonomically informative. Furthermore, bearing in mind that many plants do not produce phytoliths at all, it is often not realistic to produce a list of plant taxa used by site occupants based only on phytoliths.

One important exception is the identification of cereal taxa. Sophisticated morphological analyses have been applied for identifying subtle differences between phytoliths from different cereals (Ball et al., 1999). This makes it possible to differentiate between phytoliths from the main cereal taxa (wheat, barley, rye, oats, rice, etc.). This has important applications in reconstructing agricultural practices (Piperno, 2006).

PLANT CATEGORIES

Grasses produce many phytoliths, and these have characteristic morphologies. Furthermore, wild grasses can be differentiated from domesticated grasses (mainly cereals). Dicot leaves also produce phytoliths with characteristic features. The phytoliths from wood, in particular, and, to a certain extent, bark, have a lack of characteristic features, and very often even lack a specific morphology. They are highly variable (Figure 6.4a). This trait can be used to identify wood- and bark-derived phytoliths (Albert and Weiner, 2001). Thus phytolith assemblages can be used to reconstruct the different proportions of grasses, leaves, and wood or bark used by the occupants of a site (Madella et al., 2002; Albert et al., 2003b). This is often of much archaeological interest as these plant categories are used for quite different functions. Figures 6.2 and 6.4 show examples of phytoliths from grasses, leaves, and wood and bark.

PLANT PARTS

Phytoliths from cereals have been relatively well studied, and the different parts of the plant from which they are derived (leaves, stems, and inflorescence – the flowering part where the grains reside) can be differentiated. For example, one phytolith type (dendritics; Figures 6.2d and 6.2e) is characteristic of the inflorescence of grasses (Madella et al., 2002). Dendritic phytoliths have been observed in a Neanderthal site, suggesting that Neanderthals did collect grains from wild grasses (Madella et al., 2002). The issue of cereal storage as opposed to fodder/manure accumulations in the Iron Age strata of Tel Dor, Israel, was also addressed using dendritic phytoliths. In locations where the proportions of dendritics were approximately the same as those found in modern cereals growing in this region, cereal storage was inferred. At other locations, where fewer dendritics were present, as well as phytoliths from wild grasses, fodder/manure accumulations were inferred (Albert et al., 2008). This illustrates how phytoliths can be used to address the important issues related to the presence of grains from wild or cultivated grasses, reconstructing aspects of the use of space in a site as well as agricultural and animal husbandry practices. Note that the cereal grains themselves do not contain phytoliths, except for the outer layer (Lanning and Eleuterius, 1992).

Strategy for studying phytoliths in an archaeological context

The strategy used for phytolith analysis should clearly reflect the questions posed. There are, however, some basic considerations to take into account. No single source of information can be used to determine which plants in the area of an archaeological site produce phytoliths. Furthermore, the amounts of phytoliths produced per unit weight of plant organic material can vary by orders of magnitude (Tsartsidou et al., 2007). This means that the proportions of the phytoliths that are found on the site do not represent the proportions of the plants brought to the site. Furthermore, under certain circumstances, the phytoliths may not be preserved, or perhaps even worse, they may be differentially preserved (see the section on diagenesis), and as always in archaeology, the embedded information has to be differentiated from the diagenetic overprint.

REFERENCE COLLECTION

The starting point of a comprehensive analysis of the phytoliths from an archaeological site is the building of a reference collection of the plants that grow around the site. A good reference collection will include as many plants as possible that were not only used directly by humans, but also eaten by domestic animals maintained at the site. Furthermore, as different parts of the plants are often used in different ways (e.g., the stalks/stems of cereals for fodder and the flowering parts – inflorescence – for extracting the grains for food), the reference collection should contain analyses of different plant parts. Finally, it is essential to know the amounts of phytoliths that are produced by each plant part, or at least by the whole plant, to assess its potential contribution to the phytolith record. The phytoliths therefore need to be counted, and the number of phytoliths per dry weight of plant determined (Albert and Weiner, 2001). With this information, an estimate of the weights of phytolith-containing plants brought to the site can be made (Albert et al., 2003b).

Few so-called quantitative reference collections exist (Albert and Weiner, 2001; Bamford et al., 2006). A comparison of Mediterranean collections reveals a great deal of similarity (Tsartsidou et al., 2007). It therefore seems that one large reference collection for a whole region, such as the Mediterranean, is feasible. Such a regional reference collection should maintain all the local geographic information about the plants analyzed as potential paleoclimatic information is also

142

BIOLOGICAL
MATERIALS:
PHYTOLITHS,
DIATOMS,
EGGSHELLS,
OTOLITHS, AND
MOLLUSK SHELLS

embedded in the variations in phytolith production. I would strongly advocate the production of regional quantitative reference collections. They would open up many opportunities for obtaining invaluable information from phytolith assemblages in archaeological sites and encourage many more archaeologists to use this valuable tool, without having to invest the time in producing local reference collections.

SAMPLING AND ANALYSIS

The analysis of the phytolith assemblages in the sediments from an archaeological site mainly involves first concentrating the phytolith-rich fraction and then identifying the phytolith morphotypes with consistent morphologies, as well as counting all the phytoliths in a known weight of sediment. It is essential also to perform the same analyses on control sediments from outside the site and/or different areas within a site. Only by comparison with controls are phytolith concentrations and morphotype assemblages of the site informative.

Piperno (2006) describes the various methods usually used for extracting phytoliths from plants and soils. The amounts of starting materials used range from 5 to 50 grams, and if the amount of phytoliths per unit weight of sample is required, then all the fractions are weighed and the amount is given as a weight percent of silica in the sample. Albert et al. (1999, 2003b) developed a method that requires between 0.5 and 1 gram of sample (sediment or dried plant material) and produces quantitative information on the number of phytoliths per gram of sample. This can easily be scaled down to much smaller samples. The same extraction procedure is used to analyze the morphotypes (expressed as a percentage). Following are some pointers and comments on technical issues in phytolith analysis that are not usually described in publications:

1. Organic matter, if present in large amounts, needs to be removed. Ashing at 500°C should be avoided as this will then preclude the use of the refractive index to determine whether the phytoliths were burned in antiquity (Elbaum et al., 2003). Hydrogen peroxide heated to 70°C is an effective method for removing the organic material. Note that another commonly used powerful oxidant, sodium hypochlorite, does not oxidize cellulose and dissolves phytoliths as it has an alkaline pH.

2. In most samples, the phytoliths need to be concentrated to be analyzed. This can be done by density centrifugation using sodium polytungstate, provided that the particles are well disaggregated (sonication is most effective). Most, if not all, of the other heavy liquids used are carcinogenic and should be avoided. The particles that are denser than the liquid, form a pellet at the bottom of the centrifuge tube. As phytoliths are relatively light, they remain at the

top of the tube. The precise details for achieving an effective separation need to be adjusted to the specific minerals present in the sample.

3. After removal of the heavy liquid, followed by washing and drying, an almost pure phytolith sample can be obtained. An accurately weighed (to five decimal points) aliquot (around 1 milligram) of the phytolith-rich fraction is placed on a microscope slide. This is a crucial step that can introduce major errors if the sample is not weighed accurately. The dry sample should not be transferred by pouring, but rather, by lifting with a spatula. Pouring separates particles by size. All this can be avoided by counting the phytoliths while still in the heavy liquid. This is possible (unpublished observation), but the slide obtained will start drying within a day or so, and the sodium polytungstate will crystallize, making it impossible to see the phytoliths.

4. The number of phytoliths on the slide is counted. It is not necessary to count the whole slide, but rather, a known proportion of the slide area. To do this, however, the sample must be well mixed so that the phytoliths are evenly distributed over the whole slide. Counting requires setting some arbitrary rules that need to be clearly reported. For example, should a multicellular phytolith be counted as one phytolith, or should the number of cells bound together into a single particle be counted? Should small fragments of phytoliths be included in the count? The accuracy of the counting would be greatly improved if an internal standard were to be used – a common practice in pollen analysis.

5. The errors involved in both the phytolith concentration assay and the percentage morphotype analysis need to be defined. In the studies by Albert et al. (1999, 2003b), they are around ±20% (provided that around 200 phytoliths with consistent morphologies are counted for the latter analysis). See Albert and Weiner (2001) for more details about error analysis.

Diagenesis

The possibility that diagenesis can alter the analysis of phytoliths from an archaeological site is very real. Phytolith silica is 17 times more soluble than quartz. Silica is most insoluble at very acidic pH values (around 3), and the solubility increases with increasing pH (Fraysse et al., 2006). This means that phytoliths are relatively soluble in alkaline conditions (Benayas, 1963). Such conditions generally occur in sediments that contain calcite as calcite buffers the pH of the water in the sediment to around 8.2. Thus phytoliths may be absent from a sample because they dissolved completely. If some phytoliths are preserved, then they may show signs of etching by having pitted and rough surfaces. In our

144

BIOLOGICAL
MATERIALS:
PHYTOLITHS,
DIATOMS,
EGGSHELLS,
OTOLITHS, AND
MOLLUSK SHELLS

studies in prehistoric caves in the Levant, we frequently observed such features, and these are usually most extensive in phytolith assemblages from calcite-rich sediments (Albert et al., 2000). The presence of such etched features may mean that the assemblage has been altered to such an extent that it cannot be analyzed. In much younger, open-air sites in the Levant, the phytoliths generally do not show such features, even if calcite is present in the sediments.

A curious fact is that analyses of phytoliths in soils and sediments from a variety of "nonarchaeological" areas show very clear indications that phytoliths are rapidly recycled within hundreds of years (Alexandre et al., 1997; Derry et al., 2005). A systematic comparison of phytoliths from modern plants and those in the associated soils showed significant differences (Albert et al., 2006). In the Levant, control samples obtained from just outside the site almost always have less than 100,000 phytoliths per gram of sediment, whereas in the site, phytolith concentrations are usually higher by an order of magnitude or more (Albert et al., 1999, 2000; Madella et al., 2002). The low phytolith concentrations in control samples may be due to the phytoliths outside the site having dissolved much more than in the site. It has been postulated that phytolith dissolution occurs readily in certain soils and that the silicon taken up by plant roots is derived from the dissolution of phytoliths. Thus phytoliths are both the source and sink of silicon in soils (Farmer et al., 2005). The key question, then, is why phytoliths are preserved in archaeological sites. One possibility is the reduced activity of plants on the site. Another possibility is that the activities of domestic animals and humans concentrate the phytoliths in the site. Furthermore, a small amount of silica may dissolve and increase the silica saturation of the groundwater. This in turn will preserve the remainder of the phytoliths.

It has been shown that in "nonarchaeological" sites, certain phytolith morphotypes tend to preserve much better than others (Alexandre et al., 1997; Albert et al., 2006). This in turn implies that either these phytoliths are less soluble, or they have a more robust morphology. It has in fact been observed that the more intricately shaped phytoliths do tend to dissolve more than others (Fraysse et al., 2006). Elbaum et al. (2003) observed that different phytoliths have different refractive indices. As refractive indices reflect water content, this could, in principle, account for phytoliths having different solubilities. Albert et al. (2008) have discussed possible factors that can cause differential phytolith preservation. It is important to understand this basic issue.

These observations imply that the preserved phytolith assemblages may be altered by diagenesis. Systematic experimental studies of differential phytolith preservation are needed. At this stage, however, there are no clear-cut rules for evaluating whether the phytolith assemblage is sufficiently well preserved so as to provide reliable information.

Embedded information

FUEL USE AT A SITE

With the exception of locations where natural coal was available, the options for material to be burned as fuel were mainly wood, dung, and/or bones. If the fuel used was animal dung, then the phytolith assemblage most probably comprises morphotypes derived from a mix of wild and domesticated grasses (the major components of animal fodder; Anderson and Ertug-Yaras, 1998), and their phytoliths should have refractive indices indicating that they were indeed burned (Elbaum et al., 2003). Wood and bark do not contain abundant phytoliths but do contain other properties that can be used to identify the use of wood as fuel. Most wood phytoliths are irregular or variable in shape, and thus their presence is in itself a good indicator of a wood- or bark-derived assemblage. The ratio of variable- to consistent-morphology phytoliths has been used in this way (Albert et al., 2003a). Furthermore, wood, and especially bark, contains another characteristic biogenic component called siliceous aggregates (Figure 6.4; Schiegl et al., 1994). These are composed of various local soil minerals that penetrated into the vascular system of the wood and were then embedded in a biogenic matrix of silica. This silica, unlike the silica of phytoliths, contains, in addition to the element silicon, large amounts of other elements such as aluminum, iron, and potassium. The iron often gives the aggregate a reddish brown color, and thus the siliceous aggregates are easily confused with clay aggregates when examined in the light microscope. Their infrared spectra, however, clearly differentiate them from clays (see Overview 7 in Chapter 12). Thus the presence of siliceous aggregates, together with a high proportion of variable-morphology phytoliths that are also burned, is indicative of wood being used as a fuel.

IDENTIFYING ANCIENT IRRIGATION PRACTICES AND/OR RAINFALL

It is not easy to identify ancient agricultural fields in the archaeological record. It is thus of considerable interest to be able to infer from other materials on-site whether irrigation was being used. In an experimental study in which emmer wheat plants were grown under different irrigation regimes and in different geographic locations, it was shown that the proportion of multicelled phytoliths (also known as silica skeletons) increased significantly in the irrigated wheat stands as compared to the dry-farmed stands (Rosen and Weiner, 1994). Although this certainly demonstrates the potential of this tool for identifying ancient irrigation practices, the observed change could also reflect increased rainfall. Other criteria have to be used to differentiate rainfall change from irrigation practices (Mithen et al., 2008).

One possible criterion could be the stable oxygen isotopic composition of the phytoliths. The oxygen isotopic composition of water in the

146

BIOLOGICAL
MATERIALS:
PHYTOLITHS,
DIATOMS,
EGGSHELLS,
OTOLITHS, AND
MOLLUSK SHELLS

soil, especially in dry climates, where irrigation is necessary, should be more enriched in the heavy isotope due to evaporation during storage and application to the field, as compared to rainfall. Such differences have been measured (Webb and Longstaffe, 2000). The key question is whether the phytoliths actually record the water isotopic composition. It was shown in wheat that only the isotopic composition of phytoliths formed in tissues where no evapotranspiration took place, such as stems, recorded the water isotopic composition (Shahack-Gross et al., 1996). The leaf phytolith isotopic compositions reflect both the water isotopic composition and the extent of evaporation (Shahack-Gross et al., 1996; Webb and Longstaffe, 2000). Thus the only way to use phytolith oxygen isotopic compositions to address this issue would be to analyze samples composed only of stem phytoliths. Such samples could, for example, be obtained from mats, baskets, mud bricks, and cordages. It would be difficult, however, to perform a systematic study in this way.

GENETIC INFORMATION

Phytoliths do contain various biogenic molecules that are occluded within the mineral phase and hence may be relatively well protected over time. These include glycoproteins, saccharides, and lipids (Harrison and Lu, 1994; Elbaum et al., 2009). Unfortunately, no DNA has yet been detected in phytoliths (Elbaum et al., 2009). If indeed some DNA is present, it could be used to identify plant taxa brought to the site, even in phytoliths whose morphologies are not taxonomically informative.

IDENTIFYING PLANT TAXA BROUGHT TO THE SITE

The identification of the plants brought to an archaeological site using phytolith morphotype assemblages has been and still is the main application of phytolith analysis in archaeology (Piperno, 2006). In this respect, phytolith analysis complements well the analysis of charred seeds and other plant remains as well as the analysis of pollen. Each of these approaches has its strengths and weaknesses.

The potential of phytoliths for taxonomic identification is directly related to the plants around a site that produce phytoliths and those that do not. Not all plants and not all plant parts have phytoliths. Furthermore, many (if not most) of the phytoliths that are produced do not have morphologies that are characteristic of a specific taxon, but rather, can be found in different taxa (Piperno, 2006). Even though a comprehensive taxonomic analysis of plants in an archaeological site using phytoliths is not possible, certain plant taxa produce phytoliths that provide detailed taxonomic information.

The grasses are among the most prolific phytolith producers and hence have much potential for taxonomic applications. As the grasses, of course, include the cereals, this has provided much incentive to use phytoliths to better understand the processes of cereal domestication and subsequent development. In fact, it could well be that the major achievement of phytolith research to date is the impressive body of information that exists on the phytoliths from the wild types and domesticates of many of the most important crop plants. These include maize (*Zea mays*; Pearsall, 1978), bananas (*Musa* sp.; Mbida et al., 2000), rice (*Oryza* spp.; Zhao, 1998), barley (*Hordeum vulgare*), einkorn wheat (*Triticum monococcum*), emmer wheat (*Triticum dioccum*), bread wheat (*Triticum aestivum*; Rosen, 1987, 1992), and the squashes (*Cucurbita* spp.; Bozarth, 1987) and gourds (*Lagenaria* spp.). For an excellent overview, see chapter 3 of Piperno (2006).

Even though the phytolith morphotypes of some of these crop plants can be differentiated by inspection, the use of multiple morphological markers is often necessary to enable a definitive classification (Ball et al., 1999; Hart and Matson, 2008). This approach, together with an understanding of the shape of the phytolith in relation to its anatomical location within the plant tissue (e.g., the association of certain morphotypes with veins in the leaves of maize; Piperno, 2006), is providing a solid foundation for the use of phytoliths for better understanding plant domestication.

PALEODIET

Phytoliths that can be recovered in sufficient numbers from the residues in cooking pots can provide information on the plants that were used for cooking. It was recently shown, for example, that maize was used in cooking pots from a site in central New York from about 2,270 years ago (Hart and Matson, 2008). It has also been shown that phytoliths are trapped in dental calculus (Armitage, 1975). The calculus is a mineralized material deposited, usually, by a specialized community of oral bacteria around teeth (Chapter 5). Dental calculus is often preserved in fossils. The few applications of this approach for reconstructing aspects of diet suffer from the relatively small amounts of phytoliths that can be recovered.

PALEOVEGETATION ECOLOGY

The vegetation around a site is of much interest in terms of understanding the subsistence patterns of the site occupants as well as reconstructing the paleoclimate. Phytoliths can be used for this purpose, as was demonstrated by a comprehensive study of the phytoliths in modern plants and sediments from different strata in the Olduvai Gorge (Tanzania) region (Bamford et al., 2006). In this case, the study was combined with the analysis of silicified macroscopic plant fossil remains. Care was taken to differentiate strata in which the phytoliths were not well preserved from those in which they were – a necessary requirement, especially when relatively old sediments are being studied.

148

BIOLOGICAL
MATERIALS:
PHYTOLITHS,
DIATOMS,
EGGSHELLS,
OTOLITHS, AND
MOLLUSK SHELLS

RADIOCARBON DATING OF PHYTOLITHS

The carbon in the organic material that is occluded within the silica of phytoliths can be dated using radiocarbon. This was first demonstrated by Wilding (1967), and subsequently by Kelly et al. (1991). Piperno (2006) also reports the successful use of radiocarbon for dating phytoliths. However, radiocarbon dating of phytoliths has, to date, not become a routine method, despite the efforts of several radiocarbon laboratories. As phytoliths are often found in excellent contexts, the importance of being able to date them cannot be overemphasized (Boaretto, 2009a).

RECONSTRUCTING RELATIVE AMOUNTS OF PLANT MATERIALS USED

Phytoliths derived from stems, leaves, and the flowering parts (inflorescence) of grasses (monocots); from leaves of dicots; and from wood and bark can be differentiated (Albert et al., 2003b). Furthermore, with the use of a quantitative reference collection, the relative amounts of organic material brought to the site can be calculated. This is derived from information on the number of phytoliths present per dry weight of plant and/or plant part. As some of these phytoliths are not unique to one category, the reference collection can be used to estimate what proportions are derived from which plant types. This approach is essential as grasses, for example, can, on average, produce some 40 times more phytoliths per weight of dried material than is produced by bark and wood (Tsartsidou et al., 2007). Another difficulty in reconstructing relative plant materials used is that grass phytoliths are significant contaminants in bark (Albert et al., 2003a). Thus their presence in ash may not be related to the burning of grass, but rather, to their presence in the bark of the fuel that was burned. So a phytolith assemblage dominated by grass phytoliths does not necessarily imply that grasses were the dominant plant type brought to the site or to part of a site (Albert et al., 2003b).

USE OF SPACE

The potential for using phytoliths to reconstruct the use of space in a site is enormous. This is well demonstrated by two ethnoarchaeological studies involving phytoliths in animal enclosures in a Maasai village in Kenya (Shahack-Gross et al., 2003, 2004) and phytoliths in an agropastoral community in a village in northern Greece (Tsartsidou et al., 2008; Chapter 9).

Plants were and still are used for many different purposes, including food, in building construction, as fuel, for matting, for containers, and as fodder for domestic animals. Thus using phytoliths to identify categories of plants (as opposed to specific taxa) and plant parts has much potential to contribute significantly to identifying use of space in archaeological sites. It can also provide information on the enclosures of domestic animals, their fodder, and whether their dung was

used for fertilizer (Albert et al., 2008). For example a locality dominated by phytoliths from the inflorescence of wheat rather than the
stems of wheat, is likely to be a storage site for grains, rather than for
fodder.

Final comment

The study of phytoliths should, in my opinion, become an integral part
of most major archaeological excavations. The potential of phytoliths
for reconstructing many different aspects of the archaeobotanical record
is currently underestimated.

DIATOMS

Diatoms are single-celled photosynthetic organisms that produce mineralized cell walls, called *thecae*. A cell produces two silicified thecae,
each of which is composed of a valve and several girdle bands. The
thecae are of different sizes and fit together like a Petrie dish. As the
thecae are often elaborately and beautifully shaped and are between 20
and 200 microns in diameter, they can be readily identified using a light
microscope or a scanning electron microscope (Figure 6.5).

Diatoms are abundant in many ocean environments and are also
often found in brackish and freshwater environments. In the marine
environment, they mostly float (planktonic) in the upper water column,
whereas in brackish and freshwater environments, they are usually
located on sediment and other surfaces. In fact, they can even survive in moist soils (Hustedt, 1942). The ability of diatoms to live in
almost any moist or wet freshwater environment, and the fact that they
produce siliceous cell walls that tend to be preserved over time, make
them of interest in archaeology. Furthermore, as different genera, each
with its characteristically shaped and sculpted thecae, occupy different

Figure 6.5
Scanning electron micro-
scope images of two
diatom species: *left,
Coscinodiscus aster-
omphalus; right, Tha-
lassiosira pseudonana.*
Scale bars: 1 micrometer.
Courtesy of Dr. Nils
Kroeger.

150

BIOLOGICAL
MATERIALS:
PHYTOLITHS,
DIATOMS,
EGGSHELLS,
OTOLITHS, AND
MOLLUSK SHELLS

ecological niches, the presence of diatom thecae in archaeological sites can be used to reconstruct the local paleoenvironment.

Cell wall composition

The mineral phase produced by diatoms is the same as that of phytoliths, namely, silica (also known as opal). Occluded within the mineral phase is a complex assemblage of glycoproteins, some of which are covalently linked to polyamines (Sumper and Kröger, 2004).

Diagenesis

It can be assumed that the chemical conditions under which diatom silica will be preserved are basically the same as those for phytoliths, namely under alkaline conditions the mineral may partially or completely dissolve. The solubilities of diatom and phytolith silica are similar (Loucaidies et al., 2008). Unlike most phytoliths, many diatom thecae are rather delicate and, in certain high-energy environments, may break up into fragments. Mechanical and chemical diagenetic processes may introduce a bias in the preserved assemblages of different diatom taxa. Note, too, that diatom frustules may be transported by flowing water, and a brackish estuarine environment, for example, may also contain freshwater diatoms from another locality (Battarbee, 1988).

Embedded information

A word of caution: diatoms are very common in aqueous environments, and their thecae may be preserved for millions of years. Thus their presence in an archaeological site could be as fossils from past geological epochs and may not necessarily be related to modern natural or anthropogenic activities. Such ancient fossils should be readily recognized from their morphologies and/or from their states of preservation.

ANCIENT IRRIGATION PRACTICES

Freshwater diatoms and freshwater sponges (that produce siliceous spicules) were found in the sediments of agricultural terraces at La Quemada, Mexico (Trombold and Israde-Alcantara, 2005). As the sediments are relatively porous and pools of freshwater are not likely to form, it was concluded that these terraces were irrigated on a regular basis using water from a nearby source that contained diatoms and sponges. The diatom taxa identified usually occupy well-oxygenated shallow water such as in streams and ponds. Under certain circumstances, they can also live in soils that are saturated for long periods of time. Even though this latter possibility could imply that the terrace sediments were wet due to natural processes, the combination of sponge spicules and diatom frustules makes this unlikely.

PROVENIENCE OF POTTERY

Diatoms are sometimes present in pottery and have been used to deter-mine the source of the clay used for ceramic production (Jansma, 1982). There are many difficulties involved, but despite this, some interesting applications have been made using diatoms that show both local and nonlocal sources for clays at various sites (reviewed by Battarbee, 1988).

RECONSTRUCTING THE PALEOENVIRONMENT

As diatoms are small and abundant, they may be common in sediment samples from the archaeological site or from cores in sediments sur-rounding the site. The identification of diatom genera can be used to differentiate between freshwater, brackish, and marine paleoenviron-ments (Edwards et al., 2005). Furthermore, they can be used to differ-entiate between standing and flowing water. Some of the earlier and most comprehensive environmental reconstructions were undertaken in Neolithic coastal sites in Scandinavia (reviewed by Battarbee, 1988). The study of coastal sites using diatoms is particularly advantageous because of the diatoms' sensitivity to differences in salinity. One ques-tion that was addressed using diatoms was whether the Thames in the London area was freshwater or brackish in Roman times. The diatom assemblage clearly showed that like today, it was also an estuarine brackish environment 2,000 years ago (Battarbee, 1988). Diatoms have also been used to study changing environmental conditions in wells and travertines deposited around springs (reviewed by Rapp and Hill, 1998). A stratum rich in diatoms was found in the Upper Paleolithic layers of Kebara Cave, Israel, indicating that a freshwater pool existed in the back of the cave for some period of time (Goldberg et al., 2007). For an overview, see Mannion (2007).

AVIAN (BIRD) EGGSHELLS

Avian eggshells are fairly common in archaeological sites. The eggshells of ratites, which include the ostriches, emus, cassowaries, and rheas, are particularly common in prehistoric sites because of their relatively large size. Ethnographic analogies show that ostrich eggs are used as food and the eggshells as containers for storage or for beads (Robbins, 1973). In some cases, the beads were deliberately exposed to elevated temperatures to darken their color (Kandel and Conard, 2005). Many reptiles also produce mineralized eggshells, but these are usually small and are less likely to be of archaeological significance.

Basic morphology and structure

The characteristic curvature and smooth inner and outer surfaces of eggshells make it fairly easy to visually distinguish eggshell frag-ments from mollusk shell fragments. They can also be identified by the

152

BIOLOGICAL
MATERIALS:
PHYTOLITHS,
DIATOMS,
EGGSHELLS,
OTOLITHS, AND
MOLLUSK SHELLS

presence of many small pores that traverse the structure. These can be seen using a simple magnifying glass. Avian eggshells are composed of calcite (Cain and Heyn, 1964). A thin layer of carbonate hydroxylapatite is present in the inner cuticle of the hen's eggshell (Dennis et al., 1996).

An avian eggshell has a layered structure, but unlike mollusk shells, the layers are not well separated; rather, they tend to grade into each other (Figure 6.6). In vivo, the outer surface is covered by a thin organic cuticle, and the inner surface is covered by a relatively thick membrane. The nucleation of the calcite crystals takes place on this membrane at specific sites. After nucleation, the crystals fan out in all directions. Some quickly encounter crystals from the neighboring nucleation site and stop growing. Only the crystals that grow more or less perpendicular to the membrane surface become large. The shells thus have a characteristic prismatic structure, composed mainly of large, intergrown calcite crystals (Simkiss, 1968; Arias et al., 1993).

The organic matrix comprises about 3% to 4% by weight of the shell. It is composed mainly of proteoglycans and glycoproteins. Some of these macromolecules are occluded inside the mineral phase (Gautron et al., 2007) and therefore may preserve well over time.

Diagenesis

Avian eggshells generally preserve well as they are composed of calcite, in contrast to the more common mollusk shells found in archaeological sites, which are usually composed of aragonite. The calcite can, however, undergo changes. It can dissolve and recrystallize as secondary calcite. This can only be identified from an ultrastructural study using light or scanning electron microscopy. In fossil eggshells, trace element analyses are problematic as the pores tend to fill up with sediment, and this intrusive material cannot easily be removed (Dauphin et al., 1998).

The organic matrix tends to degrade readily (Dauphin et al., 1998), but in eggshells, some protein remnants survive for long periods, as evidenced by the presence of preserved amino acids (Miller et al., 1992). This may well be due to the presence of occluded proteins inside the relatively large calcite crystals (Gautron et al., 2007). This is supported by the observation that the more soluble components of the matrix after the mineral is removed are better preserved than the insoluble ones (Dauphin et al., 1998).

Embedded information

DATING USING AMINO ACID RACEMIZATION

Ostrich eggshells are among the few biogenic mineral phases that appear to provide reliable dates based on amino acid racemization (Miller et al., 1992). The reasons for this are not clear but may be related

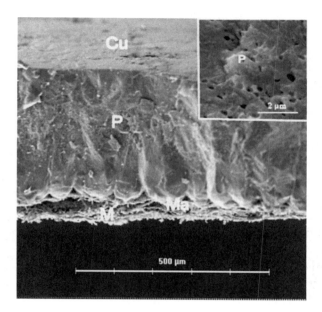

Figure 6.6
Scanning electron micro-
scope image of the cross
section of a fresh chicken
eggshell. M is the inner
shell membranes; Ma is
the mammillae where
crystal nucleation occurs;
P is the palisade com-
posed of intergrown
calcite crystals; Cu is the
outer organic cuticle.
Insert: vesicular structure
of the palisade. Courtesy
of Dr. J. Arias.

to the presence of most of the proteins inside the crystals. The proteins
are thus in a relatively uniform and protected environment.

RECONSTRUCTING THE PALEOENVIRONMENT

The stable carbon isotopic composition of eggshell calcite records the
local vegetation in terms of whether it is predominantly composed of
C_4 grasses, as opposed to C_3 grasses. This was first shown for a 10
million–year-long sequence in India (Stern et al., 1994). The use of stable nitrogen and oxygen isotopes, in addition to stable carbon isotopes,
provides more insight into the regional rainfall, as reflected in part by
the distribution of C_3 and C_4 plants (Johnson et al., 1997). The oxygen
isotopes of the mineral phase are directly related to the isotopic composition of the drinking water, which in turn indicates the extent of
rainfall. Note, however, that ostriches lay their eggs over a period of
two weeks, approximately two months after the rainy season (Bertram,
1992). Thus reconstructed paleoenvironmental information may only
be representative of a small part of the annual climatic cycle. On the
other hand, ostriches are not selective feeders and more or less sample
the local vegetation (Johnson et al., 1997).

RADIOCARBON DATING

The calcite of ostrich eggshells should, in principle, provide a reliable
radiocarbon date. In a study carried out in South Africa, it was shown
that because the laying hen eats significant amounts of limestone during
the egg-laying period, the age obtained is too old by about 180 years and
has an uncertainty of ±120 years (Vogel et al., 2001). The age offset may
vary between regions. This relatively small offset may not be important

154

BIOLOGICAL
MATERIALS:
PHYTOLITHS,
DIATOMS,
EGGSHELLS,
OTOLITHS, AND
MOLLUSK SHELLS

in older sites, and indeed, eggshells have been used for dating old prehistoric sites (Bird et al., 2003).

AVIAN GIZZARD STONES

Many, but not all, birds swallow small stones, which are retained in their gizzards (or stomach; Norris et al., 1975). These are then used for crushing food, in a manner analogous to teeth. The stones become rounded and develop a sheen or luster that makes them quite conspicuous. They are thus often found during the examination of sieved material and can easily be confused with some human activity that involved stones.

Their presence in relatively large concentrations indicates that birds roosted at the location, which may possibly have some paleoenvironmental implications. In my experience, gizzard stones are found fairly frequently in certain caves – an indication that birds, at least, occupied the cave.

OTOLITHS

Almost all animals that are mobile need to sense the earth's gravitational field. This they do using a plum-bob type of structure, comprising a heavy body that rolls around in a cavity lined with sensor cells. The heavy bodies are usually mineralized and hence are relatively well preserved (Lowenstam and Weiner, 1989). These mineralized bodies are called *otoconia* if many of them are present in the sensor chamber (e.g., most mammals have calcitic otoconia; Carlström, 1963). They are called *otoliths* if only one relatively large body is present. The most common group of living fish, the teleosts, produce relatively large (millimeter to centimeter sized) otoliths. These are thought to function in sound reception, in addition to gravity perception (Morris and Kittleman, 1967).

Otoliths are quite common in archaeological sites where fish were processed. They are usually only identified if the sediments are sieved. They do contain interesting embedded information. Otoliths from other animals that could have constituted a major part of the human diet, such as squids, may also be present in the sediments of an archaeological site, but to date, they have not been identified.

Morphology, ultrastructure, and mineralogy

Most otoliths are irregular, disk-shaped objects that exhibit a fine concentric lamination on their surfaces. This lamination is due to the fact that every day during the life of the fish, a new layer of mineral is laid down at the otolith periphery. Thus the number of such incremental growth lines reflects the number of days the fish has lived. This is widely used to estimate standing crops of fish in the temperate

6.5mm

Figure 6.7
Photographs of otoliths
from the fish *Trochorus
symmetricus*: *top*, the
smallest otoliths are
composed of vaterite
and are from the otic
chamber called the
lagena; *bottom*, the largest
otoliths are from the
sacculus, and (middle)
the intermediate-sized
otoliths are from the
utriculus. Both the intermediate and large-sized
otoliths are composed of
aragonite.

water oceans, by knowing the age structure of the population (Panella, 1971).

A teleost fish produces six otoliths, one in each of three pairs of chambers. The chamber sizes and the sizes of the otoliths inside each of the different chambers vary significantly. The largest-sized otolith, and hence the one that is almost inevitably found in archaeological sites, is composed of aragonite. The otoliths from the second largest chamber are also composed of aragonite. The otolith in the smallest chamber, in almost all teleosts examined to date, is composed of the much less stable form of calcium carbonate called vaterite (Lowenstam and Fitch, 1981; Gauldie, 1986). It is therefore very unlikely to be preserved in the archaeological record. Figure 6.7 is a photograph of otoliths from the three otic chambers.

156

BIOLOGICAL
MATERIALS:
PHYTOLITHS,
DIATOMS,
EGGSHELLS,
OTOLITHS, AND
MOLLUSK SHELLS

In cross section, the otoliths have a radiating spherulitic structure, with the aragonite crystals nucleating off a planar organic substrate in the center (Lowenstam and Weiner, 1989). Like all biogenic minerals, otoliths contain a diverse assemblage of macromolecules, including the characteristic acidic proteins (Murayama et al., 2005). It has not been proved, but is reasonable to assume, that some of these macromolecules are occluded inside the crystals and are hence relatively well protected from the environment. These will also therefore be better preserved in fossil otoliths.

Diagenesis

Because most otoliths are composed of aragonite, a polymorph of calcium carbonate that is less stable than calcite, they might well dissolve and be lost from the archaeological record. They could also partially or completely recrystallize to calcite. In such cases, the ultrastructural and chemical information embedded in the otoliths will be lost, or at least compromised. On the other hand, if the otoliths found are still composed entirely of aragonite, this is a good indication (but not proof) that the embedded information is likely to be preserved. In a study of otoliths from southern France, this was shown to be the case for ultrastructure and chemical composition, but the oxygen isotopic composition may have changed (Dufour et al., 2000). As vaterite is even more unstable than aragonite, it is unlikely that vateritic otoliths will be preserved. It should be noted that if the otoliths are roasted over an open fire or boiled, then the trace element chemistry does change (Andrus and Crowe, 2002).

Embedded information

RECONSTRUCTING THE PALEOENVIRONMENT

Stable oxygen isotopic composition. The stable oxygen isotopic composition of biogenic carbonates can record a combination of water temperature and salinity (Chapter 2), provided that the mineral was formed in isotopic equilibrium with the environment. An analysis of the growth increments of catfish otoliths from the Gulf Coast of the United States showed that these otoliths are deposited in isotopic equilibrium. Thus the oxygen isotopic composition of otoliths in an archaeological site can be used to reconstruct the environment in which the fish lived: freshwater, brackish, marine, and so on. For example, a comparison of the fluctuations in isotopic composition between a modern otolith and two from 2,000-year-old archaeological sites in the same region showed a change in the salinity of the local brackish water environment (Surge and Walker, 2005).

Trace element variations. Fine-scale analysis of the growth ring chemistry and, in particular, the trace element variations can provide detailed information on migration patterns of the fish and the environment in which it lived (Elsdon and Gillanders, 2003). This approach can, in principle, be applied to the study of fossil otoliths from archaeological sites possibly to reconstruct ancient fishing locations as well as to differentiate between fish caught in the sea versus in brackish or freshwater bodies. Analysis of the last deposited growth ring will also provide information on the location where the fish was caught. In the case of migratory fish, this could indicate whether the fish was caught in a river as opposed to the sea. To date, applications of this type in archaeology have not been made.

The changing Sr:Ca ratios within an otolith are sometimes assumed to reflect changes in environmental parameters such as temperature. A comprehensive study of the physiology of cod and the chemistry of the solution in which the otolith forms shows that this relationship is fortuitous. Changes in physiology are the major causes of these fluctuations (Kalish, 1991).

SEASON OF OCCUPATION OF A SITE

As many fish otoliths contain seasonally deposited growth rings, an examination of the last deposited growth ring can provide information on the season in which the fish was caught and hence the season of occupation of the site. It is important to verify, using modern fish otoliths, that the specific species being investigated does deposit light and dark growth rings that together constitute an annual growth deposit. In a study in New Zealand using red cod otoliths, which were first heated to enhance the differences in color of the seasonal bands, it was shown that the last deposited bands in most of the otoliths examined were from the spring (Higham and Horn, 2000). By counting the annual growth ring pairs, the age of the fish can also be determined.

MOLLUSK SHELLS

Mollusk shells are present in many archaeological sites, almost irrespective of geographic location. The shells most often found are those of land snails, freshwater snails, clams, and many different marine mollusks, provided that the site is not too far from the coast. The reasons for the presence of mollusk shells differ from site to site. The mollusks were often used as food, and the discarded shells accumulated on-site to form middens. They were sometimes used for construction purposes or as sources for producing lime. Certain mollusks were also sources of dyes. One of the most common uses of mollusk shells is for ornamentation (Bar-Yosef Mayer, 2005b). In fact, two of the very early modern *Homo*

158

BIOLOGICAL
MATERIALS:
PHYTOLITHS,
DIATOMS,
EGGSHELLS,
OTOLITHS, AND
MOLLUSK SHELLS

sapiens sites in Israel (Qafzeh and Skhul), dating to about 100,000 years BP, both have mollusk shell beads (Bar-Yosef Mayer, 2000). For more information, see Bar-Yosef Mayer (2005a).

Many land snails naturally lived and died on archaeological sites. Often, their concentrations on-site are enhanced because of the activities of rodents, which collect them and stash them underground. In some cases, humans also ate land snails, and hence large accumulations of their shells are found. Some land snails live within the sediments. Some prefer sediments with very specific properties such as sediments with relatively high humidity and that are not too compact. This often means that they occupy specific niches such as graves, the sediments that fill intact vessels, and so on (Figure 6.8).

Freshwater snails and bivalves are very common in lakes and rivers. They were often used as food, and hence their shells may also be present in large numbers in some sites (Figure 6.9). Marine mollusks were widely used for food in coastal sites, and their discarded shells form the well-known middens that have been extensively investigated all over the world since the beginnings of modern archaeology. They were also extensively used for ornaments or adornments.

Some mollusks were collected for their special properties. Members of the family Muricidae, marine gastropods, were collected in large numbers around the Mediterranean to extract a purple dye called indigo (Koren, 2005). One group of mollusks of the genus *Dentalium*, belonging to a very rare class, the Scaphopoda, were collected and used during different periods as ornamentation from at least 15,000 years ago (the Natufian period in the Levant). They were also used as currency in northwest America. Cowrie shells of a specific species, *Cypraea annulis*, were also used at times as currency in sites as far apart as China, India, and the Levant (Bar-Yosef Mayer, 2000, 2008).

Figure 6.8
Left, Sediments from a human grave from the Crusader period at Tell es-Safi, Israel. The grave contained many small shells of the terrestrial snail *Calaxis* sp. Scale bar: 20 centimeters. *Right*, Enlarged image of the area shown in the left-hand image. The white snail shells can be seen. The snail was identified by Dr. D. Bar-Yosef Mayer.

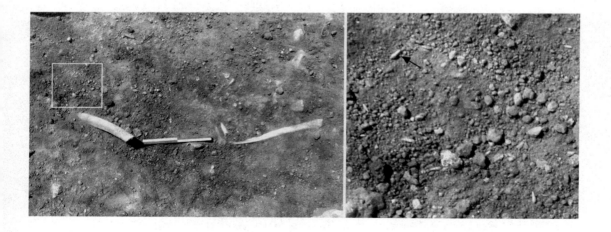

Figure 6.9
Photograph of a thick
accumulation of land
snail shells at the site of
Diyun, Guilin, China.

Taxonomy

The mollusk phylum is divided into seven classes, four of which
are relevant to archaeology: Bivalvia, Gastropoda, Cephalopoda, and
Scaphopoda. The Bivalvia include the mussels, clams, oysters, and so
on. The Gastropoda are commonly known as snails. The Cephalopoda
include the octopus, the squid, and the rare (except in the South Pacific)
chambered *Nautilus*. The Scaphopoda are very rare, but for unknown
reasons, the members of one genus, *Dentalium*, were extensively collected for some 15,000 years (Garrod, 1957). They are commonly known
as "tusk shells," and they have a curved planispiral tubular shell that is
open on both ends.

Shell ultrastructure and mineralogy

The outer layer of a modern mollusk shell is a thin, mainly organic pro-
tective coating (periostracum). The shell itself is often layered, and each
layer has its own unique ultrastructure. In some cases, layers within
an individual shell may be composed of different polymorphs of calcium carbonate, namely, aragonite or calcite. Mollusks are capable of
producing seven basic types of ultrastructure, of which perhaps the
most familiar, because of its beautiful, pearly luster, is the nacreous
ultrastructure. The most widespread ultrastructural type, however, is
the crossed lamellar structure, which is common in many gastropods.
Table 6.1 summarizes some properties of the shells of the four classes of
mollusks that are commonly found in archaeological sites. For detailed
descriptions of mollusk shells and their various properties, see Carter

BIOLOGICAL
MATERIALS:
PHYTOLITHS,
DIATOMS,
EGGSHELLS,
OTOLITHS, AND
MOLLUSK SHELLS

and Clark (1985). The definitive work on mollusk shell ultrastructures and mineralogies is that of Boggild (1930).

Mineral phase

Almost all the mollusk shells that are, in practice, found in archaeological sites at some distance from the sea are composed of aragonite. As aragonite is slightly less stable than calcite, the presence of still preserved aragonitic shells is key to reconstructing the completeness of the record at a particular site. For example, if aragonite is preserved, then it can be assumed that the more stable calcite is also primary. On the other hand, if these shells contain some calcite or are composed entirely of calcite, the preservational states of other calcitic materials, such as ash and plaster, may be poor, or they may have dissolved completely. A point to note is that in the bivalve shell, the muscles are attached to the shells via a special shell layer that the muscle cells themselves produce, called the *myostracum* (Lowenstam and Weiner, 1989). This very thin layer is always composed of aragonite and has a prismatic structure. So even in shells that are composed almost entirely of calcite, such as common oyster shells, a thin aragonitic layer is present (Stenzel, 1963). Thus if states of preservation are being investigated and the criterion for good preservation is the presence of aragonite, the myostracum can always be utilized.

The presence of carbonate minerals in general implies that the pH of the sediments is and always has been above 8, unless the carbonates formed after the sediment was deposited (e.g., as a cement). The presence of primarily deposited carbonate minerals, such as snail shells, still composed of aragonite and/or calcite in turn implies that any bones deposited in the associated sediments would not have dissolved, as this only occurs at a pH less than 7. The absence of bones means that they were never deposited at that location. In Hayonim Cave, Israel, land

Table 6.1. The basic properties of the shells of mollusks from the four classes that are most often found in archaeological sites.

Phylum	Environment	Common ultrastructure	Common mineralogy
Gastropoda	Terrestrial	Crossed lamellar	Aragonite
	Freshwater	Crossed lamellar	Aragonite
	Marine	Crossed lamellar	Aragonite
Bivalvia	Freshwater	Outer prismatic, inner nacre	Aragonite
	Marine	Crossed lamellar, prismatic, nacre	Aragonite, calcite
Scaphopoda	Marine	Crossed lamellar, homogeneous, prismatic	Aragonite

Source: Data are from Carter and Clark (1985).

snail shells composed of aragonite, calcite, and even carbonate hydroxylapatite were found in different zones (Figure 6.10). This implies that the preservation conditions varied greatly over an area of only several square meters. Significantly, in the area where the snail shells had diagenetically altered into carbonate hydroxylapatite, bones were absent (Weiner et al., 2002). As the secondary geogenic carbonate hydroxylapatite is apparently more stable and hence less soluble than the biogenic bone mineral, the apatitic snail shells were preserved, but the more soluble bone mineral had dissolved. For more information, see Chapter 3.

If the primary mineralogy is preserved, this does not necessarily imply that the original trace element or isotopic compositions are not altered (Buchardt and Weiner, 1981). There is, however, an even more sensitive method for assessing the state of preservation of a mollusk shell than mineral polymorph type. The aragonite and calcite formed by mollusks is not identical to inorganic or geological calcite or aragonite. The arrangements of the atoms within the crystals are disordered by usually less than 0.1 nanometer. These small variations can be detected both by X-ray diffraction (Pokroy et al., 2004) and by infrared spectroscopy (Gueta et al., 2007; Chapter 12). There are several possible reasons for the disorder. Many invertebrates, and for that matter, vertebrates as well, are thought to form their crystalline mature mineral phases via a transient, highly disordered phase (Weiner et al., 2005). In the case of calcium carbonate–forming invertebrates, including mollusks, this is a phase called *amorphous calcium carbonate* (ACC); (Weiss et al., 2002; Marxen et al., 2003). Thus part of the disorder could be that the crystallization from ACC to aragonite (or calcite) is not complete (Politi et al., 2008). Another source of disorder is that mollusk shells (Dauphin, 2002) and many other biogenic minerals (Cuif and Dauphin, 2005; Meldrum and Cölfen, 2008) are actually organized into nanospheres, and thus many of the atoms "feel" the surface and are thus disordered. A third source of disorder is the presence of occluded molecules and ions, such as Mg and Sr, within the crystal

Figure 6.10 Photographs of land snail shells from Hayonim Cave, composed of, *a*, aragonite and, *b*, carbonate hydroxylapatite. Scale bar: 10 centimeters.

162

BIOLOGICAL
MATERIALS:
PHYTOLITHS,
DIATOMS,
EGGSHELLS,
OTOLITHS, AND
MOLLUSK SHELLS

(see the subsequent discussion). One consequence of this disorder in archaeological applications is that if preserved, it makes it possible to differentiate, for example, between geogenic, pyrogenic, and biogenic calcites (Chapter 4). Furthermore, as the disordered mineral is less stable than its ordered counterpart, the presence of disorder can be used as an indication that the crystals have not dissolved and reprecipitated, or been heated.

If aragonite is heated to around 400°C, it converts to calcite (Lippmann, 1973). Thus heating can, in this respect, mimic diagenesis. Heated shells often have a different color. Furthermore, if some shells at a specific location are composed of calcite, whereas the others in the same area maintain their primary aragonitic composition, then this may also be a good indication that the shells were deliberately heated.

Organic matrix

Mollusk shells contain between 0.05 and 5 weight percent organic matter (Hare and Abelson, 1965). This organic matter is commonly called the *organic matrix*, and it is intimately involved in the formation of the shell. Essentially, cells in the organ responsible for shell formation (the mantle) produce and secrete the components of the matrix, and this forms a three-dimensional extracellular structure in which the minerals subsequently form. The main structural component of the matrix is the polysaccharide β-chitin. The common protein present in some, but not all, shells is silk fibroin. Mollusk shells also contain another class of proteins that is unusually rich in one of the two acidic amino acids: aspartic acid (Lowenstam and Weiner, 1989). These proteins are widely thought to be active in nucleating the crystal and controlling its growth (Addadi et al., 2006).

An important aspect of the mollusk shell organic matrix that is significant for archaeological applications is that some of the macromolecules present in the shell are occluded within the mineral phase (Addadi et al., 1991). These macromolecules are thus relatively well protected from the environment and are most likely to be preserved during diagenesis (Chapter 8). They can be extracted and analyzed for applications requiring primary organic matter.

Embedded information

Most of the information obtained from the analysis of mollusk shells in archaeological sites (*archaeomalacology*) is based on the macroscopic examination of the shells and identification of the taxa present (Bar-Yosef Mayer, 2005a). Here we focus on the information embedded within the shell itself.

DATING

Although mollusk shells should be ideal for radiocarbon dating as the carbon component of the aragonite is biogenic, in practice, radiocarbon dating of mollusk shells has proven to be complicated. The reason is that a proportion of the mineral carbonate is derived from the bicarbonate of the water, and this generally results in the age obtained being older than the correct age by hundreds of years for marine mollusks (Siani et al., 2001). Freshwater and brackish water mollusks can have much larger deviations. This so-called reservoir effect is not constant and can vary significantly between locations, and over time. This uncertainty has essentially prevented the use of mollusk shells for high-resolution radiocarbon dating.

Uranium series dating is also generally not reliable as modern mollusk shells do not contain uranium, and the date obtained thus reflects the diagenetic accumulation history of uranium into the shell (Kaufman et al., 1971).

The one dating method that has been demonstrated to work, but for unknown reasons and only for land snail shells, is amino acid racemization. Comparisons between aspartic acid racemization rates and radiocarbon dates show a correlation for the last 300 years (Goodfriend, 1992). Other amino acids can be used for earlier periods (Goodfriend, 1987). Other studies, however, have not reported such a correlation (El Mansouri et al., 1996).

RECONSTRUCTING THE PALEOENVIRONMENT

Mollusk shells are generally excellent recorders of the paleoenvironmental conditions in which they grew. Mollusk shells were used to develop and apply the method whereby the proportions of the isotopes oxygen-18 (^{18}O) and oxygen-16 (^{16}O) are used to reconstruct the past temperatures of the oceans (Epstein et al., 1953). The variations in trace elements can also provide information on the past changes in seawater temperature (Chapter 2). Both the isotopic composition and the trace elements are also influenced by the salinity of the water, and hence they can be used to differentiate seawater from brackish and freshwater environments. As some mollusks add daily and seasonal growth increments to their shells, variations in past daily temperatures and seasonal temperatures can also be reconstructed. For more information, see Dodd and Stanton (1981) and Lowenstam and Weiner (1989).

The applications of this embedded information in archaeology are diverse. In coastal sites, the configuration of the coast has often changed since the last glaciation, and mollusk shells found at the site can be used to reconstruct these changes, especially if the site is close to a river mouth or estuary. If the site is far from a river or estuary, but analysis of the mollusk shells shows that some of the shells were obtained

164

BIOLOGICAL
MATERIALS:
PHYTOLITHS,
DIATOMS,
EGGSHELLS,
OTOLITHS, AND
MOLLUSK SHELLS

from the freshwater or brackish river/estuary environment, then this information provides insight into the foraging strategies used. If the environment has been impacted by humans – by mining, for example – this, too, can be identified by analysis of mollusk shells (Nocete et al., 2005). Trading of mollusk shells often took place over very large distances, and therefore isotopic and trace element analyses of the shells may be helpful in identifying the source of the material.

SEASON OF OCCUPATION

Many mollusks, and especially those that live in the intertidal zone, form their shells by the deposition of daily and/or seasonal growth increments. Thus, by collecting mollusk shells from an archaeological site and analyzing the growth increments, the season of the last formed increment can be determined. This represents the season in which the mollusk was collected and brought to the site (Coutts, 1970). These studies often require the calibration of the growth line increments in modern shells before applying them to fossils from an archaeological site (Deith, 1983b). It is interesting to note that some mollusks also record catastrophic environmental events in their shells. This was elegantly demonstrated by individuals of the common mollusk *Mercenaria* that lived near the output of a nuclear power plant. They faithfully recorded every thermal pollution event. They also record natural shocks such as winter freezing, summer heat, strong tides, and spawning events (Kennish and Olsson, 1975). This trait of mollusks may have interesting applications in archaeological sites where it is inferred that major natural disasters occurred. For more information, see Rhoads and Lutz (1980).

SITE PRESERVATION

Most mollusk shells found in archaeological sites are composed of aragonite. As aragonite is less stable than calcite, it is most helpful to determine whether the mollusk shells are still composed entirely of aragonite, or have, in part or totally, transformed into calcite or other even more insoluble minerals. The preservation of aragonitic shells implies very good preservation conditions, and thus the various forms of calcite (such as ash and plaster) are also likely to be preserved. If the shell mineralogy is not preserved, then the calcite-containing materials in the site have also probably been altered. For more information, see Chapter 3.

7

Reconstructing Pyrotechnological Processes

Humans have used fire for at least half a million years, and possibly a million or more years (Brain and Sillen, 1988; James, 1989; Weiner et al., 1998; Goren-Inbar et al., 2004). During this entire period, the most common use of fire was presumably for cooking food, for producing light and warmth, and for protection. It was only about 15,000 to possibly 18,000 years ago that fire was used for the first time to produce synthetic materials: plaster in the southern Levant (Kingery et al., 1988; Valla et al., 2007) and ceramics in south China and Japan (Yasuda, 2002; Boaretto et al., 2009c). All deliberate uses of fire by humans are referred to here as *pyrotechnology*. This behavior is one of the unique attributes of our species. Pyrotechnological practices are therefore of much interest when reconstructing human behavior.

Pyrotechnology is based on the fact that heat causes a usually atomically ordered natural material to lose its order, change its form, and then, on cooling, adopt another arrangement of atoms that results in the new material having different properties. Cooking is perhaps the most widespread and ancient form of pyrotechnology. In the case of plaster, ceramics, metals, and glasses, the new material can also be conveniently shaped. The shaping capability, together with the advantageous material properties, are the main functional and/or aesthetic benefits of producing traditional synthetic materials.

Reconstructing pyrotechnological processes conjures up images of excavating hearths, ovens, workshops, kilns, furnaces, and so on, and in this way, deducing how the products were produced (*chaine opertiore*; discussed in the book by Henderson, 2000). Preserved structured features (installations) and hearths are, of course, invaluable for pyrotechnological reconstruction but, in practice, are not often found, and even when found, they do not easily reveal unequivocal information about their past uses. Much of the literature on pyrotechnology focuses on the synthetic products themselves and, whenever possible, the installations in which they were produced. Much less attention is spent on the waste products.

The major waste products of most pyrotechnological industries are mainly ash and charcoal. The ash and charcoal tend to spread out and cover much larger areas than the actual production site itself. Thus the identification of ash concentrations in a site may be a practical way of homing in on the installation itself. Furthermore, the characteristics of the ash, such as the fuel type used, or the presence of any associated contaminants, such as heavy metals or pottery fragments, may provide indirect information on the nature of the pyrotechnological industry involved, including common domestic fires.

It is often not appreciated just how much ash is produced by a fire. Based on measured amounts of ash yields, it has been calculated that a single fire burning for 10 years produces a pile of ash 1 meter high over an area of a square meter (Schiegl et al., 1996). Thus even a group of hunter-gatherers or the occupants of a small village could produce a very large amount of ash in a short time. A small industrial facility will also produce very large amounts of ash. Ash generally leaves a robust signal in the sediments, even if it has been diagenetically altered. Little is known about the secondary use of ash in the past, except for glass production (Henderson, 2000). If ash were used on a large scale for other purposes, this could radically change ash distribution patterns.

All materials produced at elevated temperatures are, to a greater or lesser extent disordered and are therefore, unstable at ambient temperatures. These disordered materials are less stable and more likely to undergo diagenetic change over time. Thus a central theme of this chapter is the characterization of the products of pyrotechnology, especially at the atomic level, and the assessment of their states of preservation. With this information, and given that in general, the waste products of pyrotechnological activities are also informative and tend to spread over large areas, it is hoped that more embedded information can be retrieved from the microscopic record.

BASIC CONCEPTS OF HEATING AND COOLING

When a solid material is heated, it melts to form a liquid. If the liquid is heated, it evaporates to form a gas. The atoms in a solid are, in general, more ordered than in a liquid, and in a gas, they are completely disordered. Thus heating a solid induces disorder. On slow cooling, the opposite occurs, and order is induced. If the cooling is not slow enough, then some of the disorder is "frozen in" to the solid phase.

The effect of the addition of heat is to cause the atoms to vibrate more. Even though no visible changes occur in a solid that is being heated, the atoms are vibrating more, and the material becomes more disordered. At some point, this vibration is so vigorous that the bonds that hold the atoms together are disrupted, and the solid starts to melt. The disruption process itself requires heat, so at this stage, even though more heat is being added, the temperature of the solid/liquid phase does not rise. A similar process occurs when the liquid transforms into a gas.

The cooling process is usually just the opposite of the heating process, with the transformation from a liquid to a solid occurring when the attractive forces between the atoms become dominant. Often, however, the cooling process is more complicated. For the solid to begin to form, atoms need to associate into a cluster. This does not always occur readily, and cooling can continue without the formation of the solid. The liquid is then referred to as being "supercooled." If the cooling rate is rapid, then the supercooled state can stabilize even at ambient temperatures. When this happens, we refer to the solid product as a "glass." The order of the atoms in a glass phase is more reminiscent of atomic order in a liquid, rather than of the crystalline order in a solid. Glasses therefore have many properties that differ from a crystalline solid, and the material is much less stable. Over time, the atoms in glass will tend to crystallize. This will occur when, by chance, a cluster of atoms is arranged in such a way that the attractive forces are strong. This stable nucleus can more easily attract other atoms, and the crystalline phase will grow. The result is that a glass phase can crystallize even at ambient temperatures. In fact, this same ordering process occurs in crystals as their atoms are also initially not all in their most stable configurations. If the cooling rate is slow, then the disordered phase becomes more ordered. The disordered phase hardly ever becomes completely ordered, and the defects that remain tend to reflect the manner in which the disorder was originally introduced. This phenomenon has interesting applications for reconstructing pyrotechnological practices (see the subsequent discussion). For more general information on the effects of heating and cooling, see basic textbooks on physical chemistry.

ORDER AND DISORDER IN SOLIDS

Inherent in the concept of disorder is that this does not imply one specific state, but rather, many different states. When it comes to disorder involving atoms, the situation is strongly influenced by the fact that some atoms form strong attractive forces with other atoms, and even when heated into the liquid state, these moieties do not dissociate. Examples important in archaeology are silicon, phosphorus, and carbon. Silicon and phosphorus each bind four oxygen atoms to form tetrahedral-shaped moieties (the basic building block of all silicate and phosphate minerals), and carbon, which forms a planar array with three oxygen atoms forms a carbonate moiety (the basic building block of all carbonate minerals). The silicon tetrahedron exists even in a glass phase. This means that there is local order around the silicon atoms in a glass, but the tetrahedra are misaligned, to a greater or lesser extent, over longer distances. Thus a description of atomic disorder inevitably involves the scale over which order-disorder exists. The terms *short-range order* (a few nanometers), *long-range order* (often 10 or more nanometers), and something in between (*mid-range order* or *intermediate-range order*) are often used.

Infrared spectroscopy detects short-range order as well as mid-range order very well, whereas X-ray diffraction detects mainly long-range order. Many other analytical techniques can be used for describing the extent of order of a material. In general, a good understanding of disorder-order in solid materials requires the use of more than one analytical technique.

The products of pyrotechnology are disordered, to some extent, at ambient temperatures and pressures. Thus, over time, the disordered state will slowly reorganize into a more stable, ordered state. This is the driving force for diagenetic changes that alter the products of pyrotechnology. We can therefore use the degree of disorder both to characterize the products of pyrotechnology and, by so doing, to learn about the manner in which the material was formed, and we can learn about the extent to which the material has been diagenetically altered over time. Obviously, the original disorder signal is of much more interest in archaeology than the diagenetic signal, but if the two are not somehow separated, the archaeological signal of interest may be misinterpreted. In this chapter, the common products of pyrotechnology will be discussed with these general disorder-order concepts in mind.

The focus of this chapter is on the properties of some of the common products of pyrotechnology, their instabilities over time (diagenesis), and the information relevant to archaeology that is embedded in these materials. The chapter deals with ash, charcoal, plaster/mortar, and ceramics. These are very common products of pyrotechnology found in almost every archaeological site. Metals and glass are less common but are nonetheless of much importance in archaeology. As these are materials that I know little about, I have not included them in this chapter. For comprehensive reviews of many of the common anthropogenic materials, including metals and glass, and their modes of production, ranges of variation, distributions, histories, and more, see the books by Rice (1987), Lambert (1997), and Henderson (2000).

ASH

Ash is the powdery residue that remains after the combustion of organic material. In archaeology, the common materials used for combustion are wood, animal dung, a variety of other plant materials, and occasionally, bones (Schiegl et al., 2003), peat (Simpson et al., 2003), and natural coal (White, 1978; Théry et al., 1996). Each fuel type leaves a different residue, and often, if combustion is incomplete, charred plant remains (charcoal)

Table 7.1. The components of ash produced by combusting various plant materials.

Plant materials	Source of ash component in the plant	Ash components
Wood/bark	Calcium oxalate Siliceous aggregates Phytoliths (hydrated) Bound ions	Calcite (disordered) Siliceous aggregates Phytoliths (dehydrated) Soluble salts
Leaves	Calcium oxalate Phytoliths (hydrated) Amorphous calcium carbonate Bound ions	Calcite (disordered) Phytoliths (dehydrated) Calcite Soluble salts
Grasses	Phytoliths (hydrated) Bound ions	Phytoliths (dehydrated) Soluble salts
Exceptions: *Tamarix* sp. and *Juglans regia* wood	Gypsum? (Shahack-Gross and Finkelstein, 2008)	Anhydrite (Tsartsidou et al., 2007)

are present together with the ash. Charcoal is generally not regarded as an ash component and is presented here as a different product of combustion. In this section, I will not refer to the ash of bones (see Overview 5 in Chapter 12) nor that of natural peat and coal. An excellent source of information on ash in archaeological contexts is Courty et al. (1989).

Composition of ash

Ash is the inorganic residue that remains after all the organic material has been converted into carbon dioxide. The composition of ash is thus a direct reflection of the ions associated with the organic components of the plant, the minerals in the plant, and also the minerals adhering to the surfaces of the plants used for combustion. Table 7.1 lists the major constituents of plants that contribute to their ash as well as their mineralogical forms in the ash after combustion. Well-preserved ash, in general, comprises calcite, phytoliths, and, in the case of ash from wood or bark, also siliceous aggregates. The soluble salts present in modern ash are rarely preserved in the archaeological record because they are soluble in water. In some plants, particularly those growing in the desert, they can be a major component of the ash. The freshly produced ash of these plants has been used, for example, as an additive in the production of glass (Henderson, 2000). Note, too, that the plant material used as a fuel almost inevitably contains adhering soil minerals. After burning,

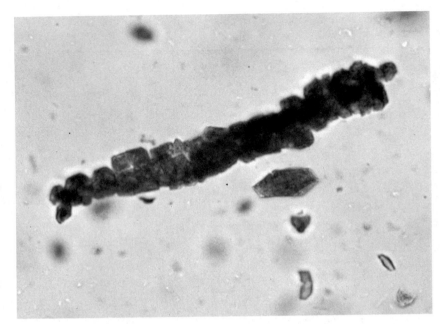

Figure 7.1
Wood ash crystals composed of calcite. Note that the crystals still retain the characteristic shape of the original calcium oxalate monohydrate crystals present in the wood prior to combustion. Width of view: 0.21 millimeters. Courtesy of Dr Ruth Shahack-Gross.

these soil particles turn a red brick color. These particles are a minor, but conspicuous part of the ash (Courty et al., 1989).

ASH FROM WOOD AND BARK

Burning of wood and its associated bark is a common source of ash. This ash is dominated by calcite produced by the degradation of the calcium oxalate crystals that are present in the wood and bark (Humphreys et al., 1987). The common mineral form of these calcium oxalate crystals is the monohydrate oxalate called *whewellite* (Scurfield and Michell, 1973). The morphologies of the whewellite crystals can vary, even within the same species. Arrays of elongated needles (raphides) are common, but crystal clusters (druses) and small, triangular-shaped crystals (crystal sand) are also fairly common (Scurfield and Michell, 1973).

On combustion of the wood, the calcium oxalate breaks down in two stages: at temperatures around 500° to 600°C, carbon monoxide (CO) is lost, and the oxalate converts directly into calcite (Ozawa, 1965). If this calcite is then exposed to higher temperatures (around 700° to 850°C), it degrades into calcium oxide (CaO) (Brochier, 1983; Brochier and Thinon, 2003). On cooling, the CaO reacts with carbon dioxide in the atmosphere, and calcite reforms. As the temperatures within a single fire can vary greatly, one or both types of calcite could be present in ash.

There are several reasons why the low-temperature form of ash calcite predominates. The low-temperature form often still retains the shape of the original oxalate crystals (pseudomorphs), although they tend to break up into small fragments (Figure 7.1). These characteristically shaped crystals are a common form of calcite in ash from wood or bark and can be recognized by examining ash in the petrographic microscope. The pseudomorphs can usually be distinguished from the rhomb-shaped crystals characteristic of inorganic calcite that form by precipitation from saturated solutions (Courty et al., 1989).

Calcite crystals formed at elevated temperatures have a relatively disordered atomic lattice. This can be identified by the ratio of the v_2 and v_4 peaks in the infrared spectrum (see Overview 2 in Chapter 12). Chu et al. (2008) reported that the ratio for modern ash is around 4, as opposed to atomically well ordered crystals of sparry calcite, which have a ratio of around 3. Modern plaster has a ratio of around 6.5. The fact that the ratio for ash is around 4 and not 6.5 implies that the predominant process responsible for ash calcite formation is the loss of carbon monoxide around 500° to 600°C, and not the formation of CaO at higher temperatures. The latter process results in a v_2:v_4 ratio of around 6.5 – the same as in plaster.

Ash also contains a small amount of minerals besides calcite. These are insoluble in acid. In the wood of trees from Israel, this fraction comprised approximately 2% by weight of the total ash (Schiegl et al., 1996). The acid-insoluble fraction of ash is composed mainly of two types of materials: siliceous aggregates and phytoliths. Siliceous aggregates is the name given to a complex material that has a matrix of silica in which soil minerals are embedded (Figure 7.2). The matrix is synthesized by the tree (mainly in the bark), and on average, only about half of its atoms are silicon. The remainder are aluminum, iron, potassium, and various other elements (Schiegl et al., 1994). When these aggregates were originally identified in wood, they were called *silica aggregates* (Bamber and Lanyon, 1960; Scurfield et al., 1974; Sangster and Parry, 1981). Because the matrix contains such a high proportion of elements other than silicon, Schiegl et al. (1994) called them *siliceous aggregates*. Silica refers to the mineral composed of almost pure SiO_2. Although it is not known how and why siliceous aggregates form, the presence of

Figure 7.2
a, Photomicrograph of a thin section of wood showing the characteristic elongated cells, together with dark granular material interspersed between the cells. These dark materials are the siliceous aggregates. Width of view: 11.4 millimeters. *b*, Back-scattered electron (BSE) microscope image of a polished surface of wood ash, showing the small calcitic crystals (bright color) and a phytolith (smooth darker color) as well as a section through a siliceous aggregate (dark heterogeneous material). Note that the latter contains a variety of different minerals, as inferred from contrast differences in the BSE mode. From Schiegl et al. (1994). Scale bar: 100 microns.

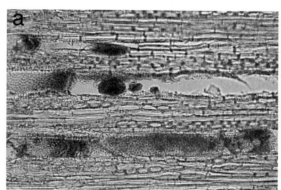

occluded soil minerals suggests that this is a defense mechanism of the tree used to remove harmful soil particles that have somehow entered into the vascular transport system. The same may be true of the silica matrix itself as it contains high concentrations of a variety of elements other than silicon. This could be a deposit of unwanted ions, and by embedding these ions in the silica, their harmful effects are neutralized. There is, however, no proof of this detoxification role for siliceous aggregates.

Silica phytoliths are the second component of the acid-insoluble fraction of wood or bark ash. Unlike the siliceous aggregate matrix, phytoliths are composed of almost pure silica. Not all species of trees produce phytoliths in their wood, and in some cases, they also do not produce phytoliths in their bark (Tsartsidou et al., 2007). Furthermore, the phytoliths that are present often have variable, irregular shapes and are not easy to identify. In fact, the presence of a large proportion of such irregularly shaped phytoliths is a good indication that the ash was derived from wood or bark (Albert et al., 1999). In general, the number of phytoliths present in wood or bark is very low per unit weight of plant material compared to other plants. As the bark is often contaminated by phytoliths from grasses, and because grass phytoliths are extremely abundant in the environment, up to 50% of the phytoliths with characteristic morphologies present in wood or bark ash may actually be contaminating grass phytoliths (Tsartsidou et al., 2007). For more details on wood or bark phytoliths, see Chapter 6.

Diagenesis

Ash can readily change its composition, and also its appearance, due to diagenesis. This makes it difficult to unequivocally identify ash in sediments, especially as fine-grained calcite from other sources may also be present. Understanding the possible diagenetic pathways of ash is therefore important. As calcite is stable above pH 8 and unstable below pH 8, it is convenient to consider diagenetic processes that affect ash above pH 8 separately from those that affect ash below pH 8.

pH ABOVE 8

If the bedrock in the local environment is composed of a carbonate mineral (dolomite and/or calcite), or if the sediments in the site contain calcite as a major component (e.g., such as in loess), the pH of the groundwater will be maintained at around 8.2 due to the buffering effect of the carbonate-bicarbonate system. Even if significant amounts of organic matter degrade, producing acid, only some of the carbonate minerals will dissolve, and the pH will still remain above 8. Under such conditions, the calcite component of ash is stable, but the siliceous components are not (Chapter 4). The calcite crystals, however, may become more ordered at the atomic level over time. This change can be monitored using infrared spectroscopy and is an indication of the state of preservation of the calcite (Chu et al., 2008; see Overview 2 in Chapter 12). The presence of pseudomorphs of biogenic oxalate in ash (Figure 7.2) is an indication of good preservation of the primary ash crystals.

The siliceous aggregates and the phytoliths can dissolve under alkaline conditions. The siliceous aggregates are expected to be more soluble and hence less stable than the phytoliths, as the silica matrix that binds the aggregate together contains very large amounts of other ions, in addition to silicon. Their presence destabilizes the silica. In fact, I have noticed that under certain alkaline conditions in the laboratory, siliceous aggregates dissolve, but the phytoliths, which are composed almost entirely of silicon and oxygen, do not.

If the phytoliths partially dissolve, their usually smooth surfaces become rough and pitted. Under more extreme conditions, they break up into smaller fragments. This was the condition of the phytoliths in the approximately 50,000- to 60,000-year-old calcitic ash dump examined in Kebara Cave, Israel (Albert et al., 2000). However, in the 12,000- to 15,000-year-old Natufian deposits in Hayonim Cave, Israel, which are also composed mainly of ash calcite, the phytoliths have smooth surfaces (Albert et al., 2003b). I doubt whether this is a function of the time elapsed; rather, it probably reflects differences in the chemical microenvironments and the local hydrologic regimes.

pH BELOW 8

The pH will decrease if organic matter degrades and releases organic acids. This will readily occur in sediments where carbonates that can buffer the system to around pH 8 were never present, or the carbonates present were totally dissolved by the production of organic acids. The degrading organic matter also often releases phosphate, which readily reacts with the unstable ash calcite to produce authigenic carbonate hydroxylapatite. If the pH drops below 7, then the carbonate hydroxylapatite dissolves and then reprecipitates as a more insoluble authigenic phosphate mineral. This reaction cascade is discussed in detail by Weiner et al. (2007) and in Chapter 3.

Each time a mineral dissolves, some of the soluble ions may be transported out of the system, and hence the volume of ash decreases. Thus, as ash calcite undergoes diagenesis, the fraction of the less soluble phytoliths and siliceous aggregates tends to increase from the initial 2% or so and, ultimately, can become the major component of the ash deposit (Schiegl et al., 1996; Weiner et al., 2002; Weiner et al., 2007). Figure 10.3 is a photograph of a section in Hayonim Cave, Israel, that is composed almost entirely of siliceous aggregates a few meters thick. Thus ash can radically change in composition, volume, and appearance and, as a result, can be very difficult to identify. Furthermore, most ash seems to spread readily from the hearth where it was produced and becomes an integral component of the sediments, making it even more difficult to identify.

Identifying ash produced by burning wood and bark

Structures that are lens shaped in section and have a somewhat circular form, usually 50 to 100 centimeters or so in diameter in plane view, may well be the remains of ash-containing hearths. If high concentrations of macroscopic charcoal and/or red brick–colored burned clay nodules are also present within the lens, there is little doubt that this represents a preserved ash deposit (Figure 7.3). Hearths, however, are not commonly preserved. Furthermore, calcite-rich white lenses resembling hearths can sometimes form as a result of local persistent dripping of water from the ceiling of a cave. Thus identifying ash only by eye, based on morphology, may be erroneous and most probably overlooks most of the ash present in the sediments of a site.

The color and texture of sediments are sometimes indications of the presence of ash. If the sediment being described is demonstrated to be almost pure calcite and has a gray color (due to the presence of microparticles of charcoal) and a powdery texture, it could well be ash. The association of the calcite or its diagenetic product with burned nodules of clay and charcoal is also a good indication that ash is present in these sediments. Proof depends on further analysis. On occasion, sediments with red, yellow, and black colors have been thought to be derived from ash. Perhaps the best-known case is from Zhoukoudian (Black et al., 1933). Analyses showed that these sediments were primarily iron-rich clays (Weiner et al., 1998).

If calcite is a major component of the sediments – and even if it is not in the form of hearths – it may well be derived from ash. This can be confirmed by identifying pseudomorphs of the original calcium oxalate crystals using a petrographic microscope (Figure 7.1) and by using the ratio of the v_2 and v_4 peaks in the infrared spectrum. The ratio should be around 4 (Chu et al., 2008). Even mild diagenesis can, however, alter these properties, and they will not help in identifying whether the calcite was derived from ash. An additional approach is to dissolve the calcite and examine the residue using a petrographic microscope. The presence of many irregularly shaped phytoliths is indicative of the presence of wood or bark ash component (Chapter 6), particularly if their refractive indices are high and hence show that they were burned (Elbaum et al., 2003). Note that the siliceous aggregates are easily confused with clay particles when examined in the petrographic microscope. An infrared spectrum of the residue will unequivocally differentiate between the two (see Overview 7 in Chapter 12). Diagenesis, however, may cause the total dissolution of the siliceous aggregates and phytoliths, especially as

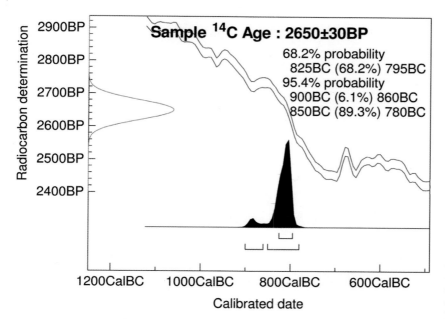

Sample ¹⁴C Age : 2650±30BP

68.2% probability
825BC (68.2%) 795BC
95.4% probability
900BC (6.1%) 860BC
850BC (89.3%) 780BC

Radiocarbon determination (Y-axis): 2900BP, 2800BP, 2700BP, 2600BP, 2500BP, 2400BP

Calibrated date (X-axis): 1200CalBC, 1000CalBC, 800CalBC, 600CalBC

Color Plate 1
Example of a ¹⁴C analysis before calibration (red curve, Y-axis) and after calibration (black-filled peaks, X-axis) using the OxCal program (Bronk Ramsey, 2003). The blue curve is the calibration curve. The red curve is a typical result obtained with a characteristic precision of ±30 years. When the red curve is projected onto the calibration curve and all the errors are taken into account, the resulting calibrated date is shown in black. The calibration curve is based on data from Reimer et al. (2004b) and the calculation using Bronk Ramsey (1995) and Bronk Ramsey (2001).

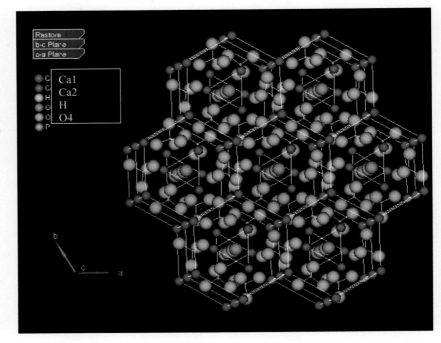

Color Plate 2
Atomic structure of hydroxylapatite. Image kindly obtained from Prof. Leng Yang from Hong Kong University of Science and Technology. It was prepared with permission using CaP Model software produced by the Hong Kong University of Science and Technology.

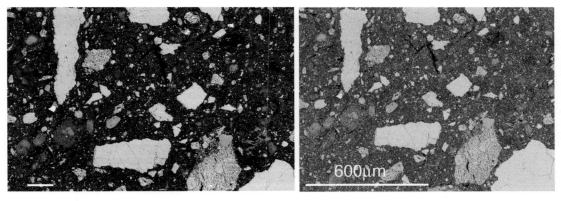

Color Plate 3 Scanning electron microscope images of a polished surface of a sample of a lime plaster. The sample was from a restoration that was performed in the Holy Sepulchre, Jerusalem, 6 years prior to sampling. *Left*. Image obtained using the back scattered electrons (BSE) detector in which different minerals have different contrasts. In this mode the binder is clearly differentiated from the aggregates. Scale bar is 100um. *Right*. The same area analyzed for chemical element concentrations using energy dispersion X-ray spectroscopy (EDS). A computer is then used to color code the different compositions. Concentrations of Ca, Si, and Al are marked on the right image by the following colors: Ca – green; Si – red; Al – blue. While the binder is primarily comprised of Ca (representing calcite), two types of aggregates are identified: calcites (green) and clays (pink, due to the red and blue combination).

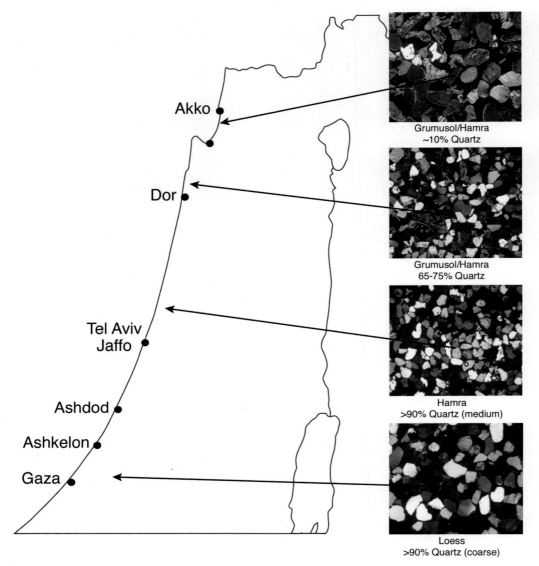

Color Plate 4 Photographs using polarized light showing the changing assemblages of clastic minerals in sediments from along the coast of Israel. The width of each photograph is 2.5mm. The changes are basically due to the fact that in the eastern Mediterranean, currents flow northward along the Levantine coast. The main source of sediments to this area is the Nile River, which drains the plutonic rock plateaus of East Africa. The most stable mineral of these rocks is quartz. This quartz sand is swept along Sinai and northward along the Israeli coast. At the same time, the inland limestone hills of the Levantine coast contribute calcareous sand to the sediments. Since Mount Carmel (Haifa) acts as a natural barrier to the Nile sand, north of Haifa the quartz sand component diminishes and the sediment becomes increasingly calcareous. Another source of clastic materials is the marine sediments. Along the Levantine coast coralline algae of the genus *Amphiroa* are a significant component of Quaternary beach deposits. The figure shows that the sediments from between Gaza and Ashkelon (lower photograph) are composed almost entirely of large rounded quartz grains, with small amounts of limestone (brown grains). Sediments from the beach at Tel Aviv about 50 kilometers north, are composed of small quartz grains that have a more uniform size. The sediments from the beach at Tel Dor on the coast near Mount Carmel contains quartz and more than 30 percent calcareous grains, some of which are identified by arrows. Finally the sediments from Akko beach north of Haifa, are almost exclusively composed of limestone grains and skeletons of marine fauna, including *Amphiroa* alga fragments (arrows). These changes are reflected in the clastic component of the locally made pottery from each area, enabling the source of the pottery along the coast to be identified. The material for the figure and the explanation were provided by courtesy of Yuval Goren. This is part of a study, made in the laboratory for comparative microarchaeology of Tel Aviv University by Yuval Goren and Nissim Golding.

the calcite buffers the pH to around 8.2. At this pH, siliceous aggregates and phytoliths may dissolve.

If calcite is absent from the sediments, but aragonitic mollusk shells are present, it can be deduced that calcite, including ash calcite, was never present (Chapter 3). As bone mineral is more stable and hence less soluble than calcite, the presence or absence of bones sheds little light on the possibility that ash calcite was once present. The absence of bones and the presence of relatively insoluble authigenic phosphate minerals implies that the pH, at some stage, decreased below 7. The ash calcite under these circumstances would certainly have dissolved along with other sedimentary carbonates. The presence of siliceous aggregates and irregularly shaped phytoliths would be a good indication that ash was once present.

Embedded information

DEMONSTRATING CONTROL OF FIRE BY HUMANS

Differentiating between the deliberate use of fire by humans as opposed to a natural fire that also engulfed the archaeological site is of much interest. Perhaps the only incontrovertible evidence for the deliberate use of fire is the presence of a hearth, or better still, a series of hearths with identifiable ash still preserved (Figure 7.3). An unanswered question is why hearths are actually preserved as such, especially when, at the same site, ash is dispersed in the associated sediments. Somehow the repeated act of making a fire at the same location causes the ash to consolidate. In the Natufian stratum of Hayonim Cave, some hearths are surrounded by circular stone structures. The ash preserved in these structures has a white color, whereas the ash all around is gray, presumably because of the presence of small fragments of charcoal. The absence of charcoal could be due to the repeated use of the hearth (Weiner et al., 2002). It would be interesting to compare more carefully the crystal disorder, crystal morphologies, and sizes, and especially to compare whether the crystals are somehow fused in the ash from the hearth, as

Figure 7.3
a, View of a series of hearths from Kebara Cave, Israel, showing their lens shape in section. Surprisingly, the major component of the sediment between the hearths is also derived from ash. For more detail, see Schiegl et al. (1996). Scale bar: 20 centimeters. *b*, Close-up view of a series of hearths in section from Kebara Cave, Israel. The speckles in the bright white layer are brick red–colored burned clay nodules. The hearths in this location are composed mainly of the phosphate minerals montgomeryite and leucophosphite as well as siliceous aggregates. The reason for the black, charred, organic-rich layer underlying the white, ash-rich layer is not understood. Scale bar: 10 centimeters.

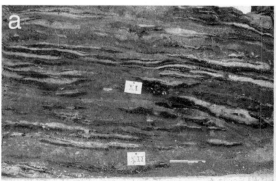

compared to the ash in the surroundings, to gain more insight into ash preservation in hearths.

The oldest hearths known to date are around 400,000 years old (James, 1989). Thus, in terms of understanding the earlier history of the control of fire, hearths are not helpful. As no other single form of evidence can be unequivocal in this matter, several lines of evidence all pointing to the deliberate use of fire, need to be obtained. These could include the identification of ash, burned flints – based on their characteristic pot-lid fracture (Goren-Inbar et al., 2004) or their thermoluminescence (Aitken and Valladas, 1992) – burned bones (using infrared spectroscopy; Shahack-Gross et al., 1997), localized paleomagnetic features (Bellomo, 1993), wood ash in a part of a cave where trees would not be expected to grow, and more. Even the presence of a combination of such features may be insufficient evidence for the deliberate use of fire as it clearly depends on the archaeological context. In the end, the evidence presented, like all scientific evidence, has to be evaluated in terms of the degree of uncertainty involved.

Layer 10 at Zhoukoudian was generally regarded as the oldest reliable proof of the controlled use of fire because of the accumulation of some 50 centimeters of so-called ash in association with artifacts (Black et al., 1933; James, 1989). A careful reexamination of this layer in the currently exposed section (Weiner et al., 1998; Goldberg et al., 2001) revealed that the deposits were not ash, and no artifacts were associated with these deposits. However, in the layer immediately above these deposits, artifacts are present and are clearly associated with an assemblage of bones. Furthermore, about 12% of these bones are burned – a proportion commonly found in much younger sites, where fire was clearly used. Obviously, the evidence would have been stronger had the underlying sediments proved to be ash, but still, the association of artifacts and burned bones in one relatively thin layer does support the controlled use of fire, especially when seen in the context of the whole 35-meter-thick section at Zhoukoudian Locality 1, which contains only one other layer with relatively abundant artifacts (Weiner et al., 1998). For more details, see Chapter 4.

FUEL TYPES USED FOR FIRES

Wood and bark, animal dung, a variety of other plant materials, bones, and natural peat are among the fuel types used traditionally. Wood and bark, and animal dung are probably the most frequently used fuel types. Different fuel types can be differentiated based on their ash compositions. The ash produced by burning wood and bark is dominated by calcite, often with characteristically shaped pseudomorphs, as well as small amounts of phytoliths and siliceous aggregates in the acid-insoluble fraction. Animal dung is composed mainly of grasses and, to some extent, leaves (Anderson and Ertug-Yaras, 1998), and the ash is therefore dominated by silica phytoliths with morphologies character-istic of grasses, leaves, or both. Furthermore, the phytoliths in wood and bark are mainly irregular in shape, whereas those in grasses and leaves have consistent morphologies (Piperno, 2006). Bone ash is com-posed of calcined carbonate hydroxylapatite and thus differs from all other forms of ash. Calcined bone can be identified by infrared spec-troscopy (see Overview 5 in Chapter 12). Peat is formed from terrestrial vegetation and therefore should contain a heterogeneous assemblage of phytoliths quite different from that of wood or bark, but possibly not easily distinguishable from animal dung ash in this respect. Peat and coal both produce about four or five times more ash by weight than the other fuel sources, mainly because of associated sedimentary minerals. The ash of coal and peat contains silicon, aluminum, and iron as the three major components, with iron sometimes being more abundant in peat than in coal (Zevenhoven-Onderwater et al., 2000). A key method for differentiating between different kinds of ash is micromorphology. This was most effectively used for identifying fuel type in a study in Iceland (Simpson et al., 2003).

RADIOCARBON DATING
Ash has not been used for radiocarbon dating, although in principle, ash should contain only carbon-14 from the atmosphere. Radiocarbon dat-ing of the wood cellulose provides a date when the wood was formed, which could be long before the wood was used and burned. Based on the v_2:v_4 ratios (Chu et al., 2008), it seems that ash calcite is derived mainly from the low-temperature form produced as a result of loss of carbon monoxide from calcium oxalate (Brochier and Thinon, 2003). If this ash calcite is well preserved, it should provide a reliable radiocar-bon date of the age when the wood formed. In practice, ash calcite is usually not stable, and dating ash may be problematic.

THERMOLUMINESCENCE AND ELECTRON SPIN RESONANCE DATING
The high potassium content of the siliceous aggregates (around 3 to 7 weight percent) (Schiegl et al., 1994) means that siliceous aggregates also contain unusually high amounts of the radioactive isotope of potassium, ^{40}K. The result is that siliceous aggregates emit relatively large amounts of gamma radiation. This can have a pronounced effect on the ther-moluminescence and electron spin resonance dating of burned flints buried in sediments rich in siliceous aggregates, as was demonstrated in Hayonim Cave, Israel (Mercier et al., 1995, 2007).

TYPE OF WOOD USED FOR FIRES
Phytoliths are a relatively stable component of wood ash. They are, however, present in relatively small amounts in wood, and the wood of some species does not contain phytoliths at all (Tsartsidou et al., 2007).

Phytoliths are more widespread and somewhat more abundant in bark (Tsartsidou et al., 2007). Even though they are not abundant in wood and bark, the production of large amounts of ash, and the diagenetic processes that often remove some or all of the relatively soluble calcite component, can result in high concentrations of ash-derived phytoliths being present in the sediments.

The majority of wood phytoliths do not have regular morphologies that are indicative of the species of tree from which they were derived (Amos, 1952). In fact, the high ratio of irregular- to consistent-morphology phytoliths in a sediment is a good indication that ash is a major component of the sediment (Albert et al., 1999). The bark of some trees contains phytoliths with characteristic shapes that are absent in the wood from the same trees. Thus the presence of these phytoliths in relatively high concentrations in the sediment can be used to infer that small branches or twigs were a major component of the fuel used, as the proportion of bark to wood is larger in small branches than in large branches or logs. The concentration of bark-derived phytoliths was used in Hayonim Cave, Israel, to show that in the Mousterian, as opposed to the later Natufian, small branches were preferentially used as fuel for fires (Albert et al., 2003b).

A method for identifying the tree species from which the wood for fuel was obtained is by examining the microstructure of the charcoal fragments (reviewed by Lev-Yadun, 2007). It should, however, be noted that in an ethnographic study of charcoal in hearths, it was shown that this may only represent the type of wood used in the last phases of the hearth, before it was abandoned (Ntinou, 2002). Although this is better than no information, it may not be representative of the overall types of wood used.

CHARCOAL AND CHARRED MATERIALS

Charred wood (charcoal) and other charred plant materials, especially seeds and fruits, are important components of the archaeobotanical record. Charcoal produced by humans may be as old as 1.5 million years (Brain and Sillen, 1988). Some of the best evidence we have for the earliest deliberate use of fire are the fire-hardened charred points of wooden sticks produced about 400,000 years ago (Thieme, 1997). Charred organic matter and phytoliths are the main materials used for reconstructing plant assemblages of a site. Furthermore, charred organic matter is the most common material used for radiocarbon dating. Despite its importance, surprisingly little is known about the structure and diagenesis of naturally charred materials. There is a vast literature on charred materials produced for industry, but the conditions of their production are more uniform, and the temperatures usually used to produce these materials are much higher than those encountered in natural fires.

Charcoal and other charred materials are produced in fires as a result of incomplete combustion. As the original organic material loses all, or almost all, of its original atomic-level structure, organisms are not able to utilize charred materials as a source of energy, and as a result, they are much more likely to be preserved than uncharred organic materials. This does not mean, however, that they are inert. On the contrary, their absence in some sites or in some locations within a site is just one indication that this is not the case. Charred materials do undergo diagenetic breakdown. This is not unexpected as charred materials are produced at elevated temperatures and in an oxygen-poor environment. They are therefore not stable when buried at ambient temperatures and in the presence of oxygen. To date, little is known about charred materials other than wood charcoal. The focus of this section will therefore be on wood charcoal.

Molecular structure of modern wood charcoal produced in natural fires

Charcoal is a charred organic material derived mainly from wood and bark. One of the first studies of charcoal formation, if not the first, was that of Priestley (1770), who showed, for example, that during the charring process, the wood initially expands and then contracts. He characterized the process by measuring the conductivity of the charred product. At elevated temperatures, the major components of the wood (cellulose, hemicellulose, and lignin) break down. They lose carbon dioxide, carbon monoxide, and other gases, and some of the remaining molecules reorganize into ringlike aromatic structures resembling graphite (Soltes and Elder, 1981). The wood pyrolysis process has been studied in detail. Briefly, loss of water begins when wood is exposed to above ambient temperatures, until about 250°C, with little other change. Above 250°C, the structure begins to change, and by 350°C, all the original components have lost their structures. Above this temperature, polyaromatic compounds, including the graphitelike crystallites, begin to form. The overall weight loss during pyrolysis is around 50%, and the dimensional contraction can vary between 20% and 40%, depending on the direction measured (Paris et al., 2005). For detailed reviews on carbonization and graphitization, see Oberlin (1984) and Lewis (1982).

Roseland Franklin (1951; of DNA fame) used X-ray diffraction of synthetic charcoal produced at high temperatures to show that the small crystallites in charcoal are similar to, but not identical to, graphite, and that a disordered carbon phase is also present. Figure 7.4 shows a schematic of this structure, adapted from Franklin (1951). This is also

Figure 7.4
Schematic of the structure of charcoal, showing graphitelike crystallites interspersed in a disordered, nongraphitic phase. The scheme was adapted from Franklin (1951).

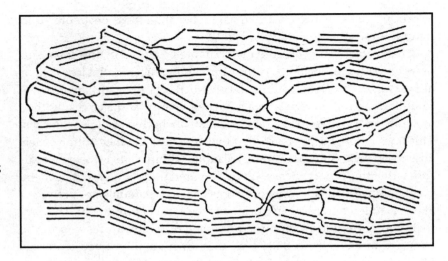

the basic structural model for charcoal produced in natural fires (Cohen-Ofri et al., 2006). The relative proportions of the two main phases, the graphitelike phase, and the nonordered phase (Franklin's terminology) are influenced by the local temperature in the fire, the amount of available oxygen, extent of burning, and probably other variables. Thus even a single fire will produce a heterogeneous assemblage of charcoal products, making it very difficult to characterize natural charcoal.

Highly resolving transmission electron micrographs clearly show the two-phase structure of modern charcoal (Figure 7.5). The ordered areas arise from the alignment of atoms within the sample (called a *lattice image*), and the spacing between the lines is consistent with this phase being the graphitelike crystals (Cohen-Ofri et al., 2006). The crystals are exceedingly small, being around 5 nanometers or so in their longest dimension. Surrounding the crystals is an unstructured material. Analysis of this unstructured material by electron energy loss spectroscopy (EELS) shows that it is very similar to amorphous carbon. Furthermore, the EELS spectra of the graphitelike phase and the amorphous phase demonstrate that in modern charcoal, oxygen is essentially absent (Cohen-Ofri et al., 2007).

Transmission electron micrograph images of modern charcoal have also revealed a minor – but very interesting – component, namely, rounded, onionlike structures (Hata et al., 2000; Figure 7.6). These are similar to multiwalled carbon nanotubes. They are composed of the graphitelike phase, but instead of being in the form of flat, crystalline platelets, they are curled up into rounded structures with no exposed edges. They can therefore be expected to be much more stable than the other graphite crystallites (Cohen-Ofri et al., 2007) as they have no exposed edges that are relatively easily oxidized. Very small amounts of rounded carbon structures with 60 carbon atoms (fullerenes) have also been found in soot (Osawa et al., 1997).

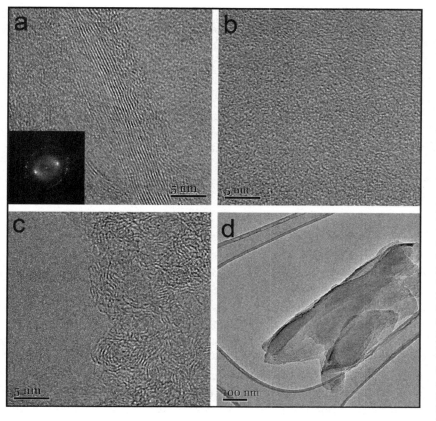

Figure 7.5
Transmission electron microscope images of small particles of charcoal: *a*, the lattice image (rows of aligned atoms) ordered crystalline phase is surrounded by a disordered amorphous carbon phase (charcoal is from *Ceratonia*); the inset is a Fourier transform of the ordered phase, which confirms that it is indeed a highly ordered phase; *b*, image of the amorphous unstructured carbon phase of *Ceratonia*; *c*, graphitelike crystallites organized into semirounded shapes (from *Quercus*); *d*, low-magnification image of a charcoal particle (*Ceratonia*), showing the layered structure. In some places, linear edges can be seen, which presumably reflect the crystalline structure of the graphitelike phase. Images were prepared by R. Popowitz-Biro and I. Cohen-Ofri.

Molecular structure of fossil wood charcoal from archaeological sites

Fossil charcoals examined to date all appear to have less of the graphite-like component and more of the disordered phase, as compared to modern charcoal (Cohen-Ofri et al., 2006). The most striking difference between modern charcoal and fossil charcoal is the presence of oxygen in the fossil charcoal, but not in the modern charcoal. This oxygen is mainly in the form of carboxylate and carbonyl groups (COO^- and $COOH$, respectively), as revealed by infrared spectra of fossil charcoal

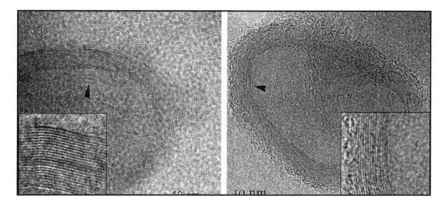

Figure 7.6
Transmission electron microscope images of rounded, onionlike structures in, *a*, modern and, *b*, fossil charcoal. The insets show high-resolution images of the areas marked by arrows. Images were prepared by R. Popowitz-Biro and I. Cohen-Ofri. Reproduced from Cohen-Ofri et al. (2007).

(see Overview 12 in Chapter 12). EELS shows that this oxygen is confined to the nonorganized phase and is absent in the graphitelike phase (Cohen-Ofri et al., 2007). At pH conditions of above 4 or so, the prevailing groups are the charged carboxylates, and thus the charcoal binds counterions, such as sodium, calcium, iron, and so on, to balance the charge. It will also readily absorb charged water-soluble molecules from the environment. Thus fossil charcoal is most likely to be contaminated with other organic molecules – a significant problem for radiocarbon dating. Fossil charcoal also contains the rounded, onionlike structures (Figure 7.6). These were particularly abundant in some poorly preserved charcoal samples from Kebara Cave, Israel (Rebollo et al., 2008).

Diagenesis

Charcoal has often been regarded as a relatively inert substance (Nichols et al., 2000), and charcoal has even been described as "almost indestructible chemically" (Leny and Casteel, 1975). This was clearly not the case for a site in Australia (Bird et al., 2002). The structural studies of modern and fossil charcoal show that oxidation is probably the most important diagenetic reaction responsible for the degradation of charcoal over time. This oxidation process converts a material that is initially relatively hydrophobic into a charged, hydrophilic material. This means that fossil charcoal can more easily disintegrate in an aqueous environment. Even though the details are not known, it seems as though the oxidation of the charcoal transforms it into a material that resembles soil humic substances, as these are also rich in aromatic groups as well as carboxylate groups (Cohen-Ofri et al., 2006). The reduction in graphitelike crystallites and the preservation of the rounded, onionlike structures in fossil charcoal (Figure 7.6) can be attributed to the effects of oxidation. The oxygen can readily attack the exposed edges of the flat, graphitelike crystallites. These, however, are absent in the rounded structures, and here the oxidation locations are probably limited to defects in the structure (Cohen-Ofri et al., 2007). Thus the most stable components of fossil charcoal are probably the rounded, onionlike structures, which are not easily oxidized.

The diagenetic oxidation process does not account for the observation in many sites that charcoal is not uniformly distributed, but rather, is concentrated in some areas and not others. This could of course be due to human activities, to the natural burning of a tree, and so on. In Kebara Cave, at least, human activities are not responsible as ash is distributed throughout the cave (Schiegl et al., 1996), whereas charcoal is restricted to the southern part of the cave. A possible mechanism for the loss of charcoal in Kebara Cave has been proposed (Rebollo et al., 2008). The mechanism is based on the observation that the authigenic phosphate mineral, taranakite, is present only in the part of the cave where charcoal is abundant (Schiegl et al., 1996). It is known that taranakite forms when the pH is between 4 and 5 (Taylor and Gurney, 1961). Rebollo et al. (2008) studied the effect of lowering the pH on charcoal from Kebara in vitro. They found that during the pH drop, the counterions present in the charcoal are removed because at low pH, the charged carboxylate groups change to uncharged carbonyl groups. Rebollo et al. (2008) postulated that when this occurred in the cave as a result of guano degradation, the counterions removed from the charcoal probably also included iron and manganese. Both these metals are known to catalyze the oxidation of graphite (Chernysh et al., 1993). As this pH drop did not occur in the northern part of the cave, the presence of the oxidative ions in those charcoals could have resulted in the conversion of the charcoal to carbon dioxide.

There are many unresolved problems regarding charcoal preservation. For example, in some sites, all the charcoal is present as very small particles distributed together with the ash, and no large chunks are preserved. Is this related to the fuel type used, the manner in which fires were managed, or preservation? In the hearths in Kebara Cave, finely dispersed charcoal is concentrated in the bottom layer of a hearth complex but is absent in the upper layers (Figure 7.3). The reason for this is not known.

Embedded information

IMPACT OF FIRES PRODUCED BY HUMANS ON THE LOCAL VEGETATION AND SOILS

The distribution of charcoal in sediments provides information on fires produced by humans (Thiebault, 1988). Wildfires ignited mainly by lightning are fairly common throughout the Phanerozoic (Scott, 2000). These can be detected by quantifying the numbers of charcoal fragments in sediment profiles (Haberle and Ledru, 2001) and can in turn be related to changing climate. Since humans developed the capability of controlling fire, the frequency of wildfires in certain areas may have increased (Carcaillet, 1998). The result is that the contribution of anthropogenic charred organic materials to the soil increased. In humid, tropical regions, where noncharred organic material degrades fairly rapidly, the presence of charred organic materials has stabilized the soil and made the soil more fertile. This is particularly prominent in the Amazon basin (Glaser et al., 2000).

INK

Ink was often produced from soot by mixing with a binder (Swider et al., 2003). Soot is composed of charred particles that become airborne during combustion. The traditional ink produced in China (known as India ink) is a suspension of soot derived from the burning of oil with a wick (lampblack) and a binder produced from skins (Lambert, 1997). The properties and preservation of the soot component should be similar to those of charred materials in general.

IDENTIFICATION OF CHARRED ORGANIC MATERIAL IN SEDIMENTS

Black-colored sediments may be black due to the presence of charred organic materials, but the black color may also be due to the diagenesis of organic materials. It is possible to differentiate between these options by identifying the presence of specific marker molecules for charred organic materials, called benzenecarboxylic acids (BPCA) (Glaser et al., 1998). In archaeological sites, this marker can, in principle, be used to identify the locations of hearths or other sites where fire was used.

RADIOCARBON DATING

Charred wood and seeds are the most common materials used for radio-carbon dating. As the seeds are short-lived, whereas the wood may be from part of a tree that was formed a hundred or more years before the time it was burned, it is preferable to date the short-lived materials. Before dating, the contaminants have to be removed and the sample prepared in the form of pure graphite to be used as a target for accelerator mass spectrometry analysis. The effectiveness of this process is influenced by the state of preservation of the charred material (Chapter 10). Charcoal was also used for rock paintings starting in the Epi-Paleolithic. This carbon can also be dated to determine the age of the drawings (Russ et al., 1990).

SEED AND FRUIT IDENTIFICATION

Charred seeds and fruit from an archaeological site are a major source of information on the archaeobotanical record (e.g., Hillman, 1996; Weiss and Kislev, 2004). The interpretation of this record should take into account the biases introduced by the differing circumstances in which plants are charred and their susceptibility to charring (Boardman and Jones, 1990), and by the fact that relatively dense, inedible plants have a higher chance of surviving (Minnis, 1981). Very little is known about whether charred seeds and fruits have the same molecular structure as charred wood, and whether their diagenesis follows the oxidation process of fossil wood charcoal.

WOOD IDENTIFICATION

Although the charring process does distort the wood structure (Paris et al., 2005), the preserved microstructure can be used to identify the species of tree from which the charcoal formed (Maby, 1932). The samples can be prepared even with a simple razor blade for examination in the light microscope (Leny and Casteel, 1975). Identification is based on a reference collection of the local trees after charring and with the help of an appropriate wood anatomy textbook such as Panshin and DeZeeuw (1970) and Lev-Yadun (2007).

PLASTER AND MORTAR

Plaster and mortar are pyrotechnology products commonly found in many archaeological sites. *Plaster* is the term used for the covering of wall surfaces and floor construction, whereas *mortar* refers to the material that binds bricks and/or stones together to form a wall or other architectural features. The term *mortar* is also sometimes used to refer to the leveling layer on the outer surface of the structure, where it serves as a base for the plaster layer. If the plaster is used to cover an exterior wall, it is often referred to as *stucco*, especially if it is used for decorative purposes.

The terms *plaster* and *mortar* thus refer to their respective functional locations. The constituents used to produce the plaster and mortar also need to be defined. The most common constituent in traditional plasters and mortars is calcium hydroxide, also known as lime. Lime plaster and mortar are mainly used together with stones or bricks. Lime plaster can, however, be mixed with sediments and used without stones or bricks to form a consolidated mass. In Mesoamerica, this is known as *lime-aggregate*. Finally, lime can also be applied with a brush, rather than a trowel, as a thin coat less than a millimeter in thickness on an exterior surface. This has been called a *wash coat*. The terminology follows Littmann (1957).

Plasters and mortars are composed of a material that binds the constituents together (binder) and added materials (aggregates) that increase the volume and improve the properties of the formed product. The compositions of the binders and aggregates as well as their relative proportions can be varied significantly to optimize the product to its function. Thus an analysis of these aspects of plasters and mortars can provide insights into manufacturing processes and functions. For more general information, see Boynton (1980) and McDonnell (2001), and for an overview of plaster and mortar in archaeology, see Gourdin and Kingery (1975).

Binders

The essential quality of all binders is that initially, they are unstable at ambient temperatures and pressures. They therefore undergo a series of reactions that usually involve the formation of a hard crystalline product that adheres strongly to the aggregate particles and to each other to form a cohesive new product in the shape desired. The three most common binders used in archaeological contexts are calcite, gypsum, and various disordered hydrated silica minerals. Only calcite and gypsum binders are the products of pyrotechnology as their precursors need to be produced at elevated temperatures to form a product that is unstable at ambient temperatures. The disordered hydrated silica minerals are traditionally derived from volcanic ash (e.g., from the area of Pozzolana in Italy in Roman times). Being the products of a volcano, they are formed naturally at high temperatures. On mixing with lime at ambient temperatures, they reform into a more stable component. In contrast to calcite and gypsum binders, which form during the drying process, the hydrated silica minerals form in the presence of water. They are thus known as hydraulic mortars or plasters. Note, too, that calcite and gypsum binders, and sometimes silicate binders as well, may be mixed into the same mortar or plaster (Luxán et al., 1995).

CALCITE BINDER

Calcite is by far the most common binder and also the first binder developed by humans some 15,000 years ago (Kingery et al., 1988; Valla et al., 2007; Chu et al., 2008). When calcite is the binder, the plaster is known as *lime plaster*. The precursor phase is produced by heating geogenic calcite, usually in the form of limestone or chalk, in a kiln to temperatures in the range of 800° to 900°C for periods of time ranging from hours to days (Boynton, 1980). This causes the $CaCO_3$ to break down into calcium oxide (CaO). This is called *quicklime*. Note that there is no specific calcination temperature for calcite as many factors influence the reaction, including the local partial pressure of carbon dioxide and the presence of small amounts of clay (Shoval et al., 2003). The CaO is then placed in water at ambient temperatures and reforms as calcium hydroxide ($Ca[OH]_2$). This is called *slaked lime*, and its mineral name is portlandite. When the calcium hydroxide dries, it adsorbs carbon dioxide from the atmosphere, and calcite forms. Even though this calcite forms at ambient temperatures, I refer to it here as pyrogenic calcite because it is the product of a high-temperature precursor phase (CaO).

This rather simple preparation procedure, in theory, is by no means easy in practice (Boynton, 1980). Perhaps the main reason why it is complicated is that the high-temperature reaction proceeds from the surface of a limestone fragment into its interior (Gourdin and Kingery, 1975). During this reaction, carbon dioxide is released and has to diffuse out of the limestone. If diffusion is retarded, then the partial pressure of CO_2 builds up, and this in turn increases the minimum temperature at which the reaction will occur, thus making it even more difficult to produce the CaO. Thus the rate of formation of CaO is a function of temperature, the size and porosity of the limestone, the sizes of the crystallites in the limestone, and the extent of impurities. An efficient conversion process is one that goes to completion and does not leave significant amounts of unconverted limestone, as well as one that requires the least amount of fuel. For this to be achieved, the person producing the lime needs to be familiar with the starting materials, the nature of the fuel used, and the characteristics of the kiln. The latter can be very large (Figure 7.7) and the production process can take days. Note that CaO can be produced in an open fire, but it is not easy and requires a large amount of fuel (personal experience).

An additional potential pitfall in CaO production is overheating. This results in large, well-crystallized aggregates of CaO that do not readily hydrate when placed in water. The product is known as *dead lime*. Thus the presence of CaO in an ancient plaster or mortar could be an indication of the production of dead lime (Boynton, 1980).

The process whereby the calcium hydroxide absorbs carbon dioxide from the atmosphere and then reacts to form calcite (known as *carbonation*) is also important in terms of the quality of the end product. It is well known from Roman times that aged slaked lime produces a mechanically improved lime plaster. In fact, the slaked lime was sometimes aged for years. Vitruvius, in his *Ten Books on Architecture*, recommended three years. A study comparing calcium hydroxide that was aged for 14 years with calcium hydroxide aged for 1 year showed that the crystals changed shape from prisms to plate shaped, and the crystal size range was significantly smaller in the 14-year aged material. The lime plaster produced from the aged calcium hydroxide also had much smaller calcite crystals and produced fewer cracks (Cazalla et al., 2000).

Figure 7.7
Photograph of a traditional, working lime plaster kiln in Hunan Province, China. Note that the kiln is in the background and the slaking pit is in the foreground.

These differences may well be preserved and could provide interesting insights into the plaster preparation technology used.

Dolomite is a common carbonate rock. In some regions, it is the dominant or even only carbonate rock available. Dolomite differs from calcite in that it is composed of roughly equal proportions of calcium and magnesium, and it has a different crystallographic structure than calcite (Lippmann, 1973). It degrades at lower temperatures than calcite (Boynton, 1980), and in this respect, it would be ideal for lime plaster and mortar production. The MgO that is produced does not hydrate readily, however, and thus remains insoluble (Boynton, 1980). It therefore has poor binding capabilities. Note that some limestones contain considerable amounts of magnesium in their calcitic structures. Thus the presence of Mg in the binder does not necessarily imply that dolomite was used as a raw material (Caró et al., 2008).

GYPSUM

When alabaster or gypsum ($CaSO_4.2H_2O$) rock is heated to relatively low temperatures (150° to 400°C), it loses most of its water. The product is called calcium sulfate hemihydrate ($CaSO_4.0.5H_2O$). This is also known as plaster of Paris. On rehydration, water is rapidly taken up, and the gypsum crystals reform into a gypsum plaster. The newly formed crystals are needle shaped, and the product is hard, but not as hard as lime plaster. If the heating is not well controlled and all the water molecules are lost, then a relatively insoluble product (anhydrite) forms that cannot easily be dissolved. Its presence thus detracts from the usefulness of the gypsum plaster. Gypsum plaster is relatively soluble in water, and thus its usefulness is restricted, particularly to regions with dry climates (Kingery et al., 1988) or for interior purposes. There are, however, certain regions, such as Spain, where gypsum plasters have traditionally been widely used for many different purposes (Luxán et al., 1995).

When gypsum plaster hardens, it expands slightly. It is therefore often mixed with a smaller amount of lime plaster, which contracts on drying. In this way, both properties are compensated and the product is improved (da Silveira et al., 2007).

HYDRAULIC PLASTER AND MORTAR

The characteristic property of a hydraulic plaster or mortar is the presence of an unstable silicate phase, in addition to the pyrogenic calcite phase. The silicate minerals are either heated together with the calcite or added after the slaked lime is produced (Borrelli, 1999). Under the relatively high pH conditions created by the $Ca(OH)_2$ slaked lime, the disordered silicate phase dissolves and reforms as a variety of calcium silicate hydrated minerals. These minerals, together with the calcitic component, act as the binder. Because the hydrated silicate phases can form in the presence of water, hydraulic plaster or mortars can harden when wet and over long periods of time. Hydraulic mortars have been reported from the 10th century BC (Furlan and Bissegger, 1975) and earlier, but they were only used on a massive scale by the Romans.

The silicate phases used include clays, which are often present in the natural limestone itself or are deliberately added. The clays are heated together with the limestone. The Romans used deposits of volcanic ash from a variety of locations, including Pozzolana – the locality that gave its name to this general category of binder component. The pozzolana is added to the slaked lime, and the two components react to form a variety of silicate phases (Branda et al., 2001). Crushed brick or ceramics (called *grog*) have also been used as silicate additives. The vitreous silicate component of bricks and ceramics is presumably the unstable silicate phase that reforms at elevated pH.

The authigenic phases produced in the hydraulic mortar are very difficult to characterize, probably because the bulk components are disordered (glassy), with no crystalline structure capable of being detected by X-ray diffraction. These have been described as calcium aluminum hydrates, calcium silicate hydrates, and a combination of both (Charola and Henriques, 1999). The infrared spectrum of a hydraulic mortar analyzed from a Roman bridge shows that the amorphous component is quite different from five volcanic tuffs known to have been used by the Romans (unpublished observation). It is thus clearly a reaction product.

Aggregates

A variety of different aggregates can be added to lime plaster and mortar and probably reflect the availability of local materials. As the aggregates can include carbonate minerals, such as dolomite, or mollusk shells, composed of aragonite, calcite, or both, it may sometimes be difficult to distinguish between carbonates added as aggregates and unburned remnants of the binding component.

PROPORTIONS OF AGGREGATES AND BINDERS

The functional properties of the lime plaster or mortar are influenced not only by the nature of the binder and the aggregates, but by the proportions of aggregates and binder and the interactions between them. This is therefore a key property for relating structure to function in these materials (Casadio et al., 2005). In a comparative study of many different mortars from Rhodes, it was shown that most of them have a proportion of calcite binder to aggregate of 1:3 (Moropoulou et al., 2000). The rule of thumb for gypsum binders is that the proportions of aggregates to binder should be around 1:1 (Luxán et al., 1995).

Many different methods have been used to estimate the proportions of binder to aggregate, including differential dissolution using acids and chelators as well as mechanical methods. In a comparative study, it was found that the most reliable method is to prepare a thin section of the plaster or mortar and, with the help of some specific stains, use digital image analysis to quantify the various components (Casadio et al., 2005). A cathodeluminescence detector is also helpful in this regard (Lindroos et al., 2007). The binder:aggregate proportions can also be estimated using the scanning electron microscope (SEM) and by taking advantage of the back-scattered electron detector, which can distinguish between minerals of the same composition but different densities such as geogenic limestone aggregates composed of calcite crystals as compared to fine-grained calcite crystals in the binder.

Identifying plaster and mortar

Plaster floors and mortars are often readily labeled as such by archae-ologists in the field, without providing direct evidence. They can, how-ever, be misidentified and confused with other mixtures of sediments that do not possess a binder, for example, mud plasters (Karkanas, 2007), soft calcareous material (Matthews et al., 1996), and phytolith-rich layers (Shahack-Gross et al., 2005). The most widely used method for identifying plasters is by examining thin sections using a petro-graphic microscope (Goren and Goldberg, 1991; Karkanas, 2007). For lime plasters, the presence of a dense, highly birefringent crystallitic fabric is perhaps the most characteristic feature, together with vari-ous transitional features (Karkanas, 2007). The presence of gypsum and the characteristic hydrated silica reaction product of hydraulic lime can also be recognized in petrographic thin sections. These minerals are also readily identified by infrared spectroscopy. Infrared spectroscopy can also be used to determine whether the calcite of the binder was derived from CaO using the ratio of two peaks in the spectrum of calcite (see Chu et al., 2008; see also Overview 2 in Chapter 12). Unless diagenetic reactions have resulted in total recrystallization of the binder, this is a helpful identification method.

Diagenesis

The calcitic binders are most likely to undergo diagenetic changes over time as they are composed of calcite microcrystals, which, at the atomic level, are relatively disordered compared to geogenic calcite (Chu et al., 2008) and have a high surface to bulk ratio. The high surface to bulk ratio implies that there are a large number of atoms that are disordered because they are located close to the crystal surface. The diagenetic trend will be toward more ordered, larger, and hence less soluble calcite crys-tals. To some extent, this is the continuation of the same crystallization process that occurred when the crystals formed. Few lime plasters or mortars can be expected to retain their original, unaltered assemblage of calcite binder crystals.

It can also be expected that the diagenetic pathway followed can differ, depending on the manner in which the lime plaster was used. Plasters used for retaining water or other liquids may undergo more extreme diagenesis than those used in a dry mode to cover walls or, to some extent, floors. To my knowledge, systematic differences have not, to date, been demonstrated.

The presence of magnesium in the calcitic binders will change the diagenetic pathway, as authigenic minerals other than calcite can form. It has been shown that a crust that formed on lime plaster statues in Mexico contained, in addition to calcite, brucite (magnesium hydroxide), hydromagnesite, and nesquehonite (another hydrated magnesium carbonate; Villaseñor and Price, 2008). Interestingly, aragonite was also detected in this crust. It is known that aragonite can form from solutions rich in magnesium (like seawater) because the magnesium specifically inhibits calcite nucleation, thus allowing the slightly less stable polymorph aragonite to form (Kitano and Hood, 1962). The source of the magnesium in these samples may have been the limestone used initially to produce the plaster or the addition of dolomitic aggregates to the plaster. Both possibilities could be rather common, and it would therefore be interesting to check for such authigenic minerals in lime plaster to better understand plaster diagenesis.

The aggregates, in principle, should be more stable, and indeed, many aggregate types probably undergo no specific change just because they are part of the plaster-mortar milieu. Some, however, are influenced by the relatively high pH conditions that are due to the presence of the pyrogenic calcitic binder. These include disordered siliceous materials, such as opal, and the various volcanic ashes.

I am not aware of diagenetic studies of gypsum plaster or hydraulic plaster that address changes in the mineral constituents with time.

Embedded information

RADIOCARBON DATING

The only reliable way, at present, to date plaster or mortar is to extract pieces of charred organic materials that may be present in the plaster and use these for radiocarbon dating. As the most likely source of these charred fragments is wood (used to heat the limestone), the date could represent the age of the wood, and not necessarily the age of the plaster (the so-called old wood effect; see Chapter 10 and Heinemeier et al., 1997).

In principle, lime plaster and mortar could be dated by radiocarbon as carbon dioxide from the atmosphere reacts with the $Ca(OH)_2$ to form the calcite binder (Labeyrie and Delibrias, 1964). Thus the ^{14}C

concentration of the calcite should provide the date when the plaster was produced. Although this possibility has been recognized for some time (Heinemeier et al., 1997), plaster still cannot be reliably dated. The difficulties are numerous. The pyrogenic calcite is disordered and therefore not stable and has the propensity to dissolve and reprecipitate. When this occurs long after the formation of the plaster or mortar, the date obtained is erroneous due to the exchange of the original carbon. If the substituted carbon in the diagenetically altered calcite is derived from geogenic aggregates, the date will be too old, or if it is derived from the atmosphere, the date will be too young. Another complication is that if geogenic aggregates are included in the analysis, then again, the dates will be too old. Finally, if the calcination of the limestone was not complete, then the binder may contain remnants of the original rock, and this, too, will result in an erroneously old date (Lindroos et al., 2007). So one solution is to analyze only the binder, and only if it is sufficiently well preserved to still maintain its original ^{14}C concentration.

Two different approaches have been used to extract mainly the binder: by mechanical grinding and sieving, in the hope that the small-sized fraction contains mainly the binder, or by differential solubilization with acids or a chelator, on the assumption that the binder calcite crystals, being small and disordered, will dissolve first. In experiments involving a combination of both approaches, it has been shown that plasters of known ages do sometimes produce the correct result if only the first dissolved fraction is analyzed (Heinemeier et al., 1997). The problem is that this is not always the case, and there is no independent method to predict which plasters are sufficiently well preserved and have the appropriate aggregates to produce correct radiocarbon dates. One approach is to semiquantitatively estimate the relative proportions of the major components and use a model to "correct" for the date obtained. Cathodeluminesence images of thin sections help to differentiate between geogenic and pyrogenic calcite (Lindroos et al., 2007).

RECONSTRUCTING PRODUCTION PROCEDURES AND FUNCTIONS

Lime plaster and mortar are used for many different purposes, including construction and decoration. Besides basic rules of thumb like using fine-grained aggregates for surface plaster, and in gypsum plaster, aspiring to a more or less 1:1 proportion of binder to aggregates (Luxán et al., 1995), many options exist for producing functional plasters. One particularly important property is the proportion of binder to aggregate as this will determine the rate of hardening (Boynton, 1980), shrinkage properties on drying, the porosity, and the microstructure. All these parameters can be adapted to different functions such as water storage, water transport, binding, and so on (Casadio et al., 2005). They can be particularly specialized in the case of preparing substrates for

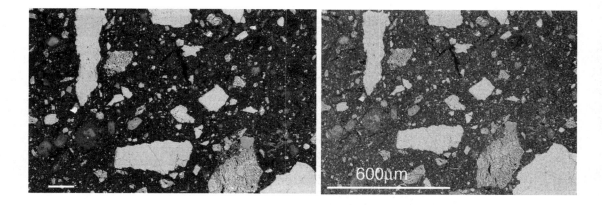

600μm

frescoes (Baraldi et al., 2006) and for hardening in the presence of water (hydraulic plaster).

The characterization of plaster components, texture, and binder to aggregate proportions is used mainly to classify different plasters, and this classification is used to compare manufacturing procedures between locations, recognize different production procedures, and develop, if possible, a chronological sequence of plaster use in a particular region (Caró and Di Giulio, 2004). The methods of characterization mainly involve the use of petrographic thin sections and/or SEM surface analyses as well as image analysis procedures to quantify the proportions of different components (Caró and Di Giulio, 2004). Figure 7.8 is an example of image analysis using an SEM. It is possible, in some cases, to try to dissolve the binder and not the aggregates and, in this way, determine their relative proportions (Casadio et al., 2005).

REFRACTORY MATERIALS PRODUCED BY HEATING CARBONATE ROCKS

Refractory materials are used to construct and line installations that operate at high temperatures. They need to retain their mechanical properties during the firing process. It is therefore of interest to characterize their mineral compositions to evaluate the firing conditions used in the past. Most refractory materials contain higher proportions of more insoluble silicates such as quartz. Some, however, can be derived from the breakdown of carbonate minerals. Magnesium oxide (MgO; also known as periclase) is a refractory material. It can be produced by extensive heating of dolomite. Calcium oxide is also produced together with small amounts of the oxides of other impurities. This refractory material is used in modern kilns (Boynton, 1980). Its use in ancient kilns is not known. The magnesium and calcium oxides are unlikely to be preserved as such and may well reform as calcite containing large amounts of magnesium. If the material were to undergo more extensive diagenesis, aragonite might form due to the presence of large amounts of Mg, which inhibits calcite nucleation (Lippmann, 1973). A layer of

Figure 7.8
Scanning electron microscope images of a polished surface of a sample of a lime plaster. The sample was from a restoration that was performed in the Holy Sepulchre, Jerusalem, six years prior to sampling. *Left*, Image obtained using the BSE detector, in which different minerals have different contrasts. In this mode, the binder is clearly differentiated from the aggregates. Scale bar is 100 microns. *Right*, The same area analyzed for chemical element concentrations using energy dispersion X-ray spectroscopy. A computer is then used to color code the different compositions. Concentrations of Ca, Si, and Al are marked on the right image by green, red, and blue, respectively. (*See color insert following page 174 for this image in color.*) While the binder is primarily composed of Ca (representing calcite), two types of aggregate are identified: calcites (green) and clays (pink, due to the red and blue combination).

aragonite was identified on certain technical ceramics used for bronze casting during the Roman period at Tel Dor, Israel (Eliyahu-Behar et al., 2009).

RESIDUE ANALYSIS

Plasters used for retaining liquids can absorb some of the organic molecules in those liquids. These can subsequently be extracted and identified. In this way, information on the function of the plaster can be obtained. This was demonstrated for stucco floors in Mesoamerica (Barba, 2007).

SPECIFIC FEATURES IN A SITE

In addition to plaster and mortar, slaked lime is used for sewage treatment in traditional latrines. The addition of lime removes foul odors, kills pathogens, and results in the precipitation of the phosphates (Boynton, 1980), presumably in the form of carbonate hydroxylapatite. Thus the presence of large amounts of calcite and carbonate hydroxylapatite in a pit may be an indication of a latrine.

Slaked lime was also used in the tanning industry for facilitating the removal of hair from the hide (Forbes, 1957). Thus slaking pits may have been part of the tanning complex and could be identified in the archaeological record as localized concentrations of disordered calcite.

CERAMICS AND POTTERY

In many excavations, ceramics are by far the most abundant macroscopic artifacts. They are therefore a very important component of the archaeological record. They have been thoroughly investigated both in terms of their macroscopic properties and their embedded microscopic properties. As a result, the literature on ceramics in archaeological contexts is large, and like all well-investigated subjects, it is also replete with contradictions and complexities.

I refer the reader to excellent treatments of ceramics by Rice (1987), Henderson (2000), Velde and Druc (1999), and Whitbread (2001). In this section, I will focus on the properties of ceramics that are key to better understanding their microscopic embedded information. Surprisingly, the issue of diagenetic change, which almost inevitably clouds the signals that we seek in almost every archaeological material, has been largely overlooked in ceramics. The few studies that have been made clearly demonstrate that ceramics do undergo diagenesis (see the subsequent discussion). If this is a general phenomenon, then much that has been written to date about ceramic provenience may need to be reevaluated, taking diagenesis into account.

Note that I use the term *provenience* to refer to the site where the raw materials were obtained or, in a broader sense, where the artifacts or archaeological materials came from. As the term *provenance* is widely used in the art world to refer to the sequence of ownership of an object, it seems preferable to use *provenience* in archaeology, even though they are regarded as synonyms by the *Oxford English Dictionary*.

The essentials of pottery manufacture

RAW MATERIALS

Basically, any sediment that has clay as its major component is suitable for ceramic production. Often additional components are added (temper) to improve the qualities of the ceramic. As all these materials are usually available within a short distance from almost any site (kilometers), ceramics are usually produced from local materials and can have variable compositions. Large stones and other components are removed, and in many cases, the fine fraction containing the clay is further concentrated by sieving or by settling in a water-filled tank (*levigation*). Furthermore, other components, such as calcite, are sometimes partially removed. This initial treatment of the raw material can thus complicate attempts to identify the source of the raw materials based on analyses of the ceramics themselves (*provenience studies*) and comparison with local raw materials.

The properties of clays that make them so useful for pottery production are mainly ascribed to the small size and platey shape of their crystals. When the clay is wet, water molecules are strongly associated with the charged surface of the clay crystal. This results in particles interacting with each other in such a way as to produce the desirable "plastic" property that makes clay-rich sediment easy to shape (Henderson, 2000). The properties of clays are discussed in a more general context in Chapter 4.

TEMPER

Temper functions to reduce cracking during drying and firing and may contribute significantly to improving the mechanical properties of the ceramic product. The temper may be organic or inorganic, and the latter can include various biogenic materials such as shell fragments, sponge spicules, and so on, as well as ground-up and discarded ceramics (grog). The addition of these materials further complicates attempts to determine the provenience of the raw materials, especially if quartz or calcite grains were added, making it difficult to differentiate between temper and primary components of the raw material.

FLUXES

The melting temperatures of the various pure clay minerals are well above 1,000°C and would be difficult to achieve in open fires and in most kilns. This technical problem usually "solves itself" naturally because most clay deposits are not composed of pure clay, but rather, contain a calcium carbonate component (usually calcite, but sometimes biogenic aragonite) that decomposes around 800°C into calcium oxide (see the preceding section on ash). This calcium oxide acts as a flux by readily reacting with the heated silicates and producing a fluid phase, which allows reactions to proceed that otherwise would have only occurred at much higher temperatures (Kingery et al., 1960). In fact, most oxides are fluxes. Other commonly used fluxes are the alkaline felspars – a suite of minerals common in many igneous rocks – and manganese and iron oxides. The extent to which the temperature is reduced is not simply a reflection of the amount of flux added, as a complex set of reactions are involved. In practice, the reduced melting temperature is very much dependent on the specific proportions of all the components present (Kingery et al., 1960; Henderson, 2000). The presence of the flux enables ceramics to be produced at temperatures as low as around 600°C (Henderson, 2000).

SHAPING AND DECORATING

The manner in which the pot is shaped and decorated is an important aspect of pottery manufacture that can, at least in part, be reconstructed from analysis of the sherds. This is, for the most part, achieved by visual inspection and/or careful measurement of the sherds (macroscopic processes). Three-dimensional reconstructions of the vessel shape based on a single sherd can be conveniently and accurately made using a special camera (Karasik and Smilansky, 2008). Hand production can be by thumb pinching, slab building, or coil building. It can also involve the use of molds. Better control over the shape and, especially, the symmetry of a pot is achieved by wheel production. Finishing and decorating the pot after it is shaped can involve beating the outside surface when the opposing side is supported by a static surface (paddle and anvil technique), smoothing, burnishing, and various forms of decoration. The surface can also be decorated by adding a liquid suspension of clay, often with a different color (*slip*). For more details, see for example Henderson (2000).

DRYING

Drying at ambient temperatures causes the clay to harden. This is due to the clay crystals coming into contact with each other. The loss of volume, however, can cause cracking, especially if the evaporation occurs mainly from the surface. The drying, therefore, has to be carefully controlled. The cracking problem can be alleviated, to some extent, by the presence of larger nonclay particles that do not contain water and hence do not change dimensions on drying, and/or by adding fibrous organic matter, which reduces crack formation. These materials are often deliberately added (temper; Henderson, 2000).

FIRING CONDITIONS

The most basic reason for exposing the clay and other components of the pot to elevated temperatures is to change the structure of the primary components in such a way that on cooling, they will interact more strongly with each other, and the result will be a material with useful properties. In the case of traditional ceramics, this can be achieved in an almost infinite variety of ways. On one hand, this enables pots to be produced under relatively unsophisticated conditions, and the products are suitable for many purposes. On the other hand, the conditions of firing and the preparation of the raw materials can be highly specialized, and the products can have unique and standardized properties. In all cases, knowledge and experience are essential – making pots is not a trivial process. This diversity of pot production processes offers many tantalizing opportunities to reconstruct aspects of the culture under investigation; in reality, it is often difficult to obtain unequivocal evidence for the use of a specific technology based on the analysis of only the final products.

The problem starts with the fact that during the firing, three interdependent parameters contribute to the properties of the product. These are the firing schedule; the temperature regime to which the specific pot, or even part of the pot, is exposed during the firing; and the atmosphere in which the pot is fired. Gosselain (1992) and Livingstone Smith (2001) have provided ethnographic-based documentations of the amazing variability in firing conditions they encountered during pottery firings in different parts of the world. These studies clearly show that it is simplistic to try to categorize firing conditions in terms of open firing versus kiln firing, firing temperature, or oxidizing or reducing conditions, based on an analysis of an assemblage of ancient sherds. We need to reduce our expectations about being able to reconstruct pottery manufacturing processes; they are far too diverse, and a similar product can be produced in different ways.

An estimate of the range of firing conditions can be obtained from the ethnographic study of Livingstone Smith (2001). He observed firings in bonfires and depressions without insulation, with light insulation and heavy insulation, as well as in pits and simple and complex kilns. He also observed the use of different types of fuel (light, heavy, dung). The size of the operation also varies greatly, as does the number of pots produced in each firing. Most of the firings were complete within an hour; some took several hours; and almost all were completed within eight hours. The maximum temperatures reached ranged from around 600°C to just over 1,000°C, but the amount of time that the fire was maintained at various temperatures (*soaking time*) varied greatly. For more discussion of this subject, see Embedded Information below.

Diagenesis

Surprisingly, little attention has been paid to the diagenesis of ceramics. The potential for diagenetic change to occur is large. For example, the clays, on heating, lose their original structure and become disordered, often to the extent that they do not diffract X-rays. These so-called amorphous clays can regain some atomic order after burial by interaction with groundwater. The more ordered clay minerals are unlikely to have the same trace element composition as the amorphous clay (Mata et al., 2002). Mata et al. also show that iron oxides form in the pores within the ceramics after burial. The glass phase of ceramics formed at high temperatures is certainly metastable under burial conditions and is therefore also likely to undergo diagenetic changes that could result in chemical composition changes (Picon, 1976; Buxeda et al., 2002).

Diagenetic changes in ceramics have unequivocally been demonstrated by comparing the surface and core elemental compositions of a set of sherds with corroded surfaces. The vast majority of these sherds had reduced calcium concentrations on their surfaces due to the removal of calcite and other calcium-containing minerals from the surface. Other elements were also leached out. Applying the standard multivariate analysis used to provenience sherds would have resulted in many of the surface samples being classified as belonging to a different group (Schwedt et al., 2004). It was also demonstrated that these changes could not be attributed to migration of elements during the drying and firing of the clay, except in the case of sodium chloride (Schwedt and Mommsen, 2007).

Clearly the subject of ceramic diagenesis has, to a large extent, been neglected. Diagenesis can alter, or even destroy, the original embedded information. Criteria for assessing ceramic preservation need to be developed and applied to determine whether the original signal is preserved. The fact that results are consistent with expectations or correlate well with some other criterion is never sufficient justification for ignoring possible diagenetic change when ancient or fossil materials are involved.

Embedded information

PROVENIENCE AND TRADE

Provenience here refers to the identification of the location where the major materials that were used to make the ceramic were obtained, as opposed to the location of the production site. Following ethnographic observations, it is generally assumed that as the raw materials are common, the source of the materials is within 10 kilometers or so from the production site (Arnold, 1985). Thus the basic strategy for determining provenience is to identify the unique characteristics of the possible sources of raw materials within the area surrounding the site. If the ceramic composition corresponds to one or more local sources, then it is assumed that it is produced locally. If not, it was brought to the site from somewhere else. If this other location can be identified, this establishes that trade and contact existed between the two sites. The trade could, of course, be in the pottery itself, or in the contents of the pottery.

There are two basic strategies for determining provenience: identify the mineral components of the ceramic in the hope that some characteristic mineral components are present (*petrographic approach*), or analyze as many chemical elements as possible in a homogenized representative aliquot of the ceramic and compare this "total" analysis to "total" analyses of possible sources of raw materials. Both approaches share a potentially serious problem, namely, if the raw materials are processed in some way as to eliminate certain constituents, or if two or more raw materials are mixed, then their primary compositions change. Another limitation for reliably determining provenience by both approaches is that the materials used are commonplace, and hence it is difficult to exclude alternative provenience options. Diagenesis can also affect both approaches. Diagenesis is probably easier to detect in the petrographic approach, based on, for example, whether voids are lined with secondarily formed crystals or reactions on mineral surfaces can be identified. The "total" elemental composition approach is probably more liable to be influenced by diagenetic changes as specific elements could be selectively leached out from more labile phases and hence bias the results. This is not easy to detect. The wide use of both these approaches with apparent success suggests that all these problems, in practice, are not major problems. A more critical approach to determining ceramic provenience is, however, needed.

Mineral constituents (petrographic approach). This is commonly achieved by examining thin sections of the ceramic in both plain light and polarized light using an optical petrographic microscope (Peacock, 1967). The use of polarized light enables materials without atomic order (glass) and with atomic order (crystals) to be distinguished. In fact, optical mineralogy can be used to identify most of the crystalline minerals present in ceramics. An excellent book on optical mineralogy is that of Heinrich (1965).

The mineral constituents can be derived from the original source material: the clay and the fragments of rocks and sediment clusters (clastics) that were present in the original deposit. The mineral components often reflect the local geology of the source material. The ceramic could also contain deliberately added materials to improve the working and shaping ability of the raw material as well as the physical properties of the end product. The application of the petrographic approach requires a detailed knowledge of the local geology and especially the sediment transportation processes. This is well illustrated in the example in Figure 7.9.

The primary constituents undergo alteration at elevated temperatures and may not be easily identifiable. The common use of calcite as a flux to reduce the firing temperature introduces another complication. If some of the flux is still present at the end of the firing process, then on cooling, it will react with the atmospheric carbon dioxide, and authigenic secondary calcite will be produced. Thus the calcite in a ceramic could be derived from the original constituents, indicating a relatively low firing temperature, or could be secondarily formed from calcium oxide. Furthermore, calcite could also form after burial as a result of diagenesis.

Despite all the variables and potential complexities, the use of petrographic thin sections to determine ceramic provenience has proved to be effective, provided, of course, that a major effort has been made to document the local and regional potential sources of characteristic source materials. An outstanding achievement in this respect is the identification of the provenience of the tablets found at El Amarna in Egypt (Goren et al., 2004). The book in which the results are described also contains an extensive explanation of the strengths and weaknesses of the method.

"Total" elemental composition approach. This approach compares a large suite of chemical elements in the ceramic with those in the possible source materials. If the latter information is absent, then even just comparing elemental compositions within a ceramic assemblage and between assemblages can provide information on whether one or more source materials were used to produce the ceramics found at a particular site. One of the first applications of this approach in archaeology was by Sayre and Dodson (1957). The two most common analytical techniques used are neutron activation analysis (NAA) (Perlman and Asaro, 1969) and analysis using an inductively coupled plasma (ICP). Both determine the concentrations of many different chemical elements, and the analyses are generally precise. Distinguishing between ceramic assemblages requires sophisticated multivariate techniques (Bieber et al., 1976), and knowledge of the local geology is not essential. Thus the approach is statistical, and many samples have to be analyzed to reliably separate the samples into different groups, if they exist. This approach has also proven to be effective for determining the provenience of ceramics, but as noted, it is subject to diagenetic change.

PRODUCTION AREAS

The macroscopic remains of ceramic production areas can include kilns, grinding implements, polishing stones, and molds. Perhaps the most

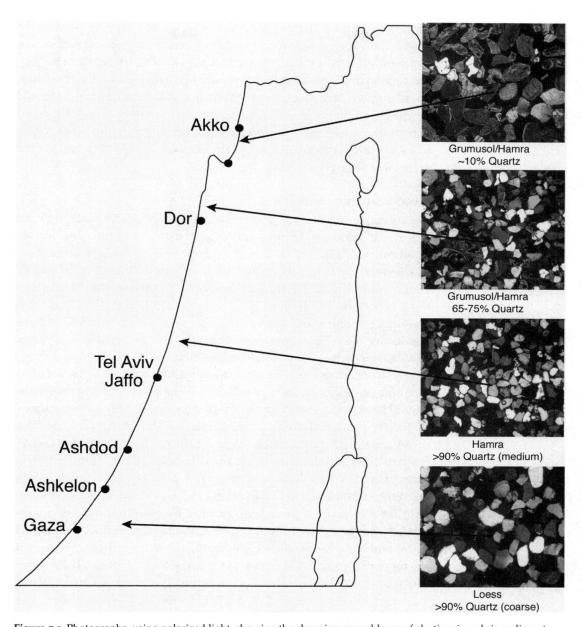

Figure 7.9 Photographs, using polarized light, showing the changing assemblages of clastic minerals in sediments from along the coast of Israel. The width of each photograph is 2.5 millimeters. The changes are basically due to the fact that in the eastern Mediterranean, currents flow northward along the Levantine coast. The main source of sediments to this area is the Nile River, which drains the plutonic rock plateaus of East Africa. The most stable mineral of these rocks is quartz. This quartz sand is swept along Sinai and northward along the Israeli coast. At the same time, the inland limestone hills of the Levantine coast contribute calcareous sand to the sediments. Since Mount Carmel (Haifa) acts as a natural barrier to the Nile sand, north of Haifa, the quartz sand component diminishes and the sediment becomes increasingly calcareous. Another source of clastic materials is the marine sediments. Along the Levantine coast, coralline algae of the genus *Amphiroa* are a significant component of Quaternary beach deposits. The figure shows that the sediments from between Gaza and Ashkelon (lower photograph) are composed almost entirely of large, rounded quartz grains, with small amounts of limestone (brown grains). (*See color insert following page 174 for this image in color.*) Sediments from the beach at Tel Aviv, about 50 kilometers north, are composed of small quartz grains that have a more uniform size. The sediments from the beach at Tel Dor, on the coast near Mount Carmel, contain quartz and over 30% calcareous grains, some of which are identified by arrows. Finally, the sediments from Akko beach, north of Haifa, are almost exclusively composed of limestone grains and skeletons of marine fauna, including *Amphiroa* alga fragments (arrows). These changes are reflected in the clastic component of the locally made pottery from each area, enabling the source of the pottery along the coast to be identified. The material for the figure and the accompanying explanation were provided courtesy of Prof. Yuval Goren.

commonly found characteristic artifacts are the wasters – the products of production errors. Microscopic remains of ceramic production areas are apparently not too informative. In fact, despite the prevalence of pottery production in almost all sites, the production areas are, for the most part, not identified. This can, in part, be attributed to the fact that household production requires little infrastructure and is usually accomplished by open firing. Thus much of what we know about ceramic manufacturing processes is based on analyses of the ceramics themselves and on the occasional remains of kilns.

MANUFACTURING PROCESSES

Macroscopic examination of sherds can usually differentiate between wheel and hand production, processes used for finishing the surface (application of slip, smoothing, and so on), and methods of decoration. Information on firing conditions is much more difficult to obtain by visual inspection. Color does contain some information (see the following discussion), but by and large, reconstructing the details of firing conditions requires the use of various analytical techniques, and the results are often equivocal. Even the most comprehensive analysis of sherds cannot result in well-substantiated information on the firing temperature, duration of firing, firing schedule, and so on, as the combination of all these factors is reflected in the product. So expectations should be realistic. For example, a well-executed, comprehensive study of pottery produced from a Late Minoan kiln in Crete, involving both mineralogical (X-ray diffraction) and ultrastructural analyses (SEM), reached the cautious conclusion that "relatively high-firing temperatures" were used (Belfiore et al., 2007, p. 640).

When reconstructing firing conditions, it is helpful to try to differentiate between processes that are controlled by the rate at which a change takes place (*kinetic control*) as opposed to changes that are essentially instantaneous (*thermodynamic control*). Kinetically controlled processes are more likely to be encountered in pottery fired at relatively low temperatures (i.e., less than about 900°C) when reaction rates are slow and are interrupted by the end of the firing process. Thermodynamically controlled processes probably dominate at higher firing temperatures, where the reactions are faster, and mineral transformations depend more on whether the temperature is high enough to cause a phase change, rather than on the amount of time spent at that temperature. The implication is that estimating actual firing temperatures is probably more reliable for pottery fired at higher temperatures, especially if it is based on the identification of a new high-temperature authigenic mineral phase.

The following paragraphs discuss the common properties of sherds that are used to provide information on firing conditions.

Color. Color (based on the Munsell color chart) is, of course, one of the most obvious properties of a ceramic that is often interpreted in terms of firing conditions. In reality, it can be misleading as it depends on many factors. If pure kaolinite is the clay type used, then the color of the ceramic is white. As most clays contain some iron and manganese, the color is either red, brown, or buff, if the firing is in an oxidizing atmosphere, or gray or black, if the firing is in a reducing atmosphere (Maniatis and Tite, 1981; Goffer, 2007). One reasonably well-substantiated generalization is that gray or black colors on the sherd surface imply that at some stage during the production process, reducing conditions were created, and this can only be achieved under controlled conditions in a kiln (Buxeda I Garrigos et al., 2003). Even this generalization has exceptions, for example, a bone powder decoration or a layer of bitumen fired at low temperatures produces a black color (Goffer, 2007), whereas a bone powder decoration fired at high temperatures can produce a white-colored decoration (Odriozola and Pérez, 2006).

Color could perhaps provide more definitive information vis-à-vis firing conditions, at least for a specific assemblage of ceramics, if a representative subcollection of the ceramics was refired at different temperatures, in oxidizing and reducing atmospheres and for varying durations, to calibrate the conditions under which the color changes; however, such refiring experiments are rarely used for color interpretation (Eiland and Williams, 2000).

Ultrastructure. Maniatis and Tite (1981) laid the foundations for reconstructing firing conditions. They first examined the fracture surfaces of the sherds using an SEM to determine the extent of vitrification and the pore structure. The sherds were then refired in oxidizing and reducing atmospheres and were again examined using the SEM to observe the development of vitrification. They noted that the behavior during firing of the raw materials containing abundant calcium carbonate was different from the behavior of low-calcium-containing material. They therefore measured the CaO contents of the sherds and identified any authigenic minerals that formed in the sherds at high temperatures using X-ray diffraction. This is an effective approach for identifying at least some of the complexities involved in reconstructing firing conditions. It involves a great deal of work and therefore cannot be applied to the study of large numbers of sherds.

Maniatis and Tite (1981) published a table on changes in the extent of vitrification that provides good guidelines for the relation between the extent of vitrification and firing temperature ranges. It is reproduced here as Table 7.2.

Difficulties in assessing the extent of vitrification arise from the fact that quantification of vitrification is impossible using the SEM. Infrared spectroscopy can provide more quantitative information based on the

Table 7.2. Vitrification stages and firing temperature ranges.

Vitrification stage	Low CaO (oxidizing)	Low CaO (reducing)	High CaO (oxidizing)	High CaO (reducing)
No vitrification	>800	>750	>800	>750
Initial vitrification	800–850	750–800	800–850	750–800
Extensive vitrification	850–950	800–900	850–1050	850–1050
Continuous vitrification		>900		

Note: Low calcium oxide (CaO) refers to less than 6% by weight.
Source: Adapted from Maniatis and Tite (1981).

shift of the major silicate absorption peak (Shoval et al., 1993; Berna et al., 2007). For more details on using infrared spectroscopy to assess temperature exposure of clay-rich sediments, and for ceramic analysis, see Overview 9 in Chapter 12.

Mineralogy. The presence or absence in the ceramic of authigenic minerals that form at specific temperatures is a helpful indicator for determining approximate firing temperatures. These are more likely to be reliable for minerals formed at higher temperatures, where thermodynamics dominates their formation. X-ray diffraction, petrography (Goren et al., 2004), and infrared spectroscopy (De Benedetto et al., 2002) can be used to identify authigenic minerals. Following is a short list of some of the more common authigenic minerals or mineral property changes commonly used for estimating firing temperatures:

1. Aragonite (usually in the form of mollusk shell temper) changes to calcite between 400° and 450°C (Maritan et al., 2007).
2. Dolomite changes into calcite at 500°C (Goren et al., 2004).
3. Mica minerals become misty in thin section at greater than 500°C (Goren et al., 2004).
4. Glauconite changes its pleochroism at around 500°C (Goren et al., 2004).
5. Calcite undergoes structural changes at greater than 700°C and decomposes around 800°C into calcium oxide (Goren et al., 2004).
6. Portlandite and periclase form above about 750°C (Maritan et al., 2007).
7. Hornblende changes to oxyhornblende at around 800°C (Goren et al., 2004).
8. Melilite forms above 800°C (Sondi and Slovenic, 2003).
9. Gehlinite forms above about 850°C (Maritan et al., 2007).
10. Mullite forms at 1,075°C (Carty and Senapti, 1998).
11. Cristobolite forms at temperatures above 1,000°C (Shoval, 1993).
12. Hematite only forms in an oxidizing atmosphere (Heimann and Maggetti, 1981).
13. Sanidine forms only when the original sediment was low in calcium-containing minerals (Maggetti, 1982).

Note that using the decomposition of calcite as an indicator of firing conditions is complicated by the fact that the decomposition temperature ranges from around 600° to 700°C for chalk and limestone, and around 750°C for monocrystalline calcite. Furthermore, on cooling the decomposed product, calcium oxide can reform to calcite (Shoval et al., 1993). Thus, unless primary and reformed calcite can be distinguished (as well as diagenetically formed calcite), inferring firing conditions from the presence or absence of calcite can be misleading.

Porosity. The porosity of a ceramic is a product of the conditions under which the ceramic was produced and is thus another useful parameter for reconstructing manufacturing conditions. In general, high-porosity ceramics are those that contain high temper concentrations and are fired at relatively low temperatures (Tite et al., 2001). These are also the conditions required to produce pottery that can resist rapid changes in temperature (an essential quality for cooking pots). The use of high firing temperatures and low temper concentrations reduces porosity and also results in a product that has increased strength (Tite et al., 2001). A rough measure of porosity can be achieved by determining the water content. More comprehensive measurements require more sophisticated techniques such as forcing mercury into the ceramic under varying pressure conditions or the infusion of liquid nitrogen into the sherd (Harry and Johnson, 2004). These techniques only measure those pores that are open to the surface. This same subset of pores will also determine to what extent the contents of the vessel will penetrate into the walls and hence is of significance in residue analysis of archaeological ceramics (see Chapter 8).

REFRACTORY CERAMICS

High-temperature installations need to be constructed of materials that can withstand exposure to firing conditions. A wide variety of such refractory materials are in use today, but relatively little is known about traditional refractory materials. In a survey of refractory ceramics, it was shown that for the most part, local clays used for ceramic vessel production were also used for producing refractories (Freestone and Tite, 1986). These were adequate for most purposes as they were able to withstand temperatures between 1,200° and 1,300°C. For the production of crucible materials, a number of specific innovations were identified by Freestone and Tite (1986), namely, the use of heavy quartz tempering, temper composed of ground-up ceramics (grog), or the inclusion of coke or graphite. In a study of Chinese celadons, the composition of the ceramics produced and the molds in which they were produced also showed little difference (Henderson, 2000). The same phenomenon was observed for furnace linings and tuyeres from a metal production facility in Cyprus that could withstand temperatures of up to about 1,200°C, based on refiring experiments (Hein et al., 2007). Here, too, the composition of these materials did not differ significantly from ceramics from the same area. The presence of relatively large voids, and perhaps a higher proportion of aggregates, probably contributed to the refractory properties of the material (Hein et al., 2007).

CONCLUDING COMMENT

The imprint of heating on minerals is manifested by a change in the extent of order of the atoms in the mineral. Heating in general introduces disorder, unless the starting material is so disordered that the heating causes the atoms to become more ordered. An example of such a starting material is bone. Cooling, on the other hand, can introduce more order, provided that the process is slow. It rarely results in the final product being totally ordered. In fact, the extent and type of disorder records how the mineral formed. Fast cooling can freeze in the disorder of the high-temperature phase. Tracking changes in mineral order-disorder can thus provide insight into pyrotechnological practices. This information has much potential for diverse archaeological applications, in the areas of both pyrotechnology and diagenesis.

8

Biological Molecules and Macromolecules: Protected Niches

Some of the most interesting questions about past human behavior can, in theory, be addressed by analyzing preserved biologically produced molecules. These biogenic molecules may contain information on absolute age based on their radiocarbon contents, genetic development using ancient DNA, migration patterns, weaning and diet using stable isotopes, and more (Chapter 2). In most environments, biological macromolecules are, however, not preserved, as exposed uncharred organic matter is efficiently and rapidly degraded, mainly by microorganisms. There are special environments, such as in frozen ice and very dry deserts, where organic materials are relatively well preserved, mainly because of the lack of biological activity (Chapter 3). Much can be learned about past human behavior from biomolecules preserved under these unusual conditions. Using only these "exotic" sources of materials, however, makes it very difficult to apply a systematic and regional approach to solving problems using biogenic molecules. For such systematic studies, we ideally need to be able to analyze biological molecules from many sites and/or many locations within a site, even when most of the organic matter has been degraded.

The only way biological molecules can survive biodegradation and chemical degradation under "normal" conditions is if they are located in protected niches that prevent microbial degradation or chemical breakdown. Some protected niches are known. Characterizing these niches is the focus of this chapter.

The search for and exploitation of preserved molecules from relatively protected niches requires an understanding of the structure of the material in which they are preserved, preservation conditions, and the application of analytical techniques capable of handling the small quantities of materials likely to be preserved. The challenge is therefore not only to find protected niches with preserved molecules, but also to be able to analyze the minute amounts of these molecular "treasures" that are likely to be available.

The last 30 years or so have witnessed a spectacular development of powerful analytical techniques in the field of molecular biology. These capabilities have had, and are still having, a major impact on the field of biomolecular archaeology. The best example is the current technology that makes it possible to obtain huge stretches of sequences from fossil (ancient) genomic DNA when just a few copies of each gene per cell are available. This seemed like an insurmountable technological barrier just a few years ago, when the state of the art involved obtaining sequences from a small section of DNA from the mitochondria, where hundreds of copies are available per cell. We now have sequences from many genes from the cell nucleus of a Neanderthal, where only one or several copies of the genes existed per cell (Green et al., 2006; Noonan et al., 2006). Such technological breakthroughs are, however, only helpful if the DNA analyzed is sufficiently well preserved so that it still maintains the original sequence information. For example, about 90% of the Neanderthal-specific sequence changes obtained in the studies by Green et al. (2006) and Noonan et al. (2006) are thought to be artifacts of damage to the original DNA and not a result of Darwinian mutations.

The old adage that "garbage in is garbage out" becomes even more telling as we acquire the technical means to extract and analyze increasingly smaller amounts of material. The intuitive scenario is that the small amounts preserved represent the remnants of much larger amounts of material, and as a result, surviving molecules have been subjected to much degradation. This, however, may not be the case. If the reason the molecules survived is that they were located in relatively protected niches, then not only will molecules be available for analysis in these niches, but they may also be relatively well preserved. This would be a dream come true!

I am optimistic and expect that the field of biomolecular archaeology will become an important part of mainstream archaeology in the future. If I am correct, then archaeologists will be paying much more attention to finding the samples that contain the best-preserved biomolecules to address fundamental questions in archaeology. These samples include eggshells, mollusk shells, bones, teeth, and also ceramic fragments that still contain preserved molecules that were once in contact with the vessel. When well-preserved samples are found, they will represent a real treasure.

Reviews of topics in biomolecular archaeology can be found in section 4 of Brothwell and Pollard (2001).

BRIEF OVERVIEW OF DIFFERENT BIOMOLECULES OF INTEREST IN BIOMOLECULAR ARCHAEOLOGY

Preserved biomolecules contain different types of information of interest to archaeology, including genetic information (DNA, proteins), information about metabolism (polysaccharides, small stable molecules such as fatty acids), paleodiet (fatty acids, polysaccharides, proteins), and radiocarbon content (all uncontaminated biomolecules). These applications differ with regard to the preservational state required to extract this information and their tolerance for contamination. For example, DNA analyses can be carried out in the presence of contaminants, but radiocarbon analyses cannot. The target DNA itself should be as well preserved as possible, whereas for radiocarbon dating, good preservation of the target molecules is less important. All applications, however, benefit enormously if the molecules are well preserved and relatively uncontaminated.

209

BRIEF OVERVIEW OF
DIFFERENT
BIOMOLECULES OF
INTEREST IN
BIOMOLECULAR
ARCHAEOLOGY

DNA

The genetic information that resides in the sequence of the four different nucleotides that constitute DNA is of prime interest for understanding molecular evolution and taxonomic affinities of the organisms from which the DNA was derived. In fact, it is usually not the sequence itself that is the main interest in these studies, but rather, the differences in the sequences that exist between samples. These differences reflect mutations that have occurred over time, some of which may have provided an advantage to the individuals in which they occurred. Thus the key to using ancient DNA sequences is the identification of these sequence changes.

The changes occur spontaneously during evolution, and whether they are maintained within the population depends on whether they provide a disadvantage or an advantage to the individual, or make no difference. The chance of a mutation occurring at a given location in the DNA is not random, but rather, is favored by local changes in DNA conformation (Gilbert et al., 2003b). Herein lies one of the key difficulties in using ancient DNA to decipher evolution, namely, that during diagenesis, the same relatively weak sites where Darwinian mutations are more likely to occur during the lifetime of the individual are also targets for preferential diagenetic change (Gilbert et al., 2003b). Thus the challenge is to somehow differentiate between changes due to damage (i.e., diagenesis) and Darwinian mutations that occur during the course of evolution. Although there may be various rules of thumb to do this, there is no absolute solution to this problem. The best, albeit partial, solution is to locate and analyze the least diagenetically altered DNA available.

The revolution that has occurred in molecular biology in general is, in one way or another, related to the development of powerful tools that enable specific stretches of DNA to be selected and copied and then, when enough material is available, enable enzymes to cleave the DNA sequentially and release the nucleotides one at a time. By analyzing the released nucleotides, the DNA sequence can be determined. This can be done for one segment at a time, or simultaneously for many different segments (Blow et al., 2008). This works very well for modern DNA as well as for ancient DNA. One problem for ancient DNA arises from the fact that the enzymes that replicate the DNA are not capable of differentiating between an intact nucleotide and one that has been altered diagenetically. Some are relatively nondiscerning and will therefore produce DNA copies even if the original molecule is badly preserved. Others are more discerning and will only copy relatively well-preserved DNA (Eckert and Kunkel, 1991). These are clearly the enzymes of choice, provided that the DNA is well preserved. The conclusion, once again, is that the original DNA must be as well preserved as possible. For more information, see Brown (2001).

Proteins

The information that defines the sequence of the 20 amino acids that are the building blocks of proteins is coded in the DNA. Thus the amino acid sequence of a protein is, in essence, a readout of the nucleotide sequence of the DNA that codes for that protein (the gene). Thus changes in the amino acid sequence also provide genetic information of interest regarding evolution and taxonomic affinities.

The amino acid sequences of preserved fossil (ancient) proteins are, however, a great deal more difficult to determine technically than the nucleotide sequences of DNA. The technology for replicating proteins does not exist so that the ancient proteins have to be extracted, purified, and sequenced using the original fossil material. This task is difficult even for a homogenate of a living cell, with all its thousands of proteins, or an extracellular tissue, such as bone, with its hundreds of proteins. The task is daunting for a fossil cell homogenate or tissue such as bone as this includes not only the surviving, intact proteins, but also all their breakdown products.

Only recently, with the advent of new sequencing methods based on mass spectrometry, has the first fossil protein been sequenced in its entirety (Nielsen-Marsh et al., 2002). It seems unlikely that in the foreseeable future, the sequencing of fossil proteins will replace or even compete with the sequencing of ancient DNA. More individual proteins may well be sequenced, provided that a source of well-preserved, intact molecules can be found. The preservation issue again looms large. For more information, see Gernaey et al. (2001).

Polysaccharides

Sugar molecules make up the complex chains of polysaccharides. The order in which the sugars are arranged is also genetically determined, but only indirectly, in that it is the product of orchestrated activities of an assemblage of enzymes that determines polysaccharide structure. Furthermore, it is technically very difficult to determine this order, even for modern biological materials, and there is little possibility that this can be done for ancient polysaccharides in the foreseeable future.

Lipids

Lipids are the major components of animal fats, plant oils, waxes, and certain resins. They are also major components of cell membranes and are commonly used for energy storage. The term *lipid* refers to an assemblage of small molecules that are characteristically hydrophobic (i.e., soluble in nonaqueous solvents). Some are constituents of larger, less stable molecules. There are many different lipid molecules, and some of them are confined to specific sources such as plant waxes, beeswax, and animal fats. Thus the presence of a particular lipid assemblage can provide information on the organic material from which it was derived. Many lipids are relatively stable and hence more likely to survive the rigors of diagenesis and microbial attack than macromolecules such as protein and DNA. This is one of the main reasons why they are of interest to archaeologists. For some reason, the analysis of lipids from archaeological contexts is commonly called *residue analysis*. For more information, see Evershed et al. (2001).

There are a variety of biologically derived molecules occasionally preserved in various materials such as the protein collagen in skin (parchment, leather) and bone; the protein keratin in hooves and horn; polysaccharides in starch, wood or bark, and chitin and pollen; complex aromatic polymers in resins (copal, gum, and amber); and more. Some of these are discussed in more detail in Chapter 12 in relation to their infrared spectra.

HISTORICAL PERSPECTIVE

The field of biomolecular archaeology has its roots in the late 1950s, when the technology for analyzing small amounts of amino acids, the building blocks of proteins, was developed (Abelson, 1956). It was subsequently demonstrated, using amino acid composition analyses, that proteins in bones and shells could survive for even millions of years (Wyckoff, 1972). Investigators at that time also performed in vitro analyses of the stabilities of these molecules to predict how long amino acids could, in theory, survive (Abelson, 1956). This two-pronged approach continued as the molecules of interest changed from single amino acids, to stretches of linked amino acids (peptides), to whole molecules composed of amino acids (proteins; Jones and Vallentyne, 1960; Hare et al., 1980; Collins et al., 1995; Gernaey et al., 2001).

In the late 1970s and early 1980s, the focus of biomolecular archaeology switched from proteins to DNA (Higuchi et al., 1984; Pääbo et al., 1989; Brown, 2001). The impetus for the analysis of fossil DNA was the availability of new and powerful analytical techniques. It was also at about this time when the first analyses of lipids in ceramics were initiated (Condamin et al., 1976). In retrospect, it seems that the search for preserved biological macromolecules and the characterization of their sequences and structures have, for the most part, been driven by the development of new analytical technologies.

Two generalizations can be made about the findings of these studies, irrespective of the specific molecules being investigated. First, as the analytical techniques improved and the analysts took more care to exclude contamination, older and older fossils containing preserved molecules were found. Second, the predictions of how long a molecule will survive based on its stability (thermodynamic considerations) usually proved to be wrong; much older molecules were repeatedly discovered. The implication is that the survival of a biological molecule is controlled not so much by its stability as by the conditions in the microenvironment in which it resides. The time elapsed since burial is not a good predictor of preservation. Thus the search for well-preserved biological molecules should focus on identifying the microenvironments (niches) that are conducive to preservation. The corollary is that if there is a rough correlation between age and survival of the molecular assemblages, then the niche in which they are located is probably open to the environment.

In this chapter, three different protected niches in which biological macromolecules are relatively well preserved will be discussed: occluded inside biogenic crystals, trapped between intergrown biogenic crystals, and adsorbed in the pores within the walls of ceramic vessels. The first protected niche is truly sealed, the second is sealed but not necessarily stable over time, and the third is open but relatively protected.

PROTECTED NICHE 1: INTRACRYSTALLINE MACROMOLECULES

The existence of organic material inside individual biogenic crystals was first demonstrated for mollusk shells, where it was shown that some organic material is occluded within individual aragonitic tablets of nacre (Watabe, 1963; Figure 8.1). It was initially assumed, however, that this material was trapped in a bubble or small cavity within the crystal (Towe and Thompson, 1972). Only in the late 1980s was it established that these occluded macromolecules are assemblages of specialized glycoproteins, when they were found inside biogenic calcite crystals formed by echinoderms (Weiner, 1985), brachiopods (Curry et al., 1991), and mollusks (Addadi et al., 1991). This was shown by grinding the biogenic mineral into a fine powder and then removing all the exposed organic material with the powerful oxidizing agent sodium hypochlorite. After dissolving the mineral, it was found that some proteins still remained. It was subsequently shown that these so-called intracrystalline molecules are common in many other mineralized tissues and are preferentially located along specific crystal planes (Berman et al., 1993). Their presence inside the crystal changes its mechanical properties (Berman et al., 1988), and this is at least one of the benefits that organisms gain from this unusual strategy.

Concurrently with the discovery of intracrystalline macromolecules in echinoderms, but quite independently, it was shown that antibodies raised against proteins extracted from modern brachiopod shells could recognize fragments of these intracrystalline proteins in very old (millions of years) brachiopods (Collins et al., 1991; Curry et al., 1991). This signal could not be eliminated by grinding the shell into a powder and removing all exposed organic matter with sodium hypochlorite. The authors inferred that the protein remnants must be located within the crystals. These studies thus demonstrated the potential of the intracrystalline niche for preserving biomolecules long after all the exposed organic material is lost (Sykes et al., 1995).

The amounts of material present in the intracrystalline niche are usually around 0.03% to 0.1% by weight (Addadi et al., 1991). The major components are proteins, many of which are rich in acidic amino acids and have covalently bound polysaccharides. These are relatively large molecules, and therefore the host crystal has to be sufficiently large to occlude these molecules. Most biogenic crystals are large enough. The one conspicuous exception is the bone family of materials (including dentin, mineralized tendon) that have crystals that are among the smallest known in the field of biomineralization (see the subsequent discussion and Chapter 5).

The more common invertebrate mineralized tissues found in archaeological contexts that are known to contain intracrystalline macromolecules are mollusk shells (Berman et al., 1993), bird eggshells (Lammie et al., 2005), and phytoliths (Elbaum et al., 2009; Chapter 6). No studies related to archaeology have, to date, been carried out specifically

Figure 8.1
a, Individual tablet-shaped crystals from the nacre of the bivalve Atrina, after treatment with sodium hypochlorite. *b*, Calcitic prisms from the same bivalve. The nacre contains an assemblage of occluded proteins rich in aspartic acid, and the prisms contain occluded aspartic acid–rich proteins and β-chitin (Nudelman et al., 2007).

on the intracrystalline macromolecules of mollusk shells and eggshells. Studies involving the stable isotopic composition and amino acid racemization of the preserved organic matrices from land snails and eggshells (Qian et al., 1995; Johnson et al., 1998) are probably mainly based on the intracrystalline component. Terrestrial gastropods are known to have an intracrystalline organic matrix in their shells (Sykes et al., 1995).

Phytoliths have 1% to 5% by weight organic matter occluded inside their opalline mineral phase (Jones and Beavers, 1963; Elbaum et al., 2009). As the mineral phase of phytoliths is amorphous and not crystalline, the term *intracrystalline* is inappropriate, but the niche type is the same. The occluded macromolecules are mainly proteins. To date, no DNA has been found (Elbaum et al., 2009). It is premature, however, to conclude that phytoliths do not contain DNA as all means of being able to detect it have not been explored. If DNA is present in phytoliths, it might be possible to partially reconstruct the local vegetation around a site using the DNA from a mixed assemblage of phytoliths.

Embedded information

AMINO ACID RACEMIZATION DATING

Despite many efforts to use the proteins in bones, mollusk shells, and eggshells for dating by racemization (conversion of L–amino acids into a mixture of D,L–amino acids; Chapter 2), success has been limited. The two mineralized tissues known to provide somewhat reliable age estimates are ostrich eggshells (Brooks et al., 1990) and terrestrial snail shells (Goodfriend, 1992). Both these mineralized tissues contain mainly intracrystalline proteins and very few intercrystalline proteins. This means that most of the proteins reside in a relatively uniform environment. Perhaps it is this uniform environment that allows the proteins to racemize in a more consistent and reproducible manner.

PALEOENVIRONMENTAL RECONSTRUCTION

The stable isotopic composition of the intracrystalline macromolecules of terrestrial snails, eggshells, and phytoliths possesses a paleoenvironmental signal. The basis for reconstructing paleoenvironments based on the stable carbon isotopic composition of plant material is that plants using the two common photosynthetic pathways, C_3 and C_4, differ in the extent to which they fractionate their isotopes. Furthermore, the relative proportions of C_3 and C_4 plants at a specific location reflect climatic conditions. A higher summer temperature and a lower soil moisture favor a higher proportion of C_4 plants (Teeri and Stowe, 1976). Terrestrial snails and ostriches both feed off the local vegetation. The carbon isotopic composition of all the organic matter in ostrich eggshells (Johnson et al., 1998) and terrestrial gastropods (Goodfriend and Ellis,

2000) does reflect the local vegetation. The macromolecules inside the mineral phase of phytoliths also carry a paleoenvironmental signal in their stable isotopic compositions (Kelly et al., 1991). As phytoliths are so common in archaeological sites, this could prove to be a fruitful avenue of research.

215

PROTECTED NICHE 2:
MACROMOLECULES
INSIDE INTERGROWN
BIOGENIC CRYSTALS
(CRYSTAL
AGGREGATES)

RADIOCARBON DATING

The macromolecules occluded inside the mineral phase represent a potential source of preserved and uncontaminated organic material for radiocarbon dating. Furthermore, these macromolecules are formed over a short period of time and therefore can provide a date that is not compromised by the so-called old wood effect (Chapters 2 and 10). Mollusk shells, ostrich eggshells, and phytoliths in particular are common in many archaeological sites. Phytoliths can be found in good contexts so their intracrystalline macromolecules should be ideal for radiocarbon dating. The probable reasons why this source of organic material has not been exploited to date for radiocarbon dating are that only small amounts of material are available and the dissolution of the mineral phase could introduce contaminants. Much effort is being made to date the occluded organic material in phytoliths, and despite some reports of success (Piperno, 2006), there are still unresolved technical problems.

PROTECTED NICHE 2: MACROMOLECULES INSIDE INTERGROWN BIOGENIC CRYSTALS (CRYSTAL AGGREGATES)

The crystals in bone and the other members of the mineralized collagen family of materials (dentin, cementum, mineralized tendon; Weiner and Wagner, 1998) are extremely small and plate shaped (Figure 8.2), with a thickness of around 2 to 4 nanometers (Weiner and Price, 1986; Lowenstam and Weiner, 1989). As a single sheet of protein is at least 1 nanometer thick, it is most unlikely that individual bone crystals can occlude

Figure 8.2
Left, Disaggregated individual plate-shaped crystals extracted from human bone after treatment with sodium hypochlorite and sonication. *Right*, The fraction of bone mineral from the same sample that does not disaggregate. They are referred to as crystal aggregates. For more details, see Weiner and Price (1986).

macromolecules such as protein or DNA. It was therefore surprising to discover that treating modern bone ground into a fine powder with the oxidizing reagent sodium hypochlorite does not remove all the collagen (Weiner and Price, 1986) nor all the DNA (Salamon et al., 2005). Examination of the powder in a scanning electron microscope shows that a large portion is composed of aggregates of intergrown crystals (Figure 8.2). It was also demonstrated that both collagen and DNA can be found inside these aggregates in fossil bone, and these macromolecules are in a better state of preservation, as compared to the bulk collagen and DNA (DeNiro and Weiner, 1988b; Salamon et al., 2005). Thus bone, like the invertebrate mineralized tissues discussed previously, also has a well-protected niche, where macromolecules are relatively well preserved.

This niche, however, is not as well protected or as stable as the intracrystalline niche because the macromolecules are, in essence, trapped between intergrown crystals, and as these crystals are thermodynamically unstable in modern bone, the smaller ones tend to dissolve and the larger crystals grow at their expense (Chapter 5). This implies that the aggregates are not inherently stable, and over time, the associated macromolecules may be exposed and consequently destroyed, or other already degraded macromolecules may be incorporated into aggregates formed during diagenesis. It would be interesting to determine whether the collagen from particularly old fossil bones, such as the collagen identified in dinosaur bones around 80 million years old or more (Wyckoff, 1972), is all preserved inside aggregates.

It has been postulated that the intimate association of the mineral and the macromolecules in bone stabilizes and hence protects some of the macromolecular constituents, such as collagen (Nielsen-Marsh et al., 2000), and proteins, such as osteocalcin (Smith et al., 2005). The mineral also effectively excludes enzymes capable of degrading collagen and other proteins (Collins et al., 1995). It is of interest to ascertain to what extent this type of protection in fossil bones is actually related to the crystal aggregates.

Vertebrates produce other mineralized tissues, in addition to bone, that also have intergrown crystal aggregates. These may be even more stable than bone. One form of dentin, known as peritubular dentin (Chapter 5, Figure 8.3), is composed of the same small, platey crystals that are present in normal intertubular dentin (or bone), but because collagen is not present or is present in very small amounts in mature peritubular dentin, peritubular dentin is more dense than intertubular dentin or bone (Miller, 1954; Weiner et al., 1999c). Thus the peritubular dentin is probably more stable than the aggregates in bone. Fresh peritubular dentin is known to occlude an assemblage of acidic proteins (Gotliv et al., 2006). To my knowledge, no one has tried to extract these proteins from fossil teeth using known methods for separating the peritubular dentin from the bulk dentin (Weiner et al., 1999c). It is conceivable that peritubular dentin may also occlude DNA. Another possible protected niche in dentin is the material that fills in the dentinal tubules in mature animal teeth (Marshall et al., 2001). As these tubules normally contain cell processes, this material may also occlude DNA.

Mature enamel is also an intergrown crystal composite (Lowenstam and Weiner, 1989; Figure 8.4). Mature enamel forms after the proteins that are present in forming enamel break down, and the crystals undergo a second growth phase that results in a very dense material with only small amounts of macromolecules (Hiller et al., 1975). Some of these macromolecules are probably trapped between crystals, but as enamel crystals are much larger than bone/dentin crystals, some may even be occluded inside the crystals. Enamel crystals are known to be relatively stable over time, as compared to dentin/bone crystals, and hence are widely used for various applications in archaeology involving the mineral phase (Chapter 5). They may also be an excellent source for fossil macromolecules.

Embedded information

As collagen and DNA are known to be preserved inside crystal aggregates, the potential embedded information is the same as for bone and tooth dentin in general, except that the preservation of these macromolecules is likely to be better. Following is a brief review of the potential embedded information in bone and teeth crystal aggregates. For more information, see Chapters 2 and 5.

PALEODIET RECONSTRUCTION
The carbon and nitrogen stable isotopic compositions of the collagen extracted from fossil bones provides information on diet (DeNiro and

217

PROTECTED NICHE 2:
MACROMOLECULES
INSIDE INTERGROWN
BIOGENIC CRYSTALS
(CRYSTAL
AGGREGATES)

Figure 8.3
Scanning electron microscope image of the fracture surface of dentin from a human tooth, showing the dense peritubular dentin surrounding the tubules and intertubular dentin between the tubule-peritubular dentin complex.

Epstein, 1978; van der Merwe and Vogel, 1978). As humans are usually omnivores, this signal is often rather similar for different individuals or between different populations. If, however, the diet changed radically and, for example, began to include C_4 plants in addition to C_3 plants, or a lot more marine-derived food, these shifts can be identified (Sealy, 2001). The collagen present inside crystal aggregates may be a good source for these analyses (DeNiro and Weiner, 1988b; Salamon et al., 2005).

PALEOGENETIC INFORMATION

DNA sequences provide invaluable information on the genetics of the animal from which the bone was obtained. In the case of human bones, this information can be used to identify the affinities of different human populations, to identify the molecular evolution of specific genes over time, and to better understand human evolution in general (Brown, 2001). The quality of this information is dependent on the DNA being as well preserved as possible. DNA and other bone proteins may also be trapped within crystal aggregates (Salamon et al., 2005). If these could be isolated and sequenced, more paleogenetic information would be obtained.

RADIOCARBON DATING

Bone collagen is widely used for radiocarbon dating. Unlike wood charcoal, it is a short-lived material and thus provides a more accurate date. It is, however, essential that the collagen be free of other organic contaminants, and hence the purity of the collagen analyzed is most important (van Klinken, 1999). Prior treatment of all the exposed parts

Figure 8.4
Scanning electron microscope image of the fracture surface of mature rat incisor enamel, showing the intergrowth of the prisms. For more information on enamel structure, see Chapter 5. Scale bar: 10 micrometers.

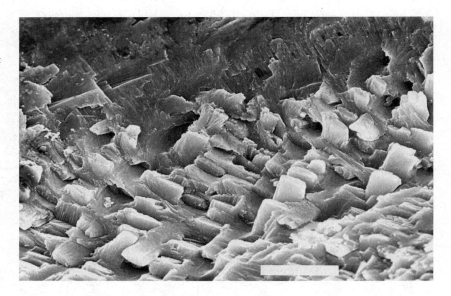

of the crushed bone with an oxidant certainly removes much of the contamination.

PROTECTED NICHE 3: MOLECULES PRESERVED IN CERAMICS

Ceramic vessels were often used to store liquids containing organic materials (food, oil, perfumes, etc.) and/or to prepare food. As the ceramic itself is porous (Figure 8.5) and many of these pores are connected to the inner surface of the vessel, some of the molecules in the jar contents penetrate into the ceramic. If some of these molecules are not destroyed with time, they can be extracted from ceramic fragments from archaeological sites and analyzed. A well-preserved assemblage of molecules can provide information mainly on the vessel contents (Condamin et al., 1976; Evershed et al., 2001) and possibly also on applied surface sealants (Heron and Pollard, 1988).

It has often been observed that these molecules are present in the ceramics but are absent or are present in very small amounts in the surroundings. Thus the pores within the ceramic constitute a relatively well-protected niche for the preservation of certain biogenic molecules. As the molecules, however, have to enter into the pores through the ceramic surface, this niche is open and not, as in the preceding two categories, sealed off from the environment.

The general approach used for analyzing these so-called residues is to focus on analyzing relatively stable molecules, sampling many ceramic fragments from a site, and determining empirically whether molecules are preserved in some or all the fragments. A first criterion for good preservation should be whether the molecular assemblages

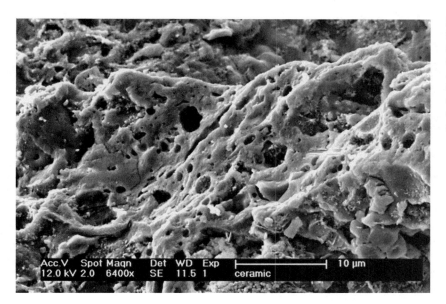

Figure 8.5
Scanning electron microscope image of the fracture surface of an Iron Age ceramic sherd, showing a wide range of pore sizes. Many, if not most, of the pores are too small to be seen.

from a specific ceramic type are the same and also consistently different from the assemblages extracted from another ceramic type in the same stratum (Namdar et al., 2009).

The state of preservation of the molecules is critical in terms of the quality of the data obtained. An assemblage that contains many highly fragmented molecules is more difficult to interpret in terms of vessel contents than one in which the original molecules, or at least large fragments of the original molecules, are preserved. Optimization of the conditions for finding the best-preserved material is thus of much importance. As very little published information is available on this subject, the following sections discuss various factors to consider.

Optimize environmental preservation conditions

The first step is to preferably analyze ceramics from sites or locations within a site where, for one reason or another, organic matter is better preserved (see Chapter 3 for a more detailed discussion). Briefly, minimal exposure of the organic molecules to oxygen and water can reduce bacterial activity and damage due to chemical reactions. Thus ceramics buried in sediments with high clay contents may, for example, have better-preserved molecular assemblages. The clay reduces the amounts of water that can pass through the sediments, and microbes within these sediments will probably use much of the dissolved oxygen for respiration before it penetrates into the pores of the ceramic.

Optimize ceramic porosity

It may also, however, be possible to a priori choose ceramics that contain better-preserved molecular assemblages. One possibility is that the organic molecules of interest may be better preserved in pores that are smaller than the size of a bacterium. This would limit degradation to chemical processes and exclude biological activity. Most bacteria are roughly around a micron in size, and if they are elongated or produce extended cellular substructures, they could probably penetrate pores with diameters around one-tenth of a micron (100 nanometers). Analyses of the size distributions of pores connected to the ceramic surface (the ones also of relevance to residue analysis) show that the range of porosity can be very large, depending on the conditions under which the ceramic was produced (Harry and Johnson, 2004). Pore size distribution can be measured by forcing mercury into the ceramic under increasing pressure. There is a good correlation between the pressure applied and the pore size (Whittemore and Halsey, 1983). Table 8.1 shows the volume of pores with diameters less than 100 nanometers in collections of ceramics of different quality, based on the data of Morariu et al. (1977).

Table 8.1. Volume of pores with diameters less than 100 nanometers in ceramics of different quality. Bacteria are unlikely to penetrate pores of this size range.

Quality of the ceramic	Volume of pores with diameters less than 100 nm (%)
Category 1 – poor quality	22–38
Category 2	22–45
Category 3	10–35
Category 4 – best quality	8–18

Source: Data are based on the study of Morariu et al. (1977).

The four categories roughly correlate with increasing firing temperature (assessed independently) and/or length of firing time. The results clearly show that the best-quality ceramics have the lowest proportion of open pores with diameters less than 100 nanometers. Thus high-quality ceramics may be less likely to contain preserved biogenic molecules. The corollary is that ceramics produced at lower temperatures and that were fired for shorter periods of time may be more likely to have preserved organic molecules. This hypothesis has not been tested.

Optimize ceramic material type

The mineral composition of the ceramic may also influence the preservation state of the organic residues. For example, the presence of calcite in the ceramic can be expected to buffer the pH to around 8. This would maintain an environment conducive to bacterial action, even if the prevailing pH in the sediments in which the ceramic is buried is lower.

Some ceramics may have pore surfaces and exposed mineral grains that bind certain molecules better than others. This would stabilize them and hence reduce the rate of chemical breakdown. If such preferential binding exists, it could introduce a bias into the results of the analysis obtained as the molecules that bind more strongly are likely to be better preserved than others. In fact, there are probably many other processes related to the manner in which the molecules penetrate into the ceramic that will favor some molecules and not others.

Heating of vessels will cause the molecules to break down and/or char. Heated vessels are therefore unlikely to contain well-preserved molecular assemblages. This implies that vessels used for cooking may, in general, have more poorly preserved molecular assemblages. Another open question is, to what extent are the preserved molecules derived from the last use of the vessel before it broke or was buried?

In conclusion, there are certainly many parameters to be systematically tested in an effort to optimize the chances of finding the best-preserved suite of molecules for residue analysis. For a review, see Heron and Evershed (1993).

Embedded information

VESSEL CONTENTS

The identification of the molecules preserved within the walls of ceramic vessels provides information mainly on the contents of the vessels, and hence on the use of the vessels. This, in turn, can contribute to a better understanding of the relation between vessel form and function, and possibly trade. This is the major interest in analyzing these molecular assemblages from ceramics. For overviews on this subject, see Heron and Evershed (1993) and Evershed et al. (2001).

By combining the analysis of the molecule types with their carbon and nitrogen stable isotopic compositions, valuable additional information can be obtained. For example, milk fats degrade in such a way that they are indistinguishable from other fats, based only on the molecular types preserved. Milk-derived fats can, however, be identified if the carbon isotopic composition of certain fatty acids is also determined (Dudd and Evershed, 1998; see also Chapter 2).

RADIOCARBON DATING

Visible charred materials on the surfaces of pottery have been dated fairly often. These, however, are not common and can easily be contaminated. A radiocarbon date from the molecules preserved within the pores of the ceramic should provide a more reliable date as the specific molecules analyzed should be free of contamination. This is technically a very challenging task as the quantities available are very small. Despite the difficulties, specific molecules have been dated (Stott et al., 2001). Although there are some inconsistencies, this study proves that it can be done. It has, however, not become a routine procedure, presumably because of the difficulties involved.

THE ENIGMATIC PRESERVATION OF STARCH GRAINS

Many studies have demonstrated unequivocally that starch grains derived from many different plants (Figure 8.6) can survive for long periods of time when associated with archaeological artifacts. This is really puzzling given the widespread prevalence of enzymes in sediments that are capable of degrading starch grains. Haslam (2004) has reviewed this subject. One conclusion is that starch grains that do survive for any length of time must have somehow been protected. In other words, they, too, must have a niche in which they are protected from these enzymes. Furthermore, the fact that the starch grains are associated with artifacts implies that the protected niche is also somehow connected to the artifact surface itself. Bearing in mind the sizes of starch grains (from 1 to 100 or so microns in diameter), it is difficult to conceive of a widespread niche of that size, such as a crack, that would actually protect them (Barton, 2007).

WHERE WERE THERE ONCE LARGE CONCENTRATIONS OF ORGANIC MATERIALS?

223

WHERE WERE THERE
ONCE LARGE
CONCENTRATIONS
OF ORGANIC
MATERIALS?

Knowing where concentrations of organic matter once existed in a site is in itself of much interest, even though the molecules themselves have long since degraded. These locations can provide important insights into different activity areas such as storage sites, garbage dumps, animal enclosures, latrines, and so on. There are several different approaches to this problem. Like all applications in archaeology, the use of two or more independent methods improves the reliability of the interpretation significantly.

Phosphate concentrations. The use of phosphorus for reconstructing activity areas in archaeological sites is perhaps the first widespread utilization of the microscopic record in archaeology (Arrhenius, 1931; reviewed by Herron, 2001). The method basically identifies locations where large amounts of organic matter were once concentrated and, in this way, reflects certain activity areas.

The term *phosphorus* refers to the element (designated P). Phosphorus is almost always associated with oxygen atoms to form various types of phosphates. Phosphate is an integral component of many biologically produced molecules. When the molecules degrade, the phosphate is released. As it is a charged moiety, it readily binds to a cation – often calcium, if available – and forms a relatively insoluble mineral (Chapter 3). These minerals tend to remain at the same location where the large accumulations of organic matter were once present. This is therefore a very useful tool for reconstructing an important part of the missing organic matter. It cannot, however, be used indiscriminately.

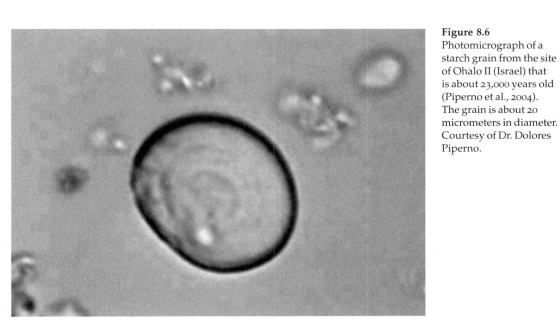

Figure 8.6
Photomicrograph of a starch grain from the site of Ohalo II (Israel) that is about 23,000 years old (Piperno et al., 2004). The grain is about 20 micrometers in diameter. Courtesy of Dr. Dolores Piperno.

Table 8.2. Phosphorus content of organic matter.

	Phosphorus content (wt %)
Cereals (Woot-Tsuen, 1968)	
Barley (*Hordeum vulgare*)	0.25
Maize (*Zea mays*)	0.30
Rice (*Oryza sativa*)	0.31
Rye (*Secale cereale*)	0.35
Sorghum sp. (*Sorghum caudatum*)	0.45
Wheat (*Triticum aestivum*)	0.32
Barley straw (Solano et al., 2001)	0.11
Other organic materials	
Citrus leaves (Esslemont et al., 2000)	0.15
Tea leaves (Esslemont et al., 2000)	0.42
White clover (Esslemont et al., 2000)	0.48
Pine needles (Esslemont et al., 2000)	0.13
Guano and manure	
Fruit bat guano (Shahack-Gross et al., 2004)	2.2
Insectivorous bat guano (Shahack-Gross et al., 2004)	8.1–18.5
Bird (pigeon) guano (Shahack-Gross et al., 2004)	5.0,3.1
Poultry manure (Kirchmann and Witter, 1992)	1.9
Pig manure (Solano et al., 2001)	0.32
Pig manure (Kirchmann and Witter, 1992)	2.9
Poultry manure (Solano et al., 2001)	0.37
Sheep manure (Solano et al., 2001)	0.77
Human sewage (Solano et al., 2001)	0.69
Cattle manure (Kirchmann and Witter, 1992)	0.9
Bone	11.5

Note: Prepared with the help of Dr. Ruth Shahack-Gross.

The extent to which phosphate mineral concentrations in sediments really do reflect areas that were once high in organic matter is first and foremost influenced by the original concentration of the phosphorus in the organic material. This can vary a great deal. Table 8.2 shows that the accumulation, for example, of cereals in storage sites, or indirectly in enclosures where animals were fed only straw, will result in sediment phosphate concentrations that are much less than for guano and manure accumulations. The concentration of phosphorus in bone mineral is also shown in the table, for comparison. Note that some of the sediment extraction methods used result in partial or complete dissolution of bone mineral, and this can confuse the interpretation of the results. Obviously, if a large amount of organic material is degraded that originally contained low concentrations of phosphorus, then the signal is enhanced. Iron Age sediments from Tel Dor (Israel) that were derived from animal enclosures did not contain large concentrations of phosphate

(Shahack-Gross et al., 2005). On the other hand, degrading bat and bird guano that accumulated in large amounts in various caves in Israel resulted in the formation of large amounts of authigenic phosphate minerals (Shahack-Gross et al., 2004).

225

POSSIBILITY OF
FINDING OTHER
PROTECTED NICHES
FOR ORGANIC
MOLECULES

There are other factors that determine whether the phosphate in the sediments faithfully maps areas that originally contained high concentrations of organic matter. If water flow through the sediments is active during the actual organic matter breakdown period, then part of the released phosphate could be transported elsewhere. If this hydrologic activity continues, then even relatively insoluble phosphate minerals will slowly dissolve.

Authigenic minerals. As the breakdown of large amounts of organic matter can cause a significant drop in pH, this will, in turn, cause more soluble minerals in the sediments to dissolve and other less soluble minerals to form. These newly formed authigenic minerals do therefore "record" the pH drop, which, in turn, marks the area where large concentrations of organic matter once existed. This pH drop probably occurred soon after the organic matter was deposited as biological degradation is a relatively rapid process. For more details, see Chapter 3.

Phytolith concentrations. As phytoliths are widespread components of plants, their presence in high concentrations in the sediments is certainly an indication that organic material was once present at a particular location in large amounts as well. For more details, see Chapter 6.

PRESERVED ORGANIC MOLECULES: ARE THEY REALLY IN CONTEXT AND NOT INTRUSIVE?

The discovery of intact, as opposed to charred, biogenic molecules and macromolecules in a site where this type of preservation is not common needs to be carefully assessed in terms of whether the uncharred molecules are intrusive. If they are not in a protected niche, every effort should be made to prove that they are indeed in an original context, before analyzing them and drawing far-reaching conclusions. The reason is that even polymers like chitin, which are chemically extremely stable, are readily digested by microorganisms (Hood and Meyers, 1977). There are very few biogenic molecules and macromolecules that can escape this fate, unless they are protected or charred.

POSSIBILITY OF FINDING OTHER PROTECTED NICHES FOR ORGANIC MOLECULES

Charcoal is a widely used industrial adsorbent for organic molecules. On the day it was produced by burning, it was certainly free of any molecules adsorbed from the environment. Charcoal then adsorbs molecules and/or ions from the environment in which it was located. Some or all of these adsorbants may have archaeological interest.

Authigenic minerals form in situ within the sediments. These are often phosphate minerals that formed as a result of the breakdown of organic matter, causing the release of phosphate. As these minerals are often highly disordered, they may well occlude various organic molecules from the degrading organic matter.

Resins provide excellent protection against bacterial activity and chemical degradation, hence the well-known phenomenon of insects and other organisms being protected within amber. Asphalt impregnated sediments may also provide protection against biological and chemical degradation. Although not common, protected niches such as these may produce some of the molecular treasures we seek.

9

Ethnoarchaeology of the Microscopic Record: Learning from the Present

The idea of using ethnographic data to better understand past societies is very old. Van der Kooij (2002) pointed out that even in 1727, Christiaan Schoettgenius made ethnographic observations to better understand agricultural methods in antiquity. The study of extant traditional societies as a key to the past started in earnest more than a century ago (Orme, 1974). In 1899, an ethnographer, Harlan Smith, appealed to archaeologists to have more awareness of ethnography as it would improve their understanding of archaeological material (Smith, 1899). This aspect of ethnography is referred to as *ethnoarchaeology*. Braidwood was among the initiators of the modern era of systematic ethnoarchaeological research, together with his two students Watson (1979) and Kramer (1982). These studies, as well as those of Binford (1983), Brain (1967a, 1967b, 1981), Gould (1980), and Yellin (1977), in many respects laid the foundations of this field.

Ethnoarchaeology can provide a reference framework for interpreting the archaeological record, and by applying archaeological methods to ethnographic contexts, it can provide a means of validating these methods (Isaac, 1968). The ethnographic context is also an excellent environment for developing new analytical tools for studying the archaeological record (Binford, 1978). Many have noted the potential pitfalls of using ethnographic observations as direct analogies to the archaeological record, but here, too, with caution, the insights gained can be helpful (Orme, 1974). To date, very little attention has been paid to the microscopic ethnoarchaeological record – the topic of this chapter.

Ethnoarchaeological studies have, for the most part, focused on the relationship between humans and their materials that results in the so-called material culture (Peregrine, 2004). The specific topics chosen for study often originate from unsolved questions in the archaeological record. When using ethnoarchaeology to gain insight into the microscopic record, this is the obvious starting point as some human behaviors also directly impact the microscopic record. It is, in addition, of much interest to study the microscopic record of the subrecent past using abandoned structures and spaces that still retain their original site structures (Gorecki, 1985; Figure 9.1). This "taphonomic" approach is particularly suitable for gaining insight into the microscopic record as the small-sized artifacts in the sediments have less tendency to be redistributed than the macroscopic artifacts. Furthermore, structures abandoned for tens of years often still maintain a "link" with their primary site structure. Thus the study of human and other activities in a traditional setting, together with associated abandoned, but still recognizable structural features, is an excellent bridge to the microscopic archaeological record.

MICROARTIFACTS: THE ETHNOGRAPHIC EVIDENCE OF THEIR USEFULNESS

Human activities can result in an initial sorting of the large artifacts from the small artifacts. O'Connell (1987) observed that the refuse produced by an Alyawaran household (Australia) is size sorted, with items larger than about 5 centimeters being tossed into the refuse zone just outside the activity area. Smaller items are usually dropped in the activity zone. Some may later be swept out into the refuse area, but other items remain in the activity area. A similar phenomenon was observed in a Bedouin camp in Jordan (Simms, 1988). The Nunamiut were observed to clean their activity areas daily. Most of the bone chips remained, but most of the splinters were removed to a dump (Binford, 1983). Binford (1978) noted that this can be informative with regard to areas where the activity takes place, as opposed to the dump. Another well-recognized

Figure 9.1
Abandoned structures in the courtyard of a house in Rajasthan, India. A family lives in the house seen in the background. Note the presence of both whole ceramic vessels (foreground) and broken ones (close to the wall that surrounds a courtyard) as well as degrading plaster on the wall.

phenomenon that affects the large bone fragments to a much greater extent than the small microscopic fragments is the activity of dogs. Dogs efficiently destroy the larger bones and bone fragments. Their gnawing preferentially destroys the ends of long bones (epiphyses; Binford, 1978). The absence of large numbers of bones in the agropastoral villages studied by Kramer (1982) and Watson (1979), as well as in a Bedouin camp (Simms, 1988), was related, in part, to the behavior of dogs.

Small artifacts, such as bone fragments, enter into the substrate far more frequently than larger artifacts (Gifford, 1978). They thus have a much better chance of being preserved, and when excavated, they also have a better chance of being found in or close to the location where they were produced (O'Connell, 1987). Good evidence for this was obtained by Gifford, who examined a site on the shore of Lake Turkana (northern Kenya) that was occupied by eight men and boys of the Dassanetch people for four days. She recorded that on the day of abandonment, nine times the number of bone fragments were recovered from the subsurface than had been visible on the surface. The subsurface fragments averaged 3 centimeters in maximum dimension, whereas those on the surface were much larger. She suspected that this size-dependent sorting may have been due to trampling (Gifford, 1978). In a follow-up experimental study, it was shown that after just a few hours of trampling by humans, obsidian fragments placed on the surface of a sandy substrate could reach depths of up to 10 centimeters (Gifford-Gonzalez et al., 1985).

One millimeter or so is the cutoff between fragments that can be discerned by the naked eye and those that cannot – a good definition of size that differentiates the microscopic and macroscopic records. During the production of obsidian tools, more than 99% of the number of fragments produced are much smaller than 1 millimeter (Fladmark, 1982). Even by weight, the so-called microdebitage (fragments 1 millimeter or smaller) can constitute up to 30% of the original material if pressure flaking is used for knapping. Even though it is not known whether the same fragment size distributions documented for obsidian also apply to flint (chert), it is reasonable to expect that numerically, the number of microscopic fragments produced during flint knapping will also be huge compared to the number of macrofragments. Thus the microscopic lithic record is, in this respect, very rich and can be used to identify knapping areas as well as use and disposal areas (Hull, 1987).

A highly skewed distribution of large and small caribou bone fragments was observed during marrow processing experiments. Binford (1983) differentiates between chips, which range in size from 2 to 3 millimeters up to 1.3 centimeters in length, and splinters, which are larger. Even though the absolute numbers probably vary greatly from process to process, the proportion of small fragments produced that are less than 1 centimeter in size is most significant. Thus, in terms of concentrations of bone fragments, the microscopic record should also be much richer

229

MICROARTIFACTS:
THE ETHNOGRAPHIC
EVIDENCE
OF THEIR
USEFULNESS

than the macroscopic record and can be used for identifying areas in which bones were broken for whatever purpose.

Artifact fragment size thus differentiates the macroscopic record from the microscopic record. These ideas have been incorporated into a model for identifying workshop and habitation sites based on size distributions of lithic artifacts (Stevenson, 1985). The microscopic record of microartifacts can therefore be rich and informative.

The obvious major weakness in terms of extracting embedded information from bone and flint fragments is that their small size complicates the possibility of identifying characteristic morphological features. The small fragments of bone and flint may, however, contain morphological information that, to my knowledge, has not been examined to date. For example, does the mechanical act of trampling alter aspects of the morphological features of these fragments, and can this possibly reflect the size of the animal responsible for the trampling? Examination of the microstructure of bone chips could be used to differentiate very young animals from older animals, as the latter have many more osteons. Young bovids have a different bone structure than older bovids (plexiform vs. osteonal bone; Currey, 2002). Even small bone chips may be used for extracting DNA and, in this way, identifying the taxon of the animal from which the bone fragment originated. One obvious strength of the microartifact record is that it can be used to reliably identify the locations of activity areas.

CONTROLS

Almost all measurements and observations need to be compared to something. This something is usually referred to as a "control." In archaeology, a common "control" in terms of the shaping of the archaeological record is what would have happened anyway in the absence of human activity – the natural process, as opposed to the cultural process (Schiffer, 1987). This important frame of reference for interpreting the archaeological record can be obtained by sampling around the site, particularly in areas that have been minimally impacted by human activities. In some regions, such controls are often not easily found but are essential for interpreting the microscopic ethnoarchaeological record.

The importance of controls is well recognized in the context of prehistoric cave archaeology. Here the problem is particularly acute, as a variety of carnivores also tend to occupy cave habitats, and many of their behaviors can impact the archaeological record of caves.

One of the first archaeologists to recognize this problem was C. K. Brain (1967b). Brain realized that to interpret the bone assemblages in the prehistoric caves of Swartkrans and Sterkfontein in South Africa, it was imperative to be able to differentiate between phenomena that could have been caused by animals that also live in caves and phenomena that are the products of humans living in caves (Brain, 1981). It is well known that hyenas, for example, concentrate bones in their lairs, which are often caves (Buckland, 1822). In South Africa, hyenas, leopards, porcupines, and owls are the main carnivorous bone-eating cave dwellers. These animals bring parts or even whole animal carcasses back to the cave, and the bones of their prey are also part of the archaeozoological record. Brain (1981) and others carried out a series of observations on the behaviors of these carnivores and drew attention to the implications of these observations for interpreting the macroscopic archaeological record of prehistoric caves (Mills and Mills, 1977). Brain noticed, for example, that when cheetahs devour an antelope, almost all the bones are left intact, whereas when they devour a baboon, only the skull is left intact. Leopards usually only leave the skull intact, irrespective of the nature of their prey. Porcupines may well be the most important agents that bring bones to caves. Such bones are often gnawed in characteristic ways. Brain thus provided a basis for differentiating between the contributions of humans (hominins) to the cave archaeological record, as opposed to the contributions of these other cave-dwelling carnivores. He applied this information to interpreting the archaeozoological record of various South African prehistoric caves. This archaeologically important line of research has been continued in South Africa and elsewhere at the macroscopic level on hyena dens (Sutcliffe, 1970; Klein et al., 1999), on vulture bone accumulations in caves (Marín-Arroyo et al., 2009), and on the activities of wolves and dogs (Binford, 1981), and other animals. This approach still however needs to be applied in a systematic way for better understanding the microscopic archaeological record. A first step has been made with the use of micromorphology for understanding the microscopic record of a prehistoric hyena den in France (Goldberg, 2001).

ETHNOARCHAEOLOGY OF THE MICROSCOPIC RECORD

Few ethnoarchaeological studies to date have been specifically directed toward understanding the microscopic record. Some of these studies will be discussed in some detail later in the chapter. Much information relevant to the primary microscopic record (the record produced during occupation) can, however, be inferred from field studies of occupied villages in which visual documentation of the macroscopic record was the only means of investigation. I will illustrate this using the classic studies of the village of Aliabad (not its real name), in the Zagros Mountains in northern Iran (Kramer, 1982), and an Eskimo winter house (Binford, 1983). Many of the characteristics of Aliabad are also present in another village (called Hasanabad) in the Zagros Mountains, described by Watson (1979). This "exercise" does not take into account the important secondary postabandonment processes that are expected to dominate many archaeological records (Hutson et al., 2007). These can be studied in abandoned parts of extant villages (see the following discussion). It is, however, helpful to consider first the primary input into the microscopic record during occupation, and then the secondary, postabandonment inputs.

Inferences on the microscopic record of Aliabad based on macroscopic observations

The main agricultural crops grown by the villagers of Aliabad are wheat, barley, chickpeas, lentils, clover, alfalfa, and a variety of fruits and vegetables. The villagers also collect some 40 different species of wild plants. The common domesticated animals in the village are sheep, goats, cattle, donkeys, horses, chickens, turkeys, ducks, geese, and bees. The livestock are free ranging. The villagers also catch fish, and their bones will probably enter into the microscopic record. It can be assumed that many of the domesticated and wild plants produce phytoliths, and these will be integrated into the microscopic record after the organic component of the plant degrades. The dung from the domesticated animals also contains phytoliths from both cereals and wild plants, and these, too, will enter into the microscopic record, mainly in the form of burned phytoliths, as the dung was used for fuel. Wood charcoal may be conspicuous in its absence. The domesticated and hunted wild animals can all potentially contribute small bones and bone fragments to the microscopic record (except, of course, the bees). It is significant that Kramer (1982) observed very few bones in the village. This in part reflects the fact that meat consumption in general is very limited, and that the bones that are discarded are scavenged by the dogs. She did note that bones were cracked with an axe to extract the marrow. This activity should produce microscopic bone fragments.

At the level of village organization, there are a number of features that should be recognizable in the microscopic record.

FEATURES OUTSIDE HOUSE COMPLEXES

Dung cake manufacturing. Dung cake manufacturing areas are located around the village periphery. Once they are dry, the cakes are stored in specific storerooms within the houses. Figure 9.2 shows a pile of dung cakes ready for use in a village in Rajasthan, India. Dung is a valuable commodity as it is used almost exclusively for fuel. The villagers of Aliabad, in fact, clearly stated that dung is the most important commodity of their animals because it is their main source of fuel. The dung of the village domestic animals, like the dung of most free-ranging domestic animals, usually comprises a mix of wild and domestic grasses, and in the case of goats, also leaves, assuming that they are available in the region. It should also contain characteristically shaped dung spherulites

Figure 9.2
A pile of flattened dung
cakes in a village in
Rajasthan, India.

(Brochier, 1983; Canti, 1997). As the organic component of the dung is rapidly degraded by organisms, only the mineral components (phytoliths and spherulites) are likely to remain as part of the microscopic record.

Ash pits. Numerous pits were dug around the periphery of the village, presumably to obtain raw materials for sun-dried mud bricks. Some of these are then used to store discarded ash, which in turn is used as a fertilizer in agriculture. As the major fuel source is animal dung, this ash should contain relatively little calcite (calcite is only the major component of wood ash; Humphreys et al., 1987), and probably only microcharcoal fragments, but many phytoliths with shapes characteristic mainly of grasses. The ash pits may be differentiated from the dung manufacturing areas as the phytoliths should all be burned.

Alleys between houses. These are generally not flat, but U-shaped, with a small gulley or ditch in the center. They are 2 to 3 meters wide. Much of the village garbage (dog excrement, animal bone, glass, etc.) accumulates in these alleys. There is no communal garbage dump. It is therefore conceivable that sediments from the alleys between houses will contain relatively high concentrations of phosphate minerals, indicative of degraded organic matter, as well as microfragments of bones and other trash. The alleys are also an obvious area for trampling, which would transfer these small fragments into the sediments. An alley may also have a characteristic microlaminated texture due to trampling identifiable in micromorphological thin sections (Wattez et al., 1990).

Other important activity areas, such as the cemetery, threshing floors, and gardens, are not within the village. The cemetery will obviously be recognizable by the graves and the preserved bones, but the threshing floor and the gardens will probably be very difficult to identify in the macroscopic and microscopic records. For more information on gardens in the archaeological record, see Greenfield et al. (2005).

FEATURES INSIDE HOUSE COMPLEXES

Most of the area of the village is covered by houses and their associated courtyards. These contain a variety of features, some of which should be identifiable in the microscopic record.

A typical Aliabad household has two floors: a ground floor, which has a courtyard surrounded by a kitchen, a general storage room, a stable, and a storage room specifically for dung cakes; and a second floor, comprising mainly living rooms and a workroom and storage area (Figure 9.3). The presence of stables, the dung cake storeroom, an animal pen, and the kitchen implies high concentrations of organic matter on the ground floor. In terms of the archaeological record, this will be reflected by high concentrations of phytoliths, dung spherulites, and bones of small mammals (mice, rats) compared to the second floor. Even after the house walls have collapsed, this difference in phytolith concentrations between floors might well be preserved in the archaeological record. Such a difference in phytolith concentrations was observed in a partially collapsed two-story house in the village of Sarakini, Greece (Tsartsidou et al., 2008). The stable floors can be differentiated from those in domestic areas using micromorphology (microlamination due to trampling), phosphate analyses, and analyses of pollen (Macphail et al., 2004).

The presence of phytoliths depends in part on the properties of the floor. A fully consolidated floor made of lime plaster will not contain phytoliths a priori and will prevent phytoliths from being trampled into the floor. A well-consolidated clay floor that is refinished periodically

Figure 9.3
A plan of a typical house complex in Aliabad. Adapted from Kramer (1982, figure 4.7).

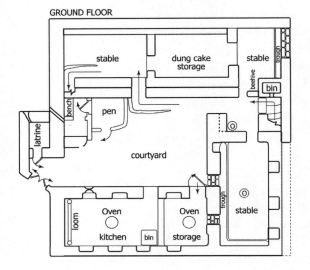

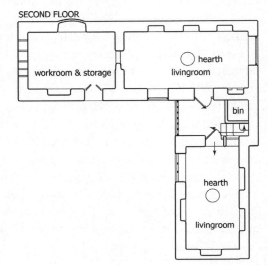

Figure 9.4
Open courtyard hearth
and cooking area in a
village in Rajasthan,
India. Note the plastered
floor and walls as well
as the structured hearth
and ash collection area in
front of the hearth.

may also have very few phytoliths as the material used may be specially selected for high clay content and, as a result, have few phytoliths. Furthermore, the effect of trampling is minimized by the repeated refinishing of the floor. A poorly made floor will almost inevitably have occluded phytoliths both from trampling and the raw materials used on the floor. In the Aliabad house, the stables have poorly prepared floors; the storeroom floors are better finished, but not as well as the floors of the kitchen and the living rooms. In this situation, the contrast in phytolith concentrations within the floors between the ground and second floors of the house should be maintained, and floors from different rooms may have phytolith assemblages and other microartifacts that reflect the activities carried out in each room.

Localities where fires are made include the kitchen oven, the courtyard, and the living room hearths. Figure 9.4 is an example of a courtyard cooking area in Rajasthan, India. These localities should be identifiable in the microscopic record by the presence of heat-altered clays, which constitute the walls and substrates of the hearth, due to the use of technical ceramics in their construction and/or due to exposure to high temperatures during operation (see Overview 9 in Chapter 12). The presence of heat-altered clays should be an effective method of differentiating between ovens and other structural features, such as storage bins or niches, that were not subjected to high enough temperatures to alter the clay structure.

The courtyards in Aliabad houses are swept daily. Their floors are composed of hardened earth. As this is a heavy-traffic area for both humans and animals and the floor is not plastered, there is a good chance that the microartifacts preserved within the floor of the courtyard will reflect the diverse activities that take place here, as compared to the more functionally specific rooms. A comparison of the base of the floor with the surface zone may distinguish between phytoliths that were from the construction materials and those that were introduced due to trampling.

Abutting the courtyard in the house shown in Figure 9.3 is a latrine. This is a hole some 25 centimeters in diameter and several meters deep. This subterranean feature should be well preserved in the archaeological record and be characterized by the presence of authigenic phosphate minerals characteristic of the degradation of phosphate-rich organic material such as human excrement. Not all houses in Aliabad have latrines. Analyses of fatty acids extracted from the sediments at the base of the latrine could yield molecules indicative of human waste (Simpson et al., 1998).

Another subterranean feature is the cereal storage bin, which is simply a hole dug in the ground. It may contain phytoliths derived from one or a few cereal types and would show no evidence of clays exposed to elevated temperatures. Many of the houses also have large subterranean stables, mainly for housing the sheep and goats in winter. The entrance is through the courtyard. These spaces should be recognizable by high phytolith concentrations, microlaminated textures in the floor sediments, dung spherulites, and phosphate concentrations (Shahack-Gross et al., 2003). Some houses also contain a well in the courtyard. There are no microscopic features of which I am aware that characterize a well in the archaeological record.

An interesting feature of the houses in this village is the presence of beehives built into the walls. In the house described in detail, the hives are located in the wall of the workroom on the second floor. The ceramic walls of the beehive may contain traces of the relatively stable alkane molecules present in beeswax (Evershed et al., 2001; Namdar et al., 2007; Mazar et al., 2008).

Kramer (1982) noted that room functions change with time, in response to differing needs. It can also be expected that after abandonment, the secondary use of the various spaces will change. These problems, together with all the other difficulties involved in reconstructing primary activity areas within households in the archaeological record, make this a daunting task. A first step, at least, is to recognize the difficulties, and then by cautiously collecting every possible bit of evidence, macroscopic and microscopic, it may be possible to arrive at one or several reasonable scenarios for the primary uses of a specific space.

Inferences on the microscopic record of an Eskimo winter house based on macroscopic observations

Binford (1983) described the organization ("site framework") of an Eskimo winter house. It included the following features: a house, a meat rack, dog tethers, hearths, a household midden, a dump of bone splinters, a dog yard, a work space, a wood pile and its associated chopping area, a children's play area, and areas of human waste disposal (p. 146). Even though Binford did not investigate the microscopic record, it is interesting to evaluate what sort of remains would probably enter into this record (assuming that during summer, microbial and fungal degradation removed most or all of the more labile organic remains).

237

ANIMAL DUNG:
MERGING OF THE
ARCHAEOZOOLOGICAL
AND
ARCHAEOBOTANICAL
MICROSCOPIC
RECORDS

WOOD PILE AND THE HEARTH

Both these features would be represented in the microscopic record by the siliceous aggregates and phytoliths present in the wood and bark of many (but not all) tree species (Chapter 6). Wood pile phytoliths could be differentiated from hearth phytoliths by the change in refractive index due to the exposure of the wood to high temperatures during burning (Elbaum et al., 2003). The hearth may also have associated charcoal, and the sediments on which the fire was made may have clays that have been structurally altered due to high-temperature exposure (Berna et al., 2007). If the camp was located above the tree line, then bones were frequently used for fuel (Binford, 1978). The ash from such fires should comprise highly crystalline carbonated hydroxylapatite (McKinley and Bond, 2001; see also Overview 5 in Chapter 12).

DUMP OF BONE SPLINTERS

This feature should be detectable by the presence of microfragments of bones in the sediments. Examination of the loose sediments using a binocular microscope and/or micromorphological techniques using stabilized thin sections of the sediments could be used to search for these fragments.

AREAS OF HUMAN WASTE DISPOSAL

Diagenetically produced phosphate nodules that formed as a result of the breakdown of phosphate-rich organic matter may well be indicative of such areas. Analyses of fatty acids extracted from the sediments could yield molecules indicative of human waste (Simpson et al., 1998).

Note that had a survey been performed of only phosphate concentrations, the dump of bone splinters, the dog yard, and the area of human waste disposal would probably all have produced locally high phosphate concentrations.

ANIMAL DUNG: MERGING OF THE ARCHAEOZOOLOGICAL AND ARCHAEOBOTANICAL MICROSCOPIC RECORDS

Kramer (1982) noted that "Aliabad's most important animals would leave little archaeological evidence in the form of bone refuse (which is not abundant, because of consumption patterns, disposal practices, and dispersal processes), but the economically important fauna might well be represented by dung both in stables and in the form of processed fuel, in wool and hair products, and more indirectly in stables, troughs, pens, coops, and hives" (p. 49). This observation, in essence, implies that access to the archaeozoological record is actually through the archaeobotanical record, particularly in relation to domestic animal dung (Anderson and Ertug-Yaras, 1998). In fact, Kramer does not report seeing bones as such in Aliabad.

In general, bones are a conspicuous macroscopic component of the archaeological record, and plants are conspicuous by their absence. Ethnoarchaeological observations of traditional villages, such as those by Kramer (1982) and Watson (1979), reveal just the opposite: plants are highly visible, but bones are not. The main reasons for the paucity of bones are that meat is a minor component of the villagers' diet, and the omnipresence of dogs more or less ensures that the few bones that are discarded will be gnawed and, in the case of small bones, totally destroyed (Brain, 1967a; Binford, 1983). A study of a pastoralist encampment (Bedouin, in Jordan) also showed that very few bones survive the gnawing of dogs, and those that do are the large bones. Interestingly, not all the large bones show signs of gnawing. The dogs also redistribute the bones from the refuse dump (Simms, 1988). So for at least the last 14,000 years or so, since dogs were domesticated (Benecke, 1987), dogs have been doing to bones what dogs know how to do, and this has certainly had a major impact on the macroscopic archaeozoological record.

The phytolith record is, of course, a record of the remains of plants. Phytoliths are usually concentrated in archaeological sites by orders of magnitude compared to the surrounding sediments. In the prehistoric caves that have been quantitatively analyzed for phytoliths, the main reason for this is the use of wood as a fuel (Schiegl et al., 1996). Even though wood and bark contain relatively few phytoliths, wood and bark are burned in huge quantities. In pastoral societies, the concentration of phytoliths is due to the animal dung that accumulates in the animal enclosures within the villages where the animals are housed at night (Shahack-Gross et al., 2003; Shahack-Gross et al., 2004), and in agropastoral societies, it is due to both the animal dung and the input from the cultivated cereals (Anderson and Ertug-Yaras, 1998; Tsartsidou et al., 2007). Note, however, that in agropastoral societies, the dung from the enclosures is often redistributed on the fields as fertilizer or is used as a fuel (Anderson and Ertug-Yaras, 1998). Thus, in pastoralist and agropastoralist societies, the phytolith record is as much about domesticated animals as it is about the use of plants by humans directly or via their domesticated animals (Miller, 1996).

The following sections describe two ethnographic studies of the microscopic record that address these issues.

Figure 9.5
Goat enclosure in a village in Rajasthan, India. The fences are composed of dry branches.

IDENTIFYING AND CHARACTERIZING LIVESTOCK ENCLOSURES

The livestock enclosure is one feature that may be preserved in the archaeological record. The livestock enclosure can be used to identify a pastoral or agropastoral way of life of the inhabitants of the site. It has been recognized in East Africa, for example, that prehistoric pastoralists and the hunter-gatherers living in the same region traded goods, and thus the presence of wild and/or domestic animal bones or cereals is not necessarily indicative of their way of life (Ambrose, 1998; Gifford-Gonzalez, 1998).

Animal enclosures are basically characterized by a fence with a gate and are areas where much animal dung accumulates. In many areas, the fence is composed of a pile of branches, often with large thorns, such as characterize the acacia tree in Africa. Figure 9.5 is a photograph of an animal enclosure in western Rajasthan, where the fences are only composed of branches. The fences are thus unlikely to leave recognizable traces in the archaeological record, except possibly in the form of postholes. The animal dung, on the other hand, contains abundant phytoliths. Thus, even though the organic fraction of the dung is readily destroyed by microbial and fungal activity, the phytoliths remain. The presence of high concentrations of phytoliths in recently abandoned animal enclosures in Maasai villages has been demonstrated (Shahack-Gross et al., 2003). These concentrations are several orders of magnitude higher than the phytolith concentrations from sediments in the surroundings (the "controls"). Furthermore, these high concentrations can be identified in villages abandoned for up to 40 years, where almost no other visible artifacts or even dark-colored, organic-rich sediments remain that would characterize the presence of an animal enclosure at that location (Shahack-Gross et al., 2003). Other features of the sediments that are characteristic of animal enclosures are a microlaminated structure of the sediments clearly evident in thin sections (Wattez et al., 1990), the presence of dung spherulites (Brochier et al., 1992; Canti, 1997), and phosphate concentrations (Macphail et al., 2004). The preserved organic matter in degraded livestock dung is characterized by high $\delta^{15}N$ values, and the $\delta^{13}C$ values of the dung may be helpful for distinguish grazing (i.e., cattle, sheep) from browsing (i.e., goats) in domestic species (Shahack-Gross et al., 2008). The combination of these five properties of animal enclosure remains in the microscopic record can be used to identify enclosures in archaeological sites. This approach has been applied to the Late Bronze and Iron Age strata of Tel Dor, Israel (Mediterranean climate), where many stratified deposits derived from animal enclosures were identified (Shahack-Gross et al., 2005; Albert et al., 2008). In arid areas, where livestock feed mostly on shrubs that do not contain many phytoliths, degraded dung is readily identifiable based on three lines of evidence: abundant dung spherulites, phosphate, and elevated nitrogen isotopic compositions of undegraded organic matter (Shahack-Gross and Finkelstein, 2008).

It has also been noted in many ethnographic settings of agropastoralists, as opposed to pastoralists, that the animal dung that accumulates in an enclosure is periodically removed as it is a valuable source of fertilizer for the fields (Brochier et al., 1992). Animal dung is also used as a fuel (Anderson and Ertug-Yaras, 1998).

PHYTOLITH AND CHARCOAL MICROSCOPIC RECORDS IN SARAKINI, NORTHERN GREECE

The village of Sarakini (Figure 9.6a) is located in the region of Thrace, in the Rhodope Mountain Range in northern Greece. The village is located at an elevation of 450 to 550 meters above seal level and has a Mediterranean climate. Sarakini is inhabited by Pomaks, who, until recently, led a traditional agropastoralist way of life. An extensive ethnographic study of the village was made previously by Efstratiou (1984, 1990; see also Tsibiridou, 2000). The village is divided into five quarters, and this division also extends to the surrounding forest and fields. Ethnoarchaeological studies on charcoal (Ntinou, 2002) and phytoliths have been carried out in this village (Tsartsidou et al., 2007).

Phytoliths

The study by Tsartsidou et al. (2008) focused on the parts of the village that were abandoned in the mid-20th century. It thus took advantage of the fact that a significant transformation, particularly of the organic remains, had already occurred, making the record more "archaeological." As the buildings and the village layout are still largely preserved, there was no doubt about the functional use of the activity areas sampled. Sediment samples from houses, barns, courtyards, paths, a mill, and a summer camp located several kilometers from the village were analyzed. The summer camp was used for threshing and for pasturing the goats and cows (Figure 9.6b). The phytoliths from plants growing in the area around the village were also analyzed (Tsartsidou et al., 2007).

As each of the 120 samples analysed contained between 10 and 50 characteristically shaped phytoliths, the amount of data generated was huge. It was thus difficult to discern characteristic trends. By normalizing the phytolith assemblages of the village sediment samples to samples obtained from both forested and open areas that were relatively unaffected by human activities, a phytolith difference index (PDI)

241

PHYTOLITH AND
CHARCOAL
MICROSCOPIC
RECORDS
IN SARAKINI,
NORTHERN GREECE

Figure 9.6 *a*, View of the village of Sarakini, located in the Rhodope Mountains, northern Greece. The houses all have the same traditional style: two stories, with a living room and storeroom on the second floor and animal stables on the first floor. See also Figure 3.2 (top left) for a photograph of an individual house. *b*, The site of a summer camp that was abandoned about 20 years before the photograph was taken. The remains of a sheep and/or goat enclosure can be seen on the hillside, and the remains of the workers' stone house are on the left foreground. The sediments in the field contained abundant phytoliths, but they were absent in the enclosure. *c*, A hole dug into the floor of the living room of the house shown in Figure 3.2. The finely laminated clay floor, about 20 centimeters thick, can be seen. The top of the floor was covered just prior to abandonment by a thin layer of lime plaster. The floor sediments contained almost no phytoliths. Scale bar: 10 centimeters. *d*, View of the section through the storeroom floor of the same house. The structured base (grayish sediment) is overlain by a finely laminated floor. The latter contained many more phytoliths than the living room floor. Scale bar: 10 centimeters. For more details, see Tsartsidou et al. (2008).

for each sample was calculated (Tsartsidou et al., 2008). A plot of this index against the phytolith concentrations correlated rather well with activity areas (Figure 9.7). Of particular importance was the fact that the PDI differentiates well between the samples of mule, cow, and goat dung and thus reflects their different diets. The mules are housed in the village most of the time and are fed fodder, composed mainly of the stalks of domestic cereals; the cows are free ranging and eat both fodder and wild grasses; and the goats are free ranging and eat fodder, wild grasses, and leaves. Interestingly, most of the samples clustered around the mule dung sample, which in itself had a PDI value rather similar to that of the stalks of rye. This is consistent with the fact that rye was the most important cereal cultivated by the villagers until recently. Rye was used to produce bread. Rye was also a major component of the fodder (together with wild grasses) for the domestic animals, particularly in the snowbound winter, and was used for thatching of the roofs of the barns where the hay was stored.

Other archaeologically relevant observations were that some of the animal enclosures (Figure 9.6b) were devoid of phytoliths, whereas the areas around them contained high concentrations of phytoliths. This is due to the fact that dung was used as a fertilizer for the fields, and the animals were often temporarily corralled around the enclosure. It is conceivable that in an archaeological site, the enclosure could be "negatively" mapped by the high concentrations of phytoliths around the enclosure and their absence in the enclosure. Most of the threshing floors were also almost devoid of phytoliths, and those that were there probably originated from the hard layer of a dung-mud mixture that was placed on the floor prior to threshing. The second floor of the houses was occupied by humans, whereas the ground floor was occupied by their animals (Figure 9.3). The floors of the second floor living rooms and storage rooms were made of clay derived from special locations that were almost devoid of phytoliths. They were also repeatedly resurfaced and thus had a finely laminated structure (Figure 9.6c). On the other hand, the floors of the storage rooms were thinner and were rarely resurfaced (Figure 9.6d). They had more phytoliths than the living room floors. The absence of phytoliths in the second floor rooms contrasts markedly with the high concentrations of phytoliths in the ground floor stables. In one house, which had partially collapsed, the two floors, now superimposed on each other, could be distinguished by phytolith concentrations. Furthermore, the PDI value of the ground floor was indicative of a fodder rich in rye stalks (Tsartsidou et al., 2008).

This ethnoarchaeological study of the microscopic record demonstrates the potential for using phytoliths not only to reconstruct activity areas in archaeological sites, but also to indirectly reconstruct much about the archaeozoological record of the domestic animals via the plant remains and other features that characterize degraded dung deposits.

243

PHYTOLITH AND
CHARCOAL
MICROSCOPIC
RECORDS
IN SARAKINI,
NORTHERN GREECE

Charcoal

The original tissue structure of charred organic material is often sufficiently well preserved to enable the identification of the taxon of the burned plant. This can be used for wood charcoal and provides information on the types of trees used for fuel and, in turn, on the local paleo-environment (Lev-Yadun, 2007). At Sarakini, Ntinou (2002) collected charcoal from different types of hearths and from waste dumps. She differentiated between confined structured hearths in the houses and gardens and those without any structure, which were located mainly in the fields. The wood types used in the structured hearths are dominated by one species, and this is often, but not always, the locally prevalent oak. This reflects the documented strategy of the villagers for supplying their winter wood fuel by collecting five or six trees from their own territory. The charcoal analyzed from hearths in the surroundings is taxonomically much more diverse and reflects the vegetation in the immediate surroundings where the hearth was built. There was no evidence for selecting wood with better burning properties. The charcoal collected from the waste dumps best reflects the local vegetation and

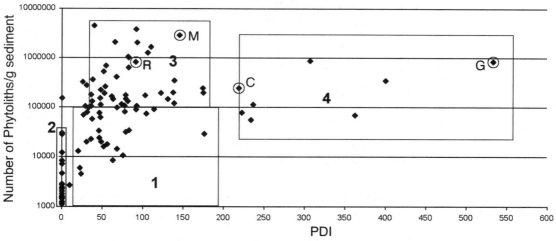

Figure 9.7 A plot of the concentration of phytoliths (number of phytoliths per gram of sediment) against the phytolith difference index (PDI). The values for the three dung samples, namely, goat (G), cow (C), and mule (M), are shown, as are values for rye (R), the dominant cereal used in the village. The data are arbitrarily assigned different boxes, as follows: box 2, very small amounts of phytoliths and very low PDI values, mainly from the floors of the living room; box 4, high phytolith concentrations and high PDI values, mainly dung-rich samples – note that the high PDI value of the goat dung reflects the goat's diet, which includes leaves and grasses; box 3, most of the samples from the village are in this box; these samples plot around the value for rye (R) and include activity areas related to rye such as storage and milling; box 1, intermediate values that also include the four regional sediment controls. For more details, see Tsartsidou et al. (2008).

would therefore be most suited for paleoenvironmental reconstructions in archaeological sites.

ACTIVITY AREAS USING PHOSPHATE CONCENTRATIONS: ETHNOARCHAEOLOGICAL VERIFICATION

Phosphate analyses of sediments in archaeological sites are widely used to identify different activity areas (Bethell and Máté, 1989; Herron, 2001). A few ethnoarchaeological studies have verified this approach. For example, phosphate analyses of the sediments in the guardhouse of the Mayan archaeological site of Aguateca, in Guatemala, clearly showed high concentrations in the kitchen area, the refuse dump, and the runoff area from the refuse dump (Terry et al., 2004). A study of two fish processing sites used by the Cupiit Eskimos in western Alaska revealed high phosphorus and other element concentrations in specific locations such as the fish drying racks (Knudson et al., 2004). The procedure used by Knudson et al. (2004) for extracting the elements from the sediments involved exposure of the sediments to 1M HCl for 14 days. This would certainly dissolve the more soluble phosphate minerals, including bone, and extract some of the small molecules to which the various elements were bound, but would probably exclude the contribution of the phosphorus from large organic macromolecules. This method would thus work better for archaeological sites where most, if not all, the organic matter was degraded and the phosphate was stabilized in the form of carbonate hydroxylapatite (Herron, 2001).

CONCLUDING REMARKS

Ethnoarchaeology provides invaluable insight into the archaeological record. Most of the information available to date is based on the macroscopic ethnoarchaeological record. The relatively few studies of the microscopic ethnoarchaeological record demonstrate that it too, can provide invaluable information for improving our understanding of the microscopic archaeological record. Furthermore, ethnoarchaeology demonstrates that the microscopic record can be a reliable guide for identifying activity areas, because microartifacts as well as chemical residues tend to remain at the locations where they were deposited.

10

Absolute Dating: Assessing the Quality of a Date

An absolute date is probably the most important information that can be obtained from the microscopic record in terms of contributing to the overall understanding of an archaeological site. Relative dating based on typologies of ceramics, coins, stone tools, glyptic objects, and epigraphic texts is still the most widely used approach for building a chronology within a site and between sites. Linking this chronology to the absolute timescale is now standard practice and essential for defining local and regional chronological frameworks. This information, in turn, can be used to track the spread of cultural changes and, in this way, significantly enhance our understanding of human cultural development.

For periods up to about 50,000 years, almost all absolute dating is based on radiocarbon – a method developed by Libby et al. (1949). For earlier periods, three related techniques, together known as *trapped charge dating* (Grün, 2001), are commonly used. These are thermoluminescence (TL) dating, developed by Aitken (1976); electron spin resonance (ESR) dating, developed by Zeller (1968) and Ikeya (1978); and optical stimulated luminescence (OSL), developed by Huntley et al. (1985). There are, in addition, a variety of other absolute dating techniques, some of which are applicable to materials found within an archaeological site, and some of which are used for dating mainly rock formations, speleothems, or sediments underlying or overlying the site. Table 10.1 lists the main dating techniques used in archaeology. For general references to dating in archaeology, see Aitken (1990) and Fleming (1976), and for more details on various dating techniques, see Chapter 2.

Each dating method has its strengths and weaknesses, and there are some weaknesses that just cannot be resolved. Perhaps the best-known inherent weakness of radiocarbon dating relates to its direct dependence on past changes in the concentration of radiocarbon in the atmosphere, and hence the need for calibration. When the rate of increase of radiocarbon in the atmosphere more or less equals the decrease by radioactive decay, the radiocarbon concentration in samples from that period are all

Table 10.1. Major dating techniques used in archaeology.

Method	Commonly used materials	Effective dating range and precision	Comments
Radiocarbon	Bone collagen, wood charcoal, charred seeds	Radiocarbon date ($\pm0.3\%$) corresponds to ±25 years for samples up to 10,000 years old; after calibration, the precision is generally around 100 years	The most powerful and generally applicable dating technique available up to 50,000 years BP
Dendrochronology	Charred or uncharred wood with rings	Generally less than ±50 years and in some cases around 10 years or less	Higher precision and accuracy than radiocarbon, but requires special wood samples
Thermoluminescence	Burned flint tools, ceramics	Absolute date ($\pm10\%$ to 15%) up to about 1 million years	Widely used in prehistory; requires special attention to burial environments and burial history
Electron spin resonance	Tooth enamel	Absolute date ($\pm10\%$ to 20%) up to about 1 million years	Widely used in prehistory; requires special attention to burial environments and burial history
Optical stimulated luminescence	Sediment grains, stones in buildings	Absolute date ($\pm10\%$ to 15%) from hundreds to around 200,000 years	Currently less used, but potential for more applications is large
Uranium series dating	Speleothems, travertine	Absolute date ($\pm1\%$) from hundreds to about 300,000 years	Used for dating prehistoric cave accumulations where authigenic calcite can be directly related to occupation levels
Obsidian hydration dating	Obsidian	Absolute date ($\pm10\%$ to 15%) up to about 100,000 years BP	Widely used in regions where obsidian tools are common and hydration kinetics are well documented
Amino acid racemization	Eggshells and land snail shells	Absolute date ($\pm10\%$ to 15%) up to about 1 million years BP	Problematic, but does seem to be reliable for eggshells and land snail shells
Archaeomagnetism	Burned clay/sediments	Thousands to millions of years	Requires local calibration curves for high-resolution dating

the same. Thus the dates obtained from such a period will be imprecise (i.e., they will cover a large range of calibrated possibilities), irrespective of how precisely the radiocarbon concentration in the sample is measured (Bronk Ramsey et al., 2001). This is illustrated in Figure 10.1.

An inherent weakness in ESR dating is that the uranium uptake history into fossil enamel cannot be determined other than by modeling, and it strongly affects the result (Schwarcz and Grün, 1992).

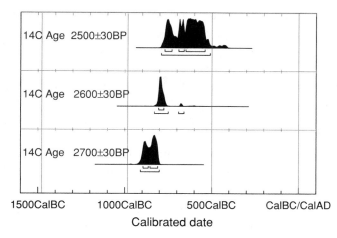

Figure 10.1 Example illustrating the effect of calibration for three theoretical dates that differ by 100 years and all have the same precision. The calibration results in the uncalibrated 2,500 BP date are relatively imprecise compared to the 2,600 BP date. Courtesy of E. Boaretto.

Dating methods that are based on chemical reactions (e.g., obsidian hydration dating and amino acid racemization dating) are influenced directly by temperature and other environmental parameters, and these are difficult to factor in to the result obtained. Ideally, if two different independent methods can be used to determine an age, this would significantly increase the reliability of the date obtained. In reality, this "luxury" rarely exists in archaeology, as the three commonly used trapped charged techniques are so similar that they cannot be regarded as independently corroborating each other, and there is no other technique that can match the precision of radiocarbon dating. On the positive side, the field of archaeology is blessed with having radiocarbon dating. It really is a fantastic dating tool that spans much of modern human cultural development. Radiocarbon dating has, for the most part, exceptionally good precision, and with the singular achievement of the establishment of the calibration curve, it is also very accurate for up to 26,000 years (Reimer et al., 2004a). There is, however, still much room for improving radiocarbon dating, especially concerning sample characterization and the way in which the dates are used (Boaretto, 2009a) – the topic of this chapter.

UNDERSTANDING A DATE: THE COMMUNICATION GAP PROBLEM

None of the dating methods can be applied in a routine manner, and all require a deep understanding of many different subjects, including archaeological context in the field and all aspects of laboratory preparation and analysis, to provide reliable results. Absolute dating today is carried out by specialists, only some of whom are familiar with and able to evaluate the field contexts from which the samples are taken. This exasperates a general problem addressed in this book, namely, that there is a knowledge and communication gap between the so-called specialist and the so-called archaeologist. When it comes to absolute dating, the damage caused by this gap is most keenly felt because of the importance of obtaining a reliable absolute chronology. One manifestation of this gap is the practice of archaeologists to evaluate the dates received based on their expectations, and if these are not met, the results are labeled "archaeologically unacceptable," filed away somewhere, and not published (Bowman, 1990). The dating specialist, on the other hand, is not in a position to counter the objections of the archaeologist, mainly because of a lack of familiarity with the context from which the samples were obtained. Furthermore, being keenly aware of all the difficulties involved in obtaining a date, the dating specialist is never sure that the date is indeed not wrong. The overall result is that there is an enormous loss of potentially valuable information (Bowman, 1990; Boaretto, 2008). The possibility that a good set of dates, and in particular, the unexpected outliers, will challenge accepted concepts in the chronology of a site or a region is often lost. Dating thus often becomes a self-fulfilling prophecy.

This chapter will mainly address ways to resolve the communication gap problem using radiocarbon dating. Where appropriate, reference will also be made to the three trapped charge techniques – TL, ESR, and OSL – which are the most widely used techniques for dating archaeological sites older than about 50,000 years: the current practical limit of radiocarbon dating. For a general overview of dating in archaeology, see Aitken (1990) as well as the reviews by Grün (2001), Hedges (2001), Schwarcz and Rink (2001), and Taylor (2001).

SOLUTION TO THE COMMUNICATION GAP PROBLEM

The process of dating can be subdivided into different steps (Boaretto, 2009a), each of which has its own uncertainties:

1. The process begins in the field with the choice of sample to be dated. This requires defining the context of the sample, choosing the type of sample, and trying to be sure that the sample is in situ and has not been secondarily deposited.
2. The next step is choosing the best samples that can provide the time resolution required, and that are sufficiently well preserved and uncontaminated such that they will most likely provide a reliable date. This involves prescreening for the best samples (Boaretto, 2008) and determining a sampling strategy that can resolve the chronological question being addressed.

3. The third step is preparing the samples for analysis by removal of the contaminants, and assessing the purity of the fraction prepared for dating.
4. Finally, the last step involves performing the analyses and determining their accuracy and precision.

Each step in this process involves uncertainties. The solution to the communication gap problem lies in the whole team (archaeologists and specialists) determining the uncertainties for every step in the dating process *independently* of the actual date obtained. Only with this information in hand should the date obtained be evaluated. The result will be that many samples that are dated today will not be dated at all. Those that are dated will have a "quality tag" attached to them before the dates are obtained. If the overall quality based on the four steps defined earlier is known to be excellent and the date obtained still does not conform to expectations, then the stratigraphic implications of the date obtained should be seriously reevaluated. In this way, the absolute dates can better contribute to a new and more reliable understanding of the chronology of the site, and some dates may radically change prevailing views on site and regional chronology.

The following section is aimed at providing information that can facilitate tagging the uncertainties onto a sample for radiocarbon dating. I deliberately describe some technical details so that all members of the excavation team can more effectively communicate about the basic issues both in the field and in the laboratory. Some comments are also made regarding evaluating the contexts of samples for trapped charged dating.

DESIGNING A PROGRAM FOR DATING A SITE

The basic rule of thumb is *not* to date a sample for which the uncertainties are so large that if the age obtained is unexpected, your conclusion will be that the context and/or quality of the sample is to blame. The main reason for not dating questionable samples is that the number of samples dated per stratum is usually small, and hence a sample that, for whatever reason, provides an unexpected date will greatly influence the overall result. Furthermore, having this dubious sample in the data set will require analyzing many more samples to prove that this sample is indeed an outlier. Once analyzed, it is part of the data set. It cannot be removed.

Calibration

A very important aspect of radiocarbon data analysis is the issue of calibration (Chapter 2). Calibration refers to a "correction" of the result that arises due to past changes in the concentration of radiocarbon in the atmosphere. In essence, calibration involves comparing past concentrations in atmospheric ^{14}C with the concentration of ^{14}C that was in the atmosphere in 1950, before the nuclear reaction tests significantly contaminated the atmosphere. This provides information on the number of years that have elapsed since 1950 and is referred to as years BP (before present), or just BP. As the concentration of ^{14}C in the atmosphere has changed in the past, it is necessary to correct the BP value by calibrating it against a curve of past ^{14}C atmospheric fluctuations as a function of BP measurements. This calibration curve is based on the measurements of ^{14}C concentrations in tree rings of known age going to back to around 12,000 years and various other annual deposits, such as marine sediment varves and coral growth increments, which extend the curve back to about 26,000 years (Reimer et al., 2004a). These changes directly affect the resolution of the radiocarbon date obtained. See Figure 10.1 for an illustration of the extent to which the calibration curve can affect the accuracy of the radiocarbon date.

In fact, the implications of the calibration curve should be discussed before the project starts as there are certain periods when the resolution is so bad that it may not be worthwhile dating the samples at all (depending, of course, on the specific chronological question being addressed). After calibration, the date is referred to as cal BP or cal BC/AD (Taylor, 2001). Almost all calibrations are made using downloadable software and data prepared by Bronk Ramsey and Higham (2003).

Context

The context in which a sample is found is probably the most critical factor in the whole dating process, and it is often also the factor that is hardest to evaluate in terms of uncertainty. Following Boaretto (2008), it is helpful to break this down into "macrocontext" and "microcontext."

THE MACROCONTEXT

Macrocontext refers to how well defined the stratum to be dated is, based on whatever parameters are available to characterize the stratum. If the stratum has good markers, such as characteristic tools or ceramic assemblages or characteristic associated architecture or sediment type, and so on, such that it can be confidently identified in different parts of the site even if the layer is not continuous, this is usually indicative of good context. Well-defined layers, such as floors that can be visually traced over a relatively large area and can be unequivocally related to specific architectures, are also regarded as good macrocontexts. Artifacts above and below such a layer clearly have a well-defined chronological relationship. There are other such well-defined macrocontexts. There is little benefit in dating a sample that is not located in a good macrocontext. Macrocontext, however, is not the only defining property of good context. The microcontext is also very important.

THE MICROCONTEXT

Within a stratum or feature that can be regarded as having a well-defined macrocontext, local features may be present that may be in good or bad contexts. For example, isolated burned seeds, sherds, or lithic tools obtained from a well-defined layer may have been introduced into the layer after it was formed or were already present in materials used for construction of the layer. The dates obtained from such materials will differ from the age when the layer was formed. A good example of a solid, reliable context would be a cluster of seeds in a constructed hearth that is in itself part of a floor (Figure 10.2, left). Even this situation has to be carefully examined as a seed cluster may have been secondarily introduced into a layer by burrowing rodents. An example is shown in Figure 10.2 (right). The burrow should identify this as a secondary deposit. Burrows, however, are not always visible. Assessing microcontext is of particular importance because there are many burrowing animals or physical processes (e.g., freeze-thaw, salt formation) that can move artifacts around locally.

Another aspect of the microcontext is the environment in which the sample to be dated is buried. For radiocarbon, this can be important as some samples may be in a chemical environment that is not conducive to good preservation, whereas others are in environments where preservation is better. The two most common materials dated by radiocarbon are the collagen of bones and charred organic materials. See Chapters 5 and 7 for more information on the stabilities of these materials during diagenesis. There are no reliable criteria for burial environments in which it can be predicted that either of these materials will or will not be better preserved, and hence, in practice, an empirical prescreening of many possible samples (see the following discussion)

Figure 10.2
Photographs of clusters of seeds and pits: *left*, a cluster of olive pits inside a well-structured hearth represents a good context (Iron Age sediments, Tel Dor, Israel); *right*, a cluster of seeds within Iron Age sediments from Tell es-Safi, Israel. These seeds were thought to be charred, until they were analyzed by infrared spectroscopy. The infrared spectrum showed that they were not charred and possibly even subrecent: clearly an intrusive context. Even after careful examination in the field, the traces of the burrow could not be seen.

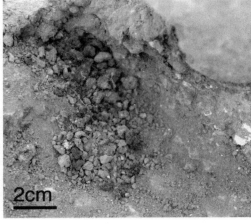

is still the best approach. There are some tentative guidelines that can be taken into account. For collagen preservation, clay-rich sediments tend to minimize the amounts of water that pass through the strata, and this in turn contributes to the better preservation of bone collagen (Weiner and Bar-Yosef, 1990). For charred organic materials, there is a tendency for poorer preservation to occur in sediments that are rich in calcite (Cohen-Ofri et al., 2006); a possible explanation for this has been proposed by Rebollo et al. (2008). There are, however, many exceptions to these generalizations.

CONTEXT FOR TRAPPED CHARGE DATING

In addition to the preceding considerations, trapped charge dating techniques have additional requirements with respect to context. TL, ESR, and OSL are all based on radiation causing charges to be trapped in the crystal structure at higher energy levels (Chapter 2). The radiation can be located inside the sample itself and/or in the environment around the sample. Thus both preservation of the sample and microcontext are crucial for choosing appropriate samples to be dated. Furthermore, the present-day radiation emission from the sediments also needs to be determined. This is done by placing radiation-sensitive materials (dosimeters) in the sediments for long periods of time. The placement of the dosimeters in terms of macro- and microcontext are as important as the locations of the samples to be analyzed. The relevant microcontext around the samples and dosimeters can be defined as a volume of sediments with a radius of some 30 centimeters from the sample. Thirty centimeters is the distance that gamma radiation can travel through wet sediments and impinge on the sample (Grün, 1989). If the mineral assemblage has changed over time due to diagenesis, then the radiation concentration measured today will not represent the dose since burial, and the date will be in error. Another key consideration is whether the sediments within this volume are homogeneous. The presence of large rocks or different mineral assemblages will cause heterogeneity, and it will be difficult, if not impossible, to accurately estimate the representative radiation dose to which the sample has been exposed. These are two factors that need to be elucidated in the field. This requires knowing a lot about the three-dimensional distributions of the mineral assemblages, and the diagenetic histories of these mineral assemblages (Chapter 3). If the samples are in dubious microcontexts, they should not be analyzed.

Thermoluminescence dating. The most common material dated is flint (chert) from tools that have been heated. The microcrystalline quartz mineral phase of which the flint tools are composed is generally stable and therefore not usually altered diagenetically. So all burned flint tools can be dated. In a study of Hayonim Cave, Israel, the proximity of different mineral assemblages close to the tool being analyzed was shown to affect the TL dating (see Figure 10.3).

Figure 10.3 View of the northern section in Hayonim Cave, Israel. The upper part of the section is dominated by ashy layers, composed mainly of siliceous aggregates (Chapter 7), whereas the lower part of the section is composed of well-defined hearths (seen as lenses in section), whose major mineral component is carbonate hydroxylapatite. Dosimeters placed in the upper and lower parts of the section measured radiation concentrations of around 950 and 400 μ Greys per year, respectively (Mercier et al., 2007). The burned flint tools used for dating came from the section that was excavated. If a tool from the siliceous aggregate environment was mistakenly linked to a dosimeter from the carbonate hydroxylapatite–dominated assemblage, this would result in an error of around 50,000 years.

Electron spin resonance dating. The material of choice for ESR dating is tooth enamel (Chapter 5). Two main sources of radiation produce the electronic charges that reside in defects (traps) in the crystal lattice – the basis for determining age. One source is the radiation emitted by uranium that is taken up into the tooth from the environment. The second source, as in TL dating, is radiation derived from the surrounding sediments. As uranium is not present in modern enamel, the date depends on the time period during which the uranium entered into the enamel crystals. This in turn reflects the diagenetic history of the crystals. The diagenetic history is usually not known and is therefore taken into account by modeling the uptake process and providing a range of possible dates. It would be interesting to better understand this complex problem by determining whether there is a correlation between the state of preservation of the enamel crystals (Chapter 5), the uranium and thorium concentrations, and the concentrations of defects in the crystals. It has been noted that at sites where other methods have been used for dating, the late uranium uptake model tends to fit most often (Schwarcz and Grün, 1992). The uptake of uranium is therefore not likely to be driven by the early diagenesis of organic matter.

The ESR signal is not as seriously affected by local variations in mineral assemblages in the surrounding sediments, as compared to TL dating. The reason is simply that the teeth themselves dissolve if the pH once dropped below 7 – the main cause for severe mineral diagenesis (Karkanas et al., 2000; Chapter 3). Thus teeth are only found in a relatively uniform mineral environment. One practical consequence is that in many caves, teeth may not be available from all the strata because in some strata they dissolved due to diagenesis. Having a nonuniform sedimentary environment for a radius of some 30 centimeters around the specimen (Grün, 1989) represents the same problem for ESR dating as it does for TL dating. This was shown to be a serious problem in the ESR dating of Hayonim Cave (Rink et al., 2004).

Optical stimulated luminescence dating. This is the newest addition to the trapped charge dating techniques. Like TL and ESR, it is based on the accumulation of trapped charge in special lattice defect sites. The unique aspect of OSL is that exposure to sunlight is the method for removing all previously accumulated light-sensitive trapped charges and "setting the clock" to zero. This resetting event should correlate with some archaeological event that is worth dating. The resetting process is very effective for dune sands and loess but can be problematic for water-deposited sediments (Prescott and Robertson, 1997). To measure the amount of trapped charge, the sample is exposed to visible or infrared light under controlled conditions. This releases the charge, and in so doing, light in the ultraviolet and visible range is released. This is the signal that is measured.

The materials that are most commonly dated are quartz and feldspar grains, and the effective dating range is from less than 1,000 years to around 200,000 years (Vafiadou et al., 2007). In an OSL study in Sibudu Cave, South Africa (Jacobs et al., 2008), it was found that the assemblage of quartz grains in the sample was mixed from two different strata and that the local mineral assemblages around individual quartz grains were heterogeneous, and hence the radiation dose to which the grains were exposed was not uniform. This introduced serious complications into the interpretation of the OSL dating results.

The main conclusions regarding context are that for dating, macro-context is important to understand the significance of the date, and microcontext is important for being certain that the sample is in situ and not intrusive or residual. Furthermore, for trapped charge dating techniques, the nature of the sediments in the immediate area can also seriously influence the date obtained.

Choice of sample type

For radiocarbon dating, there is a wide choice of materials. The ideal samples are ones that formed over a short period of time, namely, annual plants (charred or not) or bone collagen. In most bones, the collagen component is present, on average, for 10 years before it is replaced, but in some bones, this replacement could take as long as 30 years or more (Price et al., 2002). Another problem with dating human bone collagen is that if the diet included a lot of fish, the date obtained may be too old (Lanting and van der Plicht, 1998). The material most commonly found that can be radiocarbon-dated is wood charcoal. Dating wood charcoal is problematic, however, as the date records the time the wood was formed and not when it was burned. As trees can live for hundreds of years, this can introduce a serious error into the date obtained (the so-called old wood effect). Furthermore, the reuse of large wooden beams can also introduce a large error.

There are also various carbon-containing materials that are sometimes dated by radiocarbon but are problematic. The mineral phase of bone contains carbon in the form of carbonate. Some of it, however, is apparently located on the crystal surface and easily undergoes exchange. This has resulted in erroneous dates even for the more stable enamel crystals (Hedges et al., 1995). It has been shown, however, that if the bone was calcined during, for example, cremation, then the mineral carbonate does provide a reliable date (Lanting and Brindley, 1998; Lanting et al., 2001). The reason proposed is that during the heating process, the newly formed crystals are relatively large and well ordered at the atomic level, and hence are more stable.

Organic matter is present in many sediments and, in principle, could provide a date that should reflect the age of the sediments. In practice, different organic fractions extracted from sediments often provide different dates (McGeehin et al., 2001). In general, sediments cannot be dated reliably in this way. Lime plaster should also, in principle, be able to be dated as the carbonate in the calcitic binder is derived from the atmosphere (Baxter and Walton, 1970). To date, it has not been possible to reliably date plaster (Lindroos et al., 2007). The calcium carbonate phase of terrestrial and marine mollusk shells that were brought alive to the site could also, in principle, provide a reliable date, provided that all the carbon is derived from the food the animal ate and not from the seawater bicarbonate or the sedimentary carbonate. This, however, is not the case if carbonate rocks are present in the area, and dating these mollusk shells is problematic (Mangerud, 1972). In areas where no carbonate rocks are present, mollusk shells do provide reliable radiocarbon dates (Ascough et al., 2005).

Number of samples to collect and analyze

The sampling strategy is directly related to the archaeological question being asked and the resolution necessary to answer that question. The sampling strategy is also directly related to the availability of suitable materials for dating. It is *never* worth compromising on the quality of the sample (see the next section) to date more samples. If bad-quality samples are dated, then a much larger number of samples is required to minimize the impact of the poor-quality samples. When the data are published, the bad-quality samples should be clearly identified, irrespective of whether they provide anomalous results.

The first issue is to try to estimate the number of samples to be analyzed. Frustratingly, there is no straightforward answer. A single date from a particular stratum is certainly insufficient. It is always preferable to date at least two or three samples from each stratum and, in this way, directly determine reproducibility. To do this, three or four times more samples should be collected. The reason is that not all the samples will be suitable for analysis, and in many sites, many may have to be discarded (see the subsequent section on prescreening).

Even the best-planned dating project may have to be adjusted if, after the first set of dates are received, it becomes apparent that the reproducibility is not as expected and to improve statistical reproducibility, more samples need to be analyzed. Finally, every date obtained should be published, unless it is absolutely clear that a technical error was introduced.

Prescreening for sample preservation and purity

The purpose of prescreening prior to making the dating measurement is to identify the best samples for dating and to eliminate samples that, for one reason or another, are not suitable for dating. Prescreening procedures are well established for radiocarbon dating of bone collagen and are being developed for charred materials. Following is a brief review of prescreening methods.

BONE COLLAGEN

The best first approximation to determine if well-preserved collagen is present in a fossil bone is to dissolve the bone mineral in HCl, and observe whether an insoluble organic fraction remains. Insoluble bone collagen can be seen visually as a suspension in the acid solution after swirling as it does not settle rapidly (Figure 10.4). This assay can easily be performed in the field in a few minutes and is extremely useful for determining whether bone collagen is likely to be preserved, and possibly, in which parts of the site. This information can then be used as a guideline for determining how many bone samples to collect for further analysis in the laboratory.

There are several criteria for determining whether the collagen is pure. The C:N ratio of collagen is close to 2.8, and if it deviates substantially from this value, then the collagen is contaminated (DeNiro, 1985). This, however, assumes that the contaminating material has a different C:N ratio compared to collagen (which is usually the case). If very old bones are to be dated, then the C:N ratio is probably not sufficiently

Figure 10.4 Photographs of vials of acid-dissolved bone powder. The bone in the left-hand vial does not contain an insoluble fraction, whereas the one in the right-hand vial does contain an insoluble fraction, as seen by the cloudy suspension of organic particles after swirling the liquid. The rapid screening technique used is as follows: grind about 100 milligrams of bone after mechanically removing surface contaminants. Weigh the aliquot or mark a small tube with the volume equivalent of 100 milligrams bone powder. Transfer the powder to a 20-milliliter glass vial and add 10 milliliters 1N HCl. The mineral phase will dissolve within 5 to 15 minutes. After dissolution, swirl the contents and hold the vial up to the light to determine whether a suspension is present that does not settle rapidly. This is the HCl-insoluble organic fraction. Its presence is a first indication that collagen may be present, as the contaminating insoluble minerals settle quickly and the noncollagenous proteins dissolve. Using centrifugation, the suspension can be pelleted, washed a few times by resuspension, and then analyzed by infrared spectroscopy after drying. This will demonstrate whether the suspension is collagen, and if so, whether it is pure collagen (see Overview 11 in Chapter 12). The pellet can be weighed and the amount of insoluble collagen in the sample determined. A rule of thumb used in the radiocarbon dating laboratory at Oxford University is that if a bone contains more than 1 weight percent HCl insoluble fraction, then it can be assumed that this fraction is collagen, and it can be dated. In practice, this works well, at least for bones from temperate climates (van Klinken, 1999).

sensitive to prove that the collagen is pure. The amino acid composition of collagen is very characteristic as about one-third of the amino acids are glycine. If the amino acid composition is the same as for modern collagen, then the protein fraction is certainly collagen (Stafford et al., 1991). It may, however, be contaminated by other organic material that does not contain amino acids, and thus the amino acid composition is not a definitive criterion for purity (van Klinken, 1999). It has also been proposed that if a single amino acid known to be derived only from collagen, such as hydroxyproline, is analyzed, then this resolves the contamination problem (Hare and Estep, 1983). This is correct but requires a lot of collagen and is labor intensive, and therefore rather impractical. Infrared spectroscopy can be used for assessing collagen purity (Overview 11 in Chapter 12). For more information on prescreening, see Boaretto (2008, 2009a).

CHARRED ORGANIC MATERIAL FOR RADIOCARBON DATING

There is currently no simple prescreening technique for identifying better-preserved charcoal. Raman spectroscopy has been used to measure the fluorescence of the charcoal. As much of the fluorescence is derived from contaminating humic substances, this provides a measure of purity of the sample (Alon et al., 2002). One parameter that has proved to be useful for selecting the best charcoal samples for radiocarbon dating is weight loss during the purification procedure used for charcoal preparation. The samples that lose the least weight when treated first with acid, and then with alkali, are the ones most likely to provide a reliable radiocarbon date. The reason is probably that these are chemically the most stable samples, and hence the contaminating organic matter can be most effectively removed (Rebollo et al., 2008).

The bone and charcoal samples collected in the field should first be air-dried and then wrapped in aluminum foil for transport to the laboratory and for storage until the analysis is carried out. The reason for using aluminum foil is to minimize contamination, especially from paper or plastic containers, and drying minimizes the growth of microorganisms. By placing the dried samples in aluminum foil, they are kept in the dark, and this, too, discourages the growth of microorganisms.

Purifying the sample

The issue of contamination by carbon-containing molecules of a different age is crucial. It is therefore helpful to understand the basic approaches used to purify charcoal and collagen samples.

CHARCOAL PURIFICATION

After manually removing macroscopic contaminants, the sample is treated chemically for removal of carbon-containing contaminants. In the case of charred organic materials, this usually involves treating with an acid (HCl) to remove carbonate minerals and acid-soluble organic materials, followed by a series of treatments with alkali (NaOH) to remove more organic components, and finally, by a treatment again with acid (HCl) to remove any dissolved modern carbon dioxide in solution. This is commonly referred to as the acid-alkali-acid treatment (Olson and Broecker, 1958). It works well for well-preserved charred materials that are sufficiently stable to withstand these harsh treatments. Problems arise with poorly preserved charred materials, which tend to disintegrate during the process. For a detailed description of some of the chemical aspects related to this treatment procedure, see Rebollo et al. (2008). Another problem, especially for poorly preserved charred material, is that with each treatment step, major losses of the charred material are incurred. The result is that the sample that remains may become enriched in clay contaminants as they do not dissolve. As clay can also contain adsorbed organic material (Righi and Meunier, 1995) from a different period of time, the presence of large amounts of clay can result in an erroneous age (Yizhaq, 2004).

COLLAGEN PURIFICATION

Collagen also often needs to be purified after extraction. This is achieved by solubilizing the collagen at elevated temperatures in a mild acid, and then filtering the dissolved collagen to remove minerals, especially clay (Law and Hedges, 1989). The fact that the sample is treated in this way does not, however, ensure that it is not contaminated (van Klinken, 1999). The product should be characterized again by measuring the C:N ratio and/or the infrared spectrum.

ANALYZING THE RESULTS: A TEAM EFFORT

One good criterion for a successful dating program is whether the whole team – archaeologists and dating experts – change their views on the chronology of the site if unexpected results are obtained. The reason is that this requires an evaluation of the uncertainties associated with all stages of the dating procedure, from the field to the final analysis. If the uncertainties are low, then the unexpected results will change existing archaeological perceptions.

Note that the concept of defining uncertainties presented here is conceptually different from determining the error on a measurement. For the latter, all the quantifiable errors are combined together, and those that are not quantifiable are inferred from the coherence of the results of a group of replicate samples (Aitken, 1990). The idea presented here is to define uncertainties at all stages along the way, independent of the result obtained. This includes the crucial issue of context.

RADIOCARBON LABORATORY MEASUREMENTS: ARE THERE BIASES?

The radiocarbon community has a worldwide interlaboratory comparison program that is repeated every few years (Scott et al., 2003). The results are published in a way that each laboratory knows how well it performed and can thus address any problems it may have with sample preparation procedures and/or analyses that may result in biases. The results of these surveys show that in general, all laboratories are capable of carrying out precise analyses, and there are no persistent biases between laboratories. It can sometimes happen that a particular chemical or material used is contaminated, and this may cause a temporary bias in the results of a particular laboratory. The problem is usually readily discovered by the frequent analysis of standards. As the analytical quality of radiocarbon analyses is excellent, the challenge in radiocarbon dating today lies in defining the best field contexts and prescreening procedures, and in improving laboratory characterization of the samples prepared (Boaretto, 2008).

FUTURE PROSPECTS

Radiocarbon dating still has much unexploited potential for applications in archaeology (Boaretto, 2009a). One of the inherent weaknesses is that currently, the best samples for dating (charred seeds and grains and bone collagen) do not in themselves define a good context. There are common materials, such as phytoliths, wood ash, and plaster, that can be found as well-defined layers in archaeological sites and that, in principle, can be dated. So far, however, none of these materials can be reliably dated because of preservation as well as technical problems. Both ash and plaster contain an atmospheric ^{14}C signal at the time of their formation, but both are present in disordered calcite crystals that are often not stable over time (Chapter 7). The occluded organic material within phytoliths should also provide a reliable date of a short-lived material. Despite initial optimistic reports (Piperno, 1988), it is still not possible to date this material. If one or more of these materials could be reliably dated, the impact on archaeology would be enormous.

The prospect of obtaining reliable dates in the range beyond about 30,000 BP is very much dependent on our ability to remove the contaminants from charred organic materials and collagen as well as on the development of a reliable calibration curve. Effective sample preparation in turn requires an understanding of charring, the diagenesis of charred materials (Chapter 7), and the diagenesis of collagen in bone (Chapter 5). Progress is being made on the development of a calibration curve for this period (van der Plicht et al., 2004; Bronk Ramsey et al., 2006).

11

Reading the Microscopic Record On-Site

The division of the archaeological record into the microscopic and macroscopic records is based only on the fact that instrumentation is necessary to read the microscopic record. In reality, both are part of the same entity, and as such, they should ideally be exposed and investigated in an integrated manner. A very helpful approach for partially achieving this goal is to obtain some data on the microscopic record on-site during the excavation.

BENEFITS OF AN ON-SITE INTERACTIVE LABORATORY

Some benefits of an on-site laboratory follow:

1. The key element in this concept is that the results of the analyses obtained on-site are immediately integrated into the overall effort to better understand the significance of the excavation under way. This necessitates that the work on-site adopt an interactive problem-solving mode that provides answers in minutes, hours, or at most, from one day to the next. The ideal mode of operation of the on-site laboratory is to define a specific question, take a few samples that can address this question, and analyze them immediately. With the results in hand, the question can be refined or rejected. The next round of sampling can then be based on the new information. In this way, ideas can be efficiently tested, and if they appear to be well based, a full and effective sample set can be obtained for analysis off-site. This sample set will be better able to validate or negate an hypothesis, as compared to a sample set collected "blind."
2. The process of excavation is irreversible and destructive. It is therefore invaluable to have information available in "real time" so that the mode of excavation can be adjusted to the nature of the materials being exposed.
3. Many problems require producing a map of the boundaries of a feature that are not visible to the naked eye. The precise nature of

the boundary is often the key to better understanding aspects of the activities at this location, site formation processes, or difficult stratigraphic issues. The use of an on-site laboratory can be very effective in mapping such boundaries. Consider, for example, that if the area of interest is a square meter in area and the boundary should be mapped with a resolution of less than 10 centimeters to reveal its key features, 100 samples will need to be taken "blind" using a grid. Working interactively and knowing the results of every two samples before the next two samples are chosen can reduce the number of samples to one-third or less, depending on just how convoluted the boundary is. This is one of the major benefits of operating an on-site laboratory.

4. The microscopic record encountered on a day-to-day basis during the excavation is composed of the common materials and not the special finds. Thus the information obtained on-site is, for the most part, from these common materials. This in turn necessitates developing new techniques appropriate for extracting information from the common materials. This is one reason why much of this book is devoted to these materials, rather than the exotic (albeit fascinating) rare finds.

5. One important consequence of working on-site is that the archaeologists reading the microscopic record are, in practice, also reading the macroscopic record, and vice versa. This means that everyone works as a team on-site for extended periods of time. The result is that everyone is familiar with the locations of excavation squares, key loci, the stratigraphic sequence, and the unsolved problems, and all have a common basis for communication. Furthermore, both the frustrations and successes of the excavation are on the shoulders of all the team. The overall quality of the excavation thus improves significantly.

It should be noted that few problems can be fully resolved using only on-site analytical capability. Almost inevitably, analysis continues in the laboratory at the home base and involves other instrumentation. The final stage of the project involves the data analysis and the writing up of the results. This, too, brings the whole team together. Now, however, the basis for discussion of all concerned is much more solid as a result of everyone being more familiar with the "facts on the ground."

ON-SITE LABORATORIES FOR THE ANALYSIS
OF THE MACROSCOPIC RECORD

A common mode of operation at many excavations is to operate an on-site laboratory for specialists analyzing finds such as ceramics, bones, lithics, and so on. The mode of analysis is often rather similar to the mode of operation in the specialists' home laboratory environments. This type of analysis rarely produces immediate results that can be incorporated into the ongoing excavation activity in real time as it involves the examination of hundreds, if not thousands, of specimens, followed by careful analysis of the data. One major benefit is that these specialists are available on-site and do contribute significantly to the excavation. Furthermore, in many countries, the finds cannot be exported even temporarily, and therefore the analysis has to be undertaken on-site. Thus it is certainly not my intention to imply that this mode of operation is incorrect in any way; on the contrary, this approach complements well the operation of an interactive laboratory for reading the microscopic record in real time.

263

CHOICE OF
INSTRUMENTS FOR
ON-SITE ANALYSIS OF
THE MICROSCOPIC
RECORD

CHOICE OF INSTRUMENTS FOR ON-SITE ANALYSIS OF THE MICROSCOPIC RECORD

Basic considerations

The choice of instruments to operate on-site is first and foremost based on the interests and expertise of the operators. Instrumentation also has to be portable, or at least transportable. A key consideration is the time it takes to analyze the sample. Ideally, sample analysis time should be as brief as possible as the main point of being at an excavation is to be working with the materials as they are excavated, and not to be saving time spent in the laboratory after the excavation. Brief analysis times are necessary for operating in an interactive problem-solving mode. Just how brief depends on the value of having the information in the field. For example, it might be worthwhile spending a whole day preparing a thin section for micromorphological analysis, provided that the information obtained from the one slide really contributes significantly to solving a key problem. This is usually not the case. A grain mount (loose sediment smeared onto a microscope slide) contains considerably less information than a thin section but can be prepared in minutes. Grain mounts can provide information on the presence of microartifacts and phytoliths, for example. A similar consideration can be made for quantitative phytolith analysis. It currently takes several days in an off-site laboratory to prepare and analyze the phytolith assemblages in 5 to 10 samples; however, it would be very helpful to be able to map at least the variations in phytolith concentrations per weight of sediment on-site to identify areas with differing phytolith concentrations in real time. This could be indicative of variations in past behavioral activities (Chapter 6). If the initial on-site results are encouraging, then a full phytolith analysis off-site, based on a set of carefully chosen samples using the initial concentration distribution, will be far more likely to produce definitive results.

Choice of instruments

Following are the more common instruments used in on-site laboratories.

BINOCULAR MICROSCOPE

This simple microscope can be used to examine the components of the sediments up to a magnification of 50×, with good three-dimensional visualization. This allows charred plant remains, small bones and teeth, and other components of the sediments larger than a few tens of microns to be observed. These instruments are robust and can be used with a regular desk lamp as the source of illumination.

PETROGRAPHIC MICROSCOPE

These microscopes are widely used in geology to identify minerals and examine thin sections of rocks and embedded sediments. They have two polarizers above and below the sample that are aligned orthogonally to each other. Viewing the sample "between crossed Nicols" makes it possible to differentiate between crystalline and amorphous minerals. The mineral type of individual mineral grains can be identified in grain mounts using the optical properties characteristic of each mineral and by determining the refractive index of the mineral under investigation using a set of refractive index liquids. In addition to mineral identification, phytoliths can be conveniently seen and identified with this type of microscope at a magnification of 400× (Piperno, 1988). Because they are composed of amorphous silica, the capability of this microscope to differentiate between amorphous and crystalline minerals is very helpful. Furthermore, the refractive indices of the phytoliths can be used to determine whether they were burned (Elbaum et al., 2003). Small monocular petrographic microscopes are available that can be used under field conditions. The microscopes generally used in the laboratory are also transportable. For more information about mineral identification using optical mineralogy techniques, see Deer et al. (1992) and Heinrich (1965).

WET-SIEVING APPARATUS FOR CHARRED MATERIALS

A significant portion of the archaeobotanical record is in the form of charred materials. These can be extracted effectively from the sediments as they tend to float in water because of air trapped inside their structures, whereas the sediment particles sink. Note that not all charred materials do, in reality, float. There are many commercial and home-made devices for carrying out flotation, and their use, combined with the availability of a binocular microscope on-site, can greatly facilitate the exploitation of this important component of the microscopic

265

CHOICE OF
INSTRUMENTS FOR
ON-SITE ANALYSIS OF
THE MICROSCOPIC
RECORD

Figure 11.1
Flotation apparatus
for collecting charred
materials in operation at
Yuchanyan Cave, Hunan
Province, China.

archaeological record. Figure 11.1 shows an on-site flotation apparatus being operated at Yuchanyan Cave, Hunan Province, China.

FOURIER TRANSFORM INFRARED SPECTROSCOPY

Fourier transform infrared (FTIR) spectroscopy can be used to identify both crystalline and amorphous minerals as well as different categories of organic materials. It can also be used to recognize various materials exposed to elevated temperatures and for prescreening bone for radiocarbon analysis. There are many more applications (Chapter 12). Loose sediment samples or powders of consolidated samples can be readily analyzed. About 100 micrograms or less of sediment are needed. The sample preparation time (using KBr pellets) is about five minutes, and the analysis time is less than a minute. Robust portable instruments weighing about 10 to 12 kilograms are available, and they function well in the harsh environment of an excavation (Weiner and Goldberg, 1990; Figure 11.2).

X-RAY FLUORESCENCE SPECTROMETER

X-ray fluorescence (XRF) spectrometers can be used to detect concentrations of many light and heavy elements, including most of the metals of interest in archaeology. XRF spectrometers are thus an effective means of detecting past metallurgical activities based on the presence of metal concentrations in the sediments, even if the actual metal objects or workshops have not been found or preserved. Specially adapted XRF spectrometers can also detect lighter elements, such as silicon and aluminum, and can be used effectively in conjunction with infrared spectroscopy to characterize sediment mineral assemblages. Elemental compositions of ceramics can also be obtained for determining the provenience of pottery. Obtaining this information on-site can sometimes be useful (Morgenstein and Redmount, 2005).

Loose sediment samples or powders of consolidated samples are analyzed. About half a gram or so is needed. Very little sample preparation is involved; the sediments are analyzed as is, and each analysis takes a few minutes. Portable instruments (including some that are the size of a hair dryer) can be operated not only on-site, but right on the excavation section, without sampling (Williams-Thorpe et al., 1999; Morgenstein and Redmount, 2005). This is an excellent and efficient means of mapping boundaries between different structures and/or strata in real time. An analysis takes a minute or two. As these instruments are also of much use in the laboratory, the decision to operate a very small portable instrument, as opposed to a transportable, larger instrument with improved analytical capabilities, needs to be carefully considered.

RAMAN SPECTROSCOPY

Raman spectroscopy, like infrared spectroscopy, can be used to characterize materials. The major advantage of Raman spectroscopy over infrared spectroscopy is that the material does not need to be sampled; the analysis can be made directly off the sample surface. Unfortunately, almost all excavated materials produce a strong fluorescence signal that overwhelms the much weaker Raman signal. The fluorescent components (probably humic substances) can be removed by solvents, but then the major advantage over infrared spectroscopy of not having to remove or powder samples is lost. One effective solution to the fluorescence problem is to use the laser of the Raman spectrometer to remove these organic contaminants. This can be done within 10 or more minutes (Colomban, 2005). This makes it possible to nondestructively analyze glazes, pigments, ceramic surfaces, glasses, ivory, and many other materials (Colomban, 2005). Transportable instruments are available that can be used on-site. The use of fiber-optic cables makes it possible to analyze sample surfaces in a noncontact mode.

UV-VISIBLE SPECTROPHOTOMETER

Variations in sediment phosphate concentrations provide a means of identifying the locations of new sites, and intrasite variations can provide information on different activity areas. These analyses can be performed on-site using a simple spectrophotometer. Rypkema et al. (2007) have shown that samples can be prepared and analyzed rapidly and quantitatively. Very small portable spectrophotometers, weighing just a few tens of grams, are available. There may well be other potential applications in archaeology using such spectrophotometers; these include the very sensitive detection of molecules using antibodies.

267

CHOICE OF
INSTRUMENTS FOR
ON-SITE ANALYSIS OF
THE MICROSCOPIC
RECORD

MAPPING AND THREE-DIMENSIONAL RECONSTRUCTIONS

One of the major challenges of an archaeological excavation is to be able to excavate in such a way as to be able to accurately reconstruct as much of the site as possible after excavation. This reconstruction is also the basis for integrating the macroscopic and microscopic finds and analyses into the larger picture and, based on this integration, achieve a better understanding of the site. The traditional methods of recording (maps, photographs, location coordinates, etc.) are still the basis for achieving this goal. Since the early 1990s, however, major advances have been made using the sophisticated tools of computer science, together with the ability to locate objects using the Global Positioning System (Reilly, 1989). An excellent example is the three-dimensional reconstruction of the Great Temple in Petra, Jordan (Vote, 2002). Clearly the availability of tools of this type on-site during the excavation enables excavators to better adapt the excavation strategy to the features being exposed, and to improve the collection of data without slowing down the excavation process to an unacceptable pace. If information from the microscopic record is also integrated into these reconstructions, this could contribute significantly to our understanding of the entire archaeological record.

Figure 11.2
Operating a transportable Fourier transform infrared spectrometer (FTIR) in Hayonim Cave during the excavation in the 1990s. The plastic canopy is to protect the equipment from bat and bird guano falling from the ceiling. Electricity is supplied by a small generator outside the cave.

PHOTOGRAPHY

Photographs are an invaluable documentation of the archaeological record being sampled and analyzed. A good photograph may often reveal details that are not visible to the naked eye, especially if flash photography is used. There is therefore every reason for using quality photography equipment: cameras, macrolenses, wide-angle zoom lenses, and flashes.

We routinely photograph the section or surface to be studied after cleaning and before sampling. We then tag the locations where samples are taken using a dark-colored tag with dimensions around 5 × 3 centimeters (white tags reflect light and are thus difficult to read on the photograph). Figure 11.3 shows a section at Tel Dor, Israel, after sampling. The resolution of the photograph has to be such that by zooming in, the tags can be read (as in Figure 11.3b).

The on-site laboratory operated by the Kimmel Center for Archaeological Science at the Weizmann Institute (Figure 11.4) currently comprises a petrographic microscope, a binocular, an FTIR, a UV-visible spectrophotometer, and an XRF spectrometer. Note that some of these instruments are operated at the excavation, and others are operated only at the base camp.

OPERATION OF THE LABORATORY

All the equipment (microscopes, FTIR, and XRF) can usually fit into the back of a small truck. Power is supplied by a small generator, and it takes about 20 minutes to set up the laboratory in the field and 20 minutes or so to disassemble it at the end of the working day. I have air-freighted the FTIR to sites located in other countries, and this can also be done with the XRF. One group has operated an XRF in Egypt (Morgenstein and Redmount, 2005).

It is obviously beneficial to operate the laboratory during the entire field season. In reality, it may be difficult to maintain a workload for extended periods of time that involves the logistics of setting up and

Figure 11.3
a, Tagged section (AM13) from Iron Age strata at Tel Dor, Israel. *b*, Enlargement of the area marked in Figure 11.3a. Note that the tags cannot be read in Figure 11.3a, but they can be read in Figure 11.3b.

removing the laboratory each day, analyzing samples outside excavation times, and participating in the team's general activities, meetings, and so on, for a long excavation season.

Our standard mode of operation is to collect samples (ideally about 10 grams, where sample availability is unlimited) in small plastic vials or Zip-lock bags, mark the precise location with a dark-colored tag clearly showing the sample number, photograph the tags (Figure 11.3), and of course, note all relevant information in a field notebook. Then, we analyze the sample. As the FTIR requires much less than a milligram of material, very small samples can be analyzed. If large samples are obtained, care must be taken to homogenize the sample so that a representative analysis is obtained.

269

USEFUL WORK
PROGRAM FOR THE
ON-SITE
INTERACTIVE
LABORATORY

USEFUL WORK PROGRAM FOR THE ON-SITE INTERACTIVE LABORATORY

First visit to the site

It is initially most helpful to survey the range of minerals and other materials exposed during previous excavations by analyzing standing sections and balks. These have to be cleaned well, and fresh sediment needs to be exposed. This is particularly important when analyzing surfaces that have been exposed for many years as the effects of rain, wind, and the evaporation of groundwater can alter the mineral composition of the exposed surface significantly. Minerals brought to the surface by capillary action, and in particular, the common sodium nitrate, can be readily identified in an infrared spectrum (see Overview 14 in Chapter 12).

The information obtained can usually provide information on the overall mineral assemblages and preservation states of the site or areas within the site as well as whether some unknown minerals or materials need to be identified in the home laboratory using instruments such as energy-dispersive spectrometry in a scanning electron microscope (Appendix 1) and/or X-ray diffraction.

Figure 11.4

a, The on-site laboratory of the Kimmel Center for Archaeological Science being operated at Tel Dor, Israel. Both an X-ray fluorescence spectrometer (distant side of the table) and an FTIR are being operated. *b*, The on-site laboratory being operated at Tell es-Safi, Israel. A small FTIR with a built-in computer is used. A petrographic microscope (not visible in the picture) is also used.

Operation of the on-site laboratory during excavation seasons

IDENTIFYING PROBLEMS

After the initial survey, the next challenge is to identify interesting problems that will contribute to a better overall understanding of the site. This usually entails focusing on the details of specific features, mapping the distributions of certain artifacts or sediment components, solving complex stratigraphic problems by using information on sediment composition, identifying specific activities confined to certain areas, and so on. As new sediments are exposed by the ongoing excavation, the on-site laboratory can also be used to obtain immediate information on the archaeological significance of the newly exposed materials, which may also help in deciding on the most appropriate excavation strategy. In small-scale excavations, it may be possible to sample every sediment type exposed and identify their mineral assemblages, irrespective of whether a specific problem can be identified. By being systematic, inconspicuous but novel materials and/or mineral assemblages have a much better chance of being detected.

SOLVING AN IDENTIFIED PROBLEM

The next stage is to use the on-site laboratory to collect the best sample set possible for providing a well-substantiated interpretation of a particular problem. In the absence of an on-site laboratory, this stage is often compromised by not having the appropriate samples in hand for analysis in the home laboratory. It often involves using the on-site laboratory for mapping boundaries, documenting every feature, and most important, collecting the best control samples around or outside the feature or the site itself.

CONTROLS

Control samples are often the most difficult samples to obtain in a large, complex archaeological site. The controls are basically the set of data to which the feature under study is compared. This comparison will enable the differentiation of the unique properties of the feature from the properties of the sediments surrounding the feature. Choosing the controls is often problematic as in many sites, one feature interrupts another and presents its own characteristic signals. There are no general rules, except that much thought should be given to finding the best possible controls.

Controls from off-site should also be analyzed. These serve as an essential baseline for recognizing the anthropologically attributed properties of the sediments from the site. The difficulty in choosing controls is that even off-site, the sediments may have been influenced by agriculture or soil formation processes, or may simply not be representative of the regional setting.

FURTHER ANALYSES IN THE HOME LABORATORY, DATA ANALYSIS,
AND SYNTHESIS

271

EXAMPLES OF
QUESTIONS TO ASK
ABOUT THE
MICROSCOPIC
RECORD OF A SITE

Very few problems can be solved using only the on-site laboratory. In fact, it is not the purpose of the on-site laboratory to "save time" and complete the study, unless, of course, the samples cannot be taken out of the country where the excavation is located. No generalizations can be made about this stage of the project, except to emphasize that it, too, benefits from the familiarity of the investigators with all the details of the site – one of the important outcomes of the interactive, on-site operational mode.

EXAMPLES OF QUESTIONS TO ASK ABOUT THE MICROSCOPIC RECORD OF A SITE

What components are missing because they were not preserved or because they were not brought to the site?

This key question relating to preservation conditions can be assessed initially using several different approaches. What are the major mineral components of the sediments? If clay is absent or only a minor component, then the hydrological activity will be high, and it is more likely that the more soluble carbonates and possibly phosphates will have dissolved (Chapter 4). If carbonates are present, a key question is whether the relatively unstable polymorph aragonite is preserved (Chapter 3). Aragonite is the common mineral component of terrestrial and freshwater mollusk shells (Chapter 5). If aragonite is present, then the preservation conditions for other carbonates and phosphates, including bone, are good. Are bones distributed all over the site? As bones are common in most sites, their absence in the site or in parts of the site may be an indication of varying preservation conditions (Chapter 5). Finally, do the phytoliths have smooth or pitted surfaces? If they have pitted surfaces, this may indicate that dissolution of silica may have occurred, and hence the phytolith record may be biased by differential preservation (Chapter 6).

What fuel was commonly used at the site?

Since humans developed the ability to control fire, fuel has been burned at almost every archaeological site. It is thus of much interest to identify the fuel type used, and possibly to detect changes in the fuel economy, as a possible result of over exploitation of the local resources. An excellent example is the study by Simpson et al. (2003), who used micromorphology to identify the changing fuel types used by the occupants of two sites in Iceland.

Wood is the most common traditional fuel type used. Wood charcoal structure can be analyzed to identify the tree species used (Maby, 1932), and wood ash can be recognized by the presence of characteristically shaped calcite crystals (pseudomorphs) (Courty et al., 1989; Brochier and Thinon, 2003) and by disorder in the crystal lattice (Chu et al., 2008). Wood ash also contains a minor siliceous component comprising siliceous aggregates (Schiegl et al., 1994) and phytoliths. Some of the latter are formed only in the bark, and therefore a relatively high concentration of bark phytoliths may indicate that thin branches and/or bushes were used for fuel, as opposed to large pieces of wood (Albert et al., 2003b; Chapter 6).

Dung produced by domestic animals, such as sheep, goats, cows, camels, llamas, and so on, is commonly used as fuel, especially in areas where wood is scarce (Anderson and Ertug-Yaras, 1998). The dung contains mainly remnants of the plants eaten by the animals. Thus, after the organic component has been destroyed by burning, the phytoliths will remain and can be used to identify the fuel type. Their refractive indices can be determined to differentiate between those that were burned and those that were not (Elbaum et al., 2003). Furthermore, the phytolith assemblages may be indicative of the types of animal dung used (e.g., a large component of leaf phytoliths may indicate goat dung; Tsartsidou et al., 2008).

Peat is also widely used as a fuel in areas of the world where it is available. Here, too, the abundance of phytoliths and their characteristic morphotypes may well be indicative of the use of peat as a fuel (Simpson et al., 2003). It has been reported that coal was used as a fuel in two prehistoric sites in France (Théry et al., 1996). This appears to be a rare occurrence.

Natural fuels almost inevitably contain adhering sediment. When these small lumps are heated in an open fire, their clay structures readily change, and the iron-containing components tend to oxidize and become brick red in color. These burned sediment particles are often visible to the naked eye and are prominent in thin sections for micromorphology (Courty et al., 1989; Simpson et al., 2003). They are therefore useful indicators of fuel remains.

Are there indications of pyrotechnological activities other than making fires?

Macroscopic remains of the products of pyrotechnological activities (such as plaster or mortar, slags, ceramics, etc.) are obvious indications of pyrotechnological activities. Certain pyrotechnological activities may only be recorded or preserved in the microscopic record. Metallurgical activities can result in widespread pollution of a site, and hence high concentrations of a metal (such as lead or copper) in the sediments may be indicative of such industrial activities. The presence of clay that was exposed to high temperatures (Berna et al., 2007) may also indicate some past pyrotechnological practices not obvious from the macroscopic record.

Where is the site on the rural-urban continuum?

Since the domestication of animals some 10,000 years ago in the Levant (Bar-Yosef, 2001), animals have been an integral component of human lifestyles, either directly, by living with the humans (referred to here as a rural context), or indirectly, as a source of secondary products (in a more urban context). All combinations are possible, hence the use of the term *continuum*. It is of interest to characterize an archaeological site in terms of where it lies on this continuum. This can conceivably be done by quantitative analysis of the phytoliths in the sediments. High concentrations of phytoliths indicative of animal dung would point to a more rural context, whereas low concentrations of phytoliths with a high cereal component would suggest a more urban lifestyle (Albert et al., 2008).

ON-SITE ARTIFACT CONSERVATION

The presence of an on-site laboratory opens the way to more effectively limiting the irreversible damage that almost inevitably accompanies exposing and removing the artifacts from their burial environments. This removal represents the biggest environmental change that an artifact will undergo (Watkinson, 2001). The on-site laboratory can be used to identify the artifact material and any associated corrosion products so that an appropriate conservation trajectory, both on-site and later, when the object is removed for long-term storage, can be defined. This trajectory can be tailored for the specific material type, such as metal objects, or for different types of organic materials (e.g., cellulose based vs. protein based), and so on, starting in the field. The material characterization can also be used to assess the potential of the object to yield microscopic information such as DNA remnants, reliable paleoenvironmental information, organic residues, and so on. All this information can be taken into account in choosing a conservation strategy (e.g., lowering the pH will probably destroy the DNA) or before applying adhesives or other polymers for stabilization.

FUTURE TRENDS

One trend in archaeology is to excavate less, but extract more information. In fact, exploiting the microscopic record as much as possible for providing more detail about past human activities is part of this overall trend. As more tools for analyzing the microscopic record become available, the value of first probing an archaeological site by coring or digging pits for prospecting increases. These "previews" into the potential of the site can then be used to plot a more effective strategy for a focused excavation.

As many of the methods currently used to analyze the microscopic record are adapted from other disciplines, such as geochemistry, it can be predicted that in the future, more new methods will be developed to specifically address unique archaeological problems. This will be one outcome of having archaeologists trained in the natural sciences working in the field and becoming personally familiar with the major unsolved issues.

Finally, the future archaeology will resemble many other fields in the natural sciences in terms of its dependence on sophisticated instrumentation, its use of expensive reagents, and its need for employing trained laboratory and field personnel. This will necessitate funding for such projects that is commensurate with the methods used, namely, those of the natural sciences. It is hoped that funding agencies will recognize this trend sooner rather than later, and will adjust funding allocations appropriately.

12

Infrared Spectroscopy in Archaeology

The identification of materials and their characterization is, in many respects, the key to elucidating the microscopic archaeological record. Among all the methods used for this purpose in archaeology, infrared spectroscopy is one of the most useful. Infrared spectra are easy to obtain but can be difficult to interpret. The purpose of this chapter is to provide information on interpreting infrared spectra of archaeological materials as well as to review some of the more common applications. The latter are referred to as overviews in this chapter and throughout the book.

Infrared spectroscopy is a sensitive method for obtaining information on the molecular structures of crystalline and amorphous/disordered materials as well as organic materials. Infrared spectroscopy can thus be used both to identify materials and to characterize their states of atomic order and disorder. In these respects, infrared spectroscopy is similar to powder X-ray diffraction, although the latter cannot be used to identify and characterize amorphous and highly disordered materials. Amorphous and highly disordered materials are common in archaeology.

Infrared spectroscopy is based on the manner in which radiation interacts with material in the infrared range (4,000 to 250 centimeter^{-1} [cm^{-1}; wavenumbers, or the inverse of wavelength]). Some of this radiation is absorbed by the sample because it causes the chemical bonds of the sample to vibrate. The result is that less radiation reaches the detector at specific wavenumbers, and this is recorded as a series of peaks in the infrared absorbance spectrum. The wavenumber at which the peak maximum is located is characteristic of a chemical bond, or a network of chemical bonds. Thus the set of absorption peaks that make up the infrared spectrum of a specific material are characteristic of that material. Furthermore, variations in the shape of a peak, or shifts in the location of the peak maximum, may be indicative of disorder in the material or a small change in its composition. Except for artifacts due to grinding, and possibly due to hydration differences, every detail of the spectrum reflects some structural attribute of the material being analyzed. Infrared spectroscopy often requires the use of other complementary techniques to understand particular attributes of the spectrum, but once known, the information gained often proves to be invaluable. An excellent source of information on infrared spectroscopy and the infrared spectra of minerals is Farmer (1974).

Infrared spectrometers are relatively robust instruments that can be operated under field conditions. Sample preparation is simple, inexpensive, and takes only a few minutes. Infrared spectroscopy is thus a very convenient and informative analytical tool to operate on-site at an excavation (Weiner and Goldberg, 1990; Weiner et al., 1999a; Chapter 11) as well as in the laboratory. Standard infrared spectrometers cover the range from 4,000 to 400 cm^{-1}. This is perfectly adequate for most applications in archaeology. Some additional information is available in the far infrared part of the spectrum, from 400 to 250 cm^{-1}. The spectra in this chapter also include this part of the spectrum.

SAMPLE PREPARATION

There are a variety of methods for preparing samples or measuring powdered samples directly. These, however, often do not produce reproducible and undistorted spectra. In my experience, the potassium bromide (KBr) method is the most reliable and practical method for most archaeological applications. All the spectra presented in this chapter and posted on the Web in the infrared library of the Kimmel Center for Archaeological Science at the Weizmann Institute of Science (http://www.weizmann.ac.il/kimmel-arch/islib.html) were measured using KBr pellets.

KBr is used as a carrier for mounting the sample in the beam. KBr itself does not absorb in the infrared spectrum. Ultraclean KBr prepared especially for infrared spectroscopy should be used. The method for preparing a KBr pellet is as follows: tens of micrograms of a sample are lightly ground in an agate mortar and pestle, and only after light grinding is the sample mixed in the mortar with about 50 milligrams of ultrapure potassium bromide (KBr). The mixture is then transferred into a special dye and placed under pressure using either a hand-operated press or a hydraulic press. After a few minutes, a transparent disk is formed. This disk is placed in the instrument beam.

Water and water vapor absorb in the infrared region. Water vapor absorption produces myriad small, sharp peaks. Most water and water vapor absorption peaks are effectively removed because the sample spectrum is always compared to a background spectrum obtained in the absence of a sample. Water vapor peaks can be almost totally eliminated by flushing the instrument and sample chamber with dry air or dry nitrogen. The sample, however, should also be as dry as possible.

This is conveniently achieved by heating the mortar and pestle, the spatula, and the KBr under a 400-watt heat lamp for a few minutes prior to sample preparation. Note that even ultra-pure KBr does have some impurities that absorb in the infrared range. The spectrum of these impurities can be arithmetically subtracted from the sample spectrum if a pure KBr pellet is first analyzed.

POINTS TO NOTE

Sampling

Many archaeological samples are available in large quantities (grams) and are collected in vials. It is therefore imperative to remove and analyze a representative sample from the vial. In practice, this usually involves grinding and homogenizing a much larger amount of the sample than is needed for the analysis and then removing most of the ground sample. It is also important not to pour the sample into the mortar as this separates the particles into different sizes. A spatula should be used for transferring the sample from the vial to the mortar.

Grinding

Samples that are not ground well enough or are ground excessively can cause distortions and/or variations in the spectrum. Excessive grinding may release internal strain and/or cause deformation of the atomic structure of the sample. This has been demonstrated for bone mineral crystallinity (Surovell and Stiner, 2001) and for calcite (Chu et al., 2008). See the example for calcite in Overview 2.

Reproducibility

Reproducibility should be checked for individual operators by repeating the same measurement several times using a well-homogenized sample. In general, the spectra are very reproducible in terms of peak positions and shape. The relative peak heights and widths may be less reproducible, mainly due to grinding variability.

Quantification

The relative peak heights in the infrared spectra are roughly indicative of the relative quantities of the components of a mixture. In general, and without taking specific precautions, a precision of 10% to 20% can be expected. Infrared spectroscopy is therefore not a precise method for determining the relative proportions of different components in a sample. Improved quantification can be achieved by standardizing the grinding procedure using special mills (Surovell and Stiner, 2001), by internal calibration using another peak (Chu et al., 2008), and by preparing a set of standard mixtures for calibration. If all the components are crystalline, then powder X-ray diffraction is a preferred method for quantification.

Background subtraction

This should effectively remove the carbon dioxide peaks at 2,360, 2,342, and 668 cm^{-1} as well as the sharp water vapor peaks that are prominent around 1,600 cm^{-1}. If, however, a background is not taken fairly regularly, these peaks will appear and are artifacts. They usually do not complicate the interpretation of the spectrum.

Artifacts due to the quality of the KBr pellets

A KBr pellet that is partially opaque will result in a spectrum with a sloping background. The pellet can be improved by reapplying pressure and does not have to be remade. A corrugated spectrum (multiple small peaks), especially in the low wavenumber range, is usually due to the pellet being highly reflective. This causes internal reflections as the beam passes through the pellet. Buffing the surface can help, or the pellet needs to be remade.

INTERPRETATION OF THE SPECTRA: SOME GENERAL POINTERS

It takes just a few hours to learn how to produce a KBr pellet and run a spectrum. Interpreting the spectrum is the challenge. Unfortunately, the interpretation is not usually just a question of running the "search" program in the infrared software and believing the best fit between the sample spectrum and a standard. This often works well for pure compounds or simple mixtures, but even then, familiarity with the infrared spectra of the materials being analyzed is needed to make a reliable and more informative interpretation. This chapter is aimed at providing some information for interpreting the infrared spectra of materials common in archaeology. Each overview deals with a specific group of minerals, materials, or organic molecules.

Mineral, macromolecule, or small organic molecules?

Infrared spectra with broad peaks that are not well separated from each other are most likely produced by organic macromolecules such as proteins, polysaccharides, or resins. The presence of CH$_2$ and CH$_3$ peaks around 2,900 cm^{-1} will usually confirm this interpretation.

Spectra composed of broad peaks, usually above 900 cm^{-1}, and sharp peaks below 900 cm^{-1} are more likely to be derived from minerals. A broad, strong peak around 1,450 cm^{-1} indicates the presence of carbonate minerals, whereas a broad, strong peak around 1,000 cm^{-1} may be due to silicates and/or phosphates. Most silicates, however, also have a doublet just below 800 cm^{-1} and a single peak around 460 cm^{-1}. Thus the major mineral types can be readily differentiated.

Spectra composed of only sharp peaks are usually indicative of relatively small-sized organic compounds or polymers with identical repeating units. These are not often found in archaeological sites.

Mixtures of compounds

Almost all samples of sediments from an archaeological site are composed of mixtures of minerals, and occasionally, also macromolecules. The spectra are basically additive. This means that peaks from one compound are not hidden behind peaks from another compound, but rather, are overlaid. If two peaks absorb in the same region, they will overlap, and the smaller peak may be recognized only as a shoulder on the larger peak. Each component of the mixture must have its full complement of peaks before it can be positively identified. These principles are illustrated in Figure 12.1, using a sample of loess that contains the three common components of sediments in archaeological sites (clay, quartz, and calcite). The major peak of quartz (peak 4 in Figure 12.1) appears as a shoulder in the loess spectrum. This indicates that quartz is less abundant than clay. Note, too, that the peak maximum location of the shoulder (peak 10) in loess is midway between the locations of the same peak in illite and quartz. This often happens in mixtures, especially if the particular peak is relatively broad.

Shifting of peak maxima

One of the most difficult aspects of infrared spectrum interpretation is that in some classes of compounds, the peak maxima for a specific mineral do vary significantly, whereas in others, they do not. The variation is not due to irreproducibility of the measurement, but rather, to structural differences. For example, the calcite absorption peak at 712 cm^{-1} varies as a function of Mg content (Wang et al., 1997), but the peak at 875 cm^{-1} does not vary. The major absorption of quartz is almost invariably at or close to 1,084 cm^{-1}. The same peak in flint (chert), however, may be shifted up to 1,095 cm^{-1}, even though flint is also composed only of quartz (Figure 12.11 in Overview 7). Presumably, the shift is due, in part, to the fact that in flint, the crystals are very small and/or relatively disordered compared to quartz. Clays also have variable structures due to mixtures of clay types and variations in the ions that are bound to the clay surface. See Figure 12.14 in Overview 8 for an example of different spectra derived from what is thought to be the same basic clay type.

Variations in peak widths

When the same minerals are compared that differ either in the size of the particles or in the extent of the atomic order/disorder of these particles, or both, peak widths may vary (but peak maxima are the same). In some classes of minerals, such as the phosphates, these differences can be dramatic (see Overview 6). The phosphates formed in archaeological sediments are usually disordered and are composed of small crystals, compared to those derived from igneous rocks or other sources, where they were formed at elevated temperatures and pressures. One consequence is that pure standards obtained from mineralogical collections are often much more crystalline than the same mineral from an

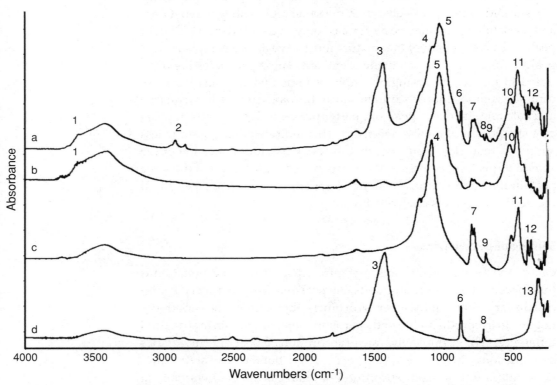

Figure 12.1 *a*, Infrared spectrum of loess from Houzhuang, China, together with the infrared spectra of the three major components of loess: *b*, clay (illite); *c*, quartz; and *d*, calcite. The contributions of each of the components can be identified in the loess spectrum. The absorbance intensities of the pure components are adjusted to their approximate intensities in the loess. The wavenumbers of the major peaks are as follows: 1, 3,618 and 3,433; 2, doublet at 2,924 and 2,853 (organic matter); 3, 1,436 (carbonate of calcite); 4, shoulder at 1,079, corresponding to the peak at 1,084 of quartz; 5, 1,031 for both loess and illite; 6, 875 (calcite); 7, doublet at 797 and 778 that is strong in quartz and weak in illite; 8, 712 (calcite); 9, 695 (quartz); 10, 519 for loess, 524 for illite, and 514 for quartz; 11, 469 present in almost all silicates; 12, 396 and 372 are two quartz peaks; 13, 314 (calcite).

archaeological site (Figure 12.10). Variations of this type are also common in calcites formed in different ways (Overview 2).

Variations in peak widths may also be induced by the grinding of the sample. Excessive grinding can cause lattice disorder and/or strain release, and this will result in a change in peak width. See the example for calcite in Overview 2.

Sharp peak at 1,384 wavenumber

This peak appears in many samples taken from existing sections that have not been freshened up. The peak is from soluble nitrate salts that precipitate due to evaporation of groundwater at the sediment surface. See Overview 14.

INFRARED MICROSCOPY

An optical microscope can be connected to certain infrared spectrometers. This so-called infrared microscope can be used to obtain infrared spectra from specific areas of a sample that can be viewed through the microscope. In this way, thin sections of embedded sediments, bones, ceramics, or any other archaeological materials can be analyzed both for texture (so-called micromorphology) and for composition of the components that make up the material. This could have wide application in archaeology.

There are numerous technical difficulties, but significant advances are being made. Berna and Goldberg (2008) have demonstrated that transmission spectra can be routinely obtained using regular slides prepared for micromorphology in the infrared region between 4,000 and 2,000 cm^{-1}. Information that can be obtained in this region includes the identification of clay mineral types and the effects of heating on clays and bone mineral. It can be predicted that infrared microscopy will have many more future applications in archaeology.

Available literature

There is no convenient source for obtaining information on interpreting infrared spectra relevant to archaeology – hence the reason for writing this chapter. For minerals in general, the book by Farmer (1974) is excellent, and for biological macromolecules, the book by Parker (1971) is most helpful.

Library of archaeologically relevant infrared spectra

To facilitate the identification of materials in archaeological sites using infrared spectroscopy, a library of spectra is available for downloading at the Web site of the Kimmel Center for Archeological Science at the Weizmann Institute (http://www.weizmann.ac.il/kimmel-arch/islib.html). Appendix B lists all the spectra available in the library as of the time of publication. This includes minerals and their chemical formulae as well as common rock types and various organic materials. Several spectra of synthetic glues and polymers that are commonly used for artifact conservation are also included, so that their presence may be identified as well. The library also includes most of the known biogenic minerals relevant to the field of biomineralization.

OVERVIEWS

Following are short overviews of 14 different topics in archaeology in which infrared spectroscopy can provide useful information.

1. Polymorphs of calcium carbonate

Problem. Calcium carbonate can exist in six different forms (polymorphs), each with its own unique atomic structure (Table 12.1). Identifying which polymorph of calcium carbonate is present in a sample can be important.

Background. Calcite is the most stable form of calcium carbonate and can be found in archaeological sites in the form of limestone rocks, wood ash, plaster, certain shells, various forms of cave deposits, cemented

Table 12.1. The known polymorphs of calcium carbonate in order of decreasing stability.

Name	Chemical formula	Relevance to archaeology
Calcite	$CaCO_3$	Very common (Chapter 4)
Aragonite	$CaCO_3$	Mainly in freshwater bivalve and gastropod shells (Chapter 6); high-temperature product (Chapter 7)
Vaterite	$CaCO_3$	Not known in archaeological sites
Monohydrocalcite	$CaCO_3 \cdot H_2O$	Formed in the intestines of some herbivores; found as spherulites in sediments (Shahack-Gross et al., 2003)
Hexahydrate	$CaCO_3 \cdot 6H_2O$	Not known in archaeological sites
Amorphous calcium carbonate	$CaCO_3 \cdot H_2O$ (stable) $CaCO_3$ (transient)	Not known in archaeological sites

sediments, dung spherulites, and probably other forms as well. Calcites formed by high temperatures can be differentiated from those formed at ambient temperatures by their $v_2:v_4$ ratios (Overview 2).

Aragonite is less stable than calcite. Aragonite is most commonly found in archaeological sites in mollusk shells. If the shell is still preserved as aragonite, this indicates that preservation conditions are relatively good and that the more stable calcite forms should also be well preserved (see Chapter 6). Aragonite can also form in boiling water (Lippmann, 1973). In fact, the white deposit that accumulates in kettles is aragonite. Thus the presence of aragonite in ancient vessels would be a good indication that water was boiled in the vessels. I have also noted small amounts of aragonite, together with calcite, in a deposit of sheep dung that was burned in historic times in Hayonim Cave, Israel. This, too, may have formed at high temperatures. Aragonite is the polymorph that precipitates out of evaporating seawater. Thus the presence of an aragonitic cement or aragonite in sediments could be indicative of a past marine environment (Milliman, 1974).

Monohydrocalcite was identified in the dung deposits of a caprine enclosure in a Maasai village in Kenya (Shahack-Gross et al., 2003). It was thought that the monohydrocalcite must have formed within the intestinal tracts of the animals. Many herbivores are known to produce spherulites composed of calcium carbonate, but their in vivo mineral form is not known (Canti, 1998, 2007).

Amorphous calcium carbonate is formed by earthworms and may therefore be a component of soils (Gago-Duport et al., 2008). Amorphous calcium carbonate, however, transforms rather easily into calcite.

The presence of any of the other polymorphs in an archaeological site, besides calcite and aragonite, would be quite exceptional. The hexahydrate is highly unstable and is unlikely ever to be found. The other three, and in particular, amorphous calcium carbonate (ACC), are proving to be more commonly formed by organisms than was previously realized (Lowenstam and Weiner, 1989; Addadi et al., 2003). With more awareness, the same might prove to be true in archaeology.

For more details on the different polymorphs of calcium carbonate, see the book by Lippmann (1973).

Infrared spectroscopy. All the polymorphs of calcium carbonate can be unequivocally identified using infrared spectroscopy (Figure 12.2). The presence of a peak between 1,400 and 1,450 cm^{-1} is almost always an indication that a carbonate phase is present, provided, of course, that it is accompanied by the other sharper peaks at lower wavenumbers. It is interesting to note that despite the fact that ACC does not diffract X-rays, the major peak (peak 2 in Figure 12.2) is split, implying that the local structural environment is ordered to some extent. In fact, this has been confirmed in both inorganic and biogenic ACC samples (Levi-Kalisman et al., 2001; Marxen et al., 2003).

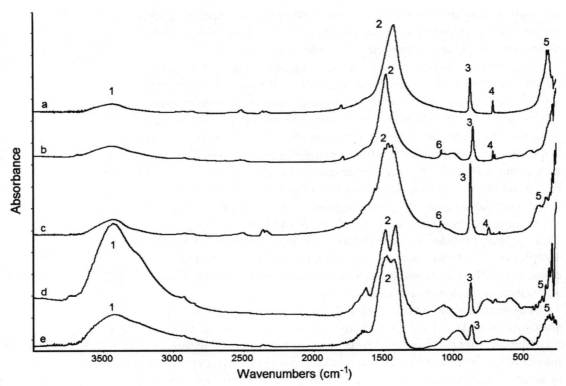

Figure 12.2
Infrared spectra of the polymorphs of calcium carbonate. The following are the locations in wavenumbers of the major absorption peaks for each polymorph. *a*, Calcite: 1, 3,400; 2, 1,421; 3, 875; 4, 712; 5, 326 and 314. *b*, Aragonite: 2, 1,476; 3, 857; 4, 712 and 700; 6, 1,084. *c*, Vaterite: 2, 1,464; 3, 875; 4, 744; 5, 383 and 339; 6, 1,087. *d*, Mono-hydrocalcite: 1, 3,400; 2, 1,483 and 1,410; 3, 874; 5, 363, 337, 313, and 292; 6, 1,087. *e*, Amorphous calcium carbonate: 1, 3,400; 2, 1,473 and 1,419; 3, 870; 5, 310.

2. Calcite disorder: Distinguishing between calcites formed by different processes

Problem. Calcite crystals can be formed by geogenic, biogenic, and pyrotechnological processes. Distinguishing among these different forms of calcite can contribute much to our understanding of the microscopic record.

Background. Calcite is an abundant and hence important constituent of the sediments of archaeological sites. Calcite, for example, is commonly found as finely dispersed crystals in archaeological sediments. These could be derived from loess, from the secondary deposition of calcite from saturated solutions of water percolating through the sediments, or from ash. A more complicated situation is when the calcitic cement that forms the matrix of a cemented sediment ("breccia") was originally ash calcite that dissolved and reprecipitated. Biogenic calcite may also be present in archaeological sites, not only in the form of shell remains and earthworm deposits (Canti, 1998, 2007), but also as the product of microbial activities, which, in certain environments, are responsible for the formation of travertine and various other calcitic cave deposits (Courty et al., 1989). Calcite in archaeological sites can thus be geogenic, biogenic, or pyrogenic in origin.

During studies of the formation of biogenic calcites (sea urchin larval spicule), it was noted that the ratio of the absorption peak at 875 cm⁻¹

(v_2 peak) to the peak at 712 cm^{-1} (v_4 peak) varies, depending on the stage of development of the spicule (Beniash et al., 1997). By correlation with X-ray diffraction reflections of the same spicule, it was demonstrated that this variation is related to the initial formation of the very unstable phase, amorphous calcium carbonate (ACC), which subsequently crystallizes into a single crystal of calcite. Theoretical calculations showed that the variation in the v_2:v_4 ratio is due to disorder of the atoms in the crystal lattice (Gueta et al., 2007). This indicated that the mature spicule does not reach its thermodynamically most stable state, where all the atoms are in their expected locations; rather, the disorder is "frozen in" to the mature crystal. It was subsequently noted that lime plaster and ash calcite have v_2:v_4 ratios that are different from those of geogenic calcite and are different from each other (Chu et al., 2008). This is assumed to reflect the fact that most ash calcite forms from the loss of carbon monoxide from calcium oxalate crystals (Brochier and Thinon, 2003), and that lime plaster calcite forms from the reaction between calcium oxide, water, and atmospheric carbon dioxide (Boynton, 1980). Thus the v_2:v_4 ratio reflects the manner in which the calcite formed – a memory effect.

Infrared spectroscopy. Figure 12.3 shows the infrared spectra of geogenic calcite and two examples of biogenic calcite. Three of the infrared absorption peaks (called v_3, v_2, and v_4) correspond to the asymmetric stretch, out-of-plane bending, and in-plane bending vibrations of the carbonate ions, respectively. Their peak maxima are located at 1,420, 875, and 712 cm^{-1}. The spectra in Figure 12.3 are normalized to the same v_3 peak heights. The v_2 peaks are very similar in height, whereas the heights and breadths of the v_4 peaks are quite different.

Figure 12.3
Infrared spectra of calcite from the test (shell) of, *a*, a sea urchin, *Paracentrotus lividus*; *b*, the shell of a brachiopod, *Laqueus californianus*; and *c*, geogenic sparry calcite. Note that the ratio of peak 2:peak 4 (v_2:v_4 ratio) of spectrum *a* is higher than that of spectrum *b*, and both are higher than the spectrum for geogenic sparry calcite.

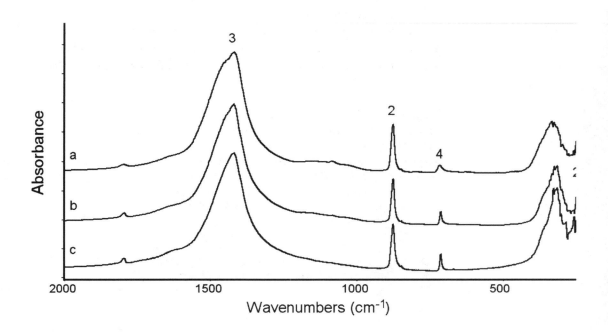

There are also differences in the peaks in the far-infrared region below 400 cm^{-1}. Using the ν_2:ν_4 ratios and following Beniash et al. (1997) and Gueta et al. (2007), it can be concluded that the sea urchin test calcite is more disordered than the brachiopod shell calcite, and the geogenic calcite crystal is the most ordered. It is interesting to note the broadening of the major peak in the far-infrared region of the disordered calcite compared to the more ordered calcites.

The manner in which the ν_2:ν_4 ratio is calculated is shown in Figure 12.4, based on Chu et al. (2008). Baselines are drawn from the lowest points on either side of the ν_2 and ν_4 peaks, even if the peaks are on the shoulders of other peaks (Figure 12.4a). Chu et al. (2008) noted that the ratio is influenced by the extent to which the sample is ground. As this also influences the width of the ν_3 peak, this parameter can be used to control for too little or too much grinding. Chu et al. (2008) proposed that the ratio should be calculated only from spectra where the full width at half maximum of the ν_3 peak is between 110 and 130 cm^{-1}. The analytical uncertainty in the measurement and calculation of the ν_2:ν_4 ratio is ±0.2.

3. The apatite family: Hydroxylapatite, carbonate hydroxylapatite, and carbonate fluorapatite

Problem. The apatite crystal can tolerate many substitutions, and each has its own atomic structure and, consequently, its own name (Table 12.2). The most common apatite mineral in archaeological contexts is carbonate hydroxylapatite. Others may also be found. As each of these minerals forms under different circumstances, they potentially have different types of embedded information. It is therefore important to differentiate between them.

Background. Because all biogenic apatite minerals (mainly in teeth and bones) as well as all authigenic apatite minerals in archaeological contexts are formed when exposed directly or indirectly to the

---

Table 12.2. List of the more common members of the apatite family of minerals, using the nomenclature of Ferraiolo (2008).

Carbonate hydroxylapatite	$Ca_5(PO_4,CO_3)_3(OH)$
Carbonate fluorapatite	$Ca_5(PO_4,CO_3)_3F$
Hydroxylapatite	$Ca_5(PO_4)_3(OH)$
Fluorapatite	$Ca_5(PO_4)_3F$
Chlorapatite	$Ca_5(PO_4)_3Cl$

Note: Note, too, that carbonate apatite is also known as dahllite (McConnell, 1952) and carbonate fluorapatite as francolite (Nriagu, 1984).

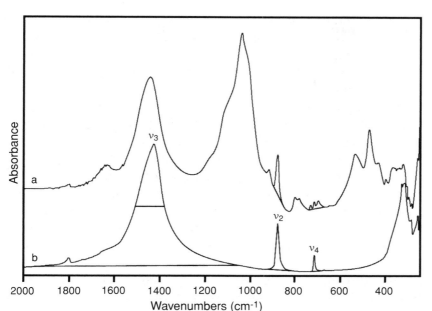

Figure 12.4
Infrared spectra of, *a*,
loess that contains calcite,
quartz, and clay and, *b*,
pure calcite. The base-
lines are drawn from the
lowest points on either
side of the v_2 and v_4
peaks (as shown), and
the full width at half
maximum of the v_3
peak is also shown in
spectrum b.

atmosphere, they all incorporate carbonate into their crystal structures.
Only geological apatites formed within the earth's crust, away from the
atmosphere, are true carbonate-free hydroxylapatites. They are therefore not likely to be found in archaeological sites, and if they are, they
could present an interesting provenience problem. Furthermore, both
the biogenic and geogenic carbonate hydroxylapatite minerals found
in archaeological sites are usually disordered and composed of small
crystals and thus produce X-ray diffraction patterns and infrared spectra with broad peaks. If, however, carbonate hydroxylapatite is heated
to around 600°C, the mineral recrystallizes, and the product is a well-
crystallized carbonate hydroxylapatite mineral (Shipman et al., 1984).
Its presence is a good indication that the mineral was heated. These
changes in crystal atomic order can also be monitored by infrared spectroscopy (Overview 4).

The carbonate component of carbonate hydroxylapatite can comprise up to about 9 weight percent of the mineral. This means that
about one in every five phosphates may be substituted for a carbonate
(Suetsugu and Tanaka, 1999). Carbonates can replace the hydroxyl
groups (A site) or the phosphates (B site) and are also in so-called
unstable locations (Rey et al., 1991). The latter may, in part, be on the
crystal surface. The amount of carbonate and its location can vary in
vivo and during diagenesis. Atomic order tends to improve during diagenesis, and the carbonate content tends to decrease (Trueman et al.,
2008). It is therefore of interest to monitor these changes to assess states
of preservation.

Fluoride is incorporated into the mineral phase of bones and teeth in small amounts during their formation, provided that fluoride is present in the drinking water. Some fish and sharks naturally produce teeth with high amounts of fluoride in their enameloid layer (Suga, 1984; Suga et al., 1991). As all biogenic apatites contain carbonate, the presence of large amounts of fluoride results in the formation of carbonate fluorapatite. Fluoridated apatite without carbonate (called fluorapatite) is almost never encountered in archaeological sites.

Fluoride can also be taken up into the crystal lattice and/or adsorbed onto crystal surfaces during diagenesis, provided that the local groundwater is rich in fluoride. The fluoride is thought to replace the hydroxyl group and/or to be associated somehow with the carbonate groups (Soudry and Nathan, 2001). This replacement reduces the asymmetry in the lattice and hence makes the mineral phase less soluble and more stable (Legeros, 1991). Fossil bones usually have either high fluoride contents or none at all, depending on fluoride availability. Few have intermediate contents (Newesely, 1989). Thus the presence of fluoride is a good indicator of bone diagenesis. Fluoride content is one of the first indicators of bone diagenesis to have been discovered.

The amount of fluoride in bone increases with age of the strata (Middleton, 1884). Oakley (1948) used this as a relative dating test. The presence of fluoride in some of the bones from Piltdown that Oakley and J. S. Weiner analyzed confirmed that this was a forgery (Weiner, 1955).

Infrared spectroscopy. Figure 12.5 shows the infrared spectra of hydroxylapatite, carbonate hydroxylapatite, and carbonate fluorapatite. The major carbonate absorption peaks are split at 1,451 and 1,414 cm^{-1}, and the minor peak at 875 cm^{-1} is usually asymmetric. These properties reflect the presence of carbonate in two different atomic sites (the so-called A and B carbonate sites; Rey et al., 1991). By deconvoluting the 875 cm^{-1} peak, the relative proportions of the carbonate molecules in these two sites can be determined (Sponheimer and Lee-Thorp, 1999). The absorption around 3,540 cm^{-1} is due to the presence of hydroxyl groups (Soudry and Nathan, 2001). This peak is usually not detectable in bone mineral, raising the question of whether bone mineral actually contains hydroxyl groups (Rey et al., 1995). The hydroxyl peak was not detectable in the spectra shown in Figure 12.5 (data not shown).

The infrared spectrum can also be used to semiquantitatively estimate the carbonate content (Lehr et al., 1968). This was also proposed by Featherstone et al. (1984) and was applied by Wright and Schwarcz (1996). Trueman et al. (2003), analyzed subrecent bones from Amboseli National Park, Kenya, and found that the method of Wright and Schwarcz (1996) overestimated the carbonate content, as the 1,415 cm^{-1} peak was superimposed on a peak of the organic matrix.

The uptake of fluoride into fossil bone has not been widely studied in bone diagenetic studies. The fluoride contents are rather small

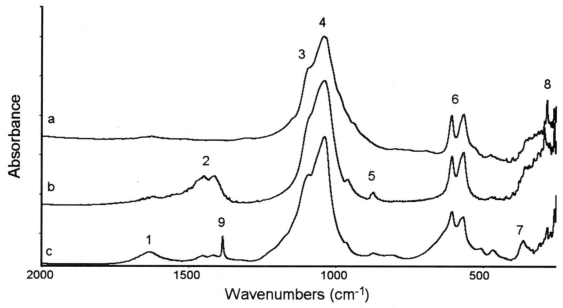

Absorbance

Wavenumbers (cm⁻¹)

and are more appropriately analyzed in fossil samples, including fossil bone, using a specific electrode (Dressler et al., 2002). Large amounts of fluoride result in the addition of two new infrared bands (around 3,643 and 3,544 cm⁻¹) and a shift in the hydroxyl absorption around 630 cm⁻¹ (Freund and Knobel, 1977). It has been proposed that the presence of the 1,096 cm⁻¹ peak in the infrared spectrum is indicative of the presence of fluoride in the lattice (Wright and Schwarcz, 1996), based on a study of sedimentary apatites (Shemesh, 1990). In the latter study, this was not explicitly claimed. In fact, I suspect that the 1,096 cm⁻¹ peak is not unique to fluoride, but rather, reflects more the increase in crystallinity that fluoride is in part responsible for.

I noted that in published spectra of synthetically produced carbonate fluorapatites (Shimoda et al., 1990) and sedimentary carbonate fluorapatites (Shemesh, 1990), the 603 cm⁻¹ peak is stronger than the peak at 567 cm⁻¹. This is not the case in carbonate hydroxylapatite, where the 603 cm⁻¹ peak is weaker than the 567 cm⁻¹ peak (Figure 12.5). This difference was confirmed by comparing the infrared spectrum of standard carbonate fluorapatite with a spectrum of carbonate hydroxylapatite (Geiger and Weiner, 1993).

Figure 12.5
Infrared spectra of three of the members of the apatite family: a, hydroxylapatite; b, carbonate hydroxylapatite (dahllite); c, carbonate fluorapatite (francolite). The absorption peaks are located at the following wavenumbers: 1, 1,633 (water); 2, carbonate doublet 1,451 and 1,414; 3, 1,092 (shoulder); 4, 1,043 in spectrum a, 1,040 in spectrum b, and 1,039 in spectrum c; 5, carbonate 872; 6, doublet at 604 and 565; 7, 361; 8, 280; 9, 1,384 is a contaminant, sodium nitrate. Note that in the doublet (labeled peak 6) in spectrum c, the peak at 604 centimeter⁻¹ (cm⁻¹) is stronger than the peak at 565 cm⁻¹ due to the presence of fluoride.

4. Crystallinity of bone, dentin, and enamel: The splitting factor

Problem. Bone and dentin crystals in vivo are extremely small and disordered at the atomic level. Thus, during diagenesis, they have a tendency to increase in size and to become more ordered, and hence more stable (Chapter 5). This combination of properties is referred to as *crystallinity*. Enamel crystals are much larger and more ordered than those in bone and dentin and hence, compared to bone and dentin crystals, are relatively stable over time. Enamel crystals do, however, also undergo diagenesis. Monitoring crystallinity provides information on the mineral preservation state.

Background. Mature bone and dentin crystals are plate shaped and have average dimensions of around $50 \times 25 \times 2$–4 nanometers (Lowenstam and Weiner, 1989). They thus have a huge surface area (around 240 square meters per gram; Weiner and Price, 1986). Being so thin, a relatively large number of atoms are close to or at the crystal surface and hence are disordered. Furthermore, the presence of carbonate causes even more disorder (Legeros and Legeros, 1984). The result is that bone and dentin crystals are relatively unstable and therefore more soluble than pure, highly crystalline, noncarbonated hydroxylapatite (Berna et al., 2003). The crystals of tooth enamel are also composed of carbonate hydroxylapatite, but they are much larger and more ordered than bone crystals. Human enamel crystals are around 70 nanometers wide and 25 nanometers thick, and their lengths may be more than 100 microns (Daculsi et al., 1984).

As bone and dentin crystals are inherently unstable, they have a tendency to dissolve and reprecipitate in a more stable form (sintering), even when the pH of the sediments is around or slightly above 7. Below pH 7, bone mineral will dissolve. The sintering process starts in vivo (Posner et al., 1965; Burnell et al., 1980) and continues postmortem. The rate at which this occurs is influenced by the availability of water and the ambient temperature. The state of the crystals in fossil bone and dentin thus varies considerably, depending on the conditions of preservation. A similar change can occur by exposure of a bone to heat (Shipman et al., 1984; Stiner et al., 1995). See Overview 5.

Crystal size variations can be monitored by direct observation of the crystals after dispersion using transmission electron microscopy (Robinson, 1952; Weiner and Price, 1986) or by high-resolution scanning electron microscopy (Wang et al., 2006). It is difficult to monitor atomic order independent of crystal size. X-ray diffraction line width broadening methods are widely used, but they reflect both crystal size and imperfections (i.e., crystallinity; Very and Baud, 1984). The sizes obtained are much smaller than those observed by electron microscopy and therefore probably mainly reflect the internal domain structure of the crystals. X-ray diffraction line width broadening has been used for the study of bone diagenesis (Person et al., 1995). Spectroscopic methods, such as Raman and infrared, are also unable to differentiate between crystal size and atomic order. The first use of infrared spectroscopy to analyze bone crystallinity was by Termine and Posner (1966). Crystallinity studies of modern enamel have been carried out (Aoba and Moreno, 1990), but studies of fossil enamel have not.

Infrared spectroscopy. The infrared spectra of modern tooth enamel and dentin are shown in Figure 12.6. The extents to which the two peaks at 604 and 565 cm^{-1} are separated are clearly different. The extent of splitting reflects the crystallinity of the mineral phase (Termine and Posner, 1966). In modern bone, the peaks are less well separated. This reflects more atomic disorder and/or smaller crystal size. The manner in which the extent of splitting is usually quantified in archaeological applications follows Weiner and Bar-Yosef (1990). This is also shown in Figure 12.6 inset. Termine and Posner (1966) initially used a different method more appropriate to the older generation of infrared spectrometers, which plotted transmittance on an exponential scale (to avoid the pen of the plotter reaching the edge of the paper).

The range of splitting factors measured for modern bone is between about 2.5 and 2.9 (Ziv and Weiner, 1994). Most fossil bones are in the range of 3 to 4 but can be as high as around 7 (Berna et al., 2003). Modern enamel has a splitting factor of about 4.1. The reproducibility

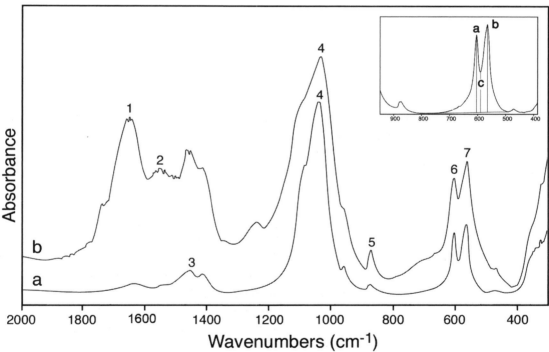

Figure 12.6 The infrared spectra of modern, *a*, tooth enamel and, *b*, dentin from a rhinoceros. The major differences are in the region from 1,700 to 1,300 cm^{-1}, due to the presence of large amounts of collagen in dentin. Collagen is not present in enamel. The 1% or so organic matter in enamel is not detected in the infrared spectrum. The two peaks around 1,450 cm^{-1} (labeled 3) and peak 5 are due to the carbonate present in the mineral phase. The remaining absorption peaks are due mainly to the phosphate. The absorption peaks are located at the following wavenumbers: 1, 1,651 (amide I); 2, 1,556 (amide II); 3, doublet at 1,456 and 1,415; 4, 1,034 in dentin and 1,040 in enamel; 5, 874; 6, 604; 7, 565. *Inset*, The splitting factor is calculated by drawing a baseline from the base of the first valley before the 565 cm^{-1} absorption peak (usually around 495 cm^{-1}) to the lowest point in the baseline after the 874 cm^{-1} peak. The heights of the, *a*, 604 and, *b*, 565 peaks and the height of, *c*, the valley between them are then measured. The splitting factor is the sum of the heights (*a* + *b*) divided by the height of the valley(*c*); Weiner and Bar-Yosef, 1990).

of the splitting factor measurement is ±0.2 if no special precautions are taken. By carefully controlling the grinding, Surovell and Stiner (2001) improved the reproducibility. Figure 12.7 shows examples of various bones from Israel with different splitting factors. It is interesting to note that spectrum e has a very high splitting factor and an extra peak at 633 cm^{-1}. This bone has either undergone severe diagenesis or was burned. As the bone had a grayish white color it was probably burned. (See Overview 5 for changes in the infrared spectra of burned bones.) Spectrum b has an extra shoulder on the 567 cm^{-1} peak, and the 605 cm^{-1} peak is almost the same height as the 567 cm^{-1} peak. This may imply that this bone contains some fluoride (Overview 4), in which case, the splitting factor would be erroneous. The reason is that it is not valid to compare carbonate fluorapatite splitting factors with splitting factors from carbonate hydroxylapatite.

The splitting factor is one of many parameters that can characterize the state of preservation of a fossil bone and dentin. Smith et al. (2005) showed that if the splitting factor is less than 3.0, the major non-collagenous protein of bone, osteocalcin, tends to be preserved (Smith et al., 2005). It has also been noted that if the splitting factor is greater than around 3.3, the bone contains very little organic matter (Trueman et al., 2008). There may be a cause and effect in this correlation (Trueman et al., 2008). Yizhaq et al. (2005) showed that at the site of Motza, near Jerusalem, Israel, most of the bones have slitting factors below 3, but collagen is either absent or present in very small amounts. The splitting factor of enamel is not expected to change much during diagenesis, but even small changes could provide information on enamel preservation.

5. Burned bones

Problem. Burned bones can have colors ranging from yellow, to black, to gray and white. Some black-colored bones may be stained black by oxides, or they may be both stained and burned (Shipman et al., 1984; Stiner et al., 1995). Identifying burned bones and the extent of burning can thus be difficult (Shahack-Gross et al., 1997).

Background. Burned bones are a common but usually minor component of the total assemblage of bones at a site. The presence of burned bones in relatively old prehistoric sites in close association with tools, such as at Zhoukoudian (Weiner et al., 1998) and Swartkrans (Brain and Sillen, 1988), has been cited as an indication of the use of fire by hominids. Bones may have been deliberately burned as a source of fuel or inadvertently burned by fires being made in their proximity. Human bones may have been cremated. There are thus diverse circumstances in which bones can be burned. Recognizing the approximate temperature at which the bones were burned and also quantifying the proportion of

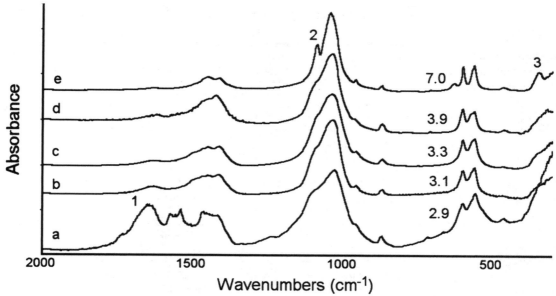

Figure 12.7
Infrared spectra of, b–e, fossil bones as well as, a, a fresh bone. The splitting factor values are shown for each spectrum. Note that the collagen peaks (1) in the fresh bone are absent in the fossil bones. In fossil bone spectrum d, the 605 cm^{-1} peak is higher than the 567 cm^{-1} peak. This indicates the presence of fluoride (see Overview 4). Spectrum e has several additional peaks located at the following wavenumbers: 2, 1,090; 3, 364. These peaks indicate that this bone mineral phase is highly crystalline.

burned bones in an assemblage can contribute toward an understanding of the circumstances of burning.

The circumstances in which bones are burned are often not clear. If the bones are burned in an open fire, where the temperatures are generally well above 650°C, they will be calcined and hence lose their mechanical integrity and disintegrate. They are thus unlikely to be preserved intact. For bones to be charred black or gray, they need to be either at the periphery of the open fire or in the sedimentary substrate beneath the fire. In the sites I have examined, I have not observed patches of burned bones that would indicate the latter circumstance. Burned bones always seem to be interspersed with the unburned bones. So burned bones may well form mainly at the periphery of the fire, in a manner similar to charcoal formation.

Infrared spectroscopy. Bones change color when they are burned, mainly due to the extent of charring of the organic matter. Stiner et al. (1995) introduced a color code to visually assess burning (Table 12.3). The colors range from a light brown to dark black, and then white. The white color corresponds approximately to a temperature of about 650°C, when all organic matter is oxidized (referred to as calcined bones). The elevated temperatures also affect the extent of atomic order of the crystals and their sizes and destroy the organic matrix. There is thus a correlation between the color changes in the bone and their infrared spectra (Figure 12.8; Table 12.3; Shipman et al., 1984; Stiner et al., 1995). Following are the major changes that can be recognized in the infrared spectra as a function of the extent of burning (Figure 12.8): by burn code 2, the organic matrix peaks (mainly the amide I of collagen [peak 1] and

Table 12.3. Changes in the infrared spectra of burned bones in relation to color changes.

Burn code	Bone color code	Matrix peaks	Key mineral peaks (cm^{-1})	Splitting factor	Carbonate content
0	Cream tan (not burned)	Prominent	1,033, 1,090 shoulder	2.8	High
1	Slightly burned	Prominent CH_3, CH_2 reduced	1,032, 1,090 shoulder	2.9	High
2	Lightly burned	Absent	1,042, 1,090 shoulder	3.3	Intermediate
3	Fully carbonized (black)	Absent	1,036, 1,090 shoulder	3.3	Intermediate
4–5	More black than white, or vice versa	Absent	1,045, 1,090 small peak	4.2	Low
6	White	Absent	1,451, 1,090 prominent, 631 prominent	6.4	Absent

Note: Color code follows Stiner et al. (1995).

associated peaks) are lost; the carbonate peaks (doublet 2 and peak 5) are totally absent in calcined bone (burn code 6); the major phosphate absorption peak (4) shifts gradually from 1,033 cm^{-1} for unburned bone to 1,048 cm^{-1} for calcined bone; the extent of splitting of the doublet (peak 7) increases with increasing exposure to temperature; and at very high temperatures, peak 6 becomes prominent. The presence of this peak is probably the most reliable indicator of calcined bone. Examples of infrared spectra of burned bones from a prehistoric cave are given in Schiegl et al. (2003).

The major problem with using only infrared spectroscopy to identify burned bones is that many of the changes that occur almost instantaneously as a result of exposure to high temperatures also occur over a long period of time at ambient temperatures due to diagenesis. Perhaps the only change that is indicative of exposure to high temperatures is the presence of a well-defined peak at 631 cm^{-1} (peak 6) in calcined bone. Note that a small peak at this wavenumber is also present in severely altered bone (Figure 12.7, spectrum e). Thus the identification of burned bone should be based on color as well as infrared spectroscopy. Color can sometimes be misleading as bones can have a black color due to the presence of oxide stains. This is usually strongest on or close to the bone surface. Infrared spectroscopy can be used to differentiate between

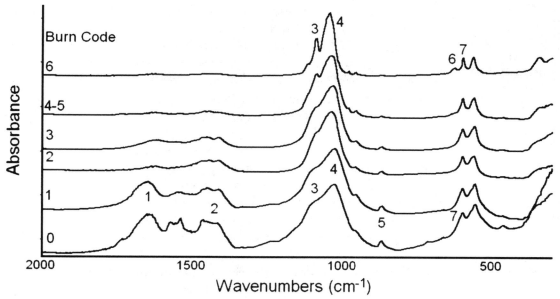

Figure 12.8
Infrared spectra of modern goat bone burned to different extents. These are the same specimens analyzed by Stiner et al. (1995), and the burn codes (numbers on left-hand side) follow Stiner et al.'s definition. Burn code 0 is unburned, and 6 is calcined. The absorption peaks are located at the following wavenumbers: 1, 1,650; 2, doublet at 1,458 and 1,419; 3, 1,091; 4, 1,033 for burn code 0 and 1,048 for burn code 6; 5, 874; 6, 631; 7, doublet at 603 and 569.

bones that are black due to burning and those that are black due to natural oxide staining, or both (Shahack-Gross et al., 1997). This is based mainly on the presence of a strong, broad peak at around 535 cm^{-1}, attributed to the presence of oxides.

6. Authigenic phosphate minerals

Problem. Phosphate minerals are relatively insoluble and hence tend to be preserved in the archaeological record. Authigenic phosphate minerals are a valuable source of information for reconstructing the paleochemistry of the site, and for indirectly reconstructing certain activity areas within a site. Phosphate minerals are often highly disordered and hence difficult to identify.

Background. Organic matter almost always contains phosphate (Chapter 8). Organic matter can accumulate in large amounts in animal enclosures, storerooms, sewers, garbage dumps, and fuel stores. In cave sites, bat and bird guano accumulates when the cave is not occupied by humans. In general, guano is particularly rich in phosphate (Hutchinson, 1950). Microbial breakdown of organic matter releases the phosphate and also releases acid, which lowers the pH (Chapter 3). The acid readily reacts with the less stable minerals and causes their partial or complete dissolution. The phosphate reacts with the released cations, especially calcium, to form authigenic phosphate minerals. The mineral that forms is a direct function of the cations available and the local chemical environment (defined as a stability field).

Thus the presence of a specific authigenic phosphate mineral is indicative of the paleochemical environment and can therefore be used to reconstruct sediment paleo-pH or paleophosphate concentrations. This in turn provides important information for assessing the completeness of the archaeological record (Karkanas et al., 2000; Chapter 3). This sequence of events can occur within tens of years (Shahack-Gross et al., 2004) and is thus "instantaneous" in terms of most archaeological applications.

Over the past 50 or so years, phosphate concentrations in sediments have been widely used for mapping activity areas in archaeological sites (Herron, 2001). This follows the same mode of phosphate production as described previously and hence essentially tracks variations in past organic matter concentrations (Chapter 8). Some of this phosphate may be present in the form of authigenic minerals and some may still be bound to organic matter.

Infrared spectroscopy. The common authigenic phosphate minerals formed in sediments can be identified using infrared spectroscopy (Figure 12.9). In general, the first mineral to form as the pH drops is carbonate hydroxylapatite (Chapter 4). This mineral is by far the most common authigenic phosphate mineral in archaeological environments. If the pH drops below 7, the carbonate hydroxylapatite dissolves, and

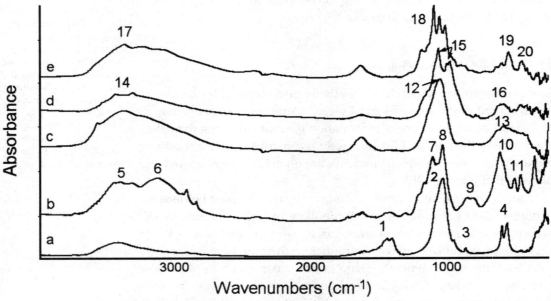

Figure 12.9 Infrared spectra of the more common authigenic minerals formed in cave sediments, presented in order of decreasing solubility. *a*, Carbonate hydroxylapatite. The wavenumbers of the characteristic absorption peaks are as follows: 1, 1,450 and 1,414; 2, 1,040; 3, 872; 4, 604 and 565. *b*, Crandallite. The wavenumbers of the characteristic absorption peaks are as follows: 5, 3,412; 6, 3,138; 7, 1,113; 8, 1,040; 9, 859 and 817; 10, 618; 11, 511 and 467. *c*, Montgomeryite (disordered). The wavenumbers of the characteristic absorption peaks are as follows: 12, 1,058; 13, 595. *d*, Leucophosphite. The wavenumbers of the characteristic absorption peaks are as follows: 14, 3,450 and 3,323; 15, 1,070 and 986; 16, 614 and 592. *e*, Taranakite. The wavenumbers of the characteristic absorption peaks are as follows: 17, 3,380 and 3,270; 18, 1,102, 1,062, and 1,020; 19, 555; 20, 456.

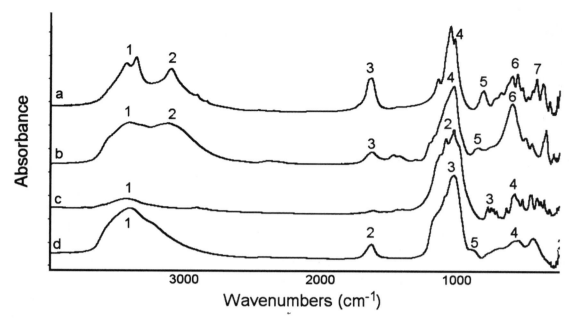

Figure 12.10 Comparison of infrared spectra of crystalline and disordered phosphate minerals. The disordered polymorphs clearly have much broader peaks: *a*, highly crystalline variscite sample from Lucin, Utah; *b*, disordered variscite nodule from Kebara Cave, Israel; *c*, highly crystalline montgomeryite from Castor, South Dakota; *d*, partially crystalline montgomeryite from Kebara Cave, Israel. The wavenumbers of the characteristic absorption peaks are as follows: for crystalline variscite, 1, 3,446 and 3,373; 2, 3,117; 3, 1,653; 4, 1,065 and 1,032; 5, 822; 6, 609 and 572; 7, 431; for disordered variscite, 1, 3,430; 2, 3,140; 3, 1,640; 4, 1,039; 5, 859; 6, 610; for crystalline montgomeryite, 1, 3,435; 2, 1,094 and 1,037; 3, 788, 762, 744, and 724; 4, 590; for disordered montgomeryite, 1, 3,413; 2, 1,643; 3, 1,036; 4, 590 to 562; 5, shoulder around 906. This flat shoulder is indicative of the presence of some leucophosphite.

at low phosphate concentrations, crandallite forms, or at high phosphate concentrations, montgomeryite forms. With a further drop in pH, and depending on available cations, minerals such as leucophosphite, variscite, or taranakite form.

A major difficulty in identifying authigenic phosphate minerals is that the crystallinity of many of these minerals (the combination of crystal size and atomic order) in archaeological environments is low, and hence the infrared spectra have broad absorptions. In fact, because of the low crystallinity, many of these minerals may not be detected at all by X-ray diffraction. Figure 12.10 compares the spectra of poorly crystalline variscite and montgomeryite from Kebara Cave, Israel, with their highly crystalline counterparts.

7. Silicon dioxide polymorphs: Quartz, flint (chert), silica (opal), and other polymorphs

Problem. The family of silicon dioxide polymorphs are among the most common and important minerals found in archaeological sites. The silicon dioxide polymorphs form under diverse circumstances (geogenic, biogenic, and pyrogenic) and can thus provide valuable information on the archaeological record.

Background. The most common members of this family in archaeological contexts are quartz, flint, and opal (Chapter 4).

Quartz is one of the most common and stable minerals in sediments in general. It is therefore often a major component of archaeological sites as well. Pure quartz is also a source material for the production of glass (Henderson, 2001).

Flint (also called chert) is another important form of quartz in many archaeological sites. This rock type is composed of fine-grained quartz crystals (often referred to as *cryptocrystalline quartz or microcrystalline quartz*). The mode of formation of flint is still not well understood, but flints formed during the last half billion years or so (Phanerozoic) are generally thought to have been derived from biogenic silica (mainly diatoms or radiolaria) that has recrystallized under elevated temperatures and pressures (Knauth, 1994).

Silica (also called opal) is another major component of many archaeological sites. Silica is mainly present in the form of phytoliths: mineral bodies formed by many plants (Chapter 6). In archaeological sites where pools of freshwater or wet soil existed, biogenic silica produced by diatoms may also be found. Diatoms are photosynthetic single-celled organisms (Protoctista) that are abundant in the oceans but also live in brackish and freshwater bodies (Chapter 6). Silica can also form as an authigenic mineral in certain sediments. Partially crystallized authigenic silica can form over long periods of time when the silica is buried (Knauth, 1994). This type of silica is known as opal-A, and if it is more crystalline, it is called opal-CT (Kastner et al., 1977).

Quartz undergoes a series of transformations at high temperatures. The polymorphs formed can be identified by X-ray diffraction. In the absence of fluxes, the stable form of quartz, namely, α-quartz, converts to β-quartz at 573°C. The latter converts to tridymite around 870°C, and at temperatures above about 1,250°C, cristobolite forms (Deer et al., 1992). As fluxes can change these transformation temperatures, the presence of a particular high-temperature polymorph can only be used as a rough indication of the temperature of formation of the polymorph (Chapter 7).

Siliceous aggregates are formed mainly in the bark of many trees and, to a lesser extent, in the wood itself. These are aggregates composed of crystalline soil minerals embedded in a biogenic matrix of silica. Unlike the silica of phytoliths, which is almost pure silicon, oxygen, and hydrogen, the matrix of the siliceous aggregates contains many other cations. In fact, in the ones analyzed, silicon only constitutes about 50% of the cation content (Schiegl et al., 1994). For more details, see Chapter 7.

Infrared spectroscopy. Figure 12.11 shows the infrared spectra of common forms of silicon dioxide and a mixed crystalline and amorphous material from wood ash (siliceous aggregates).

The peaks that characterize quartz are the prominent small peak 2 at 1,171 cm^{-1}, the location of the major peak 3 at 1,084 cm^{-1}, the small peak 5 at 695 cm^{-1}, and the two peaks 8 in the far-infrared region. Quartz is often associated with clays. Quartz can be identified by the presence of peaks 5 and 8. The main clay peak is usually around 1,035 cm^{-1}. Both have the doublet (4) and peak 7.

As flint is microcrystalline quartz, all the quartz peaks are present in flint, except that the flint quartz peaks tend to be broader because of the very small size of the crystals. Furthermore, the main peak is shifted to higher wavenumbers, sometimes even as high as around 1,095 cm^{-1}. As this shift is in the direction of the main absorption peak of opal, I assume that the shift reflects the presence of more atomic disorder compared to more crystalline quartz.

The amorphous nature of silica is readily apparent in the infrared spectrum from the broad nature of the peaks and the absence of all the peaks that are characteristic of quartz. Furthermore, the main peak (3) is located above 1,100 cm^{-1}, and the doublet (4) is not split. In many silica samples, there is a prominent shoulder between 900 and 1,000 cm^{-1} or so due to the presence of hydroxyl groups. The extent of hydration can vary even among opals. For example, a comparison of geologically produced opal and plant-produced opal (phytoliths) shows that the biogenic opal has more hydroxyl groups and water molecules (absorptions at 3,440, 1,633, and 960 cm^{-1}; Figure 12.12) than the geological opal. The numbers of hydroxyl groups can be quantified using the infrared spectrum (Schmidt et al., 2001).

Figure 12.11
Infrared spectra of various polymorphs of silicon dioxide and the composite siliceous aggregate phase from wood: *a*, siliceous aggregates; *b*, silica (opal); *c*, flint (chert); *d*, quartz. The absorption peaks are located at the following wavenumbers: 1, 1,630 (absent in c and d); 2, 1,145; 3, 1,084 for quartz, 1,087 and higher for flint, 1,102 for silica, and 1,093 for siliceous aggregates; 4, doublet at 798 and 779 for quartz, flint, and siliceous aggregates, and a single broad peak for silica at 792 to 800; 5, 695; 6, 514 (absent in b); 7, 461; 8, 396 and 372.

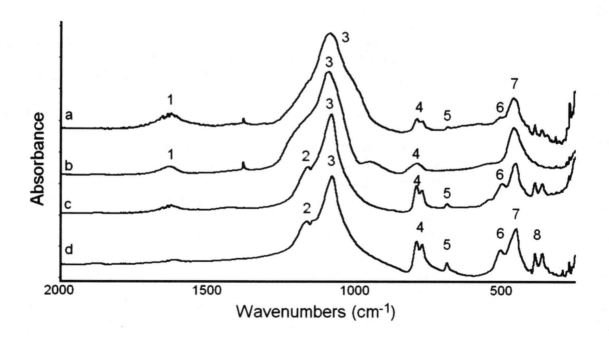

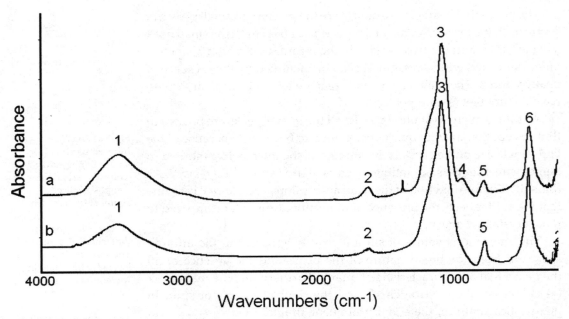

Figure 12.12 The infrared spectra of, *a*, plant biogenic silica (phytoliths from *Triticum aestivum* inflorescence after removal of the associated external organic matter by oxidants) and, *b*, precious opal formed geologically. Note the presence of stronger water absorption peaks (peaks 1 and 2) in phytoliths as compared to precious opal, and that the phytoliths have a prominent peak due mainly to hydroxyl groups (peak 4) that is very weak in precious opal. The phytolith peaks are slightly broader than those of precious opal, indicating more disorder in general. The absorption peaks are located at the following wavenumbers: 1, 3,436; 2, 1,632; 3, 1,102 for precious opal and 1,098 for phytoliths (these values vary considerably among different forms of opal); 4, 960; 5, 792 for precious opal and 800 for phytoliths; 6, 473. Note the small sharp peak in spectrum a at 1,384 cm^{-1} is due to the presence of contaminating sodium nitrate.

The presence of small amounts of quartz in the siliceous aggregates spectrum can be identified by peaks 4, 7, and 8; however, the major mineral phase has broad peaks characteristic of silica, with the major peak 3 located anywhere between 1,087 and 1,095 cm^{-1}. This spectrum can easily be confused with the spectrum of opal-CT, the partially crystalline form of silica. Examination of the material in a petrographic microscope, however, clearly differentiates between siliceous aggregates and opal-CT (Schiegl et al., 1994; Chapter 7).

Note that the crystallinity of all these polymorphs can vary significantly. This can be quantified using the small peak at 1,145 cm^{-1} (Figure 12.11, peak 2) and measuring its intensity (Shoval et al., 1991).

Two forms of silica are produced at high temperatures: cristobolite and tridymite. These can both be identified by infrared spectroscopy and can be differentiated from quartz (Figure 12.13).

8. Clays

Problem. Clays are almost ubiquitous in archaeological sites. They often constitute the major component of the sediments deposited naturally or

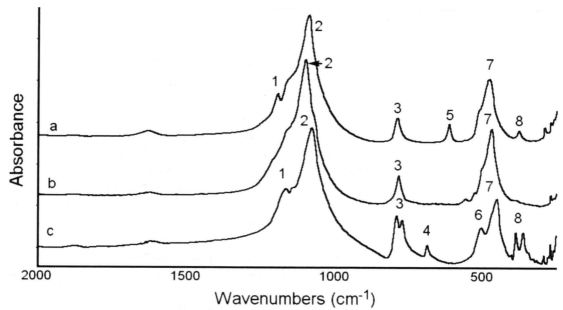

Figure 12.13
Infrared spectra of the high-temperature polymorphs, *a*, cristobolite and, *b*, tridymite, and the low-temperature polymorph, *c*, α-quartz. The absorption peaks are located at the following wavenumbers: 1, 1,198 for cristobolite, a small shoulder for tridymite, and 1,171 for quartz; 2, 1,094 for cristobolite, 1,105 for tridymite, and 1,084 for quartz; 3, 796 for cristobolite, 791 for tridymite, and a doublet at 798 and 779 for quartz; 4, 695 (unique to quartz); 5, 621 (unique to cristobolite); 6, 514; 7, 487 for cristobolite, 480 for tridymite, and 461 for quartz; 8, 386 for cristobolite and 396 and 372 for quartz.

were deliberately brought to the site. Clays are the major raw material of ceramics and mud bricks. There is therefore much to be learned from identifying the types of clays present, regarding their provenience, possible selection of clays for specific purposes, and whether they are altered in some way. The identification of clay types is challenging.

Background. The term *clay* refers to a family of hydrous silicate minerals. Each member of the family has its own unique structure. Thus each clay type is a mineral in its own right and can be identified as such (Chapter 4). Identification is, however, complicated. Different clay minerals are often intimately mixed, the crystallite sizes are very small, and clays tend to readily take up additional ions and organic molecules into their structure. Furthermore, a significant proportion of the clay minerals only have short-range atomic order (i.e., they are highly disordered at the atomic level and are therefore referred to as "amorphous" clays, also known as imogolite and allophone; Wada, 1989). For more information, see Chapter 8.

The clay family of minerals contains three groups that are common in archaeological sites: the kaolinite group, the illite group, and the smectite group. Kaolinite and illite are usually the most common clay minerals in their groups, and montmorillonite is often the most common clay mineral in the smectite group. If the clay sample being analyzed contains only one clay mineral, then it can be relatively easily identified. Often, however, several different clay minerals are mixed together. The most widely used technique for identifying crystalline clays is powder X-ray diffraction. Infrared spectroscopy is also able to identify crystalline clay types as well as those that are amorphous to X-rays.

When mixtures are present, identification using either method is difficult.

Infrared spectroscopy. Figure 12.14 shows the infrared spectra of kaolinite, illite, and montmorillonite. These can be distinguished in their pure forms. In reality, it is difficult to uniquely identify clay types based only on infrared spectroscopy as many clay-rich sediments are composed of several different clay minerals. The infrared spectra can also vary significantly, depending on the ions present within the lattice, and these do vary between localities. Figure 12.15 shows infrared spectra of a series of montmorillonites with different associated ions.

The key region for differentiating between different clay types is around 3,500 cm^{-1}. Kaolinite has hydroxyl peaks at 3,695, 3,666, 3,645, and 3,621 cm^{-1}. Al-rich smectites have a hydroxyl absorption at 3,616 cm^{-1}, and Fe-rich smectites have a hydroxyl absorption at 3,554 cm^{-1} (reviewed by Soudry and Nathan, 2001).

Clays can also undergo significant structural changes during diagenesis as a result of interactions with, for example, phosphate ions (Nriagu, 1976). The clays tend to lose their long-range atomic order.

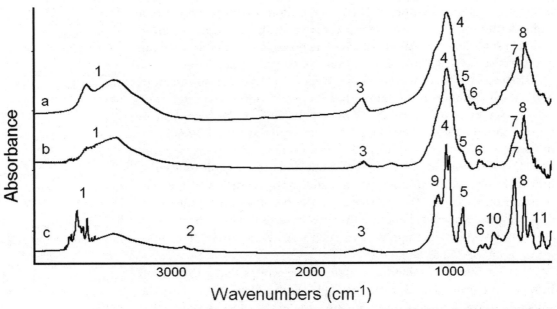

Figure 12.14 Infrared spectra of, *a*, montmorillonite, *b*, illite, and, *c*, kaolinite. Kaolinite is easily differentiated from the other two clay types. It is more difficult to differentiate between illite and montmorillonite based only on infrared spectra. The location of peak 7 is helpful in this respect. Many clays are composed of mixed clay types, and the spectra can vary, depending on the counterions (Figure 12.15). These mixtures further complicate identification. Note that the doublet (peaks 2) and some other minor peaks in kaolinite are probably due to adsorbed organic matter. The absorption peaks are located at the following wavenumbers: 1, the two peaks in montmorillonite are located at 3,625 and 3,427, and in illite at 3,735 and 3,623; the major peaks in kaolinite are at 3,735, 3,694, and 3,619; 2, 2,924 and 2,853; 3, 1,630; 4, 1,030 for montmorillonite and illite, and a doublet at 1,033 and 1,011 for kaolinite; 5, 915; 6, doublet at 798 and 778; 7, 517 for montmorillonite, 526 for illite, and 541 for kaolinite; 8, 464 to 472. Kaolinite has additional peaks at the following: 9, 1,094; 10, 693; 11, 432 and 347.

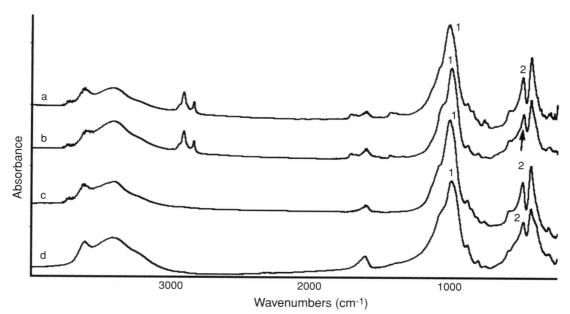

Absorbance

Wavenumbers (cm⁻¹)

Figure 12.15
Montmorillonites from different sources and with different associated ions: *a*, sodium montmorillonite; *b*, sodium montmorillonite; *c*, calcium montmorillonite; and *d*, montmorillonite with unknown counterions. The spectra are basically the same, except mainly for the major peak 1, which is located at 1,044 in spectrum a, 1,048 in spectrum b, 1,031 in spectrum c, and 1,029 in spectrum d. Peak 2 also varies from 525 in spectra a and b to 519 in spectrum c and 517 in spectrum d. Note the presence of the two small peaks around 2,900 cm⁻¹ in spectra a and b. These are due to the presence of associated organic matter.

This was observed in the lower strata of Hayonim Cave, Israel (Weiner et al., 2002). In Hayonim Cave, this loss of structure is accompanied by the formation of authigenic silica that shows some indications of being slightly ordered (cf. opal-CT). Figure 12.16 shows infrared spectra of transformed clay, the associated transformed opal, and, for comparison, a spectrum of normal clay from nearby strata. It is interesting to note that many of the changes in the spectra of these clays are similar to those observed in clays that are heated (see Overview 9).

9. Clay exposed to elevated temperatures

Problem. When fires are made or occur on clay containing sediment substrates, or when clays are exposed to elevated temperatures during various high-temperature pyrotechnological processes such as ceramic production, the clay structure is altered and becomes more disordered (Mendelovici, 1997; Chapter 7). Identifying these changes and assessing the approximate temperatures at which they took place can contribute significantly to our understanding of human pyrotechnological activities at a site.

Background. Fire has been used in a controlled manner for at least 400,000 years, and possibly much longer (Brain and Sillen, 1988; Goren-Inbar et al., 2004). In the last 15,000 years or so, fire has also been used to alter natural materials to produce synthetic materials, such as plaster, ceramics, mortar, metals, and glass, that have advantageous properties (Valla et al., 2007; Boaretto et al., 2009c). Thus, in many

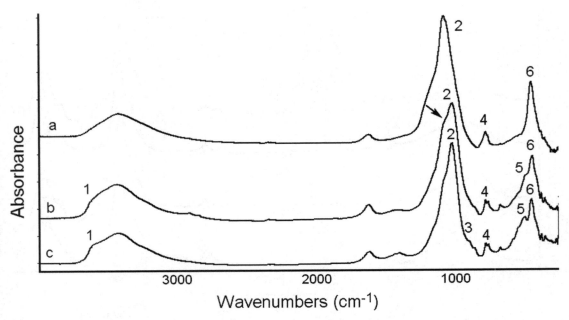

Figure 12.16 Infrared spectra of sediments from the diagenetically altered Layer F in Hayonim Cave, Israel: *a*, opal becoming somewhat crystalline, as inferred from the relatively sharp and asymmetric peak 4; *b*, transforming clay; note that peak 5 is only a shoulder, whereas in normal clay, *c*, peak 5 is prominent. Note, too, the shoulder at around 1,090 cm^{-1} (arrow), indicates the presence of associated silica. *c*, Normal clay (mainly montmorillonite) from an associated younger layer. Note that the peak 1 shoulder in normal clay is more prominent than in transforming clay, and it is absent in silica. The absorption peaks are located at the following wavenumbers: 1, 3,620; 2, 1,097 for transforming opal and 1,036 for transforming and normal clay; 3, shoulder at 915 is more prominent in normal clay; 4, the doublet at 798 and 779, present in normal and transforming clay, is a single asymmetric peak in opal centered at 798; 5, 518; 6, 468.

archaeological sites, both in prehistory and in later periods, sediments have been exposed to elevated temperatures in a variety of circumstances that relate to human activities.

Even though natural fires easily reach temperatures of up to 900°C, the temperatures of the sediments in the upper few centimeters beneath the fire are usually less than 500°C, and the sediments often do not change color (Bellemo and Harris, 1990). It is therefore not easy to recognize that the sediments were exposed to elevated temperatures. If such heat-altered sediments could be identified, this would provide another means of addressing the challenging issue of whether a fire in a prehistoric archaeological site was produced deliberately, by determining whether the altered sediments are localized beneath the area where the fire was located. It would also enable the identification of many pyrotechnological activities that do not result in the production of associated artifacts such as cooking on open fires.

When conditions for controlling the fire are such that the temperature rises above 1,000°C (usually indicating use of ovens, kilns, and/or bellows), the clay minerals alter their structure more radically, and a glassy phase is produced (Ramaswamy and Kamalakkannan, 1995; Bray

Table 12.4. Summary of the major changes that take place on heating of montmorillonite for 4 hours.

Temperature (°C)	Peak 2 (cm^{-1})	Peak 1	Peak 3	Peak 5
1,100	1,085	Absent	Shoulder (broad)	Absent
1,000	1,086 (broad)	Absent	Shoulder (broad)	Absent
900	1,080 (broad)	Absent	Shoulder (broad)	Absent
800	1,078 (broad)	Absent	Shoulder (broad)	Absent
700	1,045	Absent	Absent	Absent
600	1,046	Shoulder	Absent	Absent
500	1,049	Present	Shoulder	Present
400	1,036	Present	Present (weak)	Present
300	1,029	Present	Present	Present
Unheated	1,029	Present	Present	Present

Note: Data are from Berna et al. (2007). The peak numbers refer to the peaks in Figure 12.17.

and Redfern, 1999). It would be most helpful to be able to differentiate such high-temperature pyrotechnologies from those involving open fires.

Infrared spectroscopy. Infrared spectra of clays exposed to elevated temperatures change as a function of clay type, temperature, and duration of exposure (Farmer, 1974; Shoval, 1993; Mendelovici, 1997). The presence of fluxes, such as calcite, in the sediments may also influence the manner in which the clays alter (Chapter 7). To reconstruct the approximate temperature–exposure time combination, it is necessary to calibrate the local sediments by heating them in an oven to various temperatures and for different periods of time. The resultant calibration spectra can then be used to reconstruct past exposure temperatures for local clay mixtures of an archaeological site.

The major changes in the spectra of montmorillonite (Figure 12.17) are summarized in Table 12.4. The first identifiable change occurs when peak 2 shifts from 1,029 to 1,036 cm^{-1} at 400°C. Peak 2 shifts again to 1,049 cm^{-1} at 500°C. At 600°C, peaks 1, 3, and 5 disappear. At 800°C, peak 2 shifts to 1,078 cm^{-1}, and peak 3 broadens and develops a shoulder. At 1,000°C, peak 2 shifts again to 1,086 cm^{-1}. Thus, for a pure montmorillonite sample, the observed changes in the infrared spectra can differentiate between exposed temperatures at intervals of 100° to 200°C. The changes vary with different clay types (Berna et al., 2007), and in the presence of other minerals, such as quartz, it is not always possible to identify all the changes observed with pure clay.

Note, however, that changes in clay structure may also occur due to reactions with phosphate (Nriagu, 1976) and/or acid solutions (Madejova, 2003), and the resulting infrared spectra have features similar to clays exposed to high temperatures (Berna et al., 2007). Thus, when interpreting such spectra, one needs to take into account the context and associated minerals and artifacts.

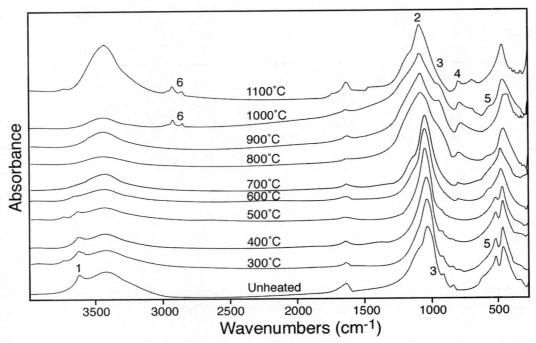

Figure 12.17
Infrared spectra of the
clay montmorillonite
(from Otay, California)
unheated and heated to
different temperatures
for 4 hours in an oven
(samples from Berna
et al., 2007, reanalyzed).
The changes as a function
of temperature are sum-
marized in Table 12.4.
The major peak maxima
are located at the fol-
lowing wavenumbers:
1, 3,625; 2, from 1,029 to
1,086; 3, 913, and at high
temperatures, a broad
shoulder around 940;
4, 779; 5, 517. Note that
the samples heated to
1,000°C and 1,100°C were
contaminated with some
organic matter, as evi-
denced by the doublet
at 2,924 and 2,853 cm^{-1}
(peak 6).

10. Calcium oxalates

Problem. Calcium oxalates are produced in huge amounts by plants and lichens but appear to be almost entirely absent in the archaeological record. Is this correct, and if it is, what is the reason for this absence?

Background. Many plants produce calcium oxalates, particularly in their leaves. These are widespread among different taxa (Lowenstam and Weiner, 1989). Being an "organic mineral" (CaC_2O_4), calcium oxalates are susceptible to biological degradation (Sahin, 2004). Calcium oxalates and various other types of oxalates are also produced by lichens (Jones and Wilson, 1986). Some bacteria cultured from rock surfaces produce calcium oxalates (Hess et al., 2008), and these bacteria may also be responsible for the formation of the oxalate-rich crusts that form naturally on rock surfaces (Watchman, 1990). Calcium oxalates are relatively insoluble and could be expected to survive in other environments as well.

Biogenic calcium oxalates are usually, but not always, composed of the monohydrate form called whewellite, as opposed to the dihydrate form, weddellite. Whewellite crystals can adopt several different morphologies, depending on the plant that produces them. These include so-called crystal sand, which is composed of micron-sized crystals; druses, which are clusters of relatively large crystals; and raphides, which are bundles of needle-shaped crystals (Webb, 1999). The latter are commonly produced in the wood and bark of many trees and are widely thought to be the major source of the ash calcite that forms when the wood is burned (Brochier, 1983; Brochier and Thinon, 2003).

Infrared spectroscopy. The two forms of calcium oxalate, whewellite $(CaC_2O_4 \cdot H_2O)$ and weddellite $(CaC_2CO_4 \cdot 2H_2O)$, can be distinguished by a small shift in one of the prominent peaks in the infrared spectrum (Figure 12.18). The 1,317 cm⁻¹ peak is characteristic of whewellite, whereas the 1,325 cm⁻¹ peak is characteristic of weddellite. There are also other characteristic differences. For example, the series of small, broad absorptions ranging from 3,486 to 3,060 cm⁻¹ is present in whewellite, but not in weddellite. Note, too, that if a mixture of the two forms is present in a sample, then peak 3 has its maximum at an intermediate value between 1,324 and 1,317 cm⁻¹. This was demonstrated by analyses of mixtures of the two types (Garti et al., 2002).

As calcium oxalates are commonly absent in the archaeological record, it would be very interesting to discover them and understand the circumstances of their preservation. Thus knowing the spectra of the common oxalates, and especially the significance of their characteristic sharp peak in the infrared spectrum at or around 1,317 cm⁻¹, might facilitate their identification.

11. Collagen: State of preservation

Problem. Bone collagen degrades during diagenesis and can be contaminated by extraneous organic matter. Paleodiet and radiocarbon analyses of bone collagen require as pure a sample as possible. Thus characterizing collagen preservation and purity is of much interest.

Background. The protein collagen is the major organic component of bone and skin (and hence parchment and leather). It has a unique

Figure 12.18
Infrared spectra of, *a*, whewellite (calcium oxalate monohydrate) and, *b*, weddellite (calcium oxalate dihydrate). The two spectra differ in several respects. Note that peak 4 in spectrum b is not part of the normal weddellite spectrum. The peak maxima are located at the following wavenumbers: 1, a series of small peaks present in whewellite at 3,486, 3,430, 3,342, 3,262, and 3,060; 2, 1,623 in whewellite and 1,617 in weddellite; 3, 1,317 in whewellite and 1,325 in weddellite; 4, 1,086 (artifact in standard); 5, 781; 6, 668 in whewellite and 613 in weddellite; 7, 517.

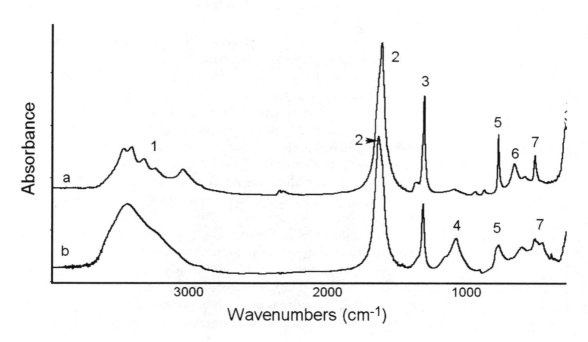

triple helical structure that, for the most part, is composed of a triplet amino acid repeat, in which every third amino acid is glycine and a large proportion of the remaining amino acids is proline (Veis, 2003). Collagen thus differs in these respects from all other proteins. Collagen in its fibrous form is not easily degraded biologically, and special protein cleaving enzymes (called collagenases) are required (Werb, 1992). When collagen loses its fibrous structure and denatures, it is called *gelatin*. Gelatin is and was widely used as a glue. The term *gel* is derived from the term *gelatin*. Gelatin, as opposed to collagen, can also be degraded by specific proteolytic enzymes (Werb, 1992).

In bone, the crystals are located within the collagen fibril and between fibrils. They thus provide some degree of protection to the collagen. It has been noted empirically that in many modern bones, a significant fraction of the crystals are intergrown, and collagen can be trapped inside these crystal aggregates (Weiner and Price, 1986). This relatively well-protected collagen can also be found in fossil bones (DeNiro and Weiner, 1988b; Salamon et al., 2005). For more details, see Chapters 5 and 8.

Some of the noncollagenous proteins (NCPs) are intimately associated with the mineral phase in bone and can only be removed if the bone mineral is dissolved (Termine et al., 1981). This NCP fraction is thus often even better protected than the collagen, and in many fossil bones, it also survives better than the collagen. The NCPs have a different protein structure, and many of them also contain covalently bound polysaccharides. The most common NCP, osteocalcin (also known as bone Gla-protein), has been identified in fossil bone, and its amino acid sequence has been determined from a fossil bone (Nielsen-Marsh et al., 2002).

Infrared spectroscopy. The infrared spectrum of collagen (Figure 12.19) reflects its unique amino acid sequence. Proline is relatively abundant in collagen, as compared to many other proteins. It has a cyclic structure not present in other amino acids and, as a result, a unique infrared absorption peak at 1,455 cm^{-1}. Thus the three major peaks of collagen (amide I, amide II, and the proline absorption) provide collagen infrared spectra with a very distinctive "stepped" pattern in the 1,660 to 1,400 cm^{-1} region. Furthermore, as collagen does not contain polysaccharides, which generally have a broad and strong absorption in the 1,000 to 1,100 cm^{-1} region, the presence of a peak in this region implies that the collagen is contaminated. The contaminants may be NCPs and/or soil humic acids, both of which have a strong absorption in this region, and/or silicate or phosphate minerals.

As bone collagen is a valuable and widely used material for radiocarbon dating (Chapter 10) and paleodiet analysis (DeNiro and Epstein, 1978), assessing its purity is of much importance. Infrared spectra can be used to assess the purity and preservational state of bone collagen after the carbonated apatite mineral has been removed by dissolution using 1N HCl. More details can be found in Yizhaq et al. (2005). See Chapter 10 for details on a rapid prescreening method for collagen in fossil bones.

12. Wood and olive pit preservation

Problem. Charred and uncharred wood are not always easy to differentiate. Furthermore, well-preserved wood may contain relatively well-preserved DNA, which can be used for genetic analysis.

Background. Wood and the outer endocarp layer of olive pits are both composed mainly of cellulose, hemicellulose, and lignin. The celluloses are polysaccharide chains composed of linked glucose moieties, whereas the lignin is a complex polymer rich in aromatic groups. Unless the wood is totally dry or charred, the main agents of degradation are fungi. White rot fungi usually degrade both the cellulose and lignin components, although some species preferentially degrade lignin (Faix

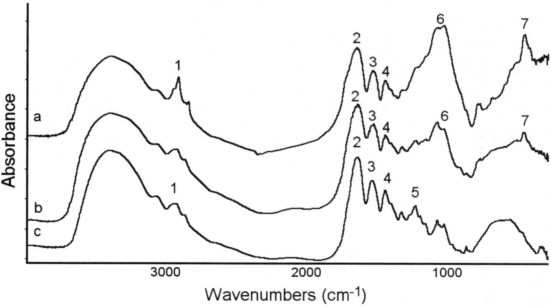

Figure 12.19 Infrared spectra of, *a*, fossil bone collagen with a large amount of contamination; *b*, fossil bone collagen with a small amount of contamination; and *c*, pure, fresh bone collagen. Peaks 2 and 3 are called amide I and amide II and are present in most proteins. Peak 4 is due to the absorption of the amino acid proline, and its presence in relatively large amounts is characteristic of collagen. Thus the presence of peaks 2, 3, and 4 in the relative proportions shown is characteristic of the presence of collagen in the sample. Peak 5 is the amide III absorption, which is also present in most proteins. The large, broad absorptions in spectra b and c (peak 6) and the presence of the silicate absorption (peak 7) show that these samples are contaminated by quartz and clay. Peak 6 in spectrum c is very broad. This, together with the prominent methyl group absorptions (peaks labeled 1), shows that this sample contains other organic material in addition to collagen and mineral. The absorption peaks are located at the following wavenumbers: 1, 2,925; 2, 1,655 for spectrum a, 1,660 for spectrum b, 1,649 for spectrum c; 3, 1,540; 4, 1,455; 5, 1,239; 6, 1,036 and 1,083; 7, 464. Note that the variable locations of the amide I peak maximum position probably reflect conformational differences.

et al., 1991). The more common brown rot fungi tend to degrade the cellulose components more than the lignin components (Genestar and Palou, 2006).

Wood is preserved in certain archaeological sites, particularly in northern latitudes and/or in waterlogged environments such as bogs and submarine environments. One of the oldest examples of wood preserved in an archaeological site is the 2.6 to 2.8 million–year-old wood from Sterkfontein, South Africa (Bamford, 1999). Fossil wood has also been found in various Acheulian sites, including the approximately 800,000-year-old waterlogged site of Gesher Benot Yaakov (Israel), which contains abundant wood specimens (Goren-Inbar et al., 2002). The approximately 400,000-year-old site of Schoningen contains spectacularly well-preserved wooden spears, with char-hardened, pointed ends (Thieme, 1997).

Olive pits are common in archaeological sites around the Mediterranean. Most are charred, but under special circumstances, uncharred pits may be preserved. These olive pits, in addition to uncharred wood, are potentially invaluable materials for genetic analysis using ancient DNA for paleoclimatic reconstructions using, in particular, the cellulose component, and for radiocarbon dating.

Infrared spectroscopy. Fossil wood is often dark in color, either because it is charred or because of the formation of colored compounds as a result of diagenesis. It is thus helpful to differentiate initially between wood charcoal and uncharred fossilized wood specimens. This can be done using infrared spectroscopy (Schultz et al., 1985). Figure 12.20 shows the infrared spectra of modern wood charcoal and fossil wood charcoal, and Figure 12.21 shows spectra of well-preserved and poorly preserved uncharred fossil wood.

Figure 12.20
Infrared spectra of, *a*, modern wood charcoal and, *b*, fossil wood charcoal. The modern charcoal spectrum is characterized by a few discrete absorption peaks. Fossil charcoal contains several peaks, the most prominent of which are due to carboxylate absorptions (spectrum b, peaks 2 and 3; Cohen-Ofri et al., 2006). These form as a result of oxidative diagenesis. The major absorption peaks are located at the following wavenumbers: 1, 3,400; 2, 1,712; 3, 1,581 for modern charcoal and 1,596 for fossil charcoal; 4, 1,384; 5, 1,256; 6, 1,108.

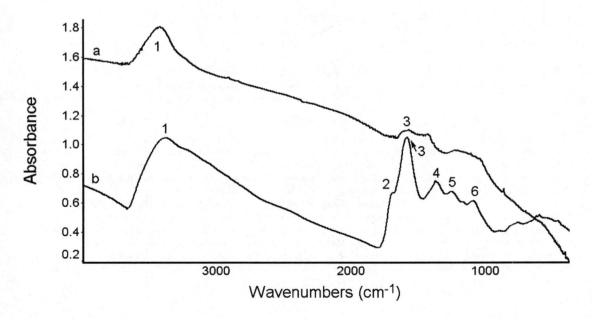

As lignin and cellulose infrared spectra are different (Figure 12.21), infrared spectroscopy can be used to estimate the relative proportions of the two major components of wood (Toivanen and Alen, 2006). Toivanen and Alen (2006) show empirically that the height of the aromatic vibration at 1,512 cm^{-1} (Figure 12.21, peak 5) is related to lignin content, and the carbon and oxygen vibrations around 1,000 and 1,100 cm^{-1} are related to the cellulose content. Thus infrared spectra can be used to monitor relative states of preservation of fossil wood. Figure 12.21 shows the infrared spectra of well-preserved and poorly preserved woods. The spectra show that cellulose and lignin are present in the well-preserved wood, whereas mainly lignin is present in the poorly preserved wood. Figure 12.21 also shows the infrared spectra of two fossil wood samples (both about 200 years old).

Infrared spectroscopy can also be used to identify well-preserved olive pits. This approach was developed in a study of ancient DNA in the Levant (Elbaum et al., 2006). Infrared spectra of both desiccated and waterlogged olive pits from several archaeological sites were obtained. This initial screening differentiated between charred and uncharred olive pits, both of which are dark in color and can easily be confused. The lignin contents of the uncharred specimens were then evaluated by measuring the area under the lignin aromatic absorption peak at around 1,512 cm^{-1}, normalized to the area under the C-H stretch absorption at around 2,927 cm^{-1}. The so-called L-ratio between the two areas was determined to be 0.20 ± 0.01 for fresh olive pits. Fossil olive pits with ratios close to 0.20 were then chosen for further screening for well-preserved DNA, and finally, the best-preserved specimens were fully analyzed and produced informative DNA sequences.

Figure 12.21
Infrared spectra of, a, pure cellulose; b, fossil wood (relatively well preserved); c, fossil wood (relatively poorly preserved); and d, pure lignin. Peaks 4 and 5 are present in lignin, but not in cellulose. The three peaks (labeled 6) and the set of peaks (labeled 8) are characteristic of cellulose. The major absorption peaks are located at the following wavenumbers: 1, around 3,400; 2, 2,902; 3, 1,732; 4, 1,640 in cellulose and 1,605 in lignin; 5, 1,512 in lignin only; 6, the triplet 1,372, 1,337, and 1,318 in cellulose; 7, broad peak in lignin centered around 1,208; 8, broad complex set of peaks in cellulose; 9, a single peak in lignin at 1,042.

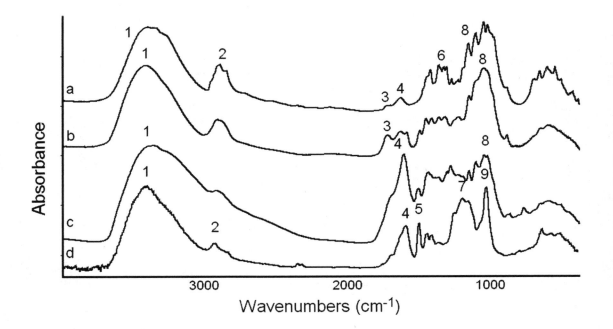

13. Natural organic materials: Resin, copal, amber, gum, bitumen, and humic and fulvic acids

Problem. Most naturally produced organic materials cannot be reliably identified based on visual inspection. Infrared spectroscopy can be used to identify many of these materials, and can also partially differentiate between different types within the same class of materials.

Background. Two different types of organic materials are grouped together in this section: preserved natural organic materials and assemblages of complex molecules that are extracted from sediments and other buried materials. The group of natural organic materials includes different compounds that were and still are used for many different purposes: adhesives, substrates for writing, incense, embalming, waterproofing, and more. Table 12.5 lists the more common archaeologically relevant natural organic materials. These materials are all highly complex in structure and variable in composition, and are hence often not easy to identify. Some are discussed in more detail in Chapter 8.

The second group comprises the macromolecular complexes that are extracted from sediments, and especially soils. They are collectively

Table 12.5. The archaeologically more relevant natural organic materials.

Major component	Basic unit	Material name
Polysaccharides	Saccharide	Gum (carbohydrate and terpenes, frankincense and myrrh) Starch Cellulose (cotton, flax, papyrus) Chitin (insect cuticles)
Proteins	Amino acid	Keratin (wool, horn, hooves) Collagen (parchment, leather, skin, gelatin, glue) Silk
Resins	Terpenes	Resin (varnish is dissolved resin) Copal Amber Pine tar
Wax	Fatty acids, alkanes	Beeswax
Petroleum residues	Complex mix of small molecules, mainly alkanes	Bitumen (also called asphalt)
Lignin	Polymers rich in aromatic moieties	Lignin
Humus (humic substances)	Polymers rich in aromatic moieties, with acidic functional groups soluble in alkali	Humic acid
	As above, but soluble in both alkali and acid	Fulvic acid

called *humus* or *humic substances* (Davies and Ghabbour, 1998) and are claimed to be the most abundant form of organic material on the earth's surface. These substances form in sediments as a result of organic matter degradation (Tan, 2003). They are also present in archaeological sediments, and they almost inevitably contaminate everything that is buried in the sediments. As they fluoresce strongly, their presence in archaeological artifacts prevents the much broader use of Raman spectroscopy for material characterization and identification in archaeology. It is interesting to note that lignin, a material produced in plants, including in the wood and bark of trees, has structures and chemical properties rather similar to humic substances, and it has been proposed that a part of the sediment humic substances is derived directly from the plant lignin (Chefetz et al., 2002).

Infrared spectroscopy. In general, infrared spectra of polymeric materials can be recognized by their relatively broad peaks, as opposed to materials that are composed mainly of small molecules with relatively few molecular groups, such as asphalt, which have sharp peaks. The more common organic materials can be divided into four different groups: polysaccharides, proteins, resins, and asphalt (also called bitumen), which is a complex mix of small organic molecules. Figure 12.22 shows representative spectra from each of these four

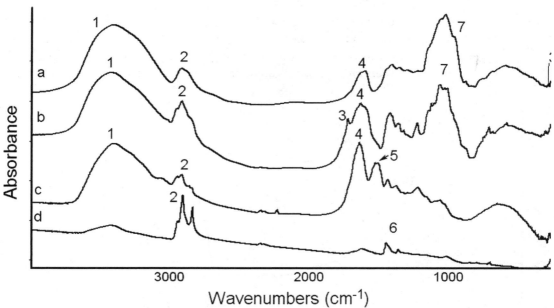

Figure 12.22 Infrared spectra of various natural polymers: *a*, gum (polysaccharide); *b*, resin (complex mixtures of polymers produced by trees); *c*, wool (protein); and *d*, asphalt (bitumen; complex mixture of small molecules including many hydrocarbons). Characteristic peaks are located at the following wavenumbers: 1, 3,430 (this water absorption peak is almost absent in asphalt); 2, peaks between 2,930 and 2,850 are mainly due to CH_3^- and CH_2^- groups (these are always present in organic materials; they are a major component of asphalt); 3, 1,737 due to COOH; 4, 1,615 in spectrum a, 1,646 in spectrum b, 1,654 in spectrum c (the latter is the amide I peak in proteins); 5, 1,541 is the amide II peak of proteins; 6, 1,455 and 1,375 are peaks characteristic of asphalt; 7, centered around 1,040. A broad peak in this region is indicative of the presence of polysaccharides. It is clearly very prominent in gum, which is composed mainly of polysaccharides, but it may also be present in proteins, which often have covalently bound polysaccharides.

groups. The polysaccharides in general contain a broad absorption band centered around 1,050 cm^{-1}. Protein spectra are characterized by three absorptions (known as amide I, amide II, and amide III) at around 1,650, 1,550, and 1,230 cm^{-1}. The spectra of resins contain prominent CH$_3$ and CH$_2$ absorptions at 2,930 and 2,870 cm^{-1} and another prominent peak at 1,716 cm^{-1} (carboxyl groups). Asphalt spectra have very strong CH$_3$ and CH$_2$ absorptions as well as two fairly sharp absorption peaks around 1,460 and 1,376 cm^{-1}. For more information, see Parker (1971).

The assemblage of polymers that is extracted from sediments under alkaline conditions and then precipitated when the solution is acidified is called *humic acid*. The fraction that remains in solution at all pH values is called *fulvic acid* (Hayes, 1998). In reality, they are a continuum of molecules (collectively termed humic substances) that are not well defined chemically (Davies and Ghabbour, 1998). Their infrared spectra are shown in Figure 12.23. They all contain prominent carboxylate absorptions at around 1,730 cm^{-1} (COOH) and 1,644 cm^{-1} (COO$^-$). Note that if the sample were to be analyzed in its acidic form, the COOH absorption would be present together with the COO$^-$ absorption. If not, then only the COO$^-$ absorption would be present. The major difference between humic and fulvic acids is the presence of the strong and broad absorption centered around 1,050 cm^{-1}. For more information, see Davies and Ghabbour (1998).

Resins are divided arbitrarily into different categories, depending on the extent to which they have undergone diagenetic changes over time. Fresh resins extracted from trees are called *resins*, and fossil resin is called *amber*. Copal is an intermediate between the two end members

Figure 12.23
Infrared spectra of, *a*, fulvic and, *b*, humic acids extracted from a soil (Masmia, Israel). The characteristic peaks are located at the following wavenumbers: 1, 3,410; 2, 2,930; 3, 1,731 and 1,644 for fulvic acid and 1,710 and 1,620 for humic acid; 4, 1,046; 5, 628; 6, triplet at 1,220, 1,114, and 1,037. Samples prepared by and provided courtesy of A. Nissenbaum.

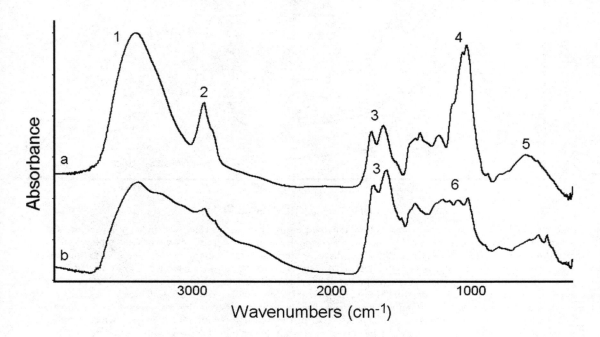

(Lambert et al., 1995). Figure 12.24 shows the infrared spectra of resin, copal, and three different types of amber. It has been shown that amber samples from different sources have unique infrared spectra (Angelini and Bellintani, 2005). This is not obvious in this (very) small sample set. See Chapter 2 for more information on using infrared spectra for determining the provenience of amber.

14. Presence of soluble salts in sediment samples

Problem. Sediment samples are often extracted from existing sections or balks in an archaeological site. If these sections were excavated several years earlier, then there is a tendency for them to dry out. The drying process results in soluble salts precipitating at or close to the surface. Salt crystal formation can cause other minerals to be dislodged. As analysis of such sediment samples can provide misleading information, it is helpful to identify these exposed samples by the presence of the salt deposits.

Background. The soil surface, balks, and sediment sections in archaeological sites often dry out over months and years. Water is drawn to these surfaces by capillary action from the interior. Thus large volumes of water pass through these surfaces. The result is that the soluble salts are concentrated close to the surface, and even though they are highly soluble, they eventually precipitate. This deposit of new crystals is not only unrepresentative of the sediment composition, but also, the growth of the crystals can mechanically displace some of the original fine-grained components of the sediments as well as artifacts. Nitrates

Figure 12.24
Infrared spectra of extant and fossil resins: *a*, extant resin; *b*, copal (Philippines); *c*, amber (Baltic); *d*, amber (Dominican Republic); *e*, amber (Dominican Republic). The major peaks are located at the following wavenumbers: 1, around 3,435; 2, 2,929 and 2,667; 3, 1,737 to 1,716 (note that the extant resin has an extra peak at 1,646); 4, 1,436 for resin, 1,448 for copal, and between 1,456 and 1,480 for ambers; 5, 1,385; 6, 1,240 in resin; 7, 1,240 and 1,172; 8, 1,079 (broad) in resin. Samples provided courtesy of A. Nissenbaum.

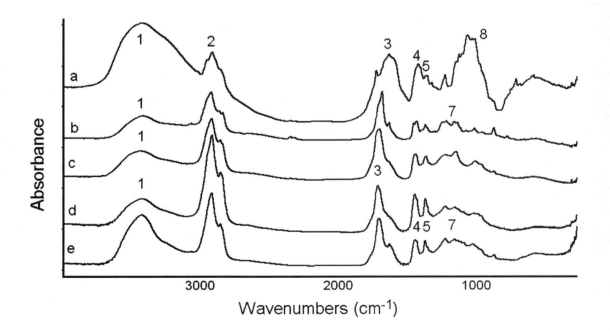

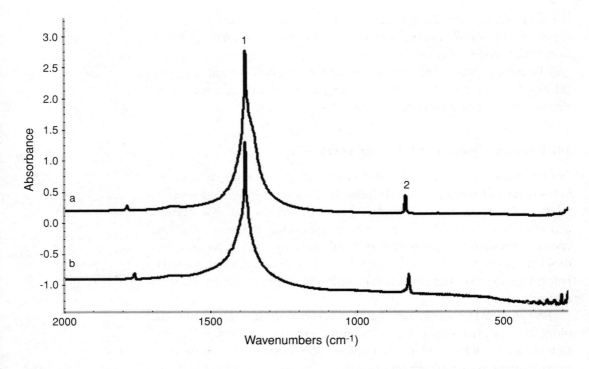

Figure 12.25
Infrared spectra of, *a,*
sodium nitrate and, *b,*
potassium nitrate. In both
spectra, peak 1 absorbs
at 1,384 cm^{-1}. Peak 2 of
sodium nitrate absorbs at
836 cm^{-1}, and potassium
nitrate at 825 cm^{-1}.

are present in small amounts in groundwater and are common constituents of this surface evaporitic deposit. In certain chalky deposits, this evaporitic deposit can reach thicknesses of several centimeters or more and, after a short time (years), can totally obliterate the surface of the original section. Sometimes this deposit actually stabilizes the section and can discourage birds and other animals from burrowing into the section. To obtain representative samples of the bulk sediment from such a surface, the original surface layer needs to be removed to expose fresh sediments.

Infrared spectroscopy. Many different salts may precipitate in this surface layer. The nitrates, however, have very simple and distinctive spectra, with a sharp peak at 1,384 cm^{-1}. The second minor peak varies, depending on the type of nitrate present (Figure 12.25). Furthermore, because the nitrate salt is a small and very simple molecule, the 1,384 cm^{-1} absorption peak is clearly visible, even if only a few micrograms of material are present.

Appendix A

Identifying Minerals Using Microchemical Analysis

Dr. Panagiotis Karkanas

The elemental compositions of minerals in embedded and polished blocks of sediments can be determined using the electron microprobe, or with energy and/or wavelength dispersive detectors (EDS and/or WDS) in a scanning electron microscope. The results are usually presented as an indication, but not a confirmation, of the mineral phase present. A detailed analysis can, however, be used to identify the mineral phase with a reasonable degree of certainty. The approach is to use the elemental analysis to calculate the chemical formula of the suspected mineral. The ideal number of oxygen atoms of the suspected mineral is used, and not the amount of oxygen analyzed. If the calculated formula is similar to the actual chemical formula, it is reasonable to assume that this is indeed the correct mineral phase.

Table A.1 is an example of the output of a typical elemental analysis of a mineral. Following are the steps used to identify the mineral phase:

1. A first check of the quality of the analysis is whether the sum of the amounts of compounds is close to 100% (column 4 in Table A.1). In the example in Table A.1, the water and volatite contents were not analyzed, so the sum cannot be 100%, but should be close to 100%.
2. A guess of the possible mineral phase is then made, based on the major elements present. In the example in Table A.1, a good guess would be the mineral carbonate hydroxylapatite. As carbon was not analyzed, the question is whether the analysis obtained corresponds to hydroxylapatite. In the software program used for elemental analysis, open the method called "stoichiometry normalized results (oxygen by stoichiometry)." Then calculate the number of oxygens from the general chemical formula of the mineral hydroxylapatite: $Ca_5(PO_4)_3(OH,F,Cl)$. Note that the number of oxygens is the number in the formula (i.e., 13 oxygens: 12 in the phosphate position and 1 in the hydroxyl position). A correction needs to be made for the cations that were not analyzed, in this case, the hydrogen of the hydroxyl group. A half oxygen needs to be subtracted as

318

APPENDIX A:
IDENTIFYING
MINERALS USING
MICROCHEMICAL
ANALYSIS

Table A.1. An elemental analysis output from the standard software for elemental analysis using EDS or WDS of a calcium- and phosphorus-rich mineral phase.

Element	Element %	Formula	Compound %	No. of ions
Si	0.10	Na_2O	0.22	0.04
Al	0.18	Al_2O_3	0.35	0.07
Ca	35.93	CaO	50.28	9.43
Fe	0.21	Fe_2O_3	0.30	0.04
Mg	0.31	MgO	0.51	0.13
Mn	0.00	MnO	0.00	0.00
K	−0.01	K_2O	−0.01	0.00
Na	1.00	Na_2O	1.35	0.46
P	17.56	P_2O_5	40.23	5.96
Ti	0.13	TiO_2	0.22	0.03
O	38.02			
Total	93.43		93.43	25.00

two hydrogens are needed for each oxygen to make a compound. As this results in 12.5 oxygens, it is better to duplicate the formula $[Ca_{10}(PO4)_6(OH,F,C)_2]$ and use 25 oxygens (anions). Another useful example of this calculation is calcite. The calcite formula, $CaCO_3$, has three oxygens, but two of them are associated with the carbon, which is usually not analyzed. Therefore the number of oxygens used for the calculation is one.

3. The next step is to calculate the formula and confirm that this is a monomineralogical phase and not a combination of minerals. The latter is a serious problem when amorphous aggregates (e.g., many phosphates) are present. For this step, the common substitutions in the chemical formula need to be taken into account. For example, the complete formula of hydroxylapatite is actually $(Ca,Na,Mg,Sr,Pb,\ldots)_{10}(PO_4,CO_3,SO_4,\ldots)_6(OH,F,Cl,CO_3)_2$. Therefore the computed formula, using the last column in Table A.1, is $(Ca_{9.43},Na_{0.46},Fe_{0.04},Si_{0.04},Al_{0.07})_{10.04}(PO_4)_{5.96}(OH)_2$. From this it can be seen that the analysis is very good, as the sum of cations in the Ca position (10.04) and in the P position (5.96) are very close to the ideal stoichiometric formula. In addition, the amounts of Si and Al are very low. This confirms that the major mineral phase is not contaminated by clays – a common phenomenon in phosphatized soils. Note that if the sum of the Ca plus the usual monovalent and divalent cations is not close to 10, and phosphorus is not close to 6, the analysis should be rejected. At this point, another guess of a possible mineral phase can be made and then checked, or it can be concluded that the mineral phase has a nonstoichiometric chemical composition. Nonstoichiometric compositions are acceptable for some minerals, in particular, poorly crystalline minerals (so-called amorphous phases), but not for the usual crystalline minerals.

A simple rule for ion substitutions is that the ions should be of equivalent strength (e.g., divalent ions for divalent ions), and if this is not possible, then monovalent ions should substitute divalent ions and trivalent ions should substitute divalent ions, and so on, but in such a way that neutrality is maintained. Note that in the example in Table A.1, carbon and hydrogen were not analyzed, so we cannot be sure of the substitutions in the phosphorus position or the actual composition of the hydroxyl position. Iron presents another problem because iron can be divalent or trivalent. By knowing the formula of the expected mineral, the correct valence of iron can be assigned.

319

APPENDIX A:
IDENTIFYING
MINERALS USING
MICROCHEMICAL
ANALYSIS

Appendix B

Identifying Minerals and Compounds Using Infrared Spectra: Table of Standard Minerals and Compounds for Which Infrared Spectra Are Available

Several complementary approaches can be useful for identifying the materials being analyzed. Perhaps the most powerful approach is to use the "search" option present in most infrared software packages and compare the unknown sample spectrum to spectra in a reference library. For this reason, the infrared spectral library of the Kimmel Center for Archaeological Science, Weizmann Institute of Science, is posted on the Web (http://www.weizmann.ac.il/kimmel-arch/islib.html). The materials in the library are listed in Table B.1. This list is also a simple "classification" of archaeologically relevant compounds. Note, too, that it contains minerals produced by organisms, many of which are less relevant to archaeology but more relevant to the field of biomineralization. Other useful libraries are available, such as that of the Infrared and Raman Users Group (http://www.irug.org/).

Perhaps the major problem with using search software for material identification is that peak positions are not invariant; rather, they depend on the local structural environment, counterions, and probably many other factors. This makes it difficult to know when a match can be accepted with confidence. A second problem relates to identifying mixtures of compounds. In this case, the library search can be focused on key peaks that are indicative of a particular compound.

Table B.1. Samples for which infrared spectra are currently available at the Kimmel Center for Archaeological Science Web site. The list includes not only archaeologically relevant samples, but also biogenic minerals. Listings in italics are samples for which no spectra are available at the time of writing.

Category	Item	Chemical formula or description
	Biogenic minerals	
Carbonates	Calcite	$CaCO_3$
	Aragonite	$CaCO_3$
	Vaterite	$CaCO_3$
	Monohydrocalcite	$CaCO_3 \cdot H_2O$
	Hydrocerussite	$Pb_2(OH)_2CO_3$
	Amorphous calcium carbonate (ACC)	$CaCO_3 \cdot H_2O$
Phosphates	Carbonate hydroxylapatite (dahllite)	$Ca_{10}(PO_4,CO_3)_6(OH)_2(PO_4)_{14}$
	Whitlockite	$Ca_{18}H_2)(Mg,Fe)^{2+}_2$
	Carbonate fluorapatite (francolite)	$Ca_5(PO_4)_3F$
	Octacalcium phosphate	$Ca_8H_2(PO_4)_6 \cdot 5H_2O$
	Brushite (DCPD)	$Ca(HPO_4) \cdot 2H_2O$
	Struvite	$Mg(NH_4)(PO_4) \cdot 6H_2O$
	Vivianite	$Fe^{2+}_3(PO_4)_2 \cdot 2H_2O$
	Amorphous calcium hydrated ferric phosphate and opal	
	Amorphous pyrophosphate	
Halides	Fluorite	CaF_2
	Amorphous fluorite	
	Hieratite	
	Atacamite	$Cu_2Cl(OH)_3$
Sulfates	Gypsum	$CaSO_4 \cdot 2H_2O$
	Celestite	$SrSO_4$
	Barite	$BaSO_4$
	Jarosite	$KFe_3^{3+}(SO_4)_2 \cdot (OH)_6$
	Calcium sulfate hemihydrate	$CaSO_4 0 \cdot 5(H_2O)$
Silicates	Silica (opal)	$SiO_2 \cdot nH_2O$
	Siliceous aggregates	Soil minerals in a matrix of impure silica
Oxides	Magnetite	$Fe^{2+}Fe_2^{3+}O_4$
	Goethite	α-FeO(OH)
	Lepidocrocite	γ-FeO(OH)
	Ferrihydrite	
	Amorphous iron oxide	
	Amorphous manganese oxide	
	Amorphous ilmenite	
	Todorokite	$(Mn^{2+},Ca,Mg)Mn^{4+}_3O_7 \cdot H_2O$
	Birnessite	$Na_4Mn_14O_{27} \cdot 9H_2O$
Sulfides	Pyrite	FeS_2
	Hydrotroilite	$FeS \cdot nH_2O$
	Sphalerite	ZnS
	Wurtzite	$(Zn,Fe)S$
	Galena	PbS
	Greigite	$Fe(II)Fe(III)_2S_4$
	Mackinawite	$(Fe,Ni)_9S_8$
	Amorphous pyrrhotite	

(continued)

Table B.1 (*continued*)

Category	Item	Chemical formula or description
Metals	Sulfur	S
Organic "minerals"	Whewhellite	$CaC_2O_4 \cdot H_2O$
	Weddelite	$CaC_2O_4 \cdot 2H_2O$
	Glushinskite	$Mg(C_2O_4) \cdot 2(H_2O)$
	Copper oxalate	$CuC_2O_4 \cdot 2H_2O$
	Manganese oxalate	$MnC_2O_4 \cdot 2H_2O$
	Earlandite	$Ca_3(C_6H_5O_7) \cdot 4(H_2O)$
	Guanine (anhydrous)	$C_5H_5N_5O$
	Sodium urate	$C_5H_3N_4NaO_3$
	Uric acid	$C_5H_4N_4O_3$
	Paraffin wax	C_nH_{2n+2}, $n = 20\text{--}40$
	Wax (bees, dark and light)	$C_{15}H_{31}CO_2C_{30}H_{61}$
	Calcium tartrate	$Ca(C_4H_4O_6)] \cdot 4H_2O$
	Calcium malate	$Ca(C_2H_4O(COO)_2$

	Geogenic minerals (common only)	
Silicates	Quartz	SiO_2
	Opal (silica)	$SiO_2 \cdot nH_2O$
	Opal-A	$SiO_2 \cdot nH_2O$
	Opal-CT	$SiO_2 \cdot nH_2O$
	Opal transforming	$SiO_2 \cdot nH_2O$
	Clay: kaolinite	$Al_2Si_2O_5(OH)_4$
	Clay: illite	$KAl_2[(OH)_2|AlSi_3O_{10}]$
	Clay: montmorillonite (Ca and Na)	$(Na,Ca)(Al,Mg)6(Si_4O_{10})3(OH)_6 \cdot nH_2O$
	Clay: bentonite	$(Na,Ca)_{0.33}(Al,Mg)_2Si_4O_{10}(OH)_2 \cdot (H_2O)_n$
	Clay: nontronite	$Ca_5(Si_7Al_8Fe_2)(Fe_{3.5}Al_{.4}Mg_{.1})O_{20}(OH)_4$
	Clay: vermiculite	$(MgFe,Al)_3(Al,Si)_4O_{10}(OH)_2 \cdot 4H_2O$
	Enstatite	$MgSiO_3$
	Hypersthene	$(Mg,Fe)SiO_3$
	Felspar: anorthite	$CaAl_2Si_2O_8$
	Alkali felspar: microcline	$(K,Na)(Al_3SiO_8)$
	Plagioclase felspar: oligoclase	$Na(AlSi_3O_8)\text{-}Ca(Al_2Si_2O_8)$
	Sodium felspar: albite	$Na(Si_3Al)O_8$
	Muscovite	$KAl_3O_{10}(OH)_2$
	Olivine	$(MgFe)_2SiO_4$
	Hisingerite	$Fe_2Si_2O_5(OH)_4 \cdot 2(H_2O)$
	Talc	$Mg_3Si_4O_{10}(OH)_2$
Carbonates	Calcite	$CaCO_3$
	Dolomite	$CaMg(CO_3)_2$
	Magnesite	$MgCO_3$
	Hydromagnesite	$Mg_5(CO_3)_4(OH)_2 \cdot 4(H_2O)$
	Strontianite	$SrCO_3$
	Cerrusite	$PbCO_3$
	Rhodocrosite	$MnCO_3$
	Smithsonite	$ZnCO_3$
Sulfates	Gypsum	$CaSO_4 \cdot 2H_2O$
	Anhydrite	$CaSO_4$
Oxides	Hematite	Fe_2O_3
	Magnetite	$Fe^{2+}Fe_2^{3+}O_4$
	Goethite	$\alpha\text{-}FeO(OH)$

Category	Item	Chemical formula or description
	Ilmenite	$FeTiO_3$
	Ochre	Hydrated iron oxides
	Cuprite	Cu_2O
Hydroxides	Brucite	$Mg(OH)_2$
Sulfides	Pyrite	FeS_2
	Pyrrhotite	$Fe_{1-x}S\ (0.2 > x > 0)$
Phosphates	Hydroxyapatite	$Ca_5(PO_4)_3(OH)$
	Whitlockite (β-tricalcium phosphate)	$Ca_9(Mg,Fe^{2+})2(PO_4)_6(PO_3OH)$
Organic "minerals"	Anthracite (coal)	C
	Graphite	C
	Authigenic minerals formed at ambient conditions	
Carbonates	Calcite	$CaCO_3$
	Siderite	$Fe^{2+}CO_3$
	Trona	$Na_3CO_3HCO_3 \cdot 2H_2O$
Nitrates	Nitratite (sodium nitrate)	$NaNO_3$
	Potassium nitrate	KNO_3
Phosphates	Ardealite	$CaHPO_4 \cdot CaSO_4 \cdot 4H_2O$
	Carbonate hydroxylapatite (dahllite)	$Ca_{10}(PO_4,CO_3)_6(OH)_2$
	Carbonate hydroxylapatite transforming	$Ca_{10}(PO_4,CO_3,Al)_6(OH)_2$
	Brushite (DCDP)	$CaHPO_4 \cdot 2H_2O$
	Variscite	$AlPO_4 \cdot 2H_2O$
	Crandallite	$(Ca,Al)_{10}(PO_4,CO_3)_6(OH,F)_2$
	Montgomeryite	$Ca_4MgAl_4(PO_4)_6(OH)_4 \cdot 12H_2O$
	Montgomeryite amorphous	
	Tinsleyite	$K(Al,Fe)_2(PO_4)_2(OH) \cdot 2H_2O$
	Newberyite	$Mg(PO_3OH) \cdot 3H_2O$
	Leucophosphite	$K_2(Fe^{3+},Al)_4(PO_4)_4(OH)_2 \cdot 4H_2O$
	Taranakite	$H_6K_3Al_5(PO_4)_8 \cdot H_2O$
	Wavellite	$Al_3(PO_4)_2(OH)_3 \cdot 5H_2O$
	Strengite	$FePO_4 \cdot 2H_2O$
	Evansite	$Al_3PO_4(OH)_6 \cdot 6H_2O$
	Struvite	$NH_4MgPO_4 \cdot 6H_2O$
	Vivianite	$Fe_3(PO_4)_2 \cdot 8H_2O$
Oxides, hydroxides	Oxides: manganese and iron	
	Brucite	$Mg(OH)_2$
Sulfates	Gypsum	$CaSO_4 \cdot 2H_2O$
	Barite	$BaSO_4$
Silicates	Transformed opal	
	Transformed clay	
	Analcite	$Na(AlSi_2O_6) \cdot H_2O$
	Authigenic minerals formed at elevated temperatures	
Carbonates	Aragonite	$CaCO_3$
	Calcite (ash of wood and bark)	$CaCO_3$

(*continued*)

Table B.1. (*continued*)

Category	Item	Chemical formula or description
Oxides, hydroxides	Portlandite (calcium hydroxide, slaked lime)	$Ca(OH)_2$
	Calcium oxide	CaO
	Copper oxide	CuO
	Magnesium oxide	MgO
Silicates	Tridymite	SiO_2
	Clay (montmorillonite; 300°–1,000°C)	Series of spectra heated at intervals of 200°C for 4 hours
	Cristobolite	SiO_2
	Mellilite	$Ca_2(MgAl)(Al,Si)SiO_7$
	Wollastonite	$CaSiO_3$
	Portlandite	$Ca(OH)_2$
	Periclase	MgO
	Gehlenite	$Ca_2Al(AlSi)O_7$
	Mullite	$3Al_2O_3 . 2SiO_2$
	Sanidine	$(K,Na)(Si,Al)_4O_8$
Organic "mineral"	Graphite	C

	Pigments	
Carbonates	Azurite (blue)	$2CuCO_3 . Cu(OH)_2$
	Huntite (white)	$CaMg_3(CO_3)_4$
	Hydrocerussite (white)	$Pb_2(OH)_2CO_3$
	Malachite (green)	$CuCO_3 . Cu(OH)_2$
Silicates	Crysocolla (dark green)	$CuSiO_3 . nH_2O$
	Epidote	$Ca_2(Al,Fe)_3(SiO_4)_3(OH)$
	Lazurite (lapis lazuli, ultramarine)	$(Na,Ca)_8Al_6Si_6O_{24}(S,SO_4)$
	Prehnite	$Cu_2Al_2SiO_3O_{10}(OH)_2$
	Wollastonite green	$(CaCu)SiO_3$
	Egyptian blue	$CaCuSi_4O_{10}$
Vanadate	Carnotite	$K_2(UO_2)_2(VO_4)_2 \cdot 2H_2O$
Chlorides	Atacamite	$Cu_2Cl(OH)_3$
Sulfates	Anhydrite	$CaSO_4$
	Barite	$BaSO_4$
	Gypsum	$CaSO_4 \cdot 2H_2O$
Oxides, hydroxides	*Anatase (white)*	TiO_2
	Goethite	$\alpha\text{-}FeO(OH)$
	Hematite (red)	Fe_2O_3
	Lepidocrocite	$\gamma\text{-}FeO(OH)$
Sulfides	Cinnabar (red)	HgS
	Orpiment	As_2S_3
	Realgar	As_4S_4

	Kohl (cosmetic eye paints)	
Carbonates	Cerrusite	$PbCO_3$
	Hydrocerrusite	$2Pb(CO_3) \cdot Pb(OH)_2$
	Malachite	$CuCO_3 \cdot Cu(OH)_2$
Phosphates	Pyromorphite	$Pb_5(PO_4)_3(F,OH,Cl)$

Category	Item	Chemical formula or description
Sulfates	Anglesite	$PbSO_4$
	Brochantite	$CuSO_4.3Cu(OH)_2$
Sulfides	Galena	PbS
	Sphalerite	ZnS
	Ochre	
Oxides	Copper oxide	CuO
Silicates	Chrysocolla	$CuSiO_3 \cdot 2H_2O$

	Bead and tool materials	
Phosphates	Turquoise	$CuAl_6(PO_4)_4(OH)_8.4H_2O$
Silicates	Enstatite	$MgSiO_3$
	Steatite (synthetic, high temperature)	
	Talc (steatite)	$Mg_3(Si_2O_5)_2(OH)_2$
	Carnelian	SiO_2

	Glass and materials for glass and metal production	
	Glass (Roman, well preserved)	
	Glass (Roman, poorly preserved)	
	Bindheimite (lead antimonite)	$Pb_2Sb_2O_6(O,OH)$
	Copper oxide	CuO
	Cuprite	Cu_2O
	Pyrolusite	MnO_2
	Cassiterite	SnO_2
	Stannite	Cu_2FeSnS_4
	Lead arsenate	$PbHAsO_4$

	Rocks, soils, and ash	
	Basalt	
	Diatomite	Biogenic silica
	Flint (chert)	Microcrystalline quartz
	Cemented sandstone (kurkar)	
	Limestone	Calcite
	Loess	Quartz, clay, and calcite
	Obsidian	
	Pozzolana (volcanic ash)	From five different sources in Italy
	Pumice	
	Terra rossa soil	Quartz, clay, calcite, and oxides
	Ash (bark and wood)	Calcite, siliceous aggregates, phytoliths
	Siliceous aggregates	Soil minerals in silica matrix

	Macromolecules	
Proteins	Collagen: fresh	
	Collagen: fossil	
	Collagen: contaminated	
	Keratin	
	Silk: spider	
	Silk: silkworm cocoon	
	Wool	
Polysaccharides	Cellulose	
	Chitin (alpha)	
	Chitin (beta)	
	Starch	

(*continued*)

Table B.1 (*continued*)

Category	Item	Chemical formula or description
	Natural polymeric mixtures	
	Amber	Terpenes, five different sources
	Anthracite	Coal
	Asphalt (bitumen)	
	Charcoal	
	Copal	Terpenes
	Fulvic acid	
	Gum	Terpenes and polsysaccharides
	Jet	
	Humic acid	
	Humic acid (extracted from charcoal)	
	Lignin	
	Resin	Four different sources
	Biomaterials (mineralized)	
	Bone: recent	Collagen, carbonate hydroxylapatite, water
	Bone: fossil	Carbonate hydroxylapatite, water, collagen?
	Bone: burned (different temperatures)	Collagen (charred), carbonate hydroxylapatite
	Dentin	Collagen, carbonated hydroxylapatite, water
	Enamel	Carbonate hydroxylapatite, protein, water
	Biomaterials	
	Beeswax (dark and light colored)	
	Bark: recent	Cellulose, lignin
	Date (fruit of a palm): fresh	From outer cuticle layer
	Date fossil	Roman period, Israel
	Ivory	Collagen, carbonate hydroxylapatite, water
	Parchment: recent	Collagen
	Parchment: fossil (Dead Sea Scrolls)	
	Pollen	
	Seeds	Starch (major component)
	Wood: recent and fossil	Cellulose, lignin
	Anthropogenic materials	
	Ceramic	
	Glass	Roman period
	Egyptian blue	
	Mortar	Roman hydraulic
	Plaster/mortar	
	Steatite beads	
	Synthetic glues and stabilizers, solvents	
	Polyethyleneglycol (PEG)	
	Perspex	
	Paralloid	
	Cyclodecane	
	Salts	
	Barium chloride	$BaCl_2$
	Ammonium carbonate	NH_4HCO_3
	Ammonium oxalate	$(NH_4)_2C_2O_4.H_2O$
	Ammonium sulfate	$(NH_4)_2SO_4$

References

Abelson, P. H. (1955). Organic constituents of fossils. *Carnegie Institution of Washington Yearbook* 54, 107–109.

Abelson, P. H. (1956). Paleobiochemistry. *Journal of American Science* 195, 83–88.

Addadi, L., Berman, A., and Weiner, S. (1991). Intracrystalline proteins from a sea urchin and a mollusk: a comparison. In: Mechanisms and Phylogeny of Mineralization in Biological Systems (ed. S. Suga and H. Nakahara), pp. 29–33. Springer, Tokyo.

Addadi, L., Joester, D., Nudelman, F., and Weiner, S. (2006). Mollusk shell formation: a source of new concepts for understanding biomineralization processes. *Chemistry European Journal* 12, 980–987.

Addadi, L., Raz, S., and Weiner, S. (2003). Taking advantage of disorder: amorphous calcium carbonate and its roles in biomineralization. *Advanced Materials* 15, 959–970.

Aitken, M. J. (1958). Magnetic dating. *Archaeometry* 1, 16–20.

Aitken, M. J. (1976). Thermoluminescence age evaluation and assessment of error limits: revised system. *Archaeometry* 18, 233–238.

Aitken, M. J. (1990). Science-Based Dating in Archaeology. Longman Group, London and New York.

Aitken, M. J., and Valladas, H. (1992). Luminescence dating relevant to human origins. *Philosophical Transactions of the Royal Society of London, Series B* 337, 139–144.

Albert, R. M., and Weiner, S. (2001). Study of phytoliths in prehistoric ash layers using a quantitative approach. In: Phytoliths: Applications in Earth Sciences and Human History (ed. J. D. Meunier and F. Colin), pp. 251–266. A. A. Balkema, Exton, PA.

Albert, R. M., Tsatskin, A., Ronen, A., Lavi, O., Estroff, L., Lev-Yadun, S., and Weiner, S. (1999). Mode of occupation of Tabun Cave, Mt Carmel, Israel during the Mousterian Period: A study of the sediments and phytoliths. *Journal of Archaeological Science* 26, 1249–1260.

Albert, R. M., Weiner, S., Bar-Yosef, O., and Meignen, L. (2000). Phytoliths in the Middle Paleolithic deposits of Kebara Cave, Mt. Carmel, Israel: study of the plant materials used for fuel and other purposes. *Journal of Archaeological Science* 27, 931–947.

Albert, R. M., Bar-Yosef, O., and Weiner, S. (2003a). Use of plant remains in Kebara Cave: phytoliths and mineralogical analyses. In: Kebara Cave, Mt.

Carmel, Israel: The Middle and Upper Paleolithic Archaeology, Part 1 (ed. O. Bar-Yosef and L. Meignen), pp. 147–164. Peabody Museum of Archaeology and Ethnology, Harvard University, Cambridge, MA.

Albert, R. M., Bar-Yosef, O., Meignen, L., and Weiner, S. (2003b). Quantitative phytolith study of hearths from the Natufian and Middle Paleolithic levels of Hayonim Cave (Galilee, Israel). *Journal of Archaeological Science* 30, 461–480.

Albert, R. M., Bamford, M. K., and Cabanes, D. (2006). Taphonomy of phytoliths and macroplants in different soils from Olduvai Gorge (Tanzania) and the application to Plio-Pleistocene palaeoanthropological samples. *Quaternary International* 148, 78–94.

Albert, R. M., Shahack-Gross, R., Cabanes, D., Gilboa, A., Portillo, M., Sharon, I., Boaretto, E., and Weiner, S. (2008). Phytolith-rich layers from the Late Bronze and Iron Ages at Tel Dor (Israel): mode of formation and archaeological significance. *Journal of Archaeological Science* 35, 57–75.

Alexander, M. (1977). Introduction to Soil Microbiology. 2nd edition. John Wiley, New York.

Alexandre, A., Meunier, J.-D., Colin, F., and Koud, J.-M. (1997). Plant impact on the biogeochemical cycle of silicon and related weathering processes. *Geochimica et Cosmochimica Acta* 61, 677–682.

Alon, D., Mintz, G., Cohen, I., Weiner, S., and Boaretto, E. (2002). The use of Raman spectroscopy to monitor the removal of humic substances from charcoal: quality control for 14C dating of charcoal. *Radiocarbon* 44, 1–11.

Al-Shorman, A. (2004). Stable carbon isotopic analysis of human tooth enamel from the Bronze Age cemetery of Ya'amoun in Northern Jordan. *Journal of Archaeological Science* 31, 1693–1698.

Ambrose, S. H. (1991). Effects of diet, climate and physiology on nitrogen isotope abundances in terrestrial foodwebs. *Journal of Archaeological Science* 18, 293–317.

Ambrose, S. H. (1998). Chronology of the Late Stone Age and food production in East Africa. *Journal of Archaeological Science* 25, 377–392.

Amos, G. L. (1952). Silica in timbers. *CSIRO Bulletin Melbourne Australia* 267, 5–55.

Anderson, S., and Ertug-Yaras, F. (1998). Fuel fodder and faeces: an ethnographic and botanical study of dung fuel use in Central Anatolia. *Environmental Archaeology* 1, 99–109.

Andrus, C. F. T., and Crowe, D. E. (2002). Alteration of otolith aragonite: effects of prehistoric cooking methods on otolith chemistry. *Journal of Archaeological Science* 29, 291–299.

Angelini, I., and Bellintani, P. (2005). Archaeological ambers from Northern Italy: an FTIR-DRIFT study of provenance by comparison with the geological amber database. *Archaeometry* 47, 441–454.

Aoba, T., and Moreno, E. (1990). Changes in the nature and composition of enamel during porcine amelogenesis. *Calcified Tissue International* 47, 356–364.

Arias, J. L., Fink, D. J., Si-Qun, X., Heuer, A. H., and Caplan, A. I. (1993). Biomineralization and eggshells: cell-mediated acellular compartments of mineralized extracellular matrix. *International Review of Cytology* 145, 217–250.

Armitage, P. L. (1975). The extraction and identification of opal phytoliths from the teeth of ungulates. *Journal of Archaeological Science* 2, 187–197.

Arnay-de-la-Rosa, M., González-Reimers, E., Gámez-Mendoza, A., and Galindo-Martín, L. (2009). The Ba/Sr ratio, carious lesions, and dental calculus among the population buried in the church La Concepción (Tenerife, Canary Islands). *Journal of Archaeological Science* 36, 351–358.

Arnold, D. E. (1985). Ceramic Theory and Cultural Process. Cambridge University Press, Cambridge.

Arnold, D. E. (2005). Linking society with the compositional analysis of pottery: a model from comparative ethnography. In: Pottery Manufacturing Processes: Reconstruction and Interpretation. (ed. A. Livingstone Smith, D. Bosquet, and R. Martineau), pp. 15–21. British Archaeological Reports, International Series 1349, Oxford.

Arrhenius, O. (1931). Die bodenanalyse im dienst der archäologie. *Zeitschrift für Pflanzenernährung, Düngung und Bodenkunde B* 10, 427–439.

Arsenault, A. L. (1991). Image analysis of collagen-associated mineral distribution in cryogenically prepared turkey leg tendons. *Calcified Tissue International* 48, 56–62.

Ascough, P. L., Cook, G. T., Dugmore, A. J., Scott, E. M., and Freeman, S. P. H. T. (2005). Influence of mollusk species on marine ΔR determinations. *Radiocarbon* 47, 433–440.

Aufderheide, A. C., Muñoz, I., and Arriaza, B. (2005). Seven Chinchorro mummies and the prehistory of northern Chile. *American Journal of Physical Anthropology* 91, 189–201.

Ayliffe, L. K., and Chivas, A. R. (1990). Oxygen isotopic composition of the bone phosphate of Australian kangaroos: potential as a palaeoenvironmental recorder. *Geochimica et Cosmochimica Acta* 54, 2603–2609.

Baillie, M. G. L. (1995). A Slice Through Time: Dendrochronology and Precision Dating. Routledge, London.

Baker, G., Jones, L. H. P., and Wardrop, L. D. (1959). Cause of ware in sheep's teeth. *Nature* 184, 1583–1584.

Ball, T. B., Gardner, J. S., and Anderson, N. (1999). Identifying inflorescence phytoliths from selected species of wheat (*Triticum monococcum, T. dicoccum, T. dicoccoides, and T. aestivum*) and barley (*Hordeum vulgare and H. spontaneum*) (Gramineae). *American Journal of Botany* 86, 1615–1623.

Bamber, R. K., and Lanyon, J. W. (1960). Silica deposition in several woods of New South Wales. *Tropical Woods* 113, 48–53.

Bamford, M. (1999). Pliocene fossil woods from an early hominid cave deposit, Sterkfontein, South Africa. *South African Journal of Science* 95, 231–238.

Bamford, M. K., Albert, R. M., and Cabanes, D. (2006). Plio-Pleistocene macro-plant fossil remains and phytoliths from Lowermost Bed II in the eastern paleolake margin of Olduvai Gorge, Tanzania. *Quaternary International* 148, 95–112.

Baraldi, P., Bonazzi, A., Giordani, N., Paccagnella, F., and Zannini, P. (2006). Analytical characterization of Roman plasters of the "Domus Farini" in Modena. *Archaeometry* 48, 481–499.

Barba, L. (2007). Chemical residues in lime-plastered archaeological floors. *Geoarchaeology* 22, 439–452.

Barber, M., Field, D., and Topping, P. (1999). Neolithic Flint Mines in England. Royal Commission on the Historical Monuments of England, Swindon.

Barton, H. (2007). Starch residues on museum artifacts: implications for determining tool use. *Journal of Archaeological Science* 34, 1752–1762.

Bar-Yosef, O. (2001). The world around Cyprus: from Epi-Paleolithic foragers to the collapse of the PPNB civilization. In: The Earliest Prehistory of Cyprus from Colonization to Exploitation (ed. S. Swiny), pp. 129–164. American Schools of Oriental Research, Boston.

Bar-Yosef Mayer, D. E. (2000). The economic importance of mollusks in the Levant. In: Archaeozoology of the Near East, vol. IV A (ed. M. Mashkour, A. M. Choyke, H. Buitenhuis, and F. Poplin), pp. 218–227. Archeological Research and Consultancy, Groningen, Netherlands.

Bar-Yosef Mayer, D. E. (2005a). Archaeomalacology: Mollusks in Former Environments of Human Behavior. Oxbow, Oxford.

Bar-Yosef Mayer, D. E. (2005b). The exploitation of shells as beads in the Paleolithic and Neolithic of the Levant. Paléorient 31, 176–185.

Bar-Yosef Mayer, D. E. (2008). Archaeomalacological research in Israel: the current state of research. Israel Journal of Earth Sciences 56, 191–206.

Battarbee, R. W. (1988). The use of diatom analysis in archaeology: a review. Journal of Archaeological Science 15, 621–644.

Baxter, M. S., and Walton, A. (1970). Radiocarbon dating of mortars. Nature 225, 937.

Beck, C. W., Wilbur, E., Meret, S., Kossove, D., and Kermani, K. (1965). The infrared spectra of amber and the identification of Baltic amber. Archaeometry 8, 96–109.

Behrensmeyer, A. K. (1978). Taphonomic and ecologic information from bone weathering. Paleobiology 4, 150–162.

Behrensmeyer, A. K., and Hill, A. P., eds. (1988). Fossils in the Making: Vertebrate Taphonomy and Paleoecology. University of Chicago Press, Chicago.

Belfiore, C. M., Day, P. M., Hein, A., Kilikoglou, V., La Rosa, V., Mazzoleni, P., and Pezzino, A. (2007). Petrographic and chemical characterization of pottery production of the Late Minoan I kiln at Haghia Triada, Crete. Archaeometry 49, 621–653.

Bell, I. M., Clark, R. J., and Gibbs, P. J. (1997). Raman spectroscopic library of natural and synthetic pigments (pre- approximately 1850 AD). Spectrochimica Acta A 53, 2159–2179.

Bellomo, R. V. (1993). A methodological approach for identifying archaeological evidence of fire resulting from human activities. Journal of Archaeological Science 20, 525–553.

Bellemo, R. V., and Harris, J. W. K. (1990). Preliminary reports of actualistic studies of fire within Virunga National Park, Zaire: towards an understanding of archaeological occurrences. In: Evolution of Environments and Hominidae in the African Western Rift Valley, vol. 1 (ed. N. T. Boaz), pp. 317–338. Virginia Museum of Natural History Memoir, Martinsville.

Benayas, J. (1963). Disolución parcial de sílice organica en suelos. Anales de Edafologia y Agrobiologia 22, 623–626.

Benecke, N. (1987). Studies on early dog remains from northern Europe. Journal of Archaeological Science 14, 31–49.

Beniash, E., Aizenberg, J., Addadi, L., and Weiner, S. (1997). Amorphous calcium carbonate transforms into calcite during sea urchin larval spicule growth. Proceedings of the Royal Society of London, Series B 264, 461–465.

Bentley, R. A., Krause, R., and Price, T. D. (2003). Human mobility at the early Neolithic settlement of Vaihingen, Germany: evidence from strontium isotope analysis. Archaeometry 45, 471–486.

Benyon, A. D., and Wood, B. A. (1987). Patterns and rates of enamel growth in the molar teeth of early hominids. *Nature* 326, 493–496.

Berman, A., Addadi, L., and Weiner, S. (1988). Interactions of sea urchin skeleton macromolecules with growing calcite crystals – a study of intracrystalline proteins. *Nature* 331, 546–548.

Berman, A., Hanson, J., Leiserowitz, L., Koetzle, T. F., Weiner, S., and Addadi, L. (1993). Biological control of crystal texture: a widespread strategy for adapting crystal properties to function. *Science* 259, 776–779.

Berna, F., and Goldberg, P. (2008). Assessing Paleolithic pyrotechnology and associated hominin behavior in Israel. *Israel Journal of Earth Sciences* 56, 107–121.

Berna, F., Matthews, A., and Weiner, S. (2003). Solubilities of bone mineral from archaeological sites: the recrystallization window. *Journal of Archaeological Science* 31, 867–882.

Berna, F., Behar, A., Shahack-Gross, R., Berg, J., Boaretto, E., Gilboa, A., Sharon, I., et al. (2007). Sediments exposed to high temperatures: reconstructing pyrotechnological processes in Late Bronze and Iron Age Strata at Tel Dor (Israel). *Journal of Archaeological Science* 34, 358–373.

Bernal, M. P., Sánchez-Monedero, M. A., Paredes, C., and Roig, A. (1998). Carbon mineralization from organic wastes at different composting stages during their incubation with soil. *Agriculture, Ecosystems, and Environment* 69, 175–189.

Bertram, B. C. R. (1992). The Ostrich Communal Nesting System. Princeton University Press, Princeton, NJ.

Bethell, P. H., and Máté, I. (1989). The use of soil phosphate analysis in archaeology: a critique. In: Scientific Analysis in Archaeology, Monograph 19 (ed. J. Henderson), pp. 1–29. Oxford University Committee for Archaeology, Oxford.

Bieber, A. M., Brooks, D. W., Harbottle, G., and Sayre, E. V. (1976). Application of multivariate techniques to analytical data on Aegean ceramics. *Archaeometry* 18, 59–74.

Binford, L. R. (1978). Nunamiut Ethnoarchaeology. Academic Press, New York.

Binford, L. R. (1981). Bones: Ancient Men and Modern Myths. Academic Press, New York.

Binford, L. R. (1983). In Pursuit of the Past. Thames and Hudson, New York.

Bird, M. I., Turney, C. S. M., Fifield, K., Jones, R., Ayliffe, L. K., Palmer, A., Cresswell, R., and Robertson, S. (2002). Radiocarbon analysis of the early archaeological site of Nauwalabila I, Arnhem Land, Australia: implications for sample suitability and stratigraphic integrity. *Quaternary Science Review* 21, 1061–1075.

Bird, M. I., Turney, C. S. M., Fifield, L. K., Smith, M. A., Miller, G. H., Roberts, R. G., and Magee, J. W. (2003). Radiocarbon dating of organic- and carbonate-carbon in Genyornis and Dromaius eggshell using stepped combustion and stepped acidification. *Quaternary Science Reviews* 22, 15–17.

Black, D. (1931). Evidences of the use of fire by *Sinanthropus*. *Bulletin of the Geological Society of China* 11, 107–108.

Black, D., Teilhard de Chardin, P., and Young, C. C. (1933). Fossil man in China. *Memoirs of the Geological Survey of China* A, 1–166.

Blackman, E. B. (1969). Observations on the development of the silica cells of the leaf sheath of wheat (*Triticum aestivum*). *Canadian Journal of Botany* 47, 827–838.

Blake, R. E., O'Neil, J. R., and Garcia, G. A. (1997). Oxygen isotope systematics of biologically mediated reactions of phosphate: I. Microbial degradation of organophosphorus compounds. *Geochimica et Cosmochimica Acta* 61, 4411–4422.

Blow, M. J., Zhang, T., Woyke, T., Speller, C. F., Krivoshapkin, A., Yang, D. Y., Derevianko, A., and Rubin, E. M. (2008). Identification of ancient remains through genomic sequencing. *Genome Research* 18, 1347–1353.

Blum, J. D., Taliaferro, H. E., Weisse, M. T., and Holmes, R. T. (2000). Changes in Sr/Ca, Ba/Ca and $^{87}Sr/^{86}Sr$ ratios between trophic levels in two forest ecosystems in the northeastern U.S.A. *Biogeochemistry* 49, 87–101.

Boardman, S., and Jones, G. (1990). Experiments on the effect of charring on cereal plant components. *Journal of Archaeological Science* 17, 1–11.

Boaretto, E. (2008). Determining the chronology of an archaeological site using radiocarbon: minimizing uncertainty. *Israel Journal of Earth Sciences* 56, 207–216.

Boaretto, E. (2009a). Dating materials in good archaeological contexts: the next challenge for radiocarbon analysis. *Radiocarbon* 51, 275–282.

Boaretto, E., Barkai, R., Gopher, A., Berna, F., Kubic, P. W., and Weiner, S. (2009b). Specialized flint procurement strategies for hand axes, scapersa and blades in the Late Lower Paleolithic: a ^{10}Be study at Qesem Cave, Israel. *Human Evolution*.

Boaretto, E., Wu, X., Yuan, J., Bar-Yosef, O., Chu, V., Pan, Y., Liu, K., et al. (2009c). Radiocarbon dating of the deposits and pottery at Yuchanyan Cave, Hunan Province, China. *Proceedings of the National Academy of Sciences of the United States of America.* 106, 9595–9600.

Bocherens, H., Koch, P. L., Mariotti, A., Geraads, D., and Jaeger, J.-J. (1996). Isotopic biogeochemistry (^{13}C, ^{18}O) of mammalian enamel from African Pleistocene hominid sites. *Palaios* 11, 306–318.

Boggild, O. (1930). The shell structure of the mollusks. *K. Dan. Vidensk. Selsk. Skr. Naturvidensk. Math. Afd.* 9, 233–326.

Bolan, N. S., Hedley, M. J., and White, R. E. (1991). Processes of soil acidification during nitrogen cycling with emphasis on legume based pastures. *Plant and Soil* 134, 53–63.

Bonani, G., Ivy, S., Hajdas, I., Niklaus, T. R., and Suter, M. (1994). AMS ^{14}C age determinations of tissue, bone and grass samples from the Ötztal Ice Man. *Radiocarbon* 36, 247–250.

Borrelli, E. (1999). Binders. International Centre for the Study of the Preservation and Restoration of Cultural Property, Rome.

Bowman, H. R., Asaro, F., and Perlman, I. (1973). Composition variations in obsidian sources and the archaeological implications. *Archaeometry* 15, 123–127.

Bowman, S. (1990). Radiocarbon Dating: Interpreting the Past. University of California Press, Berkeley.

Boyde, A. (1963). Estimation of age at death of young human skeletal remains from incremental lines in the dental enamel. *Ecerpta Medica International Congress Series* 80, 36–46.

Boyde, A. (1997). Microstructure of enamel. In: Dental Enamel, CIBA Foundation Symposium 205 (ed. D. J. Chadwick and G. Cardew), pp. 18–31. John Wiley, Chichester, UK.

Boynton, R. S. (1980). Chemistry and Technology of Lime and Limestone. John Wiley, New York.

Bozarth, S. (1987). Diagnostic opal phytoliths from rinds of selected *Cucurbita* species. *American Antiquity* 52, 607–615.

Brain, C. K. (1967a). Hottentot food remains and their bearings on the interpretation of fossil bone assemblages. *Scientific Papers of the Namib Desert Research Station* 32, 1–11.

Brain, C. K. (1967b). New light on old bones. *South African Museum Association Bulletin* 9, 22–27.

Brain, C. K. (1981). The Hunters or the Hunted? An Introduction to African Cave Taphonomy. University of Chicago Press, Chicago.

Brain, C. K., and Sillen, A. (1988). Evidence from the Swartkrans cave for the earliest use of fire. *Nature* 336, 464–466.

Branda, F., Luciani, G., Constantini, A., and Piccioli, C. (2001). Interpretation of the thermogravimetric curves of ancient pozzolanic concretes. *Archaeometry* 43, 447–453.

Bray, H. J., and Redfern, S. A. T. (1999). Kinetics of dehydration of Ca-montmorillonite. *Physical Chemistry of Minerals* 26, 591–600.

Brill, R. H., and Wampler, J. M. (1965). Isotope ratios in archaeological artifacts of lead. In: Applications of Science in the Examination of Works of Art, pp. 155–166. Museum of Fine Arts, Boston.

Britton, K., Grimes, V., Dau, J., and Richards, M. P. (2009). Reconstructing faunal migrations using intra-tooth sampling and strontium and oxygen isotope analyses: a case study of modern caribou (*Rangifer tarandus granti*). *Journal of Archaeological Science* 36, 1163–1172.

Brochier, J. É. (1983). Combustions et parcage des herbivored domestiques. *Bulletin de la Societé Préhistorique Française* 80, 143–145.

Brochier, J. É., and Thinon, M. (2003). Calcite crystals, starch grains aggregates or . . . POCC? Comment on "calcite crystals inside archaeological plant tissues." *Journal of Archaeological Science* 30, 1211–1214.

Brochier, J. É., Villa, P., and Giacomarra, M. (1992). Shepherds and sediments: geo-ethnoarchaeology of pastoral sites. *Journal of Anthropological Archaeology* 11, 47–102.

Bronk Ramsey, C. (1995). Radiocarbon calibration and analysis of stratigraphy: the OxCal Program. *Radiocarbon* 37, 425–430.

Bronk Ramsey, C. (2001). Development of the radiocarbon program OxCal. *Radiocarbon* 43, 355–363.

Bronk Ramsey, C. (2003). OxCal Version 3.9. Oxford Radiocarbon Accelerator Unit, Oxford.

Bronk Ramsey, C., and Higham, T. (2003). Towards high precision AMS: progress and limitations. Paper presented at the 18th International Radiocarbon Conference, Wellington, New Zealand.

Bronk Ramsey, C., van der Plicht, J., and Weninger, B. (2001). "Wiggle matching" radiocarbon dates. *Radiocarbon* 43, 381–389.

Bronk Ramsey, C., Buck, C. E., Manning, S. W., Reimer, P., and van der Plicht, J. (2006). Developments in radiocarbon calibration for archaeology. *Antiquity*, 783–798.

Brooks, A. S., Hare, P. E., Kokis, J. E., Miller, G. H., Ernst, R. D., and Wendorf, F. (1990). Dating archaeological sites by protein diagenesis in ostrich eggshell. *Science* 248, 60–64.

Brothwell, D. R., and Pollard, A. M., eds. (2001). Handbook of Archaeological Sciences. John Wiley, Chichester, UK.

Brown, A. (1973). Bone strontium content as a dietary indicator in human populations. University of Michigan. PhD Dissertation.

Brown, T. A. (2001). Ancient DNA. In: Handbook of Archaeological Sciences (ed. D. R. Brothwell and A. M. Pollard), pp. 301–311. John Wiley, Chichester, UK.

Bryant, J. D., Luz, B., and Froelich, P. N. (1994). Oxygen isotopic composition of fossil horse tooth phosphate as a record of continental paleoclimate. *Palaeogeography, Palaeoclimatology, Palaeoecology* 107, 303–316.

Bryant, J. D., Koch, P., Froelich, P. N., Showers, W. J., and Genna, B. J. (1996). Oxygen isotope partitioning between phosphate and carbonate in mammalian bone. *Geochimica et Cosmochimica Acta* 60, 145–148.

Buchardt, B., and Weiner, S. (1981). Diagenesis of aragonite from Upper Cretaceous ammonites, a geochemical case-study. *Sedimentology* 28, 423–438.

Buckland, W. (1822). Account of an assemblage of fossil teeth and bones of elephant, rhinoceros, hippopotamus, bear, tiger, and hyaena and sixteen other animals: discovered in a cave at Kirkdale, Yorkshire in the year 1821; with a comparative view of 5 similar caverns in various parts of England and others on the Continent. *Philosophical Transactions of the Royal Society of London* 112, 171–237.

Burnell, J., Teubner, E., and Miller, A. (1980). Normal maturational changes in bone matrix, mineral, and crystal size in the rat. *Calcified Tissue International* 310, 13–19.

Burroni, D., Donahue, R. E., and Pollard, A. M. (2002). The surface alteration features of flint artefacts as a record of environmental processes. *Journal of Archaeological Science* 29, 1277–1287.

Buxeda, J., Garrigos, I., Mommsen, H., and Tsolakidou, A. (2002). Alterations of Na, K and Rb concentrations in Mycenaean pottery and a proposed explanation using X-ray diffraction. *Archaeometry* 44, 187–198.

Buxeda, J., Garrigos, I., Jones, R. E., Kilikoglou, V., Levi, S. T., Maniatis, Y., Mitchell, J., Vagnetti, L., Wardle, K. A., and Andreou, S. (2003). Technology transfer at the periphery of the Mycenaean world: the cases of Mycenaean pottery found in Central Macedonia (Greece) and the Plain of Sybaris (Italy). *Archaeometry* 45, 263–284.

Buxton, D. R., and Russel, J. R. (1988). Lignin constituents and cell-wall digestibility of grass and legume stems. *Crop Science* 28, 553–558.

Cain, C. J., and Heyn, A. N. J. (1964). X-ray diffraction studies of the crystalline structure of the avian eggshell. *Biophysical Journal* 4, 23–39.

Calvert, S. E. (1974). Deposition and diagenesis of silica in marine sediments. In: Pelagic Sediments: On Land and Under the Sea, vol. 1 (ed. K. J. Hsü and H. C. Jenkyns). *International Association of Sedimentology Special Publications* 1, 273–299.

Canti, M. (1997). An investigation of microscopic calcareous spherulites from herbivore dung. *Journal of Archaeological Science* 24, 219–231.

Canti, M. G. (1998). Origin of calcium carbonate granules found in buried soils and Quaternary deposits. *Boreas* 27, 275–288.

Canti, M. G. (2007). Deposition and taphonomy of earthworm granules in relation to their interpretative potential in Quaternary stratigraphy. *Journal of Quaternary Science* 22, 111–118.

Carcaillet, C. (1998). A spatially precise study of Holocene fire history, climate and human impact within the Maurienne Valley, north French Alps. *Journal of Ecology* 86, 384–396.

Carlström, D. (1963). A crystallographic study of vertebrate otoliths. *Biological Bulletin* 125, 441–463.

Caró, F., and Di Giulio, A. (2004). Reliability of textural analysis of ancient plasters and mortars through automated image analysis. *Materials Characterization* 53, 243–257.

Caró, F., Riccardi, M. P., and Mazzilli Savini, M. T. (2008). Characterization of plasters and mortars as a tool in archaeological studies: the case of Lardirago Castle in Pavia, northern Italy. *Archaeometry* 50, 85–100.

Carter, J. G., and Clark, G. R. (1985). Classification and phylogenetic significance of molluscan shell structure. In: Mollusks: Notes for a Short Course (ed. T. W. Broadhead), pp. 50–71. Department of Geological Science Studies, University of Tennessee, Knoxville.

Carty, M. W., and Senapti, U. (1998). Porcelain – raw materials, processing, phase evolution, and mechanical behavior. *Journal of the American Ceramic Society* 81, 3–20.

Casadio, F., Chiari, G., and Simon, S. (2005). Evaluation of binder/aggregate ratios in archaeological lime mortars with carbonate aggregate: a comparative assessment of chemical, mechanical and microscopic approaches. *Archaeometry* 47, 671–689.

Casas, L., Linford, P., and Shaw, J. (2007). Archaeomagnetic dating of Dogmersfield Park brick kiln (southern England). *Journal of Archaeological Science* 34, 205–213.

Cazalla, O., Rodriguez-Navarro, C., Sebastian, E., and Cultrone, G. (2000). Aging of lime putty: effects on traditional lime mortar carbonation. *Journal of the American Ceramics Society* 83, 1070–1076.

Charola, A. E., and Henriques, F. M. A. (1999). Hydraulicity in lime mortars revisited. Paper presented at the RILEM TC 167-COM International Workshop, University of Paisley, Scotland.

Chefetz, B., Tarchitzky, J., Deshmukh, A. P., Hatcher, P. G., and Chen, Y. (2002). Structural characterization of soil organic matter and humic acids in particle-size fractions of an agricultural soil. *Soil Science Society of America Journal* 66, 129–141.

Chernysh, I. G., Pakhovchisin, S. V., and Goncharik, V. P. (1993). The activity of dispersed oxides on natural and exfoliated graphite surfaces. *Reaction Kinetics Catalysis Letters* 50, 273–277.

Cho, G., Wu, Y., and Ackerman, J. L. (2003). Detection of hydroxyl ions in bone mineral by solid state NMR spectroscopy. *Science* 300, 1123–1127.

Chu, V., Regev, L., Weiner, S., and Boaretto, E. (2008). Differentiating between anthropogenic calcite in plaster, ash and natural calcite using infrared spectroscopy: implications in archaeology. *Journal of Archaeological Science* 35, 905–911.

Cohen-Ofri, I., Weiner, L., Boaretto, E., Mintz, G., and Weiner, S. (2006). Modern and fossil charcoal: aspects of structure and diagenesis. *Journal of Archaeological Science* 33, 428–439.

Cohen-Ofri, I., Popovitz-Biro, R., and Weiner, S. (2007). Structural characterization of modern and fossil natural charcoal using high resolution TEM and electron energy loss spectroscopy (EELS). *Chemistry: A European Journal* 13, 2306–2310.

Cole, W. E., and Hoskins, J. S. (1957). Clay mineral mixtures and interstratified minerals. In: The Differential Thermal Investigation of Clays (ed. R. C. Mackenzie), pp. 248–274. Mineralogical Society, London.

Collins, M. J., Muyzer, G., Westbroek, P., Curry, G. B., Sandberg, P. A., Xu, S. J., Quinn, R., and MacKinnon, D. (1991). Preservation of fossil biopolymeric structures: conclusive immunological evidence. *Geochimica et Cosmochimica Acta* 55, 2253–2257.

Collins, M. J., Riley, M., Child, A. M., and Turner, W. G. (1995). A basic mathematical simulation of the chemical degradation of ancient collagen. *Journal of Archaeological Science* 22, 175–183.

Collins, M. J., Nielsen-Marsh, C. M., Hiller, J., Smith, C. I., Roberts, J. P., Prigodich, R. V., Wess, T. J., Csapó, J., Millard, A. R., and Turner-Walker, G. (2002). The survival of organic matter in bone: a review. *Archaeometry* 44, 383–394.

Colomban, P. (2005). Raman μ-spectrometry, a unique tool for on-site analysis and identification of ancient ceramics and glasses. *Materials Research Society Symposium Proceedings* 852, 1–15.

Condamin, J., Formenti, F., Metais, M. O., Michel, M., and Blond, P. (1976). The applications of gas chromatography to the tracing of oil in ancient amphorae. *Archaeometry* 18, 195–201.

Courty, M. A., Goldberg, P., and MacPhail, R. (1989). Soils and Micromorphology in Archaeology. Cambridge University Press, Cambridge.

Coutts, P. J. F. (1970). Bivalve growth patterning as a method of seasonal dating in archaeology. *Nature* 226, 874.

Crane, N. J., Popescu, V., Morris, M. D., Steenhuis, P., and Ignelzi, M. A. (2006). Raman spectroscopic evidence for octacalcium phosphate and other mineral species deposited during intramembraneous mineralization. *Bone* 39, 431–433.

Cuif, J.-P., and Dauphin, Y. (2005). The two-step mode of growth in the scleractinian coral skeletons from the micrometre to the overall scale. *Journal of Structural Biology* 150, 319–331.

Currey, J. D. (1984). The Mechanical Adaptations of Bones. Princeton University Press, Princeton, NJ.

Currey, J. D. (2002). Bones. Princeton University Press, Princeton, NJ.

Curry, G. B., Cusack, M., Walton, D., Endo, K., Clegg, H., Abbott, G., and Armstrong, H. (1991). Biogeochemistry of brachiopod intracrystalline molecules. *Philosophical Transactions of the Royal Society of London, Series B* 333, 359–365.

Daculsi, G., Menanteau, J., Kerebel, L. M., and Mire, D. (1984). Length and shape of enamel crystals. *Calcified Tissue International* 36, 550–555.

Darwin, C. (1859). The Origin of Species. John Murray, London.

da Silveira, P. M., do Rosário Veiga, M., and de Brito, J. (2007). Gypsum coatings in ancient buildings. *Construction and Building Materials* 21, 126–131.

Dauphin, Y. (2002). Comparison of the soluble matrices of the calcitic prismatic layer of *Pinna nobilis* (Mollusca, Bivalvia, Pteriomorpha). *Comparative Biochemistry and Physiology, Part A* 132, 577–590.

Dauphin, Y., Pickford, M., and Senut, B. (1998). Diagenetic changes in the mineral and organic phases of fossil avian eggshells from Namibia. *Applied Geochemistry* 13, 243–256.

Dauphin, Y., Montuelle, S., Quantin, C., and Massard, P. (2007). Estimating the preservation of tooth structures: towards a new scale of observation. *Journal of Taphonomy* 5, 43–56.

Davies, G., and Ghabbour, E. A. (1998). Humic Substances: Structures, Properties and Uses. Royal Society of Chemistry, Cambridge.

Dean, M. C., Beynon, A. D., Thackeray, J. F., and Macho, G. A. (1993). Histological reconstruction of dental development and age at death of a juvenile *Paranthropus robustus* specimen, SK 63, from Swartkrans, South Africa. *American Journal of Physical Anthropology* 91, 401–419.

De Benedetto, G. E., Laviano, R., Sabbatini, L., and Zambonin, P. G. (2002). Infrared spectroscopy in the mineralogical characterization of ancient pottery. *Journal of Cultural Heritage* 3, 177–186.

Deer, W. A., Howie, R. A., and Zussman, J. (1992). An Introduction to the Rock-Forming Minerals. London Scientific and Technical, London.

Deith, M. R. (1983a). Seasonality of shell collecting determined by oxygen isotope analysis of marine shells from Asturian sites in Cantabria. In: Animals and Archaeology, vol. 2, Shell Middens, Fishes and Birds (ed. C. Grigson and J. Clutton-Brock). *British Archaeological Reports International Series* 183, 67–76.

Deith, M. R. (1983b). Molluscan calendars: the use of growth line analysis to establish seasonality of shellfish collection at the Mesolithic site of Morton, Fife. *Journal of Archaeological Science* 10, 423–440.

Della Casa, P. (2005). Lithic resources in the early prehistory of the Alps. *Archaeometry* 47, 221–234.

DeNiro, M. J. (1985). Postmortem preservation and alteration of in vivo bone collagen isotope ratio in relation to palaeodietry reconstraction. *Nature*, 317, 806–809.

DeNiro, M. J., and Epstein, S. (1978). Influence of diet on the distribution of carbon isotopes in animals. *Geochimica et Cosmochimica Acta* 42, 495–506.

DeNiro, M. J., and Weiner, S. (1988a). Chemical, enzymatic and spectroscopic characterization of collagen and other organic fractions from prehistoric bones. *Geochimica et Cosmochimica Acta* 52, 2197–2206.

DeNiro, M. J., and Weiner, S. (1988b). Organic matter within crystalline aggregates of hydroxyapatite: a new substrate for stable isotopic and possibly other biochemical analyses of bone. *Geochimica et Cosmochimica Acta* 52, 2415–2423.

Dennis, J. E., Xiao, S. Q., Agarval, M., Fink, D. J., Heuer, A. H., and Caplan, A. I. (1996). Microstructure of matrix and mineral components of eggshells from white leghorn chicken (*Gallus gallus*). *Journal of Morphology* 228, 287–306.

Derry, L. A., Kurtz, A. C., Ziegler, K., and Chadwick, O. A. (2005). Biological control of terrestrial silica cycling and export fluxes to watersheds. *Nature* 433, 728–731.

de Vaux, R. (1973). Archaeology and the Dead Sea Scrolls. Oxford University Press, Oxford.

Dixon, J., and Weed, S. (1977). Minerals in Soil Environments. Soil Science Society of America, Madison, WI.

Dodd, J., and Stanton, R. J. (1981). Paleoecology: Concepts and Applications. John Wiley, New York.

Doner, H. E., and Lynn, W. C. (1977). Carbonate, halide, sulfate, and sulfide minerals. In: Minerals in Soil Environments (ed. J. B. Dixon and S. B. Weed), pp. 75–98. Soil Science Society of America, Madison, WI.

Douglass, A. E. (1921). Dating our prehistoric ruins. *Natural History* 21, 27–30.

Douglass, A. E. (1941). Crossdating in dendrochronology. *Journal of Forestry* 39, 825–831.

Dove, P. M., Weiner, S., and DeYoreo, J. J. (2003). Biomineralization. *Reviews in Mineralogy and Geochemistry* vol. S54.

Dressler, V. L., Pozebon, D., Flores, E. L. M., Paniz, J. N. B., and Flores, E. M. M. (2002). Potentiometric determination of fluoride in geological and biological samples following pyrohydrolytic decomposition. *Analytica Chimica Acta* 466, 117–123.

Dudd, S. N., and Evershed, R. P. (1998). Direct demonstration of milk as an element of archaeological economies. *Science* 282, 1478–1481.

Dufour, E., Cappetta, H., Denis, A., Dauphin, Y., and Mariotti, A. (2000). La diagenese des otolithes par la comparaison des donnees microstructurales, mineralogiques et geochimiques; application aux fossiles du Pliocene du Sud-Est de la France. *Bulletin de la Societe Geologique de France* 171, 521–532.

Eckert, K. A., and Kunkel, T. A. (1991). DNA polymerase fidelity and the polymerase chain reaction. In: PCR Methods and Application (eds. Bentley, D., Gibbs, R., Green, E. and Myers, R. pp. 17–24. Cold Spring Harbour Laboratory Press, New York.

Eckmeier, E., Gerlach, R., Gehrt, E., and Schmidt, M. W. I. (2007). Pedogenesis of Chernozems in central Europe – a review. *Geoderma* 139, 288–299.

Edwards, K. J., Whittington, G., Robinson, M., and Richter, D. (2005). Paleoenvironments, the archaeological record and cereal pollen detection at Clickimin, Shetland, Scotland. *Journal of Archaeological Science* 32, 1741–1756.

Edwards, N. T. (1975). Effects of temperature and moisture on carbon dioxide evolution in a mixed deciduous forest floor. *Soil Science Society of America Proceedings* 39, 361–365.

Eframov, I. A. (1940). Taphonomy: a new branch of paleontology. *Pan-American Geology* 74, 81–93.

Efstratiou, N. (1984). Ethnoarchaeological research in Thrace. *Archaeology* 13, 20–26.

Efstratiou, N. (1990). Prehistoric habitations and structures in northern Greece: an ethnoarchaeological case study. *Bulletin de Correspondance Hellénique* 19, 33–41.

Eiland, M. L., and Williams, Q. (2000). Infrared spectroscopy of ceramics from Tell Brak, Syria. *Journal of Archaeological Science* 27, 993–1006.

Elbaum, R., Albert, R. M., Elbaum, M., and Weiner, S. (2003). Detection of burning of plant materials in the archaeological record by changes in the refractive indices of siliceous phytoliths. *Journal Archaeological Science* 30, 217–226.

Elbaum, R., Melamed-Bessudo, C., Boaretto, E., Galili, E., Lev-Yadun, S., Levy, A. A., and Weiner, S. (2006). Ancient olive DNA in pits: preservation, amplification and sequence analysis. *Journal Archaeological Science* 33, 77–88.

Elbaum, R., Zaltzman, L., Burgert, I., and Fratzl, P. (2007). The role of wheat awns in the seed dispersal unit. *Science* 316, 884–886.

Elbaum, R., Melamed-Bessudo, C., Tuross, N., Levy, A. A., and Weiner, S. (2009). New methods to isolate organic materials from silicified phytoliths reveal fragmented glycoproteins but no DNA. *Quaternary International* 193, 11–19.

El Hiveris, S. O. (1978). Nature of resistance to *Striga hermonithica* (Del) Benth. parasitism in some *Sorghum vulgare* (Pers.) cultivars. *Weed Research* 27, 305–311.

Elias, R. W., Hirao, Y., and Patterson, C. C. (1982). The circumvention of the natural biopurification of calcium along nutrient pathways by atmospheric inputs of industrial lead. *Geochimica et Cosmochimica Acta* 46, 2561–2580.

Eliyahu-Behar, A., Regev, L., Shalev, Y., Shilstein, S., Sharon, G., Gilboa, A., and Weiner, S. (2009). Functional analysis of a pyrotechnological installation from the Roman period at Tel-Dor, Israel: casting pit for bronze objects. *Journal of Field Archaeology*, 34, 135–151.

El Mansouri, M., El Fouikar, A., and Saint Martin, B. (1996). Correlation between ^{14}C ages and aspartic acid racemization at the Upper Paleolithic site of the Abri Pataud (Dordogne, France). *Journal of Archaeological Science* 23, 803–809.

Elsdon, T. S., and Gillanders, B. M. (2003). Reconstructing patterns of fish based on environmental influences on otolith chemistry. *Reviews in Fish Biology and Fisheries* 13, 219–235.

Epstein, S., Buchsbaum, R., Lowenstam, H. A., and Urey, H. C. (1953). Revised carbonate-water isotopic temperature scale. *Bulletin of the Geological Society of America* 64, 1315–1326.

Ericson, J. E. (1985). Strontium isotope characterization in the study of prehistoric human ecology. *Journal of Human Evolution* 14, 503–514.

Esslemont, G., Maher, W., Ford, P., and Krikowa, F. (2000). The determination of phosphorus and other elements in plant leaves by ICP-MS after low-volume microwave digestion with nitric acid. *Atomic Spectroscopy* 21, 42–45.

Everett, D. H. (1959). An Introduction to the Study of Chemical Thermodynamics. Longmans, Greem, London.

Evershed, R. P., Dudd, S. N., Lockheart, M. J., and Jim, S. (2001). Lipids in archaeology. In: Handbook of Archaeological Sciences (ed. D. R. Brothwell and A. M. Pollard), pp. 331–349. John Wiley, Chichester, UK.

Faix, O., Bremer, J., Schmidt, O., and Stevanovic, T. (1991). Monitoring of chemical changes in white-rot degraded beech wood by pyrolysis – gas chromatography and Fourier-transform infrared spectroscopy. *Journal of Analytical and Applied Pyrolysis* 21, 147–162.

Farmer, V. C. (1974). The Infrared Spectra of Minerals. Mineralogical Society, London.

Farmer, V. C., Delbos, E., and Miller, J. D. (2005). The role of phytolith formation and dissolution in controlling concentrations of silica in soil solutions and streams. *Geoderma* 127, 71–79.

Featherstone, J. D. B., Pearson, S., and LeGeros, R. Z. (1984). An infrared method for the quantification of carbonate in carbonated apatites. *Caries Research* 18, 63–66.

Ferraiolo, J. A. (1982). A systematic classification of nonsilicate minerals. *Bulletin of the American Museum of Natural History* 172, 1–237.

Ferraiolo, J. A. (2008). A Systematic Classification of Nonsilicate Minerals. Ferraiola, J. A. jfer@erols.com, Bowie, MD, 1–457.

Feynman, R. P. (1998). The Meaning of It All: Thoughts of a Citizen Scientist. Perseus Books, Reading, MA.

Fitton Jackson, S. (1956). The fine structure of developing bone in the embryonic fowl. *Proceedings of the Royal Society of London, Series B* 146, 270–280.

Fladmark, K. R. (1982). Microdebitage analysis: initial considerations. *Journal of Archaeological Science* 9, 205–220.

Fleming, S. (1976). Dating in Archaeology. St. Martin's Press, New York.

Fogel, M. L., Tuross, N., and Owsley, D. W. (1989). Nitrogen isotope tracers. *Carnegie Institution of Washington Yearbook* 88, 133–134.

Forbes, R. J. (1957). Studies in Ancient Technology. Vol. 5. Brill, Leiden, Netherlands.

Franceschi, V. R., and Horner, H. T. (1980). Calcium oxalate crystals in plants. *Botanical Review* 46, 361–427.

Franklin, R. E. (1951). Crystallite growth in graphitizing and non-graphitizing carbons. *Proceedings of the Royal Society of London, Series A* 209, 196–218.

Fraysse, F., Pokrovsky, O. S., Schott, J., and Meunier, J.-D. (2006). Surface properties, solubility and dissolution kinetics of bamboo phytoliths. *Geochimica et Cosmochimica Acta* 70, 1939–1951.

Freestone, I. C., and Tite, M. S. (1986). Refractories in the ancient and preindustrial world. In: High-Technology Ceramics: Past, Present and Future (ed. W. D. Kingery), pp. 35–63. American Ceramic Society, Westerville, OH.

Freund, F., and Knobel, R. M. (1977). Distribution of fluorine in hydroxyapatite studied by infrared spectroscopy. *Journal of the Chemical Society Dalton* 12, 1136–1140.

Friedman, I., and Smith, R. L. (1960). A new dating method using obsidian: Part 1, the development of the method. *American Antiquity* 25, 476–522.

Friedman, I., and Trembour, F. W. (1983). Obsidian hydration dating update. *American Antiquity* 48, 544–547.

Furlan, V., and Bissegger, P. (1975). Les mortiers anciens: histoire et essais d'analyse scientifique. *Revue suisse d'Art et d'Archéologie* 32, 166–178.

Gago-Duport, L., Briones, M. J. I., Rodríguez, J. B., and Covelo, B. (2008). Amorphous calcium carbonate biomineralization in the earthworm's calciferous gland: pathways to the formation of crystalline phases. *Journal of Structural Biology* 162, 422–435.

Garrison, E. G. (2003). Techniques in Archaeological Geology. Springer, Berlin.

Garrod, D. A. E. (1957). The Natufian culture: the life and economy of a Mesolithic people in the Near East. *Proceedings of the British Academy* 43, 211–227.

Garti, J., Kunin, P., Delarea, J., and Weiner, S. (2002). Calcium oxalate and sulphate-containing structures on the thallial surface of the lichen *Ramalina lacera*: response to polluted air and simulated acid rain. *Plant, Cell and Environment* 25, 1591–1604.

Gauldie, R. W. (1986). Vaterite otoliths from chinook salmon (*Oncorhynchus tshawytscha*). *New Zealand Journal of Marine and Freshwater Research* 20, 209–217.

Gautron, J., Rodriguez-Navarro, A. B., Gómez-Morales, J., Hernández-Hernández, M. A., Dunn, I. C., Bain, M. M., García-Ruiz, M., and Nys, Y. (2007). Evidence for the implication of chicken eggshell matrix proteins in the presence of shell mineralization. In: Biomineralization: From Paleontology to Materials Science (ed. J. L. Arias and M. S. Fernández), pp. 145–154. Editorial Universitaria, Santiago, Chile.

Geiger, S. B., and Weiner, S. (1993). Fluoridated carbonatoapatite in the intermediate layer between glass ionomer and dentin. *Dental Materials* 9, 33–36.

Genestar, C., and Palou, J. (2006). SEM-FTIR spectroscopic evaluation of deterioration in an historic coffered ceiling. *Analytic Bioanalytic Chemistry* 384, 987–993.

Gernaey, A. M., Waite, E. R., Collins, M. J., and Craig, O. E. (2001). Survival and interpretation of archaeological proteins. In: Handbook of Archaeological Sciences (ed. D. R. Brothwell and A. M. Pollard), pp. 323–329. John Wiley, Chichester, UK.

Gheradi, S. (1862). Sul magnetismo polare de palazzi ed altri edifizi in Torino. *Il Nuovo Cimento* 16, 384–404.

Gifford, D. P. (1978). Ethnoarchaeological observations of natural processes affecting cultural materials. In: Explorations in Ethnoarchaeology (ed. R. A. Gould), pp. 77–101. University of New Mexico Press, Albuquerque.

Gifford-Gonzalez, D. P. (1998). Gender and early pastoralists in East Africa. In: Gender in African Prehistory (ed. S. Kent), pp. 115–137. Altamira Press, Walnut Creek, CA.

Gifford-Gonzalez, D. P., Damrosch, D. B., Damrosch, D. R., Pryor, J., and Thunen, R. L. (1985). The third dimension in site structure: an experiment in trampling and vertical dispersal. *American Antiquity* 50, 803–818.

Gilbert, M., Hansen, A., Willerslev, E., Rudbeck, L., Barnes, I., Lynnerup, N., and Cooper, A. (2003a). Characterization of genetic miscoding lesions caused by postmortem damage. *American Journal of Human Genetics* 72, 48–61.

Gilbert, M. T. P., Willerslev, E., Hansen, A. J., Barnes, I., Rudbeck, L., Lynnerup, N., and Cooper, A. (2003b). Distribution patterns of postmortem damage in human mitochondrial DNA. *American Journal of Human Genetics* 72, 32–47.

Giraud-Guille, M. M. (1988). Twisted plywood architecture of collagen fibrils in human compact bone osteons. *Calcified Tissue International* 42, 167–180.

Glaser, B., Haumaier, L., Guggenberger, G., and Zech, W. (1998). Black carbon in soils: the use of benzenecarboxylic acids as specific markers. *Organic Geochemistry* 29, 811–819.

Glaser, B., Balashov, E., Haumaier, L., Guggenberger, G., and Zech, W. (2000). Black carbon in density fractions of anthropogenic soils of the Brazilian Amazon region. *Organic Geochemistry* 31, 669–678.

Glob, P. V. (1965). The Bog People: Iron-Age Man Preserved. New York Review of Books, New York.

Goffer, Z. (2007). Archaeological Chemistry. 2nd edition. John Wiley, Hoboken, NJ.

Goldberg, P. (2001). Some micromorphological aspects of prehistoric cave deposits. *Cahiers d'archéologie du CELAT* 10, 161–175.

Goldberg, P., and MacPhail, R. I. (2006). Practical and Theoretical Geoarchaeology. Blackwell, Malden, MA.

Goldberg, P., Weiner, S., Bar-Yosef, O., Xu, Q., and Liu, J. (2001). Site formation processes at Zhoukoudian. *Journal Human Evolution* 41, 483–530.

Goldberg, P., Laville, H., Meignen, L., and Bar-Yosef, O. (2007). Stratigraphy and geoarchaeological history of Kebara Cave, Mount Carmel. In: Kebara Cave, Mt. Carmel, Israel: The Middle and Upper Paleolithic Archaeology, Part 1 (ed. O. Bar-Yosef and L. Meignen), pp. 49–89. Peabody Museum of Archaeology and Ethnology, Harvard University, Cambridge, MA.

Goodfriend, G. A. (1987). Evaluation of amino acid racemization/epimerization dating using radiocarbon-dated fossil land snails. *Geology* 15, 698–700.

Goodfriend, G. A. (1992). Rapid racemization of aspartic acid in mollusc shells and potential for dating over recent centuries. *Nature* 357, 399–401.

Goodfriend, G. A., and Ellis, G. L. (2000). Stable carbon isotopic record of middle to late Holocene climate changes from land snail shells at Hinds Cave, Texas. *Quaternary International* 67, 47–60.

Goodfriend, G. A., Collins, M. J., Fogel, M. L., Macko, S. A., and Wehmiller, J. F. (2000). Perspectives in Amino Acid and Protein Geochemistry. Oxford University Press, New York.

Gorecki, P. (1985). Ethnoarchaeology: the need for a post-mortem enquiry. *World Archaeology* 17, 175–191.

Goren, Y., and Goldberg, P. (1991). Petrographic thin sections and the development of Neolithic plaster production in northern Israel. *Journal of Field Archaeology* 18, 131–138.

Goren, Y., Finkelstein, I., and Na'aman, N. (2004). Inscribed in Clay: Provenance Study of the Amarna Tablets and Other Ancient Near Eastern Texts. Emery and Claire Yass Publications in Archaeology, Tel Aviv.

Goren-Inbar, N., Werker, E., and Feibel, C. (2002). The Acheulian Site of Gesher Benot Yaakov, Israel: The Wood Assemblage. Oxbow Books, Oxford.

Goren-Inbar, N., Alperson, N., Kislev, M. E., Simchoni, O., Melamed, Y., Ben-Nun, A., and Werker, E. (2004). Evidence of hominin control of fire at Gesher Benot Ya'aqov, Israel. *Science* 304, 725–727.

Gosselain, O. P. (1992). Bonfire of the enquiries – pottery firing temperatures in archaeology: what for? *Journal of Archaeological Science* 19, 243–259.

Gotliv, B., Robach, J. A., and Veis, A. (2006). The composition and structure of bovine peritubular dentin: mapping by time of flight secondary ion mass spectrometry. *Journal of Structural Biology* 156, 320–333.

Gould, R. A. (1980). Living Archaeology. Cambridge University Press, Cambridge.

Gourdin, W., and Kingery, W. (1975). The beginnings of pyrotechnology: Neolithic and Egyptian lime plaster. *Journal of Field Archaeology* 2, 133–150.

Green, R. E., Krause, J., Ptak, S. E., Briggs, A. W., Ronan, M. T., Simons, J. F., Du, L., et al. (2006). Analysis of one million base pairs of Neanderthal DNA. *Nature* 444, 330–336.

Greenfield, H. J., Fowler, K. D., and van Schalkwyk, L. O. (2005). Where are the gardens? Early Iron Age horticulture in the Thukela River Basin of South Africa. *World Archaeology* 37, 307–328.

Greensmith, J. T. (1963). Clastic quartz, provenance and sedimentation. *Nature* 197, 345–347.

Grögler, N., Geiss, J., Grünenfelder, M., and Houtermans, F. G. (1966). Isotopenuntersuchungen zur Bestimmung der Herkunft römischer Bleirohre und Bleibarren. *Zeitschrift für Naturforschung* 21a, 1167–1172.

Grün, R. (1989). Electron spin resonance (ESR) dating. *Quaternary International* 1, 65–109.

Grün, R. (2001). Trapped charge dating (ESR, TL, OSL). In: Handbook of Archaeological Sciences (ed. D. R. Brothwell and A. M. Pollard), pp. 47–62. John Wiley, Chichester, UK.

Grün, R., Stringer, C., McDermott, F., Nathane, R., Porat, N., Robertson, S., Taylor, L., Mortimer, G., Eggins, S., and McCulloch, M. (2005). U-series and ESR analyses of bones and teeth relating to the human burials from Skhul. *Journal of Human Evolution* 49, 316–334.

Grupe, G., and Hummel, S. (1991). Trace element studies on experimentally cremated bone. I. Alteration of the chemical composition at high temperatures. *Journal of Archaeological Science* 18, 177–186.

Gueta, R., Natan, A., Addadi, L., Weiner, S., Refson, K., and Kronik, L. (2007). Local atomic order and infrared spectra of biogenic calcite. *Angewandte Chemie International Edition* 46, 291–294.

Gujer, W., and Zehnder, A. J. B. (1983). Conversion processes in anaerobic digestion. *Water Science and Technology* 15, 127–167.

Haberle, S. G., and Ledru, M.-P. (2001). Correlations among charcoal records of fires from the past 16,000 years in Indonesia, Papua New Guinea and central South America. *Quaternary Research* 55, 97–104.

Hackett, C. J. (1981). Microscopical focal destruction (tunnels) in exhumed human bones. *Medical Science and Law* 21, 243–265.

Hagelberg, E., Sykes, B. C., and Hedges, R. E. M. (1989). Ancient bone DNA amplified. *Nature* 342, 485.

Hardy, K., Blakeney, T., Copeland, L., Kirkham, J., Wrangham, R., and Collins, M. J. (2009). Starch granules, dental calculus and new perspectives on ancient diet. *Journal of Archaeological Science* 36, 248–255.

Hare, P. E. (1980). Organic geochemistry of bone and its relation to the survival of bone in the natural environment. In: Fossils in the Making: Vertebrate Taphonomy and Paleoecology (ed. A. K. Behrensmeyer and A. P. Hill), pp. 208–219. University of Chicago Press, Chicago.

Hare, P. E., and Abelson, P. H. (1965). Amino acid composition of some calcified proteins. *Carnegie Institution of Washington Yearbook* 64, 223–234.

Hare, P. E., and Abelson, P. H. (1967). Racemization of amino acids in fossil shells. *Carnegie Institution of Washington Yearbook* 66, 526–528.

Hare, P. E., and Estep, M. L. F. (1983). Carbon and nitrogen isotopic composition of amino acids in modern and fossil collagens. *Carnegie Institution of Washington Yearbook* 82, 410–414.

Hare, P. E., Hoering, T. C., and King, K. (1980). Biogeochemistry of Amino Acids. John Wiley, New York.

Hare, P. E., Fogel, M. L., Stafford, T. W., Mitchell, A. D., and Hoering, T. C. (1991). The isotopic composition of carbon and nitrogen in individual amino acids isolated from modern and fossil proteins. *Journal of Archaeological Science* 18, 277–292.

Harrison, C. C. (1996). Evidence for intramineral macromolecules containing protein from plant silicas. *Phytochemistry* 41, 37–42.

Harrison, C. C., and Lu, Y. (1994). In vivo and in vitro studies of polymer controlled silicification. *Bulletin de l'Institut océanographique, Monaco* 14, 151–158.

Harry, K. G., and Johnson, A. (2004). A non-destructive technique for measuring ceramic porosity using liquid nitrogen. *Journal of Archaeological Science* 31, 1567–1575.

Hart, J. P., and Matson, R. G. (2008). The use of multiple discriminant analysis in classifying prehistoric phytolith assemblages recovered from cooking residues. *Journal of Archaeological Science* 36, 430–433.

Haslam, M. (2004). The decomposition of starch grains in soils: implications for archaeological residue analyses. *Journal of Archaeological Science* 31, 1715–1734.

Hata, T. Y. O., Kobayashi, E., Yamane, K., and Kikuchi, K. (2000). Onion-like graphitic particles observed in wood charcoal. *Journal of Wood Science* 46, 89–92.

Hauschka, P. V., Lian, J. B., and Gallop, P. M. (1975). Direct identification of the calcium-binding amino acid, γ-carboxyglutamate in mineralized tissue. *Proceedings of the National Academy of Sciences of the United States of America* 72, 3925–3929.

Hayes, M. H. B. (1998). Humic substances: progress towards more realistic concepts of structures. In: Humic Substances: Structures, Properties and Uses (ed. G. Davies, E. A. Ghabbour, and K. A. Khairy), pp. 1–27. Royal Society of Chemistry, Cambridge.

Hedges, R. E. M. (2001). Overview – dating in archaeology; past, present and future. In: Handbook of Archaeological Sciences (ed. D. R. Brothwell and A. M. Pollard), pp. 3–8. John Wiley, Chichester, UK.

Hedges, R. E. M. (2002). Bone diagenesis: an overview of processes. *Archaeometry* 44, 319–328.

Hedges, R. E. M., Thorp, J. A., and Tuross, N. C. (1995). Is tooth enamel carbonate a suitable material for radiocarbon dating? *Radiocarbon* 37, 285–290.

Heimann, R. B., and Maggetti, M. (1981). Experiments on simulated burial of calcareous terra sigillata (mineralogical change): preliminary results. *British Museum Occasional Paper* 19, 163–177.

Hein, A., Kilikoglou, V., and Kassianidou, V. (2007). Chemical and mineralogical examination of metallurgical ceramics from a Late Bronze Age copper smelting site in Cyprus. *Journal of Archaeological Science* 34, 141–154.

Heinemeier, J., Jungner, H., Lindroos, A., Ringbom, A., von Konow, T., and Rud, N. (1997). AMS C-14 dating of lime mortar. *Nuclear Instruments and Methods in Physics Research, Section B* 123, 487–495.

Heinrich, E. W. (1965). Microscopic Identification of Minerals. McGraw-Hill, New York.

Henderson, J. (2000). The Science and Archaeology of Materials: An Investigation of Inorganic Materials. Routledge, London.

Henderson, J. (2001). Glass and glaze. In: Handbook of Archaeological Science (ed. D. R. Brothwell and A. M. Pollard), pp. 471–482. John Wiley, Chichester, UK.

Henry, A. G., and Piperno, D. R. (2008). Using plant microfossils from dental calculus to recover human diet: a case study from Tell al-Raqa'i, Syria. *Journal of Archaeological Science* 35, 1943–1950.

Heron, C., and Evershed, R. P. (1993). The analysis of organic residues and the study of pottery use. In: Archaeological Method and Theory, vol. 5 (ed. M. B. Schiffer), pp. 247–284. University of Arizona Press, Tucson.

Heron, C., and Pollard, A. M. (1988). The analysis of natural resinous materials from Roman amphoras. In: Science and Archaeology, Glasgow 1987: Proceedings of a Conference on the Application of Scientific Methods to Archaeology, vol. 196 (ed. E. A. Slater and J. O. Tate), pp. 429–447. British Archaeological Reports, British Series, Oxford.

Herron, C. (2001). Geochemical prospecting. In: Handbook of Archaeological Sciences (ed. D. R. Brothwell and A. M. Pollard), pp. 565–573. John Wiley, Chichester, UK.

Herz, N. (1992). Provenance determination of Neolithic to classical Mediterranean marbles by stable isotopes. *Archaeometry* 34, 185–194.

Hess, D., Coker, D. J., Loutsch, J. M., and Russ, J. (2008). Production of oxalates in vitro by microbes isolated from rock surfaces with prehistoric paints in the Lower Pecos region, Texas. *Geoarchaeology* 23, 3–11.

Higham, T. F. G., and Horn, P. L. (2000). Seasonal dating using fish otoliths: results from the Shag River Mouth site, New Zealand. *Journal of Archaeological Science* 27, 439–448.

Higuchi, R., Bowman, B., Freiberger, M., Ryder, O. A., and Wilson, A. C. (1984). DNA sequences from the quagga, an extinct member of the horse family. *Nature* 312, 282–284.

Hill, C., and Forti, P. (1997). Cave Minerals of the World. 2nd edition. National Speleological Society, Huntsville, AL.

Hiller, C. R., Robinson, C., and Weatherell, J. A. (1975). Variation in the composition of developing rat incisor enamel. *Calcified Tissue Research* 18, 1–12.

Hillman, G. (1996). Late Pleistocene changes in wild plant-foods available to hunter-gatherers of the northern Fertile Crescent: possible preludes to cereal cultivation. In: The Origins and Spread of Agriculture and Pastoralism in Eurasia (ed. D. R. Harris), pp. 159–203. UCL Press, London.

Hillson, S. (1986). Teeth. Cambridge University Press, Cambridge.

Hodder, I. (1999). The Archaeological Process. Blackwell, Oxford.

Hodge, A. J., and Petruska, J. A. (1963). Recent studies with the electron microscope on ordered aggregates of the tropocollagen molecule. In: Aspects of Protein Structure (ed. G. N. Ramachandran), pp. 289–300. Academic Press, New York.

Hodson, M. J., White, P. J., Mead, A., and Broadley, M. R. (2005). Phylogenetic variation in the silicon composition of plants. *Annals of Botany* 96, 1027–1046.

Holden, J. L., Phakey, P. P., and Clement, J. G. (1995). Scanning electron microscope observations of incinerated human femoral bone: a case study. *Forensic Science International* 74, 29–45.

Holliday, V. T. (2004). Soils in Archaeological Research. Oxford University Press, New York.

Hood, M. A., and Meyers, S. P. (1977). Rates of chitin degradation in an estuarine environment. *Journal of Oceanography* 33, 328–334.

Hughen, K., Lehman, S., Southon, J., Overpeck, J., Marchal, O., Herring, C., and Turnbull, J. (2004). ^{14}C activity and global carbon cycle changes over the past 50,000 years. *Science* 303, 202–207.

Hull, K. L. (1987). Identification of cultural site formation processes through microdebitage analysis. *Antiquity* 52, 772–783.

Hull, K. L. (2001). Reasserting the utility of obsidian hydration dating: a temperature-dependent empirical approach to practical temporal resolution with archaeological obsidians. *Journal of Archaeological Science* 28, 1025–1040.

Humphrey, L. T., Dirks, W., Dean, M. C., and Jeffries, T. E. (2008). Tracking dietary transitions in weanling baboons (*Papio hamadryas anubis*) using strontium/calcium ratios in enamel. *Folia Primatalogica* 79, 197–212.

Humphreys, G. S., Hunt, P. A., and Buchanan, R. (1987). Wood-ash stone near Sydney, N.S.W.: a carbonate pedological feature in an acidic soil. *Australian Journal of Soil Research* 25, 115–124.

Huntley, D. J., Godfrey-Smith, D. I., and Thewalt, M. L. W. (1985). Optical dating of sediments. *Nature* 313, 105–107.

Hustedt, F. (1942). Aerophile Diatomeen in der nordwestdeutschen Flora. *Berigte der Deutschen Botanischen Gesellschaft* 60, 55–73.

Hutchinson, G. (1950). Survey of contemporary knowledge of biogeochemistry. 3. The biogeochemistry of vertebrate excretion. *Bulletin of the American Museum of Natural History* 96, 1–554.

Hutson, S. R., Stanton, T. W., Magnoni, A., Terry, R., and Craner, J. (2007). Beyond the buildings: formation processes of ancient Maya houselots and methods for the study of non-architectural space. *Journal of Anthropological Archaeology* 26, 442–473.

Huxley, T. H. (1863). Essays: On Our Knowledge of the Causes of the Phenomena of Organic Nature. J. A. Mays, London.

Ikeya, M. (1978). Electron spin resonance as a method of dating. *Archaeometry* 33, 153–199.

Inbar, Y., and Chen, Y. (1990). Humic substances formed during the compasting of organic matter. *Soil Science Society of America Journal* 54, 1316–1323.

Isaac, G. (1968). Traces of Pleistocene hunters: an East African example. In: Man the Hunter (ed. R. Lee and I. DeVore), pp. 253–261. Aldine, Chicago.

Jacobs, Z., Wintle, A. G., Roberts, R. G., and Duller, G. A. T. (2008). Equivalent dose distributions of single grains of quartz at Sibudu, South Africa: context, causes and consequences for optical dating of archaeological deposits. *Journal of Archaeological Science* 35, 1808–1820.

James, S. R. (1989). Hominid use of fire in the Lower and Middle Pleistocene. *Current Anthropology* 30, 1–11.

Jans, M. M. E., Nielsen-Marsh, C. M., Smith, C. I., Collins, M. J., and Kars, H. (2004). Characterisation of microbial attack on archaeological bone. *Journal of Archaeological Science* 31, 87–95.

Jansma, M. J. (1982). Diatom analysis from some prehistoric sites in the coastal area of the Netherlands. *Acta Geologica Academiae Scientiarum Hungaricae* 25, 229–236.

Jansonius, J., and McGregor, D. C. (1996). Palynology: Principles and Applications. American Association for Palynology Foundation, College Station, TX.

Jodaikin, A., Weiner, S., and Traub, W. (1984). Enamel rod relations in the developing rat incisor. *Journal of Ultrastructure Research* 89, 324–332.

Johnson, B. J., and Miller, G. H. (1997). Archaeological applications of amino acid racemization. *Archaeometry* 39, 265–287.

Johnson, B. J., Miller, G. H., Fogel, M. L., and Beaumont, P. B. (1997). The determination of late Quaternary paleoenvironments at Equus cave, South Africa, using stable isotopes and amino acid racemization in ostrich eggshell. *Palaeogeography, Palaeoclimatology, Palaeoecology* 136, 121–137.

Johnson, B. J., Vogel, M. L., and Miller, G. H. (1998). Stable isotopes in modern ostrich eggshell: a calibration for modern paleoenvironmental applications in semi-arid regions of South Africa. *Geochimica et Cosmochimica Acta* 62, 2451–2461.

Jones, D., and Wilson, M. J. (1986). Biomineralization in crustose lichens. In: Biomineralization in Lower Plants and Animals (ed. B. S. C. Leadbeater and R. Riding), pp. 91–105. Clarendon Press, Oxford.

Jones, J. D., and Vallentyne, J. R. (1960). Biogeochemistry of organic matter – I. Polypeptides and amino acids in fossils and sediments in relation to geothermometry. *Geochimica et Cosmochimica Acta* 21, 1–34.

Jones, M. K., and Colledge, S. (2001). Archaeobotany and the transition to agriculture. In: Handbook of Archaeological Sciences (ed. D. R. Brothwell and A. M. Pollard), pp. 393–401. John Wiley, Chichester, UK.

Jones, R. L., and Beavers, A. H. (1963). Some mineralogical and chemical properties of plant opal. *Soil Science* 96, 375–379.

Jowsey, J. (1961). Age changes in human bone. *Clinical Orthopaedics* 17, 210–218.

Kalish, J. M. (1991). Determinants of otolith chemistry: seasonal variation in the composition of blood plasma, endolymph and otoliths of bearded rock cod *Pseudophycis barbatus*. *Marine Ecology Progress Series* 74, 137–159.

Kandel, A. W., and Conard, N. J. (2005). Production sequences of ostrich eggshell beads and settlement dynamics in the Geelbek Dunes of the Western Cape, South Africa. *Journal of Archaeological Science* 32, 1711–1721.

Karasik, A., and Smilansky, U. (2008). 3D scanning technology as a standard archaeological tool for pottery analysis: practice and theory. *Journal of Archaeological Science* 35, 1148–1168.

Karkanas, P. (2007). Identification of lime plaster in prehistory using petrographic methods: a review and reconsideration of the data on the basis of experimental and case studies. *Geoarchaeology* 22, 775–796.

Karkanas, P., Bar-Yosef, O., Goldberg, P., and Weiner, S. (2000). Diagenesis in prehistoric caves: the use of minerals that form in situ to assess the completeness of the archaeological record. *Journal of Archaeological Science* 27, 915–929.

Karkanas, P., Rigaud, J.-P., Simek, J., Albert, R., and Weiner, S. (2002). Ash, bones and guano: a study of the minerals and phytoliths in the sediments of Grotte XVI, Dordogne, France. *Journal of Archaeological Science* 29, 721–732.

Karkanas, P., Koumouzelis, M., Kozolowski, J. K., Sitlivy, V., Sobczyk, K., Berna, F., and Weiner, S. (2004). The earliest evidence for clay hearths: Aurignacian features in Klisoura Cave 1, southern Greece. *Antiquity* 78, 513–525.

Karkanas, P., Shahack-Gross, R., Ayalon, A., Bar-Matthews, M., Barkai, R., Frumkin, A., Gopher, A., and Stiner, M. C. (2007). Evidence for habitual use of fire at the end of the Lower Paleolithic: site formation processes at Qesem Cave, Israel. *Journal of Human Evolution* 53, 197–212.

Kastner, M., Keene, J. B., and Gieskes, J. M. (1977). Diagenesis of siliceous oozes – I. Chemical controls on the rate of opal-A to opal-CT transformation – an experimental study. *Geochimica et Cosmochimica Acta* 41, 1041–1951.

Katz, E. P., and Li, S. (1973). Structure and function of bone collagen fibrils. *Journal of Molecular Biology* 80, 1–15.

Katzenberg, M. A. (1993). Age differences and population variation in stable isotope variations from Ontario, Canada. In: Prehistoric Human Bone: Archaeology at the Molecular Level (ed. J. B. Lambert and G. Grupe), pp. 39–62. Springer, Berlin.

Katzenburg, M. A., and Harrison, R. G. (1997). What's in a bone? Recent advances in archaeological bone chemistry. *Journal of Archaeological Science* 5, 265–293.

Kaufman, A., Broecker, W. S., Ku, T. L., and Thurber, D. L. (1971). The status of U-series methods of mollusc dating. *Geochimica et Cosmochimica Acta* 35, 1155–1183.

Kelly, E. F., Amundson, R. G., Marino, B. D., and DeNiro, M. J. (1991). Stable isotope ratios in carbon in phytoliths as a quantitative method of monitoring vegetation and climate change. *Quaternary Research* 35, 222–233.

Kennish, M. J., and Olsson, R. K. (1975). Effects of thermal discharges on the microstructural growth of *Mercenaria mercenaria*. *Environmental Geology* 1, 41–64.

Kenyon, K. M. (1960). Archaeology in the Holy Land. Ernest Benn, London.

Kidwell, S. M., and Holland, S. M. (2002). The quality of the fossil record: implications for evolutionary analyses. *Annual Review of Ecological Systematics* 33, 561–588.

Kingery, W. D., Bowen, H. K., and Uhlmann, D. R. (1960). Introduction to Ceramics. John Wiley, New York.

Kingery, W. D., and Francl, J. (1954). Fundamental study of clay: XIII, drying behavior and plastic properties. *Journal of the American Ceramic Society* 37, 596–602.

Kingery, W. D., Vandiver, P. B., and Prickett, M. (1988). The beginnings of pyrotechnology, Part II: production and use of lime and gypsum plaster in the Pre-Pottery Neolithic Near East. *Journal of Field Archaeology* 15, 219–244.

Kirchmann, H., and Witter, E. (1992). Composition of fresh, aerobic and anaerobic farm animal dungs. *Bioresource Technology* 40, 137–142.

Kitano, Y., and Hood, D. W. (1962). Calcium carbonate crystal forms formed from sea water by inorganic processes. *Journal of the Oceanographic Society of Japan* 18, 141–145.

Kittrick, J. (1977). Mineral equlibria in the soil system. In: Minerals in Soil Environments (ed. J. Dixon and S. Weed), pp. 1–25. Soil Science Society of America, Madison, WI.

Klein, R. G., Kruz-Uribe, K., Halkett, D., Hart, T., and Parkington, J. E. (1999). Paleoenvironmental and human behavioral implications of the Boegoeberg 1 Late Pleistocene hyena den, northern Cape Province, South Africa. *Quaternary Research* 52, 393–403.

Knauth, L. P. (1994). Silica: physical behavior, geochemistry and materials applications. *Reviews in Mineralogy* 29, 233–258.

Knudson, K. J., Frink, L., Hoffman, B., and Price, T. D. (2004). Chemical characterization of Arctic soils: activity area analysis in contemporary Yup'ik fish camps using ICP-AES. *Journal of Archaeological Science* 31, 443–456.

Koehl, M. A. R. (1982). Mechanical design of spicule-reinforced connective tissue: stiffness. *Journal of Experimental Biology* 98, 239–267.

Koon, H. E. C., Nicholson, R. A., and Collins, M. J. (2003). A practical approach to the identification of low temperature heated bone using TEM. *Journal of Archaeological Science* 30, 1393–1399.

Koren, Z. C. (2005). The first optimal all-Murex all-natural purple dyeing in the eastern Mediterranean in a millennium and a half. In: Dyes in History and Archaeology, 20, 136–149. Archetype, London.

Kramer, C. (1982). Village Ethnoarchaeology. Academic Press, London.

Kramer, I. R. H. (1951). The distribution of collagen fibrils in the dentine matrix. *British Dental Journal* 91, 1–7.

Kriasakul, M., and Mitterer, R. M. (1978). Isoleucine epimerization in peptides and proteins: kinetic factors and applications to fossil proteins. *Science* 201, 1011–1014.

Kronick, P. L., and Cooke, P. (1996). Thermal stabilization of collagen fibers by calcification. *Connective Tissue Research* 33, 275–282.

Kühl, N., and Litt, T. (2003). Quantitative time series reconstruction of Eemian temperature at three European sites using pollen data. *Vegetation History and Archaeobotany* 12, 205–214.

Labeyrie, J., and Delibrias, G. (1964). Dating of old mortars by the carbon-14 method. *Nature*, 742.

Lalueza Fox, C., Juan, J., and Albert, R. M. (1996). Phytolith analysis on dental calculus, enamel surface, and burial soil: information about diet and paleoenvironment. *American Journal of Physical Anthropology* 101, 101–113.

Lambert, J. B. (1997). Traces of the Past: Unraveling the Secrets of Archaeology through Chemistry. Perseus Books, Reading, UK.

Lambert, J. B., Johnson, S. C., and Poinar, G. O. (1995). Resin from Africa and South America: criteria for distinguishing between fossilized and recent resin based on NMR spectroscopy. *American Chemical Society Symposium Series* 617, 193–202.

Lammie, D., Bain, M. M., and Wess, T. J. (2005). Microfocus X-ray scattering investigations of eggshell nanotexture. *Journal of Synchrotron Radiation* 12, 721–726.

Lanning, F. C., and Eleuterius, L. N. (1992). Silica and ash in seeds of cultivated grains and native plants. *Annals of Botany* 69, 151–160.

Lanting, J. N., and Brindley, A. L. (1998). Dating cremated bone: the dawn of a new era. *Journal of Irish Archaeology* 9, 1–8.

Lanting, J. N., and van der Plicht, J. (1998). Reservoir effects and apparent ^{14}C ages. *Journal of Irish Archaeology* 9, 151–165.

Lanting, J. N., Aerts-Bijma, A., and van der Plicht, H. (2001). Dating of cremated bones. *Radiocarbon* 43, 249–254.

Law, I. A., and Hedges, R. E. M. (1989). A semi-automated bone pretreatment of older and contaminated samples. *Bone* 31, 247–253.

Laws, R. M. (1952). A new method of age determination for mammals. *Nature* 169, 972.

Lee-Thorp, J. (2002). Two decades of progress towards understanding fossilization processes and isotopic signals in calcified minerals. *Archaeometry* 44, 435–446.

Lees, S. (1987). Considerations regarding the structure of the mammalian mineralized osteoid from viewpoint of the generalized packing model. *Connective Tissue Research* 16, 281–303.

Legeros, R. Z. (1991). Calcium Phosphates in Oral Biology and Medicine. Karger, Basel, Switzerland.

Legeros, R. Z., and Legeros, J. P. (1984). Phosphate minerals in human tissue. In: Phosphate Minerals (ed. J. O. Nriagu and P. B. Moore), pp. 351–385. Springer, Berlin.

Legeros, R. Z., Balmain, N., and Bonel, G. (1987). Age-related changes in mineral of rat and bovine cortical bone. *Calcified Tissue International* 41, 137–144.

Lehninger, A. L. (1982). Principles of Biochemistry. Worth, New York.

Lehr, J. R., McClellan, G. H., Smith, J. P., and Frasier, A. W. (1968). Characterization of apatites in commercial phosphate rocks. *Coll. Int. Phosphates Mineraux Solides, Toulouse* 2, 29–44.

Leny, L., and Casteel, R. W. (1975). Simplified procedure for examining charcoal specimens for identification. *Journal of Archaeological Science* 2, 153–159.

Leute, U. (1987). An Introduction to Physical Methods in Archaeology and History of Art. Wiley-VCH, Weinheim, Germany.

Levi-Kalisman, Y., Raz, S., Weiner, S., Addadi, L., and Sagi, I. (2001). XAS study of the structure of a biogenic "amorphous" calcium carbonate phase. *Dalton Transactions* 21, 3977–3982.

Lev-Yadun, S. (2007). Wood remains from archaeological excavations: a review with a Near Eastern perspective. *Israel Journal of Earth Sciences* 56, 139–162.

Lewis, I. C. (1982). Chemistry of carbonization. *Carbon* 20, 519–529.

Libby, W. F., Anderson, E. C., and Arnold, J. R. (1949). Age determination by radiocarbon content: world-wide assay of natural radiocarbon. *Science* 109, 227–228.

Lieberman, D. E. (1993). Life history variables preserved in dental cementum microstructure. *Science* 261, 1162–1164.

Lieberman, D. E., and Meadow, R. H. (1992). The biology of cementum increments (with an archaeological application). *Mammal Review* 22, 57–77.

Lindroos, A., Heinemeier, J., Ringbom, A., Brasken, M., and Sveinbjornsdottir, A. (2007). Mortar dating using AMS C-14 and sequential dissolution: Examples from medieval, non-hydraulic lime mortars from the Aland Islands, SW Finland. *Radiocarbon* 49, 47–67.

Lippmann, F. (1973). Sedimentary Carbonate Minerals. Springer, Berlin.

Liritzis, I. (1994). A new dating method by thermoluminescence of carved megalithic stone building. *Comptes Rendus de l'Académie des sciences* 319, 603–610.

Littmann, E. W. (1957). Ancient Mesoamerican mortars, plasters and stuccos: Comalcalco, Part I. *American Antiquity* 23, 135–140.

Liu, D., Wagner, H. D., and Weiner, S. (2000). Bending and fracture of compact circumferential and osteonal lamellar bone of the baboon tibia. *Journal Material Sciences Material and Medicine* 11, 49–60.

Liu, D., Weiner, S., and Wagner, H. D. (1999). Anisotropic mechanical properties of lamellar bone using miniature cantilever bending specimens. *Journal of Biomechanics* 32, 647–654.

Livingstone Smith, A. (2001). Bonefire II: the return of pottery firing temperatures. *Journal of Archaeological Science* 28, 991–1003.

Longinelli, A. (1965). Oxygen isotopic composition of orthophosphate from shells of living marine organisms. *Nature* 207, 716.

Longinelli, A. (1984). Oxygen isotopes in mammal bone phosphate: a new tool for paleohydrological and paleoclimatalogical research? *Geochimica et Cosmochimica Acta* 48, 385–390.

Loucaidies, S., van Cappellen, P., and Behrends, T. (2008). Dissolution of biogenic silica from land to ocean: role of salinity and pH. *Limnology and Oceanography* 53, 1614–1621.

Lowenstam, H. A., and Fitch, J. E. (1981). Vaterite formation of higher teleost fishes. Paper presented at the 62nd annual meeting of the Pacific Division of the American Association for the Advancement of Science.

Lowenstam, H. A., and Weiner, S. (1989). On Biomineralization. Oxford University Press, New York.

Lozinski, J. (1973). Rare earth elements in fossil bones. *Mineralogia Polonica* 2, 29–35.

Lucas, P. W. (2004). Dental Functional Morphology. Cambridge University Press, Cambridge.

Luckenback, A. H., Holland, C. G., and Allen, R. O. (1975). Soapstone artifacts: tracing prehistoric trade patterns in Virginia. *Science* 187, 57–58.

Luke, C., Tycott, R. H., and Scott, R. W. (2006). Petrographic and stable isotope analyses of late classic Ulúa marble vases and potential sources. *Archaeometry* 48, 13–29.

Lux, A., Luxová, M., Hattori, T., Inanaga, S., and Sugimoto, Y. (2002). Silicification in sorghum (*Sorghum bicolor*) cultivars with different drought resistance. *Physiologia Plantarum* 115, 87–92.

Luxán, M. P., Dorrego, F., and Laborde, A. (1995). Ancient gypsum mortars from St Engracia (Zaragoza, Spain): characterization, identification of additives and treatments. *Cement and Concrete Research* 25, 1755–1765.

Luz, B., and Kolodny, Y. (1989). Oxygen isotope variations in bone phosphate. *Applied Geochemistry* 4, 317–323.

Luz, B., Kolodny, Y., and Horowitz, M. (1984). Fractionation of oxygen isotopes between mammalian bone-phosphate and environmental drinking water. *Geochimica et Cosmochimica Acta* 48, 1689–1693.

Maby, J. C. (1932). The identification of wood and wood charcoal fragments. *Analyst* 57, 2–8.

Macphail, R. I., Cruise, G. M., Allen, M. J., Linderholm, J., and Reynolds, P. (2004). Archaeological soil and pollen analysis of experimental floor deposits; with special reference to Butser Ancient Farm, Hampshire, UK. *Journal of Archaeological Science* 31, 175–191.

Madejova, J. (2003). FTIR techniques in clay mineral studies. *Vibrational Spectroscopy* 31, 1–10.

Madella, M., Jones, M. K., Goldberg, P., Goren, Y., and Hovers, E. (2002). The exploitation of plant resources by Neanderthals in Amud Cave (Israel): the evidence from phytolith studies. *Journal of Archaeological Science* 29, 703–719.

Madella, M., Alexandre, A., and Ball, T. (2005). International code for phytolith nomenclature. *Annals of Botany* 96, 253–260.

Maggetti, M. (1982). Phase analysis and its significance for technology and origin. In: Archaeological Ceramics (ed. J. S. Olin and A. D. Franklin), pp. 121–133. Smithsonian Institution Press, Washington, DC.

Mahamid, J., Sharir, A., Addadi, L., and Weiner, S. (2008). Amorphous calcium phosphate is a major component of the forming fin bones of zebrafish: indications for an amorphous precursor phase. *Proceedings of the National Academy of Sciences of the United States of America* 105, 12748–12753.

Makarewicz, C., and Tuross, N. (2006). Foddering by Mongolian pastoralists is recorded in the stable carbon ($d^{13}C$) and nitrogen ($d^{13}N$) isotopes of caprine dentinal collagen. *Journal of Archaeological Science* 33, 862–870.

Mangerud, J. (1972). Radiocarbon dating of marine shells, including a discussion of apparent age of recent shells from Norway. *Boreas* 1, 143–172.

Maniatis, Y., and Tite, M. S. (1981). Technological examination of Neolithic–Bronze Age pottery from central and southeast Europe and from the Near East. *Journal of Archaeological Science* 8, 59–76.

Mannion, A. M. (2007). Fossil diatoms and their significance in archaeological research. *Oxford Journal of Archaeology* 6, 131–147.

Marín-Arroyo, A. B., Fosse, P., and Vigne, J.-D. (2009). Probable evidences of bone accumulation by Pleistocene bearded vulture at the archaeological site of El Mirón Cave (Spain). *Journal of Archaeological Science* 36, 284–296.

Maritan, L., Mazzoli, C., and Freestone, I. (2007). Modeling changes in mollusc shell internal microstructure during firing: implications for temperature estimation in shell-bearing property. *Archaeometry* 49, 529–541.

Marshall, G. W., Habelitz, S., Gallagher, R., Balooch, M., Balooch, G., and Marshall, S. J. (2001). Nanomechanical properties of hydrated carious human dentin. *Journal of Dental Research* 80, 1768–1771.

Marxen, J. C., Becker, W., Finke, D., Hasse, B., and Epple, M. (2003). Early mineralization in *Biomphalaria glabrata*: microscopic and structural results. *Journal of Molluscan Studies* 69, 113–121.

Mason, B. (1958). Principles of Geochemistry. 3rd edition. John Wiley, New York.

Mata, M. P., Peacor, D. L., and Gallart-Marti, M. D. (2002). Transmission electron microscopy (TEM) applied to ancient pottery. *Archaeometry* 44, 155–176.

Matthews, W., French, C., Lawrence, T., and Cutler, D. (1996). Multiple surfaces: the micromorphology. In: On the Surface: Catalhoyuk 1993–95 (ed. I. Hodder), pp. 301–342. MacDonald Institute for Research and British Institute for Archaeology, Ankara, Cambridge.

Matthews, W., French, C. A. I., Lawrence, T., Cutler, D. F., and Jones, M. K. (1997). Microstratigraphic traces of site formation processes and human activities. *World Archaeology* 29, 281–308.

Mazar, A., Namdar, D., Panitz-Cohen, N., Neumann, R., and Weiner, S. (2008). Iron Age beehives in Tel Rehov in the Jordan Valley. *Antiquity* 82, 629–639.

Mbida, C. M., van Neer, W., Doutrelepont, H., and Vrydaghs, L. (2000). Evidence for banana cultivation and animal husbandry during the first millennium B.C. in the forest of southern Cameroon. *Journal of Archaeological Science* 27, 151–162.

McConnell, D. (1952). The crystal chemistry of carbonate apatites and their relation to calcified tissues. *Journal of Dental Research* 31, 53–63.

McConnell, D. (1969). The mineralogy of the apatites and their relation to biologic precipitation. *Proceedings of the North American Paleontological Convention*, 1525–1535.

McDonnell, J. G. (2001). Pyrotechnology. In: Handbook of Archaeological Sciences (ed. D. R. Brothwell and A. M. Pollard), pp. 493–505. John Wiley, Chichester, UK.

McGeehin, J., Burr, G. S., Jull, A. J. T., Reines, D., Gosse, J., Davis, P. T., Muhs, D., and Southon, J. R. (2001). Stepped combustion ^{14}C dating of sediment: a comparison with established techniques. *Radiocarbon* 43, 255–261.

McKinley, J. I., and Bond, J. M. (2001). Cremated bone. In: Handbook of Archaeological Sciences (ed. D. R. Brothwell and A. M. Pollard), pp. 281–292. John Wiley, Chichester, UK.

McNaughton, S. J., and Tarrants, J. L. (1983). Grass leaf silicification: natural selection for an inducible defense against herbivores. *Proceedings of the National Academy of Sciences of the United States of America* 80, 790–791.

Meldrum, F. C., and Cölfen, H. (2008). Controlling mineral morphologies in biological and synthetic systems. *Chemical Reviews* 108, 4332–4432.

Mendelovici, E. (1997). Comparative study of the effects of thermal and mechanical treatments on the structures of clay minerals. *Journal of Thermal Analysis* 49, 1385–1397.

Mercier, N., Valladas, H., Joron, J., Schiegl, S., Bar-Yosef, O., and Weiner, S. (1995). Thermoluminescence dating and the problem of geochemical evolution of sediments. *Israel Journal of Chemistry* 35, 137–141.

Mercier, N., Valladas, H., Froget, L., Joron, J.-L., Reyss, J.-L., Weiner, S., Goldberg, P., et al. (2007). Hayonim cave: a TL-based chronology for this Levantine Mousterian sequence. *Journal Archaeological Science* 24, 1064–1077.

Meredith, N., Sheriff, M., Setchell, D., and Sivanson, S. (1996). Measurements of the microhardness and Young's modulus of human enamel and dentin using an indentation technique. *Archives of Oral Biology* 41, 539–545.

Michel, V., Ildefonse, P., and Morin, G. (1996). Assessment of archaeological bone and dentine preservation from Lazaret Cave (Middle Pleistocene) in France. *Palaeogeography, Palaeoclimatology, Palaeoecology* 126, 109–119.

Middleton, J. (1844). On fluorine in bones, its source and its application to the determination of bone age. *Proceedings of the Geological Society of London* 4, 431–433.

Millard, A. R. (2000). A model for the effect of weaning on nitrogen isotope ratios in humans. In: Perspectives in Amino Acid and Protein Geochemistry (ed. G. A. Goodfriend, M. J. Collins, M. L. Fogel, S. A. Macko, and J. F. Wehmiller), pp. 51–59. Oxford University Press, New York.

Miller, G. H., Beaumont, P. B., Jull, A. J. T., and Johnson, B. (1992). Pleistocene geochronology and paleothermometry from protein diagenesis in ostrich eggshells: implications for the evolution of modern humans. *Philosophical Transactions of the Royal Society of London, Series B* 337, 149–157.

Miller, J. (1954). The microradiographic appearance of dentin. *British Dental Journal* 97, 7–9.

Miller, N. F. (1996). Seed eaters of the ancient Near East: human or herbivore? *Current Anthropology* 37, 521–528.

Miller Rosen, A., and Weiner, S. (1994). Identifying ancient irrigation: a new method using opaline phytoliths from emmer wheat. *Journal of Archaeological Science* 21, 125–132.

Milliman, J. D. (1974). Marine Carbonates. Springer, New York.

Mills, M. G. L., and Mills, M. E. J. (1977). An analysis of bones collected at hyaena breeding dens in the Gemsbok National Parks (Mammalia:Carnivora). *Annals of the Transvaal Museum* 30, 145–155.

Minnis, P. E. (1981). Seeds in archaeological sites: sources and some interpretive problems. *American Antiquity* 46, 143–152.

Mithen, S., Jenkins, E., Jamjoum, K., Niumat, S., Nortcliff, S., and Finlayson, B. (2008). Experimental crop growing in Jordan to develop methodology for the identification of ancient crop irrigation. *World Archaeology* 40, 7–25.

Moffat, D., and Butler, R. J. (1986). Rare earth element distribution patterns in Shetland steatite – consequences for artifact provenancing studies. *Archaeometry* 28, 101–115.

Moore, P. B. (1984). Crystallochemical aspects of the phosphate minerals. In: Phosphate Minerals (ed. J. O. Nriagu and P. B. Moore), pp. 155–170. Springer, Berlin.

Morariu, V. V., Bogdan, M., and Ardelean, I. (1977). Ancient pottery: its pore structure. *Archaeometry* 19, 187–192.

Morgenstein, M., and Redmount, C. A. (2005). Using portable energy dispersive X-ray fluorescence (EDXRF) for on-site analysis of ceramic sherds at El Hibeh, Egypt. *Journal of Archaeological Science* 32, 1613–1623.

Moropoulou, A., Bakolas, A., and Bisbikou, K. (2000). Investigation of the technology of historic mortars. *Journal of Cultural Heritage* 1, 45–58.

Morris, R. W., and Kittleman, L. R. (1967). Piezoelectric properties of otoliths. *Science* 158, 368–370.

Müller, W., Fricke, H., Halliday, A. N., McCulloch, M. T., and Wartho, J. (2003). Origin and migration of the Alpine Iceman. *Science* 302, 862–866.

Murayama, E., Herbomel, P., Kayakami, A., Takeda, H., and Nagasawa, H. (2005). Otolith matrix proteins OMP-1 and Otolin-1 are necessary for normal otolith growth and their anchoring onto the sensory maculae. *Mechanisms of Development* 122, 791–803.

Namdar, D., Neumann, R., Sladezki, Y., Haddad, N., and Weiner, S. (2007). Alkane composition variations between darker and lighter colored comb beeswax. *Apidologie* 38, 453–461.

Namdar, D., Neumann, R., Goren, Y., and Weiner, S. (2009). The contents of unusual cone-shaped vessels (cornets) from the Chalcolithic of the Southern Levant. *Journal of Archaeological Science* 36, 629–636.

Nanci, A. (2003). Ten Cate's Oral Histology. 6th edition. Mosby, St. Louis, MO.

Nash, S. E. (1999). Time, Trees, and Prehistory. University of Utah Press, Salt Lake City.

Navazo, M., Colina, A., Domínguez-Bella, S., and Benito-Calvo, A. (2008). Raw stone material supply for Upper Pleistocene settlements in Sierra de Atapuerca (Buergos, Spain): flint characterization using petrographic and geochemical techniques. *Journal of Archaeological Science* 35, 1961–1973.

Nesse, W. D. (1991). Introduction to Optical Mineralogy. Oxford University Press, New York.

Newesely, H. (1989). Fossil bone apatite. *Applied Geochemistry* 4, 233–245.

Nichols, G. J., Cripps, J. A., Collinson, M. E., and Scott, A. C. (2000). Experiments in waterlogging and sedimentology of charcoal: results and implications. *Palaeogeography, Palaeoclimatology, Palaeoecology* 164, 43–56.

Nicholson, R. A. (1993). A morphological investigation of burnt animal bone and an evaluation of its utility in archaeology. *Journal of Archaeological Science* 20, 411–428.

Nielsen-Marsh, C. M., and Hedges, R. E. M. (1997). Dissolution experiments on modern and diagenetically altered bone and their effects of the infrared splitting factor. *Bulletin de Societe Geologique Francaise* 168, 485–490.

Nielsen-Marsh, C. M., and Hedges, R. E. M. (1999). Bone porosity and the use of mercury intrusion porosimetry in bone diagenesis studies. *Archaeometry* 41, 165–174.

Nielsen-Marsh, C. M., Hedges, R. E. M., Mann, T., and Collins, M. J. (2000). A preliminary investigation of the application of differential scanning calorimetry to the study of collagen degradation in archaeological bone. *Thermochimica Acta* 365, 129–139.

Nielsen-Marsh, C. M., Gandhi, H., Shapiro, B., Cooper, A., Hauschka, P. V., and Collins, M. J. (2002). Sequence preservation of osteocalcin protein and mitochondrial DNA in bison bones older than 55 ka. *Geology* 30, 1099–1102.

Nocete, F., Álex, E., Nieto, J. M., Sáez, R., and Bayona, M. R. (2005). An archaeological approach to regional environmental pollution in the south-western Iberian Peninsula related to third millenium BC mining and metallurgy. *Journal of Archaeological Science* 32, 1566–1576.

Noonan, J. P., Coop, G., Kudaravalli, S., Smith, D., Krause, J., Alessi, J., Chen, F., et al. (2006). Sequencing and analysis of Neanderthal genomic DNA. *Science* 314, 1113–1118.

Norris, E., Norris, C., and Steen, J. B. (1975). Regulation and grinding ability of grit in the gizzard of Norwegian Willow Ptarmigan (*Lagopus lagopus*). *Poultry Science* 54, 1839–1843.

Norton, D. A., and Ogden, J. (1987). Dendrochronology: a review with emphasis on New Zealand applications. *New Zealand Journal of Ecology* 10, 77–95.

Nriagu, O. J. (1976). Phosphate-clay mineral relations in soils and sediments. *Canadian Journal Earth Sciences* 13, 717–736.

Nriagu, O. J. (1984). Phosphate minerals: their properties and general modes of occurrence. In: Phosphate Minerals (ed. J. O. Nriagu and P. B. Moore), pp. 1–136. Springer, Berlin.

Ntinou, M. (2002). Charcoal analysis at Sarakini: An ethnoarchaeological case study. In: El paisaje en el norte de Grecia desde el Tardiglaciar al Antlántico: Formaciones vegetales, Recursos y Usos. *British Archaeological Reports International Series* 1038, 115–129.

Nudelman, F., Chen, H. H., Goldberg, H. A., Weiner, S., and Addadi, L. (2007). Lessons from biomineralization: comparing the growth strategies of mollusk shell prismatic and nacreous layers in *Atrina rigida*. *Faraday Discussions* 136, 9–25.

Oades, J. M. (1989). An introduction to organic matter in mineral soils. In: Minerals in Soil Environments, vol. 1 (ed. J. B. Dixon and S. B. Weed), pp. 89–159. Soil Science Society of America, Madison, WI.

Oakley, K. P. (1948). Fluorine and relative dating of bones. *Advancement of Science* 16, 336–337.

Oakley, K. P. (1970). On man's use of fire, with comments on tool-making and hunting. In: Social Life of Early Man (ed. S. L. Washburn), pp. 176–193. Aldine, Chicago.

Oberlin, A. (1984). Carbonization and graphitization. *Carbon* 22, 521–541.

O'Connell, J. F. (1987). Alyawara site structure and its archaeological implications. *American Antiquity* 52, 74–108.

Odriozola, C. P., and Pérez, M. H. (2006). The manufacturing process of 3rd millennium BC bone based incrusted pottery decoration from the Middle Guadiana river basin (Badajoz, Spain). *Journal of Archaeological Science* 34, 1794–1803.

Olson, E. A., and Broecker, W. S. (1958). Sample contamination and reliability of radiocarbon dates. *Transactions of the New York Academy of Sciences, Series II* 20, 593–604.

Olszta, M. J., Cheng, X., Jee, S. S., Kumar, R., Kim, Y.-Y., Kaufman, M. J., Douglas, E. P., and Gower, L. B. (2007). Bone structure and formation: a new perspective. *Material Science and Engineering R* 58, 77–116.

Orme, B. (1974). Twentieth-century prehistorians and the idea of ethnographic parallels. *Man* 9, 199–212.

Osawa, E., Hirose, Y., Kimura, A., and Shibuya, M. (1997). Fullerenes in Chinese ink: a correction.*Fullerene Science and Technology* 5, 177–194.

Ostwald, W. Z. (1879). Studies on the formation and transformation of solid phases. *Physical Chemistry* 22, 289–330.

Ostwald, W. Z. (1896). Lehrbruck der Allgemeinen Chemie. Leipzig, Germany.

Ozawa, T. (1965). A new method of analyzing thermogravimetric data. *Bulletin of the Chemical Society of Japan* 38, 1881–1886.

Pääbo, S. (1985). Molecular cloning of ancient Egyptian mummy DNA. *Nature* 314, 644–645.

Pääbo, S., Higuchi, R. G., and Wilson, A. C. (1989). Ancient DNA and the polymerase chain reaction: The emerging field of molecular archaeology. *Journal of Biological Chemistry* 264, 9709–9712.

Panella, G. (1971). Fish otoliths: daily growth layers and periodical patterns. *Science* 173, 1124–1126.

Panshin, A. J., and DeZeeuw, C. (1970). Textbook of Wood Technology. McGraw-Hill, New York.

Paris, O., Zollfrank, C., and Zickler, G. A. (2005). Decomposition and carbonisation of wood biopolymers – a microstructural study of soft wood pyrolysis. *Carbon* 43, 53–66.

Park, R., and Epstein, S. (1961). Metabolic fractionation of C12 & C13 in plants. *Plant Physiology* 36, 133–138.

Parker, F. S. (1971). Infrared Spectroscopy in Biochemistry, Biology, and Medicine. Plenum Press, New York.

Parker, R. B., and Toots, H. (1970). Minor elements in fossil bone. *Bulletin of the Geological Society of America* 81, 925–932.

Peacock, D. P. S. (1967). The heavy mineral analysis of pottery: a preliminary report. *Archaeometry* 10, 97–100.

Pearsall, D. M. (1978). Phytolith analysis of archaeological soils: evidence for maize cultivation in formative Ecuador. *Science* 199, 177–178.

Peregrine, P. N. (2004). Cross-cultural approaches in archaeology: comparative ethnology, comparative archaeology, and archaeoethnology. *Journal of Archaeological Research* 12, 281–309.

Perlman, I., and Asaro, F. (1969). Pottery analysis by neutron activation. *Archaeometry* 11, 21–52.

Pernicka, E., Begemann, F., Schmitt-Strecker, S., Todorova, H., and Kuleff, I. (1997). Prehistoric copper in Bulgaria: its composition and provenance. *Eurasia Antiqua* 3, 41–180.

Perry, C. C. (2003). Silicification: the process by which organisms capture and mineralize silica. In: Biomineralization: Reviews in Mineralogy and Geochemistry, vol. 54 (ed. P. M. Dove, J. J. DeYoreo, and S. Weiner), pp. 291–327. Mineralogical Society of America / Geochemical Society, Washington, DC.

Person, A., Bocherens, H., Saliege, J. F., Paris, F., Zeitoun, V., and Gerard, M. (1995). Early diagenetic evolution of bone phosphate – an X-ray-diffractometry analysis. *Journal of Archaeological Science* 22, 211–221.

Picon, M. (1976). Remarques préliminares sur deux types d'altération de la composition chimique des céramiques an cours du temps. *Figlina* 1, 159–166.

Pike, A. W. G., Hedges, R. E. M., and van Calsteren, P. (2002). U-series dating of bone using the diffusion-adsorption model. *Geochimica et Cosmochimica Acta* 66, 4273–4286.

Piperno, D. R. (1988). Phytolith Analysis: An Archaeological and Geological Perspective. Academic Press, San Diego, CA.

Piperno, D. R. (2006). Phytoliths: A Comprehensive Guide for Archaeologists and Paleoecologists. Altamira Press, Lanham, MD.

Piperno, D. R., Weiss, E., Holst, I., and Nadel, D. (2004). Processing of wild cereal grains in the Upper Paleolithic revealed by starch grain analysis. *Nature* 430, 670–673.

Plummer, T. W., Kinyua, A. M., and Potts, R. (1994). Provenancing of hominid and mammalian fossils from Kanjera, Kenya, using EDXRF. *Journal of Archaeological Science* 21, 553–563.

Pobeguin, T. (1943). Les oxalates de calcium chez quelques angiospermes. *Annales des Sciences Naturelles Botanique* 4, 1–95.

Pokroy, B., Qunitana, J. P., Caspi, E. N., Berner, A., and Zolotoyabko, E. (2004). Anisotropic lattice distortions in biogenic aragonite. *Nature Materials* 3, 900–902.

Politi, Y., Metzler, R. A., Abrecht, M., Gilbert, B., Wilt, F. H., Sagi, I., Addadi, L., Weiner, S., and Gilbert, P. U. P. A. (2008). Transformation mechanism of amorphous calcium carbonate into calcite in the sea urchin larval spicule. *Proceedings of the National Academy of Sciences of the United States of America* 105, 17362–17366.

Pollard, A. M., and Heron, C. (2008). Archaeological Chemistry. Royal Society of Chemistry, Cambridge.

Posner, A. S., Harper, R. A., and Muller, S. A. (1965). Age changes in the crystal chemistry of bone apatite. *Annals of the New York Academy of Sciences* 131, 737–742.

Post, P. W., and Donner, D. D. (2005). Frostbite in a pre-Columbian mummy. *American Journal of Physical Anthropology* 37, 187–191.

Prescott, J. R., and Robertson, G. B. (1997). Sediment dating by luminescence: a review. *Radiation Measurements* 27, 893–922.

Price, T. D., Grupe, G., and Schröter, P. (1994). Reconstruction of migration patterns in the Bell Beaker period by stable strontium isotope analysis. *Applied Geochemistry* 9, 413–417.

Price, T. D., Burton, J. H., and Bentley, R. A. (2002). The characterization of biologically available strontium isotope ratios for the study of prehistoric migration. *Archaeometry* 44, 117–135.

Priestley, J. (1770). Experiments and observations on charcoal. *Philosophical Transactions* 14, 211–227.

Qian, Y., Engel, M. H., Goodfriend, G. A., and Macko, S. A. (1995). Abundance and stable isotopic composition of amino acids in molecular weight fractions of fossil and artificially aged mollusk shells. *Geochimica et Cosmochimica Acta* 59, 1113–1124.

Quitmyer, I. R., and Jones, D. S. (1997). The sclerochronology of hard clams, *Mercenaria* spp., from the south eastern U.S.A.: a method for elucidating the zooarchaeological records of seasonal resource procurement and seasonality in prehistoric shell middens. *Journal of Archaeological Science* 24, 825–840.

Ramaswamy, K., and Kamalakkannan, M. (1995). Infrared study of the influence of temperature on clay minerals. *Journal of Thermal Analysis* 44, 629–638.

Rapp, G., and Hill, C. L. (1998). Geoarchaeology. Yale University Press, New Haven, CT.

Rebollo, N. R., Cohen-Ofri, I., Popovitz-Biro, R., Bar-Yosef, O., Meignen, L., Goldberg, P., Weiner, S., and Boaretto, E. (2008). Structural characterization of charcoal exposed to high and low pH: implications for ^{14}C sample preparation and charcoal preservation. *Radiocarbon* 50, 289–307.

Reiche, I., Vignaud, C., and Menu, M. (2002). The crystallinity of ancient bone and dentine: new insights by transmission electron microscopy. *Archaeometry* 44, 447–459.

Reiche, I., Favre-Quattropani, L., Vignaud, C., Bocherens, H., Charlet, L., and Menu, M. (2003). A multi-analytical study of bone diagenesis: the Neolithic site of Bercy (Paris, France). *Measurement Science Technology* 14, 1608–1619.

Reilly, P. (1989). Data visualization in archaeology. *IBM Systems Journal* 28, 569–570.

Reimer, P. J., Baillie, M. G. L., Bard, E., Bayliss, A., Beck, J. W., Bertrand, P. G., Blackwell, C. E., et al. (2004a). Radiocarbon calibration from 0–26 cal kyr BP. *Radiocarbon* 46, 1029–1058.

Reimer, P. J., Baillie, M. G. L., Bard, E., Bayliss, A., Beck, J. W., Bertrand, C., Blackwell, P. G., et al. (2004b). IntCal04:Calibration issue. *Radiocarbon* 46, 1029–1058.

Reinhard, K. J., and Danielson, D. R. (2005). Pervasiveness of phytoliths in prehistoric southwestern diet and implications for regional and temporal trends for dental microwear. *Journal of Archaeological Science* 32, 981–988.

Renfrew, C., and Bahn, P. (1991). Archaeology: Theories, Methods and Practice. Thames and Hudson, London.

Renfrew, C., Dixon, J., and Cann, J. (1966). Obsidian and early cultural contact in the Near East. *Proceedings of the Prehistoric Society* 32, 30–72.

Rey, C., Collins, B., Goehl, T., Dickson, I. R., and Glimcher, M. J. (1989). The carbonate environment in bone mineral: a resolution-enhanced Fourier transform infrared spectroscopy study. *Calcified Tissue International* 45, 157–164.

Rey, C., Renugopalakrishnan, V., Collins, B., and Glimcher, M. J. (1991). Fourier transform infrared spectroscopic study of the carbonate ions in bone mineral during aging. *Calcified Tissue International* 49, 251–258.

Rey, C., Miquel, J. L., Facchini, L., Legrand, A. P., and Glimcher, M. J. (1995). Hydroxyl groups in bone mineral. *Bone* 16, 583–586.

Rheren, T., and Pernicka, E. (2007). Coins, artefacts and isotopes – archaeometallurgy and archaeometry. *Archaeometry* 50, 232–248.

Rhoads, D. C., and Lutz, R. A. (1980). Skeletal Growth of Aquatic Organisms. Plenum Press, New York.

Rhode, D. (2003). Coprolites from Hidden Cave revisited: evidence for site occupation history, diet and sex of occupants. *Journal of Archaeological Science* 30, 909–922.

Rice, P. (1987). Pottery Analysis: A Source Book. University of Chicago Press, Chicago.

Righi, D., and Meunier, A. (1995). Origin of clays by rock weathering and soil formation. In: Origin and Mineralogy of Clays and the Environment (ed. B. Velde), pp. 43–161. Springer, Berlin.

Riley, T. (2008). Diet and seasonality in the Lower Pecos: evaluating coprolite data sets with cluster analysis. *Journal of Archaeological Science* 35, 2726–2741.

Rink, W. J., Schwarcz, H. P., Weiner, S., Goldberg, P., Stiner, M. C., Meignen, L., and Bar-Yosef, O. (2004). Age of the Mousterian industry at Hayonim Cave, northern Israel, using electron spin resonance and ^{230}Th/^{234}U methods. *Journal of Archaeological Science* 31, 953–964.

Robbins, L. H. (1973). Turkana material culture viewed from an archaeological perspective. *World Archaeology* 5, 209–214.

Robinson, R. A. (1952). An electron microscopy study of the crystalline inorganic components of bone and its relationship to the organic matrix. *Journal of Bone and Joint Surgery* 34, 389–434.

Robinson, R. A. (1979). Bone tissue: composition and function. *Johns Hopkins Medical Journal* 145, 10–24.

Rogers, A. K. (2008). Obsidian hydration dating: accuracy and resolution limitations imposed by intrinsic water variability. *Journal of Archaeological Science* 35, 2009–2016.

Rollo, F., Ermini, L., Luciani, S., Marota, I., Olivieri, C., and Luiselli, D. (2006). Fine characterization of the Iceman's mtDNA haplogroup. *American Journal of Physical Anthropology* 130, 557–564.

Rosen, A. (1986). Cities of Clay – The Geoarchaeology of Tells. University of Chicago Press, Chicago.

Rosen, A. M. (1987). Phytolith studies at Shiqmim. In: Shiqmim I: Studies Concerning Chalcolithic Societies in the Northern Negev Desert, Israel (1982–1984) (ed. T. E. Levy). *British Archaeological Reports International Series* 356, 243–249.

Rosen, A. M. (1992). Preliminary identification of silica skeletons from Near Eastern archaeological sites. In: Phytolith Systematics: Emerging Issues (ed. G. Rapp and S. C. Mulholland), pp. 129–147. Plenum Press, New York.

Rosen, A. M., and Weiner, S. (1994). Identifying ancient irrigation: a new method using opaline phytoliths from emmer wheat. *Journal of Archaeological Science* 21, 125–132.

Russ, J., Hyman, M., Shafer, H. J., and Rowe, M. W. (1990). Radiocarbon dating of prehistoric rock paintings by selective oxidation of organic carbon. *Nature* 348, 710–711.

Rypkema, H. A., Lee, W. E., Galaty, M. L., and Haws, J. (2007). Rapid, in-stride soil phosphate measurement in archaeological survey: a new method tested in Loudoun County, Virginia. *Journal of Archaeological Science* 34, 1859–1867.

Sahin, N. (2004). Isolation and characterization of mesophilic, oxalate-degrading Streptomyces from plany rhizosphere and forest soils. *Naturwissenschaften* 91, 498–502.

Salamon, M., Tuross, N., Arensburg, B., and Weiner, S. (2005). Relatively well preserved DNA is present in the crystal aggregates of fossil bones. *Proceedings of the National Academy of Sciences of the United States of America* 102, 13783–13788.

Saleh, N., Deutsch, D., and Gil-Av, E. (1993). Racemization of aspartic acid in the extracellular matrix proteins of primary and secondary dentin. *Calcified Tissue International* 53, 103–110.

Sangster, A. G., and Parry, D. W. (1969). Some factors in relation to bulliform cell silicification in the grass leaf. *Annals of Botany* 33, 315–323.

Sangster, A. G., and Parry, D. W. (1981). Ultrastructure of silica deposits in higher plants. In: Silicon and Siliceous Structures in Biological Systems (ed. T. L. Simpson and B. E. Volcani), pp. 383–407. Springer, New York.

Sanson, G. D., Kerr, S. A., and Gross, K. A. (2006). Do silica phytoliths really wear mammalian teeth? *Journal of Archaeological Science* 34, 526–531.

Saxon, A., and Higham, C. (1969). A new research method for economic prehistorians. *American Antiquity* 34, 303–311.

Sayre, E. V., and Dodson, R. W. (1957). Neutron activation study of Mediterranean potsherds. *American Journal of Archaeology* 61, 35–41.

Scheffer, T. C., and Cowling, E. B. (1966). Natural resistance of wood to microbial deterioration. *Annual Review of Phytopathology* 4, 147–170.

Schieber, J., Krinsley, D., and Riciputi, L. (2000). Diagenetic origin of quartz silt in mudstones and implications for silica cycling. *Nature* 406, 981–985.

Schiegl, S., Lev-Yadun, S., Bar-Yosef, S., El Goresy, A., and Weiner, S. (1994). Siliceous aggregates from prehistoric wood ash: a major component of sediments in Kebara and Hayonim caves (Israel). *Israel Journal Earth Sciences* 43, 267–278.

Schiegl, S., Goldberg, P., Bar-Yosef, O., and Weiner, S. (1996). Ash deposits in Hayonim and Kebara caves, Israel: macroscopic, microscopic and mineralogical observations, and their archaeological implications. *Journal Archaeological Science* 23, 763–781.

Schiegl, S., Goldberg, P., Pfretzschner, H. U., and Conard, N. J. (2003). Paleolithic burnt bone horizons from the Swabian Jura: distinguishing between in situ fire places and dumping areas. *Geoarchaeology* 18, 541–565.

Schiffer, M. B. (1983). Toward the identification of formation processes. *American Antiquity* 48, 675–706.

Schiffer, M. B. (1986). Radiocarbon dating and the "old wood" problem: the case of the Hohokam chronology. *Journal of Archaeological Science* 13, 13–30.

Schiffer, M. B. (1987). Formation Processes of the Archaeological Record. University of New Mexico Press, Albuquerque.

Schmidt, M., Botz, R., Rickert, D., Bohrmann, G., Hall, S. R., and Mann, S. (2001). Oxygen isotopes of marine diatoms and relations to opal-A maturation. *Geochimica et Cosmochimica Acta* 65, 201–211.

Schmidt, M. W. I., Skjemstad, J. O., and Jäger, C. (2002). Carbon isotope geochemistry and nanomorphology of soil black carbon: black chernozemic soils in central Europe originate from ancient biomass burning. *Global Biogeochemical Cycles* 16, 70-1–70-8.

Schmidt, W. J. (1936). Uber die Kristallorientierung im Zahnschmelz. *Naturwissenschaften* 24, 361.

Schoeninger, M. J. (1979). Diet and status at Chalcatzingo: some empirical and technical aspects of strontium analysis. *American Journal of Physical Anthropology* 51, 295–310.

Schoeninger, M. J., and DeNiro, M. J. (1984). Nitrogen and carbon isotopic composition of bone collagen from marine and terrestrial animals. *Geochimica et Cosmochimica Acta* 48, 625–639.

Schubert, P. (1986). Petrographic modal analysis – a necessary complement to chemical analysis of ceramic course ware. *Archaeometry* 28, 163–178.

Schultz, T. P., Curry Templeton, M., and McGinnis, G. D. (1985). Rapid determination of lignocellulose by diffuse reflectance Fourier transform infrared spectrometry. *Analytical Chemistry* 57, 2867–2869.

Schurr, M. R., and Gregory, D. A. (2002). Fluoride dating of faunal materials by ion-selective electrode: high resolution relative dating at an early agricultural period site in the Tucson basin. *Antiquity* 67, 281–299.

Schwarcz, H. P. (1980). Absolute age determination of archaeological sites by uranium series dating of travertines. *Archaeometry* 22, 3–24.

Schwarcz, H. P., and Grün, R. (1992). Electron spin resonance (ESR) dating of the origin of modern man. *Philosophical Transactions of the Royal Society of London, Series B* 337, 145–148.

Schwarcz, H. P., and Rink, W. J. (2001). Dating methods for sediments of caves and rockshelters with examples from the Mediterranean region. *Geoarchaeology* 16, 355–371.

Schwedt, A., and Mommsen, H. (2007). On the influence of drying and firing of clay on the formation of trace element profiles within pottery. *Archaeometry* 49, 495–509.

Schwedt, A., Mommsen, H., and Zacharias, N. (2004). Post-depositional elemental alterations in pottery: Neutron activation analyses of core and surface samples. *Archaeometry* 46, 85–101.

Scott, A. C. (2000). The pre-Quaternary history of fire. *Palaeogeography, Palaeoclimatology, Palaeoecology* 164, 281–329.

Scott, E. M., Bryant, C., Cook, G. T., and Naysmith, P. (2003). Is there a fifth radiocarbon international intercomparison (VIRI)? *Radiocarbon* 45, 493–495.

Scurfield, G., and Michell, A. J. (1973). Crystals in woody stems. *Botanical Journal of the Linnaen Society* 66, 277–289.

Scurfield, G., Anderson, C. A., and Segnit, E. R. (1974). Silica in woody stems. *Australian Journal of Botany* 22, 211–229.

Sealy, J. (2001). Body tissue chemistry and paleodiet. In: Handbook of Archaeological Sciences (ed. D. R. Brothwell and A. M. Pollard), pp. 269–279. John Wiley, Chichester, UK.

Segal, I., Nathan, Y., Zbenovich, B., and Barzilay, E. (2005). Geochemical characterization of flint and chert artifacts from the Modi'in area. *Israel Journal of Earth Sciences* 54, 229–236.

Shahack-Gross, R., and Finkelstein, I. (2008). Subsistence practices in an arid environment: a geoarchaeological investigation in an Iron Age site, the Negev Highlands, Israel. *Journal of Archaeological Science* 35, 965–982.

Shahack-Gross, R., Shemesh, A., Yakir, D., and Weiner, S. (1996). Oxygen isotopic composition of opaline phytoliths: potential for terrestrial climatic reconstruction. *Geochimica et Cosmochimica Acta* 60, 3949–3953.

Shahack-Gross, R., Bar-Yosef, O., and Weiner, S. (1997). Black-colored bones in Hayonim Cave, Israel: differentiating between burning and oxide staining. *Journal of Archaeological Science* 24, 439–446.

Shahack-Gross, R., Marshall, F., and Weiner, S. (2003). Geo-ethnoarchaeology of pastoral sites: the identification of livestock enclosures in abandoned Maasai settlements. *Journal of Archaeological Science* 30, 439–459.

Shahack-Gross, R., Berna, F., Karkanas, P., and Weiner, S. (2004). Bat guano and preservation of archaelogical remains in cave sites. *Journal of Archaeological Science* 31, 1259–1272.

Shahack-Gross, R., Albert, R. M., Gilboa, A., Nagar-Hilman, O., Sharon, I., and Weiner, S. (2005). Geoarchaeology in an urban context: the uses of space in a Phoenician monumental building at Tel Dor (Israel). *Journal of Archaeological Science* 32, 1417–1431.

Shahack-Gross, R., Ayalon, A., Goldberg, P., Goren, Y., Ofek, B., Rabinovich, R., and Hovers, E. (2008). Formation processes of cemented features in karstic cave sites revealed using stable oxygen and carbon isotopic analyses: a case study at Middle Paleolithic Amud Cave, Israel. *Geoarchaeology* 23, 43–62.

Shemesh, A. (1990). Crystallinity and diagenesis of sedimentary apatites. *Geochimica et Cosmochimica Acta* 54, 2433–2438.

Shimoda, S., Aoba, T., Moreno, E. C., and Miake, Y. (1990). Effect of solution composition on morphological and structural features of carbonated calcium apatites. *Journal of Dental Research* 69, 1731–1740.

Shipman, P., Foster, G. F., and Schoeninger, M. (1984). Burnt bones and teeth: an experimental study of colour, morphology, crystal structure and shrinkage. *Journal of Archaeological Science* 11, 307–325.

Shoval, S. (1993). The burning temperature of a Persian-period pottery kiln at Tel Michal, Israel, estimated from the composition of slag-like material formed in its wall. *Journal of Thermal Analysis* 39, 1157–1168.

Shoval, S., Ginott, Y., and Nathan, Y. (1991). A new method for measuring the crystallinity index of quartz by infrared spectroscopy. *Mineralogical Magazine* 55, 579–582.

Shoval, S., Graft, M., Beck, P., and Kirsh, Y. (1993). Thermal behavior of limestone and monocrystalline calcite tempers during firing and their use in ancient vessels. *Journal of Thermal Analysis* 40, 263–273.

Shoval, S., Yofe, O., and Nathan, Y. (2003). Distinguishing between natural and recarbonated calcite in oil shales. *Journal of Thermal Analysis and Calorimetry* 71, 883–892.

Siani, G., Paterne, M., Michel, E., Sulpizio, R., Sbrana, A., Arnold, M., and Haddad, G. (2001). Mediterranean sea surface radiocarbon reservoir age changes since the Last Glacial Maximum. *Science* 294, 1917–1920.

Sillen, A. (1991). Solubility profiles of synthetic apatites and of modern and fossil bones. *Journal of Archaeological Science* 18, 385–397.

Sillen, A., and Smith, P. (1984). Weaning patterns are reflected in strontium-calcium ratios of juvenile skeletons. *Journal of Archaeological Science* 11, 237–245.

Sillen, A., Hall, G., and Armstrong, R. (1998). $^{87}Sr/^{86}Sr$ ratios in modern and fossil food-webs of the Sterkfontian Valley: implications for early hominid habitat preference. *Geochimica et Cosmochimica Acta* 62, 2463–2478.

Simkiss, K. (1968). The structure and formation of the shell and shell membranes. In: Egg Quality: A Study of the Hen's Egg (ed. T. C. Carter), pp. 3–25. Oliver and Boyd, Edinburgh.

Simkiss, K., and Wilbur, K. (1989). Biomineralization: Cell Biology and Mineral Deposition. Academic Press, San Diego, CA.

Simms, S. R. (1988). The archaeological structure of a Bedouin camp. *Journal of Archaeological Science* 15, 197–211.

Simpson, I. A., Dockrill, S. J., Bull, I. D., and Evershed, R. P. (1998). Early anthropogenic soil formation at Toft Ness, Sanday, Orkney. *Journal of Archaeological Science* 25, 729–746.

Simpson, I. A., Vésteinsson, O., Adderly, W. P., and McGovern, T. H. (2003). Fuel resource utilization in landscapes of settlement. *Journal of Archaeological Science* 30, 1401–1420.

Smith, C. I., Craig, O. C., Prigodich, R. V., Nielsen-Marsh, C. M., Jans, M. M. E., Vermeer, C., and Collins, M. J. (2005). Diagenesis and survival of osteocalcin in archaeological bone. *Journal of Archaeological Science* 32, 105–113.

Smith, H. I. (1899). The ethnological arrangement of archaeological material. Report of the Museums Association of the United Kingdom 1898.

Smith, T. M., Reid, D. J., and Sirianni, J. E. (2006). The accuracy of histological assessments of dental development and age at depth. *Journal of Anatomy* 208, 125–138.

Solano, M. L., Iriarte, F., Ciria, P., and Negro, M. J. (2001). Performance characteristics of three aeration systems in the composting of sheep manure and straw. *Journal of Agricultural Engineering Research* 79, 317–329.

Soltes, E. J., and Elder, T. J. (1981). Pyrolysis of Organic Chemicals from Biomass. CRC Press, Boca Raton, FL.

Sondi, I., and Slovenic, D. (2003). The mineralogical characteristics of the Lamboglia 2 Roman-age amphorae from the central Adriatic (Croatia). *Archaeometry* 45, 251–262.

Soudry, D., and Nathan, Y. (2001). Diagenetic trends of fluorine concentration in Negev phosphorites, Israel: implications for carbonate fluorapatite composition during phophogenesis. *Sedimentology* 48, 723–743.

Sponheimer, M., and Lee-Thorp, J. A. (1999). Alteration of enamel carbonate environments during fossilization. *Journal of Archaeological Science* 26, 143–150.

Sponheimer, M., and Lee-Thorp, J. A. (2006). Enamel diagenesis at South African Australopith sites: implications for paleoecological reconstruction with trace elements. *Geochimica et Cosmochimica Acta* 70, 1644–1654.

Stafford, T. W, Hare, P. E., Currie, L., Jull, A. J. T., and Donahue, D. J. (1991). Accelerator radiocarbon dating at the molecular level. *Journal of Archaeological Science*, 18, 35–72

Stankiewicz, B. A., Hutchins, J. C., Thomson, R., Briggs, D. E. G., and Evershed, R. P. (1998). Assessment of bog-body tissue preservation by pyrolysis-gas chromatography/mass spectrometry. *Rapid Communications in Mass Spectrometry* 11, 1884–1890.

Stanley, R. G., and Linskens, H. F. (1974). Pollen: Biology, Biochemistry, Management. Springer, Berlin.

Stein, J. K., and Farrand, W. R. (2001). Sediments in Archaeological Context. University of Utah Press, Salt Lake City.

Stenzel, H. B. (1963). Aragonite and calcite as constituents of adult oyster shells. *Science* 142, 232–233.

Stern, L. A., Johnson, G. D., and Chamberlain, C. P. (1994). Carbon isotope signature of environmental change found in fossil ratite eggshells from a South Asian Neogene sequence. *Geology* 22, 419–422.

Stevenson, M. G. (1985). The formation of artifact assemblages at workshops/habitation sites: models from Peace Point in northern Alberta. *American Antiquity* 50, 63–81.

Stiner, M., Kuhn, S., Weiner, S., and Bar-Yosef, O. (1995). Differential burning, recrystallization, and fragmentation of archaeological bone. *Journal of Archaeological Science* 22, 223–237.

Stos-Gale, Z. A., Maliotis, G., Gale, N. H., and Annetts, N. (1997). Lead isotope characteristics of the Cyprus copper ore deposits applied to provenance studies of copper oxhide ingots. *Archaeometry* 39, 83–124.

Stott, A. W., Evershed, R. P., Jim, S., Jones, V., Rogers, J. M., Tuross, N., and Ambrose, S. (1999). Cholesterol as a new source of paleodietary information: experimental approaches and archaeological applications. *Journal of Archaeological Science* 26, 705–716.

Stott, A. W., Berstan, R., Evershed, P., Hedges, R. E. M., Bronk-Ramsey, C., and Humm, M. J. (2001). Radiocarbon dating of single compounds isolated from pottery cooking vessel residue. *Radiocarbon* 43, 191–197.

Stuiver, M., Kromer, B., Becker, B., and Ferguson, C. W. (1986). Radiocarbon age calibration back to 13,300 years BP and the ^{14}C age matching of the German oak and US Bristlecone pine chronologies. *Radiocarbon* 28, 969–979.

Stumm, W., and Morgan, J. J. (1970). Aquatic Chemistry. John Wiley, New York.

Stutz, A. J. (2002). Polarizing microscopy identification of chemical diagenesis in archaeological cementum. *Journal of Archaeological Science* 29, 1327–1347.

Suetsugu, Y., and Tanaka, J. (1999). Crystal growth of carbonate apatite using a $CaCO_3$ flux. *Journal of Materials Science: Materials in Medicine* 10, 561–566.

Suga, S. (1984). The role of fluoride and iron in mineralization of fish enameloid. In: Tooth Enamel, vol. 4 (ed. R. W. Fearnhead and S. Suga), pp. 472–477. Elsevier, Amsterdam.

Suga, S., Taki, Y., Wada, K., and Ogawa, M. (1991). Evolution of fluoride and iron concentrations in the enameloid of fish teeth. In: Mechanisms and Phylogeny of Mineralization in Biological Systems (ed. S. Suga and H. Nakahara), pp. 439–446. Springer, Tokyo.

Sumper, M., and Kröger, N. (2004). Silica formation in diatoms: the function of long-chain polyamines and silaffins. *Journal of Materials Chemistry* 14, 2059–2065.

Surge, D., and Walker, K. J. (2005). Oxygen isotopic composition of modern and archaeological otoliths from the estuarine hardhead catfish (*Ariopsis felis*) and their potential to record low latitude climate change. *Palaeogeography, Palaeoclimatology, Palaeoecology* 228, 179–191.

Surovell, T. A., and Stiner, M. C. (2001). Standardizing infrared measures of bone mineral crystallinity: an experimental approach. *Journal of Archaeological Science* 28, 633–642.

Sutcliffe, A. (1970). Spotted hyaena: crusher, gnawer, digester and collector of bones. *Nature* 227, 1110–1113.

Swider, J. R., Hackley, V. A., and Winter, J. (2003). Characterization of Chinese ink in size and surface. *Journal of Cultural Heritage* 4, 175–186.

Sykes, G. A., Collins, M. J., and Walton, D. I. (1995). The significance of a geochemically isolated intracrystalline organic fraction within biominerals. *Organic Geochemistry* 23, 1059–1065.

Sykes, N. J., White, J., Hayes, T. E., and Palmer, M. R. (2006). Tracking animals using strontium isotopes in teeth: the role of fallow deer (*Dama dama*) in Roman Britain. *Antiquity* 80, 948–959.

Tan, K. H. (2003). Humic Matter in Soil and the Environment. Marcel Dekker, New York.

Taylor, A., and Gurney, E. (1961). Solubilities of potassium and ammonium taranakites. *Journal of Physical Chemistry* 65, 1613–1616.

Taylor, H. P., O'Neil, J. R., and Kaplan, I. R. (1991). Stable Isotope Geochemistry: A Tribute to Samuel Epstein. Special Publication 3. Geochemical Society, San Antonio, TX.

Taylor, R. E. (2001). Radiocarbon dating. In: Handbook of Archaeological Sciences (ed. D. R. Brothwell and A. M. Pollard), pp. 23–34, John Wiley, Chichester, UK.

Tchernov, E., and Valla, F. F. (1997). Two new dogs, and other Natufian dogs, from the Southern Levant. *Journal of Archaeological Science* 24, 65–95.

Teilhard de Chardin, P., and Young, C. C. (1929). Preliminary report on the Choukoutien fossiliferous deposit. *Bulletin of the Geological Society of China* 8, 173–202.

Ten Cate, A. R. (1989). Oral Histology: Development, Structure and Function. Mosby, St. Louis, MO.

Termine, J. D. (1984). The tissue-specific proteins of the bone matrix. In: The Chemistry and Biology of Mineralized Tissues (ed. W. T. Butler), pp. 94–97. Ebsco Media, Birmingham, AL.

Termine, J. D., and Posner, A. S. (1966). Infra-red determination of percentage of crystallinity in apatitic calcium phosphates. *Nature* 211, 268–270.

Termine, J. D., Belcourt, A. B., Conn, K. M., and Kleinman, H. K. (1981). Mineral and collagen-binding proteins of fetal calf bone. *Journal of Biological Chemistry* 256, 10403–10408.

Terri, J. A., and Stowe, L. G. (1976). Climatic patterns and the distribution of C4 grasses in North America. *Oecologia* 23, 1–12.

Terry, R. E., Fernández, F. G., Parnelli, J. J., and Inomata, T. (2004). The story in the floors: chemical signatures of ancient and modern Maya activities at Aguateca, Guatemala. *Journal of Archaeological Science* 31, 1237–1250.

Thellier, E. (1938). Sur l'aimantation des terres cuites et ses applications geo-physiques. *Annal* Institute de Physique du Globe of Paris 16, 157–302.

Théry, I., Gril, J., Vernet, J. L., Meignen, L., and Maury, J. (1996). Coal used for fuel at two prehistoric sites in southern France: Les Canalettes (Mousterian) and Les Usclades (Mesolithic). *Journal of Archaeological Science* 23, 509–512.

Thiebault, S. (1988). Paleoenvironment and ancient vegetation of Baluchistan based on charcoal analysis of archaeological sites. *Proceedings of the Indian National Science Academy* 54, 501–509.

Thieme, H. (1997). Lower Paleolithic hunting spears from Germany. *Nature* 385, 807–810.

Thompson, D. (1942). On Growth and Form. 2nd edition. Cambridge University Press, Cambridge.

Tindall, J. A., and Kunkel, J. R. (1999). Unsaturated Zone Hydrology. Prentice Hall, Upper Saddle River, NJ.

Tite, M. S., Kilikoglou, V., and Vekinis, G. (2001). Strength, toughness and thermal shock resistance of ancient ceramics, and their influence on technological choice. *Archaeometry* 43, 301–324.

Toivanen, T.-J., and Alen, R. (2006). Variations in the chemical composition within pine (*Pinus sylvestris*) trunks determined by diffuse reflectance infrared spectroscopy and chemometrics. *Cellulose* 13, 53–61.

Towe, K. M., and Thompson, G. R. (1972). The structure of some bivalve shell carbonates prepared by ion-beam thinning. *Calcified Tissue Research* 10, 38–48.

Traub, W., Arad, T., and Weiner, S. (1992). Growth of mineral crystals in turkey tendon collagen fibrils. *Connective Tissue Research* 28, 99–111.

Trigger, B. G. (1989). A History of Archaeological Thought. Cambridge University Press, Cambridge.

Trombold, C. D., and Israde-Alcantara, I. (2005). Paleoenvironment and plant cultivation on terraces at La Quemada, Zacatecas, Mexico: the pollen, phytolith and diatom evidence. *Journal of Archaeological Science* 32, 341–353.

Trueman, C. N. G., Behrensmeyer, A. K., Tuross, N., and Weiner, S. (2003). Mineralogical and compositional changes in bones exposed on soil surfaces in Amboseli National Park, Kenya: diagenetic mechanisms and the role of sediment pore fluids. *Journal of Archaeological Science* 31, 21–39.

Trueman, C. N., Field, J. H., Dortch, J., Charles, B., and Wroe, S. (2005). Prolonged coexistence of humans and megafauna in Pleistocene Australia. *Proceedings of the National Academy of Sciences of the United States of America* 102, 8381–8385.

Trueman, C. N., Behrensmeyer, A. K., Potts, R., and Tuross, N. (2006). High-resolution records of location and stratigraphic provenance from the rare earth element composition of fossil bones. *Geochimica et Cosmochimica Acta* 70, 4343–4355.

Trueman, C. N., Privat, K., and Field, J. (2008). Why do crystallinity values fail to predict the extent of diagenetic alteration of bone mineral? *Palaeogeography, Palaeoclimatology, Palaeoecology* 266, 160–167.

Tsibiridou, F. (2000). Les Pomak dans la Thrace greque: Discours ethnique et practiques Socioculturelles. L'Harmattan, Paris.

Tsartsidou, G., Lev-Yadun, S., Albert, R. M., Miller-Rosen, A., Efstratiou, N., and Weiner, S. (2007). The phytolith archaeological record: strengths and weaknesses evaluated based on a quantitative modern reference collection from Greece. *Journal of Archaeological Science* 34, 1262–1275.

Tsartsidou, G., Lev-Yadun, S., Efstratiou, N., and Weiner, S. (2008). Ethnoarchaeological study of phytolith assemblages from an agro-pastoral village in northern Greece (Sarakini): development and application of a Phytolith Difference Index. *Journal of Archaeological Science* 35, 600–613.

Tuross, N., Behrensmeyer, A. K., and Eanes, E. D. (1989a). Sr increases and crystallinity changes in taphonomic and archaeological bone. *Journal of Archaeological Science* 16, 661–672.

Tuross, N., Behrensmeyer, A. K., Eanes, E. D., and Fisher, D. L. (1989b). Molecular preservation and crystallographic alterations in a weathering sequence of wildebeest bones. *Applied Geochemistry* 4, 261–270.

Urey, H. C. (1947). The thermodynamic properties of isotopic substances. *Journal of the Chemical Society*, 562–581.

Vafiadou, A., Murray, A. S., and Liritzis, I. (2007). Optically stimulated luminescence (OSL) dating investigations of rock and underlying soil from three case studies. *Journal of Archaeological Science* 34, 1659–1669.

Valla, F. R., Khalaily, H., Valladas, H., Kaltnecker, E., Bocquentin, F., Cabellos, T., Bar-Yosef Mayer, D. E., et al. (2007). Les Fouilles de Ain Mallaha (Eynan) de 2003 à 2005: Quatrième Rapport Préliminaire. *Journal of the Israel Prehistoric Society* 37, 135–383.

Valladas, H., Reyss, J. L., Joron, J. L., Valladas, G., Bar-Yosef, O., and Vandermeersch, B. (1988). Thermoluminescence dating of Mousterian Troto-Cro-Magnon remains from Israel and the origin of modern man. *Nature* 331, 614–616.

van der Kooij, G. (2002). Ethnoarchaeology in the Near East. In: Moving Matters: Ethnoarchaeology in the Near East (ed. W. Wendrich and G. van der Kooij), pp. 29–44. CNWS, Leiden, Netherlands.

van der Merwe, N. J., and Vogel, J. C. (1978). [13]C content of human collagen as a measure of prehistoric diet in woodland North America. *Nature* 276, 815–816.

van der Plicht, J., Beck, J. W., Bard, E., Baillie, M. G. L., Blackwell, P. G., Buck, C. E., Friedrich, M., et al. (2004). NOTCAL04 – comparison/calibration ^{14}C records 26–50Cal KYR BP. *Radiocarbon* 46, 1225–1238.

van Klinken, G. J. (1999). Bone collagen quality indicators for paleodietry and radiocarbon measurements. *Journal of Archaeological Science* 26, 687–695.

Vavilin, V. A., Rytov, S. V., and Lokshina, L. Y. (1996). A description of hydrolysis kinetics in anaerobic degradation of particulate organic matter. *Bioresource Technology* 56, 229–237.

Veis, A. (2003). Mineralization in organic matrix frameworks. In: Reviews in Mineralogy and Chemistry, vol. 54 (ed. P. M. Dove, J. D. DeYoreo, and

S. Weiner), pp. 249–289. Mineralogical Society of America/Geochemical Society, Washington, DC.

Veis, A., and Perry, A. (1967). The phosphoprotein of the dentin matrix. *Biochemistry* 6, 2409–2416.

Velde, B., and Druc, I. C. (1999). Archaeological Ceramic Materials. Springer, Berlin.

Verri, G., Barkai, R., Bordeanu, C., Gopher, A., Hass, M., Kubik, P., Montanari, E., et al. (2004). Flint mining in prehistory recorded by in situ produced cosmogenic ^{10}Be. *Proceedings of the National Academy of Sciences of the United States of America* 101, 7880–7884.

Verri, G., Barkai, R., Gopher, A., Hass, M., Kubik, P., Paul, M., Ronen, A., Weiner, S., and Boaretto, E. (2005). Flint procurement strategies in the Late Lower Palaeolithic recorded by in situ produced cosmogenic ^{10}Be in Tabun and Qesem Caves (Israel). *Journal of Archaeological Science* 32, 207–213.

Very, J.-M., and Baud, C.-A. (1984). X-ray diffraction of calcified tissues. In: Methods of Calcified Tissue Preparation (ed. G. R. Dickson), pp. 369–390. Elsevier, Amsterdam.

Villaseñor, I., and Price, C. A. (2008). Technology and decay of magnesian lime plasters: the sculptures of the funerary crypt of Palque, Mexico. *Journal of Archaeological Science* 35, 1030–1039.

Vogel, J. C., and van der Merwe, N. J. (1977). Isotopic evidence for early maize cultivation in New York State. *American Antiquity* 42, 238–242.

Vogel, J. C., Visser, E., and Fuls, A. (2001). Suitability of ostrich eggshell for radiocarbon dating. *Radiocarbon* 43, 133–137.

Von Post, L. (1944). The prospect for pollen analysis in the study of the earth's climatic history. *New Phytologist* 45, 193–217.

Vote, E. (2002). Discovering Petra: archaeological analysis in VR. *Computer Graphics in Art History and Archaeology*, September–October, 38–50.

Wada, K. (1977). Allophane and imogolite. In: Minerals in Soil Environments (ed. J. B. Dixon and S. B. Weed), pp. 603–638. Soil Science Society of America, Madison, WI.

Wada, K. (1989). Allophane and imogolite. In: Minerals in Soil Environments, vol. 1 (ed. J. B. Dixon and S. B. Weed), pp. 1051–1088. Soil Science Society of America, Madison, WI.

Wainwright, S. A., Biggs, W. D., Currey, J. D., and Gosline, J. M. (1976). Mechanical Design in Organisms. Princeton University Press, Princeton, NJ.

Waksman, S. (1952). Soil Microbiology. John Wiley, New York.

Wang, L., Nancollas, G. H., Henneman, Z. J., Klein, E., and Weiner, S. (2006). Nanosized particles in bone and dissolution insensitivity of bone mineral. *Biointerphases*, 1, 106–111.

Wang, R. Z., and Weiner, S. (1998). Human root dentin: structural anisotropy and Vickers microhardness isotropy. *Connective Tissue Research* 39, 269–279.

Wang, R. Z., Addadi, L., and Weiner, S. (1997). Design strategies of sea urchin teeth: structure, composition and micromechanical relations to function. *Philosophical Transactions of the Royal Society of London, Series B* 352, 469–480.

Watabe, N. (1963). Decalcification of thin sections for electron microscope studies of crystal-matrix relationship in mollusk shells. *Journal of Cell Biology* 18, 701–703.

Watchman, A. (1990). A summary of occurrences of oxalate-rich crusts in Australia. *Rock Art Research* 7, 44–50.

Watkinson, D. (2001). Maximizing the lifespans of archaeological objects. In: Handbook of Archaeological Sciences (ed. D. R. Brothwell and A. M. Pollard), pp. 649–659. John Wiley, Chichester, UK.

Watson, P. J. (1979). Archaeological Ethnography in Western Iran. Viking Fund Publications in Anthropology. University of Arizona Press, Tucson.

Watson, P. J., LeBlanc, S. A., and Redman, C. L. (1984). Archaeological Explanation. Columbia University Press, New York.

Wattez, J., Courty, M. A., and Macphail, R. I. (1990). Burnt organo-mineral deposits related to animal and human activities in caves. In: Soil Micromorphology: A Basic and Applied Science (ed. L. A. Douglas), pp. 431–439. Elsevier, Amsterdam.

Weaver, A. R., Kissel, D. E., Chen, F., West, L. T., Adkins, W., Rickman, D., and Luvali, J. C. (2004). Mapping soil pH buffering capacity of selected fields in the coastal plain. *Soil Science Society of America Journal* 68, 662–668.

Webb, E. A., and Longstaffe, F. J. (2000). The oxygen isotopic composition of silica phytoliths and plant water in grasses: implications for the study of paleoclimate. *Geochimica et Cosmochimica Acta* 64, 767–780.

Webb, M. A. (1999). Cell-mediated crystallization of calcium oxalates in plants. *Plant Cell* 11, 751–761.

Weiner, J. S. (1955). The Piltdown Forgery. Oxford University Press, Oxford.

Weiner, S. (1985). Organic matrix-like macromolecules associated with the mineral phase of sea urchin skeletal plates and teeth. *Journal of Experimental Zoology* 234, 7–15.

Weiner, S. (2008). Archaeology, archaeological science and integrative archaeology. *Israel Journal of Earth Sciences* 56, 57–61.

Weiner, S., and Addadi, L. (1997). Design strategies in mineralized biological materials. *Journal of Materials Chemistry* 7, 689–702.

Weiner, S., and Bar-Yosef, O. (1990). States of preservation of bones from prehistoric sites in the Near East: a survey. *Journal of Archaeological Science* 17, 187–196.

Weiner, S., and Dove, P. M. (2003). An overview of biomineralization processes and the problem of the vital effect. In: Biomineralization: Reviews in Mineralogy and Geochemistry, vol. 54 (ed. P. M. Dove, J. J. DeYoreo, and S. Weiner), pp. 1–29. Mineralogical Society of America/Geochemical Society, Washington, DC.

Weiner, S., and Goldberg, P. (1990). On-site Fourier transform infrared spectrometry at an archeological excavation. *Spectroscopy* 5, 46–50.

Weiner, S., and Price, P. A. (1986). Disaggregation of bone into crystals. *Calcified Tissue International* 39, 365–375.

Weiner, S., and Traub, W. (1986). Organization of hydroxyapatite crystals within collagen fibrils. *FEBS Letters* 206, 262–266.

Weiner, S., and Wagner, H. D. (1998). The material bone: structure–mechanical function relations. *Annual Reviews of Material Sciences* 28, 271–298.

Weiner, S., Lowenstam, H. A., and Hood, L. (1976). Characterization of 80-million year old mollusk shell proteins. *Proceedings of the National Academy of Sciences of the United States of America* 73, 2541–2545.

Weiner, S., Kustanovich, Z., Gil-Av, E., and Traub, W. (1980). Dead Sea Scroll parchments: unfolding of the collagen molecules and racemization of aspartic acid. *Nature* 287, 820–823.

Weiner, S., Goldberg, P., and Bar-Yosef, O. (1993). Bone preservation in Kebara Cave, Israel using on-site Fourier transform infrared spectroscopy. *Journal of Archaeological Science* 20, 613–627.

Weiner, S., Xu, Q., Goldberg, P., Liu, J., and Bar-Yosef, O. (1998). Evidence for the use of fire at Zhoukoudian, China. *Science* 281, 251–253.

Weiner, S., Goldberg, P., and Bar-Yosef, O. (1999a). Overview of ash studies in two prehistoric caves in Israel: implications to field archaeology. In: The Practical Impact of Science on Near Eastern and Aegean Archaeology, Wiener Laboratory Monograph 3 (ed. S. Pike and S. Gitin), pp. 85–90. Archetype, London.

Weiner, S., Traub, W., and Wagner, H. D. (1999b). Lamellar bone: structure-function relations. *Journal of Structural Biology* 126, 241–255.

Weiner, S., Veis, A., Beniash, E., Arad, T., Dillon, J. W., Sabsay, B., and Siddiqui, F. (1999c). Peritubular dentin formation: crystal organization and the macromolecular constituents in human teeth. *Journal of Structural Biology* 126, 27–41.

Weiner, S., Addadi, L., and Wagner, H. (2000). Materials design in biology. *Materials Science and Engineering C* 11, 1–8.

Weiner, S., Goldberg, P., and Bar-Yosef, O. (2002). Three dimensional distribution of minerals in the sediments of Hayonim Cave, Israel: diagenetic processes and archaeological implications. *Journal of Archaeological Science* 29, 1289–1308.

Weiner, S., Sagi, I., and Addadi, L. (2005). Choosing the path less travelled. *Science* 309, 1027–1028.

Weiner, S., Berna, F., Cohen, I., Shahack-Gross, R., Albert, R. M., Karkanas, P., Meignen, L., and Bar-Yosef, O. (2007). Mineral distributions in Kebara Cave: diagenesis and its effect on the archaeological record. In: Kebara Cave, Mt. Carmel, Israel: The Middle and Upper Paleolithic Archaeology, Part 1 (ed. O. Bar-Yosef and L. Meignen), pp. 131–146. Peabody Museum of Archaeology and Ethnology, Harvard University, Cambridge, MA.

Weiss, E., and Kislev, M. E. (2004). Plant remains as indicators for economic activity: a case study from Iron Age Ashkelon. *Journal of Archaeological Science* 31, 1–13.

Weiss, E., and Kislev, M. E. (2007). Plant remains as a tool for reconstruction of the past environment, economy, and society: archaeobotany in Israel. *Israel Journal of Earth Sciences* 56, 163–173.

Weiss, I. M., Tuross, N., Addadi, L., and Weiner, S. (2002). Mollusk larval shell formation: amorphous calcium carbonate is a precursor for aragonite. *Journal of Experimental Zoology* 293, 478–491.

Werb, Z. (1992). The role of metalloproteinases and their inhibitors in matrix remodeling in mineralized tissue. In: Chemistry and Biology of Mineralized Tissues (ed. H. Slavkin and P. A. Price), pp. 321–327. Elsevier Science, Amsterdam.

Whitbread, I. K. (2001). Ceramic petrology, clay geochemistry and ceramic production – from technology to the mind of the potter. In: Handbook of Archaeological Sciences (ed. D. R. Brothwell and A. M. Pollard), pp. 449–459. John Wiley, Chichester, UK.

White, D. J. (1997). Dental calculus: recent insights into occurrence, formation, prevention, removal and oral health effects of supragingival and subgingival deposits. *European Journal of Oral Science* 105, 508–522.

White, J. R. (1978). Archaeological and chemical evidence for the earliest American use of raw coal as a fuel in ironmaking. *Journal of Archaeological Science* 5, 391–393.

Whittemore, O., and Halsey, G. (1983). Pore structure characterized by mercury porosimetry. In: Advances in Materials Characterization: Materials Science Research, vol. 15 (ed. D. Rossington, R. Condrate, and R. Snyder), pp. 147–158. Plenum Press, New York.

Wilding, L. P. (1967). Radiocarbon dating of biogenetic opal. *Science* 156, 166–167.

Williams-Thorpe, O., Potts, P. J., and Webb, P. C. (1999). Field portable non-destructive analysis of lithic archaeological samples by X-ray fluorescence using a mercury iodide detector: comparison with wavelength-dispersive XRF and a case study in British stone axe provenancing. *Journal of Archaeological Science* 26, 215–237.

Wilson, E. O. (1998). Consilience. Alfred A. Knopf, New York.

Wilson, L., and Pollard, A. M. (2001). The provenance hypothesis. In: Handbook of Archaeological Sciences (ed. D. R. Brothwell and A. M. Pollard), pp. 507–517. John Wiley, Chichester, UK.

Wilson, R. W., Millero, F. J., Taylor, J. R., Walsh, P. J., Christensen, V., Jennings, S., and Grosell, M. (2009). Contributions of fish to the marine inorganic carbon cycle. *Science* 323, 359–362.

Woods, W. I. (1977). The quantitative analysis of soil phosphate. *American Antiquity* 42, 248–252.

Woot-Tsuen, W. L. (1968). Food composition table for use in Africa. Food and Agriculture Organization of the United Nations. http://www.fao.org/DOCREP/003/X6877E/X6877E02.htm.

Wright, L. E., and Schwarcz, H. P. (1996). Infrared and isotopic evidence for diagenesis of bone apatite at Dos Pilas, Guatemala: paleodietry implications. *Journal of Archaeological Science* 23, 933–944.

Wyckoff, R. W. G. (1972). The Biochemistry of Animal Fossils. Scientechnica, Bristol, UK.

Xu, S., Sun, K., Cui, F. Z., and Landis, W. J. (2003). Organization of apatite crystals in human woven bone. *Bone* 32, 150–162.

Yasuda, Y. (2002). Origins of pottery and agriculture in East Asia. In: The Origins of Pottery and Agriculture (ed. Y. Yasuda), pp. 119–142. Lustre Press, New Delhi.

Yellin, J. E. (1977). Archaeological Approaches to the Present. Academic Press, New York.

Yenner, A. K., Ösban, H., Kaptan, E., Pehlivan, A. N., and Goodway, M. (1989). Kestel: an Early Bronze age source of tin ore in the Taurus Mountains, Turkey. *Science* 244, 200–203.

Yizhaq, M. (2004). Characterizing and dating of the Early PPNB layer at the site of Motza. M.S. thesis, Weizmann Institute of Science, Rehovot, Israel.

Yizhaq, M., Mintz, G., Cohen, I., Khalally, H., Weiner, S., and Boaretto, E. (2005). Quality controlled radiocarbon dating of bones and charcoal from the early Pre-Pottery Neolithic B (PPNB) of Motza (Israel). *Radiocarbon* 47, 193–206.

Yoshida, S., Ohnishi, Y., and Kitagishi, K. (1959). The chemical nature of silicon in the rice plant. *Soil and Plant Food* 5, 23–27.

Zaslansky, P., Friesem, A. A., and Weiner, S. (2006a). Structure and mechanical properties of the soft zone separating bulk dentin and enamel in crowns of human teeth: insight into tooth function. *Journal of Structural Biology* 153, 188–199.

Zaslansky, P., Shahar, R., Friesem, A. A., and Weiner, S. (2006b). Relations between shape, materials properties and function in biological materials using laser speckle interferometry: in-situ tooth deformation. *Advanced Functional Materials* 16, 1925–1936.

Zeller, E. J. (1968). Use of electron spin resonance for measurement of natural radiation damage. In: Thermoluminescence of Geological Materials (ed. D. J. McDougall), pp. 271–279. Academic Press, London.

Zevenhoven-Onderwater, M., Blomquist, J. P., Skrifvars, B. J., Backman, R., and Hupa, M. (2000). The prediction of behaviour of ashes from five different solid fuels in fluidised bed combustion. *Fuel* 79, 1353–1361.

Zhang, L., and Gellerstedt, G. (2001). NMR observation of a new lignin structure, a spiro-dienone. *Chemical Communications* 24, 2744–2745.

Zhao, Z. (1998). The middle Yangtze region in China is one place where rice was domesticated: phytolith evidence from the Diaotonghuan Cave, northern Jiangxi. *Antiquity* 72, 885–897.

Ziv, V., and Weiner, S. (1994). Bone crystal sizes: a comparison of transmission electron microscopic and X-ray diffraction line width broadening techniques. *Connective Tissue Research* 30, 165–175.

Zohary, D., and Hopf, M. (2001). Domestication of Plants in the Old World. Oxford University Press, Oxford.

zur Nedden, D., Wicke, K., Knapp, R., Deidler, H., Wilfing, H., and Weber, G. (1994). New findings of the Tyrolean "Ice Man": archaeological and CT-body analysis suggest personal disaster before death. *Journal of Archaeological Science* 21, 809–818.

Index

Acacia tree, 239
Acidogenesis, 57
Activity areas. *See* Site spatial organization
aDNA. *See* Ancient DNA
Aerobic degradation, 53
Aerobic environment, 57
Age at death, 132
Agricultural fields, 145
Agricultural practices, 140
Agropastoral societies, 148, 229, 238, 239
  use of dung, 238, 240
Aguateca, Guatemala, 244
Airborne dust. *See* Loess
Alabaster. *See* Gypsum
Aliabad, 232–236
  absence of macroscopic bones, 232, 238
  alleys between houses, 233
  animal dung, 232
  ash as a fertilizer, 233
  ash pits, 233
  beehives, 236
  cemetary, 233
  courtyards, 236
  dogs, 232
  dung cake manufacturing, 232–233
  dung fuel, 232
  fire locations, 235
  gardens, 233
  latrine, 236
  plants and animals used, 232
  stables, 236
  storage bins, 236
  typical household plan, 234
  wells, 236
Aliabad village, Zagros Mountains, Iran,
  232–236. *See* Aliabad
Alkaline felspars, 196
Allophane, 301
Alveolar bone, 124, 129

Alyawaran household, Australia, 228
Amazon basin
  soil charcoal, 183
Amber, 36, 211, 226, 314
  infrared spectrum, 37, 315
  provenience, 37
Amboseli, Kenya, 116, 288
Amelogenin, 125
Amino acid racemization, 214
Amino acid racemization dating, 19,
    24–25, 214, 246, 247
  eggshells, 153
  land snail shells, 163
Amino acid sequence, 210
Amino acids
  analysis, 211
  racemers, 24
Ammonium carbonate, 57
Amorphous calcium carbonate, 77, 169,
    282, 283, 285
  earthworms, 283
  mollusk shells, 161
  plants, 135
Amorphous calcium phosphate, 99
  first-formed mineral in bone, 104
Amorphous carbon, 180
Amorphous mineral structure, 89
  silica, 136
Anaerobic degradation, 50, 57, 58, 59, 114
  reconstructing site use, 58
Anaerobic organisms, 57
Anatomically modern humans (AMH)
  DNA, 33
Ancient DNA, 33–35, 208, 209
  bone, 121
  crystal aggregates in bone, 218
  damage, 34, 121, 209
  Neanderthal DNA sequence, 35, 208
  preservation in crystal aggregates, 112

Ancient DNA (*cont.*)
  replicating enzymes, 209
  Tyrolean ice man, 48
Anhydrite, 169, 188
Animal enclosures, 54, 58, 86, 148, 223,
      224, 239–240
  dung, 239
  fence, 239
  phytolith accumulations, 238
  Sarakini, devoid of phytoliths, 242
Animal husbandry, 45, 141
Anthropogenic materials
  list, 321
Anthropogenic minerals
  definition, 69
Apatite mineral family, 286–289. *See also*
      Carbonate hydroxylapatite and
      Authigenic
  phosphate minerals, 83
  biogenic vs geogenic, 87
  embedded information, 86–88
  list of minerals, 286
  mineral nomenclature, 84
Aragonite, 77, 282
  assessing mineral preservation, 78, 81,
      271
  atomic structure, 77
  cement, 80
  diagenesis, 80–81
  diagenetic indicator, 63
  embedded information, 81–83
  formation at elevated temperatures, 283
  formation from boiling water, 78, 80,
      283
  formation from sea water, 78, 80, 283
  heated, 81, 162
  mollusk shells, 63, 283
  otoliths, 42, 155
  refractory material, 193
  sources in archaeological sites, 63, 80,
      283
  transformation at elevated
      temperatures, 204
Archaeobotanical record, 16–18, 149, 238
  charred materials, 178, 184
  season of occupation, 41
Archaeobotany
  paleoenvironmental reconstruction, 31
  season of occupation, 41
Archaeological record
  how bad?, 47
  missing part, 51, 62–63
  primary vs secondary deposits, 232, 236
  pristine, 47, 48–50
Archaeological science, 5–6

Archaeomagnetism, 19, 25, 246
Archaeomalacology, 162
Archaeozoological record, 101, 108, 118,
      231, 238
  bones, 101–102
Artifacts
  for relative dating, 18
  provenience, 36
  sorting by size, 228
Ash, 168–178, 284. *See also* Wood ash, 82
  acid insoluble fraction, 171, 174
  affect on TL and ESR dating, 177
  burned bone, 177
  composition, 169–170
  criteria for preservation, 175
  definition, 168, 169
  diagenesis above pH-8, 172–173
  diagenesis below pH-8, 173–174
  embedded information, 175–178
  formation from wood, 79
  from wood and bark, calcite formation,
      170
  how much is produced?, 166
  identifying ash, 174–175
  low and high temperature forms,
      170
  phytoliths, 169, 171
  pits in Aliabad village, Iran, 233
  radiocarbon dating, 177
  reaction with phosphate, 173
  recrystallization, 83
  red brick colored soil particles, 170
  sediment color and texture, 174
  siliceous aggregates, 169, 171, 173
  soluble salts, 169
  wood, crystal morphology, 82
  ν_2:ν_4 ratios of calcite, 171, 174
Aspartic acid-rich proteins, 100, 162
Asphalt, 312, 313
Atacama desert, Chile, 49, 114
Authigenic minerals
  calcite, 78
  carbonate hydroxylapatite, 84, 86, 161
  ceramic, 204–205
  definition, 68, 69
  hydraulic plaster, 189
  list, 321
  organic matter concentrations, 225
  silica. *See* Silica, authigenic
Authigenic phosphate minerals, 295–297.
      See also Phosphate concentrations, 65,
      81, 88, 236
  bone dissolution, 64, 87
  formed at low pH, 64, 175
  guano degradation, 225

identification using infrared spectroscopy, 296
nodules, 64
organic-rich sediments, 86, 223
Avian eggshells. *See* Eggshells
Avian gizzard stones, 154

Bananas
  phytoliths, 147
Barite, 116
Bark
  grass phytolith contamination, 172
  phytoliths, 178
Barley
  phytoliths, 147
Beach rock, 80
Beach sand, 91
Beads, 36, 151
  mineral list, 321
  mollusk shells, 158
Bedouin camp, Jordan, 228
Beehives, 236
Beeswax, 211, 236, 312
Benzenecarboxylic acids, 184
Bercey, France, 114
Binders. *See* Plaster binders
Binocular microscope, 264
Biogenic minerals, 99. *See* Appendix B, *See also* Biomineralization
  assessing mineral preservation, 81
  calcite, 79, 286
  carbonate hydroxylapatite, 84
  definition, 69
  intracrystalline macromolecules, 212
  list, 321
  oxygen isotopic composition, 33
  solubility, 100
Biogenic molecules
  DNA, 209–210
  lipids, 211
  list of macromolecules, 321
  major types for archaeology, 208–211
  preservation and information content, 207, 209
  proteins. *See also* Proteins, 210
Biomaterials
  list, 321
Biomineralization, 99–101
  acidic proteins, 100
  amorphous precursor phases, 61, 100, 161, 283
  eggshells, 152
  library of infrared spectra, 282
  plants, 135

role of cells and macromolecules, 100
silica formation, 89
Biomolecular archaeology, 48, 208
  historical perspective, 211–212
  molecule types, 208–211
Biotite, 93
Bioturbation, 54, 57, 62
Bird eggshells. *See* Eggshells
Bitumen. *See also* Asphalt, 203
Bivalves, 159. *See also* Clams
Bog bodies, 50, 114
Boiling water, 78, 80, 121, 283
Bone
  ash, 177
  basic constituents, 102–106
  burned. *See* Burned bone
  cooked, 121
  embedded information, 123
  fragments, 229, 233, 237
  life history reconstruction, 123
  mineral. *See* Bone mineral
  multipurpose material, 102
  noncollagenous proteins (NCPs), 105, 112
  organic matrix, 104–106
  osteocalcin, 105
  paleodiet reconstruction, 119–120, 121
  paleoenvironmental reconstruction (REEs), 31
  paleogenetics, 121–122
  paleomigration, 118–119
  porosity, 110
  radiocarbon dating, 122–123
  remodeling, 26, 102, 108, 255
  structure. *See* Bone structure
  turnover rate, 26
Bone diagenesis
  authigenic minerals, 116
  buried bones, 114, 117
  compact vs spongy bone, 114
  crystallinity, 290
  crystals, 116
  fluoride content, 288
  microbial and fungal action, 114
  mineral, 110–112
  mineral solubility, 110
  on soil surface, 115–116
  organic matrix, 110, 112–113
  porosity, 110
  pseudomorphs, 115
  recrystallization window, 111
  timescale, 115
  tunnels, 113
  wicking of groundwater, 116
Bone family of materials, 215

Bone Gla protein. *See* Osteocalcin
Bone mineral, 102–104
    atomic disorder, 61, 64, 104
    carbonates, 104
    content, 102
    crystal aggregates, 106, 112, 308
    crystal c axis alignment, 106
    crystal nucleation and growth, 106
    crystal size and shape, 104, 290
    crystal sizes, 117
    crystallinity, 104, 289–292
    crystals, 215
    dissolution, 60, 87, 111
    nomenclature, 84
    oxygen isotopic composition, 33
    phosphate oxygen isotopic
        composition, 87
    phosphorus concentration, 224
    recrystallization window, 112
    sintering, 290
    solubility, 104
    Sr/Ca ratios weaning, 45
    surface area, 104, 290
Bone powder, 203
Bone preservation, 160
    calcitic cemented sediments, 111
    clay-rich sediments, 55, 96, 111
    crystal aggregates, 112
Bone structure
    age dependence, 230
    canaliculi, 109
    circumferential lamellar bone, 107
    compact bone, 108
    fibril array, 107
    graded material, 102
    hierarchical structure, 102–109
    lamellar bone, 107
    mineralized collagen fibril, 106
    osteonal, 26, 108, 230
    packing motifs of fibril arrays, 107
    parallel fibered bone, 107
    plexiform or fibrolamellar bone, 107,
        230
    proportions of basic constituents, 102
    spongy bone, 108
    woven bone, 107
Bone tools, 101
Bones, 101–102, 108–109
    absence in ethnographic settings, 229
    black, 117
    burned. *See* Burned bone
    cemented sediment, 83
    dissolved, 88
    distribution in a site, 271
    for combustion, 168, 237

small mammals, 234
Bones vs bone, terminology, 102
Brachiopod shells
    calcite disorder, 286
    intracrystalline macromolecules, 212,
        213
Brachydonty, 129
Breccia, 83. *See* Cemented sediments
Bricks, 92, 189
Brushite, 130
Buffer, 77
Burned bone, 76, 117–118, 121, 176,
        292–295
    calcined, 117, 118, 177, 255, 293
    cause of black color, 117, 294
    changes, color and splitting factor, 118
    circumstances of burning, 292
    color change, 117, 293
    cremation, 117
    identification by infrared spectroscopy,
        292, 294
Burrows, 251

Calcined bone. *See* Burned bone, calcined
Calcite, 76–83, 282
    ash, 82, 169
    ash $\nu_2{:}\nu_4$ ratios, 171
    ash, low and high temperature forms,
        170
    avian eggshells, 152
    calcination temperature, 186
    ceramics, 198, 200, 205
    crystal morphology variations, 82
    diagenesis, 63, 80–81
    disorder, 63, 82, 284–286
    distinguishing formation modes, 81–82,
        284–286
    embedded information, 81–83
    high Mg cement, 80
    influence on bone preservation, 111
    memory effect, 285
    plants, 135
    plaster binder, 186–188
    preservation of bones, ash and plaster,
        77
    rhomb-shape crystals, 78
    sources in archaeological sites, 78–80,
        283
    structure, 77
    transformation at elevated
        temperatures, 204
    $\nu_2{:}\nu_4$ ratios, 285
Calcitic spherulites. *See* Spherulites
Calcium aluminum hydrates. *See also*
        Hydraulic plaster, 189

Calcium carbonate
  pH buffering capacity, 77, 160, 172
  polymorphs, 282–283
Calcium carbonate mineral family, 76–83
  calcite and aragonite structures, 78
  differentiating origins of calcite, 81–82
  embedded information, 81–83
  members, 77
Calcium hydroxide, 186. *See also* Lime, 79, 185
Calcium oxalate, 306–307. *See* Whewellite and weddellite
  bacteria, 306
  biogenic crystal shapes, 82, 306
  combustion in wood, 170
  crystal shapes in wood, 170
  lichens, 306
  plants, 135, 306
  source of ash calcite, 170, 306
Calcium oxide, 63, 79, 82, 177, 186, 193, 196, 204, 285
Calcium silicate hydrate. *See also* Hydraulic plaster
Calcium silicate hydrates, 189
Calcium sulfate hemihydrate. *See also* plaster of Paris, 188
Calibration curve. *See* Radiocarbon dating, calibration
Canaliculi, 109, 113
Cancellous bone. *See* Spongy bone
Capillary action, 56, 315
Carbon isotopic composition. *See also* Stable isotopic composition
  paleodiet, 27
Carbonate bicarbonate buffering, 60
Carbonate fluorapatite, 84, 112, 286, 288
  stability, 84
Carbonate hydroxylapatite, 83–88, 286. *See also* Bone mineral
  A and B carbonate sites, 131, 287
  authigenic, 76, 296
  biogenic crystals, 63
  biogenic vs geogenic, 87
  carbonate content, 84, 287
  carbonate content by infrared spectroscopy, 288
  crystal size and shape, 87
  crystallinity, 87, 289–292
  dental calculus, 130
  dentin, 127
  diagenesis, 86
  disorder, 64
  dissolved bones, 88
  embedded information, 86–88

  fluoride replacement, 84, 288
  fossil snail shells, 161
  from ash calcite, 173
  heated, 287
  hens eggshells, 152
  identification by microchemical analysis, 317–319
  nodules, 63
  nomenclature confusion, 84
  paleoclimate reconstruction, 87
  stability field, 60, 85
  structure, 85
Carbonate rock surfaces, 64
Carbonation, 187
Carboxylate and carbonyl groups
  charcoal fossil, 181
Casts. *See* Pseudomorphs
Catastrophic environmental events, 164
Cathodeluminescence, 190, 192
Caves
  authigenic calcite, 78
  authigenic phosphate minerals, 225
  carnivore dwellers, 231
  carnivore vs human activities, 230
  cemented sediment, 83
  dating carbonate deposits, 21
  detecting roof collapse, 64
  flint procurement, 91
  gizzard stones, 154
  guano, 80
  hearths, 183
  vulture bone accumulations, 231
Celadons, 205
Cellulose, 58, 177, 179, 309, 312
Cement
  aragonite, 80
  calcite. *See* Cemented sediment
Cemented sediment, 54, 78, 82–83
  ash derived, 284
  bones, 83
Cementum, 124, 129, 215
  season of occupation, 42
  seasonal increments, 129
  structure, 130
Cephalopods, 159
Ceramics, 194–206. *See also* Pottery
  beehive walls, 236
  calcite, 198, 200
  clay sources, 96
  color, 203
  diagenesis, 194, 198, 199, 200
  early production (south China), 165
  embedded information, 198–206
  extent of vitrification, 203
  firing conditions, 197–198, 202–205

Ceramics (*cont.*)
  firing temperature, regime, duration, 197, 204
  fluxes, 196
  high temperature polymorphs of silicon dioxide, 90
  minerals formed at elevated temperatures, 204–205
  molecules in pores, 29
  porosity, 205, 219, 221
  production areas, 202
  production processes, 202–205
  protected niche for molecules, 219–222
  provenience and trade, 198–200
  proveniencing, 39, 96, 200
  raw material sources, 199
  raw materials, 92
  refiring, 203
  refractory materials, 206
  technical, 194, 235
  temper, 205
  ultrastructure, 203–204
Chaine opertiore, 165
Charcoal, 178–185. *See also* Charred material, 16, 166
  adsorbed ions and molecules, 66
  associated clays, 95
  distribution, 64
  fluorescence, 258
  in sediments, 183
  microparticles, 174
  production, 179
  radiocarbon dating, 21, 255
  Sarakini village, Greece, 243–244
  structures for taxonomic identification, 178
  weight loss and shrinkage during formation, 179
Charcoal fossil, 181–182
  2 major components, 181
  bound ions and molecules, 182
  carboxylate and carbonyl groups, 181
  cf humic substances, 182
  degradation mechanism, 183
  diagenesis, 182–183
  distribution in sites, 182
  onionlike structures, 182
  oxidation, 182
  oxygen distribution, 182
Charcoal structure, 180
  amorphous carbon, 180
  graphite crystal size, 180
  graphitelike crystallites, 179
  graphitelike phase, 180

  molecular structure, 179–180
  nonordered phase, 180
  onionlike structures, 180
Charred material, 178–185. *See also* Charcoal, 16, 58
  benzenecarboxylic acids, 184
  circumstances of charring, 17
  dating plaster, 191
  identification in sediments, 184
  plants, 16
  preservation, 179, 252
  radiocarbon dating, 184
  Raman spectroscopy, 72
  seed and fruit identification, 184
  soil stabilization, 183
  wet sieving, 265
Charred wood. *See* Charcoal
Cheetahs, 231
Chemical elemental analysis, 72
  typical analysis
Chert. *See* Flint
Chitin, 100, 312
  mollusk shells, 162
  preservation, 58
Chlorapatite, 286
Clams, fresh water, 63, 80
Clay, 300–303
  adsorbed ions and molecules, 66
  adsorbed organic matter, 94, 95
  amorphous, 94, 95, 198, 301
  atomic structures, 93
  formation, 92
  heated, 97, 198, 235, 303–305
  hydrological properties, 96
  melting temperatures, 195
  mineral classification, 94
  mineral groups, 93
  plasticlike properties, 92, 195
  provenience, 96–97
  Raman spectroscopy, 97
  reaction with phosphate, 95, 302
  structures, 93–94
  terminology, 73, 301
Clay family of minerals, 92–97, 300–303
  diagenesis, 95–96
  differential thermal analysis (DTA), 94
  embedded information, 96–97
  identifying mineral type, 94
  infrared spectroscopy, 94
  X-ray diffraction, 94
Clay-rich sediment, 66
  affect of fire, 97
  better preservation, 96
  bone preservation, 111, 252

pottery manufacture, 195
springs, 96
Coal, 145, 168
ash, 177
Coke, 205
Collagen, 211, 312
bone, 308
C/N ratio, 256
cementum, 129
degradation in bone, 115
fiber, 105
in bone crystal aggregates, 106, 112, 217,
308
molecular structure, 308
nitrogen isotope ratios, 45
paleodiet reconstruction, 28, 119–120
preservation, 123, 252, 307–309
preservation in crystal aggregates, 112
preservation in parchment, 50
purity, 307
radiocarbon dating, 122–123
triple helical molecules, 105
type I, 100, 105, 127
unfolding (gelatinization), 50, 113
Combe-Grenal, France, 131
Combustion materials. See Fuel
Compact bone, 108
Compasting. See Organic matter
degradation and Aerobic
degradation, 53
Completeness of the archaeological
record, 46–47, 81, 296
aragonite preservation, 160
assessing completeness, 62, 98
Conservation, 273
Context
samples for radiocarbon dating,
250–254
trapped charge dating, 252–254
Controls, 230–231, 270
Cooked bones, 118
Cooking, 165
Cooking pot residues
phytoliths, 147
Copal, 312. See also Resins, 211
Coprolites, 27, 76
Cosmetic eye paints (Kohl)
mineral list, 321
Cosmogenic isotopes. See also
Radiocarbon dating
beryllium 10, 91
flint, 40
flint mining, 40
Courtyards, 235, 236
Cowrie shells, 158

Crandallite, 86, 297
stability field, 60
Cremated bone
radiocarbon dating, 122, 255
Cremation, 117, 118
Cristobolite, 88, 90, 298
formation temperature, 204
Crucibles, 205
Cryptocrystalline quartz. See also Flint,
298
Crystal aggregates, 106, 215–219, 308
ancient DNA and collagen, 122, 216
bone, 215
embedded information, 217–219
paleodiet reconstruction, 218
Crystal sand (calcium oxalate), 170
Crystallinity, 289–292. See also Splitting
factor, 104
authigenic phosphate minerals, 297
definition, 290
Currency, 158
Cypraea annulis
currency, 158

Dahllite, 84. See Carbonate
hydroxylapatite
Darcy's law, 55
Darwin, C. R., 46
Dating, 18–25. See also Radiocarbon
dating
bone, 122–123
communication gap, 247–249
determining uncertainties, 249
eggshells, 153
enamel (ESR), 132
enamel, uranium series, 132
four stages, 248
mollusk shells, 163
number of samples to analyze, 255–256
plaster, 191
relative, 18, 245
Dating methods
amino acid racemization, 24–25
archaeomagnetism, 25
dendrochronology, 21–22
fluoride uptake, 23, 288
list of methods, 245
obsidian hydration, 23–24
perspective, 19
radiocarbon. See also Radiocarbon
dating, 19–21
trapped charge (TL, ESR and OSL),
22–23
uranium series, 21
Dead lime. See also Plaster binder, 187

Dead Sea Scrolls, 50
  parchment preservation, 113
Definition of science, 2
Degradation. *See Diagenesis*
Dendritic. *See* Phytoliths, dendritic
Dendrochronology, 19, 21–22, 246
Dental calculus, 130, 131
  minerals, 130
  paleodiet, 132–134
  phytoliths, 147
Dentalium, 158, 159
Dentin, 215
  abrasion by phytoliths, 137
  basic constituents, 127
  crystallinity, 289–292
  crystals, 127, 290
  embedded information, 133
  fibril arrays, 128
  growth lines, 26
  hierarchical structure, 126–129
  mineralized collagen fibril, 127
  noncollagenous proteins, 127
  peritubular dentin, 128
  root vs crown dentin, 128
  secondary, 26
  structure, 107
  tubules, 124, 127, 128, 217
  type I collagen, 127
  types, 124, 127
Dentin diagenesis, 131
Dentine. *See* Dentin
Dentin-enamel-junction (DEJ), 124, 129
Diagenesis. *See also* Organic matter
    degradation, 46
  agents of degradation, 62
  anthropogenic effects, 54
  ash above pH8, 172–173
  ash below pH8, 173–174
  bone. *See* Bone diagenesis
  calcite, 63
  calcite and aragonite, 80–81
  carbonate hydroxylapatite, 86
  ceramic, 198
  charcoal fossil, 182–183
  charred materials, 58
  chemical reactions, 54–56
  conceptual framework, 62–63
  conceptual framework applications,
    63–66
  dentin, 131
  diatoms, 150
  driving forces, 54–56
  eggshells, 152
  extent of degradation, 62
  freeze-thaw affects, 54

gelatin formation, 113
geogenic processes, 54
hydrological regime, 54–56
macroscopic versus microscopic
  records, 52
mechanical processes, 54
minerals, 59–61
mollusk shell, 161
organic matter, 57–59
organisms in soils, 57
otoliths, 156
pH decrease, 60
phytoliths, 143–144
plaster, 190–191
silicon dioxide polymorphs, 90
teeth, 130–131
time frame, 52–54, 62
water flow, 55
water, role of, 54
waterlogged environments, 114
Diagenesis bone. *See* Bone diagenesis
Diagenesis enamel, 130–131
  fluoride uptake, 131
  uranium uptake, 131
Diatoms, 89, 149–151, 298
  cell wall composition, 150
  diagenesis, 150
  embedded information, 150–151
  habitats, 150
  irrigation, 150
  paleoenvironmental reconstruction,
    151
  pottery provenience, 151
  silica solubility, 150
  theca, 149
Differential thermal analysis
  heated clays, 97
Dinosaur bone collagen, 216
Disorder in minerals, 61, 63, 81, 82, 161,
    166, 167–168, 206
  biomineralization, 99, 162
  calcite, 82, 161
  carbonate hydroxylapatite, 84, 104
  clay, 95
  effects of heating and cooling, 166–167
  scale, 168
  silica, 88
Diyun, Guilin, China, 159
DNA. *See also* Ancient DNA, 209–210
  polymerase chain reaction, 34
  sequences, 33
Dogs
  bone scavenging and gnawing, 101, 229,
    232, 238
  domestication, 238

Dolomite, 188
  plaster binder, 188
  transformation at elevated
    temperatures, 204
Domestication
  cereals, 147
  plants, 147
Dosimeters, 252
Drinking water, 33, 132, 153
  oxygen isotope composition, 35
Druses (calcium oxalate), 170
Dung, 237–238
  ash, 177
  common components, 233
  fertilizer, 242
  for combustion, 168, 232–233
  fossil dung identification, 240
  monohydrocalcite, 283
  phytolith difference index (PDI),
    242
  spherulites, 232, 234, 236, 240, 283. *See
    also* Spherulites, 44
  stable isotopic composition, 240
Dye, 158
  from mollusks, 157
  purple. *See also* Indigo

Earthworms, 283, 284
Echinoderm skeletons
  calcite disorder, 286
  intracrystalline macromolecules, 212
EDS. *See* Energy dispersive sprectrometry
Eggshells, 79, 151–154
  dating, 24
  dating, amino acid racemization, 153
  diagenesis, 152
  embedded information, 152–154
  formation, 152
  intracrystalline macromolecules, 213
  mineralogy, 152
  morphology, 152
  organic matrix, 152
  ostriches, 151
  oxygen isotopic composition, 33
  paleoenvironmental reconstruction,
    153
  radiocarbon dating, 154
  ratites, 151
El Amarna tablets, Egypt, 200
Electron spin resonance dating, 18, 23, 131,
    245, 246, 358, 371
  context, 253–254
  uranium uptake history, 246
Elemental analysis. *See* Chemical
  elemental analysis

Emmer wheat, 145
Enamel, 124
  3-dimensional structure, 126
  amelogenin, 125
  basic constituents, 124–125
  crystal size and shape, 124, 290
  crystallinity, 291
  dating, 23, 132, 253
  diagenesis, 130–131
  electron spin resonance, 23
  embedded information, 133
  fluoride uptake, 131
  graded structure, 126
  growth lines, 26
  hierarchical structure, 124–126
  intergrown crystal composite, 217
  life history reconstruction, 132
  organic matrix, 125
  preservation, 253
  prisms (crystal arrays), 126
  Sr/Ca ratios, 121
  Sr/Ca ratios weaning, 45
  strontium isotope ratios, 35
  structure, 125, 218
  surface striations, 136
Enameloid, 124, 288
Energy dispersive spectrometry, 72, 74
Eskimo winter house, 236–237
  dump of bone splinters, 237
  human waste disposal, 237
  phosphate concentrations, 237
  wood pile and hearth, 237
ESR. *See also* Electron spin resonance
    dating
Ethnoarchaeology, 48
  abandoned structures and spaces,
    228
  activity areas using phosphate
    concentrations, 244
  Aliabad village, Zagros Mountains,
    Iran. *See also* Aliabad, 232–236
  charcoal, 243–244
  controls, 230–231
  definition, 227
  dung degradation, 54
  Eskimo winter house, 236–237
  Maasai animal enclosures, 54
  merging archaeobotanical and
    archaeozoological records, 237–238
  microartifacts, 228–230
  pottery production, 197
  primary vs secondary deposits, 232,
    236
  Sarakini village, Greece, 240–244
Ethnography, 227

Fatty acids, 58, 237. *See also* Lipids and
    Residue Analysis
  latrines, 236
  site spatial organization, 44
Fertilizer, 149, 242
  ash, 233
  dung, 238, 240
Feynman, R., 2, 6
Fibrolamellar bone, 107
Fire
  deliberate control, 175–176, 178, 292,
    303, 304
  history of the use of, 165
  impact on environment, 183
  phytolith types in ash, 178
  temperatures, 304
  type of wood used, 178
Fish, 157
  environmental habitat, 156
  otoliths, 154
Fish teeth
  enameloid, 124, 288
Fishing locations, 157
Flint, 88–89, 298
  burned, 176
  dating, 22, 252
  diagenesis, 90
  formation process, 89
  infrared spectrum, 89
  mining, 91
  provenience, 40
  provenience and procurement
    strategies, 91–92
  structure, 89
Flint tools
  dating, 92
  procurement strategies, 91
Floors, 194, 250
  Aliabad village house, 235
  different types, 235
  differentiating upper and lower, 234
  microlaminated texture, 236
  plaster, 44, 185, 190
  Sarakini village, Greece, 242
Fluorapatite, 286, 288. *See* Carbonate
    fluorapatite
Fluoride
  bone mineral, 112, 288
  carbonate hydroxylapatite, 84, 85
  infrared spectrum change, 289
  uptake into enamel, 131
Fluoride uptake dating, 5, 19, 23, 288
Fluorine, 85
Fluxes, 195–196, 305
  calcite, 200

Foraging strategies, 164
Fossil charcoal. *See* Charcoal fossil
Fossil proteins
  amino acid sequences, 34, 122, 210
Fossil record
  completeness, 46
  imperfection, 46
Fourier transform infrared spectroscopy.
    See Infrared spectroscopy
Franklin Rosalind, 179
Freeze-thaw effects, 54, 251
Fuel, 166
  bones, 121, 237
  brick-red burned soil particles, 272
  common materials, 168
  dung, 145, 238, 272
  identification, 176–177, 271–272
  identification using phytoliths, 17,
    145
  peat, 272
  wood, 145, 272
Fullerenes, 180
Fulvic acid. *See also* Humic substances,
    314
Fungal degradation. *See also* Microbial
    degradation
  bone, 114

Gamma radiation, 177, 252
Garbage pits and dumps, 86, 223, 295
Gardens, 233
Gastropod shells. *See* Snail shells
Gastropods, 159
Gehlinite, 204
Gelatin, 113, 308. *See also* Collagen
  degradation, 113, 308
Genetic information, 34
Geoarchaeology, 69
Geogenic minerals
  calcite, 78
  definition, 69
  list, 321
  silica (opal), 136
Gesher Benot Yaakov, Israel
  preserved wood, 310
Gibbsite
  tropical soils, 95
Gizzard stones, 154
Glass, 168
  crystallization over time, 167
  product of supercooling, 167
Glass production, 91
  ash soluble salts, 169
  mineral list, 321
  secondary use of ash, 166

Glauconite
  transformation at elevated
    temperatures, 204
Gleaning, 52
Global Positioning Systems, 267
Glue, gelatin, 308
Goethite
  tropical soils, 95
Gourds
  phytoliths, 147
Graphite, 179, 205
  oxidation catalysts, 183
Graphitelike crystallites, 179
Graves
  land snails, 158
Gravity sensing, 154
Great temple, Petra, Jordan, 267
Grog, 189, 195, 205
Growth lines. *See* Rhythmic growth
Guano, 116, 225
  authigenic phosphate mineral
    formation, 80
  degradation, 64, 183
  pH of freshly degrading, 66
  phosphate concentrations, 224
  rich in phosphate, 295
Gum, 211, 312
Gypsum, 59
  heated, 188
  plaster binder, 188

Halite, 50
Hasanabad village, Zagros Mountains,
  Iran, 231
Haversian bone. *See* Osteonal bone
Hayonim Cave, Israel, 96, 160
  clay degradation, 303
  on-site laboratory, 267
  phytolith dissolution, 173
  TL and ESR dating, 177, 252
Hearths, 9, 96, 165, 235, 251, 253
  charcoal distribution, 183
  definition, 174
  deliberate control of fire, 175
  Eskimo winter house, 237
  Natufian, Hayonim Cave, 175
  oldest known, 176
  preservation process, 175
Heating and cooling materials,
  166–167
Heavy liquids, 142
Hematite, 204
  tropical soils, 95
Hemicellulose, 179, 309
Hexahydrate, 282

Homo erectus, 74
Hooves, 211
Horn, 211
Hornblende, 204
House, two storied, 234
Humic acid, 314
Humic substances, 58, 72, 182, 312, 313
  Raman spectroscopy, 266, 313
  resemblance to lignin, 313
Huxley, T. H., 46
Hydraulic conductivity, 55
Hydraulic mortar, 186
Hydraulic plaster, 186, 188–189, 190
  authigenic silica, 90
  authigenic silicates, 189
  definition, 189
  grog, 189
  infrared spectrum, 189
  Pozzolana, 189
Hydrogen peroxide, 142
Hydrological regime, 55, 62, 225, 271
  bone preservation, 111
  diagenesis, 54–56
Hydrolysis, 112
Hydroxylapatite, 286, 287. *See also*
  Carbonate hydroxylapatite, 84
  atomic structure, 84, 85
Hydroxyproline, 258
Hyena, 231
  prehistoric den, 231
Hypsodonty, 129

ICP-OES. *See* Inductively Coupled
  Plasma-Optical Emission
  Spectrometry
Ikkaite, 77
Illite
  iron-rich, 76
  soils in temperate zones, 95
Illite group of clays, 93, 301
Illuviation, 95
Imogolite, 301
India ink. *See* Ink
Indigo, 158
Inductively coupled plasma-optical
  emission spectrometry
  proveniencing ceramics, 39
Infrared microscopy, 71, 281
Infrared spectroscopy, 71, 275
  atomic disorder, 61
  basis, 276
  bone mineral crystallinity, 112
  clay structures, 97
  library of standard spectra, 282
  on-site, 265, 276

Infrared spectroscopy interpretation of spectra, 278–281
  major classes of compounds, 279
  mixtures of compounds, 280
  peak at 1384 wavenumbers, 281
  shifting of peak maximum, 279–280
  variations in peak width, 281
Infrared spectroscopy methods
  background, 278
  grinding, 277
  potassium bromide pellets, 276, 278
  quantification, 278
  reproducibility, 277
  sample preparation, 276–277
  sampling, 277
Infrared spectrum of
  amber from different locations, 315
  amorphous calcium carbonate, 284
  aragonite, 284
  asphalt, 313
  bone (fossil), 293
  bone (fresh), 293
  bone burned, 295
  calcite, 280, 284, 287
  calcite geogenic crystal, 285
  calcite, test (shell) of sea urchin, 285
  calcite, shell of, brachiopod, 285
  carbonate hydroxylapatite, 289, 296
  cellulose, 311
  charcoal, wood fossil, 310
  charcoal, wood modern, 310
  clay (mainly montmorillonite), 304
  clay transforming, 304
  collagen, fossil major contamination, 309
  collagen, fresh, 309
  collagen, minor contamination, 309
  copal, 315
  crandallite, 296
  cristobolite, 301
  dentin, 291
  enamel, 291
  flint (chert), 299
  fluorapatite, 289
  fulvic acid, 314
  gum, 313
  humic acid, 314
  hydroxylapatite, 289
  illite, 280, 302
  kaolinite, 302
  leucophosphite, 296
  loess, 280, 287
  monohydrocalcite, 284
  montgomeryite (crystalline), 297

montgomeryite (disordered), 296, 297
montmorillonite, 302
montmorillonite heated to different temperatures, 306
montmorillonite with different associated ions, 303
nitrate, potassium, 316
nitrate, sodium, 316
quartz, 280, 299, 301
resin, 313, 315
silica (opal), 299
silica (opal) crystallizing, 304
silica (opal) geogenic, 300
silica (opal) biogenic, 300
siliceous aggregates, 299
taranakite, 296
tridymite, 301
variscite (crystalline), 297
variscite (disordered), 297
vaterite, 284
weddellite, 307
whewellite, 307
wood fossil (poorly preserved), 311
wood, fossil (well preserved), 311
wool, 313
Ink, 184
Installations for pyrotechnology, 165, 166, 205
Intergrown crystals. See Crystal aggregates
Intertubular dentin, 124
Intracrystalline macromolecules, 100, 112, 156, 162, 212–215
  amino acid racemization dating, 214
  amounts and composition, 213
  embedded information, 214–215
  mollusk shell, 213
  paleoenvironmental reconstruction, 214–215
  radiocarbon dating, 215
Irrigation, 145–146
  diatoms, 150
Isotherms. See also Stability fields of minerals, 110
Isotope. See also Stable isotopic composition
  definition, 68
Isotope fractionation
  paleodiet reconstruction, 28

Kaolinite, 94, 203
  atomic structure, 93
  degradation product, 95
  soil in tropics, 95
Kaolinite group of clays, 93, 301

Karstic environments, 78
Kebara Cave, Israel, 65, 88
    charcoal distribution, 64, 182
    diatoms, 151
    phytolith dissolution, 173
Kenyon, K. M., 8, 47
Keratin, 211, 312
Kiln, 193, 200, 304
    dating, 25
    lime plaster, 187
Kimmel Center for Archaeological
        Science, Weizmann Institute of
        Science, 268, 282
Klisoura Cave, southern Greece, 96
Kohl
    mineral list, 321

La Quemada, Mexico, 150
Lake Turkana, Kenya, 229
Lamellar bone, 107
    circumferential, 107
Land snails. See Snail shells
Latrines, 58, 86, 223
    characteristic features in sediments, 236
    slaked lime, 194
Lead isotope ratios
    provenience, 38
Leather, 211, 307
Leopards, 231
Leucophosphite, 86
Levigation, 195
Libby, W. F., 5, 18
Lichens, 306
Life history reconstruction, 27
    bone, 123
    enamel, 132
Lightning, 183
Lignin, 18, 179, 321, 371
    content in wood using infrared
        spectroscopy, 311
    microbial degradation, 58
    preservation in fossil wood, 311
    resemblance to humic substances, 313
    structure, 58, 309
Lime, 185
Lime aggregate, 185
Lime plaster, 185, 186, 193. See also Plaster
    ageing, 187
    calcite crystal morphology, 82
    calcite $\nu_2:\nu_4$ ratios, 171, 190
    formation, 79
    mollusk shells, 157
Lipids, 36, 211. See also Fatty acids
    definition, 211
Lithic tools. See Tools, lithic

Livestock enclosures. See Animal
        enclosures
Loess, 73, 279, 284

Maasai villages, Kenya, 54
    animal enclosures, 239
    monohydrocalcite, 77, 283
    phytoliths, 148
Magnesium oxide, 188, 193
Maize
    paleodiet reconstruction, 28
    phytoliths, 147
Mandible
    alveolar bone, 124
Mantle (mollusks), 162
Manure, 224
Marble, 36
    provenience, 38
Material culture, 227
Melilite, 204
Mercenaria, 164
Metals, 36, 168, 205, 266
    provenience, 39
    site pollution, 272
Mica
    transformation at elevated
        temperatures, 204
Micrite, 75
Microarchaeological record. See
        Microscopic record
Microarchaeology, 1, 5
    integrating with macroarchaeology,
        8–9
Microartifacts, 30, 228–230
    site spatial organization, 44
    size cutoff, 229
    trampling, 229
Microbial degradation
    absence of water or oxygen, 18
    affect of climate, 114
    bone, 110, 114, 115
    compasting, 57
    deserts, 49
    gelatin, 113
    lignin, 58
    plant material, 16
Microcharcoal, 233
Microchemical analysis. See Chemical
        elemental analysis
Microcrystalline quartz. See also Flint,
        252
Microlaminated texture, 233
    animal enclosures, 240
    floors, 236
    living room floors, Sarakini, 242

Micromorphology, 30, 69, 73–76
  ash types, 177
  fuel types used, 271
  infrared microscopy, 281
  plaster identification, 190
Microscopic artifacts. *See* Microartifacts
Microscopic record, 1, 6–8, 68
  Aliabad village, Zagros Mountains,
    Iran, 232–236
  definition, 13
  Eskimo winter house, 236–237
  ethnoarchaeological contribution, 228
  information categories embedded in the
    microscopic record, 16
  merging archaeobotanical and
    archaeozoological records, 237–238
  on-site laboratory, 10
  plant remains, 16
  rich in microartifacts, 229
  Sarakini village, Greece, 240–244
Middens, 9, 41, 157, 158
Migration, 27, 35, 118–119
  fish, 157
Mineral assemblages
  diagenesis, 252
  in situ (micromorphology), 73–76
  site formation processes, 68, 97–98
Mineral formation in biology. *See*
  Biomineralization
Mineral identification, 70–72
  chemical elemental analysis, 72
  infrared spectroscopy, 71
  microchemical analysis
  optical mineralogy, 70
  petrographic microscope, 264
  Raman spectroscopy, 72
  X-ray diffraction, 33
Mineral particles
  size and shape, 72–73
  size terminology, 73
Mineralized collagen family of materials,
  215
Mineralized collagen fibril, 106
  dentin, 127
  tendon, 215
Minerals
  authigenic. *See* Authigenic minerals
  categories, 69
  classification and nomenclature, 70
  diagenesis, 59–61
  disorder, 61, 167–168. *See also* Disorder
    in minerals
  dissolution-reprecipitation, 60
  stability and solubility, 59
  stability fields, 59, 60, 80, 85, 111

Mining, 164
  flint raw materials, 91
  procurement strategies, 40
  tin, 39
Mollusk shell, 157–164
  crossed lamellar structure, 159
  dating, 163
  heated, 162
  mantle, 162
  myostracum, 160
  paleoenvironmental reconstruction, 164
  paleotemperature analysis, 33
  pearly nacreous luster, 159
  periostracum, 159
  pseudomorphs, 115
  rhythmic growth, 41
  season of site occupation, 164
  site preservation, 164
  structure, 6, 159–160
  ultrastructural types, 159
Mollusk shell mineral, 160–162
  aragonite, 63, 160
  assessing preservation, 81
  assessing preservation of calcite, 160
  atomic disorder, 161
  calcite, 80
  stability, 63
Mollusk shell organic matrix, 162
  aspartic acid-rich proteins, 162
  intracrystalline macromolecules, 212
  silk fibroin, 162
  β-chitin, 162
Mollusks
  taxonomy, 159
  uses in antiquity, 157
Monohydrocalcite, 77, 282
  dung deposit, 283
Montgomeryite, 86, 297
  bones dissolved, 88
  stability field, 59
Montmorillonite, 301
  atomic structure, 93
Mortar. *See* Plaster
  definition, 185
Mud bricks, 52, 53, 92, 233, 301
Mud plaster, 190
Mullite, 204
Munsell color chart, 203
Muricidae, 158
Muscovite, 93
Mutations, 208, 209
Myostracum, 160

NAA. *See* Neutron activation analysis
Nacre, 213

Nanotubes, 180
Natufian period, 158
Natural organic materials. *See also* Humic
    substances and resins, 312–315
  list, 321
  list of common materials, 312
Neanderthals
  dental calculus, 130
  DNA, 33, 35, 208
  phytoliths, 140
Neutron activation analysis
  proveniencing ceramics, 39, 200
Nilsson, S., 4
Nitrates, 56
  deposited on sediment surfaces,
    316
Nitrogen isotopic composition. *See* Stable
    isotopic composition
  paleodiet, 27
NMR
  clay structures, 97
Noncollagenous proteins
  preservation in bone, 112, 308
  radiocarbon dating, 122
Nunamiut, 228

Obsidian
  dating, 19, 23
  knapping, production of
    microfragments, 229
  provenience, 37
Obsidian hydration dating, 23–24, 246, 247
Occluded macromolecules. *See*
    Intracrystalline macromolecules
Octacalcium phosphate, 130
Odontoblasts, 124
Old wood effect, 191, 255
Olduvai Gorge, Tanzania
  phytoliths, 147
Olive pit, 17, 251
  ancient DNA, 310
  preservation, 309–311
Olorgesaille, Kenya, 32
Onionlike structures, 180, 182. *See also*
    Charcoal structure
On-site laboratory, 10, 11, 63, 267, 269
  analysis times, 263
  benefits, 261–262
  choice of instruments, 263–268
  conservation, 273
  examples of questions to be addressed
    on-site, 271–273
  infrared spectrometers, 71
  macroscopic record, 263
  maps of boundaries, 261

mode of operation, 261
of Kimmel Center for Archaeological
    Science, Weizmann Institute of
    Science, 268
operation, 268–269
useful work program, 269–271
Opal. *See* Silica
Opal-A, 88
Opal-CT, 88
Optical mineralogy, 70, 199
Optical stimulated luminescence dating,
    18, 245, 246
  context, 254
  materials, 254
Oral bacteria, 147
Order in minerals. *See* Disorder in
    minerals
Organic matrix
  bone, 102, 105
  bone diagenesis, 113
  diagenesis in bone, 110, 112
  eggshells, 152
  enamel, 125
  inter- and intracrystalline, 100
  mollusk shells, 162
  otoliths, 156
  phytoliths, 136
  two major groups, 100
Organic matter
  dessicated, 50
  phosphate, 59
  phosphorus concentrations, 224
  removal by oxidation, 142
  sulfur, 59
  tanning, 50
Organic matter concentrations, 59, 64,
    223–225
  Aliabad village house, 234
  alleys between houses, 233
  phytolith concentrations, 225
Organic matter degradation, 57–59, 225
  aerobic and anaerobic processes, 53
  driving force for diagenesis, 56, 57
  microbial action, 58
  pH lowering, 50, 57
  processes, 57
  rapid phase, 53
  tilted strata, 65
Organic-rich sediments, 58
  identification, 86–87
  phosphate, 44, 86
Ornamentation. *See* Beads
  Dentalium, 158
OSL. *See* Optically Stimulated
    Luminescence dating

Osteocalcin, 105, 112, 216, 292, 308
Osteon
    size, 26
Osteonal bone, 107–108
    life history reconstruction, 123
Ostriches
    drinking water, 33
    eggshells, 151, 214
Ostwald's Rule of Stages, 80
    bone, 104
Otoconia. *See also* Otoliths, 154
Otoliths, 154–157
    3 chambers, 155
    diagenesis, 156
    embedded information, 156–157
    growth lines, 154
    mineralogy, 155
    nomenclature, 154
    paleoenvironmental reconstruction, 156
    season of occupation, 42, 157
    structure and organic matrix, 156
    trace element variations, 157
Overton Down, England, 114
Owls, 231
Oxidation
    charcoal, 16, 182
    charred organic matter, 58
    organic matter, 57, 96, 114
    removal of organic matter, 142
Oxidizing agent. *See* Sodium hypochlorite
Oxygen isotopic composition. *See also*
        Stable Isotopic Composition
    drinking water, 33, 35
    migration, 27
    phosphate, 87
Oxyhornblende, 204
Oysters, 80
    shell mineralogy, 160

Paleochemical environment, 68, 296
Paleoclimate reconstruction. *See also*
        Paleoenvironment reconstruction
    carbonate hydroxylapatite, 87
    charcoal in sediments, 183
    phytoliths, 142, 147
Paleodiet reconstruction, 30
    basis for, 120
    bone, 119–121
    collagen in bone, 28
    cooked and burned bone, 121
    crystal aggregates, 218
    individual amino acids, 29
    isotope fraction, 28
    maize, 28
    marine derived food, 28

phytoliths, 147
    residue analysis, 29–30
    single amino acids of collagen, 120
    Sr:Ca ratios in bone, 120–121
    stable isotope compositions, 28–29
    stable isotopes bone collagen, 119–120
    strontium isotope ratios, 29
Paleoenvironment reconstruction, 30–31
    archaeobotany, 31
    diatoms, 150, 151
    eggshells, 153
    intracrystalline macromolecules,
        214–215
    iron minerals, 66
    micromorphology, 30
    mollusk shells, 100, 163–164
    otoliths, 156
    phytoliths, 31
    pollen, 32
    rare earth elements (REE), 31–32
    rare earth elements in bone, 122
    stable isotope variations, 32–33
Paleoenvironmental reconstruction
    charcoal, 243
Paleogenetics, 33–35, 121–122
    ancient DNA, 34
    ancient DNA in crystal aggregates, 218
    fossil protein sequences, 34
    Neanderthal DNA sequence, 35
    protein, 122
Paleomagnetic features in sediments, 176
Paleomigration, 35, 118–119. *See also*
        Migration
Paleo-pH, 296
Paleotemperature, 33
    stable oxygen isotopic composition,
        163
    trace elements, 163
Paleovegetation ecology
    phytoliths, 147
Palygorskite group of clays, 93
Parallel fibered bone, 107
Parchment, 211, 307
    collagen-gelatin proportions, 113
    Dead Sea Scrolls, 50
    preservation, 50
Parenchyma, 16
Pastoral societies, 238, 239
PCR. *See* Polymerase chain reaction
PDI. *See* Phytolith Difference Index
Pearly luster, 159
Peat, 272
    ash, 177
    combustion material, 168
Peking Man Site. *See* Zhoukoudian, China

Peptides, 211
Periclase, 204. *See also* Magnesium oxide,
    193
Periodontal ligament, 124, 129
Periostracum, 159
Peritubular dentin, 124, 128, 217
    crystal aggregates, 216
    matrix proteins, 216
Petrographic microscope, 73, 264
    micromorphology, 69
    mineral identification, 70, 199, 264
    phytolith identification, 264
Petroleum residues, 312
pH, 59
    ash diagenesis, 172–174
    carbonate buffer, 77, 160
    drop in sediments, 58, 63, 225
    microbial activity, 60, 98
    organic matter degradation, 50, 57, 64,
        66
    phytolith stability, 143
    silica dissolution rates, 90
    slaked lime, 188
Phase transformations
    heating and cooling, 167
Phosphate, 59, 223
Phosphate concentrations. *See also*
        Authigenic phosphate minerals, 44,
        60, 223–225, 296
    alleys between houses, 233
    animal enclosures, 240
    cave sediments, 88
    colorometric assay, 86
    ethnoarchaeology, 244
    fish processing site, 244
    guard house, 244
    organic matter, 224
    sediments, 59, 86
    site spatial organization, 44
    UV-visible spectrophotometers, 266
Phosphophoryn, 127
Phosphorus, 223
    content in organic matter, 224
Photography, 268
Photosynthetic systems, 214
    C_3 and C_4, 28, 153
Phreatic zone. *See* Saturated zone
Phytolith assemblages, 139–141
    identifying plant taxa, 146–147
    information on plant parts, 140, 141
    nonarchaeological sediments, 144
    plant quantities brought to site, 148
    rural-urban continuum, 273
    Sarakini village, Greece, 240–243
    taxonomic information, 140

Phytolith Difference Index (PDI), 241, 243
Phytolith record, 17, 238
Phytoliths, 135–149. *See also*
        Archaeobotanical record
    absence of occluded DNA, 146, 214
    bananas, 147
    bark, 272
    barley, 147
    burned, 17, 136, 174, 233, 237, 272
    cereal storage vs fodder storage, 140
    cereals, 140, 147
    concentrations, 141, 148, 234, 238
    consistent and variable morphologies,
        139
    cooking pot residues, 147
    dendritic, 140
    dental calculus, 147
    diagenesis, 143–144
    dissolution, 144, 173
    embedded information, 145–149
    etched surfaces (weathered), 144, 271
    floor types, 235, 242
    formation and morphology, 137–139
    fuel use, 145
    functions, 137
    genetic information, 146
    genetic vs environmental control, 138
    gourds, 147
    grasses, 140, 146, 148
    hardness, 136
    irrigation, 145–146
    location in cell, 137
    material, 137
    mechanical function, 137
    mineral solubility, 143
    morphotype classification, 139
    morphotypes (morphologies), 138
    multi-celled (silica skeletons), 145
    nomenclature, 135
    occluded macromolecules, 146, 213
    organic matrix, 136, 214
    paleodiet reconstruction, 147
    paleovegetation ecology, 147
    radiocarbon dating, 148, 260
    reference collection, 141–142, 148
    rice, 147
    sampling and analysis, 142–143
    site spatial organization, 148–149
    squash, 147
    stable oxygen isotopic composition, 145
    strategy for studying phytoliths,
        141–143
    tooth abrasion, 137
    two storied house, 242
    wheat, 147

Phytoliths (*cont.*)
   wood, 140, 148, 172
   wood and bark, 139
Pigments
   analysis, 72
   list, 321
Piltdown forgery, 5, 23, 288
Pine tar, 312
Plants. *See also* Archaeobotany
   archaeological sites, 16
   minerals produced, 135
   nitrogen incorporation, 28
   phytolith concentrations, 141
   phytolith producers, 138
   silica formation, 89
   soil formation, 94
   use of, 148
Plaque. *See* Dental calculus
Plaster. *See also* Lime plaster and
     Hydraulic plaster, 185–194
   dating problems, 192
   definition, 185
   diagenesis, 190–191
   early production (Natufian), 165
   embedded information, 191–194
   frescoes, 193
   gypsum, 185, 188
   identification, 190
   radiocarbon dating, 255, 260
   reconstructing production processes,
     193
   refractory materials, 193–194
   residue analysis, 194
Plaster aggregates, 185, 189–190
   binder to aggregate proportions, 189
Plaster binder, 185–189
   ageing, 187
   calcite, 186–188
   calcite production process, 186, 187
   gypsum, 188
Plaster floors
   fatty acid concentrations, 44
Plaster of Paris, 188
Plexiform bone. *See* Fibrolamellar bone
Pollen, 18, 32, 70, 211, 234, 338, 348, 351,
     365, 367
   outer exine layer, 18
   paleoenvironmental reconstruction, 32
   preservation, 31
   Tyrolean ice man, 48
Pollen grains, 16
Polymerase chain reaction, 34
Polymorphs, 77
Polymorphs of calcium carbonate, 282–283
Polysaccharides, 162, 211, 312

Pomaks, 240
Porcupines, 231
Porosity
   bone, 109, 110
   ceramics, 205
Portlandite, 204. *See also* Plaster binder, 186
Postholes, 239
Potassium isotope ^{40}K
   siliceous aggregates, 177
Pot-lid fracture of flints, 176
Pottery. *See also* Ceramics, 194–206
   celadons, 205
   contents, 35–36, 219
   embedded information, 198–206
   furnace lining, 193, 205
   production areas, 202
   surface sealants, 219
   tuyierres, 205
Pottery manufacture, 195–198
   bone powder decoration, 203
   cracking, 195, 197
   crucible production, 205
   drying, 197
   ethnographic observations, 197
   firing conditions, 197–198, 202–205
   fluxes, 195–196
   kinetic vs thermodynamic control, 202
   paddle and anvil technique, 196
   processes, 202–205
   raw materials, 195
   shaping and decorating, 196
   slip, 196
   soaking time, 198
   temper, 195
   wasters, 202
   wheel production, 196
Pottery provenience, 39, 151, 198–200
   El Amarna tablets, 200
   mineralogical (petrographic) approach,
     199–200
   total element approach, 200
   two approaches, 199
   XRF, 266
Pozzolana, Italy, 186
Preservation
   ash, 175
   assessing mineral preservation, 81, 160
   atomic disorder, 162
   bones, 160
   charcoal distribution, 64
   charred material, 179
   clay-rich sediments, 66, 96
   context of uncharred organic materials,
     225
   deserts, 49

dessicated, 49, 50
frozen, 48
Procurement strategies, 40–41
  cosmogenic isotopes, 40
  flint, 91–92
  mining, 40
Protected niches, 207, 208
  authigenic minerals, 226
  ceramics, 219–222
  charcoal, 226
  crystal aggregates, 106, 215–219
  enamel, 217
  intracrystalline, 100, 152, 212–215
  peritubular dentin, 217
  starch grains, 222
Proteins, 210, 312. *See also* Fossil proteins
    and Noncollagenous proteins
  brachiopod shells, 213
  enamel, 125, 217
  fossil amino acid sequences, 210
  fossil genetic information, 122
  inside crystals. *See* Intracrystalline
    macromolecules
  mineralized tissues, 100
  mollusk shells, 162
  peritubular dentin, 216
  preservation, 49
Provenance. *See* Provenience
  definition, 36, 195
Provenience, 36
  amber, 37
  clay, 96–97
  definition, 36, 195
  diatoms, 151
  flint, 40, 91–92
  lead isotope ratios, 38
  marble, 38
  obsidian, 37
  pottery, 39, 198–200
  quartz grain morphologies, 91
  soapstone, 38
  sources of raw materials, abundant,
    39–40
  sources of raw materials, limited, 37–39
  steatite, 38
  tin, 39
  trace element analysis, 39
Provenience and procurement strategies,
    36–41
Pseudomorphs, 83
  bone, 115
  bones vs shells, 101, 115
  in ash, 174
  wood ash, 82, 171, 173, 176, 272
Pulp cavity, 124

Pyrite, 59
Pyrogenic minerals
  aragonite, 81
  ash, 60, 82
  calcite, 77, 79, 82, 186, 188, 192
  definition, 69
  list, 321
Pyrolysis, 179
Pyrotechnology
  ash, 168–178
  ash and charcoal waste products, 166
  basis, 165
  cooking, 165
  definition, 165
  diagenesis of products, 168
  plaster binders, 186
  waste products, 166

Qesem Cave, Israel, 83
Quartz, 56, 88–89, 298
  along coast of Israel, 201
  beta quartz, 90
  grain morphologies, 91
  high temperature forms, 298
  provenience, 91
  soils in arid and desert zones, 95
Quicklime. *See also* Plaster binder, 186
Qumran 24 Cave, Dead Sea, 49

Racemers, 24
Racemization. *See* Amino acid
    racemization
Radiocarbon dating, 19–21, 245, 246, 259
  acid-alkali-acid (AAA) treatment, 259
  ash, 177
  biases, 260
  bone, 122–123, 254
  bone collagen prescreening, 257, 258
  calibration, 20, 245, 247, 249–250
  charred material, 184, 254
  charred material prescreening, 258
  charred material purification, 258–259
  clays associated with charcoal, 95, 259
  collagen C/N ratio, 256
  collagen in crystal aggregates, 219
  collagen purification, 259
  context, 250–252
  cremated bone, 122, 255
  effective range, 18
  eggshells, 154
  estimating uncertainties, 259
  half-life, 19
  hydroxyproline, 258
  interlaboratory comparisons, 259
  intracrystalline macromolecules, 215

Radiocarbon dating (*cont.*)
  macrocontext, 250–251
  materials, 19, 251, 254–255
  microcontext, 251–252
  mollusk shells, 163, 255
  number of samples to analyze,
    255–256
  old wood effect, 21, 255
  organic matter in sediments, 255
  phytoliths, 148, 215, 260
  plaster, 191, 255
  prescreening samples, 256–258
  reservoir effect, 163
  sample collection in the field, 258
  sample purification methods,
    258–259
Radiolaria, 89, 298
Rainfall, 153
  multi-celled phytoliths, 145
Raman spectroscopy, 72, 266
  clay structures, 97
  pigment analysis, 72
Raphides, 170
Rare earth elements
  bone, 122
  paleoenvironmental reconstruction,
    31–32
Ratites
  eggshells, 151
Reaction cascade, 60, 61, 173
Reaction rim, 64, 65
Recrystallization window, 111
  changes in bone mineral, 112
Red brick colored nodules, 174
Red soils. *See also* Soils, tropics
REE. *See* Rare earth elements
Refractive index, phytoliths, 17, 136, 144,
    237, 264, 272
Refractory material, 193–194
  aragonite, 193
  ceramic 17, 206
  magnesium oxide (periclase), 193
Reservoir effect, 163
Residue analysis, 27, 29, 36, 211
  beeswax, 236
  ceramics, 219–222
  plaster, 194
Resins, 211, 226, 312, 314
  fossil (amber), 314
Rhomb-shaped crystals
  calcite, 78, 82
Rhythmic growth, 41–42
  cementum, 129
  enamel and dentin, 132

mollusk shells, 163, 164
  otoliths, 154, 157
Rice
  phytoliths, 147
Rock paintings
  radiocarbon dating, 184
Rural-urban continuum, 273

Salinity variations
  otoliths, 156
Salt deposition on sediment surfaces, 56,
    251, 315–316
Sand dunes, 91
Sanidine, 204
Sarakini village, Greece, 234, 240–244
  animal enclosures, 242
  rye use, 242
  threshing floors, 242
Saturated zone, 55
Scaphopods, 159
Schoningen, Germany
  wood preservation, 310
Sea urchin test (shell). *See* Echinoderm
    skeletons
Sea water
  aragonite precipitation, 78
  paleotemperatures, 33, 156, 163
Season of occupation, 41–42
  archaeobotanical remains, 41
  cementum, 42
  mollusk shells, 164
  otoliths, 42, 157
  rhythmic growth, 42
Seasonal increments. *See* Rhythmic growth
Sediments
  absence of calcite, 77
  exposure to elevated temperatures, 97
  mineral assemblages and site
    preservation, 97–98
  water flow, 55
Seed clusters, 251
Sewers, 58, 86, 295
Sharpey's fibers, 129
Sherds. *See also* Ceramics, 196
  color, 203
  firing conditions, 202
  trace element analysis, 198
Sibudu Cave, South Africa, 254
Silica, 89–90, 298
  atomic structure, 88, 137
  authigenic, 90, 96, 298, 303
  biological production, 89
  bound water and hydroxyls, 136
  dehydration, 66

diagenesis, 61, 90
diatoms, 298
high temperature polymorphs, 90
luster, 136
mesostructure, 136
phytoliths, 89, 298
plants, 135
refractive index, 136
solubility, 90
Silica aggregates. *See* Siliceous aggregates
Silicates layered, 93
Silicates sheet, 93
Siliceous aggregates, 139, 145, 169, 237,
    253, 272, 298
  ^{40}K isotope, 177
  confusion with clay particles, 174
  Hayonim Cave, Israel, 173
  solubility, 173
  structure and formation, 171
Siliceous phytoliths. *See* Phytoliths
Silicon dioxide polymorphs, 88–92,
    297–300
  diagenesis, 90
  embedded information, 91–92
Silicon tetrahedra, 168
Silk, 162, 312
Sink hole, 65
Sintering, 290
Site formation processes, 42
  micromorphology, 69
  mineral assemblages, 68, 98
  size and shape of mineral particles,
    72
  transformation processes, 43
Site framework. *See* Site spatial
    organization
Site spatial organization, 43–44, 230
  fatty acids, 44
  fire locations, 235
  floor types, 235
  microartifacts, 44
  phosphate concentrations, 44, 223–225,
    296
  phytolith difference index (PDI), 242
  phytoliths, 141, 148–149
  size sorting of artifacts, 228
  two storied houses, 234
Site use
  secondary, 52
Skin, 105, 113, 184, 211, 307
Slaked lime. *See also* Plaster binder, 186
  sewage treatment, 194
  tanning, 194
Slip, 196

Smectite
  soils in arid and desert zones, 95
  soils in temperate zones, 95
Smectite group of clays, 93, 301
Snail shells, 161, 214, 215
  aragonite, 63, 80
  dating, 24
  diagenetic mineral changes, 161
  intracrystalline macromolecules,
    214
Snails
  freshwater, 158
  land, 158
Soapstone. *See* Steatite
Sodium hypochlorite, 142, 213, 216
Sodium nitrate, 269
Sodium polytungstate, 142
Soil. *See also* Sediments
  arid and desert zones, 95
  burned organic matter, 95
  charcoal fragments, 183
  definition, 73
  high latitudes, 95
  hydroxides and oxides, 95
  temperate latitudes, 95
  tropics, 95
Solubility of minerals, 59
Soot, 183
  fullerenes, 180
Speleothems
  uranium series dating, 21
Spherulites, 44
  dung, 44, 233, 234, 236, 240
  otoliths, 156
Splitting factor, 116, 291. *See also* Bone
    mineral, crystallinity
  bone collagen content, 292
  bone mineral, 291
  enamel, 291
  measurement using infrared spectrum,
    291
Sponges, 89, 150
Spongy bone, 108
Springs, 96
Squash
  phytoliths, 147
Squid otoliths, 154
Sr/Ca ratios
  bone, 120–121
  otoliths, 157
  weaning, 45
Stability fields of minerals, 59, 60, 80,
    295
  carbonate hydroxylapatite, 85

Stable isotopic composition
  collagen in crystal aggregates, 217
  dung, 240
  eggshells, 153
  fractionation, 32
  individual amino acids, 28
  intracrystalline macromolecules, 214
  marble provenience, 38
  nitrogen, 27, 28, 45
  otoliths, 156
  oxygen, phytoliths, 145
  paleodiet, 119–120
  paleoenvironment reconstruction,
    32–33
  paleotemperatures (mollusk shells), 163
  water in sediments, 146
Stables, 236
Starch, 18, 211, 312
Starch grains, 134, 222, 223
Steatite, 36
  provenience, 38
Sterkfontein Cave, South Africa, 230
  wood preserved, 310
Storage bins, 236
Storage sites, 58, 223
Strontium isotope ratios, 119
  bone mineral, 29
  migration, 26, 119
  paleodiet reconstruction, 29
  paleomigration, 35
Structural features. See Installations for
    pyrotechnology
Stucco, 194. See also Plaster, 185
Sugars. See Polysaccharides
Supercooled state, 167
Swartkrans Cave, South Africa, 230, 292

Tanning, 50
  slaked lime, 194
Taphonomy. See also Diagenesis, 53
  bones, 115, 116
Taranakite, 64, 86, 183, 297
Teeth. See also Tooth, 123–129
  abrasion by phytoliths, 136
  basic structure, 123
  brachydonty, 129
  dental calculus, 130
  design strategies, 129
  embedded information, 132–134
  fish, 288
  hypsodonty, 129
  strontium isotopes, 119
Tel Dor, Israel, 65, 224
  ancient animal enclosures, 240

aragonite refractory material, 194
  phytoliths, 140
  sediments exposed to elevated
    temperatures, 97
Tell es Safi, Israel, 158
Temper, 195
  types, 195
Tendon mineralized, 107
Terrestrial gastropods. See Snail shells
Thames River, 151
Theca, 149
Thermoluminescence, 176
Thermoluminescence dating, 92, 245, 246,
    350. See also TL, 18
  flint tools, 92
Thomsen, C. J., 4
Three-dimensional site reconstructions,
    267
Threshing floors, 233, 241, 242
Tilted strata, 65
  caves, 65
  organic matter degradation, 65
Tin
  provenience, 39
TL. See also Thermoluminescence
    dating
Tools, lithic
  dating by TL, 22
  flint, 91
  obsidian proveniencing, 37
  procurement strategies, 41
  provenience, 36
  quartzite, 74, 76
Tooth. See also Teeth, Enamel, Dentin, and
    Cementum
  development, 26
Trabecular bone. See Spongy bone
Trace elements, 68
  analysis, 37
  ceramic, 39
  flint, 40
  marble, 38
  otoliths, 157
  soapstone, 38
Trade
  pottery, 198–200
Trampling, 234. See also Microlaminated
    texture, 229, 230, 233
Trapped charge dating, 22–23, 245. See also
    Thermoluminescence, Optical
    stimulated luminescence, Electron
    spin resonance, 18, 19
  affect of siliceous aggregates, 177
  context, 252–254

dosimeters, 252
gamma radiation, 252
Travertine, 21, 80, 284
uranium series dating, 21
Tree rings
radiocarbon concentrations, 250
Tricalcium phosphate, 118
Tridymite, 88, 90, 298
Triple helical molecule. *See* Collagen
Trona, 116
Tubules. *See* Dentin, tubules
Turkana homestead, Kenya, 47
Tusk shells. *See also* Dentalium, 159
Tuyierres, 205
Tyrolean ice man, 48

Unsaturated zone, 55
Uranium series dating, 14, 19, 21, 246
enamel, 132
mollusk shells, 163
range, 21
Uranium uptake into enamel, 131,
253
UV-Visible spectrophotometers,
267

Vadose zone. *See* Unsaturated zone
Variscite, 64, 297
Vaterite, 77, 282
otoliths, 42, 155
plants, 135
Vermiculite
high latitude soils, 95
Vermiculite group of clays, 93
Vessel contents. *See* Pottery contents
Vitruvius, 187
Volcanic ash. *See also* Pozzolana, Italy,
186
degradation into clay, 95

Wash coat. *See also* Lime plaster, 185
Waste products. *See also* Pyrotechnology
pyrotechnology, 166
Wasters, 202
Water. *See also* Hydrological regime
absence restricts microbial activity, 18,
114
agent of diagenesis, 96
anaerobic conditions, 32, 50
clay-rich sediments, 93, 96
drinking, 33, 132
driving force of degradation, 52
fluoride, 23
hydrolysis reactions, 112

irrigation, 150
liquid vs vapor for preservation, 49
saturated and unsaturated zones, 55
standing vs flowing, 151
Water-logged environments, 50
Wax, 211, 312
Weaning, 44–45
age of, 121
domestic animals, 45
nitrogen isotopic composition, 45
Sr/Ca ratios, 45
Weddellite, 306
Wells, 151, 236
Wet sieving, 265
Wheat phytoliths, 147
Whewellite, 82, 306. *See* Calcium oxalate
morphologies of crystals in wood and
bark, 170
wood, 79
Wilson, E. O., 3
Wood
calcium oxalate crystals, 170
charred vs uncharred, 309
fire hardened sticks, 178, 310
fossil, 58
fuel, 145, 238
fungal degradation, 309
lignin and cellulose preservation, 311
major components, 179
phytoliths, 139, 140
preservation, 309–311
preserved in old sites, 310
pyrolysis process, 179
taxonomic identification, 184
Wood ash, 83
calcite crystal morphology, 82
calcite degradation, 79
calcium oxalate pyrolysis, 79
cemented sediment, 83
phytoliths, 178
pseudomorphs, 82
siliceous aggregates, 145
Worsaae, J. A., 4
Woven bone, 107

X-ray diffraction, 70–71, 104, 168
bone mineral, 116
ceramics, 203
charcoal, 179
clay minerals, 94, 97, 301
collagen to gelatin transformation, 113
crystallinity, 290
disorder in bone mineral, 64
disorder in carbonate minerals, 82, 161

X-ray diffraction (*cont.*)
    identifying authigenic phosphate
      minerals, 297
    quantification of mineral assemblages,
      278
X-ray fluorescence spetroscopy (XRF),
    265–266

Yuchanyan Cave, China, 265

Zhoukoudian, China, 5, 31, 75, 174,
    292
    evidence for deliberate control of fire,
      176
    fossil ashes?, 74
    Layer 10, Locality 1, 74–76
    use of fire, 75

$\nu_2:\nu_4$ ratio. *See* Calcite, $\nu_2:\nu_4$ ratio